British Politics

www.palgrave.com/foundations/leach

Palgrave Foundations

A series of introductory texts across a wide range of subject areas to meet the needs of today's lecturers and students.

Foundations texts provide complete yet concise coverage of core topics and skills based on detailed research of course requirements suitable for both independent study and class use – *the firm foundations for future study.*

Published

A History of English Literature
Biology
British Politics
Chemistry (third edition)
Communication Studies
Contemporary Europe (second edition)
Economics
Economics for Business
Foundations of Marketing
Modern British History
Nineteenth-Century Britain
Philosophy
Physics (second edition)
Politics (second edition)

Further titles are in preparation

British Politics

ROBERT LEACH
BILL COXALL
LYNTON ROBINS

palgrave
macmillan

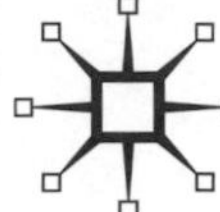

First published 2006 by
PALGRAVE MACMILLAN
Houndmills, Basingstoke, Hampshire RG21 6XS and
175 Fifth Avenue, New York, N.Y. 10010
Companies and representatives throughout the world

PALGRAVE MACMILLAN is the global academic imprint of the Palgrave Macmillan division of St. Martin's Press, LLC and of Palgrave Macmillan Ltd. Macmillan® is a registered trademark in the United States, United Kingdom and other countries. Palgrave is a registered trademark in the European Union and other countries.

ISBN-13: 978–1–4039–4922–6
ISBN-10: 1–4039–4922–0

This book is printed on paper suitable for recycling and made from fully managed and sustained forest sources.

A catalogue record for this book is available from the British Library.

A catalog record for this book is available from the Library of Congress.

10 9 8 7 6 5 4 3 2 1
15 14 13 12 11 10 09 08 07 06

Printed and bound in China

This book is dedicated to the memory of Bill Coxall

Contents

PART III

Issues and Policies

Figures

Tables

Boxes

In focus boxes

Preface

British Politics is a new book that replaces an older one, *Contemporary British Politics*, a well-established text which went through four editions between 1989 and 2003. Even the best textbooks require regular updating, and it was essential to cover such critical recent developments as the Iraq War and its aftermath, the impact of European Union enlargement, the 2005 General Election, the July 2005 London bombings, and the new leadership of the Conservative and Liberal Democrat parties. However, a new book rather than a further edition of the old one seemed necessary because of changes in the project's authorship and format, as well as ongoing but far-reaching changes in the substance of British politics.

Bill Coxall and Lynton Robins were jointly responsible for the first three editions of the earlier book. After Bill's sad death in 1999, Robert Leach joined the team to work with Lynton and coordinate the production of the fourth edition, published in 2003. When Lynton decided that he wished to play a largely advisory role on the project thereafter, it seemed to the publishers an opportune moment for a comprehensive rewrite and redesign, with new features, to be included in Palgrave Macmillan's Foundations series, alongside and complementing Andrew Heywood's very successful general introduction to *Politics*.

However, a new book is also appropriate because British politics too has been radically transformed. Familiar constitutional principles have been challenged and the institutions and processes of government transformed. The sovereignty of Westminster and Whitehall has been eroded from above and below, replaced by a still evolving system of multi-level governance. Changes in voting behaviour and the introduction of new electoral systems have assisted the emergence of a new multi-party political system. Yet active involvement in and engagement with political parties has declined markedly, to be increasingly supplemented or supplanted by other forms of political participation, including various forms of direct action, and at one extreme, terrorism.

The book is designed to provide a clear, accessible and user-friendly introduction to British politics but with a depth and breadth of coverage to appeal to the most discriminating and demanding reader. New features included in *British Politics* are chapter summaries and questions for further discussion which should prove helpful to both staff and students. Some other valuable features have been also adopted from Andrew Heywood's companion title, including 'key thinkers' boxes, and these have been supplemented by new boxes on issues of academic controversy. However, those familiar with the old *Contemporary British Politics* will find that many tried and tested features have been retained and developed, including highlighted definitions, comparative politics boxes and a mass of figures, tables, graphs and photos to illustrate the body of the text.

There is never a 'right' time to bring out a new book on British politics. Despite every effort to provide the latest information and analysis, events soon inevitably conspire to render some material outdated, even before publication, and increasingly as the years pass before a new edition. The companion website to this book – which can be found at www.palgrave.com/foundations/leach – will be regularly updated, at least every six months, to include all the critical developments in British politics that take place between editions.

Robert Leach

Acknowledgements

The authors and publishers are grateful to the following for permission to use copyright material:

EMPICS: pp. 8, 41, 61, 97, 98, 119, 137, 218, 233, 256, 279, 293, 322, 343, 355, 374, 388, 400, 415, 429, 440, 452.
Getty Images: pp. 92, 95, 103.
Photofusion: p. 395.
Reuters: p.190
Robert Leach: pp. 84, 301.

Every effort has been made to contact all the copyright-holders but if any have been inadvertently overlooked the publishers will be pleased to make the necessary arrangements at the first opportunity.

Robert Leach would particularly like to acknowledge the shrewd advice, professional commitment and sheer efficiency of Steven Kennedy, Suzannah Burywood and Barbara Collinge at Palgrave Macmillan, together with Susan Curran and Mike Fenn at Curran Publishing, who have all laboured well beyond the call of duty to assist in the production of this volume. Once more, he also wishes to pay tribute to the patient support and understanding of his wife, Judith, who was repeatedly (and generally inaccurately) assured that the book was 'near completion'.

Abbreviations

AA	Automobile Association
ACEA	Association of European Automobile Constructors
AI	Amnesty International
ALF	Animal Liberation Front
AMS	Additional Member System
APL	anti-personnel landmines
APNI	Alliance Party of Northern Ireland
ASBO	Anti-social Behaviour Order
ASH	Action on Smoking and Health
AV	Alternative Vote
AWM	Advantage West Midlands (development agency)
BBC	British Broadcasting Corporation
BMA	British Medical Association
BNP	British National Party
BSE	bovine spongiform encephalitis ('mad cow' disease)
BUF	British Union of Fascists
CAG	Comptroller and Auditor-General (of the EU)
CAP	Common Agricultural Policy
CBA	cost–benefit analysis
CBI	Confederation of British Industry
CCT	compulsory competitive tendering
CEFIC	European Chemical Industry Council
CEMR	Council of European Municipalities and Regions
CFSP	Common Foreign and Security Policy (of the EU)
CLEAR	Campaign for Lead-Free Air
CLP	Constituency Labour Party
CND	Campaign for Nuclear Disarmament
CofE	Church of England
COPA	Committee of Professional Agricultural Organisations (EU)
COREPER	Committee of Permanent Representatives (EU)
CPAG	Child Poverty Action Group
CPGB	Communist Party of Great Britain
CPRE	Council for the Protection of Rural England
CRE	Commission for Racial Equality
CSA	Child Support Agency
DEFRA	Department of the Environment, Food and Rural Affairs
DfES	Department for Education and Skills
DID	Department of International Development
DoE	Department of the Environment (now part of DEFRA)
DoH	Department of Health
DSC	Departmental Select Committee
DTI	Department of Trade and Industry
DUP	Democratic Unionist Party
ECHR	European Court of/Convention on Human Rights
EC	European Community
ECAS	European Citizen Action Service
ECJ	European Court of Justice
ECSC	European Coal and Steel Community
EEC	European Economic Community
EEDA	East of England Development Agency
EMS	European Monetary System
EMU	economic and monetary union
EP	European Parliament
ERM	Exchange Rate Mechanism of the EMS
ESC	Economic and Social Committee (EU)
ESDP	European security and defence policy
ETUC	European Trade Union Confederation
EU	European Union
EUROBIT	European Association of Manufacturers of Business Machines and Information Technology
FCO	Foreign and Commonwealth Office
FoE	Friends of the Earth
FMI	financial management initiative
FPTP	first-past-the-post (electoral system)
FSA	Financial Services Authority
GATT	General Agreement on Tariffs and Trade (now administered by WTO)
GCHQ	Government Communications Headquarters
GDP	Gross Domestic Product
GLA	Greater London Authority

GM	genetically modified
GNP	Gross National Product
GO(R)	Government Office for the Regions
GP	General Practitioner
HAT	Housing Action Trust
IMF	International Monetary Fund
IPPR	Institute for Public Policy Research
IRA	Irish Republican Army
IRC	Industrial Reorganisation Corporation (now defunct)
ITA	Independent Television Authority
LA	local authority
LEA	local education authority
LGA	Local Government Association
LSE	London School of Economics
LMS	local management of schools
MAD	mutually assured destruction
MAFF	Ministry of Agriculture, Fisheries and Food (now subsumed in DEFRA)
MEP	Member of the European Parliament
MINIS	Management Information System for Ministers
MLR	Minimum Lending Rate
MoD	Ministry of Defence
MP	Member of Parliament
MRSA	methicillin resistant staphylococcus aureas (a 'superbug')
MSP	Member of the Scottish Parliament
MWA	Member of the Welsh Assembly
NATO	North Atlantic Treaty Organisation
NDPB	non-departmental public body
NEB	National Enterprise Board
NEC	National Executive Committee (of the Labour Party)
NEDC	National Economic Development Council (now defunct)
NF	National Front
NFU	National Farmers' Union
NGO	non-governmental organisation
NHS	National Health Service
NICE	National Institute for Clinical Excellence
NNDR	national non-domestic rates
NPM	new public management
NUM	National Union of Mineworkers
NWDA	Northwest Development Agency
ODPM	Office of the Deputy Prime Minister
OECD	Organisation for Economic Cooperation and Development
Ofcom	Office of Communications
Ofgem	Office of gas and electricity markets
OFT	Office of Fair Trading
Ofwat	Office of Water Services
OMOV	one member one vote
ONE	One North East (development agency)
OPEC	Organisation of Petroleum Exporting Countries
ORR	Office of the Rail Regulator
PAC	Public Accounts Committee
PC	Plaid Cymru (Welsh nationalist party)
PC	Privy Councillor
PC	politically correct
PCA	Parliamentary Commission for Administration (Ombudsman)
PCT	Primary Care Trust
PESC	Public Expenditure Survey Committee
PFI	Private Finance Initiative
PLP	Parliamentary Labour Party
PM	Prime Minister
PMQT	Prime Minister's Question Time
PPP	public-private partnerships
PPBS	planned programmed budgetary systems
PPS	Parliamentary Private Secretary
PR	proportional representation
PSA	public service agreement
PSBR	Public Sector Borrowing Requirement
PTA	parent–teacher association
PUP	Progressive Unionist Party
QAA	Quality Assurance Agency
qualgo	quasi-autonomous local government organisation
quango	quasi-autonomous non-governmental organisation
RDA	regional development agency
RSPB	Royal Society for the Protection of Birds
RSPCA	Royal Society for the Prevention of Cruelty to Animals
SCS	Senior Civil Service
SDLP	Social Democratic and Labour Party (Northern Ireland political party)
SDP	Social Democratic Party (now subsumed within Liberal Democrats)
SEA	Single European Act
SEEDA	South East England Development Agency

SERA	Socialist Environment and Resources Association
SF	Sinn Fein
SNP	Scottish National Party
TEU	Treaty of the European Union (Maastricht Treaty)
TGWU	Transport and General Workers Union
TNC	transnational corporation
TUC	Trades Union Congress
UDA	Ulster Defence Association
UDC	Urban Development Corporation
UK	United Kingdom
UKIP	United Kingdom Independence Party
UN	United Nations
UNICE	Union of Industrial and Employers' Confederations of Europe
USA	United States of America
USSR	Union of Soviet Socialist Republics
UUP	Ulster Unionist Party
UVF	Ulster Volunteer Force
VAT	value added tax
vCJD	variant Creutzfeld-Jacob disease (human variant of 'mad cow' disease)
WA	Welsh Assembly
WTO	World Trade Organisation
YF	Yorkshire Forward (development agency)
ZBB	zero-base budgeting

People and Politics

Politics, Democracy and Power

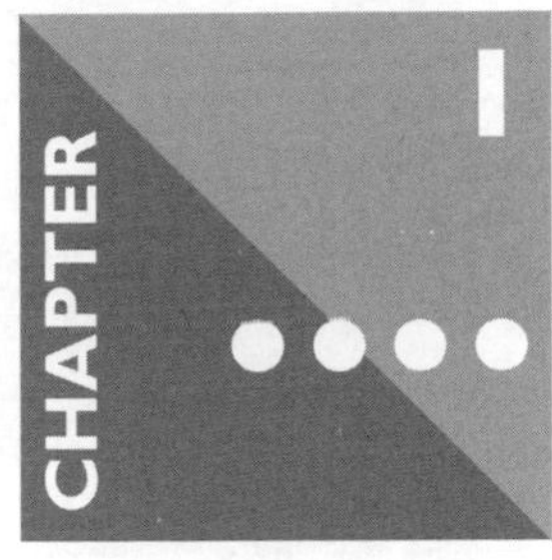

Contents

Politics is a subject that arouses conflicting emotions. Some are intensely interested in political issues and follow politics keenly. For others politics involves distant institutions, remote politicians and obscure complex issues with little direct relevance for immediate everyday life. Others again show a strong distaste towards political parties and politicians who are 'all the same' or 'on the make', and 'only interested in what they can get out of it'. Unsurprisingly such critics argue it would be much better if education, or health, or agriculture could be somehow 'taken out of politics'.

Yet politics is inescapable. Everyone is affected by it, whether they like it or not. At the very least people have to pay taxes and obey laws, or suffer the penalties. They are obliged to register births, marriages and deaths, and fill in forms for countless other purposes. They can only drive their cars, exchange their houses or travel abroad if they fulfil the necessary requirements. In some states citizens are still liable to conscription into the armed forces. All this emphasises what may appear to be the downside of politics – the restraints on individual freedom, although of course these same restraints on others might help communities to enjoy peace, security, and the pursuit of their own lives without fear. More positively, people receive various services provided or financed through the state in some form or other. Mostly these services are regarded as beneficial, although some may seem irksome or extravagant. Indeed, precisely what services should be provided by the state, the level of those services and how they should be provided and paid for are political questions, which cannot be 'taken out of politics' because they have massive consequences for individuals and communities. Even the privatisation in Britain of some activities that were formerly state owned and run (such as rail transport) has not succeeded in depoliticising them.

What is politics?

Various answers have been given to the simple question 'What is politics?' Some of them are given in Box 1.1.

The first definition links politics and government in a common sense way. Clearly politics is about government, and this book analyses at some length the institutions of government. Yet this definition implies that politics is a rather remote activity, not for ordinary people. How far does politics include the governed as well as those doing the governing? And does it just involve the government of states? Some definitions of politics suggest that it is not only a universal human activity, as the ancient Greek philosopher Aristotle argued, but can take place at very different levels and in different spheres.

Box 1.1

What is politics?

'The science and art of government'
(Shorter Oxford English Dictionary)

'Who gets what, when, how'
(H. Lasswell, American political scientist)

'The authoritative allocation of value'
(David Easton, another American political scientist)

'The art of the possible'
(R. A. Butler, British Conservative Politician)

Box 1.2

Politics, conflict and coercion

'Political power grows out of the barrel of a gun.'
(Mao Zedong, Chinese Communist leader)

'War is nothing but a continuation of politics by other means.'
(Von Clausewitz, German military strategist).

'Every state is founded on force.'
(Leon Trotsky, Russian Communist politician)

'The state is a human community that (successfully) claims the monopoly of the legitimate use of physical force within a given territory.'
(Max Weber, German sociologist)

Thus some talk of the politics of the golf club, or the board room, or the university. However, the study of politics does in practice focus largely on government and public policy rather than what is sometimes called 'micro-politics'.

The two crisp American definitions suggest (in rather different language) that politics is about choosing between alternatives. Individuals, communities and governments cannot have everything they want, but must determine their priorities. Butler hints at the constraints involved in the political process. Compromise is often necessary because different sections of the community want different and often conflicting things. It is not possible to please everyone all the time. Decisions commonly produce winners and losers. Indeed some have seen disagreement and conflict as the essence of politics, and have emphasised the role of coercion and physical force (see box 1.2).

All these quotations emphasise the coercive and violent side of politics, which is only too obvious in the modern world. 'Might' seems to matter more than 'right'. Indeed, those who have physical force on their side may determine what is right. Justice appears to be merely 'what is in the interests of the stronger party' (as the sophist Thrasymachus declared in Plato's *Republic,* one of the earliest and most celebrated analyses of politics).

Yet such interpretations of politics do not tell the whole story. Power may be used for constructive as well as destructive purposes. Politics may arise out of disagreement and conflict, which can sometimes take a violent form, but it also involves the search for a peaceful resolution of conflict through compromise. Indeed a 'political solution' is commonly seen as an alternative to violence. Winston Churchill, famous largely as a great war leader, once observed 'Jaw jaw is better than war war', while a noted French political scientist, Maurice Duverger (1972: 221), defined politics as 'a continual effort to eliminate physical violence'. Politics, he claimed, 'tends to replace fists, knives, clubs and rifles with other types of weapons', although he added sadly, 'it is not always successful in doing so'.

The scope of politics

There are disagreements also over the scope of politics. Some liberals and conservatives would draw a clear distinction between the state and civil society, between a public or political sphere and a private sphere of life from which politics should be excluded – the family and other voluntary associations. Champions of the free market would seek to exclude the state and politics from much economic activity, and place firm limits on government intervention. By contrast, many socialists have sought to establish a political system in which the state controlled the economy (see Chapter 6). Fascism was associated with a totalitarian theory of the state, under which the state was all-embracing and excluded from no sphere of activity.

Definitions

The state is a political and governmental unit – a compulsory association that is sovereign over a particular territory.

Civil society refers to the part of social life outside the control of the state, e.g. clubs, groups and associations, private business, the family.

While some of these approaches to politics have become less fashionable, other contemporary political ideologies have involved a radical reinterpretation of the scope of politics. Thus feminists insist 'the personal is political'. They are not just concerned with formal legal equality in the public sphere, but with gender relations in the family, home and bedroom, because these are seen as central to the injustice and oppression suffered by women. Consequently, interpersonal relations, sexual relations and the division of labour within the home are not purely private matters but a legitimate sphere for political engagement (see Chapter 23). At another level green ideas have politicised a whole range of issues which at one time were seen as having not much, if anything, to do with politics (see Chapter 25).

Authority, power and influence

Politics is clearly about power, but this key concept is difficult to define. 'Power' suggests a capacity to achieve desired results, and compel obedience. It may be lawful or unlawful. An armed criminal may compel his victims to do things that they would not choose. He is clearly exercising power, although unlawfully. Others, such as a government minister or a judge, may also wield effective power, but power which is generally recognised as rightful and legitimate. The term 'authority' is widely used to describe the rightful use of political power, or legitimate power. Power may compel obedience, while authority is widely accepted by those over whom it is exercised. We voluntarily obey those in authority because we accept the legitimacy of their power.

Why do we obey them? The German sociologist Max Weber distinguished between three main types or sources of authority: traditional, charismatic and legal-rational. Traditional authority rests on long-established custom – the authority of a tribal chief or hereditary monarch for example. Charismatic authority derives from the compelling personal qualities of an individual – the authority exercised by a Napoleon, Hitler or (more positively) Nelson Mandela. They are obeyed because of who they are, rather than because of what they are. Legal-rational authority is authority based on formal rules. Elected politicians or appointed government officials may be obeyed, not because of custom, nor because of their personal qualities, but because it is acknowledged that they legitimately hold their office under accepted rules and procedures. It is the office or post rather than the person who occupies the post whose authority is obeyed. Weber considered that legal-rational authority is the characteristic form of authority in the modern world. Both modern bureaucracy and representative democracy involve legal-rational authority.

Power is sometimes also distinguished from influence. While power implies a capacity to determine outcomes directly, influence suggests the ability to shape outcomes indirectly, to exert pressure on those who are taking the decisions, persuading them to change their opinion and behaviour. The study of politics involves not just examining the formal institutions and offices directly involved in government, but also the influences on government and the policy process, the role for example of business organisations and trade unions, voluntary bodies and cause groups. Many political decisions taken by politicians or civil servants may have their origin and explanation in the successful influence of groups outside government (see Chapter 8).

Definitions

Power is the capacity to achieve desired goals.

Authority is the rightful or legitimate use of power.

Influence involves the ability to shape a decision or outcome through various forms of pressure.

Democracy – power to the people?

Britain, along with most states in the modern western world, and many others elsewhere, claims to be a democracy. This near-universal approval of democracy as a system of government is relatively recent. A form of democracy flourished in ancient Athens nearly 2,500 years ago, but from then until at least the late 18th century democracy scarcely existed anywhere, and was regarded as a remote and essentially impractical system of government. While direct rule by all the people themselves was just about possible in a small city state like ancient Athens, it was impractical for the extensive empires and large nation states which have flourished subsequently. Democracy became more feasible with the development in the 19th century of representative democracy, government by the elected representatives of the people, rather than direct democracy. Today democracy has become so widely approved that even some of the most tyrannical and corrupt regimes lay claim to the title 'democratic' for form's sake. Even so, democracy has often been accorded only faint praise by some influential modern thinkers and politicians (see Box 1.3).

Whether modern representative democracy does ensure real government by the people, as Abraham Lincoln asserted, is far from clear. Indeed it does not even invariably result in a government chosen by the majority of the people (see Chapter 5). Yet at a minimum in mature democratic systems it does offer an element of real choice between rival parties and programmes, it does render opposition respectable rather than treasonable, and it does provide for the peaceful transfer of power between governments. These are very considerable benefits which should not be underrated, particularly when the alternatives are considered.

Definitions

Direct democracy involves the direct and continuous participation of citizens in government.

Representative democracy involves indirect government by the people, through representatives elected by the people.

Box 1.3

Democracy – some definitions and observations

'Our constitution is called a democracy because power is in the hands not of a minority but of the whole people.'

Pericles of Athens, 431 BC as reported in Thucydides' *History of the Peloponnesian War* (1954 trans.: 145).

'Government of the people, by the people, for the people.'

President Abraham Lincoln, Gettysburg address, 1863.

'Were there a people of gods, their government would be democratic. So perfect a government is not for men.'

Jean-Jacques Rousseau, *The Social Contract* (1968 trans.: 1762).

'Democracy substitutes election by the incompetent many for appointment by the corrupt few.'

George Bernard Shaw, *Man and Superman*, 1903.

'Democracy is the worst form of Government except all those other forms that have been tried from time to time.'

Winston Churchill, speech in the House of Commons, 11 November 1947.

'So two cheers for democracy: one because it admits variety and two because it permits criticism. Two cheers are quite enough: there is no occasion to give three.'

E. M. Forster, *Two Cheers for Democracy*, 1951.

While the British like to think they invented modern representative democracy, the Americans and the French have a rather better claim. The American rebels against the British state and crown, through their successful Declaration of Independence of 1776, and the constitution they devised for the United States of America soon afterwards, effectively created what was to become the first modern democracy. The French revolution of 1789 substituted the ideas of popular sovereignty and liberty, equality and fraternity (initially only briefly) for the autocracy of the old French monarchy.

Britain only came to terms with democracy

rather later. Although England boasts an ancient Parliament with over 700 years of near-continuous existence since it was established in 1265, even the lower house of that Parliament, the House of Commons, was not elected democratically until recently. Only a small proportion of adult males could participate in elections until a series of Reform Acts extended the vote to most men in the course of the 19th century. Women could not vote until 1918, and they only obtained the vote on the same terms as men in 1928. Even today it is questionable how far Britain satisfies all the conditions to qualify as a full and fair system of representative democracy.

How far and fully Britain satisfies these conditions will be discussed in more detail later in this book (particularly in Chapter 5), although it is generally conceded that British elections do involve a real choice and they are not patently rigged (as they are in some countries). Yet regardless of the extent of the right to vote and the mechanics of the electoral system, there are many who would question whether government 'of the people, by the people, for the people' is a reality in Britain. First, are the elected representatives of the people the real rulers of Britain? Second, and more importantly, how far do the right to vote, and other rights associated with the political system, give the people or the majority of the people real power?

If Britain is a democracy that in theory gives power to the many, not the few, how far do ordinary people have any real control or influence over those who govern them? Those who bother to use their vote may determine which of two or three rival teams of politicians occupies government posts for the next four or five years, but does this give voters significant influence over key government decisions and policies? What other opportunities do citizens have to participate in the political process? How far can 'ordinary people' hope to have a real voice in the many decisions that affect them? These questions will be addressed throughout this book but particularly in Chapters 4 to 9.

Box 1.4

Conditions for representative democracy

- Full adult franchise – that is, all adults have the right to vote.
- A secret ballot – helps ensure voting without intimidation or bribery.
- Regular elections – governments and parliaments must not be able to postpone elections.
- Fair elections – each vote should count equally.
- An effective choice of candidates and parties for voters.
- A level playing field between rival parties and candidates contesting elections.
- A free and diverse media enabling a wide expression of views.

Power in Britain

Do elected politicians make the real decisions that affect the British people? Perhaps the real decision makers are not the politicians who tend to dominate the news but relatively faceless civil servants or advisers. Alternatively, more real power and influence might be exercised by individuals who are not part of the formal political process at all – businessmen (and they are usually still 'men'!), bankers, or owners of newspapers, television companies and other media, some of whom may not even be British. Newspapers and magazines sometimes attempt to compile lists of the most powerful people in Britain. These are generally headed by the prime minister, as one might expect, but often include prominent businessmen, media magnates, appointed officials, and even sports personalities and pop idols, interspersed among some other elected politicians. Such lists are hardly scientific and may reflect little more than the highly subjective views of the journalists who compose them. However, they do suggest that power is not just confined to those who hold some formal position in government, and that business tycoons such as Rupert Murdoch or Sir Richard Branson have more power than some Cabinet ministers.

One cynical conclusion might be that 'money talks'; those with substantial wealth and income can use it to buy (sometimes literally) political

In Focus 1.1

Representative democracy in action!

A man with his dog votes at an improvised polling station in a temporary hut at Coven Heath in the constituency of South Staffordshire in the General Election of 5 May 2005. A healthy democracy is widely held to require a high participation in the electoral process. In response to declining turnout in UK elections, more accessible, voter-friendly locations for polling stations in supermarkets, pubs and even fish and chip shops have been provided. To make voting easier still there have also been trials with other means of registering votes, including telephone and internet voting. However, only easier postal voting has had much effect on turnout. (For more on voter turnout, see Chapter 4.)

Photograph: EMPICS.

influence. Yet there is no simple correlation between wealth and power. Newspapers also sometimes list the wealthiest people in Britain, but some of the names near the top of such lists, such as the Duke of Westminster or the Queen, do not figure prominently if at all in the lists of those with power. There are others, such as leading footballers or pop stars, who avoid any formal association with politics and lack significant economic power, but may have enormous influence as role models on behaviour, and perhaps contribute more to changing political attitudes on key issues than professional politicians. Yet again, it is possible that real power and influence is exercised by many who are not celebrities – 'faceless bureaucrats', or political advisers (see Chapter 12).

However, this whole approach may make too much of the power of particular individuals. Ministers and company chairs come and go, but the organisations they head generally last much longer. Perhaps we should be looking at the power of institutions or corporate power. Perhaps the civil service, or the City of London, or transnational corporations exercise far more effective power and influence in the British political process than any single personality. Alternatively, power may not lie with particular institutions but with more amorphous interests or elites, such as 'the ruling class', 'the establishment', 'big business', 'the military-industrial complex' or 'global capitalism'. The implication is that those who hold formal positions of power, the official rulers, are driven by forces outside their control.

Alternatively we can seek to identify those who are effectively excluded from power. Thus it is often suggested that certain groups or interests might be marginalised in the political system – the unemployed, ethnic minorities, teenagers, women, or those who live and work in the countryside. There may be sub-cultures, an underclass, or possibly a whole gender largely excluded from the political process.

Definitions

Elite – a small dominant group. Elite theorists argue that power is inevitably exercised by the few (or by an elite or elites), even in nominally democratic organisations or states.

The establishment – a term sometimes used to describe the British elite, an unaccountable dominant social group largely educated at leading public schools and ancient universities.

The ruling class is a term used particularly by Marxists to describe those who own and control capital, and whose economic power gives them political power.

All this implies that power may be rather or very unevenly distributed. Some, perhaps a small minority, appear to have a great deal of power, others relatively little influence, while others again may be virtually excluded from any effective participation in the decisions that affect their lives. Yet while elite theorists suggest that power is narrowly concentrated, pluralists argue that ordinary people do have the capacity to influence and even determine key outcomes, in accordance with notions of democracy.

The distribution of power may also change over time. The journalist Anthony Sampson wrote a series of books examining power in Britain, the first in 1962, the last in 2004. He suggests that over that period some institutions have lost influence, such as the trade unions and the universities, while the media are more important than ever. He thinks power has become more centralised, and the prime minister and the Treasury are more dominant, while the Cabinet and the civil service are less influential. Looking back with a more sceptical eye Sampson had become 'more impatient and intolerant of the humbug and deceptions of democracy' (2005: xii). This is, however, only one man's view, and not necessarily right.

Perspectives on power

Who then rules Britain? It is a simple question, to which a variety of simple answers may be given. Britain has cabinet or prime ministerial government, parliamentary sovereignty, an elected dictatorship, government by bureaucracy, business or corporate power, the dominance of an 'establishment' or 'ruling class'. All these answers, and others besides, have some plausibility and it is worth giving serious consideration to them. Yet although it is certainly possible to provide a wealth of relevant information and analysis which should help towards an appreciation of who rules Britain, it should be acknowledged right away that it is impossible ultimately to give an authoritative and definitive answer to the question. Those answers that are given inevitably reflect different interpretations of the facts, and ultimately fundamentally different perspectives on politics, and different underlying ideological assumptions.

The term 'model' is often used in social science to describe a simplified version of reality. We try to make sense of a wide range of possibly relevant information by constructing simple hypotheses about the relationship between key variables, and see how far the real world fits the resulting models. Some simple models of the possible distribution of power in society are given in Table 1.1. The crucial question is how far power is dispersed or concentrated in the political system, but the different models also provide alternative explanations of the institutions and mechanisms involved.

They are not the only possible models, and indeed, different names or versions of these models may be encountered elsewhere. Moreover, not all the models are mutually exclusive. 'Pluralism', 'liberal capitalism' or 'liberal democracy' are the names often given to a composite version of the first three models listed here, suggesting a model where power is dispersed through a mixture of the ballot box, the free market and the influence of group interests on the policy process. Certainly these institutions and processes can be seen as playing mutually reinforcing roles. Yet they also reflect different and sometimes competing perspectives. Some old-fashioned liberals (or those on the modern New Right) place far more emphasis on the free market than the verdict of the ballot box, particularly if that leads to interference with free market forces. Similarly, they may fear that group influences represent selfish sectional interests and illegitimate power that may distort the market. Similarly,

Definitions

Pluralism involves the belief that power is widely dispersed through society, rather than heavily concentrated in the hands of an elite or ruling class.

Neo-pluralism is a modified version of pluralism which still emphasises the dispersal of power while acknowledging the influence of key interests (e.g. business).

Democratic elitism is a modified form of elitism which still emphasises the importance of elites or leadership in politics, while acknowledging that competition between elites (e.g. through elections) encourages them to be responsive and accountable to the masses.

while pluralists assume a role for elections and representative institutions, they regard these as only providing a very limited, occasional and blunt instrument for popular political participation, and place more emphasis on the continuous influence of countless pressure groups on the policy process.

How persuasive are these models? Which is the most convincing? The obvious answer is to look at the evidence, but the problem here is that each model begins from rather different assumptions, employs different methodologies and looks at different sorts of evidence. The representative government model largely assumes that political power lies where the constitution, laws and other official documents say it does, so here it is important to examine the theory and practice of the key institutions. The market model derives its key assumptions from classical economics. It is countless individual producers and consumers operating through the market who determine the crucial questions of who gets what, when, how. The role of politics in this economic process is (and, proponents of this model argue, should be) strictly limited, as government intervention can only distort the operation of the free market and lead to a less efficient allocation of resources. Evidence in support of these assumptions comes from analysis of market forces and government intervention in practice. Pluralists cite case studies in decision making to demonstrate the role of large numbers of different groups in the process. Elitists by contrast identify key individuals or groups who dominate decision making in their communities. Marxists infer political power from economic power. They document the massive inequalities in income and wealth in modern capitalist society, and assume that it is those who control the means of production who also control the political process.

At this point an intelligent reader coming to the study of politics for the first time might think, 'Hold on! Is this description or prescription? Science or ideology?' The answer is, inevitably, both. While writers on politics may conscientiously strive to provide an accurate picture of the way in which the political process actually operates, they are inevitably influenced by their own fundamental assumptions, and sometimes also by their ideals. Marx believed he was providing a

Table 1.1 Models of the possible distribution of power

Name of model	Key players	Power	Evidence	Thinkers
Representative democracy model	Individual voters through the ballot box	Dispersed	Formal political mechanisms, electoral system, written constitutions	Bentham, J S Mill
Market model	Individual consumers and producers through the free market	Dispersed	Classical economic assumptions – evidence of working of market	Adam Smith, Hayek, Friedman
Pluralist model	Pressure groups	Relatively dispersed	Influence of groups in case studies of decision making	Bentley, Truman, Robert Dahl, neo-pluralists (e.g. Lindblom)
Elitist model	Elites (e.g. social, business, military, bureaucratic, professional elites)	Concentrated	Reputation of key figures and relationships between them	Pareto, Mosca, Michels, Wright Mills
Marxist model	Ruling class ('bourgeoisie' in a capitalist society)	Highly concentrated	Distribution of income and wealth – working of capitalist system	Marx, Lenin, Trotsky, Gramsci, Miliband, Poulantzas

dispassionate analysis of the underlying forces within capitalism, but it is difficult to divorce this analysis entirely from his condemnation of capitalism and hopes for a future socialist revolution. He wrote, 'Philosophers have only interpreted the world, the point however is to change it' (*Theses on Feuerbach*). There is a similar mixture of analysis and prescription among modern free marketeers. Like Marx, they too want to change the world, although in a quite different direction. Moreover, while much of the debate between pluralists and elitists apparently involves dispassionate social scientific research into the distribution of power, most of those involved are also defending or advancing theories of democracy, and implicitly or explicitly criticising or defending the processes they describe.

Ideas, interests and ideologies

The study of politics, from Plato onwards, assumed the importance of political ideas. It has been said that there is nothing so important as an idea whose time has come. Democracy, national self-determination, socialism, the free market, are all examples of powerful ideas that have, at one time or another, appeared to change the world. A new idea, or perhaps more commonly the revival of an old idea, may still today seem to drive political change. It is often suggested that political parties, or potential political leaders, need a 'big idea' if they are to succeed.

Yet at various levels the importance of ideas in politics has been questioned. Much modern politics seems to be more about presentation (see Chapter 9) than values, principles and ideas. Image is more important than substance. Voters judge politicians by their physical appearance, hair, clothes, voice and accent, physical mannerisms rather than their principles. Politicians and parties increasingly seem to communicate with the wider public through slogans and soundbites rather than carefully argued manifestos and reasoned speeches. Politics is reduced to manipulation and marketing, like the sale of soap powder or cornflakes.

Ideas, however, require communication, and this can take place at various levels. Soundbites are not new, but have been cogently expressed by some of the greatest political philosophers and practising politicians the world has known. Consider, for example, some of the observations by leading thinkers and politicians on democracy (see Box 1.3). They involve succinct summaries of important insights, expressed in memorable terms, like soundbites. They may contain the essence of important truths – although of course such terse statements commonly require further examination, elaboration and qualification. Similarly, politicians (like Margaret Thatcher) may be coached to improve their image and presentation, remodelling their clothes, hair, voice and posture, but this does not mean they have nothing of substance to say. Margaret Thatcher had an important message to communicate (whether one agrees with it or not).

At another level, it may be argued that the ideas we hold are conditioned by our background and circumstances. We may simply come to think that what is in our interests is fair and just. Thus our core beliefs may simply involve a rationalisation of our own self-interest. From a Marxist perspective, ideas are essentially a rationalisation of the interests of different economic classes. However, Marx also argued that 'the ruling ideas in every age are the ideas of the ruling class'. Plausibly, the dominant class (capitalists, in a capitalist society) is in a strong position to influence or condition the thinking of subordinate classes, through for example the education system and the mass media. Thus the manual working class may come to hold views that are not in their objective interests. Consequently they may reject socialism (very much in their objective interests from a Marxist perspective). By contrast, liberals and modern neo-liberals assume that individuals act in their own rational self-interest (as voters and consumers). If they reject socialism it is because they have concluded (correctly, from a neo-liberal perspective) that it is not in their interest or unworkable.

Both Marxists and neo-liberals thus in their different ways suggest that it is interests (individual or class) that drive political behaviour. Yet both paradoxically illustrate the power of ideas. Marx's ideas inspired political movements around the world, and revolutions in Russia, China and elsewhere which did much to shape the issues and conflicts of the 20th century. The revival of free market ideas by modern neo-liberals similarly transformed the government and politics of the western world, before going on to affect (with varying success) the economies and societies of the Communist world, most of which spectacularly imploded after the collapse of the Berlin Wall in 1989. Ideas can still exert a powerful grip on our collective consciousness.

Ideologies

Many modern political differences arise from rival political perspectives or ideologies, reflecting distinctive assumptions and involving different political prescriptions. Most British political controversy, and much in the western world more generally, has long seemed to focus on the arguments between and within the mainstream ideologies of liberalism, conservatism and socialism (see Chapter 6).

Typically, a political ideology provides a description and interpretation of contemporary society, explaining why and how it has come to be as it is, and how far it might be changed. Thus conservatism involves suspicion of change which may reflect broad satisfaction with the current social, economic and political system, or pessimism over the chances of securing any improvement. Socialism, by contrast, combines radical criticism of the existing social and political order with the hope and expectation that a fairer and better alternative is possible. However, some of the deepest ideological divisions are over strategy, the means to achieve desired ends. Thus socialists differ more over the means to achieve socialism than ends, greens are split between fundamentalists and realists over how far they are prepared to compromise their ideas, while even conservatives can disagree over the best way of preserving social and political stability.

> **Definition**
>
> A **political ideology** involves any connected set of political beliefs with implications for political behaviour (McLellan, 1995, Leach 2002). This is the neutral understanding of the term as it is most commonly used today. On this definition, conservatism, liberalism, socialism, fascism, nationalism and feminism are all ideologies. However, the term 'ideology' has often been used – and is still sometimes employed – in a pejorative (hostile or negative) sense, and equated with rigid adherence to political dogma, which critics have sometimes associated with Marxism. Marxists, by contrast, have interpreted ideology as the rationalisation of material interests, particularly the interests of the ruling class.

Ideologies are neither uniform nor static. While they transcend national boundaries, the particular form they take is influenced strongly by the historical context and the prevailing culture of a country. Thus the British interpretation of liberalism, conservatism and socialism is distinctive, reflecting British political circumstances. Ideologies also adapt to changing conditions, frequently reinterpreting old values and principles. All mainstream British ideologies have evolved and changed over time, although this has often involved bitter debate between modernisers and their opponents over the real meanings of conservatism, liberalism and socialism.

British politics?

This is a book that focuses primarily on British politics, although it is not wholly confined to Britain. Wherever relevant, comparisons with other countries are made, particularly with the USA and with some of the leading European states. Many features of British politics are found elsewhere, although some are relatively rare or even unique. Both the similarities and the differences with other states can be instructive. It is, for example, virtually impossible to discuss the system of voting in Britain, its advantages and disadvantages, and proposals for reform, without some reference to voting systems in other countries (see Chapter 5).

Nor does a focus on Britain preclude some discussion of politics both above and below the level of the British state. While many of the crucial decisions that affect British citizens are still resolved within Britain's central government around Whitehall and Westminster, others are taken elsewhere. Some decisions are made above the level of the British state – for example, by the United Nations, the International Monetary Fund, the World Trade Organisation, the North Atlantic Treaty Organisation or (especially) the European Union. Other decisions are taken below the level of the central United Kingdom government based

Box 1.5

Left and right

The labels 'left' and 'right' are still widely used to classify ideologies and political parties, and to describe the position of individual thinkers and politicians. The terms derive from the seating positions in the National Assembly following the 1789 French revolution, when the most revolutionary members sat on the left and the more conservative members on the right. Today on the conventional left–right political spectrum communists are placed on the far left, socialists on the left, conservatives on the right and fascists on the far right. Liberals (including the British Liberal Democrats) might be located somewhere in the centre, although the term 'liberal' today covers a wide range.

Other ideologies are more difficult to place. Nationalism is today more commonly associated with the right, although in different times and places it has been linked with ideas and parties from across the ideological spectrum. Many members of Plaid Cymru (the Welsh nationalist party) and the Scottish National Party would place themselves on the left. greens are generally linked with the left, although greens themselves often claim to be off the scale – 'not left, not right but forward'.

Indeed, if degrees of 'left' and 'right' can be marked on a scale it is by no means clear what that scale is measuring. Attitudes to change? Attitudes to authority? Attitudes to capitalism and the free market? None of these seems to fit closely the way in which the terms 'left' and 'right' are actually used (see Leach 2002: 11–13). Consequently, some argue the terms are confusing and should be abandoned (Brittan 1968). Others have suggested a more complex two-dimensional system of classifying political ideas, with attitudes to authority on the vertical axis and attitudes to change on the horizontal axis (Eysenck 1957, www.political compass.org). Whatever the merits of such more complex systems of classification of political attitudes, it is unlikely that they will ever displace the more familiar language of left and right.

Left–right conventional scale

far left	left	centre	right	far right
communists	socialists	liberals	conservatives	fascists

in Whitehall and Westminster, by devolved parliaments and assemblies (see Chapter 16) or local councils (see Chapter 17).

Needless to say, the level at which decisions should be taken is often an acutely controversial political question. Some would like to devolve or decentralise power as far down as possible to local councils or communities, to give people more say in those decisions that affect them. Others would stress the need for more cooperation between nations to resolve essentially global problems – peace and security, world poverty, population growth and resources, the future of the planet – which implies the need for decisions and compromises above state level. This raises some questions about the whole future of independent sovereign nation states in an apparently increasingly interdependent globalised world. Perhaps formerly powerful and independent states like Britain are inevitably losing real power and influence in a new global or European politics.

The European Union (EU) raises some particularly important questions about levels of decision making and indeed the whole future of British politics. Britain's membership of what is now the

Definitions

An **independent sovereign state** is a state which has a monopoly of supreme (or sovereign) power within its borders, not subject to interference in its internal affairs by any outside power.

Globalisation is a term that emphasises the increasing interdependence of people, organisations and states in the modern world and the growing influence of global economic, cultural and political forces or trends. It implies limits to state sovereignty.

EU has been acutely controversial since the British government first applied to join in 1961, and more particularly from 1973, when the Heath government signed the treaty of accession (Young 1998). Some see the EU as providing Britain with an opportunity to exert more political and economic influence, in cooperation with other member states, over decisions that affect all Britons. Others fear the absorption of Britain into a European super-state, which they see as a threat to British independence and identity. Whatever view is taken, it is clear that the institutions and processes of the EU are now an important element of the politics that affect us all. Indeed. the impact of Europe on British government and politics will be a running thread throughout this book (but see especially Chapter 15).

Yet the future of British politics is not just affected by the threat (real or exaggerated) of a European superstate. The very term 'Britain' and the notion of 'British politics' is itself increasingly contested (Davies 2000: 853–86). The official title of the state (since 1922) is 'the United Kingdom of Great Britain and Northern Ireland'. It is often described more simply as 'the United Kingdom' or by the acronym 'UK'. 'Britain' or 'Great Britain' is simply the largest of those islands, still often referred to as 'the British Isles', although the second largest of this group of islands, Ireland, is politically divided. Most of Ireland constitutes the Irish Republic, an independent sovereign state that is a member of the United Nations and the European Union. Northern Ireland remains part of the United Kingdom, although its inhabitants remain fiercely divided in their political allegiance. The majority insist they are 'British', rather more passionately than most people who live across the Irish sea in 'Great Britain'. A large minority consider themselves Irish rather than British, and wish to belong to the Irish Republic rather than remain within the UK or British state. The political future of Northern Ireland remains acutely controversial.

Even without the long-running problem of Northern Ireland, the future of Britain and the British state is an open question. England is the largest of the constituent parts of Britain in territory and by far the largest in population. Many of those who live in England describe themselves almost interchangeably as 'English' or 'British', a confusion which can infuriate those who live in Scotland or Wales. Wales was absorbed by the English crown in the Middle Ages and was formally politically united with England in 1536. Scotland was an independent state until James VI of Scotland also became James I of England in 1603, although this union of the crowns did not involve full political union until 1707. The notion of a British state and the image of 'Britannia' effectively date from then. Some inhabitants of Scotland and Wales consider themselves to be both Scots or Welsh and British. Others consider themselves primarily or exclusively Scots or Welsh, and a significant minority would prefer to be part of an independent Scotland or Wales (see Chapters 3 and 16). Indeed, some have forecast the imminent 'break-up of Britain' (Nairn 1981, 2000). This could happen. If the majority of those in Scotland and/or Wales clearly wished to be part of a separate state it would be impossible to maintain the union. 'Britain' would no longer exist as a meaningful political entity (although it would probably survive as a useful geographical term to describe the island). 'British politics' would be confined to the history books, to be replaced by the study of English (or Scottish or Welsh) politics (see Chapter 16).

■ Multi-level governance

However, the break-up of Britain has yet to take place and may never happen. For the present, and for the immediate future, the British state survives, although it has become more complicated. Scotland and Wales remain in a political union with England, although since 1999 Scotland has had its own Parliament and Executive, and Wales an Assembly and Executive. This involves what is described as a 'devolution' of power, rather than the total separation sought by nationalists or a fully federal system of government (as exists in the USA or Germany). Some people in England would like to see an English Parliament or the delegation of some functions to elected regional assemblies (although voters in the north-east voted overwhelmingly against this in 2004). This trend to devolve power away from central government to the regions is a feature of several other European states (Keating 1998).

Whatever the future of devolved government, there has long been some form of local government in Britain. A complex system of elected local authorities in England, Wales and Scotland employs large numbers of people, spends considerable amounts of public money and presides over important public services. However, it is widely alleged that local government has less discretion and effective control of services than it used to (Wilson and Game 2002). Local councils are now increasingly expected to enable others to provide services that they previously provided themselves. Thus alongside elected local authorities there is a bewildering range of more specialist appointed public agencies, publicly funded partnerships and voluntary organisations. Yet this new and more complicated world of 'local governance' still has massive implications for the quality of people's lives (see Chapter 17, and also Leach and Percy-Smith 2001).

Thus government and politics operate at a number of levels, both above and below the more familiar world of Whitehall and Westminster (see Chapter 18). These levels are far from self-contained, as is evident from any major policy area. For example, there is a significant local, regional, devolved national, UK and European input into British transport policy, as well as cross-cutting inputs from specialist government agencies, business interests, political parties, pressure groups and advisers. Here we are concerned with the whole political process that affects public policy and the delivery of public services in Britain. The UK government remains particularly crucial in determining policy and allocating resources for most functions and services. Thus it is inevitably still Whitehall and Westminster, rather than Brussels or Edinburgh or Cardiff or the local town hall, which remains the principal focus of a book on British politics. Yet British politics involves them all and more besides.

■ Policies – who gets what, when, how?

Older books on politics concentrated on political institutions and processes, but often neglected the decisions, policies and services that are the product of the political process. This is like watching a game but ignoring the result. Who wins and who loses is crucial, in politics even more than in sport. So a study of politics must include not just the policy-making process, but the outputs and outcomes of that process.

'It's the economy, stupid!' was the catch phrase of former US President Bill Clinton's Democrats, suggesting that politicians and governments are judged by how they run the economy. Of course it is possible that some of the most important economic developments are outside politicians' control, the consequence of national or global trends which may not be fully understood. Governments claim credit for the good times or pay the price for failure, when they may sometimes have little to do with either. Yet governments by their actions or inactions can help or hinder national prosperity (see Chapter 20).

Public services such as health and education are now at the centre of political debate in Britain. Upon the quality of these services depends an important element of the quality of life of individuals and communities. Poor education in schools, colleges and universities ultimately affects everyone, not just the unfortunate recipients. Thus it has long been recognised that such services cannot be left to the free market. Yet how far the state should intervene, the level of service, and the method of control, delivery and finance of services remain acutely controversial (see Chapter 21).

Can governments eradicate poverty? If the rich are getting richer, is that necessarily a bad thing? How far is it the role of government to promote equality and social justice? Such questions are at the centre of debate between socialists, liberals and conservatives, and the answers depend inevitably on ideological assumptions as well as economic analysis. Yet the relative poverty of some can affect people generally, obviously from the payment of taxes to fund social security benefits, less directly from the possible knock-on effects on national economic prosperity, health, education and crime. Child poverty, the problems of low income and one-parent families, run-down housing estates and deprived urban areas are problems which successive British governments have tried to tackle in different ways. The proposed remedies often reflect different perspectives on the nature of the problem (see Chapter 22).

Whole categories of people may be more systematically excluded from power and a share of general prosperity as a result of blatant or more subtle forms of discrimination, injustice and prejudice. British women were long excluded from the most basic civil and political rights, and from the opportunity to enter the main professions or compete on equal (or sometimes any) terms with men. Although women now enjoy formal political equality, they remain under-represented in parliament and government, and despite equal pay and anti-discrimination legislation, women generally still earn less than men, and find it difficult to rise to the highest positions. They continue to shoulder a disproportionate share of domestic and child care duties. Some suffer physical violence, or constraints on their lives arising from the fear of violence. Feminists argue that women remain grossly unequal in a male-dominated society (see Chapter 23).

The rising number of black and Asian Britons often suffer more blatant forms of discrimination and prejudice (see Chapter 24). Most of the ethnic minorities have lower levels of pay and higher levels of unemployment than the majority white community. Although they are far more liable to be stopped by the police, they are more likely to be victims of many forms of crime than whites. They remain grossly under-represented in politics, and in higher professional and managerial jobs. As a consequence, some feel excluded from British society and have problems with their political identity. In some urban areas this has resulted in tension, a breakdown in community relations, and sometimes violence. It remains a serious and potentially explosive political problem Ethnic divisions are often further complicated by religious differences. The attack on the twin towers in New York on 11 September 2001 and more recently the London bombings of 7 July 2005, exacerbated what has come to be called Islamophobia.

11 September 2001 provides a sharp reminder, if a reminder is needed, that politics transcends national boundaries. Any country may be profoundly affected by remote events and crises in far corners of the world. While the UK has not been involved in a major war since 1945, British troops have been engaged in active combat in Korea, the South Atlantic, the Persian Gulf, Kosovo, Afghanistan and most recently Iraq. British foreign policy has been guided by three main associations and interests; the 'special relationship' with the USA, the continuing (though declining) association with the Commonwealth, and the steadily increasing importance of the EU. Balancing the cross-Atlantic ties with the USA and the cross-channel ties with nearer neighbours in an expanding EU is likely to remain a dilemma for future British foreign policy. Yet a more fundamental problem for Britain and other advanced capitalist countries is the gross and intensifying differences in living standards across the world. It is global inequality rather than inequality within Britain that could now threaten a political explosion (see Chapter 26).

It is no longer only the threat of violent conflict between the 'haves' and the 'have nots' which now endangers the future of the planet. The relationship of humankind with its environment has only been widely recognised as a serious issue in relatively recent times, but for some this has become the supreme political problem facing this country and the world generally. Finite resources are being used up, and various forms of environmental pollution threaten irreversible changes to soil and climate. At best, future generations may suffer a heavy burden from our extravagance. At worst, 'spaceship earth' could be heading for catastrophe. The politics of the environment has added a new dimension to ethical and political debate (see Chapter 25).

All this is politics. All these issues are on the agenda of British politics, whether the problems originate in Britain or elsewhere. They are all addressed further in the last part of this book. The issues are far from trivial. Indeed they may appear so frighteningly large and intractable that some may prefer to cut themselves off from politics and concentrate on their immediate lives and concerns. Yet ultimately we cannot exclude politics, unless we deny our common humanity, for we are political animals, as the philosopher Aristotle maintained. There is no subject more difficult, more important and ultimately more fascinating.

■ Summary

- Politics involves far more than government and party politics. It is about power and decision making which affect all our lives, and it determines how scarce resources are allocated – 'who gets what, when, how'.
- There are disagreements over the legitimate scope of politics. Some distinguish between a public or political sphere, and a private

sphere, between the state and 'civil society'. Others would deny that politics can or should be excluded from many areas previously considered private.

- Although politics is clearly about power, this is difficult to define and measure. A distinction can be drawn between power and authority (or legitimate power). Those without formal power may still have influence over decisions that affect them.
- Britain is called a representative democracy, implying that the people or the majority have effective influence over government and over decisions that affect them. Britain satisfies most of the conditions commonly laid down for representative democracy.
- Yet there is disagreement over the distribution of power in Britain. Some argue that it is effectively concentrated in the hands of the few, others that it is widely dispersed. Theories or 'models' of power reflect conflicting underlying assumptions and look at different kinds of evidence.
- Although politics is about the conflicting interests of different social or ethnic groups, it is also about ideas. Political differences commonly reflect contrasting underlying ideological assumptions.
- While a focus on British politics may appear narrow, as many crucial political decisions are made both above and below the level of the British state, which is itself undergoing substantial change, British central government still dominates most policies and services affecting people living in Britain. British politics must, however, be examined within the wider context of multi-level governance.
- The study of politics should focus not just on political institutions and processes but on policy issues and outcomes – 'who gets what, when, how'.

Questions for discussion

- What is politics? Why do many people seem to show a distaste for politics?
- Is it possible, or desirable, to take such issues as education, health, defence or law and order out of politics?
- Should we distinguish between a political (or public) sphere and a private sphere from which politics should be excluded?
- What do you understand by democracy? Is Britain a democracy?
- Who governs Britain? Where does power lie in Britain? Is power highly concentrated or relatively widely dispersed?
- What do you understand by the terms 'left' and 'right'? How far are these terms still relevant to the analysis of contemporary British politics?
- Does it still make sense to study British politics, when the British state is apparently in process of being eroded from both above and below?

Further reading

There are few good accessible general introductions to the study of politics that can be recommended. The first chapter of Andrew Heywood's *Politics* (2002) is a good starting point: it has a particularly useful brief discussion of power. Bernard Crick's *In Defence of Politics* (1964, fourth edition 1993) is thought-provoking, if a little idiosyncratic. The French political scientist Maurice Duverger's *The Study of Politics* (1972) is still worth reading.

Anthony Arblaster (1987) provides a readable short introduction to *Democracy*. C. B. Macpherson's almost as brief *The Life and Times of Liberal Democracy* (1977) might also be consulted. Fuller and more ambitious is David Held (1996), *Models of Democracy*.

The distribution of power in Britain is inevitably a controversial subject. One readable personal view is provided by the journalist Anthony Sampson in *Who Runs This Place?* (2005), the last version of a series of studies of the 'Anatomy of Britain' which he began in 1962.

The rest of this book explores some of the themes discussed briefly in this chapter, and reading on each topic is recommended at the end of each chapter.

The Shadow of the Past: British Politics since 1945

Contents

All countries live in the shadow of their own past, and Britain is no exception. Much of British politics can only be understood in the light of history, distant episodes beyond living memory, and more recent developments which generations still alive today experienced, and which helped to shaped their own political ideas. Thus in early 21st-century Britain there remain millions who lived through the Second World War – some who fought in it, many more who experienced the bombing and the wartime shortages and privations of the civilian population. Others grew up in the post-war years, when the welfare state was established. Then Britain still appeared to rule an extensive empire abroad. Those growing up subsequently experienced the rapid, sometimes painful, disengagement from empire and partial engagement with Europe, as well as the sexual revolution of the 1960s, and the economic and industrial problems of the 1970s. A later generation, sometimes dubbed 'Thatcher's children', reached maturity in the long period of Conservative rule from 1979 to 1997.

Young adults in Britain today, voting for the first time, have grown up under New Labour, with no personal memory of the government of Margaret Thatcher and only a shadowy recollection of her successor, John Major. They may, however, pick up impressions of periods they have not lived through, from family, school and the media: the 'spirit of the blitz', wartime and post-war rationing and controls, the Irish troubles, the miners' strike. Political leaders may seek to keep alive partisan interpretations of their own past triumphs, such as the Falklands taskforce (1982) or, more commonly, their opponents' disasters – the 'three day week' (1974), the 'winter of discontent' (1979) and 'Black Wednesday' (1992).

As these examples may suggest, some perceptions of the past (for example, the Dunkirk spirit) involve a widely shared vision, part of 'being British' while others (such as the miners' strike) may be far more divisive (see below for further details). This is particularly obvious in Northern Ireland, where the Unionist and nationalist communities have their own highly distinctive interpretation of historical events. Battles and personalities of 300 years or more ago remain sources of bitter political division, celebrated or denigrated in contemporary street theatre, murals and graffiti. Yet elsewhere in Britain perceptions of past events may also be strongly coloured by distinctive class, religious or ethnic backgrounds.

If the past shapes everyone's political attitudes and behaviour, it also strongly influences ministers, civil servants and others actively involved in making policy and taking critical political decisions. British economic and social policies in the post-war period were strongly shaped by experience of

Box 2.1

Comparative politics: continuity and change in Britain and other countries

British politics appears a model of stability and continuity when compared with the politics of many other states. France, for example, has experienced a succession of revolutions and regime changes, including several forms of monarchy, two periods of empire and five republics. Italy and Germany, which only became nation states in the late 19th century, went through similar upheavals, culminating in fascist and Nazi dictatorships, before the restoration of parliamentary democracy following the military defeat of those regimes in 1945. Spain, Portugal and Greece have only more recently reestablished democracy after periods of dictatorship. Eastern European countries only escaped from Communist dictatorship with the fall of the Berlin Wall in 1989. Most states now represented at the United Nations did not even exist in 1945; many were former colonies that have since gained their independence, while others (such as Bangladesh, Slovakia and Slovenia) have emerged from the partition of larger states.

Britain experienced religious upheavals in the 16th century and violent civil war and political revolutions in the 17th century, but from then onwards its politics has evolved largely peacefully with no revolutions or dramatic regime changes. British political history over the last three centuries is often presented as an unbroken succession of administrations headed by a prime minister and cabinet, backed by (normally) a parliamentary majority. The bullet has not generally been a feature of the politics of mainland Britain (although Ireland is another matter). Violence has rarely erupted (at least until the London bombings of 7 July 2005). Revolution has sometimes been feared or threatened, but most crises have been resolved without bloodshed. Even so, the appearance of stability and continuity is in some respects illusory. Britain retains a monarchy, a Cabinet, two Houses of Parliament, and (more questionably) a two-party system, but none of these operate in remotely the same way as they did in the 18th or 19th centuries. Under the surface power has shifted, and the substance of British politics has profoundly changed. In many ways Britain is not the same country it was 100, 50 or even 25 years ago.

the inter-war years, particularly mass unemployment. British post-war foreign policy was conditioned by the 'appeasement' of dictators, which failed to avert the Second World War. The economic policies of the Thatcher government were shaped by the perceived economic problems of the previous decades. Each new political crisis evokes parallels with the past. The Blair government's handling of the 2001 foot-and-mouth disease outbreak was partly conditioned by, and inevitably compared with, the handling of the last major outbreak in the 1960s. Sometimes, of course, the 'lessons of the past' may mislead. Circumstances change. Politicians, like generals, may be trying to 'fight the last war' rather than confront altered conditions. Yet as the philosopher George Santayana (1863–1952) once observed, 'Those who cannot remember the past are condemned to repeat it'.

Britain after the Second World War – the end of empire and the Cold War

Britain emerged from the Second World War as a victor, escaping the defeat and occupation that was the fate of much of continental Europe. Britain still appeared a great power, one of the 'big three' (along with the USA and USSR) determining the shape of the post-war world. Yet Britain's great power status was largely illusory. The British economy, already for half a century or more in relative decline, was further damaged by the war, and British manufacturing industry was ill-equipped to compete effectively with the USA, and subsequently with the fast-recovering economies of western Europe and Japan. The British Empire, still extensive in the maps hung on classroom walls, was to be substantially liquidated within 20 years, although it continued to influence political attitudes, and was a factor in Britain's failure to engage more positively with continental Europe.

The conversion of the former British Empire into a Commonwealth of independent states proceeded rapidly. The white-settler-dominated former colonies of Canada, Australia, New Zealand and South Africa had long gained 'dominion' status and effective independence.

Table 2.1 British Prime Ministers from Attlee to Blair

1 Clement Attlee	1945–51
2 Sir Winston Churchill	1951–5
3 Sir Anthony Eden	1955–7
4 Harold Macmillan	1957–63
5 Sir Alec Douglas-Home	1963–4
6 Harold Wilson	1964–70, 1974–6
7 Edward Heath	1970–4
8 James Callaghan	1976–9
9 Margaret Thatcher	1979–90
10 John Major	1990–7
11 Tony Blair	1997–

Although they actively supported Britain in two world wars, they otherwise looked after their own economic and political interests, effectively resisting pressure from Conservative-led British governments to pursue 'imperial preference' in trade. India and Pakistan became independent in 1947 and Burma and Ceylon (now Sri Lanka) followed in 1948. Elsewhere British governments tried for a time to preserve colonial rule, sometimes in the face of nationalist revolts (as in Kenya and Cyprus), but ultimately lacked the will and the means to resist the anti-colonial tide. Most of the rest of the British Empire was rapidly liquidated, with the granting of independence to most former colonies in Asia and Africa in the 1960s, leaving a few remaining trouble spots. These included Rhodesia (where a white-settler minority government made a unilateral declaration of independence in 1965, a rebellion not ended until 1980, when a new black majority state of Zimbabwe finally emerged), and some anomalous survivals (such as the Falklands, Gibraltar and, until 1997, Hong Kong).

Loss of empire was regretted by many, particularly on the right of the Conservative Party, although it was celebrated by some Britons, active in organisations such as the Movement for Colonial Freedom. However, transition from Empire to Commonwealth, while it involved some violence and bloodshed, was largely achieved peacefully, without the traumatic consequences for domestic politics that were seen in France's painful disengagement from Indo-China and Algeria. Even so, there was a painful process of adjustment. As an US Secretary of State, Dean Rusk, famously observed, 'Great Britain has lost an empire and not yet found a role'.

Britain's post-war foreign policy was largely shaped by the emerging reality of the 'Cold War' between the two superpowers of the USA and the USSR. Although both had been wartime allies, there was never any doubt that Britain would side with the USA, becoming one of the founding members of the North Atlantic Treaty Organisation (NATO) which was established in 1949, and the USA's most reliable ally. However, the special relationship with the USA was always an unequal one, with Britain very much a junior partner. Although Britain became a nuclear power, its 'independent nuclear deterrent' became in practice increasingly dependent on US rockets and submarines. The one occasion when a British government engaged in a foreign policy adventure opposed by the USA, the Anglo-French attack on the Suez Canal in 1956, it was forced into a humiliating climb-down, which entailed the resignation of Eden, the prime minister responsible.

The illusion of world power status, the 'special relationship' with the USA, and the continuing

Box 2.2

The end of empire

Dates when some former British colonies became independent

1947	India, Pakistan
1948	Burma (Myanmar), Sri Lanka
1957	Malaysia
1960	Cyprus, Nigeria, Ghana, Lesotho
1961	Sierra Leone, Tanzania
1962	Jamaica, Uganda
1963	Kenya
1964	Malta, Malawi, Zambia
1965	Singapore, Gambia
1966	Guyana, Barbados
1967	Aden and Yemen
1970	Fiji
1971	Gulf states
1980	Zimbabwe*
1997	Hong Kong

* Date when independence was recognised. The white settler government of Ian Smith had earlier made a unilateral declaration of independence in 1965.

Definition

The term **Cold War** describes the long conflict from the end of the Second World War to the fall of the Berlin Wall between the Union of Soviet Socialist Republics (USSR) and its allies on the one hand, and the United States of America (USA) and its allies on the other. It was a 'cold' war because it never involved direct armed conflict between the two major powers, despite periodic crises when the Cold War threatened to become a hot war. Some argue this was only prevented by the fear of 'mutually assured destruction' (MAD) in such a war between the two major nuclear powers.

concern with the empire and commonwealth effectively deterred British governments from closer engagement with continental Europe. Although Winston Churchill took a benevolent interest in closer European cooperation, British governments, both Labour and Conservative, were not interested in joining the European Coal and Steel Community, set up by the 1951 Treaty of Paris, nor the European Economic Community, established by the 1957 Treaty of Rome. Britain thus missed the opportunity to help shape the new Europe. Significantly it was only after the Conservative Prime Minister Harold Macmillan acknowledged the end of empire in his celebrated 'wind of change' speech in 1960 that he launched the first attempt by a British government to join the European Economic Community the following year (see Chapter 15).

Post-war Britain: the welfare state and the mixed economy

The end of war and Labour's unexpected landslide election victory in 1945 seemed to mark a decisive break with the politics of the past. Attlee's government promised a new dawn, particularly for the less affluent majority. Yet the new government both built on and was constrained by the legacy of the past. All parties were determined to turn their backs on the policies of the inter-war years, which had failed to deal with unemployment at home or the rise of the fascist dictators abroad. It was no accident that it was first Labour and then former Conservative rebels such as Churchill, Eden and Macmillan who dominated the politics of the early post-war years. At the same time many of the policies pursued had their roots in the past, in the experience of war and the wartime coalition government. There was indeed a substantial consensus (or agreement) between the major parties on economic and social policies in the post-war period.

The post-war consensus in Britain was based on widespread acceptance of the economic ideas of the economist John Maynard Keynes and the social reformer William Beveridge (both of them incidentally liberals, with a large and small 'l'). Hence it is sometime described as the 'Keynes-Beveridge consensus'. Key elements of agreement included the system of government, the welfare state, the mixed economy, Keynesian full employment policy, and in most respects foreign and defence policy. However, the extent and even the reality of the post-war consensus has been questioned (see Chapter 6).

Definition

Consensus means agreement. The term 'consensus politics' implies a fundamental agreement among the governing elite, the major parties and (more questionably) the wider public over assumptions, ideas and policies.

Box 2.3

William Beveridge

William Beveridge (1879–1963) after an early brilliant academic career devoted himself to social reform. As a young civil servant he helped the then Liberal president of the Board of Trade, Winston Churchill, to establish labour exchanges. After the First World War he moved back into academic life, becoming director of the London School of Economics, and subsequently master of University College, Oxford, but continuing to serve on a number of public committees. Recalled to the civil service in the Second World War, he chaired the Committee on Social Insurance and Allied Service, which reported in 1942. It was this Beveridge Report, proposing a system of national insurance 'from the cradle to the grave' which made him a household name. Churchill's wartime government was initially reluctant to endorse such radical reform, but was effectively bounced into its acceptance by public enthusiasm. Beveridge became briefly a Liberal MP from 1944–5 and subsequently a Liberal peer until his death in 1963. His name is closely associated with that of Keynes, as the cost of Beveridge's scheme for national insurance could only be kept within reasonable bounds by the pursuit of Keynesian full employment economic policies.

Box 2.4

The welfare state: key developments

1942	Report on Social Insurance and Allied Services (the Beveridge Report)
1944	Education Act
1944	White Paper on Employment Policy (high and stable level of employment)
1945	Family Allowances Act
1946	National Insurance Act (implemented Beveridge Report)
1948	Inauguration of National Health Service

The welfare state was effectively established by the post-war Labour government, which substantially implemented the 1942 Beveridge Report, providing social security 'from the cradle to the grave' (Dutton 1997: 17–20), paid for by national insurance contributions, and created the new National Health Service (NHS) providing universal free health care paid for largely by national taxation. Labour also expanded education, social services, housing and planning. Later Conservative governments embraced the welfare state, including the NHS, which they had earlier opposed. Indeed, by the 1950s the welfare state was almost universally approved (Coxall and Robins 1998, ch. 10).

Ironically it was Attlee's Labour government which was responsible for the first significant exception to free health care. Charges for teeth and spectacles were introduced by the Chancellor of the Exchequer, Hugh Gaitskell, to help pay for the Korean War in 1951. This provoked the resignation of the left-wing socialist Aneurin Bevan, the architect of the NHS, together with Harold Wilson, a future Labour leader, and initiated the split between Bevanites and Gaitskellites which continued to affect the party long after its leading figures died (Bevan in 1960, Gaitskell in 1963). The new health service charges foreshadowed later concerns over the escalating cost of the NHS in particular and the welfare state in general, and the implications for the burden of taxation. The post-war decades involved a growth in both state spending and taxation that was unprecedented in peacetime.

Labour's policy of nationalisation involved a more contentious extension of state intervention. Attlee's Labour government brought into public ownership the Bank of England (1946), coal (1947), electricity, gas, and rail (all 1948), and finally steel and road haulage (1949), thus establishing a mixed economy with a substantial state sector. Yet this fell well short of the wholesale introduction of 'common ownership of the means of production, distribution and exchange' to which Labour was apparently committed in Clause IV of its own constitution. Moreover, of these measures only steel and road haulage were acutely controversial. The other industries that were nationalised were either already substantially municipally owned (electricity, gas) or declining (railways, coal). The Conservatives on coming to power in 1951 partially denationalised steel and road haulage, but otherwise maintained the mixed economy with a substantial state sector.

Labour's general management of the economy involved the continuation of some wartime rationing in the face of post-war shortages, but beyond that Labour did not attempt detailed controls of production and labour. While there were those in the Labour Party who favoured a more interventionist form of socialist planning, Attlee's government adopted Keynesian economic management, and this was maintained by its Conservative successors. Indeed, there appeared so little difference between the economic policies pursued by the Labour Chancellor Hugh Gaitskell, and the Conservative Chancellor R A Butler, that the *Economist* in 1954 coined the term 'Butskellism' to describe their approach (Dutton 1997: 57). Commonly, this involved increasing demand in the economy whenever unemployment appeared to be rising above politically acceptable levels by reducing taxation and/or increasing government spending (if necessary running a budget deficit). However, these policies apparently succeeded in maintaining close to full employment, in marked contrast to the inter-war period (Coxall and Robins 1998, ch. 9).

Box 2.5

John Maynard Keynes

John Maynard Keynes (1883–1946) had been a brilliant critic of interwar government policy, notably in his damning indictment of the post First World War peace settlement, *The Economic Consequences of the Peace*, and his attack on Chancellor Winston Churchill's return to the gold standard in 1925. His great contribution to economics came in 1936 with the publication of *The General Theory of Employment, Interest and Money*. Keynes believed in government management of the economy to achieve desirable economic objectives, including full employment, stable prices, steady economic growth and a healthy balance of payments. This was to be done by influencing total (or aggregate) demand for goods and services, through fiscal and monetary policy, without requiring direct intervention or controls on particular firms or industries. This 'managed capitalism' was attractive to radical politicians across the political spectrum: to the Liberal Lloyd George, to Conservatives such as Macmillan and Butler, and to Labour modernisers such as Hugh Gaitskell and Tony Crosland.

In the Second World War Keynes joined the Treasury, and his economics became the new orthodoxy. After the war both Labour and Conservative governments pursued Keynesian demand management policies to secure full employment. Subsequently, Keynesian policies were blamed by the New Right for increasing government spending and fuelling inflation, although Keynes himself died in 1946, and can hardly be blamed for the (mis?)interpretation of his theory by politicians, who tended to manipulate the economic cycle for political advantages.

The under-performing economy, 'stagflation' and crisis: 1964–79

Despite continuing political stability coupled with the establishment and maintenance of full employment, a mixed economy and the welfare state, all did not seem well with the British economic and political system in the period from 1964–79. Although the Conservative premier Harold Macmillan (1957–63) boasted 'You've never had it so good', Britain's economic growth, admittedly higher than in the past, was only modest in comparison with that of major competitors in North America, western Europe and Japan. Low growth was blamed on 'stop-go' policies, under which expansion led to inflation and a balance of payments crisis, followed by cuts in public spending, recession and increased unemployment, sparking reflation and a recurrence of excess demand and rising prices (see Figure 2.1). Thus governments seemed incapable of pursuing steady growth. Britain's competitiveness also appeared to be undermined by relatively low labour productivity, exacerbated by strikes and other problems with industrial relations, and outdated management.

Figure 2.1 The 'stop–go' cycle of the political economy

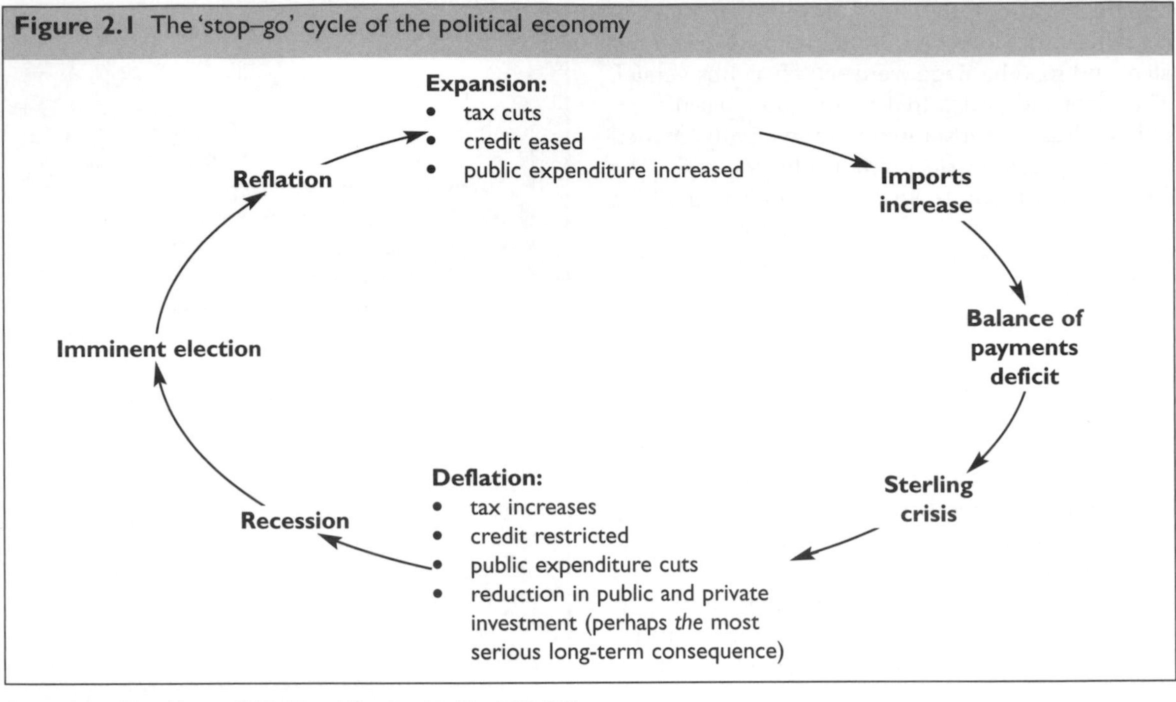

Source: derived from Thomas (1992: 55) and Coxall and Robins (1998: 217).

After 13 years of Conservative rule a new Labour government under Harold Wilson was elected in 1964, pledged to modernise the economy and secure an annual rate of economic growth of 4 per cent to pay for further social reform and increased spending on public services. Yet the government proved unable to produce the required rate of economic growth, while public spending continued to rise, largely because of the escalating cost of the welfare state. Although the government seemed packed with talent, it proved unable to make an impact on Britain's long-standing economic problems. It was handicapped by a deteriorating balance of payments and increasing pressure on the exchange rate of the pound sterling, which eventually forced devaluation in 1967, an event from which Wilson's reputation never quite recovered. Both his government and the following Conservative government under Heath (1970-4) attempted to reform trade unions and industrial relations, but failed. Increasing numbers of days were lost to industrial action, culminating in the miners' strike of 1973–4 which effectively brought down the Heath government.

The Keynes-Beveridge consensus was increasingly challenged. The rising cost of the welfare state and the accompanying burden of taxation were beginning to be questioned by some critics, while others questioned its effectiveness. Problems such as homelessness, failing schools, child poverty and inner city decline showed that the system was not providing effective social security 'from the cradle to the grave'. Moreover Keynesian economic policies no longer seemed to be working as theory suggested they should. Keynesian theory recommended contrasting policy remedies to cope with inflation on the one hand or economic stagnation with rising unemployment on the other. However, by the 1970s governments were confronted with rising prices and rising unemployment: an unlikely combination, according to Keynesian orthodoxy. Journalists coined the term 'stagflation' to describe this apparently new phenomenon.

Politicians from both parties concluded that unreasonable wage increases were pushing up prices. Thus governments from Macmillan to Callaghan tried to restrain inflationary pressures through various forms of incomes policy. This entailed striking deals with the leaders of business and organised labour, leading to a new

Definition

Stagflation was a term coined in the 1970s to describe simultaneous inflation and economic stagnation, a combination previously considered almost impossible from Keynesian assumptions.

policy process involving government, the Confederation of British Industry (CBI) and the Trades Union Congress (TUC), a process described as 'tripartism' or 'corporatism'.

The terms described who was involved but said little about the power relationships between them. While some saw corporatism as a new political system involving partnership with business and labour, others saw it as an essentially top-down process, bypassing Parliament and people. Some socialist critics thought the apparent participation of the unions in policy making was essentially cosmetic, concealing restraints on workers' wages in the interest of business profits. By contrast, critics on the right thought the unions has been given too much power, and that incomes policies were inflationary, interfering with free market forces, and further damaging Britain's competitiveness. In practice, incomes policies helped restrain wage rises in the short term, but were difficult to maintain on a longer-term basis.

The Heath government's attempts to control inflation were not helped by the 1973 energy crisis which involved a quadrupling of oil prices. This underlined the continued importance of Britain's coal industry, and the industrial muscle of the miners, who began a national strike in 1973. Heath responded by imposing a three-day week to save energy costs. The crisis provoked an early election in February 1974 which the government narrowly lost, allowing Wilson to return as the prime minister of a minority Labour government, which acquired a slim majority in a second election the same year.

Definitions

Corporatism in Britain is taken to mean a process of policy making involving government and the major economic interests, capital and labour.

Tripartism is a term with a similar usage to describe decision making by three major partners: the government, the Confederation of British Industry (representing employers) and the Trades Union Congress (representing workers).

Inflation continued to rise steeply to 27 per cent in the first year of the incoming Labour government (Dutton 1997: 102). The government initially sought to maintain its spending plans by borrowing. In 1976, after Callaghan had replaced Wilson as prime minister, mounting debts forced the government to seek a massive loan from the International Monetary Fund (IMF) under conditions which involved major cuts in public spending. Confidence in Keynesian solutions was undermined, as Callaghan mournfully acknowledged to the Labour Party Conference in 1976:

> We used to think that you could just spend your way out of recession and increase employment by cutting taxes and boosting Government spending. I tell you, in all candour, that that option no longer exists, and that in so far as it ever did exist, it only worked ... by injecting a bigger dose of inflation into the economy, followed by a higher level of unemployment as the next step.
>
> (Callaghan 1987: 426)

Savage deflationary policies did eventually enable the Labour government to control spending and reduce inflation but at considerable political cost, alienating voters and many in the unions, and dividing the Labour Party. The last version of incomes policy introduced by the Callaghan government culminated in strikes by key public sector workers, a 'winter of discontent' leading to Labour's defeat at the polls in 1979.

The apparent failure of governments of both parties to solve Britain's economic problems was a factor in the decline of their support. The combined two-party vote which had reached 97 per cent in 1951 fell to 75 per cent in two elections in 1974. An immediate beneficiary of this loss of confidence in the two major parties was the old Liberal Party, which had been one of two main parties until the First World War but had been reduced to a mere six seats in Parliament in the 1950s. A Liberal revival culminated in the party winning close to a fifth of the votes in 1974, but because of Britain's electoral system, this only secured a doubling of their parliamentary representation. It was a similar story later in 1983, when the Liberals, allied with the new Social Democratic Party formed largely from Labour right-wing dissidents, secured a quarter of the votes but only 23 (or 3.5 per cent) of the seats in Parliament. Even so, the two-party monopoly of British politics had been challenged.

■ From Empire to Europe

Both Conservative and Labour governments had failed to deal with Britain's persistent economic problems. Both came to see entry to the European Economic Community (EEC), or 'Common Market' as it was then widely called, as a possible solution to those problems. The six countries that had formed the EEC in 1957 were all apparently growing much faster than Britain. British membership of the EEC was increasingly seen as a potential answer to slow growth and lack of competitiveness. Macmillan's Conservative government applied to join in 1963, and Wilson's Labour government in 1967, but both attempts were effectively vetoed by the French President, De Gaulle. Heath's government successfully negotiated entry in 1973, after De Gaulle's departure from office, and this was subsequently endorsed by two-thirds of British voters in a referendum in 1975, after some minor renegotiation of the terms of entry by the incoming Labour government.

The time finally seemed ripe for Britain to engage with Europe. Major earlier obstacles to membership, including ties with the British Empire, Commonwealth and wider world, no longer seemed so important. Most former colonies had achieved, or would very soon achieve, full independence. The new Commonwealth states were disinclined to follow Britain's lead. British forces had been withdrawn from east of Suez, in line with a scaling-down of defence commitments, and sterling was no longer an important reserve currency. The leaders of all three parties had supported entry, and those politicians who had opposed it largely accepted that the 1975 referendum had settled the issue for the immediate future.

However, the British commitment to Europe was less than wholehearted. The debate over entry focused almost wholly on the economic costs and benefits of membership rather than the political implications, although these were obvious enough to anyone who had followed the development of European integration. Yet entry into the EEC provided no instant answer to Britain's economic problems. The timing was unfortunate. The UK missed out on the years of growth and rising living standards that the original six member states had experienced, and joined in the year of the energy crisis which precipitated an economic downturn. Moreover, the UK had joined the club too late to affect the development of its rules, which did not suit British needs. Thus Britain's small but comparatively efficient agricultural sector did not benefit much from the cumbersome Common Agricultural Policy, which initially consumed three-quarters of the Community's total budget. This led to early complaints that Britain was paying far more to Europe than it was getting in return, and Mrs Thatcher's demand for a budget rebate, a demand which was ultimately successful, but at some cost to the UK's relationship with its European partners.

Only the then tiny Liberal Party was consistently in favour of membership. Labour was divided. Broadly speaking the social democratic right were in favour, and the more socialist left, who regarded the EEC as a rich man's club, were against (although there were significant exceptions to this generalisation on both wings of the party). Wilson had finally and reluctantly agreed to a referendum on the issue to paper over the cracks in his own party. Under the leadership of Michael Foot, the biographer and keen disciple of Nye Bevan, Labour fought the 1983 election committed to withdrawal from Europe without a referendum. Meanwhile, the end of empire made it easier for many Conservatives to accept European engagement as a practical alternative, but there was a significant minority opposed to the implications for Britain's national sovereignty. This number was to grow from the early 1990s, until the Conservatives became a largely Euro-sceptic party. Ironically over the same period the majority of the Labour Party became more positive, but with a minority still hostile to Europe.

Northern Ireland, Scotland and Wales

To many observers in the 1970s the main threat to the integrity and sovereignty of the United Kingdom came not from Europe but within, from the resurgence of nationalist feeling and agitation in Northern Ireland, Scotland and Wales, aimed at breaking away from Britain. This support for separatist nationalism may in part also be linked with the relative political and economic decline of Britain, now neither a world power, nor the centre of an extensive overseas empire. Some Scots and Welsh felt they were no longer partners in a great imperial enterprise, but neglected second-class citizens of a shrunken British state. Economic problems hit the more peripheral areas of the British state particularly hard – Northern Ireland shipbuilding, the coal and steel industries of south Wales, and the industrial belt of central Scotland. Those nationalists who had always questioned union with England now had additional economic arguments to support their case.

Northern Ireland posed the first and most immediate threat to the British state. From the late 1960s onwards, for the first time since the Irish Treaty had partitioned Ireland in 1922, the Union of the United Kingdom of Great Britain and Northern Ireland seemed under threat. The majority of the province of Northern Ireland were Protestants, who maintained a fierce allegiance to the British crown, while the loyalty of most of the substantial Catholic minority was to Irish nationalism, and the unification of the six counties with the Irish Republic. Even so, despite periodic disturbances the province had been fairly quiet since the war. It had retained its own devolved government and parliament (based at Stormont), but also sent 12 MPs to Westminster. The Ulster Unionist Party, then affiliated to the Conservatives, dominated both the Stormont Parliament and the Northern Ireland representation at Westminster. The nationalist party Sinn Fein won some seats in predominantly Catholic areas, but declined to take them up, as it did not recognise British rule. Unionist (and Protestant) domination of the province seemed complete, while Catholics were a disadvantaged minority.

From the mid-1960s Catholics dissatisfied by their second-class status demanded civil and political rights, leading to political disturbances. The moderate Ulster Unionist Prime Minister Terence O'Neill announced reforms, which upset many Protestants without winning support from Catholics. The two communities became increasingly polarised. Sectarian riots led to the fall of O'Neill and the rise of a new hard-line Protestant unionism, of which Ian Paisley was to become a key leader. The troops that the British government sent in to restore order in 1969 were at first welcomed by the Catholics, who had suffered attacks by loyalists, but perhaps inevitably these troops soon became targets for nationalists, who saw them as representatives of an alien occupying force. The Provisional Irish Republican Army (IRA) began a violent campaign to secure first the withdrawal of British troops, and ultimately a united Ireland. In 1972 British troops fired on demonstrators, killing 13 civilians. The events of 'Bloody Sunday' led to the resignation of the Unionist government and the imposition of direct rule on Northern Ireland. Violence, involving sectarian murders, revenge attacks and bombings, was to remain a feature of Ulster life for a quarter of a century, and was periodically exported to the mainland. A series of political initiatives failed to end the cycle of violence. Finally, John Major's government secured a temporary IRA ceasefire, and Tony Blair's a more lasting if still uneasy peace.

The Good Friday agreement (1998) provided for a new devolved assembly and government for Northern Ireland involving power sharing between representatives of the two communities. The intransigence of Paisley's Democratic Unionists, coupled with the failure of the IRA to disarm, has led already to four suspensions of the new devolved institutions, although the ceasefire still holds. The Union of Britain and Northern Ireland may last while this is the wish of the majority in the province, but its long-term future seems questionable (see Chapter 16).

The Irish nationalist challenge to the Union was paralleled by a resurgence of Scottish and Welsh nationalism, although these have been almost entirely non-violent. Parliamentary by-election victories for nationalists led to a marked advance for the Scottish National Party and (to a lesser extent) Plaid Cymru in the two General Elections of 1974. Disturbed at the threat to its support in Scotland and Wales, Labour promised a new elected Scottish Parliament and Welsh Assembly, involving some devolution of power rather than the independence pursued by nationalists. This first attempt at devolution foundered with the failure to secure sufficient votes in referendums in 1979, an outcome which precipitated the fall of Callaghan's Labour government. The Conservatives had long been the party of the Union, and the governments of Thatcher and Major made no concessions to nationalism. It was only after Labour's 1997 election victory that new referendums secured a majority for devolution, elections and the emergence of a Labour–Liberal Democrat coalition government in Scotland, and Labour government in Wales. It remains to be seen whether devolution is a long-term solution which preserves the union, or a half-way house on the road to separation. Yet it has already helped to transform the politics of Scotland and Wales. British politics and government have become more multi-layered and complex.

Social change and the politics of protest

Prime Minister Harold Macmillan (1957–63) once famously boasted, 'You've never had it so good'. Despite Britain's relatively low growth and other economic problems (see above), living standards still rose continuously in the post-war decades. Following the end of rationing and wartime shortages there was a greater range of goods on which to spend money, including durable consumer goods such as cars, washing machines and television sets, increasingly within the range of ordinary working people. Some argued that increased prosperity was affecting political allegiances. Workers in the then flourishing car industry acquired middle-class lifestyles, and perhaps attitudes, for the middle-class vote was then overwhelmingly Conservative. A 1959 election slogan capitalised on the sense of well-being: 'Life's better under the Conservatives. Don't let Labour ruin it'. The accompanying pictures showed a happy middle-class family with father, mother and two children, enjoying their new home and car.

Increasing prosperity was accompanied by other social change, less consistent with traditional family values. It was becoming easier for both men and women to choose alternative lifestyles. The 1960s have been associated with increased sexual liberation. Contraceptive pills enabled couples to plan or avoid parenthood. More couples lived openly together without marrying. Illegitimacy lost much of its earlier stigma. Abortion was legalised in 1967. Divorce law was reformed, making divorce easier and cheaper. Homosexual acts, previously punishable by law, were legalised between consenting adults, although it took longer for public attitudes to homosexuality to be affected. Some deplored increased permissiveness and the effects it had on the traditional family, and particularly on children. It is more difficult to generalise about the effect on women. While easier divorce enabled some men to abandon middle-aged wives for younger partners, it also enabled some women to escape from bad marriages. Women's increased earning power gave them more freedom to choose and control their own lives.

The families portrayed in election posters, in commercial advertising, and in the media generally remained overwhelmingly white until the last years of the 20th century. Yet one largely unintended consequence of empire had been substantial immigration into Britain from its former colonies, particularly from the West Indies, the Indian subcontinent and parts of Africa. The growing black and Asian population faced considerable prejudice and discrimination, and in the largely inner urban areas where most of them settled there were ethnic tensions and sometimes serious riots. It was only gradually that sportsmen and women, comedians, professionals and politicians from ethnic minorities have obtained a still sometimes grudging acceptance by the majority, but over a period Britain has clearly become a multi-cultural society, accommodating a range of different religions, languages and lifestyles. Ethnic minorities have undoubtedly brought a new dimension to British politics, yet there is still tension and conflict. The children and grandchildren of immigrants, while often assimilating much of British culture, have been less prepared to accept the casual discrimination and prejudice their elders ignored.

Social change provoked political change. Largely outside the parties, the politics of protest grew in the 1960s and the 1970s. The Campaign for Nuclear Disarmament (CND), in which young people were heavily involved, organised a series of massive marches against the bomb, while they and other groups demonstrated against the US war in Vietnam, as part of a growing peace movement. Others became active participants in the developing green movement. A feature of both the peace movement and the green movement was the strong involvement of women, still marginalised in mainstream politics. The continuing economic, social, legal and political inequality suffered by women inspired a powerful feminist movement, which helped secure significant changes in the law and some real advances in employment opportunities, child care and political representation. In response to the racist agitation stimulated by some far-right groups, and tacitly endorsed by a few mainstream politicians, the Anti-Nazi League and ethnic minority groups sought to counter racial prejudice and discrimination, and champion the rights of minorities. Much of this politics of protest involved a reaction against the political mainstream and the established traditional parties, and cut across old class divisions. The relative homogeneity of British society and culture, proclaimed by some earlier British and foreign observers, seemed to be breaking down.

Conservative dominance: Thatcherism and the free market (1979–97)

However, the impact of the new politics can be exaggerated. In some respects, the Conservative election victory in 1979, which inaugurated 18 years of Conservative rule, can be seen as a reaction against much of the social and political change outlined above. Britain's new prime minister, Margaret Thatcher, spoke the language and reflected the values of the white English middle classes. She was to prove the most controversial figure in British post-war politics. Her legacy is still hotly contested. To her admirers she was a great leader who restored the British economy, confronted and defeated enemies at home, while resolutely defending and advancing Britain's interests abroad. To her critics, including not only Labour and the trade unions but some Conservatives (e.g. Gilmour 1992), her government was harsh and divisive, with disastrous implications for Britain's social harmony, its manufacturing industry and its public services.

There are rarely sharp breaks in history, and the 1979 election was not the only nor perhaps even the principal cause of the changes in the British state, economy and society which took place in the last decades of the 20th century. As noted above, the Labour government had already largely abandoned Keynesianism and introduced public spending cuts. Both the Wilson and Heath governments had attempted to reform industrial relations, anticipating some of the Thatcher curbs on trade unions. To an extent what came to be called Thatcherism was a response to changing economic conditions in Britain and the wider world. Western governments of various political colours pursued similar policies. Yet despite these reservations, it is worth recording the verdict of Nigel Lawson, Thatcher's former chancellor and once close ally, who resigned after quarrelling with his chief over exchange rate policy. She had, he said, 'transformed the politics of Britain – indeed Britain itself – to an extent that no other government has achieved since the Attlee government of 1945–51'.

Thatcher broke decisively from consensus politics. She declared in 1979, 'I am a conviction politician. The Old Testament prophets did not say, Brothers I want a consensus' (quoted in Dutton 1997: 110). She rejected Keynesian economics, not sorrowfully like her Labour predecessor, but because she was a convinced supporter of the free market economics of Hayek, Friedman and ultimately the founder of classical economics, Adam Smith (see the discussion of Thatcherism and the New Right in Chapter 6). Like Friedman she saw control of the money supply as the key to controlling inflation, and early on, the term 'monetarism' was used to describe her philosophy.

In practice the Thatcher government was not particularly effective in controlling the money supply, and the importance of this was subsequently played down, although not before high interest rates had damaged manufacturing industry and substantially increased unemployment. Moreover, although Mrs Thatcher's rhetoric was anti state, anti big government, and anti public spending, her government was not particularly successful in cutting total state spending, partly because the rise in unemployment increased the cost of welfare benefits. Yet her free market views

Definition

Monetarism in the narrow sense involves controlling inflation by controlling the money supply. In a broader sense it involves the rejection of interventionist Keynesian policies and increased government spending which, monetarists argued, fuelled inflation, particularly if spending was financed by budget deficits and borrowing. Monetarism emphasised the need to 'roll back the state' and reduce government spending to promote free enterprise and a healthy economy.

Box 2.6

Some of the principal privatisations involving former public enterprise

Date	Company or undertaking
1981 onwards	British Aerospace
1984 onwards	British Telecom
1986	British Gas
1987	British Airways
1988	British Steel Corporation
1989	Water authorities
1990	Electricity distribution
1991	Electricity generation
1995	British Rail

did inspire the policy with which she became most associated, privatisation.

Privatisation involves the transfer of ownership of assets from the public sector to the private sector. The major nationalised industries – British Telecom, British Gas, British Airways, the British Steel Corporation, the water authorities and the electricity industry – were sold off under the Thatcher government, while British Rail was to follow under her successor, John Major. How far privatisation made economic sense is still debatable – advocates claimed significant gains in economic efficiency, although critics suggested these public assets were undervalued, and thus sold at a loss. However, privatisation was thought to produce some political dividends for the Conservatives, by extending a 'property-owning democracy' as well as promoting 'popular capitalism'. Another massive transfer of property ownership from the public sector into private hands was secured by legislation obliging local authorities to sell council houses at substantial discounts to tenants who wanted to purchase them. In 10 years 1.3 million council houses were sold under the 'Right to Buy'.

While there were some real cuts in public services, the welfare state was not substantially reduced. Margaret Thatcher declared that 'the NHS is safe in our hands', and spending on education per pupil was slightly increased. However, these services were exposed to increased competition, through the introduction of an internal market in the health service, and similar developments in education. Moreover, some 'ancillary' health and local government services were subjected to compulsory competitive tendering (CCT), which involved putting some services, including cleaning, catering, laundry, refuse collection and ground maintenance out to tender to the lowest bidder, which was sometimes a private-sector firm.

The Thatcher government also took on the trade unions. Curbs on trade union powers were initially not unpopular, because of a fairly widely held view that strikes were harming British industry and hurting the public. Indeed the 1979 'winter of discontent' in which many public-sector workers had gone on strike, dramatised by media images of rubbish piling up in the streets, had been a significant factor in the Conservative election victory. Thus compulsory strike ballots and other new restrictions on picketing had public support. Moreover, rising unemployment weakened effective trade union resistance. Yet when the government's fight with the unions reached its climax with the miners' strike of 1984–5, public sympathy began to switch to the coal miners, when it became clear that the government was intent on their total defeat, perhaps in revenge for the humiliation the National Union of Mineworkers (NUM) had inflicted on a previous Conservative government in 1974.

It was Thatcher's image and record in foreign affairs that earned her the nickname 'Iron Lady'. She demanded and secured a rebate in the British contribution to the European Community budget, establishing a reputation for standing up for British interests abroad, although her style of diplomacy hardly endeared her to the UK's European partners.

This provided an early indication of her increased Euro-scepticism, although she had earlier supported Britain's entry to the EEC, and later signed the Single European Act, and even, near the end of her premiership, allowed British entry into the Exchange Rate Mechanism (ERM). More to her taste was the special relationship with the USA and her own close personal relationship with her political soul mate, US President Ronald Reagan, to whom she was a reliable ally in the last years of the Cold War. The end of the Cold War appeared as much a triumph for her as for Reagan, a victory for their joint vision of free market capitalism over communism.

Without Reagan's strong tacit support it is unlikely that Britain could have recovered the Falkland Islands. This dramatic episode in Thatcher's first term as premier could have brought down her government, which had been caught totally unprepared by the Argentine invasion of the remote British south Atlantic colony in early 1982. The entire Foreign Office team of ministers accepted responsibility and resigned. The government equipped a substantial task force to sail to the Falklands and recapture the islands. This cumbersome expedition might easily have ended in disaster, and did involve substantial losses of men and ships, but the aim was in the end accomplished. Thus what began as a political disaster became a personal triumph for the prime minister, if an expensive and divisive one. Thatcher took the salute at the victory march past, and went on to win the 1983 election by a landslide.

The Falklands and the miners' strike came to typify Thatcher's leadership style as warrior rather than healer. Although she could be persuaded to accept compromise (for example, over Zimbabwe and Northern Ireland), she was more commonly reluctant to make concessions. She was also essentially an English politician, whose support came from the England of the shires and suburbs rather than the cities, and she showed little sympathy or understanding for Scottish and Welsh interests and susceptibilities. Thus she opposed devolution, while support for her party steadily declined in Scotland and Wales. She also took on local government, which was largely in the hands of opposition parties, abolishing the Greater London Council led by Ken Livingstone and the metropolitan counties. Functions were removed from local government, and a succession of measures were introduced to curtail local government spending, culminating in the ill-judged poll tax, a policy disaster which provoked riots and substantial electoral reverses, and was a major factor in Thatcher's eventual fall in 1990.

By then she had won three elections and served as premier for over 11 years, a longer continuous tenure of office than any of her predecessors since Lord Liverpool in the early 19th century. She might have lasted longer still had she not succeeded in antagonising not only the political opposition, but a substantial section of her own party, including some of her former leading allies, especially Michael Heseltine, Nigel Lawson and Geoffrey Howe, whose devastating resignation speech precipitated the challenge to Thatcher's leadership.

Her successor, John Major, had a difficult act to follow, and his six-and-a-half year premiership in retrospect seems little more than a prolonged coda to Thatcherism, although his style was more consensual. Major effectively inherited from his predecessor the US-led first Gulf War, launched in response to Saddam Hussein's invasion of Kuwait. In domestic policy, although the Major government replaced the poll tax with the council tax, it otherwise maintained and extended Thatcher's competition and privatisation policy, selling off the railways. While he declared he wanted Britain to be at the heart of Europe, Major reflected growing Conservative doubts over some aspects of the European agenda. Thus he negotiated opt-outs for Britain from the single European currency and the Social Chapter at the Maastricht Treaty, although this was not enough to satisfy the growing number of Euro-sceptics in his party.

Britain's role in Europe had been a Conservative achievement, yet opinion in the party increasingly moved against the European Union, at the very time when the previously divided and substantially hostile Labour Party was moving in the other direction. One catalyst for Conservative Euro-scepticism was Britain's forced exit from the ERM and the effective devaluation of the pound in 1992 in the dramatic events of Black Wednesday. Thatcher had reluctantly been persuaded to accept British membership of the ERM in the last months of her premiership, following the urging of her chancellor and foreign secretary. In retrospect, the UK joined at the wrong time and at the wrong level. Shortly after Major had secured in 1992 a largely unexpected election victory which had enhanced his standing, Black Wednesday dealt a blow to his government and party from which it was never able to recover. Previous economic crises had occurred largely on Labour's watch, while the Conservatives had enjoyed a reputation for economic competence. This was shattered almost overnight. Black Wednesday fatally weakened the government and contributed to the growing divisions within the Conservative Party.

Major's government was also weakened by a series of scandals involving low-level corruption ('cash for questions') and sexual misbehaviour (although Major's own affair with Edwina Currie was not revealed until much later). This was rendered more serious by Major's call to 'get back to basics', widely interpreted to mean traditional family values. Major delayed the election as long as he could, and the economy did substantially recover, but it was too late. Labour, whose chances of ever returning to power had once been almost written off, swept to victory with the biggest election landslide since the war.

New Labour in power (1997 onwards)

As much of this book is necessarily concerned with analysis of the system of politics and government that has emerged since 1997, it is hardly necessary to anticipate much of that analysis here, although it is useful to review some of the political changes which that election involved and foreshadowed.

Certainly the 1997 election involved a massive reversal of party fortunes. After losing four consecutive elections leading to 18 consecutive years of Conservative dominance, a divided Labour Party had seemed fated to permanent opposition. Instead a transformed party under its new leader Tony Blair returned to power with a huge majority. None of Labour's new Cabinet had served in a Cabinet before. Most had not even been in Parliament when the last Labour government fell. The Conservatives, by contrast, long accustomed to government, ended up with far fewer MPs than Labour's worst post-war defeat in 1983. Some leading former ministers lost their own seats; others, like Major himself and his deputy Michael Heseltine, retired to the back benches. A shell-shocked much reduced parliamentary party went on to elect the relatively unknown former Welsh secretary William Hague as leader. Somewhat obscured by this transformation in the relative position of the major parties, the Liberal Democrats doubled their parliamentary representation (on a smaller proportion of the total vote), becoming a credible third parliamentary force.

The dramatic changes in the relative strength of parties make 1997 a landmark election on those grounds alone. The swing in support from Conservative to Labour was a massive 10 per cent, an unprecedented figure in post-war elections. The political geography of Britain was transformed. The Conservatives won no seats in Scotland or Wales, while Labour won seats in parts of the south of England which had previously been alien territory for them (see Chapter 5). The ensuing 2001 election only served to confirm the change in the party-political landscape, securing another landslide majority for the Labour government, and the prospect of a full second term, for the first time in the party's history. The Liberal Democrats made further modest advances, while the Conservatives failed to make any appreciable recovery. Hague immediately resigned, to be replaced briefly by Iain Duncan Smith, and then in 2003 by Michael Howard. A third consecutive election defeat in 2005 involved a small gain in seats but no significant rise in the Conservative share in the vote. Howard immediately announced that he would resign once there was an agreed new system in place for electing a new leader. Three Conservative leaders in succession had failed to become prime minister (compared with just one in the whole previous century, Austen Chamberlain). The former party of government had already spent an unprecedented period in the political wilderness, with no guarantee of any early return to power.

Yet it is too early to say whether the huge reversal in party fortunes from 1997 to the present marks a similarly massive change in British government and policy. The obvious comparison here is with the Conservative victory in 1979, or the Labour landslide of 1945, both of which in retrospect changed Britain. It is still unclear how far the 1997 election will be seen by future historians to mark a similar turning point. While some of Labour's constitutional reforms, most notably devolution to Scotland and Wales, are far-reaching and almost certainly irreversible, economic and social change has appeared more modest, with substantial elements of continuity. Economic management has been more generally successful than that of past Labour governments. Blair's foreign policy has been much more controversial, not least for his own party, and its impact on the future shape of British politics could prove significant. (Much of this is discussed in much more detail in later chapters.)

British politics today compared with 1945

Much on the surface appears unchanged. To judge from the images in the media, power still revolves around Westminster and Whitehall as it did in 1945. The daughter of George VI, Britain's wartime monarch, celebrated her golden jubilee in 2002, still Queen and head of the Commonwealth. Yet much has been transformed utterly. The empire has gone, and Britain is now a member of a still-expanding European Union which did not exist even in embryo in 1945. Power has been devolved to Scotland, Wales and, more precariously, Northern Ireland. The British government contains a significant minority of women, some Black and Asian ministers and others who are openly gay, partially reflecting more extensive changes in a society where women are more equal than they were, and where there are substantial and growing ethnic and religious minorities. Some of this is mirrored in party representation in the European Parliament, Westminster, devolved assemblies and local councils, and some is more obvious in politics outside the parties. Politics reflects new issues and involves new divisions. Even so, much of the legacy of the past lives on in the style and substance of modern British politics.

Summary

- British politics has been shaped by past history. Yet while apparently showing marked stability and continuity, the British political system, like that of other countries, has been massively transformed by economic, social and political developments.
- British politics in the immediate post-war period was shaped by the development of a welfare state and mixed economy at home, and the Cold War abroad.
- Although people enjoyed rising living standards and low unemployment, Britain continued to suffer relative economic decline, causing political difficulties for successive governments.
- The fast shrinking British empire and the special relationship with the USA were obstacles to earlier close engagement with Europe. Britain joined the European Community too late to shape its rules or share early benefits, and the commitment was less than wholehearted.
- From the late 1960s onwards the United Kingdom faced threats to the maintenance of the Union from nationalist movements in Northern Ireland, Scotland and Wales, culminating in the introduction of devolved assemblies and governments in all three countries. It is not clear yet whether devolution will preserve the Union or lead to separation.
- Changes in population, living standards and lifestyles raised new political issues, and involved some rejection of traditional values. They helped spark a politics of protest largely outside the traditional party system.
- The Thatcher government involved a marked shift away from the politics of the post-war decades, with a rejection of Keynesian economics and a renewed emphasis on market forces.
- Politics under New Labour shows elements of change and continuity with the past. Labour's constitutional reform programme has however transformed the system of government, with unclear implications for the future.

Questions for discussion

- How far was Britain's great power status an illusion after the Second World War?
- Was there a political consensus in the period after the Second World War, and if so, on what was it based?

- How successful was the application of Keynesian economics by British governments? Why did politicians lose faith in Keynesian remedies from the 1970s onwards?
- Why were British governments not involved in closer European integration in the 1950s?
- How and why was the unity of the United Kingdom threatened from the 1970s?
- Why do Margaret Thatcher and Thatcherism still inspire so much controversy?
- How far has the election of a Labour government in 1997 involved a turning point in British history, comparable to the election of the Attlee government in 1945 or the Thatcher government in 1979?

Further reading

There are several useful books on post-war British politics. Sked and Cook (1979) provide a useful survey of the earlier periods and Dutton (1997) a good chronological account up to the dying days of the Major government, with particular emphasis on consensus politics. Morgan and Owen (2001) give an excellent overview of the whole period. Coxall and Robins (1998) adopt a more thematic approach, with chapters on different topics and policies.

On particular periods, Hennessy (1993) provides a vivid account of politics and life in 1945–51. Pimlott (1992) has written a reliable, sympathetic account of Harold Wilson, while Crossman's diaries (1975, 1976, 1977) provide a fly-on-the-wall insider account of Wilson's 1964–70 government. Campbell (1993) is useful on Heath. The literature on Thatcherism has become voluminous. Kavanagh (1990) provides a very readable introduction, while Hugo Young (1990) gives a lively biography of Thatcher herself. Kavanagh and Seldon (1994) provide a very useful survey of the early part of Major's government, while Major's own autobiography (1999) is frank and readable. The literature on Blair and new Labour is expanding fast. See especially Rawnsley's (2001) blow-by-blow account of the first term, Seldon (2001), and Ludlam and Smith (2004) for analysis of policies and issues. Rentoul (2001) and Seldon (2004) are interesting on Blair himself.

Contemporary British Society and Politics

In Chapter 2 we saw how the politics of the present is shaped and influenced by the politics of the past. Yet that same chapter also drew attention to some of the major changes that have taken place in Britain since the Second World War. In this chapter the focus shifts towards an analysis of contemporary Britain and the new contours of British society and politics. We explore some of the major divisions in British society, and their implications for the way people see themselves, for their identities and allegiances, and for their political behaviour. We begin by examining the political geography of Britain, the nations and regions that make up the United Kingdom of Great Britain and Northern Ireland, the so-called 'north–south divide', the differences within and between cities and between town and country. We go on to look at other divisions within society which cut across territorial divisions, such as gender divisions, age divisions, ethnic and religious divisions, which all have implications for political attitudes and behaviour. Finally, and crucially, we explore the extent of inequality of income and wealth in Britain and the ongoing changes in class structure and their implications for political allegiance and behaviour.

Contents

Political geography – nations, regions, town and country

Although the United Kingdom is made up from four main component territories and national groups, most of its inhabitants (50 million out of close to 60 million) live in England. Thus the Union inevitably perhaps appears a rather lop-sided affair between the English and the much less numerous peoples inhabiting Scotland, Wales and Northern Ireland (see Table 3.1). The preponderance of 'England' within 'Britain' and the 'United Kingdom' helps explain why these terms are often incorrectly used interchangeably, to the annoyance of Scots and Welsh. England is also much more densely populated than the other parts of the United Kingdom, particularly Scotland.

There are differences in culture and institutions arising out of past patterns of settlement and distinctive historical influences. Each country has its own religious traditions and divisions. Wales has its own language and a distinctive culture associated with that language. Scotland has its own legal and educational system. There are also important economic differences between the countries. Agriculture is rather more important to Scotland and Wales than England, although central Scotland, south Wales and Belfast were dependent on heavy industries that were adversely affected by Britain's industrial decline. However, although levels of income per head in Wales and

Table 3.1 The population of the United Kingdom of Great Britain and Northern Ireland, 2004

	Population	% UK population
England	50,093,800	83.7
Wales	2,952,500	4.9
Scotland	5,078,400	8.5
Northern Ireland	1,710,300	2.9
United Kingdom	59,834,900	

Source: population estimates taken from National Statistics on line, September 2005.

Northern Ireland are substantially below the average of the UK as a whole, levels in Scotland are close to the average.

There are also some significant differences in income and other economic indicators (such as unemployment) between English regions. They show some marked variations in regional prosperity, between a wealthy London and south-east and the north-east, which on 2003 figures is clearly not only the poorest English region, but worse off than Scotland and similar to Wales and Northern Ireland. Regional disparities are a subject of some concern to economists and they also have political implications, fuelling demands for more favourable treatment by the centre, assistance for inward investment, improvements to basic infrastructure, and also sometimes for more political autonomy.

These economic disparities in the performance of Britain's nations and regions have some implications for political allegiances. The north–south divide has become something of a cliché, but it is a cliché which has some basis in economic and political reality. Not only is the south richer than the north, but Labour's main political support still comes from the industrial north of England, central Scotland and south Wales (even after the 1997, 2001 and 2005 elections), while Conservative strength lies in the south of England and particularly the south-east. The industrial midlands of England are politically contested. However, although the distinctive political allegiances of Wales, Northern Ireland and some areas of Scotland can partly be explained in terms of economic inequality and relative deprivation, cultural factors and the politics of identity and allegiance have always been more significant in Northern Ireland and are increasingly significant in Scotland and Wales (see below).

It should be appreciated, however, that there remain more significant differences in economic activity and thus in income and wealth within than between nations and regions. Yorkshire and the Humber, for example, is among the poorest of Britain's regions, but it contains Leeds which is relatively booming as a major financial, commercial and administrative centre, at least compared with Sheffield, Hull and neighbouring Bradford. Bradford is now unhappily known for its deprivation, racial tension and riots rather than the wool on which its former wealth was based. Yet contained within the boundaries of Bradford Metropolitan District is the small commuter town of Ilkley, overwhelmingly white, middle class and as comfortably prosperous as parts of the Surrey stockbroker belt. Ilkley in turn is part of the parliamentary constituency of Keighley, a formerly prosperous woollen town now shared between poor working-class Asian and predominantly working-class white communities which do not interrelate much. Similar comparisons between prosperity and deprivation, often close together, could be drawn all over Britain.

There are generally marked differences in wealth and living standards between inner urban areas on the one hand and outer suburbs and 'dormitory' towns on the other. Some of the political implications of these economic differences can be charted in the party representation of parliamentary constituencies and local government wards (see Waller and Criddle 2002). It is still broadly true that the more deprived urban areas are more likely to be represented by Labour, and the more prosperous outer suburbs and semi-rural areas by Conservatives. However, where economic deprivation is particularly significant there may be more serious political consequences in terms of alienation, anti-social and criminal behaviour, disturbances to public order, inter-community conflict and the rise of anti-system parties and movements, such as neo-fascist groups.

Allegiance and identity

Where people live is less significant for politics than how people think about where they live, and the nations or communities to which they think they belong. The national identity of the substantial majority of those who live in England is for the most part unproblematic, but there are divided loyalties among the non-English parts of the United Kingdom (see Curtis, in Hazell 2000). This is particularly evident in Northern Ireland where the majority of Protestants (72 per cent in 1999) see themselves as British, and only 2 per cent see themselves as Irish, whereas among Catholics the figures are almost reversed: only 9 per cent think of themselves as British while 68 per cent consider themselves Irish.

In Scotland opinion is rather less polarised, and many acknowledge a dual identity as Scots and British.

These felt identities clearly may be significant for political behaviour. Thus the figure for those who think of themselves as 'Scottish not British' (33 per cent) is not far from the level of support (29 per cent) recorded for the pro-independence Scottish National Party in the 1999 Scottish Parliament elections (although it went down to 24 per cent in 2003). Rather more of those in Wales acknowledge a dual Welsh and British nationality – there was only a bare majority for a Welsh national assembly in the 1997 referendum (although support for it has increased somewhat since) and only 11 per cent supported Welsh independence in 2000 (Curtis, in Hazell 2000: 238). Of course, such felt identities and allegiances can shift over time, but they have some clear implications for the future of United Kingdom and British politics generally.

Regional consciousness remains relatively weak over most of England (with the partial exception of the north-east and south-west), which is one reason that there has, to date, been little popular demand for elected regional assemblies. There is rather more identification with the ancient counties (which go back a thousand years or more) in some parts of England at least. However, county loyalties generally have more to do with sport than politics, and the counties (some would argue) make little sense as political and

Figure 3.1 National identity in Scotland

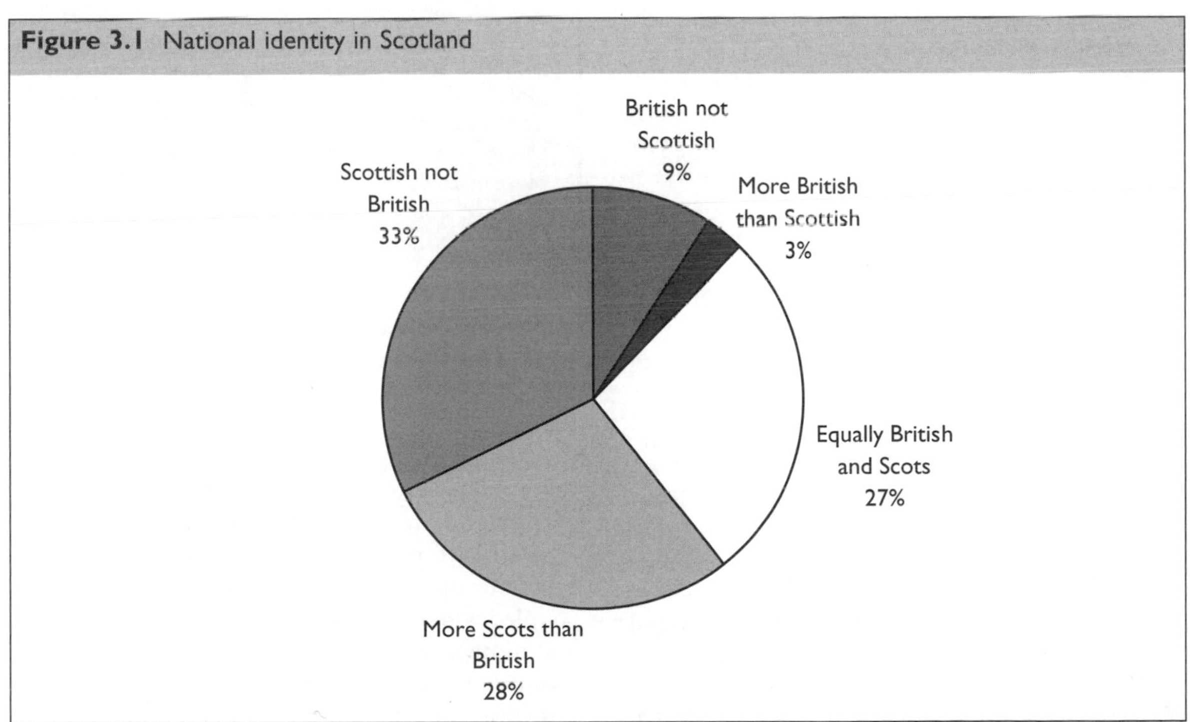

Source: adapted from Curtis in Hazell (2000: 236).

administrative units, as they hardly reflect the pattern of life and work in 21st-century Britain.

The cities may be rather more important in this respect, and city identities and loyalties may be stronger today. Rivalries between neighbouring cities are a feature of sub-national politics – between Glasgow and Edinburgh, Cardiff and Swansea, Manchester and Liverpool, Leeds and Sheffield. There are also significant differences in identities and allegiances within urban areas. Some suburban dwellers, who may work in a city and depend on it for shopping and recreation, still strenuously resist the notion that they are part of the city, preferring to identify with the dormitory towns and 'villages' where they are housed. Yet this may sometimes have more to do with financial self-interest and the fear of higher local government tax bills in city-dominated local authorities than any real sense of community identity. There are also continuing perceived differences between 'town' and 'country', even though only a tiny percentage (1 per cent) of the UK working population is engaged in agriculture. However a rather larger number live in and/or identify with the country, which helps explain the apparent political strength and influence of bodies such as the Council for the Protection of Rural England, and more recently the Countryside Alliance.

Thus where people live sometimes gives rise to a sense of belonging to a particular community, and a sense of identity and allegiance. Yet some have no strong sense of allegiance to the place in which they just happen to live. Instead, they may have a greater sense of attachment to other kinds of community, bound together not by physical proximity, but by some other shared membership, for example of a particular ethnic group or faith community (see Box 3.1).

Box 3.1

Identity politics: an illustration

Imagine, for example, a disabled woman of Pakistani descent who heads a one-parent family and is employed as a manual worker in Scotland, and has been brought up as a Muslim. All these aspects of her life may be fed into a range of statistical tables. Some may change over time, so she may appear in different categories when the next census is taken. Yet the bald facts do not tell us what she thinks about herself, and which of the various categories to which she belongs are important to her. Does she think of herself as British, Scottish, Asian or Pakistani, or a mixture of these identities? Is her Muslim religion the most important part of her self-identity or is it more incidental to her life? Is it her gender, her family circumstances, her disability or her social class that is more significant for her political attitudes and behaviour? How she thinks about herself will be influenced by all kind of factors – family upbringing, education, work and social contacts, peer group pressure, the mass media. Her self-identity may change over time, depending on her experiences and contacts. She may decide, or be persuaded, to join a trade union, or a woman's group, or a support group for those who share her disability, and each of these may alter her outlook on life. Equally of course, how she is perceived and treated by others may affect her own sense of identity. If she suffers discrimination and prejudice as a 'Paki' or a Muslim, she may find it difficult to see herself as a Scot, or to experience a strong sense of solidarity with the working class or with her own sex.

Ethnicity

The definition of 'ethnicity' and how it is distinguished from terms such as 'nation', 'culture', 'community' and (most contentious of all) 'race', is, to say the least, problematic. The 'English' or 'British' are sometimes referred to as a 'mongrel' people, the product of waves of invasion and immigration from different ethnic groups over the centuries – Celts, Angles, Saxons, Vikings, Norman French and so on. Some of these different ethnic origins can be evidenced in place names in different parts of the country, and in surviving surnames, yet they generally have no lasting political implications. When people talk of 'ethnic minorities' today, they are referring largely or exclusively to 'non-white' ethnic groups. These are mainly the product of immigration over the last half-century, because of persecution, or simply poverty and poor economic opportunities in their country of origin, coupled with labour shortages in particular regions and industries in the United Kingdom. Until very recently nearly all the immigration was from the territories of the former British Empire (now Commonwealth) and might be described as a legacy of empire. While in the early post Second World War period there was free entry to citizens of the British Commonwealth, from 1962 onwards there was a progressive tightening of immigration restrictions, on grounds which were effectively racist, to reduce the growth of what was becoming a substantial non-white ethnic minority population. By the year 2000 this totalled just over four million, compared with nearly 55 million 'whites' out of a total of 59 million inhabitants.

Figure 3.2 involves some problematic issues of definition, and excludes 'white' groups who are sometimes categorised as ethnic minorities – Jews, Irish, Poles and so on – and who may suffer some of the discrimination and prejudice experienced by non-white minorities. Indeed, the reason that 'ethnic minorities' are significant for politics is not because they are observably different (although many are, on the crude criteria of skin colour and dress) but because of the way they think and behave and, more critically, the way they are treated by other ethnic groups and particularly the 'white' majority.

Issues of identity and allegiance can be complicated for ethnic minorities. It is hardly surprising that many relatively recent immigrants and their immediate descendants should have some continuing positive sentiments towards their country of origin, particularly where they retain contacts with relatives there. The USA, which has long had a fairly successful programme of education to integrate immigrants into the American way of life and mould them into US citizens, still has thriving Irish-American, Spanish-American, Polish-American and Jewish-American communities. Similarly, there are thriving Polish, Italian and Ukrainian communities in some British cities. These hyphenated identities suggest that allegiances are not mutually exclusive – it is possible to be Irish and American. Similarly it is possible to black or Asian and British, and such a dual allegiance is clearly felt by many.

Yet a more exclusive allegiance may be felt, perhaps as a consequence of rejection, prejudice and discrimination on the part of the majority, of which there is unfortunately considerable evidence. Thus ethnic minorities have generally been the first casualties of an economic downturn and unemployment. Today, unemployment levels remain significantly higher for most ethnic minorities (see Figure 3.3) with black and Asian

Figure 3.2 Non-white ethnic minorities in Britain (total 4,140,000) in the year 2003

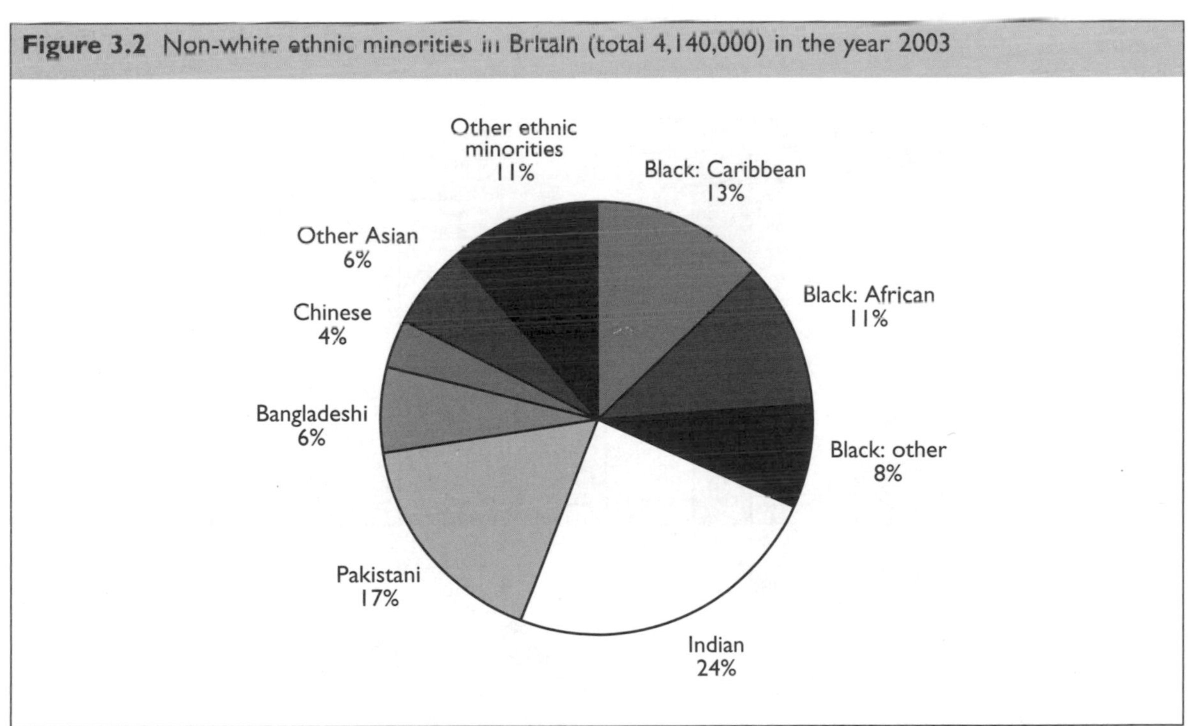

Source: derived from *Annual Abstract of Statistics*, 2005.

Figure 3.3 Unemployment levels by ethnic groups

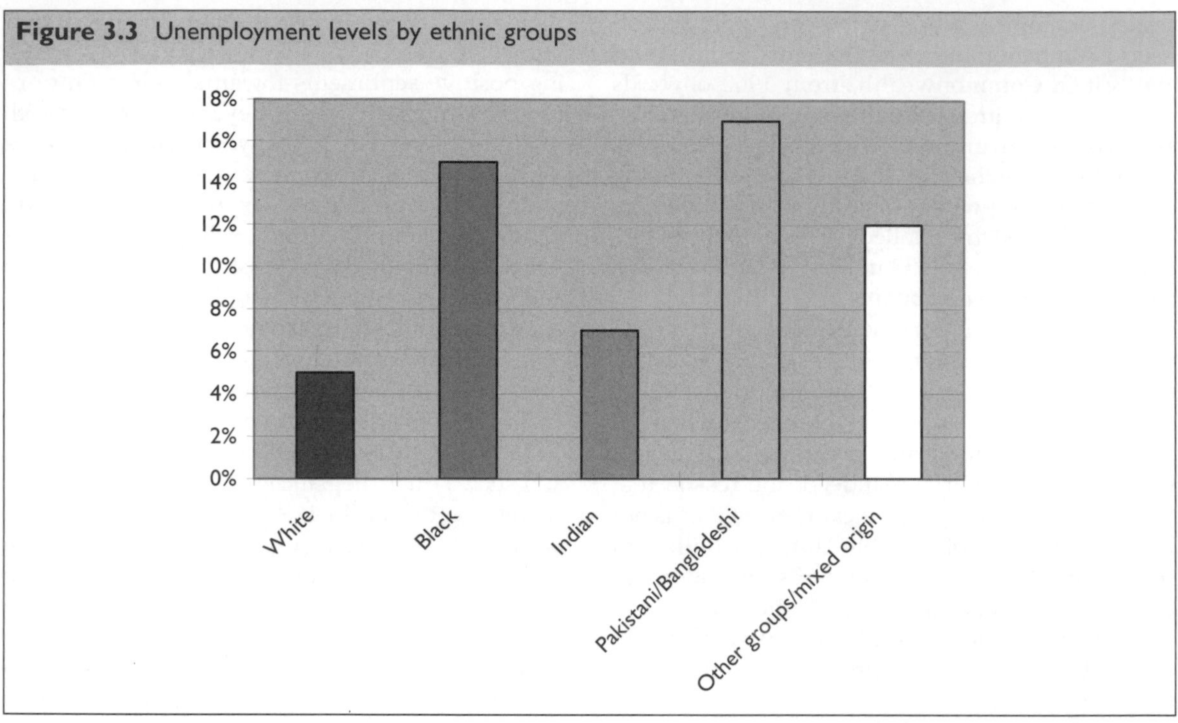

Source: derived from *Social Trends*, 2002.

Figure 3.4 Unemployment levels among 18-24 year olds by ethnic groups

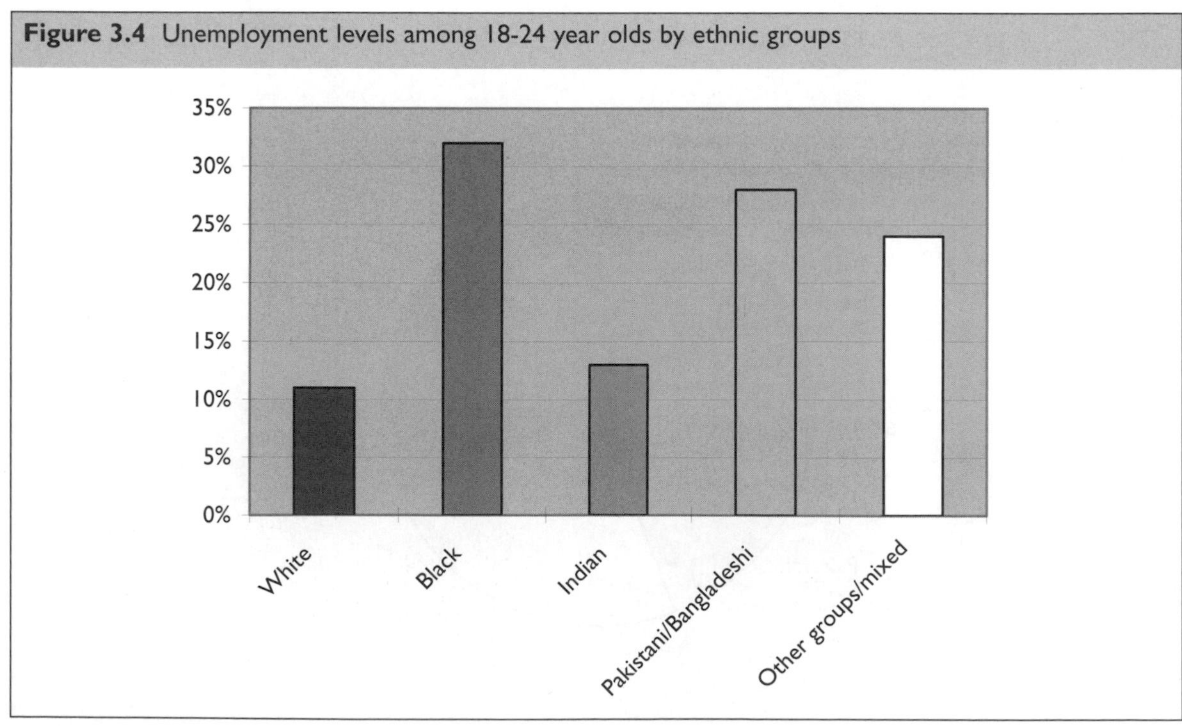

Source: derived from *Social Trends*, 2002.

school leavers in particular finding it much more difficult to secure jobs than their white counterparts (see Figure 3.4).

Other economic indicators tell a similar story. Blacks and Asians are less likely to be employed in occupations appropriate to their qualifications, and are more likely to be employed in part-time or casual labour, often involving working unsociable hours. They also encounter discrimination in the housing market, and are more likely to be victims of certain kinds of crime, while they are far more likely to be stopped by the police and questioned.

While parts of Britain, particularly some areas of London, have become multi-ethnic and genuinely multi-cultural, more commonly ethnic differences are reinforced by residential, social and educational segregation. In some urban areas adversely affected by the decline of a staple industry and rising unemployment, economic deprivation has sharpened mutual suspicions and antagonisms between the white and ethnic minority population, and increased ethnic tensions. After 11 September 2001, and still more after 7 July 2005, prejudice and discrimination against some ethnic minorities was further complicated by Islamophobia. As a consequence it seems that ethnic divisions and tensions will have increasing rather than diminishing significance for British politics, certainly in terms of mainstream political activity – voting, representation, participation in pressure groups – but more seriously perhaps in terms of riots and violent disturbances.

Religion

Religion was once a major source of political division and conflict in Britain. Religious differences were a running thread in political history from the 16th century through to the 19th century. Yet apart from the persecution of the relatively small Jewish minority, religious divisions then were between variants of Christianity. Following the Protestant reformations in both England and Scotland in the 16th century, Roman Catholics became a feared, hated and persecuted minority in Britain, and an oppressed majority in Ireland. The further division between high Anglicanism and Puritanism or non-conformism in the 17th century was the major cause of Civil War and a leading element among the subsequent political differences between the rival Tory and Whig parties. Later, while the Church of England was dubbed the 'Tory Party at prayer', it was the 'non-conformist conscience' which was the bedrock of British 19th-century Liberalism, and a key strand in the early Labour Party.

Yet if religion was once very important as a source of political inspiration and conflict, it was of

In Focus 3.1

Multi-cultural Britain

The Queen (and head of the Church of England) visits a local Islamic Centre in Scunthorpe in July 2002. When she succeeded to the throne in 1952, nearly all her UK subjects were 'white' and they were predominantly Christian. Fifty years later Britain has become considerably more diverse in ethnicity and religion. This has significant implications for British society and politics, and particularly for people's sense of who they are and what they believe in. While earlier policies emphasised the need for the assimilation and integration of minority communities, the positive benefits of ethnic and religious diversity are increasingly stressed in what has become multi-cultural Britain. (For more on this subject see Chapter 24.)

Photograph: EMPICS.

fast-declining political significance for most of the 20th century. Today Anglicans, non-conformists, Catholics and Jews can be found among the supporters of all modern mainstream political parties (in Britain, if not Northern Ireland). Religion ceased to be an indicator of political allegiance for most of England, with the partial exception of areas such as Liverpool, where the Protestant/Catholic divide remained important in sporting loyalties and had a significant if diminishing influence on party support. Such divisions were more important in Scotland, especially Glasgow and parts of Edinburgh, where religious differences remained a key factor in explaining political allegiances, and also the rejection of separatist nationalism by working-class Catholics. However the obvious exception to generalisations on the declining significance of religion for politics remains, of course, Northern Ireland, where religious affiliations continue to correlate closely with political loyalties – particularly for the fundamental Unionist/Nationalist divide (see above). A problem for Unionists is that the number of Catholics is steadily if slowly increasing as a proportion of the total population, to the extent that, on current trends, the Catholic minority could eventually become a majority, with political consequences that hardly need spelling out.

Leaving Northern Ireland aside for the moment, there are some signs that religious differences may become of rather more political significance in 21st-century Britain, not, as formerly, because of divisions within Christianity, but as a consequence of the enhanced importance of other religious faiths. Of these the Jewish faith (0.5 per cent of the population) continues to retain a high profile, and a strong Jewish identity is still felt by many of Jewish descent, even by those who retain little or no religious belief, partly as a consequence of the persecution Jews have suffered over the centuries. Muslim, Hindu and Sikh temples also now appear in British cities, providing additional physical evidence of the multi-faith society which Britain has become. Of these faiths, Islam is the most visible and important, in terms of numbers of adherents, places of worship and political significance. Following 11 September 2001, and more particularly 7 July 2005, Britain's Muslims have been subject to scrutiny, much of it hostile and ill-informed, stimulating the growth of what has been termed 'Islamophobia', and reinforcing racist prejudice among some of the white population. Inevitably, prejudice and discrimination has led some among the Muslim community to reconsider their own political allegiance and identity. The Iraq War has created further difficulties and tensions, and significantly weakened the former strong Muslim support for the Labour Party, as became evident in some parliamentary constituencies in the 2005 election.

Until recently these new and renewed religious affiliations still had only marginal significance for politics. Yet recent political events have sharpened some religious antagonisms, while the demands of some religious groups for their own faith schools, following the precedent of 'church' schools and Catholic schools, may increase segregation and mutual suspicion between religions.

Figure 3.5 provides evidence for the increased variety of religious faith in Britain, without however really denting the assumption that Britain has become a predominantly secular society. Thus a quarter of the population either do not state their religion or belong to no religion. Many of those who still routinely claim to be Christian do not attend church services. Religion may be more important in the lives of those belonging to the small but growing non-Christian faith groups. However, all the non-Christian religions put together still only amount to only 6 per cent of the population, and Muslims to just 3 per cent, underlining the absurdity of the fear of a British Islamic state promoted by British National Party propaganda.

Gender

The division between 'male' and 'female' is in many ways both the most obvious and the most persistent of social divisions. Although the position of women within British society and western society generally has been considerably transformed over the last two centuries in ways which are too familiar to require repeating, and the equality of women is now formally recognised, females continue to suffer discrimination and inequality in many spheres. Gender remains a social division of considerable importance for politics in general, although not especially for party allegiances.

Women slightly outnumber men in the overall population, by 30,446,000 to 29,108,000 (2003 figures, *Annual Abstract of Statistics*, 2005). Men

Figure 3.5 Religious affiliation, Great Britain, 2001

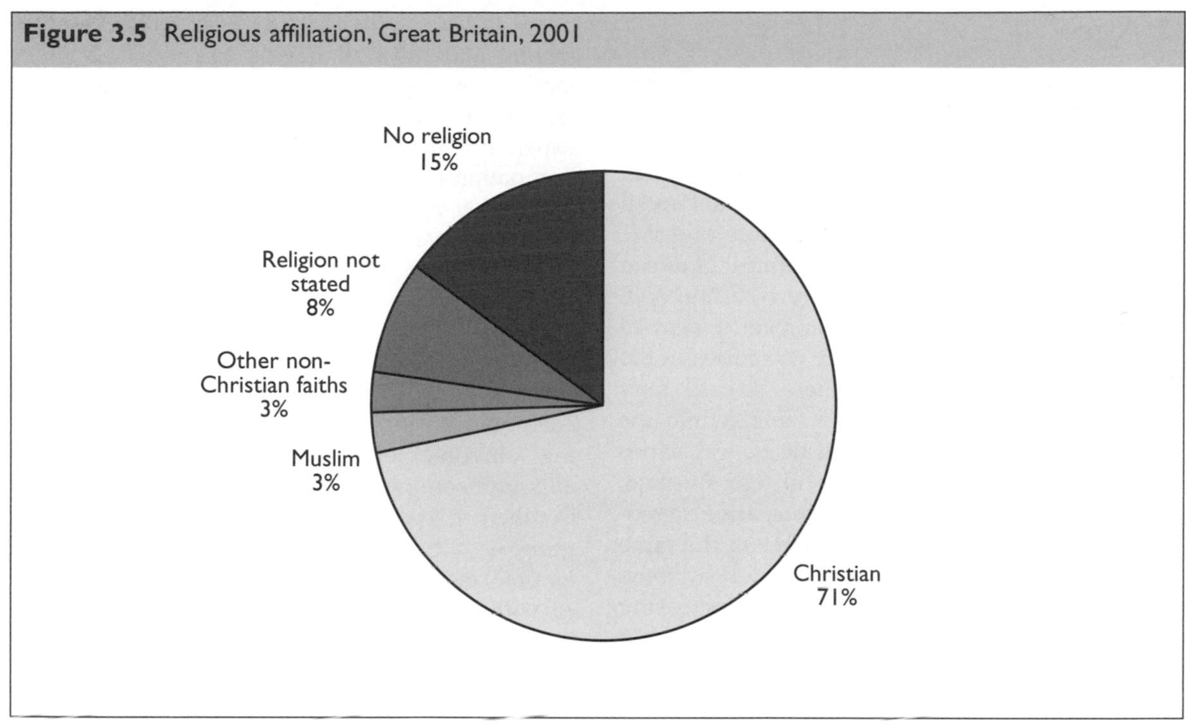

Source: figures derived from *Social Trends*, 2005.

continue to outnumber women in the workforce, however, although the gap is fast closing, as women workers are up from 10 million in 1971 to 13 million in 2004, while the male labour force has remained relatively static at 15.4 million (figures from *Social Trends*, 2005). However, these figures which show close to equal participation in paid work are rather misleading as women are far more likely than men to be undertaking part-time work (5.2 million compared with 1.2 million). Moreover, women are still expected to undertake a disproportionate share of the burden of domestic work and child care. They are also far more likely to be involved in the care of elderly relatives (who themselves are more likely to be women, as they outnumber men by three to one among the population aged 85 and over). This dual burden of outside and domestic work may be one reason (besides prejudice) that relatively few women reach the highest and most well-paid managerial and professional posts. Women's average pay still lags well behind that of men, despite equal pay and equal opportunities legislation. As we shall see in more detail in subsequent chapters, men still substantially outnumber women in formal involvement in politics and government. One consequence of this continued male dominance of the political process, feminists would argue, is that policies are still skewed towards male interests and male economic dominance.

While gender divisions are not expressed in terms of separate political parties, they have been politically expressed in a number of other ways. Thus women have worked in pressure groups, through and across existing parties and through the women's movement as a whole, to secure better representation in politics and government, and to secure specific reforms to improve the position of women. One problem for the women's movement is that many women feel that there is no longer a need for this kind of activity, or that other interests and causes are more pressing. The gender divide is cut across by numerous other divisions, including class, age, ethnicity and religion, and inevitably women find themselves on opposite sides on many political issues. (Feminism and the women's movement is discussed further in Chapter 23.)

Age

Different age groups are an obvious social division. Members of a particular arbitrarily defined age group may have some interests and attitudes in common. Yet as John Vincent (in Payne 2000: 150) points out, age groups are an unusual social division, 'as we anticipate moving from one side of the division(s) to the other'. Thus most of us can expect to experience infancy, puberty, adulthood, parenthood, grandparenthood and retirement as we move between statistical age categories in the course of an average lifecycle. The old may remember how it feels to be young, while the young may anticipate how their needs, capacities and circumstances will change with age. Even so, the elderly can be the victims of negative stereotypes, and they may experience some of the same kind of discrimination and prejudice felt by some other social categories. There are now increasing complaints over 'ageism' as well as over sexism and racism.

There have been significant changes in the age structure of the British population from the 19th century and even from the mid-20th century, with considerable implications for politics. 2003 figures indicate that those aged over 65 (9.5 million) are nearly as numerous as those under 16 (11.7 million), and current projections suggest that the numbers of the over-65s will exceed the under-16s from 2013. The implications of an ageing population are particularly obvious for pensions and health, and it is no accident that these two issues have shot up the political agenda in recent years. Adequate pensions and good health care are critical for the quality of life of the elderly, but have massive implications for public expenditure and taxation.

The elderly have potentially growing political weight. In the USA, for example, there is talk of 'grey power', involving the tacit assumption that the elderly have some interests in common which they seek to advance. In Britain 'grey power' is less evident, but already elderly voters outnumber young voters, and are more likely to use their vote (see Chapter 4). They also have the time and leisure to involve themselves in other political activities, in political parties and in a range of pressure groups (see Chapters 7 and 8).

Yet it should not assumed that the elderly, or for that matter any age group, have homogeneous interests. They will differ in family circumstances, mental and physical health, but most of all in income and wealth. Thus the elderly who are largely or wholly reliant on state benefits may experience real poverty, while those with good occupational pensions and their mortgage paid off may enjoy a very comfortable retirement, often including several holidays abroad each year, regular use of a car, frequent meals out and entertainment. They may indeed enjoy a better quality of life than when they were younger.

Young adults constitute a smaller proportion of the population than formerly. Their political influence may be further reduced by their relatively low involvement in conventional politics, although some would argue that this is balanced by their participation in single-issue pressure group activity. Yet the relative political apathy and ignorance of the young has aroused some concern. As with the elderly, generalisations are dangerous, as there are many significant divisions among young adults: between the growing number of university students and graduates and those not involved in higher education, and between the full-time employed, casually employed and unemployed, along with differences associated with gender and ethnic divisions. Thus there is some active resentment of students among some poor working-class communities among whom relatively few have attended or expect to attend university. While some young adults are much more comfortable within a multi-cultural environment than their elders, others from both the white majority and from ethnic minorities are attracted to more extremist or exclusive political involvement, such as racist parties or various forms of religious fundamentalism.

There are clear differences of attitude between age groups on a range of issues, some essentially economic, others based on formative influences when young (such as drugs, crime, sexual orientation and race relations). Some of the differences in attitudes witnessed among older people may simply be the consequence of the ageing process. Thus it is often assumed that, as they age, people become more set in their ways, less open to change, and conservative (with a small 'c', but perhaps with a large 'C' as well). There is some evidence to support the assumption, although there are some conspicuous exceptions to the generalisation. It may also be the case that different generations, or age cohorts, may have different expectations because of the experiences they have gone through. Thus 'war babies' born in the Second World War may have markedly different expectations and attitudes from the '1960s generation', or 'Thatcher's children' born into the 1980s. Prevailing values in society when people were young may condition their own attitudes for a lifetime. The convictions of anyone who is now over 65 and born and bred in Britain were formed at a time when the population was overwhelmingly white, when there remained a stigma attached to illegitimacy, when homosexuality and abortion were still crimes, and when most of today's 'recreational' drugs were largely unknown. This goes some way to explain the often considerable gap between the generations on issue of personal morality and freedom.

Inequalities in income and wealth

Some of the social divisions referred to above clearly have an economic dimension. Some nations or regions within the UK may have a lower standard of living than others. Above-average unemployment and lower than average wages are experienced by some ethnic minorities. Women are more likely to experience economic deprivation than men, while poverty is more prevalent among some age groups than others – particularly children and the elderly. Yet although poverty may be unevenly distributed between these different social categories, it is hardly gender, or ethnicity or age or geographical location which largely explains poverty. The manifestation of poverty within some of these social divisions reflects a more fundamental division in economic circumstances.

A feature of almost all past and present societies has been gross inequality in income and wealth. The division between the rich and the poor has been seen as the crucial political divide, at least from the time of Plato and Aristotle onwards. Commonly, the rich have constituted a tiny minority, and poverty has been the common experience of the majority. Indeed, Plato and Aristotle assumed that democracy, the rule of the many, would be the rule of the poor, while the rule of the few – oligarchy – involved in practice the rule of the rich minority in their own interests. Until recently gross inequality, and poverty for the majority, was widely assumed to be an unalterable aspect of human society. The early classical economist Thomas Malthus (1766–1834) argued that any improvement in the living standards of the poor would lead to an increase in population and a reduction in their circumstances to subsistence levels. While industrialisation raised the living standards of whole nations, including the poor, thus apparently disproving the gloomy assumptions of Malthus, and redistributed income and wealth between groups, it did not reduce inequality within society as a whole, and indeed may have increased it. However, it was no longer necessarily assumed that governments could or should do nothing about poverty and inequality. Indeed, it was widely reckoned that progressive taxation on the one hand and state welfare provision on the other were significantly reducing inequality and poverty in countries like Britain in the period after the Second World War.

This comfortable assumption of progress towards a more equal society was dented by revelations of the failures of the welfare state in certain areas: the rediscovery of child poverty, and the recognition of the economic deprivation suffered by some declining industrial urban areas from the 1960s onwards. It was more severely shaken by the economic problems of the 1970s, which not only involved the return of large-scale unemployment, but led to a more fundamental questioning of the role of the state. Some argued that it was the growth of government that was largely responsible for Britain's economic problems. Governments should not be in the business of redistribution. State welfare and high taxation sapped individual initiative and enterprise and created a dependency culture. Market forces, left alone, would create more wealth and prosperity for the nation as a whole, including the poorest. Attempts to reduce inequality were counter-productive. While this new orthodoxy was never fully acted upon, the growth of public spending was checked and the burden of taxation of the better off was substantially reduced. There is fairly clear evidence that some apparent progress towards a more equal society in Britain was checked in the last quarter of the 20th century, and partially reversed, because income inequality has grown.

Britain continues to be characterised by wide disparities in the distribution of wealth (which has

Table 3.2 The distribution of marketable wealth (adults aged 20 or over), year 2002

Stratum of society by wealth	Percentage of wealth owned
Most wealthy 1 per cent	23
Most wealthy 5 per cent	43
Most wealthy 10 per cent	56
Most wealthy 25 per cent	74
Most wealthy 50 per cent	94

Source: adapted from *Social Trends*, 2005.

changed little in recent years). The poorest half of the population own only 6 per cent of total marketable wealth (see Table 3.2). For much of the population the only significant wealth they own is bound up with their houses. If these are excluded from marketable wealth the figures are even more stark. In 2002 the top 1 per cent owned 35 per cent of marketable wealth excluding dwellings, and the top 50 per cent owned 98 per cent, leaving just 2 per cent of wealth to the other half of the population.

While it is difficult to make accurate comparisons with previous periods, it does appear that inequality in Britain is as marked as it ever was, and that democracy, involving the assumption of political equality, has not resulted in much greater economic and social equality. The sources of wealth may have changed considerably over the last 200 years, and there has been some significant social mobility, but the gulf between rich and poor remains. In so far as valid comparisons can be made with other countries, it does appear that inequality in Britain is more marked than some other advanced industrial nations.

However, poverty in Britain today is clearly a relative concept. The poor in Britain suffer relative deprivation rather than absolute poverty. People feel deprived because they lack commodities or facilities that the bulk of the population take for granted. Where car ownership is almost universal, lack of access to a car does appear to have a severely adverse effect on the quality of life, yet poor Britons clearly do not lack the basic necessities of life. In the mid-19th century it is reckoned that around a million people in Ireland died as a result of the potato famine, and the population was reduced by some 20 per cent as a result of starvation and emigration. This level of poverty is unthinkable in modern Britain or Ireland or any developed nation, although it is unfortunately common enough elsewhere. The problems of global inequality dwarf those within Britain, yet it is inequality in Britain that is more relevant for British politics and government. Thus it is important to examine in rather more detail the nature and extent of these social divisions by exploring the contentious concept of social class.

Occupation and social class

Sometimes it is suggested that Britain is already, or well on the way to becoming, a classless society. Others suggest not only that class differences are persistent, but that social inequality is increasing. Some foreign observers are struck by the extent to which Britain remains a class-conscious country. Class remains an important concept in social science in general and political science in particular. It is, for example, still regarded as an important factor in explaining voting behaviour and party allegiance (see Chapters 5 and 7). But if class is important it is difficult to define. It is most commonly operationalised in terms of occupational categories, but different categories are used for different purposes, and these different categories hint at problems and ambiguities in fundamental concepts.

Class is a particularly important aspect of the Marxist perspective on power and state (discussed in Chapter 1). 'The history of all hitherto existing society is the history of class struggles' (*Communist Manifesto*, Marx and Engels, 1848). Marx, however, used the term 'class' in a distinctive way, linking it with the ownership of productive wealth rather than occupation. He assumed there was a fundamental conflict of interest in a capitalist society between the class who owned and controlled the means of production – the capitalists or bourgeoisie – and those who owned only their own labour, the proletariat. These were the two key classes that mattered in a modern capitalist society – others such as the old landed gentry, the petty bourgeoisie and the peasants, were becoming progressively less significant. Yet the actual ownership of the means of production may be less important in a modern capitalist society, where ownership may be divorced from effective control, and the key decisions are made by managers. Marx may also have underestimated the power of the professions and the growing state bureaucracy. These developments were more fully appreciated by Max Weber, writing rather later. While Weber acknowledged that the ownership of property was a key element in understanding social inequality, he also attached importance to differences in status between groups, particularly occupational groups.

Our modern understanding of class owes rather more to Weber than to Marx. In popular usage it is closely linked to hierarchies of social status. A simple three-class distinction – upper, middle and lower (or 'working') – is long-established, although the 'upper class' is often relatively ignored. In so far as it is seriously treated it is either linked with the old aristocracy and landed gentry, or used in a quasi-Marxist sense to mean those who are sufficiently wealthy not to have to depend on their own labour for a more than adequate income. The distinction between the middle and working class is most commonly associated with the division between 'white collar' (or non-manual) work and 'blue collar' (or manual) work.

The distinction between manual and non-manual work, although it is bound up closely with the popular understanding of class in Britain and also underpins some formal classifications for statistical purposes and much academic analysis, is not necessarily closely aligned with differences in income and wealth. Some 'white-collar' jobs (such as junior clerical workers) are relatively poorly paid, while some manual workers (plumbers and builders in some parts of Britain) enjoy comparatively high wages. Moreover, it should be noted that the distinction between a manual working class and a non-manual middle class in no way corresponds to the Marxist distinction between the working class and the 'bourgeoisie' (although this term is often translated as 'middle class'). From a Marxist perspective both blue-collar and white-collar workers are 'working class'. The (essentially non-Marxist) British Labour Party similarly both referred to the familiar distinction between manual and non-manual

Box 3.2

Some social or occupational class categories commonly used in Britain

Registrar General's classification formerly used in official surveys:

- I Professional
- II Intermediate
- III Skilled (subdivided into non-manual and manual)
- IV Semi-skilled
- V Unskilled

System of classification used by Institute of Practitioners in Advertising (IPA) and commonly adopted by social scientists and political scientists, particularly in the analysis of voting and party allegiance:

- A Higher managerial, administrative or professional
- B Intermediate managerial, administrative or professional
- C1 Supervisory or clerical, and junior managerial, administrative or professional
- C2 Skilled manual workers
- D Semi-skilled and unskilled manual workers
- E State pensioners or widows (no other earnings), casual or lowest-grade workers, long term unemployed.

New official classification used for government statistical purposes:

1 Higher managerial and professional occupations (e.g. company directors, barristers)
2 Lower managerial and professional occupations (e.g. nurses, police, journalists)
3 Intermediate occupations (e.g. clerks, secretaries)
4 Small employers and own-account workers (e.g. publicans, farmers, decorators)
5 Lower supervisory, craft and related occupations (e.g. printers, plumbers, train drivers)
6 Semi-routine occupations (e.g. shop assistants, bus drivers, hairdressers)
7 Routine occupations (e.g. waiters, building labourers, refuse collectors)
8 Never worked and long-term unemployed.

work, but rejected its significance, in the phrase 'workers by hand or by brain' in the old Clause 4 of its constitution. Academic commentators have often grouped junior white-collar workers with the working class, along with various categories of manual workers, and this makes a great deal of sense in terms of income and economic inequality. Even so, the distinction in assumed social status between white-collar and blue-collar work has proved remarkably persistent, with implications for political behaviour. Thus many poorly paid white-collar workers have declined to identify themselves with the 'interests of labour' which the Labour Party and its trade union allies claimed to champion.

The terms 'working class' and 'middle class', particularly the latter, cover too wide a range to be of much practical value unless they are broken down into further sub-categories. Thus the middle class is commonly taken to include business owners and directors, both salaried and self-employed professionals, clerical workers, shop-keepers and own-account workers (such as small builders). While some work in the private sector and some own their own businesses, many others work in the public sector. It should be clear that many of this diverse group scarcely share the same economic and political interests. Some of the 'middle class' have a strong interest in low taxation and reduced regulation of business enterprise, others have a vested interest in high public expenditure and thus high taxation. Some are professionally involved in the state intervention and regulation that other members of the middle class complain about. Similarly the manual working class is conventionally subdivided into skilled, semi-skilled and unskilled, and as with the middle class there is a cross-cutting distinction between those employed in the public and private sectors.

Yet it is increasingly questionable whether the old and familiar distinction between manual and non-manual work means much any more. Because of the decline of mining and heavy manufacturing industries, and the increased application of technology, much less work involves heavy physical labour. Many occupations require some manual and some non-manual labour. At the same time, some white-collar and blue-collar occupations have experienced an element of 'deskilling', while others require more complex skills and training than formerly.

Box 3.3

Self-assigned class?

The classifications described in Box 3.2 and elsewhere are for the most part objective – depending on occupational category. But individuals may think of themselves as working class or middle class, and this self-assigned class may not correspond with the categorisation of statisticians. Thus a manual worker who earns high wages, owns his own house and car, and adopts a middle-class lifestyle, may think of himself as middle class. Similarly, a university lecturer (middle class by most objective qualifications) may have left-wing political convictions and come from a manual working-class family background, and proudly proclaim himself working class. Self-assigned class may be significant for political behaviour. For example, a manual worker who considers himself middle class may be more likely to vote Conservative, while it is probably safe to assume that the self-proclaimed working-class lecturer will be on the left politically.

Changing class structure?

There has been much academic debate on how Britain's class structure may be changing. Thus it is widely argued that class is not as important as it was. In particular the old manual working class is now relatively far smaller and more fragmented (*class fragmentation*). Others would claim that inequalities in income and wealth are as significant as ever and the basic class structure of Britain has not altered (*class persistence*). Others again would argue that old class divisions are being replaced by new ones (*class realignment*).

One of the reasons that there is so much disagreement about what is happening to the British class system relates back to differences in theoretical assumptions and classifications (discussed above). If the working class is identified with the old manual workers employed in mining and manufacturing, it is clear that numbers have declined, because these industrial sectors have declined, both relatively and absolutely, within the British economy. Moreover, many of the new jobs that have been created are in the services sector, and most of these jobs are commonly counted as middle class, because they appear to be 'white collar' and 'non-manual'. However, it is at best questionable whether, for example, work in call centres (one major growth area) should be regarded as 'middle class'. It is poorly paid, relatively unskilled work often undertaken on a short-term or casual basis. Yet if the decline of the working class is exaggerated, it is certainly true that there is a larger proportion of the population now employed in management and the professions. Moreover it is also true that the working class appears more fragmented – between employed and unemployed, part-time and full-time, public sector and private sector, as well as along increasingly important gender and ethnic lines. These differences have clearly affected working-class homogeneity and reduced traditional working-class solidarity, with political repercussions.

Indeed, new social divisions may be becoming rather more important. It has been persuasively argued that there are now significant new divisions or 'cleavages' in British society, based not on differences within the production process but on differences in the consumption of goods and services. Thus it is claimed that there are significant differences in interest between those who are substantially reliant on public services – particularly public transport, and state-provided education, health and housing services – and those who are more reliant on their private cars, private health care and private schools, and privately owned houses. The former have a vested interest in public services and in higher public spending and taxation, while the latter have a vested interest in lower public spending and taxation. Indeed, the poorer public services are, the more their decision to opt out of them seems justified.

Housing tenure and the distribution of property

One of the most significant of these 'consumption cleavages' used to be housing tenure. A key division, with social class and political implications, was between 'home owners' (those who owned their house outright and those who were buying their house on a mortgage) and those who were renting a house from the local authority. While many from the 'working classes' lived in council houses, owner occupation was a badge of middle-class respectability. The 'council estate' was among the most reliable source of Labour votes, while home owners were far more likely to vote Conservative. However, the sale of council houses and the transfer of substantial local authority housing to other landlords (largely voluntary housing associations), both encouraged by Conservative governments after 1979, has substantially altered the pattern of housing tenure (see Figure 3.6).

Thus the number of council houses has been more than halved, a trend which has continued under Blair's Labour government, as some remaining council estates are in the process of being transferred to the favoured 'third force' of housing associations. Owner occupation has become easily the majority form of housing tenure. It was widely anticipated that this would have politically damaging implications for the core vote of the Labour Party, and indeed there was evidence of increased Conservative voting (initially) among those who had bought their council homes. However, in the longer term it seems that these major changes in housing tenure have not led to commensurate changes in party allegiance (see Chapter 5).

Economic inequality and political power

The growth of home ownership is one aspect of what might be seen as a deliberate attempt to give more people a stake in property, not just in bricks and mortar but in stocks and shares. Indeed a growing proportion of the population has now acquired a large if indirect stake in the stock market through the investment of pension and life insurance funds. Further encouragement was provided by the growth of the unit trust movement and government-sponsored investment schemes. However, the most high-profile stimulus to wider share holding was provided through the heavily promoted privatisations and flotations of shares in former nationalised industries. The initial flotations were so successful that they were substantially over-subscribed. The cumulative effect was that share owners soon outnumbered (the declining number of) trade union members, which would not have been anticipated in the

Figure 3.6 Changing patterns of housing tenure in Britain

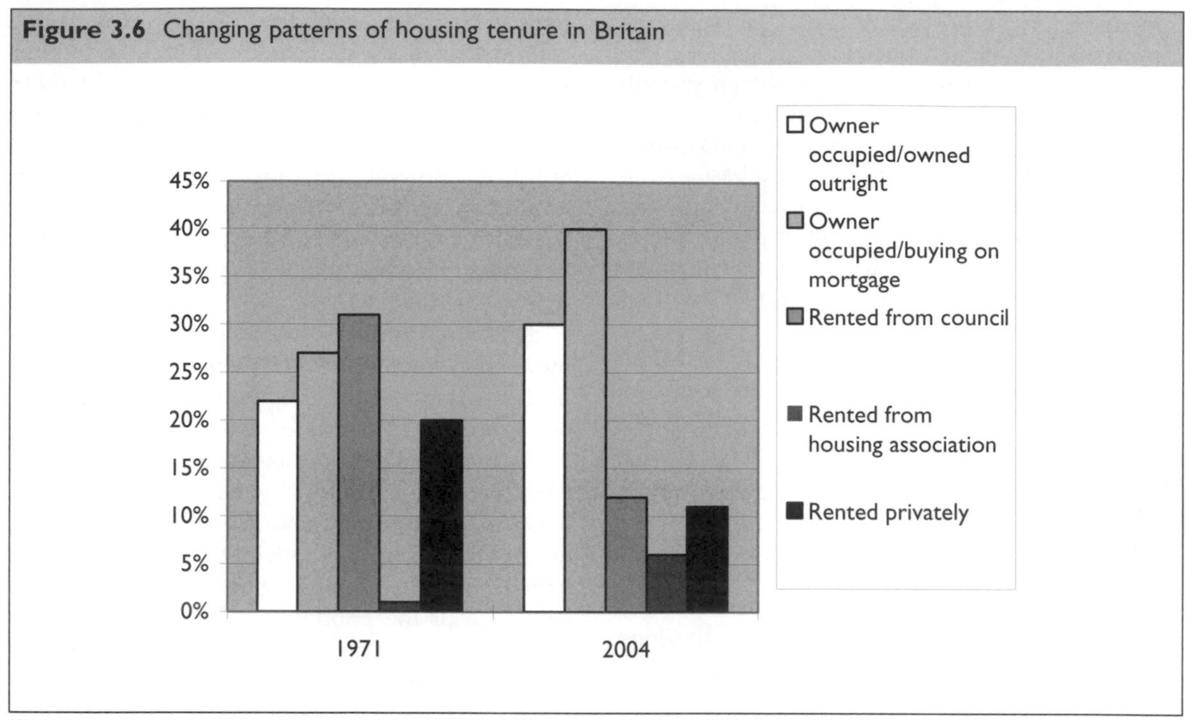

Source: Office of the Deputy Prime Minister (ODPM).

very different economic and political climate in the years immediately after the Second World War.

This suggests that 'popular capitalism' has arrived. Yet the extent of the change can be exaggerated. While many more people seemed to have acquired a stake in property or capitalism, for most of them that stake has remained very small. As Table 3.2 on the distribution of wealth indicates, property ownership has not been significantly spread, but remains heavily concentrated. Income inequality if anything has widened. Little significant progress has been made towards either the old Labour ideal of a more equal society or the Conservative 'property-owning democracy'.

The relationship between economic inequality and political power remains contentious. The norms of representative democracy – one person, one vote, one value – suggest political equality and the rule of the majority. To Marxists, the marked concentration of the distribution of income and wealth in the hands of the few reflects the effective concentration of political power in the hands of the ruling class. To neo-liberals, this inequality in income and wealth simply reflects market forces and the effects of the unequal distribution of talents and enterprise and initiative in society – thus the massive earnings of some company directors, and a few footballers and pop stars, is simply the price placed on their scarcity. Both Marxists and neo-liberals assume the primacy of economics over politics. Social democrats, by contrast, implicitly assume that the political power of the majority can be mobilised to create a more equal society through the ballot box and representative government .

Economic and social divisions – the time dimension

The focus of this chapter has been contemporary Britain, but it is worth reemphasising how much Britain has changed over the period since the Second World War (the subject of the preceding chapter). Here is a brief extract from a book, first published in 1941, written by a leading expert on British politics in the mid-20th century, Sir Ivor Jennings.

> Great Britain is a small island with a very homogeneous population. Few think of themselves as

> primarily English, Scots or Welsh. The sting has long been taken out of religious controversy. The country is so interdependent that there is little economic agitation on a regional basis, as there sometimes is in a large country like the United States. There are class divisions and (what is often the same thing) economic divisions, but they are not wide or deep, and they are tending to disappear through heavy taxation at the one end and high wage rates at the other. We are a closely knit economic unit, with a large measure of common interests and a long political tradition.
>
> (Jennings 1966: 8–9)

Anyone with a basic acquaintance with contemporary British politics (and anyone who has read this chapter) will realise that this description is hardly valid today. The population now no longer appears 'very homogeneous'. Scottish and Welsh identities and allegiances have significant political implications. Some consider that the importance of religion in politics is again on the increase. Jennings' assumptions over diminishing economic and class divisions seem questionable.

Equally significant are the divisions Jennings ignores. Understandably, he made no observations about ethnic divisions, as multi-racial and multi-cultural Britain and some of the associated political controversy is substantially (although not wholly) a product of post-war immigration. He also ignored gender divisions, then more glaring than today (although war briefly provided nursery facilities and wider employment opportunities for women), yet this oversight reflected a then fairly common complacent view that 'votes for women' had secured their political equality.

The point is not to denigrate Sir Ivor Jennings, an outstanding writer on politics of his time, but to emphasise how social divisions, and the importance attached to them, can change so markedly over a relatively short period. His description, when it was first written, reflected reasonably accurately the mood of national unity at the height of the Second World War. Moreover, it preceded many of the substantial changes in society and changes in political attitudes that have taken place in Britain since the Second World War, often reflecting global change. These have included large-scale immigration into Britain and the emergence of a multi-ethnic and multi-faith society, second-wave feminism and the women's movement, the rise of nationalism and devolution, the decline of mining and manufacturing, together with manual trade unionism, and massive changes in the management of the economy. Politics is not static but dynamic. British society and British politics have changed dramatically in the 60 years or so since the Second World War. It is still changing, and will continue to change, perhaps in directions that it is difficult to foresee.

■ Summary

- Although the bulk of the population of the United Kingdom live in England, Scotland, Wales and Northern Ireland retain their own distinctive cultures and identities.
- Average incomes are lower than the UK average in Northern Ireland and Wales, and there are substantial inequalities between the English regions. The 'north–south divide' has some validity in terms of both economics and politics. There is, however, more significant inequality within regions and cities than between them.
- A growing ethnic minority population has resulted from immigration from the 'new Commonwealth' and more recently from eastern Europe. Ethnic differences reinforced by social and educational segregation have fed prejudice and discrimination, and created some political tension between communities.
- Political differences related to variants of Christianity have declined in significance. Non-Christian faiths are practised by a small but increasing minority. Following 9/11, the Iraq war, and 7/7 Muslims have suffered from 'Islamophobia' and some have felt divided loyalties.
- The role of women continues to change in the workplace, but less in the home. Gender divisions have had only a limited impact on party political allegiances, but women continue to suffer discrimination in many fields, including politics, and there is an ongoing struggle to secure equal rights and justice for women.

- Changes in the age structure of the UK population mean that pensioners now comfortably outnumber children. The 'grey vote' is of increasing political significance.
- Income and particularly wealth remain very unequally distributed in Britain. While economic inequality has some obvious implications for political power, the relationship remains contentious.
- Changes in occupational class structure overlaid by other social differences have had contentious implications for politics. Differences based on the consumption (public or private) of key goods and services (particularly housing) may be of increased significance.

Questions for discussion

- Why are more people in Scotland and Wales identifying themselves as Scots or Welsh rather than British? What might be the political implications?
- How politically significant are economic differences between the nations and regions of the United Kingdom?
- How far do ethnic minorities suffer continuing prejudice and discrimination in Britain? Are ethnic tensions rising or declining?
- Should politicians pay more attention to 'faith politics', and if so, why? What are the causes and consequences of 'Islamophobia'?
- How far does the more extensive participation of women in the paid workforce indicate there is no longer significant discrimination against them? Why might gender differences remain important for politics?
- What are the possible political implications of increased 'grey power'? Is there a danger that the political voice of the young may be relatively unheard (and, if so, why)?
- Is social class still important for British politics? How might changes in the class structure have affected political allegiances?

Further reading

More extensive analysis of economic and social divisions in Britain can be found in standard textbooks on sociology, such as Tony Bilton *et al., Introductory Sociology*, 4th edition (2002), or Anthony Giddens, *Sociology*, 4th edition (2001). Geoff Payne (2000) has edited a thoughtful collection of essays on *Social Divisions*, which examines in far more detail some of the theoretical and practical issues raised in this chapter.

Many of the implications of the social and economic divisions explored here for British politics as a whole are addressed in later chapters of this book. The more specific implications of these divisions for parliamentary constituencies and local government are explored in fascinating detail in Waller and Criddle, *The Almanac of British Politics* (2002).

The most easily accessible source for up-to-date statistics is via the website www.statistics.gov.uk. A wealth of official statistical information is regularly published in the *Annual Abstract of Statistics* and *Social Trends*. A useful one-volume reference book is Briscoe, *Britain in Numbers: The essential statistics* (2005).

Participating in Politics

Contents

This chapter is the first of several that examine aspects of the British political process in more detail. It focuses on participation in politics, and both serves as an introduction to the succeeding chapters and inevitably touches on some of the topics explored in those chapters; elections and voting (Chapter 5), political ideologies (Chapter 6), political parties (Chapter 7), pressure groups (Chapter 8), and political communication and the mass media (Chapter 9).

The first part of this chapter explores the extent of political participation in Britain today. We look at levels of involvement in politics. We ask, what are the main forms of political participation? What proportion of the population can be considered active in politics, and who are the active participants? Are the patterns of political participation changing? What are the causes of falling turnout in elections, and how might this trend be reversed? How far is the decline in some traditional forms of political behaviour offset by a rise in more direct political action of various kinds? We then turn to the beliefs and attitudes shaping political attitudes and behaviour, examining political culture and political socialism, and the extent to which British political culture may have changed. We go on to explore the meaning of citizenship and community in contemporary society, and conclude with a brief discussion of the academic controversy around the term 'social capital'. How far is a perceived decline in political participation linked to a wider decline in social interaction and engagement in modern society?

Political participation

While other political systems may not necessarily involve extensive participation by ordinary people in politics beyond obeying the government, democracy presupposes active citizen involvement. Yet political participation in Britain is limited. Figure 5.1 divides the population into three main types of participant: a small number of activists; the majority – just voters – whose participation in politics is limited to voting in elections; and a substantial minority who are almost inactive, and scarcely participate at all. The diagram is derived from distinctions made by Milbrath (1965), but also reflects findings on political participation in Britain (Parry, Moyser and Day 1992, Bromley *et al.* 2001, 2002), and recent joint research by the Electoral Commission and the Hansard Society (2004, 2005).

Definition

Political participation is citizen involvement in politics through, for example, voting or pressure group and party activity aimed at influencing government and public policy.

Political knowledge and interest

Although political participation is central to democracy, a readiness to participate presupposes some knowledge of, and interest in, politics. In the 5th century BC Pericles spoke of the extent of participation in Athenian democracy.

> Here each individual is interested not only in his own affairs but in the affairs of the state as well: even those who are most occupied in their own business are extremely well-informed on general politics – this is a peculiarity of ours: we do not say that a man who takes no interest in politics is a man who minds his own business; we say that he has no business here at all.
> (From Pericles' funeral oration, Thucydides, 1972 trans.: 147)

Ancient Athens was of course a direct democracy, arguably requiring a rather higher level of political involvement among citizens than a modern representative democracy. Even so, if Britain can be regarded as a democracy in a meaningful sense, and if ordinary people do have some real power, then it is still necessary that they should have some knowledge of, interest in and engagement with politics. Yet today there is some concern at the extent of political ignorance and apathy in modern Britain.

Most British citizens could hardly be described as 'extremely well-informed' on politics. A joint report by the Hansard Society and the Electoral Commission (*An Audit of Political Engagement 2*, 2005) has found that more than half the Britons polled felt they knew either 'not very much' (44 per cent) or 'nothing at all' (10 per cent) about politics. Women, young voters, manual workers and members of ethnic minorities particularly felt less knowledgeable. Unsurprisingly perhaps,

Figure 4.1 A hierarchy of political participation

Activists
The very small percentage of the electorate who are actively involved in political parties, pressure groups and other political organisations.

Just voters
The much greater percentage of the electorate who play a basically passive political role, but who may discuss politics, read political coverage in newspapers and watch political programmes on television. Passive membership of trade unions and pressure groups. Will turn out and vote.

Almost inactive
This includes many of the 39 per cent of non-voters in the 2005 general election as well as non-voters in local and European Parliament elections. It contains a disproportionate number of younger people, who may actively avoid talking about politics, reading about it or watching political programmes on television.

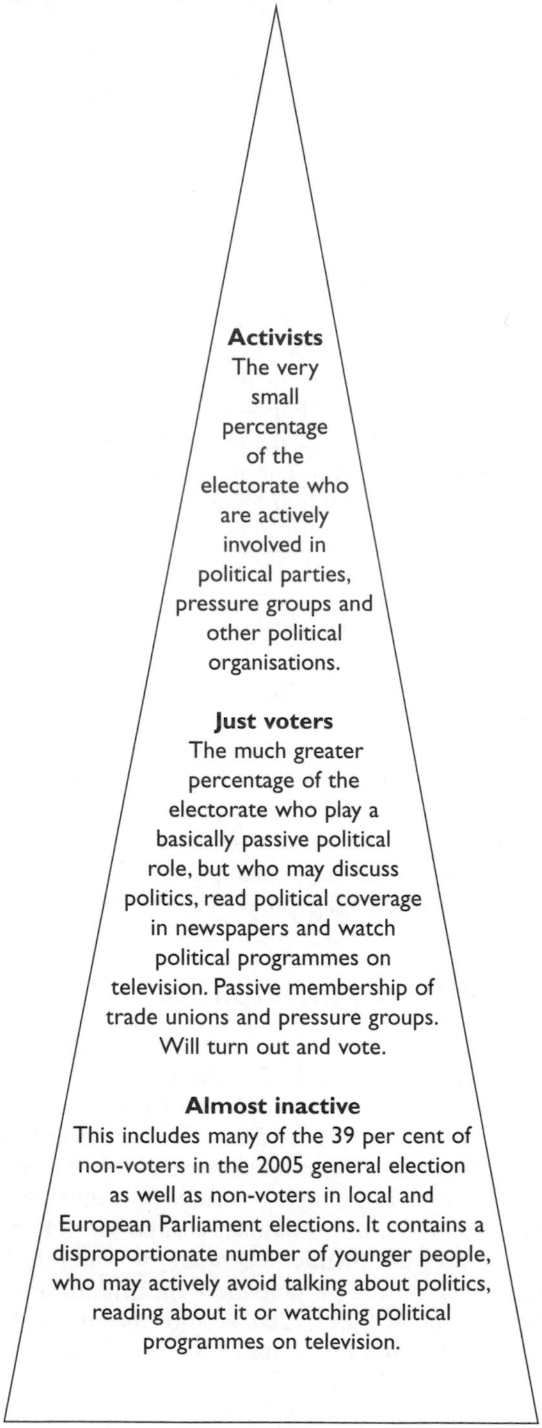

Source: adapted from Milbrath, 1965: 16–22.

those with higher educational attainment were more knowledgeable. As might be expected, there was a strong correlation between knowledge of and interest in politics. A bare majority of respondents were either 'very interested' (13 per cent) or 'fairly interested' (40 per cent) in politics, compared with 28 per cent who were 'not very interested' and 19 per cent who were 'not at all interested'.

Interest in issues, local, national and international, was found to be significantly higher than interest in politics, indicating 'that many of those who say they are uninterested in politics do so because of how they interpret the concept'. The report observes that politics 'tends to be seen as something done by, and for, others' and is 'closely identified with "politicians" and with the formal political process'. It concludes that there was 'an urgent need to rebuild the relevance of "politics" as a concept and as an activity worth taking part in'. (Electoral Commission/Hansard Society 2005: 3.12).

Thus rather more people may be interested in politics if it is defined broadly (see the discussion on the meaning of politics in Chapter 1). Even so, this survey and previous research indicate that at least a very substantial minority of the population feels alienated and excluded from the political process. These feelings are most evident among the poorest sections of society. Among residents in the most deprived 10 per cent of areas in the country only 35 per cent declared an interest in politics, compared with 69 per cent in the most affluent areas.

Voting and non-voting

The most basic form of political participation in a representative democracy is voting. The political system depends on the readiness of people to exercise their right to vote. Substantial non-voting reduces the legitimacy of any elected individual or authority. Low turnout in elections has become a matter of concern in Britain. Turnout in General Elections has declined since the 1950s, when it averaged over 80 per cent. In 1992 turnout was 77.7 per cent, in 1997, 71.5 per cent, and in 2001, 59 per cent, improving only slightly to 61 per cent in 2005. Voting turnout is lower still at all other types of election, including referendums, and is especially low in Euro elections and local elections (see Table 4.1).

Britain is hardly alone in registering low and generally declining levels of electoral participation. Indeed, they appear to be a feature of most western democracies (Hague and Harrop 2001: 133). Even the election of the US president (arguably the most important elected role in the world) only secures the involvement of around half of eligible US citizens (52 per cent in 2000). Although it is sometimes argued that non-voting reflects contentment, the more general view is that low turnout is a serious cause of concern. Whiteley *et al.* (in Norris 2001: 222), reviewing the drop in turnout in the General Election of 2001, observe, 'If this is not a crisis of democratic politics in Britain, then it is hard to know what would be'. For Bill Jones (2003: 24), large-scale abstentions indicate that 'worryingly large numbers of people have little faith in the political system'. Suggested remedies for low and declining electoral turnout depend to a degree on some very different perceptions of the causes of non-voting (see Table 4.2).

All the suggested causes of non-voting have a certain plausibility and most of these suggested remedies have already been tried, many in Britain, and others elsewhere. Thus we have already seen that over half the electorate feel they know little or nothing about politics. Those who are better educated are more interested and more likely to vote. There have been efforts to improve the level of political education in Britain, through the national curriculum and through the efforts of campaigning individuals and societies. Political education is intrinsically controversial. Many are

Table 4.1 Recent levels of turnout by British voters

General election, 2001	59%
Scottish Parliament elections 2003	49%
Welsh Assembly elections 2003	38%
European Parliament elections 2004	38%
General Election, 2005	61%

Table 4.2 Falling electoral turnouts: possible causes and remedies

The cause?	The cure?
Voter ignorance of politics and government in general and particular ignorance of local government and the European Union	More political education in schools and colleges. Improved media coverage of government and politics
Lack of confidence that voting changes anything, particularly for non-Westminster elections. Lack of a clear impact of voting on government.	More powers for local and devolved government Increase accountability of European institutions to the elected European Parliament
Potential voters put off by 'low-tech' antiquated and inconvenient means of registering choice, by marking a ballot paper in a remote polling station	Penalties (e.g. fines) for non-voting More convenient polling stations (e.g. in supermarkets) Reform voting methods by introducing more postal voting, telephone voting and internet voting.
Potential voters deterred by limited effective choice in British elections and 'unfair' relationship between votes cast and the result in terms of seats won	Reform the electoral system to provide a more proportionate relationship between votes cast and election outcomes, and more effective choice
Citizens disillusioned by party politics, elections and the processes of representative democracy	More direct democracy (e.g. through referendums, focus groups, citizens 'juries'). New forms of politics involving more direct action and involvement.

worried that it could involve political indoctrination. Yet if it is confined to the safer ground of the political system and process rather than more controversial political issues, it risks being boring. The impact of more political education can only be judged in the longer term, but to date the results are unimpressive. The youngest age group in the electorate, those aged between 18 and 24, remain the least knowledgeable, the least interested and the least likely to vote.

Arguably low knowledge of, and interest in, politics may be blamed more on the mass media than any deficiency in political education. Certainly there is evidence of reduced political coverage in the tabloid press and on the main television news programmes. Much of the coverage is also superficial and, in the case of the press, nakedly partisan. Yet those involved in the media might reasonably claim only to be reacting to demand, or in this case the lack of it. The public has shown clear signs of being 'turned off' by the saturation coverage of politics in election campaigns (see Chapter 9 for more on the media and politics).

Some non-voting might reflect not so much political ignorance as a (reasonably accurate?) belief that voting is unlikely to make much difference for anything other than Westminster elections (and even here the low turnout in 2001 could be blamed on the widespread assumption that the result was a foregone conclusion). Thus low turnout in local elections may be because local councils do not seem to have much power, and perhaps also in many cases because elections are unlikely to lead to a change in party control (see Chapter 17 for more on local elections). Voters may also perceive that the European Parliament lacks power. Although it has gained increased influence over legislation, the budget and even the composition of the European Commission, it does not control the government of Europe (see Chapter 15). Thus voting in European elections does not appear to make much difference to political decisions in the European Union. Nationalists would argue that one reason for the lower turnout in elections for the Scottish Parliament, and particularly the Welsh Assembly, is that these bodies still do not have enough power (see Chapter 16). Whether turnout would be markedly higher in elections for local councils, devolved assemblies and the European Parliament if these bodies had more power seems debatable, however.

Voting might be encouraged by the use of

carrot or stick reforms. To deal with the latter first, some countries, like Belgium, fine non-voters. Unsurprisingly this encourages very high turnout. Yet such a solution has not generally found favour. Compulsion involves some interference with freedom. Moreover, the constrained voter may vote arbitrarily or perversely. However, some consider there may be some merit in allowing positive abstention as an option in elections, for example allowing voters to put a cross next to 'none of the above' under the parties or candidates listed.

In Britain more emphasis has been placed on modernising and simplifying voting procedures, through the trial use of extended postal voting, and experiments with telephone voting, text messaging and internet voting. While it is plausible that a generation used to communicating through mobile phones and the internet should find marking a ballot paper with a pencilled cross in some remote schoolroom requisitioned as a polling station both antiquated and inconvenient, there are continuing security concerns. Among alternative methods of recording votes, only the relatively 'old-tech' postal voting has led to significantly higher turnout levels, at the cost of increased allegations of electoral fraud, which the Electoral Commission and in some cases the police have investigated. There have also been experiments with rather more user-friendly polling stations, sited in supermarkets. Having elections on a Sunday or public holiday instead of a working day is another option, widely used elsewhere, which might encourage higher turnout in Britain.

Electoral reform might do more to ensure that each vote counts, and thus increase the incentive to vote. At present, turnout is higher in marginal constituencies, and lower in those unlikely to change hands. Thus it is at least plausible that a more proportional electoral system would lead to a higher turnout. Yet more proportional electoral systems introduced for elections for the European Parliament, Scottish Parliament and Welsh Assembly have not produced high turnouts. It is even possible that these more complicated electoral systems have confused some electors and put them off.

More direct democracy?

Finally it is at least possible that the kind of politics that seems inseparable from representative democracy is a turn-off for a section of the electorate. Thus polls indicate that people distrust politicians and dislike adversarial party politics. More direct democracy might be the solution. One possibility would be increased use of the referendum, occasionally used in Britain for issues of a constitutional nature, and more commonly employed in some countries like Switzerland. A similar device is the initiative, used in some US states (such as California), where if an issue is raised by a sufficient number of voters it can be placed on the ballot paper. However, not everyone approves of referendums, and many politicians are less than enthusiastic, as they undermine their representative role (see Box 4.1).

However, while many party politicians dislike referendums, they make extensive use of opinion polls to guide their own policies and commitments. Local councils and other public bodies frequently engage in public consultation exercises to ascertain people's wishes and preferences. Further insights into public thinking may be gained using a focus group, in which a small broadly representative sample of people discuss a particular issue or policy in more depth. Local councils or health authorities sometimes use citizens' juries (or citizens' panels) to consult public opinion on key issues in a similar but more thorough and systematic way. Yet although focus groups or citizens' juries may involve a representative cross-section of the population, they have not been chosen by the people and cannot properly represent them. They may enable decision makers to become better informed on public opinion, but they do not transfer power to the public. They are supplements rather than alternatives to the ballot box.

Political participation beyond voting

Voting is only the simplest and most basic form of political participation in a modern representative democracy. A rather higher level of political commitment than voting is registered by joining a political party. The modern political parties that developed and flourished in the 20th century had substantial mass membership, and most voters strongly identified with specific parties. Both active party membership and strong party

Box 4.1

The merits and disadvantages of initiatives and referendums

In favour of votes on a single issue, it may be said that:

- They give people a chance to vote on specific issues that affect their lives, whereas in a General Election they can only offer a general verdict on the performance and promises of governing and opposition parties.
- They may help educate citizens on key political issues and stimulate more interest in public policy.
- They may exert pressure on elected representatives to act responsibly, and in the general public interest rather than specific interests with which representatives may be linked.
- Elected representatives may sometimes be out of touch with the views of those they claim to represent.

Against such consultation, it may be said that:

- There are commonly problems in framing questions, as it is seldom that an issue can be simplified sufficiently for a yes/no answer. It is not easy to accommodate shades of opinion.
- Frequent referendums arguably require more political knowledge and interest than elections. Although they may help to educate the public, it is equally possible they will produce voter fatigue and apathy.
- Campaigns can be expensive and therefore to the advantage of well-funded groups; business interests have far more scope to influence the outcome.
- Initiatives and referendums weaken the role of political parties in the democratic process and undermine the responsibility and accountability of parliaments and other representative bodies.
- They encourage single-issue politics, rather than debate based on a conflict of broad principles.
- The majority view can work to the disadvantage of minorities, for example, blacks and gays.
- Referendums can be used by voters to voice general discontent with the government of the day rather than provide an answer to a specific referendum question.
- Dictators or charismatic leaders have often used referendums not to transfer power to the people but to legitimise their own power and policy.

loyalty have declined markedly over the last half-century over most of the western world, and in Britain in particular. The Labour Party had only 208,000 individual members in 2004, the Conservative Party less than 300,000, and the Liberal Democrats 73,000. Altogether only between 1 and 2 per cent of voters are party members, fewer still are actively involved in party meetings, fundraising and canvassing (see Chapter 7 for further analysis). Party membership thus does not necessarily indicate active participation in politics. Many members do no more than pay subscriptions by banker's order, and some join for the social facilities offered by Conservative or Labour clubs.

It is sometimes argued that the decline in involvement in political parties has been balanced by a rise of participation in single-issue pressure groups. Indeed, the membership of some groups runs into millions, and far exceeds the membership of political parties. Yet again, some of these membership figures are hardly reliable indicators of active participation in politics. Most of the three million or so who have paid to join the National Trust have done so to secure free access to National Trust properties. Similarly, many RSPB (Royal Society for Protection of Birds) members simply wish to visit its bird sanctuaries. A more reliable indicator of political activism is perhaps provided by membership of campaigning groups such as Greenpeace, Friends of the Earth or Amnesty International (all between 100,000 and 200,000).

How many people, then, are more actively engaged in politics? Parry and Moyser (1990) found that 23.2 per cent were involved in some political activity other than voting, but only a very small minority (1.5 per cent) were real political

Box 4.2

Comparative politics: the referendum in France on the European Constitution, 29 May 2005

France has long used referendums on constitutional issues, although French voters have sometimes used them to vent their displeasure with the government of the day. In May 2005 they voted to reject the proposed new EU constitution by a margin of 55.6 per cent to 44.4 per cent. According to Timothy Garton Ash:

> the French did not just say no to a particular, cumbersome constitutional treaty, despite the fact that its main architect was a Frenchman. They said no to what the EU has become since the fall of the Berlin wall, no to a much-enlarged EU where France is no longer in the driving seat. No to the prospect of Turkish membership. No to Anglo-Saxon style economic reform: deregulation, free-market liberalism, Thatcherism imported via Brussels. And, of course, no to lupine Jacques Chirac (the French President) and the Parisian governments and elites they feel have failed them. This was a no of fear. Fear of losing your job to the now proverbial Polish plumber. Fear of immigration. Fear of change.
> (*Guardian*, 30 May 2005)

This interpretation of the vote may not necessarily be correct, but it does illustrate how a vote on a particular issue can perhaps be swayed by a complex combination of emotions and views, some of little real relevance to the referendum question.

activists, involved in a wide range of political behaviour, including party campaigning, pressure group activity, demonstrating and protesting, and contacting elected representatives. More recently the joint survey commissioned by the Electoral Commission and the Hansard Society (2005) concluded that 'one adult in six (16 per cent) are political activists, defined as having done at least three from a list of eight political activities (excluding voting and other related activities) in the last two or three years' (see Table 4.3). This working definition of political activism hardly requires extensive participation. Yet even on this relatively loose and generous definition, it is clear that only a relatively small minority of the population are political activists.

Who participates, and why?

Political activists are found disproportionately among the higher social classes. Thus those from social classes A, B and C1 (managerial, professional and other white-collar workers) are twice as likely to contact their elected representatives than those from classes C2, D and E (manual workers, casual workers, unemployed and state pensioners

Table 4.3 Political activism: responses to question, 'Which, if any, of the things on this list have you done in the last two or three years?'

Political activity	Percentage taking part
Signed a petition	44
Boycotted certain products for political, ethical or environmental reasons	20
Presented my views to a local councillor or MP	7
Urged someone to get in touch with a local councillor or MP	16
Been to any political meeting	6
Taken part in a demonstration, picket or march	6
Taken an active part in a political campaign	3
Taken part in a strike	2
None of these	44
Three or more activities	16

Source: poll conducted by MORI for the Electoral Commission and Hansard Society (2005).

with no other income). Political participation increases with levels of education. Education builds self-confidence, increases political knowledge and provides communication skills, all of which are necessary for significant political participation. Gender differences in political participation, once significant, have largely disappeared. Women are as well represented as men among the politically active, although not at elite level. The traditional view that women participate in politics less than men 'is no longer valid today as women and men are remarkably similar in their mass behaviour and attitudes across all modes of participation' (Norris 1991: 74). Young adults (see Box 4.3) are much less likely to be active than older generations, although for perhaps obvious reasons political activism beyond voting falls away among the over-65s (Electoral Commission/Hansard Society 2005: 2.18).

Why do some people participate more in politics than others? Political activists may be more confident that their efforts may make a difference. When the Electoral Commission survey (2005) asked people how far they agreed with the statement 'When people like me get involved in politics they really can change the way that the country is run', 36 per cent agreed, 41 per cent disagreed (with the remainder expressing no opinion either way). Those believing political participation is futile and ineffective may not even try to influence decisions that affect them. They are thus unlikely to have their interests taken into account, confirming the view that 'No one takes any notice of people like us'. Yet they may be right, at least in part. Governments may be more responsive to some interests than others, while some sections of the population have fewer resources and skills for effective participation (see Chapter 8). However, there seems to be a fairly widespread dissatisfaction with popular influence on government and policy. According to the same survey, while 67 per cent of people wanted to have a say in how the country was run, only 27 per cent felt that they had a say. Moreover, 'People in affluent areas were only a little less likely than those in deprived areas to feel they have no say at the moment' (Electoral Commission/Hansard Society 2005: 3.20).

Higher than average political participation may also be related to political values. Those holding strong or extreme political views tend to participate well above average, with overall participation in all fields of political activity highest on the extreme left. By contrast, those in the moderate centre tend to under-participate. This may be because they are more satisfied with the way the country is run, and so less inclined to indulge in political activities to secure change. (The 2005 Electoral Commission

Box 4.3

Apathetic young adults?

Surveys indicate that young adults are less interested in politics, less knowledgeable about it and less likely to vote than older generations. Just 39 per cent of eligible 18–24 year olds voted in 2001, and only 37 per cent in 2005. This has aroused considerable concern over the alleged political apathy and alienation of young adults, and the prospects for democratic politics in Britain, although some argue that this is simply a lifecycle problem – young people will become more politically engaged as they grow older. Another possible explanation is that the young are turned off conventional party politics but are interested instead in a new political agenda involving single-issue pressure groups and new social movements.

A survey of young people eligible to vote in elections for the first time found that they had a rather narrow view of politics, involving government, running the country, politicians and political parties. They considered the government unresponsive to the needs and wishes of young people, and had little confidence in their ability to influence parties or the government. Although the research indicated that young people 'had a general attachment to and confidence in the democratic process', they were sceptical on the outcome of elections, and showed 'a deep-seated scepticism towards the political parties and politicians who vie for their votes and political office'. However, the young adults surveyed showed similar interests to the population as a whole in political issues (public services, war, the economy, law and order and so on). The researchers concluded that:

> at the heart of young people's declining election turnout and their apparent disenchantment with Westminster politics is a strong sense of political alienation rather than political apathy – the political system in Britain is failing to provide the stimuli necessary for young people to take a greater role in political life.
>
> (Henn, Weinstein and Forrest 2005)

survey found that only a third of the public, 34 per cent, felt that the present system of governing the country worked well while 63 per cent felt it needed improving.) Political values associated with the 'new' or 'post-materialist' politics of environmentalism, peace and feminism are linked to higher than average participation, although this may be expressed through collective and direct action far more than through more conventional forms of participation (see Box 4.4 and Chapter 8). Civil disobedience strategies have been most evident in animal rights, anti poll tax, and anti road and other environmental protests in the 1990s. While a majority only support orderly, peaceful methods of political protest, willingness to engage in more threatening forms of direct action such as site occupations, destruction of crops, refusals to pay taxes, and blocking roads appears to have increased. The London bombings of July 2005 show that a small minority are even prepared to countenance indiscriminate violence against ordinary members of the public in pursuit of political objectives.

Political culture and socialisation

Some would link the changes in political participation described in the first part of this chapter with a broader change in political attitudes and behaviour, or what is sometimes described as political culture. It used to be argued that Britain had a political culture characterised by moderation, mutual toleration and respect for the law. Almond and Verba (1965), in a comparative study of five cultures, suggested that Britain enjoyed substantial political participation, social trust and civic organisation. More recent analysis suggests this culture has changed. Social trust and more specifically trust in government and politicians has declined markedly. There is now less readiness to defer to authority. There has been a corresponding reduction in traditional forms of political participation (voting, party membership and identification), perhaps offset by a rise of participation in direct action (see Box 4.4), and an increasing resort to illegal and even violent behaviour.

Definition

A **political culture** is the pattern of understandings, feelings and attitudes that dispose people towards behaving in a particular way politically. It is the collective expression of the political outlooks and values of the individuals who make up society.

In Focus 4.1

The London bombings of 7 July 2005

Terrorism involves a form of political participation that had been largely absent from the British mainland (although Ireland is another matter) until the events of 7 July 2005. In theory, democracy provides extensive opportunities for peaceful participation, without the need to resort to violence and murder. Yet some British Muslims evidently felt so alienated and aggrieved that they were prepared not only to die themselves but to kill and maim indiscriminately their fellow citizens. Although the bombings were roundly condemned by almost all Muslims, they intensified Islamophobia, and damaged community relations.

Fear of terrorism has also led to restrictions on civil liberties and, some would argue, rights to freedom of expression.

Photograph: EMPICS.

Box 4.4

The new politics of participation

The **Anti-poll tax movement** employed a wide range of methods of protest, including lobbying of MPs and councillors, petitions and demonstrations; on occasion, it was involved in violent disturbances such as the riot in March 1990 at Trafalgar Square which ended with over 140 being injured. More significant still, its massive campaign of non-payment 'tapped into' a long tradition of civil disobedience in Britain. In the first six months of 1992 alone, nearly four million people were summonsed for failing to pay the tax. This popular non-cooperation 'fuelled by an admittedly rare combination of moral outrage and material self-interest' forced the government to back down and withdraw the tax.

Anti-roads protests were coordinated from 1991 by Alarm UK, an umbrella organisation for 250 groups, involving direct action against a large number of road schemes, including extensions to the M3, M11 and A30. 'Eco-warriors' engaged in a large variety of obstructive activities on new road sites, including occupation of houses and treehouses, barricading themselves in tunnels, chaining themselves to concrete lock-ins and occupying offices of construction companies.

Protests against the export of live animals in 1995, involving demonstrations and obstruction, succeeded in reducing the number of ferry companies and ports handling the trade, but protesters were far from satisfied with the new EU rules on the live transport of animals agreed in July 1995.

Protests against genetically modified (GM) crops (1999 onwards). Greenpeace and other environmental groups opposed trials of GM crops by the company Monsanto, fearing cross-pollination with native plants and other damaging environmental effects. Protests included the trashing of GM crops. Hostile public opinion led to a moratorium on the commercial growing of GM crops.

The fuel protests (September 2000). In September 1999 militant French road hauliers blocked fuel supplies in a protest against the rising cost of diesel. This encouraged British farmers, lorry drivers, taxi drivers and in some places fishing operatives to take similar action with blockades at oil refineries and fuel distribution depots. The Opposition leader described the blockade as a 'taxpayers' rebellion' which appeared to be supported by 95 per cent of public opinion. The fuel protesters revealed that, using the new technologies of communication, relatively few activists could create disproportional national disruption. It was estimated that only 2000 individuals were involved directly in the fuel blockade, yet within days the country was plunged into crisis. Panic buying by the public left garages without fuel and created food shortages in supermarkets. The government was clearly taken by surprise by both the speed at which the crisis developed and the free fall in the government's popularity with the public (a fall which, however, proved short-lived).

What can explain this apparent change in political culture? The process by which people come to understand and mentally absorb the culture of their society is referred to as *socialisation*, and the process by which they acquire knowledge of their political culture is known as *political socialisation*. The notion of political socialisation holds that people's political knowledge, values, attitudes and beliefs are informally learned in a process which begins in childhood and continues throughout their adult lives. Although political socialisation is best seen as continuous, certain phases seem to be particularly important. Because of the malleability of the young and their greater exposure and susceptibility to influences, it is generally held that the pre-adult years are of critical significance to political socialisation, even though political attitudes learned when young may be modified or changed as a result of later experiences and pressures.

Key agencies that influence political socialisation include the family, local community, peer groups, education, workplace experience and the media. The manner in which these agencies combine varies for each individual. Often, because of the depth and intensity of the emotional relationships it involves,

Definition

Political socialisation is the process by which political beliefs and attitudes are learned or acquired by experience and are transmitted from one generation to the next.

the family is the predominate influence. It passes on an ethnic, religious and class identity, which normally is associated with a particular set of political orientations, and it powerfully shapes a child's attitude to authority, to gender roles, and to values which have clear implications for political behaviour. But no influence, however powerful, can determine totally political outlooks. Even in the case of the family, people may rebel as teenagers or gradually grow away from its values as adults.

Often the political 'messages' emitted by the various agencies of political socialisation overlap and mutually reinforce each other. They may be all the more influential as a result. But sometimes – from books, films or television, from friends or at work – an individual receives and has to accommodate a 'message' that conflicts with the overall view of the world derived from the other agencies. If it cannot be reconciled with the existing cultural perspective, it may bring about a change in attitude.

The main agencies of political socialisation are themselves continually evolving. The considerable increase in recent decades of divorce and birth outside marriage may be weakening the family, thereby undermining its effectiveness as a mechanism for transmitting political culture. In recent decades, also, the proportion of the population with qualifications at all levels has risen steadily, and in the longer term an educated population may be expected to be a more participatory one. However, the young are more likely to participate in unconventional ways (protest politics) than conventional ones (voting in general elections). Changes in the media may also have had an impact on the political socialisation process. The period since the 1970s has been characterised by the growing predominance of television as the major source of public information about politics, although the political agenda remains strongly influenced by the (still predominantly right-wing) tabloid press. The new media seem likely to be increasingly significant over time.

Finally, an important theory of social change is the generation theory: the idea that the political outlook of each generation is powerfully shaped by the dominant ideas and institutions of the age into which it is born. In seeking to understand political attitudes and behaviour, it makes sense to consider the often sharply contrasting experiences of political 'generations'. Thus successive generations may have been moulded by the carnage of the First World War, the 1930s Depression, the post-1945 welfare state, the 'permissive society' of the 1960s, and the Thatcherite era of free markets and 'enterprise' (see Box 4.5).

Citizenship

A key term in the debate on political participation is citizenship. Citizenship implies full membership of a particular nation or state. To be a subject

Box 4.5

A Thatcher generation?

Anthony Heath and Alison Park (1997) compared the 'Thatcher generation' of the 1980s with previous generations socialised in the 1920s/1930s, the 1940s/1950s and the 1960s/1970s. They concluded that the Thatcherite crusade for a fundamental change in values had failed. Despite the Thatcherite attack on the state and government spending, support for state welfare provision remained undiminished among the general public and among the young in the late 1980s and the 1990s. Thus, the generation socialised in the 1980s was less likely to identify with the Conservatives than any previous generation, and there was little evidence to support the notion that it was more materialistic in its economic attitudes than its predecessors. Yet while there was little evidence that Thatcherite values had had a formative effect on the 1980s generation, there were real differences between the generations in attitudes towards traditional British institutions and Britain's place in the world. Support for the monarchy fell through each successive generation, reaching its lowest support with the youngest age group, while the generations growing up in the 1960s and 1980s were more likely than those growing up before or just after the Second World War to favour a closer relationship with Europe.

Other political differences, Heath and Park thought, were more likely to reflect lifecycle than generational differences. Thus, they attribute the greater apathy towards conventional politics among young voters not to 'a fundamental generation gap' but rather to their stage in the lifecycle. In other words, 'political interest increases with age', and is likely to do so for the 1980s generation too (Heath and Park: 4–18).

implies passive obedience to government and the state; to be a citizen implies willing active involvement in a political community. Citizenship is widely taken to involve a common identity with fellow citizens, a core of shared values, generally agreed rights and responsibilities, including an entitlement to participate in the nation's affairs.

In some countries, such as the USA, citizenship is only granted after formal tests in which applicants demonstrate their knowledge of a country's history, culture and political institutions, and take an oath of allegiance. In Britain there are no such formal requirements, although more recently courses and ceremonies have been introduced for new British citizens, reflecting a growing concern that citizenship in Britain does not necessarily involve a common identity and shared values. Some British citizens may identify with part of the territory of the United Kingdom only, and a minority may reject any allegiance to the British state. Yet quite apart from these ambiguities over the very nature of the British state, many British citizens (as we have seen) may fall short of the ideal of active citizenship, and full membership of the political community.

Citizenship is generally considered to involve both rights and obligations. Marshall (1950) categorised citizen rights under three headings: civil rights, political rights and social rights. Civil rights are rights necessary for individual freedom: freedom of speech and conscience, property rights, equality before the law. Political rights involve the right to participate in political life, through the rights to vote and stand for election. Social rights include the right to education, health treatment, housing and so on. These rights were progressively recognised over different periods in Europe – civil rights in the 18th century, political rights in the course of the 19th century and social rights with the growth of the welfare state in the 20th century. Yet rights carry with them obligations, not simply to obey orders, but to participate willingly and conscientiously in the political community. High levels of citizen participation have often been considered a necessary condition for democracy (see Box 4.6).

Although many British politicians and thinkers and all mainstream British political parties have favourably invoked the term 'citizen', it remains a hotly contested concept, used in different ways. Thus socialists have stressed social rights of citizens to adequate levels of education, health and housing, effectively requiring extensive state intervention. Neo-liberals, however, have tended to deny or minimise social rights, and downplay rights to political participation, emphasising instead the civil rights of the citizen against the state, the rights of individuals to live their own lives free from state interference, and their right to choose as consumers of public services.

Margaret Thatcher saw the right to own property and the working of the free market as best protecting the rights of individuals. 'Big government' was a threat to individual liberty, and ideally the state should be confined to performing minimalist functions of providing internal order and external defence. Welfare entitlements were not part of the Thatcherite view of citizenship.

Box 4.6

Political controversy: participation and democracy

Political theorists have long disagreed over the extent of participation that is necessary for a functioning democracy. Some argue that individuals should not only participate to the maximum in politics, but also should participate in family decision making, and in college/school and workplace decisions. In other words, participation and democracy should form a way of life rather than just a narrow form of political behaviour (Mill 1861, Pateman 1970). Others argue that a high level of political participation from every individual is neither a realistic nor a desirable expectation in a modern industrial society. In fact, it has only been in totalitarian societies that the importance of politics has been elevated so as to dominate over the individual. Apathy marks the limits of politics and should, in this sense, be recognised as a democratic value (Oakeshott 1962). Since a fully participatory democracy is not feasible in contemporary Britain or any other liberal democracy, it is more realistic to accept that much political decision making is done by a political elite. Indeed all that representative as opposed to direct democracy requires of the masses is the periodic election of an elite to represent them, and this does not necessarily require much interest in or knowledge of politics (Schumpeter 1943).

However, concern over increasing social disintegration led some 'one-nation' Tories such as Douglas Hurd to argue that those who had benefited from the free-market economy had a moral duty to become 'active citizens' and volunteer help to their local communities. The conception of citizens as consumers in the marketplace was developed by John Major's Conservative governments. The Citizen's Charter was concerned with the delivery of public services to the consumer citizen. Increasing numbers of league tables were published on the performance of public services as a means of informing consumer choice, a practice extended by Labour.

New Labour's view of citizenship involved cultural engineering to end social exclusion, with a new pay-off between rights and duties. Described by some commentators as a 'tough love' formula, the state would provide resources for community development. Parenting classes, homework clubs, child-care facilities would be resourced in exchange for a reduction in youth crime, higher educational attainment and improved employment prospects. Poor parents who allowed or encouraged their children to truant would be punished. The shock to Labour's designs for constructing new citizenship values came in the prolonged rioting in Bradford, Burnley and Oldham, and the apparent rejection of British society by significant numbers of young Muslim males. It was feared that some were excluding themselves from citizenship through choice rather than circumstance. The immediate political response was a set of proposals for requirements to speak English, citizenship tests and an oath of allegiance. In schools, citizenship education has already become a compulsory part of the curriculum.

■ Community

While citizenship relates to the rights and duties of individual men and women, community is about groups of people and wider social interaction. Although it commonly conjures up images of small face-to-face local communities, such as a village or neighbourhood, it is also applied to much larger collective bodies – the national community, the European Community, the international community. Moreover, community is not invariably linked with territory. Thus in other contexts we have professional communities, the academic community, ethnic minority communities or the Catholic community. There may be distinctive communities living alongside each other within a specific area, as in Northern Ireland.

Community, like citizen, has positive connotations, so much so that it is sometimes employed as an all-purpose sanitising term to promote particular initiatives (community care, community policing), institutions or even taxes (the community charge, the official description of the poll tax). More positively, it is linked with certain values and ideas, such as cooperation, fellowship and solidarity. It implies that people do have interests in common, that they are not just a mere aggregate of individuals motivated exclusively by their own self-interest, but capable of fellow feeling, group loyalty and a sense of social obligation.

Indeed a whole communitarian school of political thought has grown up to counter the narrow individualism associated with classical liberalism and, more recently, the neo-liberal New Right (Mulhall and Swift 1996). These ideas have been popularised by Amitae Etzioni (1995) among others, and briefly taken up by politicians like Tony Blair. Community in this sense is highly compatible with the notion of active citizenship, involving wider social engagement and mutual rights and obligations. Both citizenship and community are terms which have acquired a strong normative flavour, recommending how people should behave.

Some however would suggest that a sense of community, and obligations to the community, have declined markedly in the modern world. Thus we no longer live, work and interact within small face-to-face communities, but live fragmented, isolated lives, loosely linked to a range of barely related 'communities' with which we may feel little identity or loyalty. We do not necessarily know or care for our neighbours, having nothing in common beyond physical proximity. Robert Putnam (2000) in particular has linked the decline of political participation with a reduction in 'social capital', a more general decline in social interaction and engagement in the modern western world (see Box 4.7).

Box 4.7

Political controversy: social capital, and a decline in social and political engagement?

Robert Putnam (1995, 2000) has developed a complex theory linking a decline in political participation with a general reduction of what he calls social capital. Basically, social capital reflects how much individuals interact with each other face-to-face as neighbours, members of clubs and other forms of association. A result of high levels of interaction is the development of civic attitudes that will include the likelihood of voting in elections. The more individuals play passive, isolated roles in society, such as staying at home, watching television and videos, and surfing the internet, the more likely they are to withdraw from public activities such as voting, and from active involvement in political parties and pressure groups. Putnam supports his theory with a wealth of research in the USA, indicating a strong correlation between a decline in social capital and decline in active citizenship and political engagement.

Some critics suggest that Putnam's American findings do not necessarily apply to Britain. Thus Hall (1999) concluded that social capital had not declined in Britain, with men showing some marginal increase in community involvement while women's involvement had doubled. Others have been more sceptical over the extent and implications of the new forms of social and political engagement in Britain charted by Hall (Margetts in Dunleavy *et al.*, 2002). Indeed, it may be that the social and political trends charted by Putnam in the USA may over time be replicated in other western societies, as has been commonly the case with other political developments.

Others suggest that Putnam has been too pessimistic and one-sided over the social changes he has described. Social capital theorists have tended to see the new media such as television, mobile phones and the internet as a threat to participatory democracy, through the reduction in face-to-face communication and social interaction. Yet it can be argued that they offer new forms of communication and opportunities for increased participation, through for example internet chat rooms and interactive television (Margetts in Dunleavy *et al.*, 2002).

At another level, it may even be questioned whether high levels of social capital necessarily promote a healthy functioning democracy. Thus Northern Ireland appears to combine high levels of social capital with sectarian violence and conflict and marked problems in operating democratic institutions and procedures.

■ Conclusion

This chapter began by charting an apparent decline in various forms of political participation in Britain, listing some of the possible causes and the remedies that have been tried or proposed. The second half of the chapter has attempted to deepen the debate through an examination of underlying relevant theory, exploring briefly political culture and socialisation, the key concepts of citizenship and community, and the current controversy over the importance of social capital. While these theories may enlarge understanding of the processes involved, and clarify some of the terms used in debate, it is doubtful how far they have advanced the debate over the extent of political participation required for a healthy democracy or over practical measures to encourage increased political involvement.

■ Summary

- Democracy appears to require higher levels of political interest, knowledge and involvement than other political systems.
- Nevertheless up to half British adults have little knowledge of and interest in politics. A substantial and growing minority do not even vote, and a majority of the population do not participate in politics beyond voting.
- Various practical remedies have been tried or proposed to counter this apparently widespread political ignorance and apathy, including more political education, making it easier to register the vote, electoral reform and the encouragement of other forms of political involvement.
- Some argue that a decline in traditional political engagement through voting, parties and

representative institutions has been offset by a rise in new forms of political activity involving more direct action.

- Changes in political behaviour may be related to wider changes in British political culture and in political socialisation.
- Democracy may be felt to require active citizenship. In practice the term 'citizen' has been extensively but very variously used in political debate in Britain.
- Community is another key term in the debate over political participation, although it is a term that is imprecise, but carrying strong normative overtones, freely applied to different levels and types of social organisation.
- Social capital theorists have linked declining political participation with reduced levels of social interaction and engagement more generally in modern society. The analysis is suggestive but contentious.

Questions for discussion

- How far do low and declining turnout figures in elections suggest a crisis for democracy?
- Should voting be compulsory? How else might people be encouraged to vote? Does voting change anything?
- How else can individuals participate in politics beyond voting? How many do in fact participate significantly beyond voting?
- How far are there significant differences in the political outlook and behaviour of different generations? Are younger people less interested in politics, and if so, why, and how might it be remedied?
- Does the apparent increase in the politics of direct action involve a threat to rational democratic debate, or a healthy alternative to outdated and limited traditional means of political involvement?
- Should there be more education in citizenship? Should language or other tests be a requirement for British citizenship? What does, or should, citizenship involve?
- Has there been a general decline in social interaction and engagement in modern Britain, and what are the implications for politics?

Further reading

On political participation, a key source is still Parry, Moyser and Day, *Political Participation and Democracy in Britain* (1992). This should be supplemented by the *British Social Attitudes* series, produced annually, and the reports produced for the Electoral Commission and the Hansard Society (2004, 2005, best consulted on the website www.electoralcommission.org.uk). For a valuable survey of participation, citizenship and associated academic debates see the chapters by Margett and Fraser, in Dunleavy *et al.*, *Developments in British Politics 6* (2002). For more specific analysis of political culture and voting participation see Evans in Dunleavy *et al.*, *Developments in British Politics 7* (2003). A useful recent short article is Bill Jones, 'Apathy: why don't people want to vote? (2003). Lynch discusses new voting methods in 'Goodbye ballot box, hello post box' (2002). For a discussion of non-participation by the young see O'Toole *et al.* (2003) and Henn, Weinstein and Forrest (2005).

On political culture, the classic work is Almond and Verba, *The Civic Culture* (1965). On social capital see Putnam, *Bowling Alone: The collapse and revival of the American community* (2000). For a discussion of citizenship and education, see Greenwood and Robins, 'Citizenship tests and education: embedding a concept' (2002).

Elections and voting

Contents

Elections decide who governs in modern representative democracies. The 2005 General Election confirmed Blair's government in power with an unprecedented third successive Labour majority, although one secured with only 35 per cent of the votes cast. This emphasises that it is not just how people vote, but precisely how their votes are counted and converted into parliamentary majorities and governments that determines electoral outcomes. Reformers question the fairness of the British first-past-the-post electoral system, used for elections to the Westminster Parliament and local councils. Alternatives are no longer theoretical. A variety of more proportional systems have already been introduced for devolved government in Scotland, Wales and Northern Ireland, for London government and for British elections to the European Parliament. These new systems have produced markedly different results in terms of voters' behaviour, the choice of representatives, relative party strengths and the nature and style of government. They raise some fundamental issues over the future of democracy in Britain.

Even without electoral reform, there have been some significant trends in voting in recent elections, including a marked fall in turnout, an increase in tactical voting and a decline in support for the two major parties. The electorate has become more volatile. Party loyalties appear weaker. The formerly marked correlation between voting and occupational class has declined, although it remains more significant than other social divisions. There are some indications of a rise in issue voting.

The 2005 General Election

On 5 May 2005 the British people went to the polls to elect 646 Members of Parliament at Westminster, and effectively to determine which party should govern Britain for the next four or five years. The outcome was a third successive victory for Blair's Labour Party, but with a much reduced majority. Both the Conservatives and Liberal Democrats made gains at Labour's expense (see Table 5.1)

Anyone unfamiliar with the workings of the UK electoral system might be surprised that Labour managed to win 55 per cent of the seats at Westminster and a comfortable overall majority on just 35 per cent of the vote. Of the other parties, the Conservatives gained 30 per cent of the seats on 32 per cent of the vote, while the Liberal Democrats won less than one tenth of the seats on 22 per cent of the vote. Some of the other parties whose strength was concentrated in particular parts of the United Kingdom, such as the nationalist

Table 5.1 The result of the 2005 General Election

Party	% votes	Number of seats*	% seats
Labour	35.2	356	55
Conservative	32.3	197	30
Liberal Democrats	22.0	62	10
Others**	10.5	30**	5

* The results in 645 seats were declared in May 2005. The poll in Staffordshire South was postponed following the death of one of the candidates in the campaign. (It has since been retained by the Conservatives.)

** Those parties that won seats include Northern Ireland parties (18), SNP (6), Plaid Cymru (3), Respect (1), Independents (2).

parties, did reasonably well in terms of representation. Other parties like the Greens, the UK Independence Party and the British National Party, whose support was more dispersed, elected no MPs. There is obviously a markedly disproportionate relationship between votes cast and seats won in 2005. Yet British General Elections often throw up some strange results (see Box 5.1).

The first-past-the-post electoral system

To understand some of these strange statistics it is necessary to examine the British electoral system, a system that is now relatively rare in the western world. It is most accurately described as a single member simple plurality system (Curtis, in Dunleavy *et al.* 2003), although more familiarly known as the 'first-past-the-post' system. The United Kingdom is divided into 646 electoral areas (or parliamentary constituencies) which each elect a single Member of Parliament, who

Definition

The **first-past-the-post electoral system** (also known as the single member simple plurality system) involves the election of a single representative for each electoral area (or constituency) into which the country is divided. The candidate for election who gains more votes than any rival candidate wins, regardless of whether he or she has a majority of the total votes cast.

Box 5.1

'Strange but true!' Some surprising facts and figures on past British General Elections

- No party has won over half the votes in any election from 1945 onwards, but in only one election (February 1974) has the leading party secured less than half the seats.
- In 1951 Labour won 200,000 more votes than the Conservatives, who won a majority of the seats and went on to form the government.
- In February 1974 Labour won fewer votes but more seats than the Conservatives and went on to form the government.
- In 1983 the Labour Party received 27.6 per cent of the popular vote and won 209 seats. The recently formed Liberal-SDP Alliance, close behind with 25.4 per cent of the popular vote, won only 23 seats. Margaret Thatcher's Conservatives secured a massive Commons majority on 42.4 per cent of the vote, less than the 43.4 per cent gained by Sir Alec Douglas-Home's Conservatives when they lost in 1964.
- In 1997 the Liberal Democrats' total vote and share of the vote fell, compared with 1992, yet they more than doubled their number of seats (from 20 to 46).
- The number of viewers who voted in the final night of Channel Four's *Big Brother* television programme in 2001 was greater than the combined Labour, Conservative and Liberal Democrat vote in the General Election of that year.

needs to win only a plurality (more than any other candidate) rather than an overall majority of the votes cast in the constituency. To see how this can work out in a single constituency, consider the result for Ochil and South Perthshire in 2005 (see Table 5.2).

It will be seen that the victorious Labour candidate won with less than a third of the votes cast (31.4 per cent), because the rest of the vote was divided between seven other candidates, of whom the SNP secured 29.9 per cent and the Conservative 21.5 per cent. Voters could only put a cross against one of eight candidates. Had voters been able to express their preferences in order, with votes for the bottom candidates being progressively eliminated and their votes transferred to second or subsequent preferences until one candidate emerged with an overall majority, the final result might have been different. It is a fairly extreme but far from unique example of what can happen under Britain's first-past-the-post system. Thus in 2005 the Scottish National Party won the Angus constituency on 33.7 per cent of the vote and the SDLP won Belfast on 32.3 per cent. In recent elections only around half of MPs have won with the support of more than half the voters.

Yet this is not the main reason for the disproportionate relationship between the votes cast and seats won for parties over the UK as a whole. Imagine first a hypothetical example. Just two parties contest the election with candidates in every constituency. One party wins 51 per cent of vote everywhere, the other 49 per cent. All MPs would be elected on a majority of the votes cast in their constituency but the first party would win all the seats, the second none at all. In practice of course party strengths vary considerably from area to area, so such an outcome would be most unlikely. Yet it does emphasise the point that the distribution of votes can be crucial. A third or minor party whose support is significant but widely dispersed may not win a single seat. In elections for the European Parliament in 1984, then held under the first past the post system, the Liberals and their SDP allies won 19 per cent of the vote and no seats. In 1989 the Greens won 15 per cent of the vote, still by far the highest percentage they have achieved in any UK-wide election, and no seats. On the other hand nationalist parties and others whose support is concentrated in particular parts of the UK may do quite well out of the system. In the 2005 General Election George Galloway won a seat for Respect, a party that only contested a handful of constituencies, while an independent held Wyre Forest on the single issue of maintaining Kidderminster Hospital. This emphasises that the British electoral system is designed to secure the election of individual representatives for each of 646 parliamentary constituencies, not the proportional representation of political parties over the country as a whole.

Table 5.2 Votes cast for candidates in the Ochil and South Perthshire parliamentary constituency, 2005*

Candidate	Party	No. of votes	% of votes
Gordon Banks	Labour	14,645	31.4
Annabelle Ewing	SNP	13,957	29.9
Elizabeth Jane Smith	Conservative	10,021	21.5
Catherine Whittingham	Liberal Democrat	6,218	13.3
George Baxter	Scottish Green Party	978	2.1
Iain Campbell	Scottish Socialist Party	420	0.9
David Bushby	UK Independence Party	275	0.6
Maitland Kelly	Free Scotland Party	183	0.4

* Labour majority 688 (1.5%) Turnout 66%.

Definition

Proportional representation is an electoral system that delivers for each political party a share of elected representatives proportionate to its share of its total national vote. Thus a 20 per cent share of the vote should lead to a 20 per cent share of the seats in the elected parliament, assembly or council.

While the first-past-the-post system in the UK has generally exaggerated the strength of the leading party, turning a small lead in votes over its main rival to a much bigger lead in seats, it has produced a much more disproportionate relationship between votes and seats since 1974. Although the system can work tolerably where there are only two parties in contention, it becomes more capricious and apparently unfair in an era of multi-party politics. The Liberals and their Liberal Democrat successors have been the main losers. Since 1974 they have averaged around a fifth of the votes cast in British General Elections. Such support would make them a sizeable party, with the expectation of a share in government, in almost any other country in Europe. Their fortunes may usefully be compared with those of a comparable party in Germany, the Free Democrats (see Box 5.2).

Box 5.2

Comparative politics: the German Free Democrats in comparison with the British Liberals and Liberal Democrats

The German Free Democrats (FDP) have generally secured between 5 per cent and 10 per cent of the vote in elections in the German Federal Republic since 1949, and under the German electoral system they always received a broadly comparable proportion of seats in the German Bundestag or federal parliament. Because it has been rare for a single party to secure an overall majority of seats the FDP have held Cabinet seats in a coalition government for most of the period since 1949. From 1949–57 and 1961–5 they were in coalition with the Christian Democrats and from 1969–83 they partnered the Social Democrats, returning to share government posts with the Christian Democrats from 1983–98. The period from 1998 onwards has been the longest period they have been out of office.

The British Liberal Party and its successors have consistently won a larger share of the national vote than the German Free Democrats since 1974, sometimes achieving twice or three times the FDP's share of the vote. Yet the Liberals and their successors have been substantially under-represented at Westminster, and never shared in government nor held a single Cabinet post since 1945.

Should the system be changed? The charge sheet against the first-past-the-post system is extensive.

- It produces a grossly disproportionate result between votes cast and seats won for parties, normally over-representing the leading party and particularly penalising third and minor parties whose support is widely dispersed rather than concentrated. It can also penalise major parties in parts of the UK. Thus the Conservatives won no seats at all in Scotland and Wales in 1997, and have not improved their representation much since.
- Under the system most votes are effectively wasted. All votes for losing candidates and all surplus votes for winning candidates may be considered wasted as they do not contribute to the election of representatives. (To win, a candidate only needs one vote more than that received by any other candidate. A majority of 20,000 or more may be impressive, but does not make any difference to a party's representation.)
- Because most parliamentary seats are considered 'safe', as there is a substantial majority for the party that won last time, there is little incentive to vote in such seats. Only more marginal seats are likely to change hands. This is one explanation for low turnout. Turnout is often much lower in safe seats than marginals.
- The system can distort voter's preferences. Voters may fear to vote for their main preferred candidate or party for fear of 'letting in' the party they most dislike. Thus voters may vote 'tactically' for their second or third

choice. Such tactical voting has increased markedly since 1997.

Yet despite these criticisms there is not much evidence of major public dissatisfaction with the voting system. It has not apparently affected confidence in British democracy, nor the legitimacy of governments elected under it. Electoral reform has not figured significantly among the concerns of voters in election campaigns, and even the Liberal Democrats, the main losers under the current system, did not focus on the issue much in 2005. Even so, the result of that election – a comfortable majority for Labour with the support of only just over a third of voters and a fifth of the electorate – does raise questions.

Those who defend the current electoral system for Westminster make the following points:

- It is a simple and readily understood system, unlike most other electoral systems producing more proportional representation. It produces a clear result quickly.
- It preserves a strong link between the electors in each constituency and their Member of Parliament, who has a strong incentive to listen to constituents and represent their interests and that of the area in Parliament.
- Because first past the post normally exaggerates the winning margin of the leading party and delivers a clear majority of seats in the House of Commons, it provides stable government (see Box 5.3).

The case for more proportional representation is bound up with the debate over the relative advantages and disadvantages of single party and coalition government. Some argue that coalition government involves too many compromises, and often too much influence for small (sometimes extremist) parties on whose support the coalition depends for survival. Thus coalition government may appear weak and unstable, unable to take tough decisions. Alternatively, there may be a virtually permanent governing coalition with opposition parties effectively locked out of power and no effective choice. Others argue that concession and compromise are vital parts of the democratic process. Single-party governments with large majorities can behave in high-handed ways, ignoring popular opposition to policies, and riding roughshod over minorities. Critics point out that policies such as the poll tax or university top-up fees would probably not have been implemented by a coalition government (although the Iraq war might still have proceeded).

Box 5.3

Comparative politics: coalition government in Britain and elsewhere in Europe

Since 1945 Britain has had nothing but single-party government, and most of those governments have enjoyed a fairly comfortable majority in the House of Commons. Had British elections been conducted under a system of strict proportional representation no party would have won a majority of seats because none secured a majority of votes over the whole period. The consequence would have been minority or coalition government, which has been rather rare in Britain outside wartime. (The Lloyd-George wartime coalition continued into peacetime, until it broke up in 1922, and there was a Conservative-dominated National Government from 1931 which became more Conservative with time.) More recently, British politics has had more experience of coalition politics, for example in the devolved government of Scotland (under a more proportional electoral system) and on many local councils (still elected under first past the post).

Coalition government is the norm rather than the exception elsewhere in Europe. Germany and the Netherlands have long provided examples of stable and generally successful coalition government. (The September 2005 elections in Germany, however, seemingly failed to produce a credible coalition government with prospects of reasonable stability.) By contrast, France under the Fourth French Republic, and Italy for a rather longer period, experienced weak, unstable coalition government, sometimes only lasting for weeks before collapse. Further afield, proportional representation in Israel has left coalition governments sometimes dependent for their survival on the votes of tiny extremist parties.

Electoral reform

The case for electoral reform depends not only on the perceived defects of the first-past-the-post system, but on the alternatives available. Ideally an electoral system should deliver the following:

- real choice for voters – involving a range of candidates and parties
- simplicity – a system that is readily comprehensible to voters
- fair treatment of parties and candidates – each vote as far as possible should count equally
- effective representation of electoral areas (or constituencies)
- effective representation of the gender, age, ethnic, religious and occupational class divisions in the population at large
- parliaments or assemblies that can sustain stable governments
- accountable government, with a clear link between elections and the making and breaking of governments.

Yet in practice there is no ideal system that can meet all these objectives. Instead there is a range of options, each of which offers advantages and disadvantages. These options are not theoretical. There is long experience of a range of different electoral systems operating in other countries. More recently some of these systems have been introduced in the UK, not for Westminster or local elections, but for elections for the European Parliament, for devolved parliaments and assemblies in Scotland, Wales and Northern Ireland, for the Greater London Assembly and for mayoral elections. As Curtice (in Dunleavy *et al.* 2003: 100) has observed, 'Britain has become a laboratory of electoral experimentation and change'. Some of the main systems are outlined below.

The alternative vote

Voters register their preferences for candidates in order. If no candidate wins an overall majority of first-preference votes, the candidate coming last is eliminated and his or her second-preference votes are distributed among the remaining candidates. The process continues until one candidate has an overall majority of the votes cast. This system is used in Australia. It is not used in Britain for elections to any formal level of government, although a more limited form of preferential voting involving just second preferences (called the supplementary vote) is now used for mayoral elections (such as the election of the London mayor).

The advantage of the alternative vote is that representatives can no longer be elected on a minority of the vote, and electors do not have to resort to tactical voting, They can vote for their first-choice candidate and party without fearing this would 'let in' a feared opponent. It is also relatively simple. The obvious disadvantage is that it does not deliver a proportionate relationship between votes and seats. A party obtaining 20 per cent of first-preference votes over the country as a whole might still end up with no seats.

The second ballot

In countries using this system, if no candidate receives an overall majority on the first ballot, there is a subsequent second ballot. This either involves the leading two candidates (as in Mali, Ukraine and the French presidential elections) or only allows those candidates with more than a set proportion of the votes to proceed (as with French Assembly elections). In practice this works much like the alternative vote or supplementary vote, although the period between ballots gives parties, candidates and voters some time to absorb the implications of voting on the first ballot and adjust their preferences accordingly. In elections for the French Assembly there are often informal deals between parties after the first ballot. French voters, it is sometimes said, vote 'with their hearts' on the first ballot and 'with their wallets' on the second. This system has not been used in Britain for any level of government, although a succession of ballots has sometimes proved necessary for the election of party leaders (e.g. for the Conservative leadership in 1975, 1990, 1997, 2001 and 2005).

The second ballot system may ensure that the winning candidate has an overall majority, albeit with some sacrifice of voter choice. It does not deliver a proportionate relationship between seats and votes any more than the alternative vote.

National or regional party list systems

Such systems can deliver a very close relationship between votes for a party and seats. Each party draws up a list of its candidates in order. Thus in a national list system involving a 100-member legislature a party securing 40 per cent of the vote would see its first 40 candidates elected. Many larger countries that use the list system divide the country into regions, where each party has its own regional lists of candidates. Voters may be given the option of expressing their own order of preferences for candidates within parties (**open list systems**) or simply have to accept the official party list order (**closed list systems**). National or regional party list systems are widely used in continental Europe and Latin America. A closed regional party list system similar to that used by most other EU member states was introduced in Britain for the election of Members of the European Parliament from 1999 onwards (see Chapter 15).

The system is fairly simple and delivers proportional representation. It does not provide effective constituency representation, and critics suggest it gives too much power to the party nationally (or regionally) since it is responsible for drawing up lists of candidates, and marginalises local party members. It may also lead to the representation of a number of small and possible extremist parties, rendering the formation of stable government more difficult.

The single transferable vote (STV)

This is the most complex system that can produce results close to proportional representation. Under the system the country is divided into a number of electoral areas that each elect a number of representatives (multi-member constituencies), but where each voter only has a single vote that is transferable between candidates. To secure election, a candidate has to win a proportion of the total vote in the electoral area or constituency, according to the following formula:

$$\frac{\text{Total number of votes cast}}{\text{Number of seats} + 1} + 1$$

Initially, only first preferences are counted. Any candidate who achieves the quota is deemed elected, and any surplus votes above the quota are redistributed according to second (and later subsequent) preferences. If no candidate achieves the quota on the first or subsequent count, the bottom candidates are progressively eliminated and their second (and subsequent) preferences are distributed until all the seats are filled.

It sounds complicated (and is), but can be best illustrated with reference to Northern Ireland assembly elections, where the system was used in 1998 and again in 2003. Each constituency elects six members of the Northern Ireland Assembly. To be elected a candidate needs (according to the formula above) one vote more than a seventh of the total number of votes. In practice the leading parties put up not one but several candidates, hoping to get as many as possible elected in each constituency. Thus in Antrim South in 2003 two Ulster Unionists (UUP) were elected, two members of the Democratic Unionist Party (DUP), one member for the Social Democratic and Labour Party (SDLP) and one for the Alliance Party. In Fermanagh and South Tyrone there were two Sinn Fein candidates elected, two Ulster Unionists and one each for the DUP and SDLP.

The system combines constituency representation with overall results close to proportional representation. Broadly speaking, the more members elected for each constituency, the more proportional the whole system will be. The Irish Republic has used STV for many years, but most constituencies only elect three members, leading to a less proportionate relationship between a party's seats and votes than in Northern Ireland. There the system was adopted to ensure that all communities and shades of opinion were represented, as part of the ongoing peace process. There was also hope that moderate parties might profit, and indeed the small non-sectarian Alliance Party managed to retain six seats in 2003, while it would not have come close to winning any under first past the post. Yet in 2003 the moderate and constitutional nationalist party, the SDLP, lost out to Sinn Fein, while Ian Paisley's DUP overtook David Trimble's Unionists to become the largest party. (For more on elections in Northern Ireland, see Chapter 16.)

The additional member system (AMS)

Under the additional member system (sometimes called the German system) voters have two votes, one for their local constituency, and a second vote, designed to compensate parties that are under-represented in the constituencies, by electing additional members through national or regional party lists. It is often referred to as a hybrid system, combining a clear link between directly elected representatives and constituencies with overall results close to proportional representation. It has long been used in Germany, where however parties can only gain additional members if they secure more than 5 per cent of the national vote, a threshold designed to exclude small parties and prevent the fragmentation of representation in the German parliament.

The AMS has already been used in the United Kingdom for elections to the Scottish Parliament, Welsh Assembly and Greater London Assembly. In Scotland the results provide a contrast with the General Election, where Scottish MPs are still elected under first past the post. In General Elections from 1997 to 2005 Labour has won a comfortable overall majority of seats in Scotland, while the Conservatives won no seats at all in 1997 and only one in 2001 and 2005. Yet in elections for the Scottish Parliament under AMS Labour fell well short of a majority in both 1999 and 2003, and formed a coalition with the Liberal Democrats. The Conservatives only won three constituency MSPs, but a further 15 MSPs on the regional list vote, giving them a total of 18 out of 129, close to the 16 per cent of the vote they secured. Other parties that gained were the Scottish Socialist Party (six seats) and the Greens (seven seats). The AMS may also make it easier to secure a more equal share of seats by gender. In 2003 half the members of the Welsh Assembly were women. (For more on elections in Scotland and Wales see Chapter 16, and for London see Chapter 17.)

■ Further electoral reform in Britain?

Electoral reform only seems to excite political anoraks, and has never been much of an issue with most voters. Yet electoral systems can make a crucial difference to the fortunes of parties and the form and nature of government, as some of the examples above indicate. Were proportional representation ever to be introduced for Westminster elections, it would lead to minority government or coalition government, if current voting patterns were maintained. In practice it might also change voting behaviour, perhaps encouraging more support for minor parties, as in Scotland. What then are the prospects for further electoral reform in Britain, particularly for General and local elections still conducted under first past the post?

In 1997 Labour had promised a commission on electoral reform with a subsequent referendum. The commission was appointed. It was chaired by Lord Jenkins, a former Deputy Leader of the Labour Party, and the former Leader of the Social Democratic Party (SDP). Its report in 1998 recommended the introduction of the alternative vote (AV) to elect 80–85 per cent of the Commons, with the rest elected by a list system. This system would have led to increased representation for other parties had it been in place in 1997, although Labour would have had a smaller, but still comfortable, overall majority on 44 per cent of the vote. Thus it fell well short of proportional representation. In practice the report was ignored and there was no referendum.

The introduction of new more proportional systems for the European Parliament, Scotland, Wales, Northern Ireland and London might appear a spur to further reform, particularly as they have produced such markedly different results from those conducted under first past the post. Yet the public seem unfazed by the experience of voting under different rules with very different outcomes. There is pressure from Labour's coalition partners in Scotland for the introduction of proportional representation for Scottish local elections, but less agitation elsewhere.

Although some might argue that the case for electoral reform is now stronger following the election of a government with a clear majority of seats on just 35 per cent of the vote, the immediate prospects for significant change seem weaker. There are Labour MPs who still favour a more proportionate system, but the majority fear it would ensure that a majority Labour government would never hold office again. The Conservatives, the main beneficiaries of the first-past-the-post system for most of the 20th century, have been most hostile to reform. Ironically, they have benefited most from the introduction of AMS in Scotland and Wales. Yet they still hope to be able to form a majority government at Westminster in the future. Thus the big two retain a vested interest in the existing system (which is perhaps why Labour ignored the Jenkins Report). The situation might change if the Liberal Democrats held the balance of power in the House of Commons and made electoral reform a condition of their participation in a coalition government.

> **Definition**
>
> **Swing** measures the shift in support between parties between elections. The two-party swing between elections can often be measured simply by adding the increase in votes for one party to the decrease in vote for the other and dividing by two. It becomes slightly more complicated if the votes for both parties increase or decrease (because of changes in votes for other parties). Here swing is measured by the formula
>
> $$\frac{(C2-C1) + (L1-L2)}{2}$$
>
> where C1 is the percentage of Conservative votes obtained in the first election and C2 the percentage at the second, and L1 and L2 are Labour's share of the vote in the two elections.
>
> The 'swing' needed for a party coming second in one election to win the next is more easily measured: simply halve the difference in the percentage of votes of the leading two parties. Thus if Labour had 40 per cent and the Conservatives had 34 per cent at the previous election, the Conservatives would need a 3 per cent swing to win next time. In other words three voters in 100 would have to switch support between the two parties.
>
> Note, however, that in elections where several parties are competing, the two-party swing can be misleading. In 2005 there was a 4 per cent swing from Labour to Conservative, but most of this was the result of defections from Labour to other parties rather than a positive swing to the Conservatives, whose proportion of the vote scarcely increased.

Persistence and change in voting behaviour

We move now from considering the mechanics of electoral systems to examine why people vote as they do. It has long been argued that most people are habitual voters who support the same party from one election to the next, and relatively few are floating voters, prepared to changed their vote. Indeed, many people seem to determine their party allegiance young, perhaps at their first election, or maybe even earlier, and stick with that party through its fluctuating fortunes subsequently, in much the same way as many people continue to support the same football team, regardless of success or failure. Indeed, most elections in Britain since the war have involved a relatively small shift in votes from the previous election, with the 'swing' between the parties commonly being less than 3 per cent.

There is some evidence that fewer people than in the past identify strongly with a particular party, and that more are prepared to change their vote. Thus the electorate may be becoming more volatile. The 1997 General Election was a political earthquake, with an almost unprecedented swing of over 10 per cent from Conservative to Labour, a huge turn round, although subsequent elections have involved more modest shifts in party support.

One recent trend in British General Elections is towards more variation in swings between different regions and between individual constituencies. Back in the 1960s and 1970s a leading political scientist, Robert McKenzie, used a 'swingometer' to predict the results of General Elections on television after the first handful of seats had been declared. The predictions were generally very accurate, because then the whole country appeared to swing together, and there were only minor variations between the swing in particular constituencies. More recently there have been more marked differences in the size of the swing. In 2005 the average swing from Labour to Conservative of around 3 per cent masked huge variations. Thus there was an 8.7 per cent swing from Labour to Conservative in Enfield Southgate, but some seats registered a small swing to Labour. There were also some massive swings from Labour to the Liberal Democrats, particularly in seats with a large student population and/or a substantial Muslim population: 20.1 per cent in Birmingham Ladywood, 17.3 per cent in Manchester Withington (where the Iraq war and student top-up fees may have been important issues). Overall, however, the anti-Labour swing was larger in and around London than in the rest of Britain. Even so, an exit poll predicted Labour's final tally of seats and overall majority almost exactly before any seats had been declared, with the aid of a more sophisticated version of McKenzie's old swingometer, indicating that it is not yet redundant.

Definition

A **correlation** measures the strength of the association between two variables. Correlation coefficients can be calculated between –1 and +1. A negative score indicates a negative or inverse correlation between two variables (e.g. reading the *Daily Mirror* and voting Conservative). A positive score indicates a positive correlation. A score close to zero (e.g. between – 0.2 and +0.2) suggests a weak association that may not be statistically significant.

The shaping of party allegiances

Why do people support a particular party? In many cases childhood socialisation (see Chapter 4) will play an important part. Attitudes and behaviour (including political attitudes and behaviour) may be learned from the family, peer group, schooling and local community. Thus those brought up in a Labour household are more likely to support Labour themselves. They are even more likely to support Labour if other influences from peer group, neighbourhood and education reinforce family influence. Yet some young adults may have received mixed messages if there are divided allegiances in the immediate family or if there are conflicting influences among other primary agents of socialisation. In other instances experiences at university or in work may expose people to different interests and ideas, and cause them to change their attitudes. Some may rebel against their background and adopt diametrically opposed political views. Even so, it still appears that most people determine their political allegiance relatively early, perhaps by the time they cast their first vote, and stick with it. However, there is also some evidence for the widespread assumption that some people become more conservative, with a small 'c' and perhaps with a large 'C' also, as they grow older (see below).

Much of this is common sense, once some of the jargon is decoded. However, voting is also a topic that can be subjected to some sophisticated statistical analysis. Voting has been correlated with a wide range of social characteristics and divisions – housing tenure, car ownership, newspaper readership, age, gender, religion, ethnicity, region, and above all social class. Some of the analysis should be interpreted with care. A correlation does not prove a cause. Thus there may be a significant correlation between owning two cars and voting Conservative, but this does not necessarily mean that owning two cars makes someone a Conservative. It is perhaps more likely that the occupation and income that enables someone to own two cars may make them rather more likely to vote Conservative. The direction of causation may also be problematic. Thus there is a significant positive correlation between reading the *Daily Mirror* and voting Labour. Does this mean the *Daily Mirror*, a paper long committed to the Labour cause, influences its readers to vote for that party? It is certainly quite plausible. Yet is also possible that those whose background and interests incline them to Labour choose to buy a Labour paper. Perhaps a little of both goes on, and reading the *Daily Mirror* and voting Labour are mutually reinforcing. (There are also of course many exceptions to even fairly strong positive correlations. Thus some two-car owners vote Labour, and some *Daily Mirror* readers vote Conservative.)

Social class and voting behaviour

Social class has long appeared a key factor explaining voting in Britain, although there is evidence that it is less important than previously. Labour, as the name implies, was the party established to represent the interests of the working class, particularly the manual working class who were members of trade unions affiliated to the

Labour Party. The Conservative Party was associated with the interests of the property-owning middle class. Indeed, back in 1967 a British political scientist Peter Pulzer (1967) could observe that 'class is the basis of British politics; all else is embellishment and detail'. Analysis of voting by class then provided substantial justification for Pulzer's bold assertion. What Table 5.3 indicates is a strong correlation between class and voting in the middle of the 20th century. The further down the social scale, the greater the support for Labour, while the professional and managerial classes were then overwhelmingly supporters of the Conservatives, and white-collar workers (the 'C1s') were twice as likely to vote Conservative as Labour.

Even then, however, it will be noted that significant minorities did not support the party associated with their class. Thus around a fifth of the middle class in post-war elections voted Labour, while around a third of the manual working class voted Conservative. Political scientists sought to explain this 'deviant voting', particularly the working-class Conservatives. Some saw the explanation in terms of the deference of some workers to their social superiors. Others considered that affluent workers (such as Midlands car workers) were increasingly acquiring middle-class characteristics and attitudes (including voting Conservative). Indeed left-wing analysts feared that growing affluence was, over time, eroding Labour's working-class vote.

Subsequently class allegiances have become more blurred. Margaret Thatcher made a particular pitch for the skilled working-class vote (the C2s), with some success, although there was always a substantial minority of skilled workers who supported the Conservatives right through the 20th century. From a Labour perspective there were worrying social trends (see Chapter 3). The manual working class was not only declining as a proportion of the population, but also appeared increasingly fragmented on lines of ethnicity and gender, and between the public and private sectors. Labour could no longer hope to win elections by securing most of the vote of the manual working class, but had to appeal to a wider cross-class constituency if it was ever to return to power. This it seemed to achieve spectacularly in 1997, making dramatic gains across all social classes, but particularly among the C1s and C2s. This middle-class support for Labour was further consolidated in 2001 with small swings to Labour among the ABs and C1s, while the Conservatives made gains among the C2s and DEs. In 2005 there was a swing to the Conservatives among all social classes, but this was more marked among the working classes than the middle classes, further reducing the association between support for parties and social class (see Table 5.4).

Table 5.4 indicates that there is still a correlation between social class and voting. The proportion of votes for Labour still increases, while the Conservative vote decreases, the further one moves down the social scale. Yet the correlation is markedly weaker than it was. The ABs, the managerial and professional classes, split three ways, with the Conservatives having only a single-figure lead over the other two parties. Among C1s, white-collar workers, the Conservatives have regained a narrow lead (4 per cent) over Labour, and among skilled workers (C2s) they are again narrowing the gap. Only among the Ds and Es does Labour retain a strong lead. Support for the Liberal Democrats varied substantially less by

Table 5.3 Voting by social class 1945–58

	AB	C1	C2	DE
Conservative	85	70	35	30
Labour	10	25	60	65

Source: Tapper and Bowles (1982: 175).

Table 5.4 Voting by social class 2005

	AB	C1	C2	DE
Labour	28	32	40	48
Conservative	37	36	33	25
Liberal Democrat	29	23	19	18
Other	6	9	8	9

Source: MORI poll, reported in the Observer, 8 May 2005.

class than among the two leading parties, although they did rather better among the middle classes.

Age and voting

Conservative support increases, and Labour's decreases, with age. The only age group in which the Conservatives led Labour in 1997 and 2001 was the over-65s. Because people are living longer, older people are an increasing proportion of the population. By 2005 35 per cent of the UK population was over 55, but they constituted 42 per cent of those who actually voted in the General Election. This was because they were far more likely to vote than the younger age groups (a 75 per cent turnout, double the 37 per cent of young voters aged from 18–24). Thus 'grey power' is becoming increasingly significant.

Two explanations are advanced for this apparent link between age and Conservative voting. One is the familiar notion that people become more conservative (with a small and large 'c') as they grow older. They may be increasingly disturbed by change. They may become better off, with more to lose. The second explanation is linked to the notion of political generations. If most people forge their political allegiance as they reach adulthood and tend to stick with the same party, they may be particularly influenced by the prevailing political climate when they first have the right to vote. Those who first voted in the 1950s during a period of Conservative dominance might be more inclined to remain with that party subsequently. Those who came of age in the mid-1960s when Labour under Harold Wilson came to power might maintain a Labour allegiance. Others, who reached maturity in the late 1970s and 1980s, were more likely to be 'Thatcher's children', their political attitudes shaped by free-market ideas hostile to state intervention. Finally, of course, others will have been influenced by the political climate surrounding the Labour landslides of 1997 and 2001. There is something in this argument, first advanced by Butler and Stokes in 1969. However, more recent research suggests increased electoral volatility, with more voters prepared to switch their votes between elections, and party identification correspondingly weaker. Thus the notion of political generations with enduring preferences seems rather less persuasive (Denver 2003: 182–3).

Gender and voting

A higher proportion of women used to support the Conservatives than men. This gender effect almost disappeared when Britain acquired its first woman prime minister in Margaret Thatcher, briefly reappeared when Major succeeded Thatcher, then disappeared again in 1997 and 2001. However in 2005, polls suggested that among men both major parties were neck and neck on 34 per cent, while women backed Labour, with 38 per cent to the Conservatives 32 per cent. This suggests it was women who helped to keep Labour in power with a comfortable overall majority (see Table 5.5).

Religion and voting

Back in the 19th century there were close links between religious and party-political affiliations. The Church of England, it was humorously suggested, was 'the Tory party at prayer', while Protestant non-conformists (e.g. Baptists, Methodists, Congregationalists) provided the Liberal Party's core support. In the 20th century the Labour Party inherited much of the nonconformist vote – it was sometimes said that Labour owed more to Methodism than Marxism. However, with the growth of a more secular society, religion became of decreasing political importance, outside Northern Ireland of course, and with some significant exceptions elsewhere – especially Liverpool and parts of Scotland. Catholics are more likely to support Labour in Liverpool, Glasgow and Edinburgh, although it does not necessarily follow that those with other faiths will favour Labour's opponents in these areas. Outside these areas, the religious convictions of election candidates were regarded as almost totally irrelevant. Anglicans, Roman Catholics, nonconformists, Jews and atheists were found across all parties.

Today religion is becoming of more political importance in some parts of Britain as a result of the increased allegiance to non-Christian faiths associated with some ethnic minorities, for whom ethnicity and religion are inseparably bound

Table 5.5 Gender and voting, 1987–2005

		Conservative	Labour	Liberal Democrat
1987	Men	44	33	25
	Women	44	31	25
1992	Men	38	36	19
	Women	44	34	16
1997	Men	31	44	17
	Women	32	44	17
2001	Men	33	42	18
	Women	33	42	20
2005	Men	34	34	22
	Women	32	38	23

Sources: Guardian 15 June 1987, Daily Telegraph 14 April 1992, Sunday Times 4 May 1997, Observer 10 June 2001, Observer 8 May 2005.

together as part of their identity. Following the 'war on terror' and more especially the war in Iraq, some Muslims have deserted Labour for the Liberal Democrats or other anti-war parties such as Respect.

Ethnicity

Ethnicity hardly figured in past analyses of voting for the obvious reason that ethnic minorities were then insufficiently numerous to make much difference. Today ethnic minorities of various kinds amount to between four and five million in a total population of 60 million. While this is still a relatively small minority in the country as whole, the proportion in some cities is much higher, and in a few parliamentary constituencies the ethnic vote constitutes the majority. Until very recently this ethnic vote was overwhelmingly a Labour vote (as can be seen from Table 5.6 on Black and Asian voting in 2001).

What has happened since 2001? Perhaps not much for Afro-Caribbeans and non-Muslim Asians, although it is clear that the Muslim vote has become much more unpredictable and fragmented. Many older Muslims, particularly those who have become actively involved with Labour, have remained with the party. Indeed four Muslim MPs were elected in 2005, all for Labour, twice the number in the previous Parliament. On the other hand it is clear that some younger Muslims have been alienated by the Labour government's war in Iraq, and many clearly deserted Labour MPs who supported the war. The most dramatic example was the defeat of Labour's Oona King, herself the black daughter of an American civil rights leader, at the hands of George Galloway, standing for Respect (after his expulsion from the Labour Party) in Bethnal Green and Bow. By contrast, some Labour MPs fighting seats with a substantial Muslim electorate but who voted against the war, like Ann Cryer in Keighley, survived comfortably.

Table 5.6 Black and Asian voting in the 2001 general election

	Black	Asian
Conservative	9	11
Labour	76	69
Liberal Democrat	4	4
Other	1	2
Refused an answer	10	14

Source: courtesy of Operation Black Vote.

However the pattern is confusing. Clare Short, who resigned from the Cabinet over the Iraq War, had a huge swing against her in Birmingham Ladywood. It will take some time for the complex changes in voting in 2005 among ethnic minorities in general, and Muslims in particular, to be fully analysed.

A north–south divide? Regions and neighbourhoods

The notion of a political north–south divide has some basis in reality. Even a casual perusal of the political map of Britain reveals substantial Conservative strength south of a line from the Bristol channel to the Wash. Back in the 1980s Labour only held a handful of seats outside London below this line. Now it holds rather more, but this is still predominantly Conservative territory. Labour controls south Wales and the central industrial areas of Scotland, and nearly all the cities of northern England. The Midlands are contested territory. The main Liberal Democrat territory used to be the Celtic fringe – the south-west of England, rural Wales, and northern Scotland. Its more recent advance has seen gains in middle-class suburban areas and some inner-city areas. Its support is now more evenly scattered over different types of constituency in England, Wales and Scotland (where in 2005 it came second to Labour in what amounted to a four-horse race).

Generalisations about regional party strengths conceal substantial intra-regional differences. There is also something of an urban–rural divide. Even though only some 2 per cent of the British workforce derive their living from the land, there are many more rural dwellers, some commuting into the cities, others retired or working from home. Many identify with the countryside even if they work, shop and seek entertainment in the towns. Such semi-rural areas are predominantly Conservative, with a Liberal Democrat challenge in some constituencies. Thus there are strong Conservative areas in parts of a predominantly Labour north.

Some of these regional differences reflect class differences. Thus there are rather more manual workers in the north of England and Scotland, rather more professional and managerial workers in the south. Yet there may also be a neighbourhood effect. Those living in strongly Labour or Conservative neighbourhoods may be influenced by the locally prevailing political attitudes. Thus manual workers in Bournemouth may be more likely to vote Conservative than manual workers in Barnsley. Similarly, doctors or solicitors in Barnsley may be more inclined to support Labour than their fellow professionals on the south coast. Yet it is impossible to be sure about the causal connection. It may simply be the case that doctors and solicitors with Labour sympathies are more likely to end up in places like Barnsley.

Issues, values and preferences

Much earlier analysis of voting suggested that it did not involve a dispassionate analysis of party programmes by rational voters. Indeed research indicated that most voters were not even aware of some of the issues that politicians debated, and if they were, this did not seem to affect their choice of party. Thus in the 1950s and 1960s, according to opinion polls a majority of those who supported Labour opposed its 'central policy of nationalisation' (Denver 2003: 98). More recently, some political scientists have argued that issues, values or preferences are increasingly affecting voting.

Thus issues such as health, education, and law and order not only loom large in election campaigns but, research indicates, may have a significant impact on the choice of parties. Even so, not all elections have confirmed the importance of issues. Thus in 1992 polls showed that Labour was ahead on what were then perceived as the key issues of health, education and unemployment, but still lost the election. However, in 1997 Labour had a substantial lead on five key issues, and won by a landslide. Sceptics suggest that this does not mean that voters necessarily have much grasp of party policy on key issues. They may simply make up their mind which party they are supporting, and then declare that they have the best policies on particular issues (Denver 2003: 99–104). Others argue that it is broader principles, values or ideologies that lie behind party choice. Issues are transitory, values or principles or ideological outlook are more enduring, and can be related to more or less accurate perceptions of where the parties stand on, for example, the promotion of greater equality or the defence of individual freedom (see Chapter 6).

Some argue that there is one issue that tends to dominate all others – the government's handling of the economy, or people's perception of general economic prospects and their own sense of well-being – the so-called feel-good factor. People may tell pollsters that the most important issue is health, or education, or unemployment, and may claim that they would be prepared to pay more in taxes for better services or more effective policies. However, in the privacy of the polling booth they vote according to what they perceive is in their economic self-interest. Thus David Sanders (1995) found a close correlation between economic expectations (strongly influenced by changes in interest rates) and the popularity of the government in the period 1979 to 1994. Yet in 1997 the Conservative government plunged to its worse defeat for over a century, despite a fast-improving economy. Even so, as Denver (2003: 117) points out, economic considerations remained important in that election. 'Following the ERM disaster the Conservatives simply lost their longstanding reputation for being competent managers of the economy and they never recovered it.' Reputation and perception may be more important than reality. The economy was Labour's trump card in 2005. Brown's established reputation as a prudent and successful manager of the economy drowned out warnings of underlying economic problems and troubles on the horizon.

It is worth noting that most analysis of voting focuses on the electorate as a whole, understandably, because it is how the mass of voters behave that determines the outcome of elections. Yet particular sections of the electorate may be strongly influenced in their choice of parties by issues that matter to them, and this can make a critical difference in individual constituencies. Thus polls indicated that Iraq was well down the list of most voters' concerns in 2005 (14th on one assessment), yet it clearly was the decisive influence in some constituencies with a substantial Muslim population. Similarly, the huge swings from Labour to the Liberal Democrats in constituencies with a large student population seemed to reflect opposition to top-up fees and perhaps the Iraq War also. The issue of immigration and asylum seekers clearly exercised voters in some constituencies, as indicated by the BNP vote, even if the strong Conservative focus on immigration may have alienated many floating voters. More questionably, hunting, an issue that barely surfaced in the 2005 campaign as a whole, mattered rather more in some rural constituencies. There are even (admittedly very rare) occasions when voters were prepared to reject all the main parties over a particular local issue, such as concerns over the Kidderminster hospital in the Wyre Forest constituency in 2001 and again in 2005. Thus voters can show a healthy disregard for scientific forecasts of their behaviour based on the most sophisticated statistical analysis.

Party leaders

The media have long tended to treat elections as gladiatorial contests between rival leaders and prospective prime ministers. In recent elections both television and the press have focused on party leaders, to the exclusion of even their closest colleagues (the prominence of Gordon Brown in Labour's 2005 campaign is only a partial exception to this generalisation). A key poll question is 'Who would make the best prime minister?' Leaders of the opposition not publicly perceived as potential prime ministerial material are likely to lose the election for their party (Foot and Kinnock for Labour in 1983, 1987 and 1992, Hague for the Conservatives in 2001). All this seems to indicate that elections are becoming more presidential, with voters choosing between individual leaders rather than parties.

Yet the party with the most popular leader does not always win. Wilson remained more popular than Heath in 1970, but lost. Callaghan was preferred to Thatcher as prime minister by the margin of 44 per cent to 33 per cent in 1979 (Denver 2003: 120), but it was the Conservatives led by Thatcher that decisively won the election. Nevertheless, these are exceptions. Denver (2003: 122) concludes on the basis of the available evidence that 'party leaders exert a considerable "pull" (or, when they are disliked, "push")'. It certainly seems difficult to deny the importance of the 'Blair factor' in recent elections. He heavily outscored the other party leaders in the premiership stakes in 1997 and 2001, and retained a clear lead in 2005, despite the widespread view that he had become a liability for his party.

In Focus 5.1

Election manifestos of the major parties in 2005

At elections political parties publish manifestos, placing their different programmes and pledges before voters. Only a tiny minority of voters ever read these documents, but rival parties and the media dissect and interpret them, calculating (and often exaggerating) the tax implications of specific proposals, or the damage to services from promised tax cuts. The party that wins the election is expected to implement its manifesto and will face severe criticism if promises are not met. Thus in practice, manifestos are often long on images, uplifting slogans and general aspirations, but short on specific costed commitments.

In 2005 the Conservatives chose a slim, highly polished brochure to emphasise six hand-written pledges, amplified in just 28 glossy pages of colour photographs and brief accompanying text. Labour, perhaps seeking to avoid damaging accusations of spin, in 2005 preferred a deliberately plain style in a small red book with 112 pages of detailed text and just one black and white photo of Blair.

Party images

Whatever people think of leaders, parties conjure up associations and images that influence people's attitudes towards them. An internal *post mortem* into why the Conservatives were soundly defeated in a second successive election in 2001 concluded that the party suffered from an unflattering image. It was seen as nasty, racist, narrow, intolerant, anti-women and homophobic. Although xenophobia and intolerance may be attitudes found in the ageing party membership in the country, they were not the attitudes on which election victories could be won in a progressive society. Some political commentators drew unflattering contrasts between the middle-class, mostly male and all white body of Conservative MPs and the composition of wider society. This is a problem that the new Conservative leader David Cameron has sought to address, with some success. However in 2005 a black and an Asian Conservative MP were elected, while, remarkably, an Asian was selected to fight Enoch Powell's old seat of Wolverhampton South West.

In the aftermath of a third election defeat there was an internal debate over the changes still needed in the party. David Cameron has tried to achieve a Conservative 'make-over' on the lines of the successful transformation of the Labour Party between 1983 and 1997. In the early 1980s Labour was widely perceived as unelectable. Its policy commitments and values seemed at variance with those of the majority of the electorate. Its public image was not far removed from the cloth cap, macho, northern working-class cartoon character, Andy Capp. Under Kinnock, Smith and above all Blair, the image of the party was progressively modernised and transformed, enabling it to appeal to 'middle Britain', as well as the old Labour heartlands. Labour selected many more women for winnable seats, as well as some blacks and Asians. Its more receptive attitude to different lifestyles and sexual orientations also help to make more it appear more inclusive, reflecting changes in modern British society more successfully than its Conservative opponents. However, some feared that Labour was neglecting its core supporters, while others concluded that the changes were more about image (or spin) than substance.

The campaign

The conventional wisdom is that election campaigns generally make little difference to the outcome. Most voters, it seems, have made up their minds before the start of the campaign, and recent elections indicate only minor fluctuations in party support leading up to polling day. Even so, the campaign may make a crucial difference where the parties are seen to be neck and neck, as in 1964, 1974 or 1992. Thus particular incidents or perceived mistakes made in the course of these campaigns figure prominently in accounts of these elections.

In one respect at least, the conduct of election campaigns does clearly affect voters' behaviour. It has long been recognised that the outcome of elections is determined by the outcome in key marginals. Most parliamentary constituencies are 'safe seats' where it would take a political earthquake for them to change hands. Both nationally and locally, party resources are directed towards marginal seats that they must hold or win, away

In Focus 5.2

Party election posters, 2005

Party posters figure prominently in election campaigns. These posters were all photographed close together on prominent billboard sites in the marginal constituency of Keighley, West Yorkshire, but they were displayed all over Britain. Such posters, glimpsed fleetingly from passing cars, require simple visual images and few words. Labour chose to play what it considered its trump card, the National Health Service, but with a sideswipe against the Conservative alternative. Charles Kennedy, then party leader, dominates the Liberal Democrat poster, which highlights the issue of tuition fees and student debt, damaging for Labour. The Conservative poster was unashamedly negative, assuming Blair was by then an electoral liability. Poster campaigns can help stimulate interest in elections and raise turnout, although some critics suggest that negative advertising, knocking rival politicians and parties, can have a corrosive effect on public faith in democratic politics.

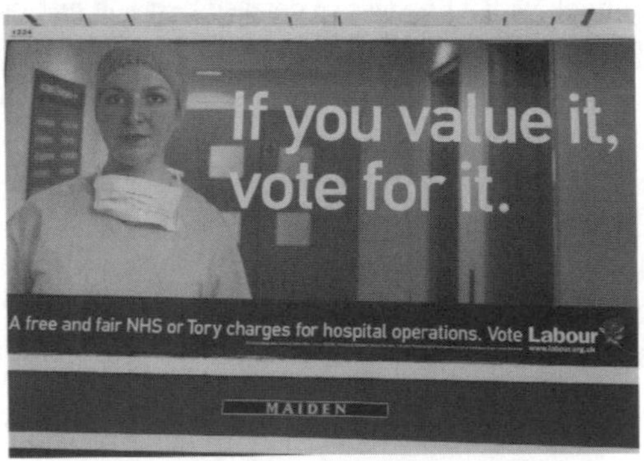

Photographs: Robert Leach.

from other seats where the outcome is virtually certain. Party leaders and other prominent figures tour the marginals, zigzagging round the country by helicopter, train or coach. Within marginal seats parties seek to ensure that their own core supporters vote, ignore their opponents' core support, and concentrate their main efforts on possible swing voters, with the help of sophisticated computer analysis and market research indicating where these potential swing voters live and what they care about. The consequence is that the mass of voters, particularly those in safe seats, are relatively neglected, to the extent that there are few signs that an election is in progress, while targeted voters in marginal constituencies are deluged with visits, phone calls and mail. This differential party activity may not always have much effect on relative party support, but it does seem to have an appreciable impact on turnout. While the overall turnout in 2001 dropped to 59 per cent and only marginally rose to just over 61 per cent in 2005, these figures conceal massive variations between constituencies. Some more marginal constituencies had nearly twice as many voters going to the polls as in some safe Labour seats with turnout percentages in the low 40s.

It is, however, the electoral system rather than the conduct of electoral campaign that is ultimately responsible for low turnout in safe seats. Indeed it may be argued that what is surprising is not how few people turn out to vote in safe seats, but how many do, in spite of the clear evidence that their cross on the ballot paper will almost certainly not affect the result.

Electoral trends: the decline of the two-party system

Fewer people today identify strongly with political parties. As party loyalties have weakened, so electoral volatility has increased. More voters are prepared to switch to another party or decide not to vote at all. There has been a more or less steady decline in the percentage of the total vote won in general elections by the Conservative and Labour parties. For example, in 1951 nearly 97 per cent of voters supported either Labour or Conservative. After touching a low point of 72 per cent in 1983, the percentage rose to 78 per cent in 1992, and fell back to 74 per cent in 1997 and 75 per cent in 2001. The combined two-party vote reached its lowest level in 2005 – under 68 per cent.

The corollary of the decline in support for the two major parties has been growth in support for the Liberal Democrats, and for other parties, most notably the nationalists. Even with the existing first-past-the-post system which penalises third and smaller parties, particularly those whose support is relatively dispersed, three-party politics has clearly arrived in Britain. This was symbolised by the new three-party graphics used by Peter Snow in BBC television coverage of the 2005 election to supplement the old two-party 'swingometer.' The Liberal Democrats more than doubled their seats in 1997 and have made further advances in 2001 and 2005. In the earlier elections their advance was largely at the expense of the Conservatives, although in 2005 nearly all their gains came from Labour. They look set to establish themselves as a permanent and sizeable third force at Westminster.

A new style of politics has also long been evident in local government, where there are many 'hung' or 'balanced' councils with 'no overall control', again despite the first-past-the-post electoral system. Yet change is more obvious in Scotland, Wales, and to a degree London, partly as a consequence of new electoral systems. Thus Wales, where Labour now has a bare overall majority, has become used to four-party politics, while in Scotland the party system has become more fragmented still, with Green and Scottish Socialist MSPs alongside the Scottish Nationalists and the three main British parties. This provides a hint of things to come elsewhere in Britain, particularly if there is further electoral reform.

Tactical voting

One explanation for the growth of three or multi-party politics despite the first-past-the-post electoral system is the emergence of tactical voting. Election analysts used to be sceptical about the real extent of tactical voting, not least because it seemed to require rather more political sophistication than they assumed most voters had. Yet tactical voting had long been evident in parliamentary by-elections, enabling disgruntled voters to use opinion polls to discern which opposition candidates were best placed to beat the governing party's candidate and 'send a message to Number Ten'. However, tactical voting was used for the first time on a large scale in the 1997 General Election. Both the size of Labour's majority and the increase in Liberal Democrat seats (on a smaller national vote) can be attributed to tactical voting against the Conservatives, encouraged by pressure groups and some media publicity. Thus:

> in Conservative seats where Labour was in second place in 1992, Labour's share of the vote went up by 13 per cent on average, while the Liberal Democrat share declined by about three per cent. In sharp contrast, in marginal seats where the Liberal Democrats were in second place in 1992, the Liberal Democrat vote increased by about two to three per cent, while the Labour share rose by less than average.
>
> (Norris 1997)

Tactical voting along similar lines also occurred in 2001, but to a lesser extent.

More complex patterns of tactical voting appear to have taken place in 2005, and Labour was no longer the main beneficiary. Several internet sites advised on tactical voting in various interests. Paid newspaper advertisements suggested how those opposed to the Iraq War might reward or punish particular MPs and parties. Liberal Democrats in some areas clearly benefited from former Labour voters switching to them over the war. Yet in constituencies where the Liberal Democrats were challenging Conservatives there was a continued squeeze on the Labour vote regardless of candidates' stands on the war, indicating that many normally Labour supporters were still prepared to 'lend' their votes to the Liberal Democrats to defeat the Tories.

Before the 2005 election result was declared some observers commented that what voters really seemed to want was a Labour government with a smaller majority, to 'send a message' to Blair, but this option was not on the ballot paper. Yet this was what the election achieved, so somehow the electorate had secured the result most of them wanted. This would appear to have happened more by accident than design, but it does seem that some voters at least are prepared to use their votes with more rational calculation than commentators give them credit for. Perhaps this is not so surprising. Voters adapt their behaviour to the rules of the game (as Scottish voters in particular have shown with the additional member system). If the first-past-the-post system is retained for Westminster elections, tactical voting will continue to thrive.

The future

Labour's third election win in succession in 2005 was unprecedented, even if it involved a substantial reduction in its previous huge majority. Labour has never before managed to govern for two whole terms, let alone three. It could be that Labour has replaced the Conservatives as the natural party of government, set to dominate the politics of 21st-century Britain as the Tories dominated the 20th century. Those who consider that Blair had become a liability to his party assume that his replacement (presumably Gordon Brown) will restore the party's fortunes and enable it secure a fourth term, and perhaps an even longer period of political hegemony.

An alternative scenario suggests that 2005 marks for the Conservatives an equivalent advance to that secured by Labour in 1992, enough to provide a springboard for victory in 2009, say, when a rejuvenated party under David Cameron will be well placed to profit from increased disillusion with Labour. Independent forecasters suggest that Labour's trump card, the economy, may no longer look so impressive in four of five years, particularly if there is a prolonged decline in consumer confidence and/or a world recession. A boundary review will inevitably remove some of the inbuilt Labour advantage associated with current constituency boundaries, and benefit the Conservatives. Thus the political pendulum could swing again. Yet the Conservative share of the vote barely increased in 2005, and the party has a long way to go to win enough seats to form a majority government.

The Liberal Democrats still have much further to go if they are to mount an effective challenge to the big two, and break through to become a potential party of government. The 2005 election, with its gains from Labour, present the party with both an opportunity and a dilemma. Until the 2005 election it seemed that the only real prospect for Liberal Democrat advance would be at the expense of the Conservatives, in almost tacit alliance with Labour. Now they have the opportunity to advance on two fronts at the expense of both the other parties. Yet in seeking to do this they may have an image or identity problem. If they pursue the apparent opening to the left, and seek to outflank Labour, they may alienate the voters they have patiently won from the Tories, and risk losing rural and suburban seats to a reviving Conservative party. They may also antagonise Labour supporters, to the extent that these become far less willing to vote tactically for Liberal Democrats as the occasion demands. Behind such tactical considerations, there are ideological divisions within the party that further complicate the debate over its future direction (see Chapter 6). At some stage or other it is more than possible that the Liberal Democrats will be faced with a more immediate dilemma, what to do if they hold the balance in a hung Parliament. In Scotland they have opted for coalition with Labour. Such a 'progressive alliance' may still seem the more likely outcome if there is a hung House of Commons, but whatever is decided will profoundly affect how voters perceive them thenceforward. These are problems facing the new Liberal Democrat leader.

Summary

- Single-party majority government has been the norm in Britain since 1945, but depends on an electoral system that involves a markedly disproportionate relationship between the votes and the seats won by political parties.
- Since 1997 a variety of new electoral systems have been introduced for elections for the European Parliament and the Scottish Parliament, other devolved assemblies and mayoral elections. These have further stimulated a trend towards multi-party politics in Britain.
- There has long been a close link between social class and support for the two main parties. This has declined markedly, but there is still a clear if diminished correlation between party support and class.
- Some other social divisions are also significant for party support. Older people are more likely to support the Conservatives. Women, once slightly more likely to vote Conservative, are now slightly more supportive of Labour. The ethnic minority vote has been overwhelmingly Labour, although the Iraq War has alienated some Muslims, who have switched to the Liberal Democrats or other candidates.
- There is still a pronounced north–south divide in British politics, with the Conservatives stronger in the south of England, and Labour in Wales, Scotland and the north of England, with the Midlands more closely contested. Urban Britain is more Labour, suburban and rural Britain more Conservative.
- Issue voting appears to be on the increase, although it is difficult to measure with any precision.
- Party leadership and party image can exert a significant influence on party support.
- In recent General Elections tactical voting has helped increase the parliamentary strength of the Liberal Democrats and the development of three-party politics. Further electoral reform might accelerate the trend towards multi-party politics in Britain.

Questions for further discussion

- How far does the result of the 2005 election advance the case for electoral reform?
- Why have so many different kinds of electoral system been introduced for various levels of government in the United Kingdom?
- What have been the effects of different electoral systems on party politics?
- How far and why does the association between voting and social class appear to be declining?
- What social divisions seem to have important implications for voting?
- How far do issues and ideas influence voters?
- How much difference do leaders make to

party support? What other factors may make a difference to the fortunes of political parties?

- How significant is tactical voting? In what circumstances can it be effective?
- What are the prospects for the next General Election?

Further reading

David Denver, *Elections and Voters in Britain* (2003) is the best short guide to this subject. It is fuller on voting behaviour than electoral systems, although it does give a brief account of the different electoral system now operating in the UK, with a succinct criticism and defence of first past the post. Dunleavy (in Dunleavy *et al.* 2002) looks at trends in voting up to the 2001 election and the impact on party politics. Curtice (in Dunleavy *et al.* 2003) and Leach (in Lancaster 2004) provide a critical appraisal of the effects of different electoral systems in the UK. See also Game (in Lancaster 2001).

Past election statistics are available from a range of sources, including Butler and Butler, *Twentieth Century Political Facts* (2000). Full accounts of particular elections are provided in the Nuffield series, with which David Butler has been associated since 1951. Recent books in the series include Butler and Kavanagh *The British General Election of 1997* (1997), Butler and Kavanagh, *The British General Election of 2001* (2001) and Butler and Kavanagh, *The British General Election of 2005* (2005). There are many other accounts of specific elections that can be consulted for comparison. Also very useful are the increasing number of publications of the Electoral Commission, some of which can be consulted on its website: www.electoralcommission.org.uk

Political Ideologies

The importance of political ideas and rival perspectives on politics was briefly explored in Chapter 1. This chapter seeks to explore in more depth the competing mainstream ideologies in British politics in relation to the parties with which they are associated. The core ideas and principles associated with the distinctive British interpretation of liberalism, conservatism and socialism are examined and contrasted, along with the internal tensions and differences within each ideology as they have evolved over time. Much British political controversy has long seemed to focus on the arguments between and within these mainstream ideologies, and this is our primary focus here. We go on to review the renewed debate over ideological consensus in British politics. We conclude with a brief discussion of ideological perspectives that cut across or transcend the traditional 'left–right' ideological spectrum (see Chapter 1). However, we reserve a fuller discussion of nationalism, feminism and green thinking for later chapters, where these ideologies will be examined in the context of relevant political developments, issues and policies.

Contents

Mainstream ideologies and political parties in Britain

Accounts of political ideologies may include creeds such as nationalism, fascism, feminism, anarchism and environmentalism (or green thinking), but they commonly focus on three 'mainstream' ideologies: liberalism, conservatism and socialism. In Britain these ideologies can be linked clearly with three significant political parties: the Liberals (and today's Liberal Democrats), the Conservatives and Labour. Yet the ideologies should not be identified fully with the parties with which they are linked. The ideas associated with liberalism are not confined to the values and policies adopted by the Liberal Party and its more recent Liberal Democrat successors. Indeed, liberalism is sometimes perceived as a 'hegemonic ideology', a system of ideas so influential that it has pervaded modern politics to such an extent that most modern ideologies, including the British interpretations of conservatism and socialism, may seem just 'variants of liberalism'. The very breadth of liberalism suggests the extent of divisions within it. Similarly, there are significant internal differences within conservatism. Thus Margaret Thatcher's brand of conservatism departed markedly from the conservatism of her immediate predecessors. Moreover the relationship between the Labour Party and socialism has long been contentious.

All this suggests that perhaps it would be preferable to examine political ideologies without linking them to parties. Yet this would not do either. The key point about political ideologies, as opposed to traditional political theory, is that they are 'action-oriented', they have implications for political behaviour. Political parties are one of the vehicles for translating ideas into practice. Thus parties that call themselves 'socialist' seek to bring about, over time, their own version of a socialist society.

Moreover, political ideologies are not just articulated by a handful of great thinkers through recognised great books. Ideologies are expressed at a number of other levels – by practising politicians who adapt the ideas of more original minds in speeches and slogans, by parties in election manifestos and programmes, and by the masses, if often in simplified and perhaps vulgarised form. Indeed, some ideologies, such as nationalism and fascism, are fairly thin in terms of sophisticated elaboration in key texts. While there are some important theoretical sources for British conservatism, much of it has to be inferred from the policy and practice of the British Conservative Party

So it is neither possible nor desirable to separate the study of political ideologies from their distinctive and sometimes highly contested expression by political parties. Yet it is also a mistake to identify ideologies wholly with the parties with which they are linked. Herbert Morrison, a leading Labour politician from the 1930s through to the 1950s, once declared that socialism is what the Labour government does. Yet those who call themselves socialists, both within and outside the British Labour Party, often disagree passionately over the nature and definition of socialism. Indeed, some would deny that Labour is, or ever has been, a socialist party. Similarly, both Conservatives and Liberals sometimes agonise over the true meaning of conservatism and liberalism. All this argument would be totally pointless if it was not possible to envisage some ideal conception of conservatism, liberalism and socialism against which the programmes, policies and performance of parties can be measured.

Liberalism – core interests and values

With liberalism it is particularly important not to confuse the political ideology entirely with the expression of liberal ideas by the British Liberal Party and modern Liberal Democrats. Liberal ideas have been so influential that they have permeated all mainstream British political parties. Thus it can be argued that liberalism has conquered while its former political vehicle, the Liberal Party, came close to extinction, before managing a partial recovery.

The term 'liberalism' was not commonly used until the 19th century. However, the foundations of European liberal thought are much older, springing from the religious reformations of the 16th and 17th centuries, the 18th-century enlightenment, the French revolution, but most of all from the economic, social and political transformation brought about over time by industrialisation. Indeed the growth of liberalism is closely linked with the growth of capitalism, representative democracy and the modern world. In that sense it is the hegemonic ideology of the modern age.

Liberalism has been closely linked with the class interests of the industrial bourgeoisie (capitalists, or more loosely, the middle class). In early 19th-century Britain, following the arguments of classical economists such as Adam Smith and David Ricardo, liberals championed the free market and free trade, and opposed government intervention in the economy. Thus they saw a very limited role for the state, summed up in the French expression *laissez faire* – suggesting government should refrain from interfering with the beneficial operation of market forces and individual freedom. Their political programme involved an extension of the vote and parliamentary representation to the new industrial centres, leading to a gradual transfer of power and influence from the old landowning aristocracy to the manufacturing classes.

Yet to achieve power Liberals increasingly had to appeal to a wider constituency, including the growing ranks of the professions and the skilled working class. Gladstone, who began his political career as a Conservative minister under Robert Peel, became a great Liberal Chancellor of the Exchequer, and served four times as prime minister, seemingly becoming more radical with age, and earning the nickname 'the People's William'. Yet the Liberal Party that he led contained an awkward coalition of old Whig landowners and successful businessmen, supported by radical nonconformists who favoured sweeping political reform. This helps to explain some of the tensions

Box 6.1

Core liberal values

- **Individualism.** Liberal analysis starts with individual men and women, rather than nations, races or classes. Individuals, it is assumed, pursue their own self-interest. The interests or rights of individuals take priority over society or the state, which is only the sum of individuals composing it at any one time. Thus social behaviour is explained in terms of some fairly basic assumptions about individual human psychology.
- **Liberty or freedom.** Individuals must be free to pursue their own self-interest. One practical application is the liberal demand for full freedom of thought and expression, and particularly religious toleration. Yet there have been some key differences between liberals over the interpretation and implementation of liberty. Early liberals emphasised freedom from tyranny and oppressive government (negative liberty) and followed Adam Smith and the classical economists in championing the free market. In the late 19th and early 20th centuries New Liberals sought freedom to fulfil individual potential (positive liberty), which might require state welfare provision and state intervention to secure full employment.
- **Rationalism.** Liberals also assume that humans are rational creatures and the best judge of their own self-interest. No one else, not rulers, priests or civil servants can decide what is in the individual's interest. Liberals followed Jeremy Bentham in assuming that if all individuals pursued their own rational self-interest this would lead to the greatest happiness of the greatest number.
- **Political and legal equality**. Liberals have generally emphasised an equality of worth, advocating equality before the law and political equality. In the economic sphere liberals have advocated equality of opportunity, but not equality of outcome. Indeed freedom in the economic sphere has commonly resulted in marked inequality.

within British liberalism as it evolved in the course of the 19th century.

Ideologies evolve over time and can subdivide into different, and sometimes sharply conflicting, tendencies. While early, or classical, liberalism advocated limited constitutional government and free markets, subsequently British liberalism became identified with full representative democracy, as advocated by John Stuart Mill (see Box 6.2). However, the extension of the vote to the working classes increased pressures for more state intervention, for example, to provide free education for all children. Some liberals, such as Herbert Spencer (1820–1903), still vehemently opposed such state intervention.

Mill was a transitional figure between the classical free-market liberalism dominant in the first half of the 19th century and the interventionist New Liberalism of the late 19th and early 20th century. New Liberals such as T. H. Green, Leonard Hobhouse and John Hobson argued that state intervention was not a restriction on freedom, but would enlarge the freedom of all individuals to make the most of their own potential. Radical Liberal politicians were responsible for increasing public intervention in local government, particularly in the major cities like Birmingham, while the Liberal government of 1906–14 introduced old age pensions, labour exchanges, and health and unemployment insurance, and laid some of the foundations for the welfare state.

The First World War and its aftermath led to splits among Liberals and the party's rapid decline. Many former Liberals moved to the Conservatives or Labour, and by the 1950s the party was reduced to just six MPs in the House of Commons. Yet New Liberal ideas permeated the other parties. Keynes and Beveridge, whose work and thought underpinned the post-Second World War political consensus, were both small and large 'l' liberals. Much of the inspiration of the policies pursued by both Labour and Conservative governments arguably owed more to New Liberalism than to traditional conservative or socialist thinking.

Ironically, when this ideological consensus was challenged in the 1970s, the challenge came from a revival of an older version of liberalism, the free-market liberalism derived from Adam Smith and

Box 6.2

Key thinker: John Stuart Mill

Photograph: Getty.

John Stuart Mill (1806–1873) survived an intensive education supervised by his father, James Mill, which turned him into a young infant prodigy and provoked an early mental breakdown, to become the leading 19th-century liberal thinker, and a continuing source of inspiration to modern liberalism. His most celebrated work is his essay *On Liberty* (1859), a passionate plea for full freedom of expression and toleration of difference. His *Considerations on Representative Government* (1861) provided a thoughtful advocacy on the principle and practice of representative democracy, which Mill thought required extensive citizen participation beyond simply voting. Unlike his father, Mill argued that the vote and political rights should not be confined to the male sex, and in a brief period as an MP introduced a bill to give votes to women. His feminism was influenced by his intellectual partnership with Harriet Taylor, whom he subsequently married. In his essay *The Subjection of Women* (1869) he compared the condition of Victorian wives to that of black slaves, denounced the violence and abuse suffered by many women, and advocated full and equal partnership between the sexes. His writings on political economy are less studied today but show some development in his ideas over time, from free market classical economics towards some sympathy with trade unionism and even socialist ideas.

the classical economists. This 'neo-liberalism' (not to be confused with New Liberalism!) was energetically promoted by key thinkers such as Hayek and Friedman, and taken up by Conservative politicians such as Keith Joseph and Margaret Thatcher (see below). Thus the second half of the 20th century in Britain can be interpreted as much as a conflict between different versions of liberalism as a battle between conservatism and socialism.

Liberalism and the Liberal Democrats

Meanwhile the Liberal Party achieved a modest revival of fortunes, initially on its own and then, from 1981, in alliance with a breakaway party from Labour, the Social Democratic Party (SDP). This culminated in a merger to form the current Liberal Democrats, which after an uncertain start has become an established third force in British politics. The Liberal Democrats retain a characteristic liberal interest in individual rights and civil liberties, support for New Liberal-type welfare policies, a strong commitment to constitutional reform (particularly devolution and electoral reform) and an internationalist, humanitarian approach in foreign affairs. They preserve links with other liberal parties around the world and form part of the Alliance of Liberals and Democrats for Europe in the European Parliament.

The Liberals and their Liberal Democrat successors have long been associated with the centre ground of British politics, occupying a middle position on the ideological spectrum (see Chapter 1) between the Labour left and Conservative right. A centre party can sometimes appear to occupy a rather difficult and uncomfortable position in politics (see Box 6.3).

Yet some leading Liberal and Liberal Democrat

Box 6.3

Maurice Duverger on the problems faced by centre parties

The French political scientist Maurice Duverger (1964: 215) has trenchantly observed:

> The fate of the Centre is to be torn asunder, buffeted and annihilated: torn asunder when one of its halves votes Right and the other Left, buffeted when it votes as a Group first Right then Left, annihilated when it abstains from voting.

Duverger's point applied to centre parties in general. It is certainly a fair description of the unhappy predicament of the British Liberal Party from the 1920s through to the 1960s.

politicians, and many party activists, would see themselves on the left rather than the centre. Indeed, the progressive New Liberal tradition of the British party has long appeared to place them well to the left of some of their continental cousins. This perception has been somewhat strengthened by the Liberal alliance and subsequent merger with the SDP, by the Liberal Democrats' cooperation with Labour on devolution and constitutional reform both before and after the 1997 election, and by their involvement in formal coalitions with Labour in Scotland (and for a time in Wales) and on many local councils. Liberal Democrat party activists would now see the party as well to the left of New Labour. They can cite in support of this claim party pledges to raise taxes to fund public services, opposition to student loans both at Westminster and more particularly in Scotland, and their consistent opposition to the Iraq War.

Yet the problem for the Liberal Democrats is that while their own activists are on the left, their voters, at least until 2005, have come predominantly from former Conservatives. Most of the parliamentary seats they have gained were formerly held by the Conservatives, and most of the marginal seats they have targeted have also been Conservative. (Here they have been helped by Labour supporters voting tactically to defeat the Conservatives – see Chapter 5.) In order to win and hold former Conservative seats, the Liberal Democrats need to appeal to voters whose concerns and interests may be very different from the party's left-wing activists. Moreover, if the Liberal Democrats are ever to break through to become a party of government, they will need to overtake and displace one of the existing big two parties. Back in the days of the Liberal-SDP alliance there were prospects of replacing Labour. Since 1997 overtaking the Conservatives has appeared a more feasible objective, yet the Liberal Democrats would find it difficult to displace the Conservatives on a radical left-wing programme. Some of its policies, such as a 50 per cent top rate for income tax, the replacement of council tax with local income tax, and consistent support for the European Union are hardly designed to appeal to Conservative interests and preferences.

Tactical electoral considerations are linked with the continuing ideological debate within the party, which has echoes of the argument between free market Liberals and New Liberals a century or more ago. Thus a party pressure group Liberal Future has challenged the commitment to tax-and-spend policies. Vincent Cable, the party's Treasury spokesperson, has supported private-sector involvement in public services and argued in favour of the private finance initiative. David Laws has called for a return to economic liberalism. After the 2005 election there were some suggestions that the party might drop local income tax as part of a general review of taxation policy, which, remarkably, would include consideration of a flat-rate tax system. This, as Mark Rathbone (2005b) has observed, would mark an 'astonishing U turn' for a party previously committed to a progressive tax system with a 50 per cent upper income tax rate. There have also been calls for the party to adopt a more Euro-sceptic tone, in marked contrast to its consistently pro-Europe approach, maintained for half a century.

Both the 2005 General Election and recent local election results indicate that the Liberal Democrats can now win votes and seats from disillusioned former Labour supporters as well as former Conservatives. They can advance on two fronts. Yet to hold on to their former Conservative seats and to win more seats from Labour they are appealing to very different sets of voters with sharply contrasting interests and assumptions.

The Liberal Democrat dilemma was dramatised by David Cameron's emergence as

Conservative leader and that party's apparent return to the centre ground. This was one catalyst for renewed pressure on Charles Kennedy as Liberal Democrat leader. Kennedy was forced out in January 2006, ostensibly because of his alleged problem with alcohol, although the new threat from Cameron (who had made a provocative appeal to Liberal Democrat voters) sharpened concerns over Kennedy's 'laid-back' style. Some critics accused him of ducking the choice over the party's direction, effectively between the 'economic liberalism' favoured by some of his leading colleagues in the parliamentary party and the 'social liberalism' supported by most party activists. Yet there are high risks attached to either strategy. A return to economic liberalism would alienate its most committed activists and recent converts from Labour. The alternative prospect of outflanking Labour on the left, although appealing to the party's radicals, and both recent and potential converts from Labour, would risk losing votes in the bulk of Liberal Democrat seats taken from the Conservatives. Labour abandoned its left-wing platform because it appeared to involve electoral suicide, and it is difficult to see how the Liberal Democrats could succeed where Labour failed. Thus the Liberal Democrats under new leadership have little real choice but to continue to contest the centre ground of British politics, a centre ground rendered more congested than ever by David Cameron's new Conservative Party.

Traditional conservatism

There are significant internal tensions and contending schools of thought within all major ideologies, which may evolve and change considerably over time. This should be borne in mind in relation to modern conservatism. Those more familiar with the free market ideas embraced by leading modern British Conservatives may be surprised to learn that in the 1950s and 1960s Conservative governments accepted the principles of Keynesian demand management, the welfare state, the mixed economy and even a form of economic planning (including incomes policy). Margaret Thatcher and her successors rejected much of this 'one nation' conservatism in pursuing neo-liberal or New Right free-market ideas. While there are important elements of continuity between the ideas of the modern party and older conservative thinking, Thatcher's leadership marks a watershed in the development of British conservatism. However, older interpretations of conservatism are not just of historical interest, but reflect continuing strands of thought within the party which could be important under new leader David Cameron. This section will concentrate on traditional conservatism, while the next section will focus on the New Right and contemporary conservatism.

Whereas early liberalism favoured change and reform, 19th-century conservatism was generally suspicious of, and resistant to, change. The Conservative Party in Britain grew out of the old Tory Party which originated in the 17th century. Tories supported the monarchy and the Church of England, and defended the rights and interests of landowners. While liberalism was a product of the 18th-century enlightenment, the American and French revolutions, and, most of all industrial capitalism, Toryism and subsequently conservatism involved a reaction against all these. They were suspicious of the 'age of reason' and the threat this seemed to present to traditional religious and secular authority. They were hostile to the language of freedom, equality and fraternity. They were fearful of many of the changes resulting from industrialisation and the ideas associated with it. Many of these ideas were expressed by the 18th-century politician and writer, Edmund Burke, who has become an acknowledged source of inspiration for conservatism (see Box 6.4).

If liberalism was (initially at least) the ideology of the rising capitalist class, Toryism and conservatism reflected the interests of the declining but still powerful landed interest. Conservatives sought to maintain the current economic, social and political order against the pressures for change that could

Definition

Conservatism suggests 'conserving', keeping things as they are, resisting radical change. It implies a defence of the existing social and political order and of traditional institutions. However, in practice conservatives are prepared to accept limited reform that grows out of the past.

Box 6.4

Key thinker: Edmund Burke and the Conservative tradition

Photograph: Getty.

Edmund Burke (1729–1797), although a Whig politician in his lifetime, has come to be regarded as one of the founding fathers of British conservatism. Like all Whigs he celebrated the 'Glorious Revolution' of 1688 which expelled James II and established a constitutional monarchy, and like many Whigs he supported the American revolution. However he broke with the leaders of his own party with his horrified reaction to the French revolution, which he condemned in his critical essay *Reflections on the Revolution in France* (1790). Here he argued for gradual reform which would grow out of tradition, rather than radical revolution inspired by 'naked reason'. His hostility to radical change, reverence for tradition and suspicion of rationalism became key elements of conservative ideas, as for example outlined by the 20th-century conservative thinker Michael Oakeshott (1901–1990).

only result in a decline in their influence and power. Yet had conservatism remained wedded to a declining landed interest it would have fast faded as a political creed. Instead it held its own in conflict with liberalism in the 19th century and proceeded to dominate the 20th century in Britain. It achieved this remarkable success by flexible adaptation to new circumstances, although it can also be argued that some of its core principles have been maintained fairly consistently.

Thus although British Conservatives have opposed radical change, they have not generally been reactionary. They have often subsequently accepted changes introduced by their political opponents rather than seeking to put the clock back, and indeed have sometimes initiated gradual reforms themselves. Flexibility, gradualism (a preference for gradual rather than radical reform) and pragmatism have been key aspects of British conservatism in action for most of the last two centuries.

To survive, Conservatives had to seek a wider base of support as the franchise was progressively extended to the middle classes, skilled workers and then the entire adult population. Increasingly, the Conservative party came to be identified with the interests of property in general, rather than landed property, winning the support of many businessmen who would have once supported the Liberals. Moreover, from the late 19th century the Conservatives under Benjamin Disraeli and subsequent leaders made a determined attempt to woo the working classes, particularly skilled workers, through social reform at home, combined with the pursuit of British national and imperial interests abroad (Beer 1982a). In the course of the 20th century they also sought to give the workers an increased stake in property through encouraging home ownership and wider share ownership.

Much of this was dismissed by political opponents as a patent 'con trick', to persuade those with little or no property to support the cause and the party of substantial property, and to reject policies of extensive social reform and redistribution advocated by socialists. Conservatives themselves have generally argued that the various classes are bound together by ties of mutual dependence in an organic society, which is more than the sum of its individual parts. This organic theory of society and the state has often been contrasted with the individualism of liberalism. Disraeli had sought to transcend class differences and create 'one nation'. He argued that wealth carries with it obligations, including an obligation to assist those less fortunate. This 'paternalism' might entail a duty of voluntary charity, or an acceptance of state-sponsored social reform.

Such an approach marks off traditional conservatism from older forms of liberalism. While early liberals thought individual human beings could achieve social progress by pursuing their own rational self-interest in a free market, traditional conservatives did not generally share this optimistic faith in human reason, goodness and progress. Conservatism has been described as a 'philosophy of imperfection' (Quinton 1978). Most conservatives do not believe in the perfectibility of humankind, but rather assume that there is an 'evil streak' (which Christians might describe as 'original sin') in human nature. This implies a need for authority – a strong state and strong government to maintain law and order, and restrain violent and anti-social behaviour (Leach 2002: 53–6).

Thus conservatives were far from being enthusiastic supporters of the free market and free trade. They supported the protection of British agriculture and 'fair trade' as opposed to 'free trade' in the 19th century. In the early 20th century the party was converted by Joe Chamberlain to tariff reform and 'imperial preference', a policy which his son Neville Chamberlain sought to put into practice as chancellor and later prime minister in the Conservative-dominated 'National Government' of the 1930s (Beer 1982a: ch. 10).

In the post-Second World War era modernisers in the Conservative party adopted Disraeli's 'one nation' slogan to embrace social reform and state intervention. This 'one nation' conservatism became the new party orthodoxy. Thus Conservative governments between 1951 and 1964, particularly that of Harold Macmillan (1957–63), appeared to have been fully converted to policies of Keynesian demand management, state welfare provision, the mixed economy, consensus and compromise in industrial relations. These policies did not seem far removed from those of the Labour Party. Indeed, Macmillan had written a book entitled *The Middle Way* in the 1930s and had once provocatively declared that conservatism was a kind of paternal socialism. For some modern Conservatives this whole period is an aberration in the long history of the party, although for some others it remains the very essence of the authentic Tory and Conservative tradition (Gilmour 1992, Gilmour and Garnett 1997).

Conservatism, according to one influential interpretation, involves an ongoing tension between two rival libertarian and collectivist strands of thought, with each appearing to be dominant at different periods (Greenleaf 1973, 1983). Indeed, such tensions and contradictions can be found in all mainstream ideologies. For others the contradictions are perhaps more apparent than real, and the core elements of conservatism remain much as they have always been, although they have required some adaptation and reformulation over time.

■ Thatcherism, the New Right and modern Conservatism

The controversy over the nature of conservatism (outlined above) is at the heart of the continuing debate over Thatcherism and the New Right. Although ideologies are about ideas and interests rather than personalities, it is difficult to discuss conservatism after 1975 without extensive reference to the lady who gave her name to a political doctrine. Controversy surrounds Margaret Thatcher. For some, she and her allies hijacked the Conservative Party, and introduced alien individualist free market ideas at odds with the One Nation tradition of social reform (Gilmour, 1978, 1992, Gilmour and Garnett 1997). For others, Thatcherism involved the rediscovery of true conservatism. Yet both critics and true believers have perhaps exaggerated the break with the immediate past.

Margaret Thatcher is widely regarded as a conviction politician, who broke with the consensus politics of the post-war era, and rejected traditional conservative pragmatism for the ideology of the free market and competition. There is clearly some truth in this picture. Under Thatcher's leadership the neo-liberal ideas of Friedrich von Hayek (see Box 6.5) and Milton Friedman became the new orthodoxy. Keynesian demand management was rejected and Adam Smith's 'invisible hand' of the free market restored to favour. Mrs Thatcher and her leading colleagues certainly embraced these ideas with some enthusiasm. Many of the policies pursued by her governments, such as the sale of council houses, the privatisation of the nationalised industries, the injection of competition into the public sector, and the attempts to 'rein back' the state and cut public spending and taxation, reflected free market ideas (Kavanagh 1990).

Yet Thatcherism can be seen as the consequence rather than the cause of the breakdown of Keynesianism and the post-war consensus. Keynesian policies had been applied with some apparent success in the post-war decades, but by the late 1970s they no longer seemed to work, and had been effectively abandoned by Callaghan's Labour government. Similarly, concerns over the growth of government, the cost of the welfare state, trade union power and poor industrial relations were already widespread before Thatcher became leader of the Conservative Party in 1975. The party and its new leader adapted to altered circumstances as British Conservatives had managed so successfully in the past.

Moreover, while in office (1979–90) Thatcher was generally a more pragmatic and cautious Conservative than is sometimes imagined. Thus although she embraced the rhetoric of the free market with some fervour, she declared that the National Health Service is 'safe in our hands', rejected the privatisation of British Rail and the Post Office, and continued policies of state-financed urban regeneration (while slashing regional aid). Despite some real cuts in spending programmes and significant changes in the distribution of taxation, Conservative governments after 1979 were not particularly successful in reducing public spending and the overall burden of taxation. The state was restructured rather than 'reined back'. It was only more towards the end of her premiership that she dogmatically and disastrously pursued policies such as the poll tax (incautiously described as 'the flagship of Thatcherism') which ultimately helped to bring her down.

Indeed, the ideology of Thatcherism or the New Right is best seen not as a pure free-market doctrine but as a blend of these ideas with some traditional conservative elements, a mix of neo-liberalism and neo-conservatism, 'the free economy and the strong state' (Gamble 1994). Thus 'reining back the state' in the economic sphere did not entail weakening government. On the contrary, Thatcherism involved a reaffirmation of the traditional Tory

Box 6.5

Key thinker: Hayek, neo-liberalism and the New Right

Friedrich von Hayek (1899–1992), born in Austria, spent much of his working life teaching in Britain at the London School of Economics. He was a fervent opponent of economic planning, not only the kind practised by the Soviet Union but the state intervention favoured by moderate social democrats, New Liberals and 'one nation' Conservatives. All state interference with the free market involved *The Road to Serfdom* (1944). His ideas were relatively ignored in the immediate post-war decades, but were later taken up with enthusiasm by Margaret Thatcher, Keith Joseph and the New Right in both Britain and America. Significantly, Hayek described himself as a liberal rather than a conservative, but his liberalism (or neo-liberalism) resembled the free market *laissez faire* liberalism of the 19th century, rather than the liberalism advocated by 20th-century liberals.

Photograph: EMPICS.

In Focus 6.1

Margaret Thatcher

Margaret Thatcher addresses the Conservative Party Conference in 1980. She led her party for 15 years and the British government for 11 and a half (1979–90) – a longer unbroken stretch in Number Ten than any of her predecessors since Lord Liverpool (1812–27). Although she gave her name to an ideology, 'Thatcherism', she was not a particularly original thinker herself. She grafted the free-market ideas of others (such as Hayek and Friedman) onto more traditional Conservative themes, such as leadership, authority and the assertion of British interests abroad. She dominated British politics for most of the last quarter of the 20th century, continuing to influence the Conservative Party after her fall in 1990, and, some would argue, Blair's New Labour also. Her achievements and her legacy remain hotly contested.

Photograph: EMPICS.

commitment to strong government, leadership, defence, law and order and the authority of the state. Thatcher and her successors continued to exploit the sentiments of nationalism and patriotism which had appealed so well in the past to the British electorate, most obviously in relation to the Falklands, the Gulf War and Europe. Both Thatcher and John Major strongly opposed devolution and continued to champion the union of the United Kingdom. Both also employed the rhetoric of traditional family values that always played well with the Conservative Party.

For a period Thatcherism played well with the electorate also. Ideologies are held at various levels. While the elaborate sophisticated version of Thatcherism reflected the economic theories of Smith, Hayek and Friedman, the popular version was more about vivid imagery and slogans – 'The Iron Lady', 'Stand on your own two feet', 'The nanny state', 'Get on your bike' (to look for work). Some of this rhetoric appealed to sections of the working class as well as the Conservative Party rank and file, although the popularity of Thatcherism can be exaggerated. Indeed, the Conservative parliamentary landslides depended more on the electoral system and weaknesses and divisions in the opposition than on positive support for Thatcher's brand of conservatism.

Moreover, this blend of neo-conservative and neo-liberal ideas inevitably involved some tensions and contradictions (see Figure 6.1). One important illustration of the problems of reconciling free market and traditional conservative ideas was over Britain's relations with the European Community (and later European Union). Margaret Thatcher had supported joining the European Community and was an enthusiastic advocate of the 'Single Market', which seemed to fulfil her own free-market values. Indeed, membership of the EC had been sold to the Conservative Party and the British people as a 'common market' entailing economic benefits for Britain. However, closer European integration threatened another core Conservative value, national and parliamentary sovereignty. Conservative schizophrenia over Europe was intensified by the Maastricht Treaty, signed by John Major, and subsequently the issues of monetary union and the European constitution.

Altogether, Thatcherism and Margaret Thatcher herself were rather more compatible with the mainstream Tory and Conservative tradition than is sometimes imagined. Even so, in one respect at least Thatcher was atypical. Her instincts were radical rather than gradualist. She was a warrior rather than a healer. She was impatient with dissent to the extent of quarrelling not only with her ideological opponents within her party but with many of her earlier allies, including

Nigel Lawson and Geoffrey Howe. Ultimately she was brought down by a coalition of the enemies she had made in the Cabinet and on the back benches, yet the bitterness caused by the circumstances of her departure has left a legacy of internal division in a party whose unity was once declared its secret weapon.

The strength of conservatism in the past has been its flexible pragmatism, its ability to adapt to new circumstances. While it might be fairly claimed that Thatcher successfully reinterpreted conservatism for a new age, she made it more difficult for her successors to perform a similar feat. Her own influence helped tip the scales against candidates for the party leadership who might have changed direction – Heseltine, Clarke and Portillo – and in favour of those more likely to protect her legacy – Major, Hague, Duncan Smith and Howard.

John Major's political style was more consensual, but otherwise his premiership did not mark a significant break from Thatcherism, although Thatcher herself became sufficiently disappointed with her chosen successor to effectively disown him. Yet apart from scrapping the poll tax, Major continued and extended his predecessor's policies, privatising the railways, developing the internal market in the health service and competition in schools, pursuing managerial centralisation through executive agencies in the civil service, and resisting devolution. Of his own initiatives the Citizen's Charter was widely if not entirely fairly dismissed as an essentially cosmetic exercise, 'back to basics' was misinterpreted, and local government reorganisation backfired disastrously, but none of these could be interpreted as a departure from the Thatcher legacy. He received most criticism over Europe from Thatcherite loyalists who conveniently forgot that it was Thatcher who had signed the Single European Act and accepted UK entry into the Exchange Rate Mechanism (Kavanagh and Seldon 1994).

John Major's successors have not wished or dared to challenge the Thatcher legacy. Hague sought to make the party more internally democratic, while attempting also to promote a more caring, inclusive conservatism. The two aims proved mutually incompatible, aimed at two very different audiences, a socially diverse electorate and a dwindling, ageing and unrepresentative party membership whose views on most issues were diametrically opposed to those of the disillusioned

Figure 6.1 Tensions within Thatcherism and the New Right

Neo-liberalism	**Neo-conservatism**
ideological conviction	consensus politics
individualism	organic society
reason	religion
self-interest	duty
freedom	authority
free market	state intervention
populism	paternalism
equality of opportunity	natural hierarchy
challenge vested interests	defend tradition
radical reform	cautious pragmatism
minimum state	strong state
internationalism	nationalism
global commerce	

The New Right
'Authoritarian populism'
'The free economy and the strong state'
Reining back the state
Privatisation and competition
Reasserting the authority of government
Law and order
Defending Britain's national interests abroad

Areas of tension
Role of state
liberty versus authority
globalisation versus nationalism
European Union
moral issues (abortion, censorship)
addiction issues (smoking, alcohol, drugs)

Source: adapted from Leach, 2002: 199.

ex-voters and new voters the party had to woo. Subsequently neither Duncan Smith nor Howard managed to revive significantly their party's fortunes. Obliged to disown any apparent retreat from Thatcherism, the party leadership has so far failed to reinvent conservatism and present a credible alternative message, although David Cameron appears to offer real change.

Margaret Thatcher successfully changed the terms of political debate to the extent that Labour was eventually obliged to accept much of her free market ideology. Since 1997 Labour has dominated the political agenda, and the Conservatives in turn have felt constrained to accept much of Labour's programme, including Bank of England independence, the minimum wage, devolution and increased spending on public services. On other issues, such as foreign policy, student loans and identity cards, they have criticised without conviction, or presenting credible alternatives. After a third successive election defeat and the resignation of a third leader who has failed to restore Conservative fortunes, there is a growing acceptance within the party that it needs to change if it is to win back support, allowing new leader David Cameron more freedom to manoeuvre.

Box 6.6

Mainstream ideologies and industrialisation

Toryism and traditional conservatism harked back to a pre-industrial, ordered society. Tories sought to protect traditional landed interests and agriculture, were wary of the upheavals involved with industrialisation and urbanisation, and suspicious of the rising manufacturing and mercantile interests.

Liberalism was essentially the ideology of industrial capitalism, and reflected the interests of manufacturing and commerce. Liberals were critical of traditional institutions and values, and favoured reforms that would increase the political influence of growing towns and cities, and remove restrictions on trade and enterprise.

Socialism, like liberalism, was essentially a product of modern industrial capitalism, but socialism reflected the interests of the growing industrial workforce rather than capital, and sought to overthrow or transform capitalism. While not normally hostile to industrialisation as such, socialists sought a radical redistribution of income and wealth, and favoured a planned rather than a free market economy.

British socialism or labourism

While conservatism involved a defence of traditional social arrangements, and liberalism a justification for moderate constitutional and social reform, European socialism developed as a radical or revolutionary ideology involving a fundamental challenge to both traditional interests and industrial capitalism. As Britain was the first country to industrialise, at some initial cost to the living conditions of the labouring poor, it might appear a fertile environment for revolutionary ideas. Yet the British working class largely rejected the periodic revolutionary movements which swept through much of the European continent.

Robert Owen (1771–1858) secured some popular support for his early version of socialism, derived initially from his own experiences of running a model factory, but subsequently from his involvement in early British trade unionism in the 1830s and the cooperative movement from the 1840s. His socialism depended on grassroots working-class self-help rather than the total overthrow of the existing economic and political system demanded by revolutionary socialists. Thus he was criticised by Marx as a 'utopian socialist' with no realistic strategy for achieving socialism. Yet Marx's own socialism found less support in Britain (the country where he spent the bulk of his working life) than in Germany, France, Italy or even (but ultimately especially) Russia. British workers gave more support to the political reforms demanded by Chartists from the 1830s through to the 1850s, and then the practical improvements in wages and conditions pursued by moderate trade unionism in the latter half of the 19th century.

The mainstream British version of socialism, the socialism of the Labour Party, developed relatively late and was distinctly unusual. Indeed, some question whether it should be called socialism at all. The Labour Party was effectively formed in 1900 as the Labour Representation Committee, from an alliance between some trade unions seeking parliamentary representation to protect trade union rights and interests and three small socialist societies, of which one, the Marxist-inspired Social

Democratic Federation, left within a year. The other two were the tiny Fabian Society, committed to gradual, evolutionary, parliamentary state-sponsored socialism, and the Independent Labour Party, which preached a quasi-religious ethical socialism based on the universal brotherhood of man rather than the revolution arising from inevitable class conflict taught by Marxists. In practice, Labour's reformist ideas were not so dissimilar from those of radical Liberals, some of whom were to switch subsequently to the new party.

Trade union ideas and interests dominated the early history of the Labour Party, which had 'emerged from the bowels of the trade union movement' in Ernie Bevin's graphic phrase. The Parliamentary Labour Party had been established to serve the wider interests of the labour movement rather than other way around. Yet the bulk of trade unionists seemed more concerned with improvements in wages and conditions through 'free collective bargaining' within the existing capitalist economic system, rather than the overthrow of capitalism. Beyond that, the largely moderate trade union leadership was content to leave parliamentary tactics and policy to the Parliamentary Labour Party and its leaders.

While socialists of sorts were part of the broad labour coalition from the start, the Labour Party only became formally committed to a socialist programme in 1918 with the adoption of Clause IV, and the celebrated commitment to the 'common ownership of means of production' (see Box 6.7). However, the detailed plans for implementing this ambitious goal were never formulated. Instead the Labour Party in practice remained committed to gradual parliamentary reform rather than a fundamental transformation of the economic, social and political order. This was demonstrated by the cautious record of the two minority Labour Governments of 1924 and 1929–31, as well as the whole labour movement's peaceful and constitutional record in the General Strike of 1926. Socialism for the Labour Party was a distant aspiration, dependent on the achievement of a parliamentary majority, and step-by-step gradual reform. Other variants of socialism, including Marxism, syndicalism, guild socialism, cooperation and local socialism, were rejected or marginalised. Critics suggested the Labour Party was always more committed to parliamentarism than to socialism (Miliband 1972), and that its moderate trade unionist and reformist programme was better described as 'labourism' rather than 'socialism' (Saville 1988).

The record of the Attlee government after the party achieved its first parliamentary majority in 1945 has come to define the Labour interpretation of socialism, both what it was and what it was not. Common ownership of the 'commanding heights of the economy' (largely fuel and transport) involved an extensive and controversial extension of the role of the state, although not the wholesale nationalisation envisaged by some socialists. Some of the industries taken into state ownership were already largely municipalised (electricity, gas) and/or perceived to be declining (gas, rail, iron and steel). Left-wing critics complained that the method of nationalisation (through public corporations) involved state capitalism rather than workers' control. Labour's economic policy followed the principles of Keynesian demand management rather than the detailed socialist planning of a command economy. Labour operated a mixed but essentially still capitalist economy, albeit with more government regulation. Thus Labour pursued town planning, established New Towns and tried to influence the location of industry. The government's most important achievement was the establishment of the welfare state. It not only largely implemented the welfare proposals of the 1942 Beveridge Report, but also established the National Health Service, and expanded municipal housing.

The second half of the 20th century saw a long battle between the Labour left and right for the soul of the party. The split effectively began with the resignation of Bevan, Wilson and Freeman

Box 6.7

Clause Four of the Labour Party Constitution (1918–95)

To secure for the workers by hand or by brain the full fruits of their industry and the most equitable distribution thereof that may be possible, upon the basis of the common ownership of the means of production, distribution, and exchange, and the best obtainable system of popular administration and control of each industry and service.

Figure 6.2 Influences on the ideology of the Labour Party

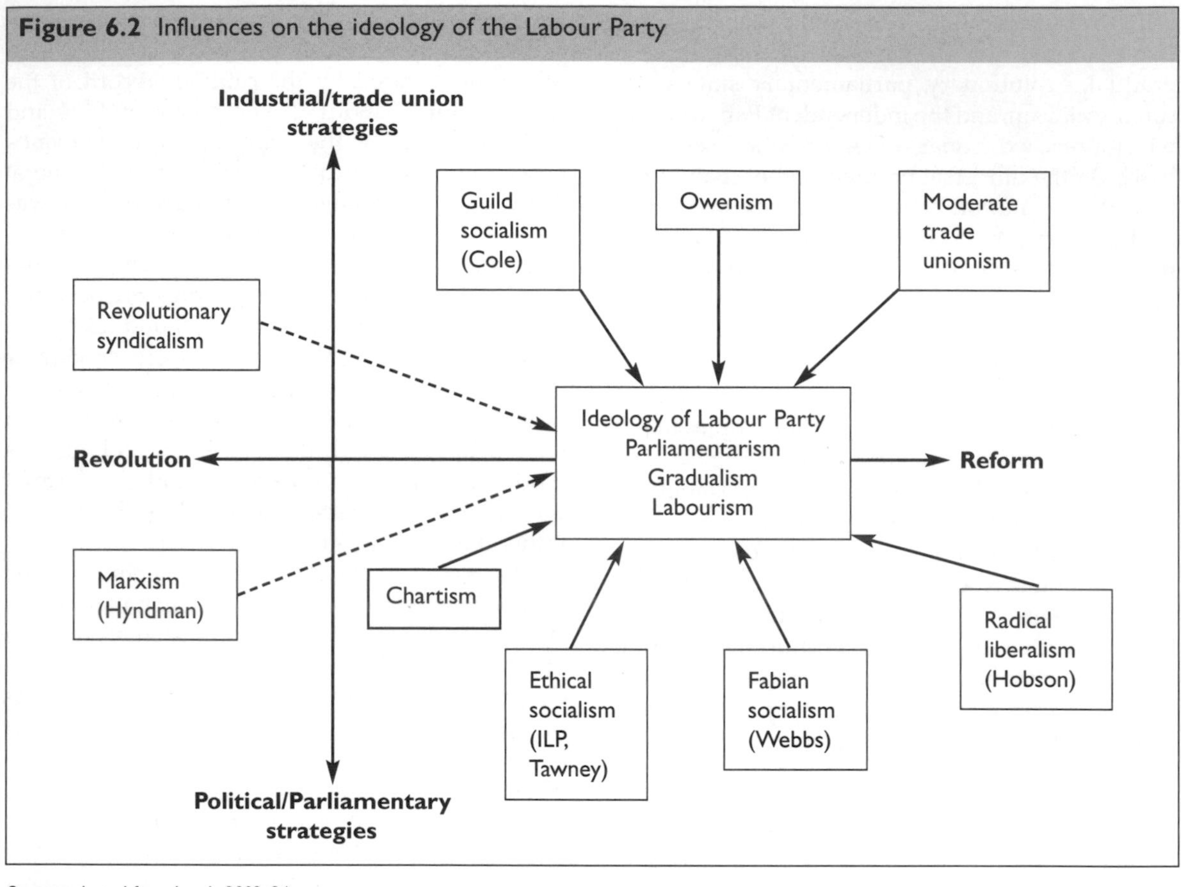

Source: adapted from Leach, 2002: 84.

from the Attlee Government in 1951, in protest against the Labour Chancellor Gaitskell's imposition of charges for teeth and spectacles on the health service that Bevan had created. Bevan became the unofficial leader of the left, which championed more nationalisation at home and opposition to German rearmament and Britain's independent nuclear deterrent. Revisionists or social democrats on the right (see Box 6.8 on Crosland) were convinced that the party had to modernise, and abandon further nationalisation, which was considered electorally unpopular. Gaitskell, who defeated Bevan for the leadership of the party in 1955, sought to scrap Clause IV, and even considered changing the party's name. He fought to reverse a party conference decision in favour of unilateral nuclear disarmament.

The conflict if anything became more bitter following the death of Bevan in 1960 and Gaitskell in 1963, after which Harold Wilson, the candidate of the left, became leader, while Roy Jenkins eventually emerged as the standard bearer of the Gaitskellites. The problems faced in government by the Wilson and Callaghan administrations further polarised opinion within the party. The left-wing socialists favoured more nationalisation, unilateral nuclear disarmament and internal party democracy, and mostly opposed membership of the European Community. The right supported NATO, nuclear weapons and EC membership while opposing further nationalisation. After the election of the old Bevanite Michael Foot as leader in 1980, some of the 'moderates' left Labour to form the Social Democratic Party (Crewe and King 1995), while others such as Healey and Hattersley stayed to fight from within. Healey narrowly defeated Tony Benn (by now the standard bearer of the left) for the deputy leadership in 1981, but

Box 6.8

Key thinker: Anthony Crosland and revisionism in the Labour Party

Anthony Crosland (1918–1977) was the most influential thinker on the social democratic right of the Labour Party. In his seminal book *The Future of Socialism* (1956) he was dismissive of Marx who, he wrote, 'has little to offer the contemporary socialist either in respect of practical policy, or of the correct analysis of our society, or even of the right conceptual tools or framework'. Capitalism in the 19th-century sense no longer existed, and had been replaced by a mixed economy. Socialism thus needed revising and updating. Ownership of industry was irrelevant. Instead, socialists should pursue greater equality through progressive taxation and improved welfare provision.

Crosland served as a minister under Harold Wilson, promoting comprehensive schools and the expansion of higher education. He died in office as foreign secretary under Callaghan. He opposed cuts in public spending at the time of the 1976 IMF loan crisis.

Photograph: Getty.

the party went on to its most disastrous defeat in 1983 on a left-wing manifesto which included commitments to further nationalisation, nuclear disarmament and leaving the European Community.

From Old to New Labour

Under the leadership of Neil Kinnock (1983–92), John Smith (1992–4) and finally Tony Blair, the Labour Party gradually restored its electoral fortunes. Kinnock faced down the hard-left Militant Tendency which had infiltrated the party, instituted a policy review which led to the abandonment of the pledges that some considered had lost the party support, and modernised the image and presentation of the party (including the introduction of the red rose logo). Smith introduced 'One person one vote' for the trade union membership rather than the old system of block votes, and Blair daringly persuaded the party to change Clause IV (see Box 6.9), which Gaitskell had earlier sought and failed to scrap. Blair's modernisation programme involved an (unofficial) rebranding of the party as New Labour.

Much has been written on the transition from old to New Labour. The party's programme clearly changed considerably after the election defeat in 1983. Some would see the change in terms of a shift from socialism to social democracy. Indeed, New Labour has embraced many of the policies of the old SDP. Others argue that Blair has abandoned not only socialism but social democracy as well, and is effectively Margaret Thatcher's heir. Certainly Blair

Box 6.9

From the New Clause Four (adopted 1995)

The Labour Party is a democratic socialist party. It believes that by the strength of our common endeavour we achieve more than we achieve alone, so as to create for each of us the means to realise our true potential and for all of us a community in which power, wealth and opportunity are in the hands of the many not the few, where the rights we enjoy reflect the duties we owe, and where we live together, freely, in a spirit of solidarity, tolerance and respect.

accepted the free market, has not reversed the Conservative privatisations, and has made controversial use of public–private partnerships and the private finance initiative to fund public sector investment. Yet at the same time the Blair government has pursued many policies that the Conservatives opposed. Thus it pursued devolution as part of a radical programme of constitutional reform, introduced a national minimum wage, ratified the Social Chapter of the Maastricht Treaty, instituted the new deal of welfare into work, and incorporated the European Convention of Human Rights into UK law.

The rejection of 'old Labour' involves the rejection not just of old left-wing socialism but of 'labourism', the moderate trade-unionist and working-class values and interests which permeated the old Labour Party. In this sense, the most symbolic change was not the redrafting of Clause IV, which had never really reflected the aims of Labour in practice, but the dropping of the old Labour Party logo with its manual workers' tools for the red rose. While the party had never preached class conflict, it had been mainly identified with the interests of (largely male-dominated and white) manual workers and trade unionists, although it was increasingly led by middle-class graduates and professionals. The problem for Labour was that the working class was a smaller proportion of the population than it had once been, and more fragmented on gender and ethnic lines, as well as between skilled and unskilled, public and private sector workers (see Chapter 3). It was no longer possible for Labour to win elections by appealing to the old manual working class of Britain's industrial heartlands. Blair's repositioning of his party to win the votes of middle England was thus an electoral necessity. The party has also become more sensitive to consumer rather than producer interests.

It is perhaps easier to explain how and why Labour has changed than to indicate what the party now stands for. Blair himself has used 'buzz words' which have been part of Labour's vocabulary since its beginnings – 'society', 'community', 'solidarity', 'cooperation', 'partnership', 'fairness'. He has argued that Labour's values are unchanged, but they need reinterpretation in the modern world. A number of fashionable concepts and strands of thought have been attached to the New Labour project (see Box 6.10).

Yet despite his flirtation with these ideas, Blair has been criticised for lacking a clear political philosophy. To some critics, New Labour involves a retreat from ideology, and a search for the political middle ground. New Labour has borrowed extensively not only from the socialist and social democratic tradition but from other ideologies. Thus there is much in common between New Labour and the New Liberal ideas of a century

Box 6.10

New Labour ideas

- **Communitarianism** – a school of philosophy critical of liberal individualism, and stressing the importance of community interests and values. Communitarian ideas were developed by a number of thinkers but popularised by Amitae Etzioni (1995).
- **Stakeholding** – a concept made fashionable by the political economist Will Hutton (1995) and taken up for a time by Blair (1996: 291–321). It goes beyond the concept of shareholding to suggest that consumers, workers, and the wider community are all 'stakeholders' in companies and states. 'Inclusion' is a key buzz term.
- **Ethical (or Christian) socialism** – hardly a new idea but a revival of a strand of thought which was particularly important in Labour's early years. The ethical basis of Labour thinking has been reaffirmed. Within the modern Labour Party there is a flourishing Christian Socialist Movement (members include the late John Smith and Blair). Yet in the context of a modern multi-faith and multi-cultural Britain more emphasis has been placed on a broader 'faith politics'.
- **The third way** – again, an old idea given some new substance, particularly by Anthony Giddens (1998), although it has been very variously interpreted and much criticised. Giddens treats the third way as an updating of social democracy. It has also been seen as a middle way between the command economy of old socialism and the unrestrained free market of neo-liberalism.

ago. Before the 1997 election Blair spoke of the need to rebuild the 'progressive alliance' between Labour and the Liberals. Although the project for coalition with the Liberal Democrats failed to materialise at Westminster, it did take shape in the devolved governments in Edinburgh, and briefly Cardiff. Blair has also drawn on the ideas of one-nation Conservatism, and on the pragmatism which was once a hallmark of conservatives. 'What matters is what works.'

It is Labour's foreign policy that, perhaps surprisingly, has provoked most controversy within the party, as well as the country. Blair's wars (Kampfner 2004), particularly the war in Iraq, have divided Labour. There has long been an important quasi-pacifist or neutralist strand within the party. MacDonald and Snowden declined to support the First World War. Lansbury, who briefly led the party in the 1930s, opposed rearmament to counter the threat from Nazi Germany. In 1960 the Labour Conference voted for nuclear disarmament against its own leader. Many Labour MPs were critical of the close support offered to US foreign policy. Blair's alliance with Clinton, a Democrat whose party had traditional links with Labour, was tolerated. His continued close support for the right-wing Republican George W Bush in the 'war against terror' has alienated a substantial section of his own followers. Some erstwhile Labour supporters have switched to the Liberal Democrats, others to a variety of left-wing groups.

By the time of the General Election of 2005 Gordon Brown was established as Blair's heir presumptive, leading to some speculation about the ethos and direction of a Labour Party led by Brown compared with Blair. While the style and the rhetoric might be different, it is far from clear that Brown would pursue a markedly different direction. Indications are that he would continue the programme of modernisation promoted by Blair, perhaps with some slight shifts in emphasis.

Towards a new ideological consensus?

Although the main British political parties draw inspiration from what were originally very different ideologies serving different interests, their ideas have appeared to converge at various times. In the decades immediately after the Second World War there appeared to be a considerable overlap between the ideas of leading Labour and Conservative politicians – the revisionist social democracy of Gaitskell and Crosland on the one hand, and the 'one nation' Conservatism of Macmillan and Butler on the other. Both Conservatives and Labour largely accepted the existing constitution, the mixed economy managed in accordance with Keynesian theory, and the welfare state, and there was much

Box 6.11

Political controversy: consensus politics

There has been a long debate about the nature and extent of Britain' post-war consensus, a term suggesting considerable common agreement within the British political establishment on ideas and policies. Even before the term 'consensus' was much used, the Canadian Robert McKenzie (1955) claimed there were minimal differences between the major British parties, while British observers saw much in common between the social democracy of Gaitskell and Crosland and the 'one nation' Conservatism of Macmillan and Butler. Two Americans provide some explanation why this should be so (without relating their arguments specifically to Britain). Anthony Downs (1957) argued that, within a two-party system, parties seek to maximise their vote by competing for the support of the median voter in the middle ground. Daniel Bell (1960) suggested that the west was witnessing the 'end of ideology'; policy makers used modern social science to find practical solutions to problems, rather than relying on old ideological assumptions. Marxists, however, argued that apparent consensus values reflected the inevitable dominance of business values in a capitalist system.

While some critics (Pimlott 1994, Jones and Kandiah 1996) have denied the existence of consensus politics, others have assumed that it did exist, and have gone on to explain how and why the consensus ended with a widening gulf between free-market conservatism and a revived left-wing socialism (Kavanagh 1990). Still others, more recently, have pointed to the re-establishment of a new, or 'Blairite' consensus (Fielding 2003). Much of the debate is summarised in Dutton (1997) and Coxall and Robins (1998).

common ground on industrial relations, foreign and defence policy. The two major parties appeared to be competing for the support of the median voter in the middle ground (McKenzie 1955, Downs 1957).

Political consensus (in so far as it existed) appeared to break down completely in the late 1970s and early 1980s, as the Conservatives under Mrs Thatcher moved to the right, and the Labour Party appeared dominated by the left. By the 1983 election the two major parties once more appeared to stand for strongly contrasting principles and programmes, allowing a third grouping (the SDP-Liberal Alliance) considerable ideological space in the centre ground. Subsequently successive Labour leaders abandoned much of the party's left-wing programme and edged back to the centre, while John Major adopted a more consensual style after Thatcher's departure. Today it is sometimes suggested that there is a new Blairite consensus. Much inevitably depends on the ideological standpoint of the observer. From the perspective of a free market enthusiast, or from that of a socialist resolutely opposed to capitalism in any shape or form, there was as little to choose between the Labour Party of Gaitskell and Crosland and Macmillan's Conservatives, as there is today between New Labour and the official Conservative opposition. Yet leading members of both parties continue to see major differences of principle between their respective positions (see Table 6.1).

■ Beyond left and right

Whatever is thought of the notion of consensus politics, mainstream British parties often seem to offer only a restricted choice. A marked feature of British politics over the last 40 years or so has been the development of new or revived movements and ways of thinking, that cut across the traditional left–right ideological spectrum. Some of these, such as nationalism and green ideas, are associated with political parties which have gained some support, while others which are not linked to specific parties have nevertheless affected political attitudes and policies. Most of these ideological currents have little in common, except that they are not primarily concerned with the interests and values of traditional ideologies centred on attitudes to state intervention. They reflect other issues and priorities, and transcend the old left–right political spectrum.

Feminism is one example. Although most of its leading figures are associated with the left, feminists can also be found on the right and centre, bound together by the common aim of securing justice for women. Feminism in some shape or form has been around for a long time, fuelling ultimately successful demands for property rights and wider career opportunities as well as votes for women. However, in Britain as in most of the western world a 'second wave' of feminism from the late 1960s onwards drew attention to the continuing severe disadvantages suffered by women despite their formal political and legal equality. Thus few women reached the top in business, government or the professions, while average women's pay lagged well behind that of men. This second wave of feminism has not only had a significant impact on public policy, it has transformed the way in which people think about politics. Indeed it has changed the way politics is defined. No longer is politics confined to the public sphere. Radical feminists argued that much of women's oppression takes place in the private sphere – in the family and in personal and sexual relationships. A particular concern remains continuing violence against women, especially rape (including rape within marriage). Thus for radical feminists 'the personal is political'. (See Chapter 23 for further discussion of feminism and gender policy.)

Nationalism has also been around for a long time, although its impact on British politics has changed significantly over the last 40 years or so. The core idea of nationalism is very simple – a nation, however defined, should form an independent state. In practice nationalism was associated with liberalism in the early 19th century, and more closely linked with conservatism and the right subsequently. Over the last century it has sometimes been associated with racism and fascism, although anti-colonial nationalism was often socialist and sometimes explicitly Marxist. Thus nationalism is something of a chameleon ideology, taking colour from the political context in which it develops. In Britain nationalist ideas were absorbed into the mainstream parties, particularly the Conservatives, and at one time seemed to reinforce the British political system and

Table 6.1 Britain's changing political consensus

Basis of the old consensus (c. 1945–70)		**Basis of the new consensus (1997 onwar**	
'Old Labour' 'Labourism' and social democracy	**Old Conservative** One-nation Toryism	**New Labour** Third way	**New Right** Neo-liberal New Right
Socialism and collectivism to advance the interests of the working class	Paternalist concern by ruling elite to provide welfare for all	'Cooperative self-help' involving community but also individual responsibility	Populist pro-market individualist philosophy
'Labourism' – protecting the interests of workers, their trade unions and the poor	Serving the interests of property owners but also protecting the poor	Protecting consumers and citizens (especially 'middle Britain')	Assisting wealth producers and entrepreneurs – benefits 'trickle down' to poor
Large welfare state to create more equal society with more opportunity for all	Pro welfare state to incorporate poor into society and provide mobility for most able	Pro new-style welfare state with increased spending, but more diversity, competition and choice	Reformed welfare state to reduce the 'culture of dependency'. Increased role for private provision
Pro planning with more public ownership	Pro capitalist but accepting mixed economy and some control of free market	Pro free market and partnership with the private sector but with increased regulation	Pro market and anti regulation
Nationalist, but with international rhetoric	Nationalist and unionist	Cosmopolitan nationalism, pro EU	Assertive British nationalism, Eurosceptic

culture. From the late 1960s, however, support for separatist nationalism in Northern Ireland, Scotland and Wales posed an increasing threat to the survival of the British state. How far this threat has been reduced by the ongoing but now stalled peace process in Northern Ireland and by devolution in Scotland and Wales remains to be seen. (See chapter 16 for further analysis.)

Separatist nationalism within Britain, coupled with anti-European and anti-globalisation sentiments, have fuelled an English backlash, manifested in support for the UK Independence Party and the British National Party. Despite their names, these have secured the bulk of their support in England. Significantly, the cross of St George has increasingly displaced the Union Jack as a nationalist symbol. Some of this English nationalism (particularly that associated with the BNP) is explicitly racist, feeding on hostility to ethnic minorities and 'asylum seekers'. This racism is commonly linked with fascism, and indeed some far-right racists have embraced the full fascist ideology. However fascism has never had much appeal for most British voters, partly because it is associated with Britain's wartime enemies. In so far as extreme right-wing parties have achieved significant support in parts of Britain from time to time, this has been because of their racism rather than other elements of fascism.

While racism is officially repudiated by mainstream parties and politicians, there is abundant evidence that racism is important in British politics. Thirty-two per cent of Britons surveyed have described themselves as 'very or quite racist' (Parekh 2000a: 119). More recently, particularly since the attack on the Twin Towers on 11

September 2001, and the bomb attacks in London in July 2005, religious differences have exacerbated racist suspicions and fears. The term 'Islamophobia' has been employed to describe hostility to Muslims. Thus for many members of minority ethnic and religious communities racism remains part of their everyday lives, as they continue to suffer substantial discrimination and prejudice.

While racism is generally associated with the extreme right, much of its rhetoric is anti-establishment. Some of its support in Britain has come from former Labour voters among deprived sections of the white working class. Once the orthodox official answer to ethnic tension was to stress the importance of integration and assimilation. The more recent response has been to celebrate difference within a multi-cultural society, and the benefits to be derived from diversity. 'Multiple identities are a natural feature of the human condition' (Davies 2000: 874). People can be both 'black' and 'British', or 'Muslim' and 'British' unless discrimination and prejudice over time renders these identities less compatible. (See chapter 24 for further discussion of racism, ethnicity and multiculturalism.)

Green thinking draws inspiration from diverse older sources, but is a relatively new ideology, prioritising the interests of the environment over specific human interests based on class, nation or gender. Although most green activists are associated with the left, the movement draws support across the political spectrum. The green slogan 'not left, not right but forward' claims to transcend conventional political divisions. The green movement in Britain was previously manifest largely in pressure group politics, but more recently the Green Party has made some gains in local, devolved national, London and European elections, although it is unlikely to secure representation at Westminster under the current first-past-the-post electoral system. While some green thinking has permeated all major parties and sections of big business, radical greens suggest this is relatively superficial 'greenspeak', which falls well short of the massive changes in policy and lifestyles they feel are necessary to avoid further irreversible damage to 'Planet Earth' (see chapter 25).

None of the ideologies discussed in this section are concerned primarily with the relationship of the individual to the state, or the argument over how far the state can and should interfere with free-market forces, which are major concerns of the traditional mainstream ideologies. In so far as these ideologies which transcend the politics of left and right are concerned with equality and social justice, it is with other divisions of the human race than social class, or in the case of greens, future generations, other species and the planet. Together they have enlarged political discourse, suggesting a rich diversity of ideological debate extending well beyond the confines of the established two-party debate.

Summary

- Much political disagreement reflects different ideological assumptions. In Britain the mainstream ideologies of liberalism, conservatism and socialism (or labourism) have developed within a British context, and show distinctive features, with some important internal differences and tensions.
- British liberalism is a broad ideology which has evolved over time, with some tension between older free market liberalism and the more interventionist New Liberalism of the late 19th and 20th centuries. These ideas have not only been important for the Liberal Party and the modern Liberal Democrats, but have influenced both Conservatives and Labour.
- British conservatism has generally sought to preserve the existing social and political order and resist radical change, emphasising tradition, authority and the interdependence of classes against the individual freedom and rational self-interest of liberalism. Conservatives often advocated protection and fair trade rather than free markets. From Disraeli onwards Conservatives have favoured limited social reform to benefit the less fortunate. Margaret Thatcher combined some traditional conservative themes (patriotism, leadership, law and order) with free market liberalism (competition and privatisation).
- British socialism (or 'labourism') has been gradualist rather than revolutionary, influenced by progressive liberalism and moderate trade unionism, although there has long been

a tension between its more socialist and reformist (or social democratic) wings. From 1945 onwards Labour was associated with the welfare state and a mixed economy (with some state ownership). New Labour under Blair has formally abandoned its commitment to nationalisation, and embraced market competition, but has increased spending on public services and pursued constitutional reform.

- In the process of adaptation, there has been some ideological convergence in Britain. Sometimes the parties appear to be converging to establish a political consensus. Some argue that a post-war consensus has been replaced by a modern Blairite consensus, incorporating elements of social democracy and Thatcherism.
- Outside the traditional mainstream, other political perspectives that prioritise different concerns are attracting increasing interest and support.

Questions for discussion

- How did the New Liberalism differ from older liberalism?
- What exactly do Liberal Democrats stand for today?
- What are the core values of traditional conservatism?
- How far was Margaret Thatcher more a 19th-century liberal than a traditional conservative?
- What is socialism? Has the British Labour Party ever been a socialist party?
- What is New Labour and how might it be distinguished from old Labour?
- When, and in what respects, has there appeared to be a political consensus in Britain in the period since 1945?
- Where do other ideologies, such as nationalism, feminism and green thinking, fit on the left–right ideological spectrum
- What is meant in politics by the terms 'left' and 'right'? Are they still meaningful?

Further reading

McLellan (1995) has written a good brief introduction to the contentious concept of ideology. For a fuller analysis see Seliger (1976) and Freeden (1996). Definitions of key terms and brief accounts of important thinkers can be found in specialist dictionaries of politics and political thought (e.g. Williams 1976, Bullock and Stalybrass 1977, Scruton 1996, Bottomore 1991). There are now many useful books on political ideologies in general, such as Heywood (2003). Leach (2002) relates ideologies specifically to British politics, as does Adams (1998). More extensive interpretations of British political thinking can be found in Beer (1982a), Greenleaf (1983) and Freeden (1996).

The literature on specific ideologies is massive. Among useful readers are Eccleshall on liberalism (1986) and conservatism (1990), and Wright (1983) on British socialism. Readable general accounts of specific ideologies include Gray (1986) on liberalism, and Davies on the ideas of the Labour and Conservative Parties (1996a, 1996b). On more recent developments in mainstream ideologies, it is difficult to select one or two titles from the daunting literature on Thatcherism and the New Right – Gamble (1994) and Kavanagh (1990) are among the more accessible. Ideas in the post-Thatcher Conservative Party are discussed in Ludlam and Smith (1996) and Gilmour and Garnett (1997). The literature on New Labour already almost rivals that on Thatcherism – see especially Blair's own collection of speeches (1996), Driver and Martell (1998, 2002), Ludlam and Smith (2001, 2004), Fielding (2003) and Coates (2005). On the third way see Giddens (1998, 2001). On the ideological divisions within the Liberal Democrats a short article by Mark Rathbone (2005b) is helpful. For the most recent expression of party policy and ideas see the main party websites (listed at the end of Chapter 7).

This chapter has concentrated on the traditional mainstream ideologies of liberalism, conservatism and socialism. For more on nationalism, feminism, racism and multi-culturalism, and green thinking see the later chapters of this book and the further reading recommended there.

Political Parties

Contents

Politics for many people today means purely and simply 'party politics', a specialist and rather unsavoury activity undertaken by party politicians. This very narrow interpretation of politics is misguided, yet it does underline how important parties have become in modern political systems. The ideas of major British parties and some of their policy implications were discussed in Chapter 6. This chapter explores briefly why parties are necessary, and goes on to review the rather unusual party system in Britain. It explores some conventional distinctions between different types of parties, as a prelude to an analysis of the organisation and distribution of power in major British parties, and some of the issues involved. The topical problem of party finance is considered in a separate section. The chapter concludes with an examination of the future of mass parties, and more specifically of the British party system.

Why parties?

It is not immediately obvious why political parties are necessary in a modern democratic political system. Why could not voters simply choose the best men and women for the job? Parties may seem to bring more division than necessary to politics. Often it is suggested that a certain issue should be 'taken out' of party politics, or that party politics should play no part in, for example, local government. Could we not do without parties altogether? The answer to that question is almost certainly no. Parties have developed in just about every political system involving representative democracy, which suggests that they are necessary for the operation of the system (see Box 7.1).

Party systems

Competition for power between political parties has become almost a defining condition of modern western democracy. In most modern democracies this involves a contest between several parties, while government is generally in the hands of a coalition of parties. (See Box 7.2 for the range of party systems in other countries.)

Note that an important question is how far a party system is the product of a particular electoral system (such as first-past-the-post elections leading to a two-party system, and proportional representation leading to a multi-party system), and how far it is a product of significant divisions or cleavages in society.

Box 7.1

The functions of political parties

- **Political choice** – parties are the principal means by which voters are given an effective choice between different teams of leaders, and between policy programmes and ideas. Without parties it would be very difficult for voters as a whole to have much influence on the shape of the government to emerge or the policies to be pursued.
- **Political recruitment** – parties recruit and train people for political office and government. Virtually all MPs and most councillors are first nominated by political parties, which also recommend individuals for appointment to other posts such as school governors or Justices of the Peace.
- **Political participation** – belonging to and taking an active role in political parties is one way in which ordinary citizens can participate in the political process besides voting. As party members they can help to choose candidates for public office, join in the election of party leaders and other party positions, and influence party policy, both directly through party conferences and policy forums and indirectly through other channels of communication with the party leadership.
- **Reconciling and aggregating interests** – parties involve coalitions of interests. They bring together various sectional interests in society, and assist in transforming a mass of demands into a coherent programme that can be placed before voters at election times. They resolve conflicting interests arising from the many issues with which governments are confronted.
- **Communication** – parties provide a two-way channel of communication between political leaders and their supporters. The party leaders use various channels of communication including speeches, websites and party publications to persuade members and voters they are doing their best to meet their needs and aspirations. Members and supporters can express their concerns through, for example, representations to MPs and councillors, resolutions to party conferences, and views voiced in party meetings, surveys and focus groups.
- **Accountability and control** – parties effectively take control of the government of the United Kingdom and other levels of government. Thus it is through parties that the government, at various levels, is held accountable for its performance, particularly at elections. Through parties, voters can clearly identify who is in charge, and either reward them by giving them another term in office or reject them and elect a government of another party or parties.

Until recently the United Kingdom could be fairly described as a two-party system.

- Only two parties have formed governments since 1945. Labour has governed from 1945–51, 1964–70, 1974–9 and 1997 to the time of writing. The Conservatives governed from 1951 to 1964, 1970–4 and 1979–97.
- Through most of British history over the last 200 years there has appeared to be a two-party duopoly – Whigs and Tories, then Liberals and Conservatives, more recently Labour and Conservatives.
- Most of the seats in the House of Commons (and sometimes nearly all of them) have belonged to the two major parties since 1945.
- The whole British system of government assumes a confrontation between two parties. There is a Government and Opposition, a Cabinet and a Shadow Cabinet, a House of Commons with two sets of benches facing each other (compared with semi-circular assemblies elsewhere).

It could be argued, however, that Britain's two-party system was in part a product of an electoral system which severely penalises third parties, particularly those (like the Liberal Democrats) whose support is not concentrated in particular areas. The introduction of more proportional representation in elections for the House of Commons and local councils would almost certainly lead to a multi-party system and more

Box 7.2

Comparative politics – party systems in other countries

- **No-party systems** – now relatively rare and confined largely to traditional autocracies dominated by a ruling family (e.g. Saudi Arabia).
- **One-party systems.** In most former Communist states only one party was permitted. In some former colonial states a nationalist party associated with the struggle for liberation from colonial rule achieved a virtual monopoly of political life. In both cases there is no competition between parties, although there may be competition between candidates within parties.
- **Dominant party systems.** In some states more than one party may contest elections, but one party dominates membership of the legislature and government, and there seems little real prospect of a change in power (in the short term at least). This was the position for many years in post-independence India, where the Congress Party dominated, and in Japan until recently, where the Liberal Democratic Party seemed to be permanently in power.
- **Two-party systems** – where two parties win most of the seats in the legislature and alternate in government, as with the competition between Democrats and Republicans in the USA. (Note that third-party groups or candidates have sometimes challenged in US elections, but have not succeeded in changing the two-party duopoly.)
- **Two-and-a-half-party systems** – where there are two major parties but normally neither can govern alone without the support of a smaller third party. This was the position in Germany for several decades. Christian Democrats (CDU/CSU) and Social Democrats (SPD) are the two major parties who relied on the smaller Free Democrats (FDP) for support in coalition governments. (However German politics became more complex with the rise of the Greens and more recently the Left Party, including former Communists.)
- **Stable multi-party systems.** Although many parties are represented and normally none can command a majority in the legislature, it is relatively easy to form stable coalition governments between parties, perhaps because ideological differences are not too deep. Until recently, both the Netherlands and France under the Fifth Republic might be included in this category.
- **Unstable multi-party systems.** It is difficult to form coalition governments, and once formed such governments often prove short-lived. Examples include France under the Fourth Republic, Italy and Israel. One problem may be the existence of substantial anti-system parties which are excluded from coalition building (e.g. Communists and Gaullists under Fourth French Republic, Communists and extreme right parties in Italy, until recently).

coalition government, as in most of continental Europe (see Chapter 5). However, even without further electoral reform there has already been a marked trend away from two-party politics.

- An increasing number of voters are no longer opting for the two major parties, Labour and Conservative. The combined two-party share of the vote has declined markedly from a high point (97 per cent) in 1951 to around 75 per cent in more recent General Elections, and 68 per cent in 2005. Liberals and Liberal Democrats have averaged just under a fifth of the vote in elections since 1974.
- The number of MPs not formally attached to the two major parties at Westminster has increased from 9 in 1951 to 92, including 62 Liberal Democrats, in 2005.
- Multi-party politics is already well established in Scotland, Wales and Northern Ireland, and is evident in General Elections and local elections, and more particularly in elections for new devolved assemblies, involving proportional representation.
- In parts of England the main conflict today is not between Labour and Conservative, but between Conservative and Liberal Democrat (e.g. in suburban and rural areas of the south and south-west), or between Labour and

Liberal Democrat (e.g. some northern towns and cities such as Sheffield, Liverpool and Newcastle).

- Some relatively new parties (such as the Scottish Socialist Party, the UK Independence Party and Respect) and some older fringe parties (like the Greens and the British National Party) are attracting more support and electoral success.
- In local government there are virtual one-party systems (e.g. much of South Yorkshire and the north-east), dominant party systems (e.g. Labour in Manchester), two-party systems (e.g. Bradford), multi-party systems (e.g. Stockport, Calderdale) and even no-party systems (e.g. rural Wales, Lincolnshire, parts of North Yorkshire).

Party politics in Britain today seem more fluid and unpredictable. Some of the trends noted above may not be sustained. New parties now attracting publicity and support may prove ephemeral. Even the substantial Liberal Democrat advance may ultimately share the fate of past Liberal revivals. A two-party system of some sort may be re-established. However, multi-party Britain is the current reality.

Mass parties?

British political parties developed in the 18th and early 19th centuries as cadre parties based on Parliament, with only rudimentary organisation in the country. The growth of a mass electorate in the 19th century made it far more important for the Liberal and Conservative parties to recruit and identify supporters in the constituencies, and ensure those eligible were registered to vote. Both the existing major parties went on to establish national organisations to look after their new mass membership. By contrast, the Labour Party was actually founded outside Parliament (as the Labour Representation Committee in 1900).

Both Conservative and Labour could at one time fairly claim to be mass parties. Party membership figures rose to a peak in the early 1950s, but have declined significantly since. Conservative Party membership has plummeted from nearly three million then to below 300,000 in the early 21st century. The decline is particularly marked at the younger end. Once there was a thriving Young Conservative membership. Now half the party's members are retired (*Guardian*, 18 November 2004). Comparisons with Labour are complicated by the question of affiliated organisations in the Labour Party. However, Labour's affiliated membership has declined, together with trade union membership in general, from the 1980s onwards. Individual membership has fallen more sharply, from a peak of over a million in the early 1950s to around 200,000 in 2005. The long decline was briefly halted and partially reversed in the run-up to the 1997 election, but many of the new members recruited then failed to renew their subscriptions. The Liberal Democrats have fewer than 100,000 members.

The problem is perhaps worse than the bald (but still probably inflated) membership figures suggest. Only a relatively small proportion of the members are active, while many do nothing beyond paying their annual subscription by bankers' order. Local political meetings are commonly too poorly attended to be worth the time and expense of organising, and social events are not well supported. Some constituency parties are effectively run by a handful of members. Indeed, it may be questioned whether parties are in any sense still 'mass parties'.

Does this matter? It has serious consequences for the parties themselves. Members bring in money through subscriptions and other fundraising. They provide invaluable unpaid voluntary labour, particularly at election times. Although their contribution to the party's ideas and policies may be more contentious, at the very least members provide an important sounding board

Definitions

In the analysis of political parties a distinction has been made between **'cadre' parties**, based around loose groups of MPs and local notables, and **mass parties**, with an extensive active party membership in the country (Duverger 1964). In many western countries early parties were of the cadre type, while subsequently socialist and social democratic parties were organised as mass parties. Many (but not all) older parties then developed their own mass organisation.

both for MPs and for the leadership. Yet there are more fundamental concerns for the health of democracy. Some of the key functions of parties within a system of representative democracy, notably recruitment, participation, reconciling and aggregating interests, and two-way communication (see above) can only be performed effectively by parties with a substantial membership.

British parties: ideological or pragmatic?

Another distinction is sometimes drawn between ideological (or 'programmatic') parties and pragmatic parties. This analysis has been applied to British political parties. In the past, Labour was seen as an ideological party, with its socialist objectives defined in the old Clause 4 of its constitution. The Conservative Party, by contrast, was perceived as essentially pragmatic, mainly interested in the pursuit of power, and thus avoiding ideology and theory. More recently, it is commonly argued, the distinction has been reversed. While Margaret Thatcher introduced ideology and 'conviction politics' into the Conservative Party, Blair has subsequently transformed Labour into a pragmatic 'catch-all party', prepared to steal the opposition's clothes. Yet the argument can be overstated. Both parties have always involved a blend of ideology and pragmatism, particularly when in office (see Chapter 6).

Indeed, the distinction between ideological and pragmatic parties is, at most, relative. Parties can hardly avoid ideological assumptions. More positively, they need ideals and a message to enthuse their supporters. They also need to show some consistency if they are to be taken seriously. Their ideas may have to evolve and change with the times, but too many sharp reversals of position in pursuit of votes cause confusion and mistrust. But while parties are inevitably ideological, if they are to succeed they have to interpret their ideology flexibly, and adapt to changed circumstances or face permanent exclusion from power and thus lose the opportunity to implement any of their ideas and policies. There are numerous instances of British parties behaving pragmatically – Labour ditching previous commitments to leave the European Community and to renationalise privatised industries, the Conservatives abandoning their previous opposition to devolution and the minimum wage after 1997. More recently David Cameron has taken this process further, accepting New Labour policies on health and education.

Definitions

An **ideological party** is a party explicitly committed to a specific ideology and political programme. This might be stated in the party's name, formal objectives and constitution. Such a party will not be prepared to compromise its ideals and principles in pursuit of popularity or power, but rather will seek to convert voters to its own ideology and programme.

A **pragmatic party** is more concerned with the pursuit of power than the implementation of programmes, and is prepared to adjust policies to the perceived preferences of voters, relying on 'common sense' or 'what works' rather than theoretical assumptions. One influential interpretation of party competition is that in order to maximise votes, parties need to seek the middle ground, and must carry any ideological baggage lightly (Downs 1957). Such parties seeking to maximise electoral support are sometimes termed **'catch-all' parties**.

Parties and pressure groups

Distinctions are commonly drawn between political parties and pressure groups. Parties pursue power by fighting elections and forming governments. Groups seek influence over government and public policy. Moreover, while groups commonly represent a single interest, parties, if they are to be successful, must involve coalitions of interests. Thus, to use the jargon, groups articulate interests while parties aggregate interests. Once more the distinction is hardly water-tight. Some parties seem more concerned with protest than power, and some are linked closely with a particular interest (for example, the UK Independence Party and Respect). By contrast, some interest groups may put up candidates at elections, but often more to win publicity than with the expectation of victory (although some single-issue groups have recently been successful in winning seats at Westminster and for the Scottish Parliament).

The British Labour party from its origins has

had a close relationship with a particular interest – trade unions. As they used to provide nearly all the party's membership and money, the relationship was a source of considerable strength to Labour, although it also provided ammunition for Labour's opponents, who argued that the unions controlled the party and its policies. The unpopularity of unions, particularly in the 1970s, the reduction in size and the fragmentation of the old manual working class, and the decline in union membership, rendered the trade union connection a fast-depreciating asset. Moreover, the unions now only provide some 30 per cent of Labour's income. In seeking to reassure business and appeal to 'middle England', Labour leaders from Wilson to Blair have sought to distance the party from the unions, to the extent that some unions have increasingly questioned the value of the Labour Party link. Yet the 'contentious alliance' (Minkin 1992) between Labour and the unions survives because, on balance, both sides have more to lose than to gain from a break-up.

The Conservative Party has been (less formally) linked with landed interests and subsequently business interests, and more broadly the middle classes. Such interests provided the party with much of its finance and active membership. Yet had the party allowed itself to become too closely associated with these interests it would never have won power and dominated government as it did for most of the 20th century. If Labour needs to reach out beyond its class base to win and retain power, this was even more obviously true for the Conservatives, as the interests with which they linked involved a far smaller proportion of the electorate. To win power the Conservatives needed to appeal to at least a sizeable minority of the working class, including trade union members. For much of the 20th century it was the breadth of the party's appeal that brought it considerable success.

Party cohesion – factions and tendencies

Any successful party arguably needs to involve a broad coalition of ideas and interests. Too narrow a focus will restrict its appeal and limit its chances of winning support. This is particularly the case in Britain, where the electoral system heavily penalises smaller parties. Thus the main British parties have involved a wide range of interests and ideas. However, the range of interests and ideological perspectives within a single party can be a constant source of tension, with the periodic threat of open dissent, rebellion and even a fundamental party split. The appearance of party unity is important, as there are many examples of voters rejecting divided parties. Yet maintaining some semblance of unity and cohesion is not easy when there are so many pressures threatening to blow a party apart.

There are significant divisions within all major British parties. These sometimes arise over particular issues (such as the European Union for Conservatives). Sometimes they have more to do with immediate tactics or medium-term strategies (for example, Liberal Democrat attitudes to coalition with other parties). Sometimes they reflect deeper ideological differences (such as between free market and one-nation Conservatives, or between socialists and social democrats in the Labour Party). Not infrequently, personal differences and rivalries complicate other divisions (as with Blair and Brown in the Labour Party).

If internal tensions and divisions within a party develop, a split may result. Needless to say splits can be very damaging, perhaps even leading to the demise of the party as a serious political force. One cause of the rapid decline of the old Liberal Party was a series of damaging divisions, in 1886, 1916–18 and 1931–2. Labour's internal divisions, long a source of electoral weakness, led to a major split in 1981 when some leading Labour 'moderates' left the party to form the Social Democratic Party (Crewe and King 1995). Some commentators concluded that the Labour Party was effectively finished as a credible party of government. More recently, divisions within the Conservative Party severely weakened John Major's government and led to the party's debacle in 1997. Although there was no major split, some Conservative MPs 'crossed the floor' to Labour or the Liberal Democrats (see Table 7.1), a few former Conservatives switched to the Referendum Party or the UK Independence Party, and some former Conservative MEPs fought the 1999 European Parliament elections as a separate party. Although the bulk of pro-Europe Conservatives have remained within the party, they have increasingly appeared an embattled minority.

Definitions

A **party tendency** is sometimes defined as a loose and informal group within a party sharing a particular ideological perspective or policy stance.

A **party faction** is a more stable, enduring group, sometimes with a constitution and formal organisation and membership.

Moreover the Labour Party in particular has been periodically concerned about the dangers of infiltration or 'entryism' by groups or tendencies that do not share the party's commitment to parliamentary methods and its own moderate interpretation of socialism. Apart from the internal divisions and conflict caused by such groups, the perception that a party has been infiltrated by 'extremists' can be electorally damaging. Although the Labour Party has suffered most from association with extremists ('reds under the beds'), instances of former BNP and National Front activists working within the Conservative Party have sometimes undermined its recent attempts to appear more inclusive and welcoming towards ethnic minorities.

The organisation of parties: power and decision making

The above analysis suggests it is very important for a party to manage internal divisions and maintain an appearance of unity and cohesion. One of the problems here is that modern political parties are extremely complex organisations which operate at a number of levels. Key elements of their organisation normally include:

- A clearly identified party **leadership**, including a single acknowledged leader who has considerable prestige and authority, and commonly a deputy leader, surrounded by a team (of ministers or shadow ministers or party spokespersons) which together constitute the collective party leadership.
- A **parliamentary party** (presuming it has parliamentary representation) with appropriate organisation for its effective functioning – including party committees and a whip system to maintain party unity and discipline.
- **Party conferences** and a **national organisation** to represent the party as a whole.

Table 7.1 'Crossing the Floor': recent changes of party by sitting MPs

Date	Name	From (party)	To (party)
1995	Alan Howarth	Conservative	Labour
1996	Emma Nicholson	Conservative	Liberal Democrat
1996	Peter Thurnham	Conservative	Liberal Democrat
1997	Sir George Gardiner	Conservative	Referendum Party
1998	Peter Temple-Morris	Conservative	Labour
1999	Shaun Woodward	Conservative	Labour
2001	Paul Marsden	Labour	Liberal Democrat
2003	George Galloway	Labour	Respect
2004	Andrew Hunter	Conservative	Democratic Unionist Party (DUP)
2005	Robert Jackson	Conservative	Labour

- A **party bureaucracy** involving both full and part-time officials who serve the party and provide it with administrative, promotional and often research support.
- A **mass membership** in the country (which for the major parties is organised at regional, constituency and ward levels).

Key questions arise over the inter-relationship between these various parts of a modern political party.

The party leadership – choosing leaders

A credible and popular leader can make a substantial difference to the fortunes of a political party (see Chapter 5). The leader of a majority party who is also prime minister wields considerable power and responsibility, and may change the course of history. It follows that the method of choosing leaders is extremely important both for parties and for the country as a whole. The selection or election of leaders has often been controversial, and the major parties have all changed their rules, in some cases several times.

For most of the 20th century the Parliamentary Labour Party (PLP) elected its own leader and (subsequently) its deputy leader also. Where there were more than two candidates a series of ballots was held, with the bottom candidate dropping out, until one candidate emerged with an overall majority. Some of these elections were very closely contested. Thus when Harold Wilson resigned as prime minister in 1976 there were six candidates to succeed him, and James Callaghan eventually emerged as party leader and prime minister in the third ballot.

The Conservative Party did not have a formal system for electing its leader until 1965. When a Conservative prime minister resigned other than because of an election defeat, the monarch invited another leading Conservative to head a new government, normally after consultation with senior figures in the party. This informal system operated without significant difficulties until Harold Macmillan suddenly announced his resignation as prime minister on the eve of the 1963 Conservative Party conference. The resulting frantic competition for support by candidates for the succession and a somewhat flawed process of consultation led eventually to the emergence of Sir Alec Douglas-Home as prime minister and leader – and the refusal of two Cabinet ministers to serve in his government in protest against his appointment. This shambles reflected badly on the party, which in opposition moved to a system of formal election by MPs, as in the Labour Party, although with rather different rules (see Box 7.3).

There were several close and bruising leadership contests involving this system. It was first used in 1965 to elect Edward Heath, who went on to become prime minister in 1970 and then to lose two close elections in 1974, after which his leadership was successfully challenged by Margaret Thatcher in 1975. She in turn, after three election victories, faced challenges to her leadership first in 1989 and then more seriously in 1990 from Michael Heseltine, who had dramatically resigned from her Cabinet over the Westland affair in 1986. Although Thatcher won more votes than Heseltine in the first ballot, she narrowly failed to secure the simple majority plus 15 per cent votes required in the party rules. She was persuaded to stand down for the second ballot, when John Major and Douglas Hurd entered the contest, leading to a decisive victory for Major. In 1995 John Major himself, frustrated by attacks on his leadership, challenged his critics to 'put up or shut

Box 7.3

How the Conservative Party elected its leader, 1965–98

First ballot: Winner needed an overall majority of Conservative MPs plus a 15 per cent lead over the nearest rival. If not achieved by any candidate, the contest went to a second ballot.

Second ballot: New candidates could now stand. Original candidates could continue or withdraw. The winner required an overall majority. If this was not achieved, candidates were allowed 24 hours to withdraw, and if a third ballot was required only the top two names went forward.

Third ballot: In the event of a tie, a fourth ballot was to be held unless the candidates could 'resolve the matter between themselves'.

up', and defeated his former Cabinet colleague, John Redwood, who however secured enough votes (89) and abstentions (20) to further damage Major's weakening position.

The last time this system was used was in 1997, after John Major resigned as leader following the Conservative defeat at the General Election. Five candidates contested the first ballot, in which none came close to a majority. The two lowest-placed candidates withdrew for the second ballot in which Kenneth Clarke retained a narrow lead over William Hague, with John Redwood a distant third. With Redwood eliminated, William Hague secured a clear victory with 92 votes against Clarke's 70.

By this time the other parties had moved to a system of election involving their wider membership. The Liberal Party was the first to broaden its election process. In 1975 David Steel was elected in a postal vote of Liberal Party members voting in constituency associations. When the Liberals and the short-lived Social Democratic Party (SDP) merged to form (ultimately) the Liberal Democrats, Paddy Ashdown was elected as leader in a postal ballot of members in 1988. After Ashdown's resignation as leader in 1999 Charles Kennedy defeated Simon Hughes in a similar election, followed by another election after Kennedy's own resignation in 2006.

Following considerable pressure for more internal party democracy within the Labour Party, a new leadership election process was adopted after a special conference held at Wembley in 1981. One problem for Labour was that the party had both individual members, attached to parliamentary constituencies, and affiliated members (mainly from trade unions affiliated to the Labour Party). The rather clumsy solution was an electoral college in which originally trade unions had 40 per cent of the votes, constituency parties 30 per cent and the Parliamentary Labour Party 30 per cent. The system was first used in a contest for the deputy leadership in September 1981, when Dennis Healey very narrowly defeated Tony Benn. It was subsequently used when Neil Kinnock and Roy Hattersley were elected leader and deputy leader in 1983, and again in 1988, when they were unsuccessfully challenged. Using the same system, John Smith and Margaret Beckett were elected leader and deputy leader in 1992.

After the 1993 Labour Party conference the system of election was further modified. The proportions in the electoral college were adjusted to give one third of the votes to each of the constituent elements (Parliamentary Labour Party, constituency associations, unions). More significantly, unions and constituency parties were obliged to ballot members individually and divide their votes accordingly, thus meeting the demand for 'one member, one vote' (OMOV). Using this modified system Tony Blair and John Prescott achieved a clear majority in the 1994 elections for leader and deputy leader in each category as well as overall (see Table 7.2).

Thus the Conservative Party, which had been slow to introduce a formal system of electing its leader by MPs in 1965, became the only major party restricting its choice of leader to MPs alone after 1981. As part of a process of party reform aimed at giving more power and influence to ordinary members, William Hague introduced a new method of election that gave them the final decision on the leadership. MPs would nominate candidates for the leadership, followed by ballots within the parliamentary party to narrow the choice down to two, with the final decision involving a ballot of ordinary party members. This system was used for the first time in 2001, when Hague resigned after the 2001 General Election defeat. Five initial candidates were reduced to three, and in the final MPs' ballot Kenneth Clarke won 59 votes, Iain Duncan Smith 54 votes and

Table 7.2 Labour Leadership election 1994 (first and only ballot)

	Trade unions %	Constituencies %	MPs %	Total %
Tony Blair	52.3	58.2	60.5	57.0
John Prescott	28.4	24.4	19.6	24.1
Margaret Beckett	19.3	17.4	19.9	18.9

Box 7.4

Conservative revival? The Conservative Party leadership election, 2005

David Cameron, initially an outsider, established his credentials in the Conservative leadership election at his party's annual conference in October. He went on to build a commanding lead among Conservative MPs in early rounds that eliminated Kenneth Clarke and Liam Fox, and eventually triumphed by a margin of two to one over the early front runner David Davis, in the final poll of party members on December 6, 2005. It was a victory for youth over relative experience. Cameron, aged 39, had only entered Parliament in 2001. The party in effect skipped a generation. It was represented also as a victory for those in the party who advocated change. Inevitably, comparisons were drawn with Blair, another young leader who had transformed his party. Just as some, both admirers and critics, saw Blair as Thatcher's heir, others hailed Cameron as Blair's heir.

Following his election, David Cameron moved swiftly to strengthen the Conservative team. William Hague, sidelined since his resignation as party leader in 2001, was brought back as shadow Foreign Secretary. Liam Fox, who had performed unexpectedly well in the leadership election, was given the defence brief. David Davis and George Osborne were retained to shadow the Home Office and the Exchequer respectively.

More significant than these appointments were new policy initiatives, suggesting a return to the political centre ground. Cameron signalled an interest in topics not previously strongly linked with the Conservatives, such as gender equality, the environment and global poverty, (on which Bob Geldof was secured as an adviser). He affirmed his party's commitment to the NHS, ditching former proposal to introduce 'health passports'. He also indicated some softening of the traditionally hard Conservative line on immigration.

David Cameron is the first Conservative leader to escape from Margaret Thatcher's long shadow. Although some discern a return to 'one nation' Conservatism, others argue the changes are essentially cosmetic, more about image than substance. Leading colleagues, such as Davis, Hague and Fox are linked with the party right, and Cameron himself shares their strong Eurosceptic views. The party will be seen to have changed only with clear new policy commitments.

The Conservative revival under new leadership provoked some panic in the other parties. The impact on the Liberal Democrats was immediate and dramatic, precipitating the virtually forced resignation in January 2006 of Charles Kennedy as party leader (effectively David Cameron's first major scalp), and much soul-searching over the party's future. Labour was uncertain whether to hail Cameron's conversion to New Labour policies, or condemn him as an unreconstructed old Conservative wolf in sheep's clothing. Although Cameron's style appeared consensual, avoiding opposition for opposition's sake, he also shrewdly exploited Labour's divisions, offering support to Blair in his projected reforms of public services, but targeting Gordon Brown, his probable opponent at the next election, as an obstacle to change. While Brown's supporters reiterated demands for Blair to step down sooner rather than later, critics wondered whether the chancellor was best placed to counter the threat from this new young challenger. Whoever succeeds, all three parties will contest the next General Election with different leaders from those who fought in 2005.

David Cameron

David Davis

Photographs: EMPICS.

Michael Portillo 53 votes. Portillo was thus eliminated, and Duncan Smith went on to win the members' ballot by 61 per cent to 39 per cent.

Party members had chosen a leader who was the first choice of neither Conservative MPs nor ordinary voters (according to opinion polls). Opposition to Duncan Smith's leadership grew when he failed to make an impact in Parliament or the country. In October 2003 he faced a vote of no confidence within the parliamentary party, and went on to lose by 90 votes to 75. This seemed to pave the way for another bruising leadership contest, yet after some discussions within the parliamentary party only one candidate, Michael Howard, was nominated, and party members were effectively denied a choice (Dorey, in Lancaster 2004). There were, however, few howls of outrage. The party rallied behind their new leader, who had come a poor fifth in the 1997 contest and had not even stood in 2001. It seemed Duncan Smith might prove to be the last and only leader to be elected by Conservative members. By late 2004 there were moves to change the method of election once again to give the final say to MPs. Following the 2005 election Howard announced that he would resign once a new system for electing a leader was in place. However, a ballot in September 2005 produced insufficient support for a rule change, and the Conservative leadership election proceeded under the system introduced under William Hague, resulting eventually in David Cameron's victory.

Box 7.5

The authority of Labour and Conservative leaders compared

Labour leaders have appeared weaker in theory than their Conservative counterparts – because:

- they have less often also been prime minister
- they are bound by conference decisions according to the Labour Party constitution
- they are constrained by the National Executive Committee (NEC) between conferences, and have not always enjoyed a majority on the NEC
- they do not control the appointment of their own deputy who is separately elected
- they can not even choose their own Shadow Cabinet in opposition, which is formed from a parliamentary committee elected by a vote of the Parliamentary Labour Party
- they do not fully control the party bureaucracy.

However, in practice Labour leaders have generally enjoyed considerable power over their parties – at times ignoring conference decisions. When Labour leaders have also been prime minister they have enjoyed all the considerable constitutional powers associated with that office, and have had as much authority as their Conservative counterparts.

The power of party leaders

While the Conservative Party has traditionally emphasised the importance of leadership, Labour historically was suspicious of the leader's power and has sought to restrain it. Yet in practice Labour leaders from Wilson onwards have been less vulnerable to formal challenges within the party. The only sitting Labour leader who faced a leadership contest over the last 40 years was Kinnock, who easily saw off a challenge from Tony Benn. Over the same period Heath, Thatcher, Major and Duncan Smith have all faced challenges, which all but Major went on to lose. Perhaps one reason for the greater vulnerability of Conservative leaders is that their party has grown accustomed to success, and is unforgiving of failure, or the prospect of failure.

It should not be forgotten that while most of the media attention is focused on the individual who is party leader, he or she is normally surrounded by other politicians with their own positions, power bases and popularity within the party. The leader has to try to satisfy the political ambitions of those who may be real or potential rivals, but also needs to draw on their talents so as to present a credible collective leadership of actual or potential ministers, and convince the voters of their collective competence. Within the leadership group, some politicians may come to seem indispensable, as Whitelaw was to Thatcher and Heseltine became to John Major. Both these were disappointed candidates for the leadership who gave full loyalty to the victors. In Blair's government, Gordon Brown, who was reluctantly persuaded to forgo his own leadership hopes in 1994, evidently retained ambitions to lead the party in which he remained a hugely important figure, with real power in his own right. Blair announced before the 2005 election that this would be the last election he would fight as leader. Brown remains Blair's heir apparent and the clear favourite to succeed, although he will presumably have to win a leadership election under the party's existing electoral college system, unless there is no rival candidate.

Parliamentary parties

While most of the media and public attention is focused on the party leadership (both individual and collective) it should not be forgotten that parties began in Britain in Parliament, and these parliamentary parties flourished long before any formal party leadership roles were acknowledged. Although it is sometimes suggested that modern parliamentary parties are mere 'lobby fodder', coerced to troop through the division lobbies at the behest of their powerful leaders, they still retain a crucial role at the very centre of the modern party system. The most gifted politicians are powerless without a significant parliamentary party behind them. Lloyd George, perhaps the ablest orator and administrator in 20th-century British politics, was effectively forced out of office in 1922, at the height of his powers, never to return, because he did not have a united parliamentary party with a majority behind him. His position depended on the support of the Conservatives, a party not his own, and this was withdrawn once Conservative backbenchers voted to fight the election as a separate party, against the advice of most of their leaders, who wanted to maintain the Lloyd George coalition. The power of ordinary Conservative backbenchers, revealed then, was subsequently formally recognised with the establishment of the 1922 Committee, which consists of backbenchers when the party is in government, and whose elected officers remain figures of real status and influence within the party. It is the 1922 Committee that acts as the sounding board for ordinary Conservative MPs, alerts the leadership to the concerns of the backbenchers, and organises leadership elections.

The Parliamentary Labour Party (PLP) continues to form a similar function within the Labour Party. When the Labour party is in opposition the PLP elects a Parliamentary Committee, which becomes in effect the Shadow Cabinet. The leader is obliged to offer shadow posts to all those elected, although others who are not elected may be given a front bench role as well. When the Labour Party is in government, the leader chooses his own Cabinet (although he or she is normally constrained initially to offer Cabinet posts to former elected Shadow Cabinet members), and the PLP chooses a small Parliamentary Liaison Committee to provide a link between the parliamentary party and the government.

Both the Labour and Conservative parties have their own system of specialist party committees covering a range of government functions, and these allow MPs to use and develop specialist interests and expertise. These party committees provide an additional channel of influence as well as a pool of more experienced MPs who may become members of key all-party Parliamentary Select Committees, or gain reputations which may earn them a government post when the party is in office.

Party cohesion and discipline is promoted by the party whips, who play a key role in the modern parliamentary party (although the name and post date back to the 18th century). Today both major parties have a whip's office, led by a chief whip assisted by junior whips. The whips may use a combination of threats, bribes and cajolery to keep members of their party in line. A disaffected MP may risk losing some valued perks of the job – for example trips abroad on parliamentary delegations, or membership of prestigious parliamentary committees, or an honour, or the prospect of promotion. In more extreme circumstances, the whips may threaten to communicate their displeasure to an MP's constituency association (which could lead to his or her deselection as party candidate at the next election), or to withdraw the party whip, so that the MP is no longer considered a member of the parliamentary party. For offences which are regarded as particularly heinous an MP may be expelled from the party, as George Galloway was from the Labour Party in 2003. Yet the party cannot expel an MP from Parliament. Only the House of Commons, or ultimately the voters, can do that.

Yet such weapons are not always effective, particularly against MPs who have no further political ambitions or no realistic expectations of promotion. Even the withdrawal of the whip may not prove too damaging to an MP who retains the support of his or her constituency party. In 1994 the whip was withdrawn from eight Euro-sceptic Conservative MPs who had consistently refrained from voting with the party on European issues. They were joined by one sympathiser who voluntarily resigned the whip, and these 'whipless nine' continued to constitute a separate parliamentary grouping until the whip was restored without promises of future good behaviour a year later. Rebellion has not always proved a bar to promotion, and in retrospect has sometimes appeared a good career move. Former rebels who have gone on to become party leaders include Winston Churchill, Harold Macmillan and Iain Duncan Smith among Conservatives, and Harold Wilson and Michael Foot on the Labour side.

Altogether the power of the party whips should not be exaggerated. Indeed much party discipline is self-discipline, as the futures of individual MPs and the party are closely bound up together. Party splits are perceived as damaging to a party's electoral prospects and hence to the prospects for re-election of individual MPs, who normally owe their position almost completely to party endorsement. Whips will use such arguments to help persuade MPs to support the party despite any reservations they may feel on a particular issue, but often such persuasion is superfluous as MPs are already well aware of the dangers of division.

However, party discipline has weakened of late, with more backbench rebellions. One possible explanation is that large government majorities (enjoyed by both Thatcher and Blair) both allow the luxury of rebellion without any risk to the survival of the government, and makes it more difficult to satisfy the political ambitions of increased numbers of MPs, who may consequently become restive. Blair's government has faced huge backbench revolts on some of its policies, notably on the Iraq War and student top-up fees (Cowley 2005a, 2005b).

Yet the power of ordinary backbench MPs is not to be measured by the size and frequency of rebellions. Much of their influence springs from the leaders and whips anticipating what the backbenchers will not stand for, and altering course accordingly. While most MPs want their party to succeed and want to remain loyal, they all have a 'bottom line', issues of principle on which they are not prepared to budge, as the party whips realise. Indeed the whips' job is not just to persuade or coerce recalcitrant backbenchers, but often, more importantly, to convey backbench feeling to the party leaders, and warn them against proceeding (or sometimes failing to proceed) with policies or decisions in the teeth of substantial opposition from their own MPs. A celebrated example was when Wilson's Labour government backed down from its proposed trade union reforms after the chief whip informed the Cabinet that he could not get the reforms through the parliamentary party. More recently, Blair was persuaded to honour the commitment to legislate on the 'right to roam' providing access to the countryside for walkers, after inclining to a voluntary agreement with landowners.

Party conferences

Each party holds an annual conference for a week in the autumn, together with other occasional or more specialised conferences. In theory there is a massive difference between the role of the Labour Party conference as the party's own 'parliament', supreme over party policy, compared with that of the conference in the Conservative Party with no constitutional power. Indeed one past Conservative prime minister, Balfour, said he would rather take advice from his valet than the party conference. Yet in practice the Labour conference was never as powerful as the party constitution suggested, while Conservative conferences were often influential despite their lack of formal power (McKenzie 1955). Labour leaders could, and effectively did, disregard conference decisions that they opposed, while the Conservative leadership was sometimes influenced by strong expressions of conference opinion, not always in the party's longer-term interest. Thus the enthusiasm of the Conservative conference for the proposed local government poll tax persuaded ministers not to phase it in gradually (which had been the original intention) but to introduce it fully and immediately in place of the old domestic rates. The tax proved unpopular with the public and was a significant factor in the declining fortunes of the Conservative Party and the fall of Margaret Thatcher.

Even so, until recently there were still considerable differences between the parties in the way in which the conferences were conducted. Labour Party conferences often involved furious rows and party splits. The party leadership lacked effective control of proceedings. They did not control the agenda, or who could speak (even leading Cabinet ministers had no right to speak). One celebrated example was in 1960, when the leader Hugh Gaitskell defiantly declared, to the jeers of his audience, that he would 'fight and fight and fight again' to reverse a Labour conference decision in favour of unilateral nuclear disarmament. Another came in 1985 when Neil Kinnock denounced Labour's (Militant-dominated) Liverpool Council to a mixture of cheers and boos. All this made for dramatic television, but also reflected badly on a divided party. By contrast, Conservative annual conferences were generally carefully stage-managed and relatively docile. Contentious motions and issues were kept off the conference agenda. Essentially they were viewed as rallies of the party faithful, rewarding loyal members with an opportunity to meet their leaders in a friendly social setting, and more importantly, allowing leading politicians to display some effective platform oratory and secure abundant valuable free publicity for the party.

This contrast between the two major parties in the handling of their conferences is much less obvious today. Labour conferences, particularly under Blair's leadership, have been more carefully managed. For all parties, conferences now seem to be more about public relations than policy. A successful conference for any party can result in a significant (if often only temporary) boost in its poll ratings. The Liberal Democrats, who have particular problems in securing publicity for their politicians and policies, have learned the value of the conference shop window, and significantly have also sought to impose more discipline and control over delegates, so as to appear more moderate and responsible. Yet ironically party conferences now attract less media coverage and have less impact on the public, partly because they no longer seem to decide important political issues. In October 2003 a carefully organised Conservative conference demonstration of loyalty to Iain Duncan Smith did not prevent Conservative MPs passing a vote of no confidence in his leadership later in the same month.

■ Party bureaucracy

Parties with a substantial mass membership require complex organisational structures to manage the relationship between the parliamentary leadership and the extra-parliamentary party, operating at various levels in the country. Major parties now require extensive permanent bureaucracies to meet their needs. This has meant employing increasing numbers of paid staff – particularly at the centre, but also in the regions and in constituencies – as well as using large numbers of unpaid voluntary party activists. Professional expertise is required for a range of purposes – raising money and controlling spending, marketing and advertising, policy-oriented research, legal advice, party management and administration. All major parties retain paid permanent agents in marginal constituencies, and these play a crucial role in maintaining the party organisation at constituency level, and maximising the party's vote at election times.

At national level the Conservative Party is organised from Conservative Central Office, founded in 1870. The party's chair is directly appointed by the leader, and Central Office has been described as 'the personal machine of the leader'. Its main tasks are money-raising, the organisation of election campaigns, assistance with the selection of candidates, research and political education. While Central Office has enjoyed substantial power and prestige in the past, it has become increasingly subject to criticism following poor election results and other evidence of the party's decline. Some party activists (such as those in the Charter Movement) would like to see Central Office become more accountable and subject to democratic control. Pressure for reform and more internal democracy in the party following the landslide defeat in 1997 led William Hague to introduce a range of changes (*The Fresh Future*), although the increased power given to members has proved problematic (see above and below).

The organisation of the Labour Party nationally has been subject to extensive change in recent years. Labour headquarters were long located at

Transport House, in the offices of the Transport and General Workers Union, symbolising the close links of Labour with the trade unions. The party's organisation was not always efficient. Back in 1955, Harold Wilson famously described the Labour Party machine as a rusty penny-farthing bicycle in the era of the jet plane, in one of a series of critical reports (Pimlott 1992: 194). In 1980 the party moved to its own modest headquarters in Walworth Road (subsequently renamed John Smith House after the death of the leader in 1994), but it was still criticised as ineffective, until a substantial reorganisation started under Kinnock's leadership (Minkin 1992: ch. 19). From 1995 key staff moved to a new campaign and media centre at Millbank Tower, which came to symbolise New Labour's slick public relations and 'spin doctoring'. Both the expense and the (increasingly unfavourable) image of Millbank led in 2002 to another move, to more modest but central premises in the heart of Westminster at Old Queen Street.

Labour leaders in the past lacked the same control over party organisation enjoyed by Conservative leaders, partly because the party's official governing body (between conferences) is not the Cabinet or Shadow Cabinet or even the Parliamentary Labour Party, but the NEC. This in the past was dominated by the trade unions, and, to a lesser degree, members chosen by constituency associations (largely left-wingers). In the 1970s and early 1980s the majority of the NEC was hostile to the party leadership. As the NEC had to approve the party manifesto and controlled key appointments in the Labour Party, including the post of general secretary, there was often division at the top.

In 1997 there was a significant reorganisation of the party's central machinery. The membership of the NEC was overhauled. The unions retained 12 seats, but on an NEC increased from

Table 7.3 The new National Executive Committee of the Labour Party

Number	Who?	How selected?	Women?
2	Leader, deputy leader	Ex officio (previously elected through an electoral college)	
1	Treasurer	Elected at annual conference	
12	Trade union members	Elected at annual conference	At least 6 women
6	Constituency party members	Elected by all members	Cannot be MPs, at least 3 women
3	Government ministers	Chosen by Cabinet	
3	MPs/MEPs	Elected at annual conference	At least 1 woman
2	Labour councillors	Elected from Association of Labour Councillors	At least 1 woman
1	Young Labour representative	Elected at youth conference	
1	Representative of socialist societies	Elected at annual conference	
1	Leader of the European Parliamentary Labour Party	Elected by Labour MEPs	

Source: adapted from official Labour Party material.

29 to 32 members. Party members could vote for six constituency party members, who could no longer be MPs (MPs and government ministers are represented separately). Separate women's representatives were abolished and replaced by new rules requiring a minimum number of women in different categories of NEC members. The new NEC has caused fewer problems to the leadership (particularly after the introduction of postal ballots for party members), and the party has appeared less divided.

Whereas the Labour Party national organisation in the past often appeared divided and shambolic while the Conservative organisation seemed ruthlessly united and efficient, the image of the two parties has almost reversed. Thus the Conservative organisation has been subjected to criticism, as the party seeks to imitate aspects of Labour's successful electoral machine. Yet Labour has paid a price for its new-found organisational unity and efficiency. The Labour leadership are accused of acting like 'control freaks', seeking to manipulate all key roles in the party, while the party's slick public relations have become increasingly identified with manipulation and 'spin'. Significantly, Labour's more celebrated or notorious spin-doctors are no longer directly concerned with party or government communication. Alastair Campbell is no longer the prime minister's director of communication, following his resignation in 2003. Peter Mandelson, long seen as a key influence on Blair and New Labour, departed for Brussels as a member of the new European Commission in 2004. Following the Phillis Report (2004) the party already seems to be relying less on 'spin' by anonymous spokespersons and more on direct communication by ministers in televised press briefings.

The party membership and constituency parties

All major parties have recently sought (ostensibly at least) to give more power and influence to ordinary members. Party members have always had one very significant power – to choose party candidates for local and general elections. Although in certain circumstances the national party may seek to influence the choice of parliamentary candidate, and exceptionally may block the selection of a particular candidate, in general it is the members voting at constituency level who choose. Moreover, particularly in the Labour Party, members have sometimes exercised powers to deselect sitting MPs with whom they have become dissatisfied. Beyond that, as we have seen (above), all major parties over the last 30 years or so sought to involve party members in the choice of the party leader, and made some show of involving them more in the policy-making process.

Internal party democracy may not necessarily help a party to win elections, however, and can be positively detrimental, particularly as active members become fewer and less representative of potential party voters. Most people who vote for a party are not party members. Joining a political party has become very much a minority hobby. Active party members almost by definition are unusual creatures with views and preferences that may be similarly untypical. Thus the problem for parties is that they serve two very different political 'markets'. Policies that please active members may not appeal to ordinary voters. Labour Party members in the 1980s wanted left-wing policies (including more nationalisation and unilateral nuclear disarmament) which the electorate rejected. Today, Labour's constituency activists and candidates are increasingly middle-class professionals, often out of touch with the party's core manual working-class voters in northern urban housing estates. There are also often marked differences between Liberal Democrat Party members and voters.

The problem for the Conservatives may be worse. Hague, Duncan Smith, Howard and Cameron have all sought a broader, more inclusive party. However, its existing dwindling membership is elderly, overwhelmingly white and middle class. Although women are well represented among party activists, many hold very traditional views on gender relations and the role of women in society and the workplace. While the leadership would welcome more women and ethnic minority candidates, that seems unlikely to happen while unrepresentative constituency parties control the selection process. Moreover, the policies that appeal to them (such as zero tolerance on drugs, a hard line on asylum seekers, and support for 'family values') alienate some of the new target voters the party is trying to attract, including ethnic minorities, unconventional families, gays, and young people generally.

All the main parties seem to have a problem recruiting and keeping younger members. Recent research suggests that Liberal Democrat activists are predominantly male, middle class with an average age in the late 50s. Perhaps the real problem is that older forms of political activity no longer appeal. Increasingly the parties are pursuing other methods of communicating with their members, through postal ballots and surveys and interactive websites. Yet it seems most unlikely that the long-term decline in active party membership will be reversed.

One pessimistic answer is that people are not interested in more participation in politics. There are more diverting ways for people to spend their leisure time in a modern consumer society. Another possible answer is that in so far as people have the energy and inclination to participate in politics, it is increasingly in single-issue pressure groups rather than political parties (see Chapters 4 and 8). Parties, involving coalitions of interests, inevitably require compromise. Those whose ideals motivate them to become involved in politics may be turned off by the messy and sometimes grubby processes of accommodation within mainstream parties. For them, political parties are

Box 7.6

Liberal Democrat leadership crisis

In May 2005 Liberal Democrats secured 62 seats, their best result for eighty years, an apparent triumph. Yet critics thought the party should have performed better against a government facing increasing problems and a still mistrusted Conservative opposition. Some colleagues blamed Charles Kennedy's 'laid back' style for the failure to achieve a bigger breakthrough, although he remained popular with party members and voters.

The threat from a revived Conservative party under new leader David Cameron precipitated a crisis in December. Kennedy was eventually forced to admit a 'drink problem' he had previously denied. Although he vowed to fight on, his position became untenable once it was clear he had lost the confidence of the parliamentary party. He resigned on 8th January. Most Liberal Democrat MPs wanted the respected deputy leader Menzies ('Ming') Campbell to succeed. However, a contest was essential in a party that prided itself on its democracy, and Campbell soon faced three rivals, Simon Hughes, the party's president, Mark Oaten, home affairs spokesperson, and the young, relatively unknown, Chris Huhne.

If Liberal Democrats hoped a leadership contest would attract favourable publicity, they were soon disabused. Initially, Kennedy's messy removal hardly helped. Then Campbell's lacklustre performance as acting leader raised doubts over his age (64) and old-fashioned image, particularly in comparison with Cameron. As a foreign affairs specialist, Campbell's views on economic and social issues were unfamiliar. There were also concerns over his past enthusiasm for coalition with Labour, back in 1997. Hughes, distrusted by leading colleagues but popular with party members, began more effectively, raising the prospect of a new leader lacking the full confidence of his parliamentary party.

Worse was to come. First, Mark Oaten suddenly withdrew, confronted with a newspaper story that he had paid for sex with a rent boy. Then, following another press investigation, Simon Hughes admitted his own homosexual inclinations, but stayed in the contest. His admission was not necessarily damaging by itself. Public attitudes had changed and several MPs had openly 'come out'. But Hughes had publicly denied he was gay. Ironically, he had first entered Parliament in a homophobic by-election campaign against the gay Labour candidate Peter Tatchell. The Liberal Democrats, normally starved of publicity, were now talked about for all the wrong reasons. The party's clean image, once largely unsullied by 'sleaze' or 'spin', was tarnished. Poll ratings dropped to the lowest for years.

The decline could prove short-lived. Leaders can make a difference, particularly in a party whose other politicians are largely unrecognised by voters. Their new leader may or may not prove more effective than Kennedy. Some changes in policy and a shift in ideological emphasis might follow. Unfortunately for Liberal Democrats these could prove largely irrelevant to a party whose fluctuations in support commonly reflect the voters' verdict on their rivals, almost irrespective of their own programme. At the next election they may find themselves squeezed between reinvigorated Conservative and Labour parties, both under new leaders free of past baggage, and competing over the increasingly crowded centre ground.

part of the problem rather than the solution, contributing to the alienation of ordinary people from the political process rather than offering an opportunity for involvement. Whatever the explanation, the UK political system depends to a degree on competition between mass political parties, which hardly any longer exist. It is not a problem confined to the UK, as a decline in party membership seems to be an almost universal problem in modern western democracies, affecting parties across the political spectrum, from communist and socialist parties on the left to Christian democrat parties on the right.

The finance of political parties

The financing of political parties has become such an important and controversial issue that it requires a separate section. Parties need money for many purposes: for example, servicing their permanent organisation, paying administrators and agents, commissioning policy research, financing elections, political advertising and market research. There are three main possible sources of finance: subscriptions from ordinary members, donations from organisations and individuals, or state funding (Outhwaite 2004).

Ideally perhaps, money should come from party members, through ordinary party subscriptions, but it is virtually impossible for a dwindling membership to provide the funds required. Much higher membership fees would deter potential recruits at a time when all parties are desperately seeking to encourage a larger and wider membership. Many 'unwaged' members (not least the large number who are retired) do not pay the full membership rates.

Thus additional sources of finance are solicited, from individual donors, from business organisations, trade unions and other friendly bodies. Yet this can cause problems for parties, as has been only too evident in recent years. How far are contributors to party finances effectively buying influence or status? There is a long history of allegations of the award of honours in return for donations to political parties. Lloyd George, the Liberal leader and coalition prime minister (1916–22), sold honours almost openly. More recently there have been charges that knighthoods and peerages have been given by Conservative governments to individual donors and directors of companies that have made donations to the Conservative Party.

More damaging are allegations of influence on policy. The Conservative Party received contributions from particular sectors of business, such as brewers, tobacco companies and construction companies, and there were suggestions that it was particularly open to influence in these areas as a result. Particularly controversial were contributions from wealthy foreign businessmen. Until Hague's leadership most large donations to the Conservatives were secret, so there were allegations of hidden influence. Labour had long openly depended financially on contributions from trade unions, provoking accusations that the party was effectively run by the unions. More recently, Labour has courted business, and Blair's Labour government was embarrassed by a large donation from Bernie Ecclestone, the Formula One (F1) boss, in 1997. The subsequent exemption of F1 events from bans on tobacco companies sponsoring sporting events was thought to reflect his influence. The problems surrounding party donations led to the Labour government establishing the Neill Committee on party funding, which reported in 1998.

Most of the Neill Report recommendations were implemented. Labour hoped that more transparency would end allegations of sleaze. Instead, the publication of donations has made it easier for journalists to allege some connection between gifts and a possible impact on policy. Publicity given to some donors has also sometimes upset party members. Thus in 2002 the revelation that the new owner of the Express group of newspapers had given the Labour Party £120,000 aroused anger from party members (including some ministers) that the party had accepted money from an individual who also owned a number of pornographic publications.

Such scandals have led to renewed interest in another possible source of party funding – state funding, ultimately out of taxation. Some countries already use such state funding. In fact, in the UK there is already some limited state financial help for opposition parties to fund policy research. While the government of the day can rely largely on the work of the regular civil service, paid special advisers and appointed commissions and

Box 7.7

Recommendations of the Neill Committee on party funding, 1998

- Public disclosure of donations to parties of more than £5,000 (or more than £1,000 to parties locally).
- A £20 million cap on parties' General Election campaign spending.
- An end to 'blind trusts'.
- A ban on foreign donations by non-citizens.
- A ban on anonymous donations to political parties of more than £50.
- Scrutiny of nominations for honours where nominees have donated more than £5,000 to a party within the last five years.
- An independent and impartial Election Commission to monitor the new regulations.
- More public money to finance political parties in parliament (see below).

committees of enquiry, opposition parties formerly had to rely largely on their own party resources and sympathetic independent research bodies. Either way it costs money. The consequences of under-financed, and possibly ill thought out, research in opposition may be manifesto commitments which prove unworkable if the party exchanges opposition for government. This problem was addressed in 1975 by the then Labour government, which introduced payments to opposition parties to enable them to carry out their parliamentary role more effectively.

More controversial is the notion of state funding for party election expenditure and party propaganda generally (which is already provided in some countries). Particularly with the current emphasis on image and marketing it may be argued that the best-financed parties have a distinct advantage. In the past the Conservative Party regularly outspent the Labour Party in election campaigns, but these two far exceeded other party spending. New rules administered by the Electoral Commission place limits on campaign spending. Even so, in the 2005 General Election, both Labour and the Conservatives spent nearly £18 million, compared to the Liberal Democrats £4,324,574 (see Figure 7.1). Minor parties spent much less: UKIP £648,397, Respect £320,716 and the Greens £160,224.

The future of the British party system

1997 was a landmark election which redrew the British political map, in ways which were seemingly confirmed in 2001 and, with some significant exceptions, 2005. A long period of Conservative Party dominance has given place to a similar period of Labour dominance, with a growing third party presence. Yet the party system could be on the verge of another transformation. Two of the three leaders of major parties who contested the 2005 election have already been replaced, while the third, Prime Minister Blair has pledged that he will not seek another term of office. The three main parties that contest the next General Election, perhaps in 2009, will all have new leaders. Changes in leadership are already beginning to impact on party images and programmes, and this process could go much further, transforming the way voters feel about the parties, and party allegiances.

A less immediate but more insidious and longer term threat to Labour dominance could be provided by the ongoing devolution process. Labour in the past has depended on Scottish and Welsh seats to give it an overall majority (although Blair unusually won a majority of English seats in 1997 and 2001). If devolution leads ultimately to the break-up of the United Kingdom, this would damage Labour severely, not only because of the direct loss of Scottish and perhaps Welsh seats but from the loss also of the inspiration and leadership its Welsh and Scottish politicians have long provided. Yet even if devolution does not result in separation it has already led to the loss of some seats in Scotland (as the result of the recommendations of the Scottish Boundary Commission). More seriously it has already weakened the cohesion and unity of the Labour Party in Britain, and provoked some serious rifts particularly between the UK leadership and the Welsh and London Labour parties (see Chapters 16 and 17). Such differences between UK Labour and the party in Scotland and Wales may grow, if only because the latter may seek to distance themselves from a UK

Figure 7.1 Spending by parties, 2005 General Election

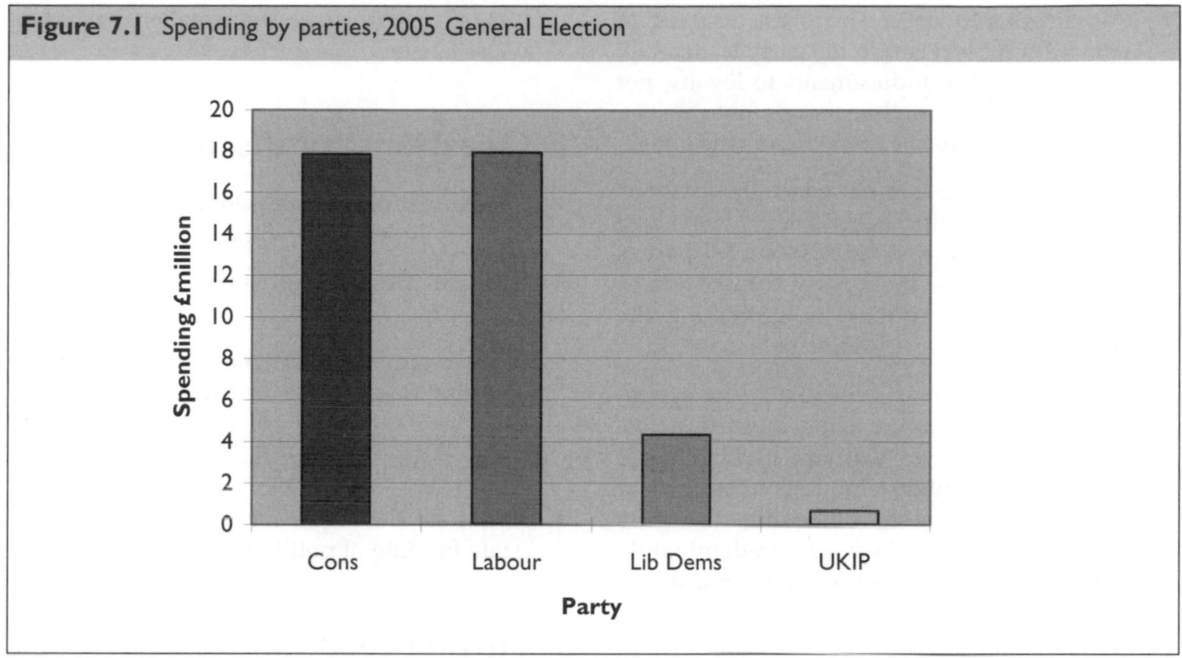

Labour government's policies which are perceived to be unpopular.

Devolution has been accompanied by electoral reform, and proportional representation has also been introduced for elections to the European Parliament. The consequence has been increased representation for nationalist parties and smaller groups such as independent socialists, greens and the UK Independence Party. Ironically, a major beneficiary of devolution and electoral reform has been the Conservative Party, which strenuously opposed both. It was rewarded by significant representation in 1999 in Edinburgh and Cardiff following its wipe-out in the General Election of 1997 in both Scotland and Wales (just one Scottish seat was won back in 2001). Electoral reform for elections to Westminster has been placed on the back burner since the report of the Jenkins Commission (see Chapter 5), but if it is ever reactivated, it could transform the UK party system, as it has already transformed the Scottish and Welsh party systems. The consequences could include the end of the traditional UK two-party system and the emergence of coalition government as the norm rather than the exception, as is already the case over much of the European continent. Within a more proportional electoral system and a multi-party system smaller parties such as the Greens might find increased space to operate. However, it is also possible that other minority parties, such as the BNP, might gain a stronger role in a more fragmented party system.

Summary

- Political parties fulfil important functions in modern democracies.
- Although the Conservative and Labour Parties still largely dominate politics at Westminster and have monopolised control of the UK government since the Second World War, multi-party systems and coalition government are now a feature of devolved parliaments and assemblies and many local councils.
- Party leaders have considerable influence over policy and strategy. An effective and credible leader seems to be crucial for a party's electoral prospects. Methods of choosing new leaders and challenging existing leaders are therefore important and often controversial. All major parties have moved towards involving ordinary members in leadership elections.

- Parliamentary parties are often accused of being too subservient to the party leadership. There are strong inducements to loyalty, not least because divided parties do not prosper. Even so, MPs are becoming more rebellious.
- Party conferences are not generally occasions for important political decisions, and now only rarely involve major controversy. All parties now seem to use their party conferences as primarily opportunities for promoting the party, its policies and leading personalities.
- Parties in Britain, as elsewhere, have experienced a significant decline in their active membership. Fewer than one in 40 voters is now a party member. It is questionable how far British parties can still be described as mass parties. Party members are predominantly elderly, and in other respects unrepresentative of the wider population.
- Local constituency members normally choose candidates for parliamentary and other elections, and have more recently been given a role in leadership elections. Their influence on policy is less easy to assess. In so far as members are influential they may damage a party's electoral prospects, as the views of party activists are generally atypical of those of voters.
- Parties need money to compete effectively, but their finances are very unequal. Subscriptions from a diminishing membership are inadequate, and parties rely on donations from corporate bodies (particularly business firms and trade unions) and from rich individuals, leading to concerns over the purchase of influence. Reforms have made party funding more transparent, but this has raised further questions about the sources of party finance. One possible solution is state funding of political parties.
- Although smaller parties have made gains largely at the expense of the big two, Labour and Conservative, the prospects for a broader party realignment in British politics remain unclear. The first-past-the-post electoral system remains a significant obstacle to a major breakthrough by smaller parties at Westminster.

Questions for discussion

- Could modern representative democracy operate successfully without political parties?
- How far does Britain still have a two-party system?
- Why might more internal party democracy possibly risk adverse electoral consequences?
- In what sense, if any, are British political parties still mass parties?
- What are the arguments for and against the state funding of political parties?

Further reading

Useful and reasonably up-to-date books on British political parties include Garner and Kelly, *British Political Parties Today* (1998), Ingle, *The British Party System* (2000) and Webb, *The Modern British Party System* (2000). The chapter by Baston in Seldon (2001) provides a review of the British party system in the light of Blair's first term, and several chapters in Dunleavy *et al.* (2002, 2003) touch on developments since 1997 and the second Labour landslide in 2001.

More specialist books include a dissection of Conservative Party members, *True Blues* (1994) by Whiteley, Seyd and Richardson, Lewis Minkin's monumental study of the *Contentious Alliance* (1992) between the Unions and Labour, and Eric Shaw's analysis of *The Labour Party since 1945* (1996). New Labour can be explored through Fielding (2003), Ludlam and Smith (2001, 2004) and Coates (2005). Useful sources for updating include journals such as the *Political Quarterly, Politics Review* and *Talking Politics*. For example, a useful article on party finance by Outhwaite (2004) can be found in *Politics Review*. Party websites can also be consulted, including:
www.conservative-party.org.uk
www.labour.org.uk
www.libdems.org.uk

Pressure Groups

Contents

Pressure groups perform a vital role in modern democracies. While elections and parties are crucial to the theory and practice of representative democracy, they do not necessarily involve much popular participation in day-to-day government and decision making. Elections are infrequent and blunt instruments, offering only a restricted choice between rival teams and programmes. Political parties are no longer mass parties, and provide limited opportunities for participation. By contrast, pressure groups offer almost limitless opportunities for ordinary people to participate in the political process on a continuous basis over specific issues that concern them. Pressure groups seek influence rather than power, yet pluralists argue that power is effectively dispersed through the widespread influence of countless groups on government and policy making. Others suggest that some groups are vastly more influential than others, both in Britain and in modern capitalist society more generally, and that power remains effectively concentrated in the hands of the few. Thus analysis of pressure group behaviour is closely tied up with theories about the distribution of power. There are also concerns over some forms of pressure group activity, which may either be almost invisible or only too visible. While some criticise the sinister influence of powerful 'hidden persuaders' behind the scenes, others point to the potential of small special interests that are strategically placed to 'hold the country to ransom'. One important question is how far protestors are justified in pursuing forms of direct action, sometimes involving breaking the law, in pursuit of a cause in which they passionately believe.

Starting with the definition and classification of pressure groups, this chapter analyses their role in the political system and considers recent trends in their activities, as well as the emergence of new social movements. We consider the various targets for pressure group influence and the factors affecting their success. We conclude with an analysis of the contribution of pressure group activity to the theory and practice of democracy.

What are pressure groups?

A simple definition (overleaf) will serve as an introduction, but some aspects are not unproblematic. Many pressure groups are highly organised, with formal constitutions, containing clearly stated aims and objectives, rules and procedures, including the election of officers and the management of resources. Yet some groups may begin with a much looser informal structure, while others may prefer to retain more informal procedures from ideological

> **Definition**
>
> A **pressure group** is any organised group that seeks to influence government and public policy at any level. Pressure groups thus
>
> - are organised; they are not just a section of the public with an interest in common
> - seek influence rather than formal positions of political power (unlike political parties)
> - are outside rather than inside government.

preference or practical considerations. Thus radical green or feminist groups may consciously reject formal structures with leadership roles for a more loose and democratic means of operating, while groups on the fringe of the law (such as some animal rights groups) might rely on informal and clandestine procedures.

Similarly, the distinction between influence and power is at best relative. While pressure groups (unlike parties) do not normally contest elections, they may seek to influence elections (for example, advising voting against particular candidates) and occasionally may fight (and even win) elections in pursuit of a particular interest or cause. Thus the Campaign for Nuclear Disarmament (CND) did sporadically put up candidates for elections, while more recently members have been elected to the Westminster Parliament and the Scottish Parliament on pressure group platforms. Moreover, some formally constituted political parties are effectively single-issue pressure groups (such as the Referendum Party which contested 547 seats in the 1997 election and Respect, which fought 25 seats in 2005).

Finally, although pressure groups are formally outside government, some groups work so closely with government that they are part of the process of governance. Government, at both national and local level, may seek the active cooperation and partnership of business groups and voluntary organisations, and may even delegate important tasks to them. Such groups may continue to put pressure on government, but as recipients of government grants and other benefits they are also clients of government. Decisions may emerge as a result of an ongoing debate within a network of public, private and voluntary organisations, all with an interest in a particular area of policy. (See the discussion of policy networks in Chapters 17 and 18.) It may even be possible on occasion for a government department or agency to be effectively captured by the interests it is responsible for. (Such 'agency capture' has sometimes occurred in the USA.) It is also worth noting that some parts of government seek to influence other parts of government, often using familiar pressure group tactics. Thus local councils and local government in general (through the Local Government Association and appropriate professional bodies) often seek to influence the decisions of central government and the European Union.

■ Types of pressure group

Pressure groups are so numerous and varied that many attempts have been made to distinguish between types of group, to bring some order into the analysis of a very crowded field. One fundamental distinction for political scientists is that between groups with a clear political purpose (such as the Countryside Alliance or the League Against Cruel Sports) and groups which exist primarily for social purposes, and may engage in politics rarely, if at all. Yet even an allotment association or sports club, ostensibly non-political, may from time to time seek political influence, over ground rents or council grants for example, or more seriously over plans for roads or buildings which might threaten their survival. Charitable organisations, such as Oxfam or the RSPCA, may frequently engage in political lobbying as part of their primary purpose (although they have to be careful not to endanger their charitable status).

Another simple distinction might be made about the level at which groups operate. Some are purely local, seeking to influence decisions and services in the immediate community. Others are national, although they might have local or regional branches (such as the National Farmers' Union (NFU), the National Union of Students (NUS) and the National Union of Teachers (NUT)). An increasing number of groups operate at the European level (like the Association of European Automobile Constructors). Some of these European groups act

Definition

Peak or **umbrella groups** involve formal associations of a large number of similar groups. The most well known of these are the Trades Union Congress (TUC), to which nearly all British trade unions are affiliated, and the Confederation of British Industry (CBI), of which most (but not all) large and medium-sized firms are members.

as peak or umbrella groups for long-established national groups in EU member states. Finally, some groups are genuinely international in their membership and concerns (such as Amnesty International and Greenpeace), although such groups commonly have links with national organisations or national branch structures.

Two systems of classifying groups have been used widely by political scientists: the first describes groups in terms of what or who they represent, the second in terms of their strategies and relations with government.

Interest and cause groups

The first approach distinguishes two main types of pressure group: first, interest groups, seeking to defend the interests of a particular section of the population (alternatively, these may be described as 'sectional' or 'defensive' groups); and second, cause (or promotional) groups.

Interest groups include business firms, trade associations, professional bodies and trade unions, and other groups involved with industry and employment. Examples include the CBI, the TUC, the British Medical Association (BMA), the Law Society and the NUT. Members of churches, sports bodies, residents' associations and groups representing particular minority communities may also be described as groups concerned primarily, although not exclusively, with defending their own interests.

Cause groups in contrast come into existence to promote some belief, attitude or principle. They are also referred to as promotional, attitude, ideological or preference groups. Examples are Greenpeace, the Child Poverty Action Group, Amnesty International, Shelter and Charter 88.

Definitions

Interest groups are concerned to defend or advance the interests of its members, whereas **cause groups** are based on a shared attitude or values.

There are two main differences between the two types of group. First, whereas membership of a sectional group is limited to those with a shared background, membership of a cause group is open to all those sharing the same values. Second, whereas the purpose of the sectional group is to protect the interests of its own members, the aim of the cause group is generally to advance other interests (the environment, children, animals, prisoners of conscience) or the public welfare as perceived by its members.

Yet the distinction between interest and cause groups is not always clear cut. First, interest groups may pursue causes. The BMA, for example, not only looks after the professional interests of doctors but also campaigns on more general health issues such as drinking and smoking. Second, while in terms of their overall goals and motives many groups are clearly cause groups, such groups also often have material interests to defend. A charity such as Oxfam owns property and employs professional staff with careers to advance.

Many groups may combine a mixture of self-interest and more altruistic concerns. Thus groups opposed to specific developments (such as a new airport runway or a bypass) can involve both those promoting the broad cause of environmental conservation and others with a more self-interested objection to the proposed development's impact on their personal well-being and their property values. While some opponents reject almost all new roads or airports as part of a radical alternative transport strategy, others simply want the proposed development somewhere else – 'not in my backyard' (NIMBY). Moreover, as a matter of tactics, to win wider public support, particular sectional interests often proclaim they are acting in the wider public interest. University lecturers seeking salary increases stress the benefits to higher education and the country.

Foxhunters defending their leisure pursuits broaden the debate to encompass the cause of countryside protection.

Despite these complications, the straightforward classification of groups into sectional and cause remains important, valuable and widely used. However, an additional typology, based on the distinction between insider and outsider groups is also widely employed (see Definitions below).

Insider and outsider groups

Wyn Grant (1995) argued that insider and outsider groups could each be subdivided into three sub-categories:

- 'High-profile insider groups': prepared to reinforce their frequent behind-the-scenes contacts with government by using the media to influence public opinion – e.g. CBI, NFU, BMA.
- 'Low-profile insider groups': concentrate on regular contacts with government, and generally do not seek to influence wider public – e.g. Howard League for Penal Reform.
- 'Prisoner groups': find it difficult to break away from their insider relationship because of dependence on government (e.g. for finance or accommodation), or because they represent parts of the public sector – e.g. Local Government Association.
- 'Potential insider groups' or 'threshold groups' which seek insider status but have yet to achieve it
- 'Outsider groups by necessity' which lack the political knowledge and skills to become insider groups.
- 'Ideological outsider groups' which do not expect or want to influence government, perhaps because their aims are fundamentally opposed to those of government and prevailing opinion. Thus they choose unconventional methods (often involving direct action, law-breaking and sometimes even violence) to put their message across – e.g. Animal Liberation Front.

Definitions

Insider groups are consulted on a regular basis by government while **outsider groups** either do not want to become closely involved with government or are unable to gain government recognition.

One important virtue of this typology is that it sets groups firmly within *a relationship with government.* It refers both to the *strategy* pursued by a group – whether or not it seeks acceptance by government – and to the *status* achieved or not achieved as a result of its efforts. Some outsider groups may lack the contacts and skills to become insiders, while others may be potential insiders, who seek to be consulted and may achieve this over time. Ideological outsider groups may suspect their aims and methods will make them unacceptable to government in any case, but they also may fear that a close relationship with government could jeopardise their independence and blunt their capacity for radical criticism and action. While insider groups operate mainly behind the scenes, rather than indulging in the politics of protest, in part because they do not want to put at risk their good relations with government and their influence in the 'corridors of power', they may on occasion campaign publicly. Some groups that are too powerful or important to ignore, such as the BMA and NFU, regularly use both behind-the-scenes influence and public campaigns.

This classification cuts across the interest/cause distinction. Interest groups are perhaps rather more likely to be insiders than cause groups. However, some cause groups have managed to achieve insider status (such as MENCAP and the Howard League for Penal Reform), while some interest groups have been conspicuously excluded from government consultation (the National Union of Mineworkers, and trade unions generally under the Thatcher government). This illustrates the obvious point that status can change over time. The TUC was regularly consulted on employment issues, incomes policies and economic and social policy generally by both Labour and Conservative governments up until 1979, when it lost insider status. It has only recovered some (but by no means all) of its extensive former influence under New Labour. By contrast, all radical environmental groups began as outsiders, but while Greenpeace remains an outsider group, Friends of the Earth seems to have acquired a degree of insider status. Questions of definition and perception as well as apparent changes over time illustrate some problems with the insider/outsider distinction as a basis for classifying groups. Thus Grant (2000) has largely abandoned it in his more recent work.

Pressure group targets and methods

Who do pressure groups seek to influence and what methods do they use? It is reasonable to consider these together, as the methods adopted may clearly depend on potential targets. Moreover, when groups are choosing their strategy, much depends on the aims and resources of the particular group and the level at which it is operating.

Potential targets include:

- the 'core executive' – government ministers (including the prime minister) and civil servants (Whitehall)
- Parliament (both Houses)
- political parties
- informed opinion (more disrespectfully described as 'the chattering classes')
- wider public opinion (mainly through the mass media)
- local institutions, including local government
- the European Union.

Influencing the government

Why do groups seek to influence the government, and why is the government ready to listen? The answer to the first question is perhaps fairly obvious. Groups seek to defend and advance their own interest or cause, and government policy or specific decisions may affect them adversely or beneficially. Therefore they have a strong motive to seek to influence government, especially as power in the British political system is heavily concentrated with the core executive (see Chapter 11). Thus a change in taxation may significantly affect business profitability or the living standards of particular sections of the population. A change in the law may similarly affect business costs, employment opportunities or individual freedom. As law-making is largely an executive function in Britain, the natural target for influence is again the government.

Government decisions on benefits, grants and subsidies and on specific projects such as hospitals, schools, roads and airports may profoundly affect particular sections of society and specific communities. Those groups affected want information on the government's early thinking and draft proposals, because it is often easier to influence the government before it has gone public and committed itself. They want the chance to influence both the substance and detail of government policy, for if they cannot change the government's mind on the principle, they will want to ensure that the detailed implementation damages their interests as little as possible. Once a law is passed or a tax introduced, affected interests may continue to seek its amendment or repeal. Influence on the core executive is commonly the most direct and effective way to look after those interests, and groups may only seek to influence Parliament, political parties or public opinion when this direct route fails.

There can be risks involved in becoming too close to government, however. Groups may fear to criticise the government for fear of losing their valued insider status. In so doing they may risk upsetting some of their own members, who may feel their interests and views are being ignored or unrepresented. Something of this sort happened to the NFU in the 2001 foot-and-mouth disease outbreak, although its difficulties were increased by differences of interest within the farming community (see Box 8.1).

It is perhaps less easy at first sight to see what the government gains from contacts with pressure groups, although this is at least as important. Government needs, first, information and specialised knowledge and advice, which is not generally available in Whitehall. Second, government will want some idea of the likely reaction to specific initiatives from those who may be affected. Prior consultation may avoid potential trouble later. Third, if possible, government wants

Box 8.1

The National Farmers Union (NFU)

The foot-and-mouth disease crisis which struck British agriculture in 2001 led to divisions among farmers and their union, the NFU. Many farmers were distressed by the government's policy of slaughtering animals to stop the spread of the disease. Often this meant killing healthy animals that were not infected, as a precaution. Some farmers wanted to have these healthy animals vaccinated against foot-and-mouth disease rather than slaughtered. The NFU leadership argued that there was no satisfactory alternative to the slaughter policy. The leadership was accused of representing the interests of big farmers and agri-businesses, and not the interests of small stock farmers. It was argued that 60,000 farmers were members of the NFU, most of them small farmers, yet it was the minority of big farmers that most influenced NFU official policy.

Small farmers complained that the NFU had never consulted them to find out their views, and consequently the union was not representing them in a democratic manner. Resulting from this, a number of small farmers left the NFU because other rival agricultural organisations represented their interests more accurately. A dilemma for large interest groups such as the NFU is that its membership is diverse. In the case of the NFU it speaks for big farmers and small farmers, arable farmers and livestock farmers, and they each have different interests and priorities, and want different policies.

support from relevant interests. If a minister can claim that those with an interest in a particular policy or initiative have been fully consulted and support the proposals, this will help win the argument in Parliament, the media and the country. Finally, on many issues the government needs the active cooperation of outside bodies, if it is to be successful. Thus a reform of the National Health Service (NHS) should preferably have the support of health service professionals.

Much effective influence may involve not high-profile meetings with ministers, but routine behind-the-scenes discussions with officials. Many group representatives sit with civil servants on the large number of committees advising government. Many group spokespersons will have frequent formal and informal contacts with their 'opposite numbers' in Whitehall.

Influencing Parliament

Attempts by pressure groups to influence Parliament often secure more media publicity than attempts to influence the executive (because much of this is behind the scenes). Thus the main television news frequently broadcast pictures of particular groups lobbying Parliament, and occasionally more dramatic interventions, such as the purple dye 'bombing' by Fathers 4 Justice of the Commons Chamber, and its invasion by protestors against the ban on hunting. Although Parliament has long been seen by most established groups as a less effective target for influence than the executive (see section above), survey evidence suggests a growing use of parliamentary channels. Reasons for this include the increase in backbench independence and the growth in size and number of the backbench revolts, the increasing importance of departmental select committees which provide another channel for influence, and the growth of Westminster-based professional consultancies, often employing MPs or their researchers. The semi-reformed House of Lords has also become an increased target of pressure group influence, particularly as it has demonstrated more readiness to amend and delay government legislation (see Chapter 13).

Groups may seek to influence Parliament by submitting petitions, lobbying Parliament and individual MPs, circulating all MPs and peers with letters and information packs, and using friendly MPs to ask questions, raise issues, and introduce amendments to legislation, or sometimes even a bill (through private members' legislation). Much of this activity is open and legitimate, although sometimes it has involved more questionable inducements, which have led to scandals and increased scrutiny, particularly from the recently established Parliamentary Commissioner for Standards Committee.

Groups may seek to influence the legislative process at every stage. As nearly all the laws passed by Parliament are government bills, much of this influence is targeted at the executive, particularly in the formative pre-parliamentary stages when the need for new legislation is

In Focus 8.1

A stunt by a Fathers 4 Justice campaigner

An activist dressed as Batman scales Buckingham Palace with a slogan to advertise his cause. Fathers 4 Justice was established by fathers separated from their former partners and aggrieved by their restricted access to offspring for whom they were required to pay high maintenance by the Child Support Agency. The group has shown that it is possible to attract extensive media publicity without mass demonstrations by using eye-catching stunts. Not all publicity is necessarily good publicity, however. Thus stunts that have inconvenienced the public or raised security concerns (such as the flour-bombing of the House of Commons chamber) have perhaps been counter-productive. An alleged plot to kidnap Tony Blair's son by an offshoot of the original group led to an announcement of the end of the Fathers 4 Justice campaign in January 2006.

Photograph: EMPICS.

discussed and the government is consulting outside interests. However, while a bill is going through Parliament, groups will seek to target both government and Parliament, particularly with regard to the details of legislation, often at the committee stage, using sympathetic MPs or peers to introduce amendments drafted for them. On controversial bills groups will hope to influence the votes of MPs, particularly backbench MPs on the government side, who may be persuaded to defy the government whips. Even after a bill is passed and becomes an Act of Parliament, groups may often be involved in the crucial implementation of the Act, and in influencing delegated legislation (although much of this influence will be directed at the executive rather than parliament). If a group remains dissatisfied with the law as it stands, it will campaign for new legislation, using the channels of influence, and the whole process may start again (see Figure 8.1).

Groups may particularly target Parliament and individual MPs and peers on private members' legislation (bills introduced by MPs who are not members of the government). Although very few of these succeed, certain controversial political areas, particularly those involving moral issues, have often been left to private members' legislation (for example changes in the law on homosexuality, divorce, and abortion), partly because these cut across normal party lines. Because such issues are normally left to a free vote of MPs, there is more scope for pressure group influence. Sometimes outside groups draft whole bills and seek to persuade MPs who have won a place in the annual ballot for a chance to present private members' bills to introduce their measure. (For more on pressure groups and Parliament see relevant sections of Chapter 13.)

Influencing political parties

Influencing Parliament and individual MPs inevitably involves influencing parties, as almost all MPs and most peers belong to parliamentary parties. Groups may also seek to influence parties more directly. They may do this in a number of ways. The most obvious way is to make donations to political parties, as do both the trade unions (to Labour) and business (formerly mainly to the Conservatives, but now increasingly also to Labour). In the last two decades, trade union contributions to the Labour Party declined (from three-quarters to under a third of its total funds, 1986–2005) whilst business contributions have grown. Since 1997 New Labour's desire to attract

Figure 8.1 Pressure group influence on Whitehall and Westminster: the main stages

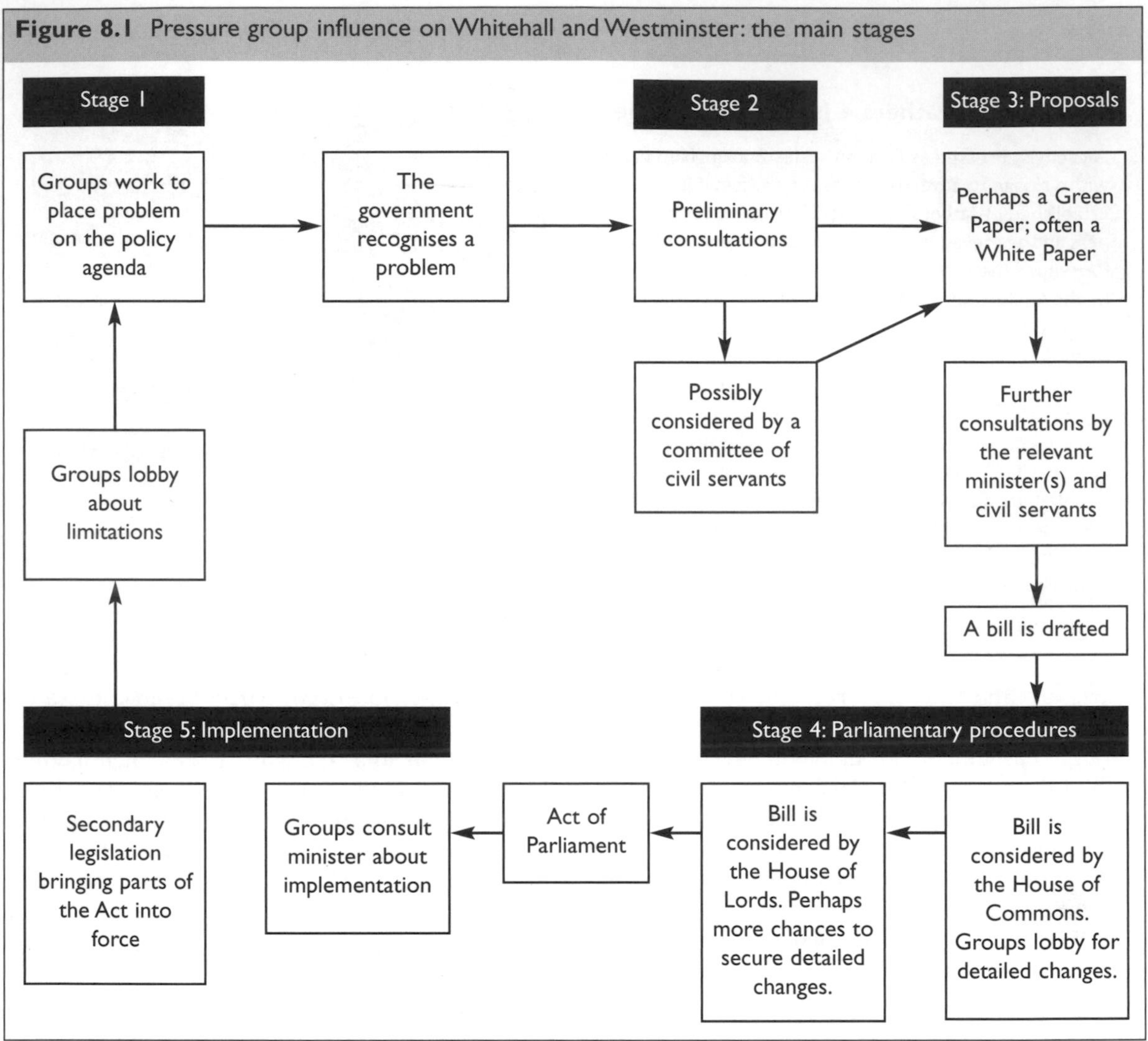

Source: adapted from Grant, 1995: 48.

business funds produced embarrassment for the party, for example over its exemption of Formula One (F1) from its proposed tobacco advertising ban after FI boss Bernie Ecclestone donated £1 million to Labour (see Box 8.2).

Another method is to sponsor candidates, as the trade unions did before 1995 in the Labour Party. Some cause groups – such as the anti-hunting and anti-abortion lobbies – try to influence parties' choice of parliamentary candidates. Others again attempt to persuade parties to place detailed commitments in their manifestos. In return for influence, such groups campaign for the party supporting their cause. Sometimes group and party membership overlaps, and this may help the groups achieve a favourable reception from parties. For example, most Labour MPs belong to trade unions. In addition, the Labour Party also contains many members of campaigning organisations such as CND, Greenpeace, Friends of the Earth and the League Against Cruel Sports, and of local community action groups.

Targeting a particular party may have drawbacks for a group. It may alienate opinion in other parties. Moreover, it is only likely to be successful if

Box 8.2

Labour and the Ecclestone affair

Labour's exemption of Formula One (F1) motor racing from its tobacco advertising ban in November 1997 led to a public furore after it simultaneously leaked out that the party had received a pre-election gift of £1 million from the F1 chief, Bernie Ecclestone. Ecclestone had had talks with Blair a few weeks before the decision was announced. F1 argued that tobacco sponsorship was vital to the sport. A ban would lead to the loss to Britain of 50,000 full time jobs and £900,000 a year in exports as well as the possible removal of F1 to Asia (from where the same tobacco advertising on placards and cars would be broadcast by television to British homes). Against this, the anti-smoking lobby, which included Action on Smoking and Health (ASH), the BMA and several charities, countered that the association of tobacco advertising with motor racing glamorised smoking and helped make it attractive to young people.

The key political issues involved the suspicion of party favours on policy in return for funding, and the power of powerful commercial interests to sway government decisions by behind-the-scenes lobbying. Labour was particularly vulnerable to such allegations in view of its pre-election attacks on Conservative sleaze and its criticisms of Conservative governments for failing to cut teenage smoking by banning tobacco advertising and their receipt of large contributions to Conservative party funds from the tobacco industry.

In retreating from the ban, Labour argued that it had not been the victim of insider lobbying but rather had been won over by the strength of the argument that the global nature of the sport made a ban counter-productive. The upshot of the affair was that, on the advice of the chairman of the Committee on Standards and Privileges, the party returned the money to Bernie Ecclestone. The EU directive's ban on sports advertising exempted F1 from the ban until 2006.

the party is in power or has reasonable prospects of reaching power. This may be one obvious reason why Labour has attracted more business donations from the 1990s onwards, while contributions to the Conservative Party have declined. Moreover, a party that gains power may not necessarily honour all its previous commitments. Even so, Labour has proved receptive to some interests (such as unions, ramblers and groups opposed to blood sports), and it made sense for relevant groups to target especially Labour MPs and the party generally to fulfil commitments on the minimum wage, access to the countryside, and hunting legislation.

Influencing informed opinion

Because many public policy issues are relatively specialised and do not attract much interest from the mass media or the wider public, it may often be more important to target what might be called 'informed opinion', or what are sometimes more disrespectfully called 'the chattering classes'. This may be achieved, for example, through influencing important professional bodies, and through more specialist media, including minority television channels and programmes, the 'quality' daily press, and weeklies (such as the *Economist, Spectator* or *New Statesman*). Such bodies and media outlets may be far more influential than their membership or audience figures may suggest, as they are noticed by those who matter. Winning the argument among leading opinion formers may often prove decisive in the long run in swaying the decisions of ministers, civil servants and MPs, even sometimes where the mass media and wider public opinion is pushing in another direction. For example, while the mass media dramatised a possible link between the triple MMR (measles, mumps and rubella) inoculation programme and autism, health professionals and informed opinion reached a clear consensus that there was no such link and the government held firm, despite an initial panic.

Influencing wider public opinion

Much of the most visible pressure group activity involves influencing public opinion, although this can be time-consuming and expensive in resources, and may be less effective than other channels. Thus groups can seek to raise public awareness of an issue by various forms of protest and direct action (Jordan and Mahoney 1997). These include legal and non-violent methods such as public petitions, marches and demonstrations (such as those by the Countryside Alliance or the Stop the War Coalition), or consumer boycotts of goods. But they can also include the illegal but non-violent non-payment tactics used by the Anti-Poll Tax Federation, the sit-ins employed by the anti-roads protesters and the disruptive methods deployed by hunt saboteurs and anti-whalers. More rarely the use of violence and intimidation is employed; for example supporters of the Animal Liberation Front break into laboratories, release animals, and target the persons and property of any individual remotely connected with experiments on animals.

Some experienced pressure group campaigners, like Des Wilson, make only very sparing use of public demonstrations, because they can be not only ineffective but even counterproductive, particularly if they get out of hand and alienate public opinion and decision makers. Thus the mobs that went on the rampage attacking suspected paedophiles (often wholly innocent victims of mistaken identity) harmed the cause they were seeking to advance. Yet more disciplined peaceful mass demonstrations can have relatively little effect. CND annually organised massive four-day marches between the nuclear research establishment at Aldermaston and London from the late 1950s onwards without having any appreciable impact on government defence policy. More recently, what was estimated to be the largest public demonstration ever, that against the Iraq War in March 2003, did not succeed in its objective of stopping the war.

Rather more successful in influencing public opinion have been much smaller more targeted demonstrations, such as those employed by Greenpeace. One of the most successful of these was the brief occupation by protestors of the Brent Spar oil rig, in protest against proposed plans to dump it at sea. The episode was filmed and shown on the main television news. The publicity embarrassed the Shell Oil Company and the government to such an extent that the plans to dispose of the rig at sea were abandoned. Whether this was the right decision is still subject to debate. However, there can be little doubt that the demonstration was successful in changing policy (Jordan 2001).

This example illustrates the importance of the mass media if a pressure group demonstration is to be effective in influencing public opinion. Without the free publicity given by the media, only those few people directly involved would have known about the occupation of the Brent Spar oil rig. Other protests have been taken up extensively and amplified by the tabloid press, particularly those by the Countryside Alliance from 1997 onwards, the fuel protests of September

Box 8.3

The Countryside Alliance

The Countryside Alliance organised its first rally in London in 1998. Around 280,000 people from rural Britain marched, primarily to defend the right to carry on hunting, but also to draw attention to other countryside concerns, including farmers' grievances, the loss of countryside to urban development, and declining rural services such as transport, schools and shops. Reflecting this, the Countryside Alliance was supported by organisations such as the British Field Sports Society, the NFU, the Clay Pigeon Association, the British Horse Society, the Country Landowners' Association, Timber Growers' Association and the Trout and Salmon Association. A second 'Liberty and Livelihood' march in 2002 was supported by over 400,000. A series of further demonstrations has since taken place, mostly peacefully within the law, although government ministers have been roughly treated, and a number of pro-hunt protestors invaded the House of Commons. Despite the protests, after delays and some compromises the hunting bill completed its parliamentary stages, and was implemented in 2005. Most hunts are still operating, but with the difference that cornered foxes are not finally torn apart by dogs but shot, which seems to be technically within the law. Many hunters, however, have declared they are prepared to defy the law if necessary.

The Countryside Alliance has successfully capitalised on a number of rural grievances, besides its main concern over hunting. It has certainly secured substantial publicity for its cause. It has arguably delayed legislation, and caused it to be somewhat modified, yet it was ultimately not able to stop the bill becoming law. Some argue that Labour can ignore rural interests, since it won a little over a quarter of the vote in the most rural seats and had only a dozen MPs from agricultural constituencies.

2000, the anti-council tax protests of 2003–4, and the 2005 protests against gypsy camps. Some critics argue the tabloid press is not so much reflecting public concerns as fanning the flames of protest, and determining the political agenda (Milne 2005).

Influencing local government and other local institutions

Many important decisions that affect people's lives are still made locally (see Chapter 17). Small local community groups with relatively few resources can sometimes be very effective in influencing these local decisions, such as the proposed closure of a school or hospital, or decisions on planning applications, or policy on roads and traffic regulation. An organisation can spring up very quickly, and can often tap local expertise to mount a professional campaign. There are some clear targets for influence. The local MP may be a potentially useful and influential ally, even if the issue involves local institutions rather than central government. Individual councillors, local government officers and the council as a whole are obvious targets for issues that are a local authority responsibility, although sometimes a government department may also be contacted if a minister has the final say. Doctors, nurses and other health service professionals, together with affected patients, readily attract sympathetic coverage on any health service issue. Meetings and demonstrations can invariably get free publicity from the local press and radio, and sometimes also regional television if there is a story that is newsworthy.

Influencing the European Union

At the other extreme, many decisions that affect people in Britain are made by the European Union (EU) (see Chapter 15). Although this seems to many Britons a remote body, it is still highly susceptible to influence from organised groups. Business and farming interests, trade unions, professional associations such as the BMA and the Law Society, and environmental groups all lobby at EU level. Some British groups have offices in Brussels and lobby directly. Many others employ consultancy firms to lobby on their behalf. Commonly British groups seek allies in other EU member states and work through Europe-wide umbrella groups such as UNICE (the Union of Industrial and Employers' Confederations of Europe), ETUC (the European Trade Union Confederation), COPA (the Committee of Professional Agricultural Organisations), BEUC (the European Bureau of Consumers' Associations) and EEB (the European Environmental Bureau). A potential disadvantage of such Eurogroups, however, is that they sometimes find it hard to agree on policy because of national differences.

Pressure groups have long sought primarily to influence the European Commission, but as the powers of the European Parliament have increased, that too has become an important target. It is rarely possible for groups to have any direct influence on the Council of Ministers, so here they have to rely on their national government to protect their interests. However they may be able to influence the Committee of Permanent Representatives (COREPER) which serves the Council of Ministers, and prepares papers on which Council decisions are made. Relatively few groups seem to make much use of the Economic and Social Committee in Brussels, which was an institution designed to reflect the interests of employers, employees and consumers.

Some British interests (such as trawler operatives) undoubtedly feel they have little or no influence over decisions made in Brussels which affect their livelihoods. Other groups, however, make use of EU directives and regulations to put pressure on their own government, and cite examples of practices in other EU member states to demand improved services and higher standards in Britain. (See Chapter 15 for more on pressure groups and the EU.)

■ New social movements

The term 'social movement' has been employed to describe a much looser informal and less organised coalition of individuals or groups supporting a broad interest or cause. It is customary to define a pressure group as an organisation which aims to influence policy by seeking to persuade decision makers by lobbying rather than by standing for election and holding office. Paul Byrne described a social movement as something that is relatively disorganised (Byrne 1997). While a pressure group is a formal organisation which has members, a social movement may be an informal and loosely organised network, with supporters rather than members. Examples of what are termed 'new social movements' are the women's movement, the peace movement, the green movement and the anti-capitalist movement. All these include some specific organised groups, and many individuals who may be members of one or more such groups, but also others who may not belong to any organised group but still identify strongly with the interest or cause. Thus the women's movement is much more than a coalition of interest groups, but represents a broad swathe of interests and opinion in society that has already promoted significant social change.

A loose informal movement may be preferred to a formal organisation for ideological reasons. Some feminists associate formal organisations, with their rules and hierarchies, with a male preference for order, authority and status, and seek less directed, more spontaneous and cooperative methods of working. Similarly, some peace campaigners and green activists positively reject leadership roles. This may be seen as part of a wider rejection of the existing social and political order based on traditional values. Social movement supporters are more likely to favour alternative ways of organising politics and society, and thus want changes that will fundamentally change the existing order. While pressure group members may work through parliamentary parties, social movement supporters are more likely to reject such traditional institutions and lead their own private lives in ways shaped by their alternative values and ideologies. Whereas members of pressure groups are likely to recognise government by a parliamentary elite as legitimate and simply attempt to influence their decisions, supporters of a social movement may challenge the values of the governing elite, question its authority and replace 'conventional' politics with the 'new' politics of direct action.

Until relatively recently nearly all protest movements challenging the legitimacy of government and parliament, and prepared to use direct action, sometimes involving deliberate breaches of the law, were clearly associated with the left. Since the advent of a Labour government with a

Box 8.4

The anti-capitalist movement

Anti-capitalist protests and direct action against transnational companies have grown. This new social movement has no established leaders, and no organisation in the sense of having a headquarters staffed by office workers, but involves a loose international network linked by the internet. It has been described as a 'global, anarchic and chaotic' body, but nevertheless has become a significant political force. Much campaigning takes place against the 'iron triangle' of global capitalism: the World Trade Organisation, the International Monetary Fund and the World Bank. Much additional 'grassroots' campaigning takes place against transnational companies such as McDonald's, Coca-Cola, Nike, Texaco, Shell, Microsoft, Disney and Gap. The protesters' causes range from anti-consumerism, environmentalism, anti-slavery and the promotion of human rights. Some successfully oppose advertised junk food replacing locally produced real food. Some oppose the use of 'sweatshop labour' by women and children in the third world to produce expensive designer-label products in the West.

May Day 'anti-capitalist' or 'anti-globalisation' demonstrations in London as well as similar events in Seattle and Quebec, are seen as 'pro-democracy' protests by many participants. Naomi Klein, for example, has criticised newspaper journalists for describing these events in terms of violence and extremism whereas really they should be seen as a healthy part of democracy (Klein 2001). For example, a consumer boycott was organised against Esso in 2001 in order to persuade the oil company to change its attitude towards global warming. Esso had suggested that there was no actual proof that global warming is caused by burning fossil fuels, and that those scientists who have made the link are scaremongerers. The Stop Esso campaign noted that Esso provided George W. Bush with more than US$1 million towards his presidential election campaign, and appeared to be repaid when the new president pulled the USA out of the Kyoto agreement (see Chapter 25).

Box 8.5

The rise of right-wing protest movements

The politics of protest used to be predominantly associated with the left in Britain (for example CND, the anti-Vietnam War protests, anti-apartheid demonstrations, the miners' strike, the anti-poll tax riots, protests against global capitalism). The massive demonstrations organised by the Stop the War Coalition in protest against the Iraq War are a recent example of such left-inspired and dominated activities. However, a relatively recent trend has been the growth of essentially right-wing protest groups, often tacitly or openly supported by the Conservative Party. These include the Countryside Alliance, the fuel protests of September 2000, and the anti-council tax protests, which unlike the campaign against the poll tax originated among those with relatively high-valued properties in middle-class rural and suburban areas. One obvious explanation is that previously the interests of the rural gentry and farmers, motorists and the road transport lobby, and middle-class home owners were reasonably well served by a Conservative government. Since 1997 some of these interests sense they are on the outside of the political mainstream under a Labour government, and resort to the methods of protest and direct action traditionally used by those who feel excluded from power and influence.

substantial majority in 1997, however, a number of right-wing protest movements have shown a willingness to defy the elected government and Parliament, employing tactics on the fringes of the law, and sometimes a readiness to defy the law (see Box 8.5).

Pressure groups, power and democracy

The debate over the role of pressure groups in the political process is closely bound up with arguments over the distribution of power and the extent of democracy, both in Britain and in other modern western political systems. (Refer back to the discussion in Chapter 1.)

Pluralists argued that power is effectively dispersed in modern western democracies, in large part through the activities of countless freely competing groups. They point to the apparent influence of pressure groups in numerous case studies of decision making. They claim that pressure groups promoting one interest or cause (such as legalised abortion, a ban on blood sports or 'green' taxes on motoring) stimulate the growth of rival groups to counter their arguments, as has happened in Britain. These rival groups, through their activities, promote democratic debate, help educate the public on the issues and lead to better-informed decisions which reflect the net sum of influence and the balance of public opinion. Thus pressure group activity is the very essence of a free democratic society. Indeed, some modern theories of democracy (notably those of Robert Dahl) depend heavily on the role of pressure groups.

Elitists argue by contrast that power remains concentrated in the hands of the few. The contest between groups, they claim, remains profoundly unequal, in part because of massive differences in resources. Some have abundant finance, effective leadership and communication skills, but above all access to decision makers, while others do not. Much of the most effective influence takes place behind the scenes rather than in the open. Government listens to some interests and ignores or rejects others. Within a capitalist system business groups have much more influence than groups representing labour or consumers, not only because of their greater resources and access to government, but because their role is crucial if the economy is to be managed successfully. Some interests – the poor, the sick, the elderly – are more difficult to organise than others.

From a democratic perspective, although the numbers involved in pressure groups are impressive, and far larger than those involved in parties, group policy is commonly determined by leaders and spokespersons. Some group leaders are elected by members, but most are not, and they can be virtually self-appointed. Although some, like the once influential Mary Whitehouse and her National Viewers and Listeners Association, claim to speak for the 'silent majority', while it remains silent there is no way of testing such claims. It is also sometimes questionable how far some groups really represent those whose interests they are ostensibly serving

Box 8.6

Who really represents the disabled?

In lobbying government, disabled people are represented by numerous voluntary-sector charities and agencies. These are very fragmented, and there is no single influential voice but rather many competing forces. Even so, these groups have greater resources and access to government than 'newer groups led by disabled people themselves' (Drake 2002: 373). A crucial issue for disabled people is how far a voluntary body staffed by people who are not disabled can really represent the disabled themselves. Some charities are almost as concerned with helping the families and relatives of disabled people as with helping disabled people themselves. In other words, the interests of the carers and the disabled become combined, yet what serves the best interests of relatives might not be in the best interests of the disabled. Furthermore, some charities provide services based on their professional judgements rather than on the needs expressed by disabled people. The problem might be resolved if disabled people held positions in charities for the disabled, but in reality disabled people have found it very difficult to get established and hold positions in the most powerful charities.

Drake argued that governments 'hear only what they want to hear', and may exclude certain strands of opinion, effectively controlling the type of advice it is likely to receive (Drake 2002). Large traditional charities are always likely to be included but smaller groups, especially if they are radical and out of line with government thinking, are more likely to be excluded. Since disabled people are more likely to be involved in the latter type of group they tend to be excluded from the political process. This results in the political agenda concerning disability being controlled more by professionals such as social workers and therapists than the disabled.

(see Box 8.6 on the representation of the disabled). Moreover, much of the most effective influence (as noted above) is behind the scenes in the 'corridors of power' rather than in the open. Thus some of the most effective pressure groups are 'hidden persuaders' rather than contributors to a democratic public debate.

While some of the criticism of the role of pressure groups in modern politics has come from the left,

Box 8.7

The rise and decline of corporatism

Corporatism is a term used to describe a system of decision making in some European countries involving partnership between the government and the interests of capital and labour. Corporatism or 'tripartism' is the label commonly given to a pattern of economic decision making evident in Britain in the 1960s and 1970s under both Labour and Conservative governments. It involved government determining policy in consultation with the CBI, representing employers, and the TUC, representing workers, particularly on incomes policy, but also at times covering broader economic and social policy. Thus the 1974–9 Labour Government agreed a 'social contract' with business and the unions.

Corporatism, like pluralism, assumed group influence on government decision making, but instead of the pluralist vision of countless groups freely competing, corporatism involved a few peak or umbrella groups working in close cooperation with government. It was not entirely clear who was driving the process and benefiting from it. Critics on the left argued that the interests of workers and unions were sacrificed to business profits. The social contract was a social 'con trick'. The right argued that trade unions were too powerful and holding the country to ransom. Others suggested that Parliament was being bypassed, and that the representatives of business and labour did not necessarily speak for their members. Decisions were being made by elite groups rather than people. Those defending corporatism countered that it had worked effectively in other countries, reducing industrial conflict and promoting growth.

The election of the Thatcher government virtually ended corporatism. Lord Young, a leading member of her Cabinet, claimed, 'We have rejected the TUC; we have rejected the CBI. We do not see them coming back again. We gave up the Corporate State' (*Financial Times*, 9 November 1988). Left-wing critics suggested that while the influence of the unions had declined markedly, the Thatcher government remained open to business interests. Corporatism in its earlier form has never returned. However, it has been argued that the theory of 'stakeholding', sometimes associated with Blair and New Labour, shares some features of corporatism.

because of marked inequalities in group resources and influence, some has come from the right, particularly the New Right. New Right thinkers and politicians have argued that increases in public spending and taxation have been pushed by an alliance of unions of public sector workers and dependent client groups with a vested interest in higher spending, against the interests of the broad mass of voters and taxpayers. The excessive influence of these groups, it was argued, interfered with the operation of free market forces, to the detriment of economic efficiency and prosperity. The Thatcher government also reacted against a particular form of economic decision making involving peak organisations representing employers and workers, known as tripartism or corporatism (see Box 8.7).

Finally, it may be noted that pressure groups are viewed variously in other political cultures, influenced by their own traditions of thought and practice. Thus while pressure groups are widely seen as integral to the process of democracy in the USA, they tend to be viewed rather differently in a country like France (see Box 8.8).

Summary

- Pressure groups offer more scope for direct involvement in the political process than political parties.
- Pressure groups may operate at various levels. Distinctions are commonly made between interest (or sectional or defensive) groups and cause (or promotional) groups, and between insider and outsider groups.
- Insider groups may enjoy a mutually beneficial relationship with government, although there may be a risk that groups get too close to government and become effectively emasculated. Government departments or agencies may sometimes be effectively captured by their client groups.
- Groups make have a variety of targets, including ministers, civil servants, Parliament and the wider public. In the British political system influence on the executive is generally seen as more effective than influence on the legislature, although some policy areas can be exceptions.
- A recent phenomenon has been the growth of broad, loosely organised 'new social movements', often involving the politics of direct action. Although these have generally been associated with the left, under the Labour government there has been increased use of direct action by groups and movements on the right.

Box 8.8

Comparative politics: pressure groups in the USA and France

The academic study of pressure groups goes back a long way in the USA, at least as far back as the work of Bentley (1908), and they have very substantially been viewed as not only a necessary but a highly beneficial part of the political process, increasing competition and spreading influence. Under Robert Dahl they have become the vital ingredient of a modern theory of democracy, or 'polyarchy' as he preferred to call it. Among the pressure groups that have been reputedly particularly well supported and influential in the American political system are the National Rifleman's Association (NRA), the National Organisation of Women (NOW), and the American Association for Retired Persons (AARP).

In France the political culture seems less compatible with pressure group politics, perhaps reflecting a tradition of thought going back to Rousseau, who saw special interests as articulating a 'partial will' as opposed to the 'general will' of the French people. Thus the Fifth French Republic 'one and indivisible' is less responsive to special interests than the US political system with its elaborate checks and balances. Groups representing labour and business are smaller and weaker than elsewhere in northern Europe. Although some French workers are often involved in disruptive action, such as strikes, obstruction and boycotts, this may reflect their relative lack of influence in government circles. However, farmers remain an important exception to the relative lack of influence of special interests in French politics.

- While some claim that competition between countless pressure groups helps to disperse power (pluralism) and enhance democracy, others claim that group resources and influence are grossly unequal, and the system favours established interests. The New Right by contrast has argued that vested interests can interfere with free market forces, and encourage high government spending and taxation.

Questions for discussion

- How far is the distinction between interest groups and cause groups valid and useful?
- How far do most pressure groups have a choice whether to become an insider or outsider group? Are there any disadvantages to insider status?
- Why do most pressure groups prefer to target the executive rather than the legislature in the British political system? What exceptions are there to this general rule?
- Why do governments bother with consulting pressure groups? How far is government an impartial arbiter of group pressures?
- What purposes might a public demonstration or protest seek to serve? Why might they sometimes be ineffective or even counterproductive?
- What is a 'new social movement' and how might such a movement be distinguished from a pressure group?
- Are there more right-wing protests and demonstrations than in previous times, and if so, why?
- How far is power effectively dispersed and democracy assisted through the activities of pressure groups?

Further reading

Good recent texts on pressure groups in Britain are those by Grant, *Pressure Groups and British Politics* (2000), Byrne, *Social Movements in Britain* (1997) and Coxall, *Pressure Groups in British Politics* (2001). Baggott (1995) remains useful. Jackson (2004) provides a useful brief overview. Jordan and Richardson (1987), Marsh and Rhodes (1992a), and Smith (1995) all illustrate the policy networks approach, and Smith a more recent one. Mazey and Richardson's *Lobbying in the European Community* (1993) provides valuable insights into the developing world of Euro-lobbying, whilst Richardson's *Pressure Groups* (1993) affords a useful comparative perspective. See also Grant (2001).

Some further examples of pressure group activity are provided in later chapters of this book, for instance in Chapter 15 on the European Union, and in the issues and policies chapters in Part 3.

More information on specific groups can be found from their websites: for example the British Medical Association www.bma.org.uk, the Campaign for Nuclear Disarmament www.cnduk.org.uk, the Confederation of British Industry www.cbi.org.uk, Countryside Alliance www.countryside-alliance.org, Friends of the Earth www.foe.co.uk, Greenpeace www.greenpeace.org.uk, the Howard League for Penal Reform www.howardleague.org.uk, the Law Society www.lawsociety.org.uk, the League Against Cruel Sports www.league.uk.com, the National Farmers Union www.nfu.org.uk, Stop the War Coalition www.stopwar.org.uk, the Trades Union Congress www.tuc.org.uk

Political Communication and the Mass Media

Communication is inseparable from politics, and a vital part of any political system in any age. However, the development of the mass media in the course of the 20th century hugely enlarged the scope of political communication. Dictators like Hitler, Mussolini and Stalin, with almost exclusive control of the press, film and radio, as well as the education system, could monopolise public debate, and substantially influence how people thought about politics. Yet the same mass media were equally important for the functioning of a democratic system which assumed effective two-way communication between political leaders and people.

The new media (including cable, satellite and digital television, and particularly the internet) have dramatically expanded further the potential for interactive public debate, enabling all kinds of special interest groups to communicate with each other and with the wider public in a globalised communication system. While a free and diverse media enabling a wide expression of views is a necessary condition for democracy (see Chapter 1), it is debatable how effectively the media in Britain meet that condition. They may be substantially free from direct government censorship, and they may offer a range of views, yet they are inevitably subject to other forms of bias, arising from their relatively restricted ownership and control. Moreover the nature of each medium of communication substantially influences the message that is transmitted, while content is ultimately determined by market considerations in a capitalist economy where profit, circulation and market share are more important considerations than the wider public interest.

This chapter examines the role of the mass media (including the new media) in modern political communication in Britain. It also explores the role of government and political elites in shaping the nature and extent of political debate, and influencing opinion.

Contents

The mass media and society

Political attitudes and behaviour are partly influenced by people's direct experience of life and work in their own immediate environment. Individuals may know something of the effect of inflation or recession, or high interest rates, or taxation, on their own lives and standard of living. Sometimes this direct personal experience may contradict the messages received through the mass media. Those unable to find work will find it difficult to believe there is full employment. Those whose personal experience of the health service is extremely positive may be unconvinced by stories of NHS failures.

Definition

The **mass media** refers to all those forms of communication where large numbers of people are exposed to an identical message. The mass media include the press, film, radio and television and the internet. The mass media provide the ideas and images which help most people to understand the world they live in and their place in that world.

Alternatively, they may conclude that their own experience is untypical. Their schools, their hospitals may appear to work well, but these are fortunate exceptions to the general rule. For inevitably, most of what people think they know about government and politics comes through the mass media. Relatively few people are politically active (see Chapter 4). Government and politicians do not, most of the time, communicate directly with voters, but through the prism of the mass media. The mass media enable government and politicians to reach far more people, but their message is shaped and sometimes transformed in the process. Moreover, those who own and control the media may have their own political agenda.

The new media

The mass media include not only newspapers, magazines, cinema, video, radio and terrestrial television, but also, more recently, multi-channel satellite, cable and digital television, the internet and mass text messaging. This growth implies greater choice for the individual as well as easier access to global mass communication. New media channels allow individual access to a far wider range of information, including political information, and also provide scope for new ways of political involvement. Recent advances in media technology have increased opportunities for more specialised individual political participation. For example, the move from analogue to digital has reshaped television. Through the 'compression' of broadcast signals, many more channels have been, and are still being, made available. An expansion of sub-genre themed interactive channels has replaced what was once a choice from only a few national or regional channels. In other words, 'narrowcasting' allows transmission of political and other content to 'niche or even individualised consumer segments' of the public audience (Cornford and Robins, in Stokes and Reading 1999: 109).

Some political scientists have speculated that driven by this technological change, the world of media conglomerates (see Table 9.1) will be replaced by 'a perfect marketplace of ideas' leading to a massive growth in decentralised, grassroots politics. In this new media world, some have argued, any individual with media access has the same potential political power as the *Sun*. Add to this the mobilising impact of the internet for bringing together individuals who share political values, then it is possible to argue that technological change in the media will result in a new, more democratic political order.

However, while the new media have the capacity to transform political communication and encourage different forms of political behaviour, it has to be said that only a small minority use the new media for political purposes. Most of the population still receive their political messages from more traditional media, including particularly terrestrial television and the national press. The new media have also, more disturbingly, provided a platform for cranks, extremists and terrorists to disseminate propaganda, and a message of hate and violence. There may be an absence of effective censorship on the internet, but there is also an absence of quality control. Garbage can be accessed as readily as wisdom.

The medium is the message?

Although the nature, power and influence of the whole mass media are commonly discussed and analysed together, it is important to appreciate the distinctive features of particular media. A celebrated media guru from the 1960s, Marshall McLuhan, coined the snappy formula 'the medium is the message'. What he meant by this is that each medium of communication has its own distinctive characteristics which influence and perhaps determine the message that is put across. There are some obvious differences between the media. Some are wholly or largely visual, for example posters or silent films, while radio is wholly aural – your mind has to supply the pictures. Some, like film and television, are both visual and aural, although arguably the main message comes through the visual images rather than the soundtrack, and pictures have more impact than the spoken word. Thus it has been argued that radio manages serious political debate better than television. Yet radio abhors silence, even for a few seconds. Questions have to be answered instantly – there is no time for reflection or rephrasing. Ideas and complex arguments may be better expressed in print, where the writer has time to develop and refine his ideas, perhaps through a succession of drafts, and readers can digest matter at their own speed, rereading what they may not have grasped initially.

There are also major differences in the circumstances in which the audience receives communications. Although the term 'mass media' implies a mass audience, that mass is generally made up of countless individuals and small groups. A national newspaper may have a huge circulation but each copy is usually read by just one person at a time. Radio and television normally broadcast into households, reaching perhaps one, two or three people in each household. The Conservative Prime Minister Harold Macmillan commented about his own television broadcasts, 'Someone once said to me "there will be twelve million people watching tonight". I just had the sense to say to myself, no, no, two people, at the most three. It is a conversation, not a speech.' He had correctly grasped that the then novel medium of television was essentially an intimate domestic medium. It was necessary to talk to people in a quiet relaxed fashion, as if he was a guest in the room with them, rather than speak at them as if he was addressing a mass meeting.

Television may be contrasted with films, viewed by large audiences in cinemas, at least before the video age. Hundreds and sometimes thousands in cinemas all over Germany would have viewed together Leni Riefenstahl's film of the Nazi party rally at Nuremberg, *Triumph of the Will*, moved by collective emotion, as if they had been part of the crowds at the rally themselves, carried away by Hitler's oratory. Yet it has been observed 'Hitler's demonic manipulation of the masses would not have been possible today because his performance would have looked ridiculous on television' (Henry Porter, *Guardian*, 12 October 1995).

Each medium works differently. Politicians adept at one form of communication may never master another that requires a different approach. The Labour leader Michael Foot was a powerful platform and parliamentary orator, and an engaging writer, but he never mastered television. By contrast, the more relaxed conversational style of James Callaghan or John Major was well suited to the box. Harold Wilson became a good television performer after his advisers persuaded him to replace his emphatic hand gestures with a calming pipe that became his trademark. Margaret Thatcher's appearance, clothes and strident voice were initially off-putting, until she sought advice, learned to soften her image and became an effective television communicator. Looking and sounding good on television has become a crucial skill that ambitious politicians have to learn.

The British press

Despite the rise of radio and television, and more recently the new media, most adults in Britain still read newspapers (although circulation is now generally declining). While over 1000 newspaper titles are published in Britain, more than half being 'free papers' wholly dependent on advertising for revenue, the press remains dominated by ten national daily papers plus linked Sunday papers. Scotland has its own dailies alongside the London press, but the few regional morning dailies elsewhere in Britain have a relatively small circulation. This is in marked contrast to some other countries, where the regional press is stronger than the national press.

The rack of papers seen outside any newsagents symbolises the British class system. *The Times*, the *Daily Telegraph*, the *Guardian*, the *Independent* and the *Financial Times* are read overwhelmingly by the higher socio-economic groups. These papers used to be known as the 'broadsheets' from the size of paper used, although this term is no longer applicable, as some of them are now printed in tabloid format. There are two papers (the *Daily Mail* and the *Daily Express*) competing in the mid-market area for the middle and lower-middle class readers, whilst the mass-circulation *Sun*, *Mirror* and *Star* have predominantly working-class readers. There is relatively little crossover in readership between these different titles (Sparks, in Stokes and Reading 1999: 47–50), and thus little effective competition.

Treatment of the news varies enormously between papers. The quality papers contain much more of what might be described as 'hard news' in addition to comment and editorial. The mass circulation papers more closely resemble adult comics, and are designed for 'looking at' rather than 'reading', containing 'soft news' and features that have interest but not immediate newsworthiness. Much space is taken up with photographs and large-print headlines. Where the quality press focuses on international events and city news, the mass circulation papers rarely fail to devote considerable space to 'scandal' of one sort or another.

The number of national dailies declined steadily until the 1980s, when the introduction of new technology destroyed the power of the old print unions, and seemed for a time to enable new papers to start and thrive. However, only one of the new titles launched then, the *Independent,* still survives rather precariously (although its circulation has recently improved after a steady decline). The other papers have enjoyed mixed fortunes (see Table 9.1). The *Daily Mirror, Daily Express* and *Daily Telegraph* have all suffered a marked decline. The relatively new *Sun* remains the market leader, followed by the long-established *Daily Mail,* whose circulation has held up better than its main rivals in an era of overall decline. The so-called 'quality press' has gained readers, particularly *The Times* and the *Financial Times*. They and the *Guardian* and *Independent* can survive on a much smaller circulation than the 'tabloids' because their readers come predominantly from the higher social classes and enjoy more income and spending power, which is significant for advertising revenue.

Ownership of the press is concentrated in the hands of a few major groups, often with an influential controlling proprietor, such as Rupert Murdoch, Lord Rothermere and Richard Desmond. Some of these have other extensive media interests. Thus Rupert Murdoch's News International owns papers in many other western countries, and also has major interests in satellite and digital television, radio, cinema and books. The Mirror group has extensive magazine interests, and also controls many regional and local papers. Richard Desmond also has a major stake in magazines (including a number of 'soft porn' titles).

Does the concentration of media ownership matter? Editors have responsibility for the overall style and content of papers, but owners appoint (and can sack) editors, and this alone gives them substantial influence. Some owners, like Rupert Murdoch, have a more hands-on approach, and enjoy the power they wield, which extends to the party political allegiance of their papers (see below).

Table 9.1 National daily newspaper circulation and ownership (2004)

Title	Circulation	Group	Proprietor
Sun	3,378,000	News International	Rupert Murdoch
The Times	609,000	News International	Rupert Murdoch
Daily Mirror	1,817,000	Trinity Mirror	
Daily Express	879,000	Northern and Shell	Richard Desmond
Daily Star	919,000	Northern and Shell	Richard Desmond
Daily Mail	2,320,000	Daily Mail & General Trust	Lord Rothermere
Daily Telegraph	871,000	Press Holdings International	Barclay brothers
Guardian	345,000	The Scott Trust	
Independent	228,000	Independent News & Media	Sir Anthony O'Reilly
Financial Times	395,000	Pearson	

British radio and television

Radio and television began in Britain as state-sponsored services financed by a licence fee paid by listeners and viewers, controlled by an arms-length public corporation, the British Broadcasting Corporation (BBC) with a charter and statutory obligation to show balance in its political reporting. The BBC monopoly was broken in the 1950s with the inauguration of commercial television and radio, with programmes financed by advertising revenue, although the statutory obligation on the Independent Broadcasting Authority (from 1990 replaced by the Independent Television Commission) to balanced political coverage remained. Effectively, as far as television was concerned, the BBC monopoly was replaced by a BBC/ITV duopoly. This was only marginally affected by the slow emergence of new television channels, BBC2, Channel 4 and finally Channel 5, before the arrival of satellite, cable and digital television considerably expanded the range of choice open to viewers. In the context of this explosion of options, the continued survival of the BBC as a public service broadcaster with a global reputation is remarkable. In most other countries public service broadcasting has shrivelled in the face of competition (Curran and Seaton 2003: 231).

The television audience is now more far more segmented than it was. At one time a large part of the population viewed the same national events and news at the same time, often as a family, in front of the single set in the house. This helped to create what was substantially a shared national political culture. Today many households have several television sets, with individual household members viewing programmes geared to their tastes in separate rooms, with video recorders and other playback facilities enabling them to watch programmes at different times. Thus television no longer brings the nation together, as it once did. It is now also much easier to avoid material that individuals may prefer not to see. Thus the mute button on the remote control or the fast speed on the video can silence or eliminate commercials or party political broadcasts, or news programmes. Alternatively, they can be avoided by simply switching channels. Thus it is possible for those who are apathetic or antagonistic towards politics to avoid overt political communication almost completely, because there is always something else to watch, even for those who rarely consider the drastic alternative of switching the set off.

The British media, political bias and democracy

A free and diverse media expressing a range of political views is widely seen as a necessary condition for democracy (see Chapter 1). The media assist the working of a democratic system through facilitating free speech and unrestricted public debate. In Britain a variety of political opinions are aired in the media, and many of them are hostile to the government of the day. However, it is often argued that there is a political bias in the media which inevitably influences public opinion.

Much of the debate over media bias is around the issue of overt or covert party-political bias. Here there is a clear difference between the press and the electronic media. British national newspapers are often vehemently partisan in their coverage of politics. This partisanship is exhibited not just in editorials and comment columns, but in news coverage, and even or especially in the visual portrayal of politicians in photographs or cartoons. Bias is also blatant in the treatment of political issues, such as the European Union or the Iraq War. Anyone who regularly reads the *Daily Telegraph*, the *Daily Mail*, the *Mirror* or the *Guardian* can have little doubt about their political allegiance and party preference. However, both commercial radio and television as well as the BBC are bound by charter and by law to show balance between parties and impartiality in reporting and treating the news. This is interpreted to mean balance between the major parties and opinions within the political mainstream. The only programmes exempted from this requirement to political impartiality are the party political broadcasts and party election broadcasts (see Box 9.1).

Despite the obligations to political balance, smaller parties and minority interests often feel broadcasters disregard their views. Even the major parties sometimes allege party bias in individual broadcasters or programmes. The left has long been critical of television's coverage of political news, particularly industrial disputes, where they detect an anti-union bias. By contrast, some in the Conservative Party have portrayed the BBC as the 'Bolshevik Broadcasting Corporation', a

Box 9.1

Comparative politics: political advertising in Britain and the United States

A marked feature of US election campaigns is the volume of political advertising on US television. Candidates, parties and special interests can buy television time to promote themselves, just like the advertising of commercial goods and services. Thirty-second or one-minute political commercials are a familiar feature of the American political scene. Candidates who run out of cash to finance advertising campaigns lose visibility. Well-funded groups like the National Rifle Association, or those with a vested interest in private medicine, are able to purchase substantial airtime to put across their message in debates over gun control or health care. However, not all groups have the financial resources to enable them to put across their case.

In Britain, parties, candidates for elections and political groups are not allowed to buy advertising time on radio and television. British political parties are, however, allotted a number of party political broadcasts (and, during an election campaign, party election broadcasts), on a formula that takes into account the seats they contest and the votes they secure at elections. (Thus the British National Party qualified for a party election broadcast during the 2005 election campaign.) The broadcasting time and basic studio facilities are free, although parties may purchase the services of film-makers, advertising agencies or public relations consultants to secure more professional promotion of their cause. A few party election broadcasts have made sufficient impact to become important news stories, with a measurable immediate effect on party support. Normally they have little impact, and are generally treated by viewers as a 'kettle opportunity' – to take a break from viewing to make coffee or tea. Some question their continuing value. They do however continue to provide an opportunity for relatively poorly financed parties (like the Liberal Democrats) to put their case to the public, helping to provide a more level playing field between competing parties.

hotbed of radicalism, hostile to mainstream conservative values. This bipartisan criticism might suggest that the BBC is indeed fulfilling its statutory obligation to balance, although clearly not everyone agrees.

In 2003 a major and bitter conflict between the Labour government's director of communications, Alastair Campbell and the BBC arose over its coverage of the government's case for war with Iraq. This conflict resulted in the resignation of Gavyn Davies, the BBC's chairman, and Greg Dyke, its director general, after the publication of the Hutton Report (see Box 9.2).

The press has no obligation to impartiality, and indeed most British national newspapers make no secret of their own political sympathies and party preferences, freely selecting and interpreting the news in accordance with their own assumptions and allegiances (see Table 9.2). The political bias of newspapers often reflects the established preferences of its readers. Most *Daily Telegraph* readers are Conservative, while *Guardian* readers are predominantly Labour. Thus editorial policy arguably reflects market considerations. Any attempt to turn the *Daily Telegraph* into a staunch Labour paper would spell disaster for its circulation.

Yet most people do not buy papers for their politics, and may notice subliminally, if at all, shifts in their political stance. Thus although the *Sun* arose from the ashes of the old *Daily Herald*, and was a Labour paper when Rupert Murdoch acquired it in 1974, he turned it into a highly partisan supporter of Margaret Thatcher's Conservatives, an allegiance initially maintained when Major succeeded Thatcher. By 1997 however, Murdoch had switched to support Blair and New Labour, and the *Sun* endorsed Labour again in 2001, and once more in 2005. The shift in allegiance of the *Sun*, still the market leader, largely explains how a substantially pro-Conservative press in 1992 became pro-Labour from 1997 onwards. The story exemplifies the power of a single newspaper proprietor. However, it can be argued that the shifts in the *Sun*'s party allegiances reflected to a degree changes in wider public opinion and thus market considerations. Plausibly also, Murdoch wanted to retain influence with what seemed certain to be a future Labour government.

Box 9.2

Alastair Campbell, the BBC and the Hutton Report

In the events leading up to the invasion of Iraq, Alastair Campbell, the government's director of communication and strategy, had a key role in the presentation of the government's case for war. A political storm broke after a BBC journalist, Andrew Gilligan, alleged on the *Today* programme on 29 May 2003 that the government had embellished or 'sexed up' the case for war based on intelligence reports. Gilligan alleged specifically that the claim that Saddam Hussein could launch chemical and biological weapons within 45 minutes was included although the government 'probably knew' it was wrong.

Campbell, appearing before the Commons Foreign Affairs Committee, denounced Gilligan, declaring 'If that is BBC journalism, then you know, God help them'. In a subsequent interview on Channel 4 he demanded that the BBC 'should accept for once that they got it wrong'. Instead the BBC rejected a suggested compromise solution to the row, and the chairman, Gavyn Davies and director general, Greg Dyke, stood by their reporter. The row became a major crisis after the source of Gilligan's allegation, David Kelly, a scientific adviser to the Ministry of Defence and a former weapons inspector, committed suicide, shortly after giving evidence to the Commons Foreign Affairs Committee. An official Inquiry was set up under Lord Hutton to investigate the circumstances surrounding Kelly's death. A lengthy examination of papers, emails and cross-examination of witnesses ensued. The stakes were high; a critical report could bring down Blair.

Hutton's report, when it eventually appeared at the end of January 2004, exonerated the government, and criticised the BBC. Blair was relieved, but cautiously refrained from demanding resignations. Campbell was not so inhibited. 'What the report shows very clearly is this: the Prime Minister told the truth, the government told the truth, I told the truth. The BBC, from the Chairman and Director General down, did not.' In the subsequent turmoil, Davies resigned, followed shortly by Greg Dyke, a consequence that the government had not initially expected or desired. Ironically, the earlier appointment of both men had been criticised by the Conservative Party because of their known Labour connections.

Davies and Dyke thought they were defending the political independence of the BBC, although they should perhaps have recognised that Gilligan's report went rather beyond the evidence from his source. An allegation that the government had deliberately and knowingly lied could be made by a newspaper journalist, but not by a BBC correspondent, without very clear evidence. Events proved the 45-minute claim was wrong, although the government continued to argue it was based on available intelligence. Some feared that the outcome would inhibit BBC political reporting in the future.

So far bias has been explored almost exclusively in terms of party bias. Yet it has often been alleged that other forms of political bias are routinely shown by the British media. Feminists have long complained that the media portray women in a demeaning or degrading way, reinforcing and perpetuating their inferior status in society, sometimes even stimulating, through pornography, the degrading or violent treatment of women. Ethnic minority groups used to complain that they were invisible in the media, or shown in subordinate, stereotypical roles, although this is less evident than before. Gays were shown, if at all, as comic figures. 'BBC English' reflected southern middle-class accents, in a way that appeared to marginalise other parts of Britain and other social backgrounds. Some of this has changed, although there are still grounds for complaint.

More generally, the media, it has been argued, inevitably reflect dominant interests in society and the economy, the views of the establishment, of business rather than the workers, of 'the haves' rather than 'the have nots' and of private enterprise and free market values in a capitalist society. This is perhaps more particularly the case for newspapers and commercial television, substantially dependent on advertising revenue, and both directly and indirectly celebrating commercial values. Some have claimed that a globalised media reflect the interests of global capitalism.

The British media are far from neutral, since they remain substantially (despite globalisation) the product of Britain's culture, a culture which is biased like any other culture, with assumptions and

Table 9.2 Changing party support of national daily newspapers

Newspaper	1992	1997	2001	2005
Mirror	Labour	Labour	Labour	Labour
Express	Conservative	Conservative	Labour	Conservative
Sun	Conservative	Labour	Labour	Labour
Daily Mail	Conservative	Conservative	Conservative	Not Labour
Daily Star	Pro-Conservative	Labour	Labour	No declared preference
Daily Telegraph	Conservative	Conservative	Conservative	Conservative
Guardian	Labour/Lib Dem	Labour	Labour	Labour
The Times	Conservative	'Euro-sceptics'	Labour	Labour
Independent	None	Labour	Not Conservative	More Liberal Democrat
Financial Times	No endorsement	Labour	Labour	Labour

Sources: derived from Butler and Kavanagh (1992, 1997, 2001, 2005).

prejudices of its own. News does not just happen, rather it is made. News items are selected and placed in order, in an implicit hierarchy of importance. Selection and ordering inevitably reflects bias of some kind. This may be a bias in favour of home rather than foreign news, of stories with a 'human interest', and, for television, a bias in favour of visually interesting material. Some of this bias may substantially reflect what it is assumed readers, listeners and viewers want. Thus the sex life of a minor British celebrity, particularly if accompanied with revealing pictures, may command more media space and time than a humanitarian disaster in a remote continent, and this both reflects and in turn influences people's values.

The power and influence of the media

The Conservative leader Stanley Baldwin once famously observed that newspaper proprietors aimed at 'power without responsibility, the prerogative of the harlot throughout the ages' (a phrase apparently suggested by his cousin, the writer Rudyard Kipling). Few would deny that the press and the media generally do have political power and influence, although there is considerable debate about its nature and extent (see Box 9.3).

How far does media bias translate into real media power and influence? On one interpretation, perhaps not as much as might be imagined. It has been persuasively argued that people do not just passively accept the political communication imparted by the media, but 'filter out' messages that do not match their own preconceived ideas, and only accept communications that reinforce those ideas. They do this through a process of selective exposure, selective perception and selective retention. Thus people tend to read newspapers or watch programmes that support their own political viewpoints. They reinterpret the hostile material they do encounter to fit in with their own preconceptions. Moreover, they remember selectively, only recalling evidence and arguments that fit in with their own ideas and forgetting those that do not (Trenaman and McQuail 1961, Blumler and McQuail 1967, Denver 2003: 132–4).

Yet as Denver (2003) points out, the key research supporting the filter model was carried out a long time ago, and largely focused on television, and more specifically on party election broadcasts and their influence on voting. The bias in party election broadcasts is both transparent and generally unsubtle, and perhaps consequently less influential. Outside the special case of party broadcasts, television coverage is constrained by obligations to balance, particularly in election

Box 9.3

The role and power of the media

Pluralist model: this suggests that Britain has a free press, with other media not controlled by the government. The media presents a wide diversity of views, aiding public debate and the democratic process, enabling people to make up their own minds on important political issues. The media also has an important 'watchdog' role on behalf of the people, over government and powerful interests in society, and promotes more effective public accountability.

Dominant values model: this model suggests that the media portray news and events in such a way as to support the dominant values of political elites. As Marx claimed, 'The ruling ideas in every age are the ideas of the ruling class.' Ownership and control of the media is heavily concentrated, reflecting the concentration of wealth, income and power in society. The media reflect only a relatively narrow range of views, and minority perspectives are given little space or airtime. The media also 'scapegoats' minority social groups perceived as 'deviant' from prevailing norms – single mothers, social security scroungers, striking workers, asylum seekers.

Market model: this suggests that the media are driven largely by market or commercial considerations. Owners, editors and producers seek to maximise profits by increasing circulation or audience share. Thus the media deliver what the public wants. The reduction of serious political content and overseas news in the press and mainstream news programmes reflects public taste and preference.

campaigns, and thus largely follows the parties' own agendas, rather than the independent judgement of television programme producers and reporters. However, television may still influence political choice in some respects. Because television is primarily a visual medium, voters may be influenced, consciously or unconsciously, by the physical appearance, clothes and body language of candidates and leaders. In a television era politicians need to 'look good on the box'. Increasingly this is a factor that influences election campaigning and even the choice of party leader.

Although most people trust television more than newspapers as a reliable source of news, the press may still be more politically influential, in part because it is uninhibited by any obligation to balance. Moreover, it is not just editorials and comment columns that show bias, but the way in which news is selected and interpreted. Even those who turn straight to the sport or 'page 3' can hardly help registering, if only subconsciously, headlines that carry a strong political message. While people may believe they are uninfluenced by papers showing a manifest bias, they also think they are not influenced by commercial advertisements. If this was the case, companies could save money by scrapping their extensive advertising budgets. They advertise because their market research indicates it is effective, if sometimes subliminally. It is difficult to believe that the drip drip drip of political propaganda has no effect on readers over a period of years, rather than the three or four weeks of an official election

Box 9.4

Case study of press influence on voting: the 1992 General Election

One election outcome that might have been influenced by the press was in 1992, when opinion polls were predicting victory for Labour and its leader, Neil Kinnock. The *Sun* campaigned ruthlessly against Labour and particularly Kinnock himself. On the eve of the election the *Sun* published a nine-page special, fronted with the banner headline 'Nightmare on Kinnock Street', graphically predicting the horrors to come if Labour won. On polling day itself the *Sun* announced to its readers that if Kinnock won, 'We'll meet you at the airport'. After Major won, and Kinnock resigned the Labour leadership, some analysts found evidence that the Tory tabloids, and particularly the *Sun*, influenced a late and decisive swing to the Conservatives, prompting Murdoch's paper to boast 'It was the *Sun* wot won it'. However, even 1992 is not a clear-cut example of press influence. It is far more difficult to make a case for decisive press influence at other recent elections when the outcome has generally been much more decisive and predictable. The most that the *Sun*'s switch to Labour in 1997 could have achieved was a larger Labour win, but as that record majority was in line with earlier poll predictions, even that would be difficult to prove.

In Focus 9.1

Tabloid front pages, polling day, 5 May 2005

The British popular press is sharply partisan, as these polling day front pages show. The *Sun,* once a fervent supporter of the Conservatives, urged its readers to get behind 'the Reds' with their two strikers, Blair and Brown (portrayed in a more harmonious partnership than has always been evident). The *Daily Mirror,* a consistent Labour paper, invoked the 'fear factor', providing a hostile image of Conservative leader Michael Howard as Dracula. The *Express,* a traditionally Conservative paper that flirted with Labour in 2001, used a long-nosed Pinocchio picture of Blair, to imply he had forfeited the trust of voters. Significantly, the consistently pro-Conservative *Daily Mail,* perhaps despairing of a Howard victory, chose another first lead, with only a passing reference to the election.

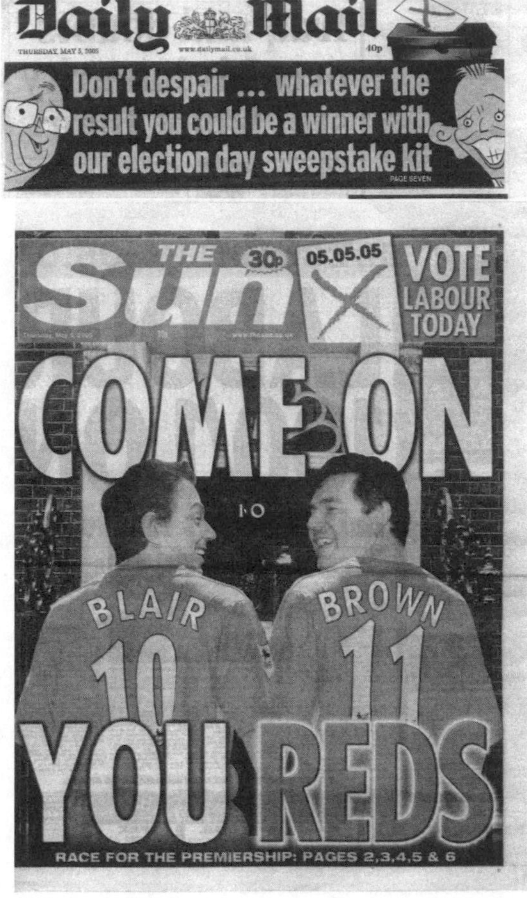

Daily Mail

THURSDAY, MAY 5, 2005 www.dailymail.co.uk 40p

Don't despair ... whatever the result you could be a winner with our election day sweepstake kit

PAGE SEVEN

THE Sun 30p 05.05.05 VOTE LABOUR TODAY

COME ON YOU REDS

BLAIR 10 BROWN 11

RACE FOR THE PREMIERSHIP: PAGES 2,3,4,5 & 6

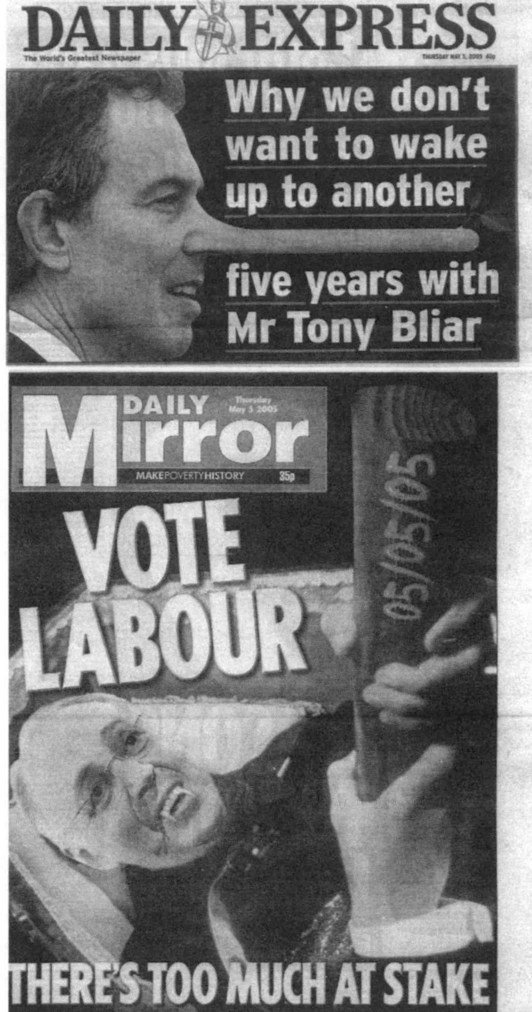

DAILY EXPRESS

The World's Greatest Newspaper

Why we don't want to wake up to another five years with Mr Tony Bliar

DAILY Mirror Thursday May 5 2005

MAKEPOVERTYHISTORY 35p

VOTE LABOUR

05/05/05

THERE'S TOO MUCH AT STAKE

campaign. As Denver (2003: 143) points out, this influence is likely to be stronger still now that fewer people identify strongly with particular parties. He concludes that 'the conditions are ripe' for increased media influence on voters' opinions 'with the development of a more free-floating and easily mobilised electorate'.

It is however plausible that the press helps to determine the political agenda, and influences public opinion on specific issues, such as the European Union, crime and asylum seekers. The capacity of television to shape the political agenda is limited by the obligation to balance, particularly during election campaigns. Thus television news coverage and most current affair programmes tend to follow the parties' own agenda or the press agenda. If the press has managed to raise an issue that the parties have ignored, then it becomes 'news' and television can report it. Otherwise, if television producers choose to raise issues that parties have deliberately avoided, they risk accusations of bias. On particular issues the press can distort, publish scare stories and plain untruths. Examples include allegations that 'loony left' councils had banned black bin-liners as racist, that the European Union was going to ban curved bananas, and that the triple measles, mumps and rubella vaccine caused autism. Some such stories are harmless nonsense; others, like the vaccine scare, can cause real damage. The relentless hostility of most of the press towards the European Union goes some way towards explaining the prevailing Euro-scepticism in Britain.

■ The 'dumbing down' of politics?

Some suggest that the media, and particularly the press, influence more general attitudes towards politics and government in Britain. Thus the media have been blamed both for 'dumbing down' political coverage, and encouraging a cynical negative attitude to parties, politicians and politics generally, with damaging consequences for political participation and the democratic process (Lloyd 2004).

There is today more political information in the public domain than ever before, as a consequence of both the proliferation of new media channels, and the continuing pressures for more open government. Yet while there is far more information out there for those who want to access it, paradoxically the majority of the public are less exposed to politics than they were, and unsurprisingly feel less well informed (see Chapter 4). For all the growth of new media channels, and new sources of information, most people still learn about politics from newspapers and mainstream television news programmes. However, serious political coverage by the popular press has declined markedly in recent decades, to be replaced by gossip, scandal and features. The private life of politicians can attract a vicious media feeding frenzy, while their ideas and policies are relatively neglected, unless they upset the prejudices of journalists or readers. Even the so-called quality press devotes far less space to some aspects of politics than previously, most notably parliamentary business. Full coverage of parliamentary proceedings, including summaries of speeches, has been replaced by short jokey reviews of (most commonly) question time, particularly prime minister's questions.

The main television news programmes have also moved down-market, devoting more time to celebrities, sport and idiosyncratic items, often featuring furry animals. Most members of the public have scarcely ever heard a full-length political speech involving a developed argument, only very short 'soundbites' – memorable sentences or phrases plucked out of context (Franklin 2004). Some consider the mass media have steadily reduced the intellectual demands made on readers, listeners and viewers. Americans call this process 'dumbing down'. Serious political coverage is reduced to increase market share. Within ITV, for example, 'there are undoubtedly pressures to reduce and popularise news output' (Crisell, in Stokes and Reading 1999: 69). The BBC is affected by similar pressures, despite its role as a non-commercial 'public service' broadcaster, partly because if its market share declines significantly it becomes politically more difficult to justify finance through the licence fee. Of course, it can be argued that far more news is now available on a 24-hour basis on minority channels for those who want it. Yet the channels that most people watch have cut their serious news content, and it is much easier for the politically apathetic to avoid informing themselves about political crises or disasters.

Others argue that the growth of cynical hostile interrogation of politicians and negative reporting

Definition

Soundbites are short snappy memorable phrases, frequently extracted from the broader context of a speech or document. Thus mainstream television rarely broadcasts whole speeches or even substantial extracts from speeches but brief soundbites. Research suggests that soundbites are becoming shorter.

has encouraged a general distrust of the political process and democracy (Lilleker, Negrine and Stanyer 2003; Lloyd 2004). If interviewers seem to assume that all politicians are crooks or liars, it is hardly surprising that viewers and listeners come to share the assumption. Politicians have hardly helped to improve their own image by the strategy they commonly adopt when confronted by sneering cross-examinations by 'rottweiler' interviewers, simply repeating their own prepared 'soundbites', almost regardless of the questions posed. Such confrontations may sometimes make good television but rarely contribute much to the sum total of public political knowledge.

Politicians and the media – the uses and abuses of 'image' and 'spin'

So far the emphasis in this chapter has been on the power and influence of the media on government and the political process. Yet government and political leaders generally are far from being helpless victims of the mass media. As they inevitably make news by their pronouncements and decisions, they can seek to control the news, by the timing and manner of the release of information. They can seek to manage the media, to use whatever channels of communication are available to put their message across.

They and their advisers can also manage the presentation of their own image. Graham Wallas (1920: 31), a pioneer social scientist, grasped in 1906 the value of photographs in projecting a favourable image of candidates for political office. 'Best of all is a photograph which brings his ordinary existence sharply forward by representing him in his garden smoking a pipe or reading a newspaper.' The casual, seemingly spontaneous appearance would in reality be carefully posed, the background, clothes, and 'props' deliberately chosen, the 'body language' conveyed by expression and posture considered. Later, the posed photograph was replaced by the 'photo-opportunity', with the context providing an appropriate political message: Margaret Thatcher cuddling a day-old calf, John Major visiting a DIY store, Tony Blair beginning an election campaign at a school, all professionally stage-managed to create an impression of informal spontaneity. More recently politicians and their advisers have learned how to project their own image more effectively through websites. The technology may change, and some of the skills, but the essential art of image projection is as old as politics.

Similarly, skilful leaders and politicians have always grasped the importance of putting a favourable gloss on events, of getting their version of the story accepted. This is essentially what 'spin' is about. 'Spin doctors' are those skilled in presentation and interpretation. The use of the term in British politics is relatively new, but the activity is very old. Thus although 'spin' has become particularly associated with New Labour, it was effectively practised in British politics long before. Indeed, one of the old Labour Party's problems was that it was not as good at political communication as its opponents. While the Conservatives hired the best advertising agencies available to put their message across, Labour was distrustful of advertisers and 'selling politics like cornflakes'. Moreover, Labour had to contend with a generally hostile press, particularly in the 1980s and early 1990s. Labour's 'spin machine' grew from the bitter experiences of opposition. The party learned the importance of good political communication, of party unity and 'staying on message' – agreeing the story and sticking to it. It also appreciated the need for better relations with the media, particularly the press. While many in the party loathed Rupert Murdoch and the *Sun* newspaper, Blair and his advisers actively sought to win and retain Murdoch's support, in the process converting a substantially anti-Labour press into a generally supportive press.

All Labour's 'spin doctors' sought to do was to present the party and its leaders in a positive light, which is only what other parties, and indeed business companies and countless other organisations, have tried to achieve, through good communication and public relations. Moreover radio and television commentators and newspaper journalists are constantly putting their own interpretation, or 'spin', on news stories. Confronted with a complex mosaic of facts and unsubstantiated rumour, journalists try to reveal the 'real story'. Often the first in the field determines what the story is, unless a rival can provide a convincing new interpretation. Far from being some kind of New Labour invention, 'spin' may be seen as a universal activity.

The excesses of New Labour 'spin' essentially resulted from over-reaction to the failures of the past. A party previously rendered unelectable by internal divisions and a disastrous public image became a party of 'control freaks' with no place for those who appeared 'off message'. The party became associated with 'spin' rather than 'substance'. Labour's own communication experts, brought into government as high-profile special advisers, were critical of the more traditional approach to communication and media relations of permanent civil servants, leading to clashes within departments. Ultimately New Labour 'spin' became counter-productive. The most successful and effective 'spinning' is that which is so unobtrusive as not to be noticed; people are led to believe that they are given the plain unvarnished and incontrovertible truth, rather than a selective and partisan interpretation of events. The problem with Labour's spin doctors was that they became too high profile. Rather than anonymously and successfully purveying good stories, they themselves became the story, and in the process damaged the product they were hired to promote (see Box 9.5), as Campbell for one seemed to appreciate.

Political communication is important in any political system, but particularly crucial in those states claiming to be democratic. Democracy requires more than effective government communication, for it implies a two-way interactive communication between government and people. A government that does not listen is unlikely to remain long in power. However, western democracy also assumes a continuous

Box 9.5

'Becoming the story': New Labour's 'spin doctors'

Peter Mandelson has been credited with successfully rebranding the Labour Party as New Labour, and making it electable. A very successful backroom operator, he had political ambitions of his own, becoming Labour candidate for Hartlepool, which he won in 1992. He played a key role in the emergence of Blair as leader in 1994, and in the revision of Clause 4 of Labour's constitution. Curiously, he was much less effective in spinning himself than his party, and was twice obliged to resign Cabinet posts in controversial circumstances in 1998 and 2001. He was subsequently nominated by Blair to become a member of the European Commission.

Alastair Campbell became a key adviser to Blair in opposition, later the prime minister's press secretary and after 2001 his director of communications and strategy, before resigning in 2003 shortly after the David Kelly affair and the Hutton Report (see also Box 9.2). An outspoken, belligerent, but generally effective champion of Labour and its prime minister, he antagonised many journalists by his bullying, threatening manner. A former journalist himself, he reportedly wore a baseball hat emblazoned with the words 'MEDIA SCUM' (Kampfner 2004: 343). He continued to advise Blair more informally.

Charlie Whelan was Gordon Brown's extremely partisan and rather truculent spin doctor, and as such antagonistic to Blair, to Campbell, and particularly to Mandelson. Whelan was instrumental in bringing to light Mandelson's secret home loan from a fellow minister, which led to his first resignation in 1998. Soon afterwards, Brown was persuaded that the provocative Whelan had to go. 'He had become far too notorious for his own or his master's good' (Rawnsley 2001: 233).

Jo Moore served as Stephen Byers's spin doctor, and was responsible for an infamous email sent on the occasion of the attack on the Twin Towers on 9/11. This, she suggested, was a good day to publish and 'bury' departmental bad news. Releasing bad news under cover of some bigger story is a familiar technique, but this was an appallingly insensitive example. Byers unwisely stood by his adviser (although eventually she had to go). Her misjudgement contributed to events leading to his own resignation in 2002.

competitive struggle for power and influence by individuals, interests and parties, in which those who manage to put across the most persuasive stories are more likely to prevail. The stakes can be high, helping to determine 'who gets what, when, how' in Lasswell's terse definition of politics (see Chapter 1). Effective communication of the message of a politician, party or group may make the difference between winning and losing. In a complex world there are inevitably many sides to difficult questions, not a single version of the truth. Effective communication generally requires selection, simplification and graphic illustration, which can easily to lead to accusations of manipulation and 'spin'. While the media can perform a watchdog role, they are also participants, with their own interests to defend and their own conflicting but strongly held interpretations of the public interest to advance. In such circumstances it is difficult for the public to know who to believe. Routine accusations of deliberate deception on the part of government or the media undermine public trust, are corrosive of democracy, and increase alienation from the whole political process (Lloyd 2004).

Summary

- Most of what people think they know about politics and government does not come from direct personal experience. Political communication between government and people is largely through the mass media.
- Each media channel has its own particular characteristics (and limitations) strongly influencing the messages it transmits. Thus television is primarily a visual medium; the pictures rather than sound commentary convey the main message.
- The British press is dominated by ten national dailies (and associated Sunday papers) competing in segmented markets. Ownership of the press is substantially concentrated, and some proprietors have other extensive media interests.
- British radio and television have charter and statutory obligations to political balance, unlike the highly partisan national press.
- The extent of media power and influence is

Box 9.6

The Phillis Report on government communication, 2004

The understandable criticism of aspects of New Labour's news management, particularly after the Jo Moore email (see Box 9.5), led to the appointment of an independent review of government communication under the chairmanship of Bob Phillis. While this review was in process a bigger storm broke over the government's use of intelligence information to justify the war in Iraq (see Box 9.2). The Phillis Report, when finally published in January 2004, described the diminishing public trust in both politicians and the media (particularly the press) with damaging consequences for public engagement in politics and the democratic process. Yet the report, while critical of government 'spin', also endorsed some of Labour's dissatisfaction with the traditional approach to communication in the civil service and government generally. There was a 'narrow view of communication ... often limited to media handling'. The Government Information and Communication Service did not cover all those in communication, lacked resources and status, and was defective in recruitment and training. There was poor coordination of communication across departments, and there was still a pervasive culture of secrecy that needed to be replaced by a culture of openness, particularly in view of the Freedom of Information Act (2000, implemented 2005). The report acknowledged that special advisers performed a useful role and were here to stay, but there was an urgent need for new guidelines to clarify their relationship with the permanent civil service. Among other specific recommendations were clearer rules on the release of statistical information and more direct government communication with the public. Most of these recommendations were accepted. One development has been to rely less on government spokespersons, and the release of unattributed briefings on lobby terms, more on televised briefings by the prime minister and other ministers. The government's communication staff now play a less obtrusive role. They are no longer household names.

contentious. Thus it has been argued that media influence on voting is very limited, although not everyone agrees. Others suggest that there is a pervasive media bias in favour of the establishment or free market capitalism.

- The media have been accused of reducing and 'dumbing down' political coverage, and more recently encouraging alienation and apathy.
- The handling of party and government communication and management of the media has also come under increasing criticism. Blair's Labour government has become associated with 'spin', putting a favourable interpretation on events and developments.
- Yet effective political communication remains of critical importance particularly in a political system that claims to be democratic.

Questions for discussion

- How far do different media require different political communication skills? In what ways might television trivialise political debate?
- How far does the concentration of ownership of the press and media generally pose problems for democracy?
- How far and in what ways are the British press and British television biased?
- How much real political power and influence do the media have?
- What evidence is there that the British press, or the media generally, have significantly influenced political views and party choice?
- To what extent has media coverage of British politics been 'dumbed down'?
- How far and what ways might the new media encourage more political participation and interactive public debate? Does the new media pose any problems for politics?
- What is spin and how new is it? How far has New Labour spin been effective?

Further reading

There are two useful very short articles on political communication in Britain – Lilleker *et al.* (2003) and Jackson (2004), both in *Politics Review.* Duncan Watts, *Political Communication Today* (1997) and Brian McNair, *An Introduction to Political Communication* (2003) treat with much more detail the subject matter of this chapter. The sixth edition of Curran and Seaton, *Power Without Responsibility: The press, broadcasting and new media in Britain* (2003) remains one of the best guides to the British media. This can be supplemented by Stokes and Reading (eds), *The Media in Britain: Current debates and developments* (1999).

On media influence on British politics, and specifically voting, see the discussion in chapter 6 of Denver (2003). The influence of the media on recent General Elections is discussed in chapters in the Nuffield studies edited by David Butler and Denis Kavanagh. On the growing literature on government communication and news management see Franklin (1994, 2004), N. Jones (1996, 1999) and the extracts from Gaber, Franklin and Jones in *The New Labour Reader* edited by Chadwick and Hefferman (2003). Lloyd (2004) is critical of the influence of media political reporting on the style and content of British politics. The Phillis Report (2004) is published by the Cabinet Office and can also be accessed on www.gcreview.gov.uk

Government and Governance

The Changing British System of Government

There is no official guide to the British system of government. Unusually in the modern world, Britain lacks a written constitution. Indeed British government is unusual in many other respects, a point reinforced by comparisons with other countries. Yet if British government is unusual, it has also long appeared a model of stability in a changing world. Britain has not thus experienced the sharp regime changes that have characterised, for example, French government and politics for over 200 years. Instead the British system of government has evolved gradually over the centuries. Reforms have been grafted onto traditional institutions. The new is painlessly absorbed into the old and familiar. This system of government was once widely revered at home, and admired and sometimes emulated abroad.

More recently the British system of government has seemed to some rather less admirable. Criticisms of core institutions and even fundamental constitutional principles fuelled a strong movement for constitutional reform for a decade before the election of a government pledged to radical changes in 1997. Many of these changes have since been implemented and appear virtually irreversible, while others remain unaccomplished or incomplete. Already, however, textbooks on British government (including this one) have required extensive rewriting, and will almost certainly need further radical revision. Yet the general public has insufficiently appreciated the extent of change. This is partly because constitutional reform does not seem to excite the public, or win elections. However it also partly reflects the Labour government's rather low-key and fragmented approach to its own reform programme. A series of radical initiatives have been pursued almost in isolation from each other and, critics suggest, uninformed by any overall vision. New institutions have been grafted onto the existing system of government. Old constitutional principles survive intact, at least according to the official interpretation. Thus the full significance of the reforms and their potential implications for the British system of government have not been generally grasped. The end result of the process remains unclear. It may in future be celebrated as a new constitutional settlement for Britain. Alternatively it could lead to the disintegration of the British state and the end of British government and politics.

This chapter examines Britain's unwritten constitution, its sources, and the main principles and features that have been attributed to it. It explores the attitudes of political parties to the constitution, and the criticisms that have fuelled demands for constitutional reform. It proceeds to examine and assess Labour's constitutional reform programme, and the implications for traditional constitutional principles. Finally, the case for a written constitution is

Contents

considered. More detailed analysis of particular aspects of the British system of government will be the subject of later chapters.

The constitution

A constitution is more than just a simple description of the government of the country. It provides clear limits on the powers of state institutions and the rights and responsibilities of citizens, and generally involves underlying assumptions and principles. Normally today for most states these are contained in a single written document. Britain remains a conspicuous exception. Yet if Britain lacks a single authoritative document on its system of government, this does not mean that Britain lacks a constitution, in the sense of well-established rules for the conduct of government and underlying constitutional principles. Some of these rules *are* written down, as part of the law of the land, contained in Acts of Parliament, or decisions on cases decided in the courts. Thus strictly speaking, the British constitution is uncodified (in the sense that it has not been collected into a single document), rather than unwritten. Some key aspects of the British system of government however are unwritten, as they are not contained within any formal written document, but rest on conventions, agreed usages which are so widely accepted they are virtually undisputed. However,

> **Definition**
>
> A state **constitution** is simply a set of rules and conventions that lays down the powers and functions of state institutions and their relationship with each other.

Box 10.1

The major sources of the British constitution

- **Statute law** – law passed by Parliament, some of which is of a constitutional nature – e.g. Acts determining the composition of the electorate and the conduct of elections, and Acts laying down the powers and composition of the House of Lords.
- **Common law** – theoretically the immemorial law of the people, in practice the law as determined by decisions of courts. The remaining 'prerogative powers' of the crown (now exercised by the government of the day) derive from common law.
- **Conventions** – unwritten rules of constitutional behaviour which are widely accepted and observed, largely because of the political difficulties which would follow if they were not. Most of the powers relating to the prime minister depend on convention. Conventions may evolve over time, and may be difficult to date precisely (e.g. the convention that a prime minister must sit in the House of Commons).
- **The law and custom of Parliament** – many of the rules relating to the functions, procedures, privileges and immunities of each house are contained in resolutions of both houses, conventions and informal understandings. These have been definitively listed and described in Erskine May's *Treatise on the Law, Privileges, Proceedings and Usages of Parliament.*
- **Works of authority** – in the absence of other authoritative written sources, works by eminent experts on the British constitutions are consulted – e.g. Walter Bagehot, *The English Constitution* (1867), A. V. Dicey, *The Law of the Constitution* (1885), and Sir Ivor Jennings, *The Law and the Constitution* (1966).
- **EU law.** Since the UK joined what was then the European Community in 1973, EC/EU law has been binding on the UK and applied by British courts. This has implications for the constitutional principle of parliamentary sovereignty. Additionally, some specific EU rules are of a constitutional nature.
- **The European Convention on Human Rights.** This was (in effect) incorporated into UK law by the 1998 Human Rights Act, which came into force in 2000

if these conventions are 'unwritten', in the sense that they have not been authoritatively recorded in some law or charter, they have been extensively recorded and written about by constitutional lawyers and political scientists. (For the major sources of the British constitution see Box 10.1.)

Many argue, on the principle 'If it ain't broke, don't fix it', that Britain does not need a written constitution as its system of government works well enough without one. Indeed, written constitutions are generally imperfect guides to political reality – to the actual as compared with the supposed distribution of power within a state. For example, many constitutions either omit or scarcely mention the roles in the political process of such institutions as parties, pressure groups and public bureaucracies. Much important political behaviour occurs outside the formal legal framework. Many bald statements in constitutions require supplementing by a body of custom and practice. Some provisions may be positively misleading or rendered ineffective (such as the electoral college to choose the US President). Moreover some constitutions have proved hardly worth the paper they were written on, torn up or simply ignored by usurpers and dictators.

Yet while written constitutions are incomplete as guides to political practice, they do matter for a number of reasons. They commonly include the most important procedural rules of a political system. They frequently also contain statements of key political principles and commitments to basic rights and freedoms. Alongside moral codes and cultural norms, they provide a means of restraint on politicians and civil servants. And finally, they are the major way of giving legitimacy to a particular system of government, and to the distribution of power within a state.

■ The separation of powers

In the analysis of any system of government the powers of the state are widely grouped under three headings: legislative, executive and judicial. These can be related in many countries to distinctive institutions, whose functions are kept separate. In Britain, however, there is no clear separation of powers, particularly between the executive and legislature. Eighteenth-century British government appeared to involve a separation of powers between king, Parliament and an independent judiciary. Yet in practice the executive was not the king but increasingly a Cabinet dependent on a parliamentary majority, involving a fusion of executive and legislative powers. Moreover, the upper house of the legislature, the House of Lords, was also Britain's highest court. The position of lord chancellor in particular long emphasised the absence of any clear separation of executive, legislative and judicial powers in the British system of government. As a senior minister in the Cabinet, the lord chancellor was a key member of the executive. He presided over the House of Lords, an integral part of the legislature, and he was also head of the judiciary. This confusion of functions has been a target of constitutional reformers.

> **Definitions**
>
> The **executive** is charged with the day to day government of the country, responsible for making policies and administering laws.
>
> The **legislature** is responsible for making laws.
>
> The **judiciary** is responsible for adjudicating on the law and legal disputes.

In many other countries the separation of legislative, executive and judicial powers has been established as an important constitutional principle. Thus it is a key feature of the US constitution, and of many other constitutions that have been established since. Thus in the USA the executive is the Presidency, the legislature is Congress, while the Supreme Court heads an independent judiciary. There are 'checks and balances' in the American Constitution that are designed to prevent any part of government from becoming too powerful.

■ Changing the constitution

Constitutions vary in the ease with which they can be changed. A common characteristic of written constitutions is that constitutional law has the status of a higher form of law, only alterable by special procedures. However, although all written constitutions lay down set procedures for constitutional

Box 10.2

Comparative politics: the US Constitution

The US Constitution was originally drawn up in 1787. Much of the text still accurately describes features of the US system of government, including the separation of legislative, executive and judicial powers.

- 'All legislative Powers herein granted shall be vested in a Congress of the United States, which shall consist of a Senate and a House of Representatives' (Article 1, Section 1).
- 'The Executive Power shall be vested in a President of the United States ...' (Article 2, Section 1).
- 'The Judicial Power of the United States shall be vested in one Supreme Court ...' (Article 3, Section 1).

Although the Constitution was proclaimed in the name of 'We the people of the United States' it was not a document originally designed to give much real power to the people. Yet over time the USA became more democratic, in part because some features of the system, such as the electoral college for choosing the President, never operated as the Founding Fathers intended. A conspicuous flaw in American democracy was the survival of slavery until the American Civil War, and the treatment of blacks as second-class citizens for more than a century afterwards.

The constitution continues to be treated with reverence by US politicians and citizens. It is a constant reference point when major disputes over government arise. Even so, it is not always an accurate guide to US government and politics. On other important issues such as the rights of the states, city and local government, political parties and organised groups, the Constitution is vague or silent.

(The text of the US constitution and its amendments is printed in many books on US politics e.g. Hames and Rae (1996) or Denenberg (1996).)

change, they differ in flexibility. In many countries more than a simple parliamentary majority is required for a constitutional amendment – commonly a two-thirds majority in each house of parliament. Some constitutions additionally stipulate the support of the people in a referendum. Federal systems of government additionally will normally require the support of all or most of the member states for a constitutional amendment.

An unwritten (or uncodified) constitution like Britain's is highly flexible. Interpretation of the constitution may alter almost imperceptibly over time. Thus at one time a prime minister could come from either house of Parliament, and in the 19th century most came from the House of Lords. In the 20th century this seemed incompatible with democratic assumptions, and over a period it has become a convention that the prime minister must sit in the House of Commons, although this has not been officially laid down in any Act of Parliament. Although some parts of the British constitution can be found in statutes (such as those relating to the powers of the House of Lords), a law with constitutional implications can be changed using the same process as for ordinary law, effectively by a simple majority in the House of Commons.

A flexible constitution may enable a system of government to evolve with the times, but could appear more vulnerable to ill-considered change, or subversion. By contrast, a constitution that can only be changed with great difficulty may lack the capacity to adapt to new pressures and altered circumstances, perhaps of a kind that its original designers could hardly anticipate. Yet changing judicial interpretation can lead to significant change even in countries with an apparently 'rigid' constitution. Thus the US Supreme Court has allowed its interpretation of the Constitution to evolve with the times, with, for example, considerable implications for racial segregation and civil rights.

Key features or principles of the British constitution

Written constitutions of states commonly contain some statements of principle, for example a commitment to democracy, or a republic or an

Box 10.3

Comparative politics: amending constitutions

Procedures for amending the **US Constitution** are described in Article 6 of the Constitution. Congress can propose amendments that have been approved by a two-thirds majority in each House. Any such amendment must also be approved by three-quarters of the state legislatures before it takes effect. Thus amending the US Constitution is very difficult. Even so, a number of important amendments have been passed. These include:

- The Bill of Rights, the name given to the first ten amendments, ratified in 1791, which includes a number of basic citizen rights including free speech and religious toleration, the right to a fair trial and the celebrated (or notorious) second amendment, the right to bear arms.
- The abolition of slavery (13th amendment, 1865).
- Prohibition of the manufacture, sale, or transportation of intoxicating liquors (18th amendment, 1920, subsequently repealed in the 21st amendment, 1933).
- The enfranchisement of women (19th amendment, 1920).
- The limitation of the Presidential period of office to two terms (22nd amendment, 1951).

In **Australia** constitutional amendments require the support of both Houses of Parliament, then a referendum which must receive majority support overall and in a majority of states.

In **Japan** constitutional amendments need a two-thirds majority in both Houses of Parliament, and majority support in a referendum.

France has two methods for making constitutional amendments:

- Amendments can be made by a majority in both houses of the French Parliament voting on an identical motion, followed by ratification of three-fifths of Congress (the two houses combined). The constitution of the Fifth Republic has been amended seven times using this method.
- Amendments can also be made by a constitutional referendum, after an identical motion passed in both Houses of Parliament.

established religion. In Britain there is no authoritative statement of the principles on which the (unwritten) constitution rests, and these in practice have been inferred by constitutional lawyers and other experts from various sources. The British constitution displays the following characteristics:

- a unitary state (rather than a federal state)
- a constitutional monarchy (rather than a republic)
- parliamentary sovereignty (rather than a separation of powers)
- representative democracy (rather than direct democracy
- the rule of law.

All of these characteristics require some further explanation and discussion. Some are increasingly contentious.

A unitary rather than a federal state?

Besides the separation of executive, legislative and judicial powers, some constitutions divide the functions of the state between different levels. Under a federal system sovereignty is deliberately divided between two (or conceivably more) levels of government. Each level of government is, in theory, sovereign (or supreme) in its own sphere. The Founding Fathers of the United States of America virtually invented federalism. Some earlier political thinkers like Thomas Hobbes had declared that sovereignty (or supreme power) could not be divided. However, it was important for the Founding Fathers to reconcile the rights of the original 13 American states with the need for some overall coordination of (especially) defence, foreign policy and inter-state trade. Thus powers were effectively divided between the federal government and state governments. This solution was attractive to other countries where there was a similar need to accommodate both unity and

Definitions

Sovereignty means supreme power. Within a state it refers to the ultimate source of legal authority. When used of states in their external relations, sovereignty means a state's ability to function as an independent entity – as a sovereign state.

Federalism involves the division of sovereignty between two or more levels of government. In a federal system each level of government is sovereign (or supreme) in its own sphere.

Definition

Devolution is a term coined to describe the delegation of powers in the United Kingdom downwards to institutions in Scotland, Wales, Northern Ireland and (to a more limited extent) English regions. Devolution is distinguished from federalism because it does not, in theory, involve any transfer of sovereignty, nor any breach of the constitutional principle of the unity of the United Kingdom. However, some argue that devolution in practice involves a quasi-federal system of government.

diversity, particularly where different ethnic, cultural and national groups were located within the same territories. Thus today there are many federal states, including the USA, Canada, Switzerland, Australia, Germany, India and Belgium (Hague and Harrop 2001: 202–6).

A federal state virtually requires a written constitution. If each level of government is supreme in its own sphere, there has to be some authoritative document determining those spheres, laying out the functions of the federal and state governments. This could involve listing the functions of each (perhaps with some powers exercised 'concurrently'), or merely listing the functions of one level, and ascribing all remaining powers to the other level. Thus the US Constitution details the powers of the federal government, reserving all other powers to the states. Inevitably, this does not preclude tensions between the levels of government. A major theme of the history of US government has been the alleged encroachment of the federal power on states' rights.

Most states are not federal states. Some particularly emphasise their unity. Thus the French Fifth Republic is 'one and indivisible'. This does not preclude other levels of government (regional and local), but these are legally subordinate to the sovereign state. Britain (like France) is still a unitary state, at least in legal form. The United Kingdom of Great Britain and Northern Ireland is a political union of several countries, each with a different constitutional status. Legally, it consists of the Kingdoms of England and Scotland, the Principality of Wales and two-thirds of the province of Ulster (Northern Ireland), which remained subject to the British Crown in 1922 when the rest of Ireland split away to form what eventually became the Republic of Ireland (1949).

Yet it is now questionable how far the UK remains a unitary state. The recent devolution of power to Scotland, Wales and Northern Ireland in theory affects neither the unity of the United Kingdom nor the sovereignty of the Westminster parliament. However, political realities begin to suggest otherwise and perhaps foreshadow the development of a quasi-federal, or ultimately fully federal, system of British government, or alternatively the break-up of Britain. (See Chapter 16 for a fuller discussion of the constitutional implications of devolution.)

Constitutional monarchy

The United Kingdom, as the name implies, remains a monarchy, but a limited or constitutional monarchy. Thus it is generally reckoned that the Queen 'reigns but does not rule' and has little or no political power. The personal political power of the monarch has been eroded gradually over the centuries and is now vestigial. Constitutional experts used to debate the monarch's discretion over the choice of a prime minister, or a requested dissolution of Parliament, but the circumstances in which there might be scope for discretion now seem remote or far-fetched. The Queen, in the words of Walter Bagehot, the 19th-century authority on the constitution, retains the right to be consulted, the right to encourage and the right to warn. The prime minister still has regular meetings with the sovereign, and it is possible that the present Queen's experience of successive governments and prime ministers from Churchill onwards might sometimes make her advice worth listening to.

However, if the personal power of the monarch is too negligible to be a live political issue, the institution of the crown and the issue of the royal prerogative are more contentious. Ministers, members of the armed forces and civil servants are officially servants of the crown rather than the public or 'the state'. Official communications are 'On Her Majesty's Service'. This may seem a quaint archaism, but it serves a negative function; there is no positive injunction to serve the public interest. Indeed civil servants who have leaked information which they considered ought to be made available in the public interest have been prosecuted. Until recently it was not even possible to sue the Crown or servants of the Crown. Moreover some of the powers of the sovereign, which are no longer exercised by the Queen, have not been abolished but transferred, mainly to the prime minister. Thus it is the prime minister who effectively exercises the former 'royal prerogative' powers to declare wars, make treaties and dissolve Parliament. A prime minister can involve Britain in war without seeking ratification from Parliament – although politically it would be very damaging to take such a step without the assurance of parliamentary support.

Until recently the future of the monarchy has rarely been a political issue, but it is now more openly debated. Criticism of the monarchy as an institution in Britain, and increased debate over its financial costs and benefits, has been exacerbated by scandals and by the perceived personal shortcomings of some members of the royal family. Moreover, the removal of the principle of heredity from the second chamber (although as yet incomplete) may be thought to have implications for a hereditary monarchy. However, the funeral of the Queen Mother, followed soon afterwards by the royal golden jubilee celebrations (both in 2002) suggested substantial continued public support for the monarchy, and have for the moment taken the wind out of republican sails. No major political party had dared propose the abolition of the monarchy, although some maverick MPs have done so. If Britain were to become a republic, a president or formal head of state would probably be necessary, in addition to the prime minister as head of government, as in most other modern democratic republics (see Box 10.4).

Box 10.4

Comparative politics: constitutional monarchies and republics

In **France**, the **USA**, and in most other countries which are regarded as democratic, republicanism is regarded as the natural corollary of democracy, and the retention of the principle of heredity for filling the post of head of state appears incompatible with democratic values. The US president is both head of state and head of government. More commonly, there is a separate formal head of state with little effective power, either directly elected by the people, or indirectly elected by parliament.

However, while the retention of the institution of monarchy is rare, it is not unique among countries with a reasonable claim to democracy. **Belgium**, the **Netherlands, Sweden, Denmark** and **Spain** are among examples in Europe of democratic states that retain hereditary monarchs, who in all cases have negligible personal political power. In addition, several Commonwealth countries still acknowledge the Queen as their head of state (although the issue has become politically contentious in **Australia**).

Parliamentary sovereignty

Parliamentary sovereignty has long been considered a key British constitutional principle. Parliamentary sovereignty, it should be noted, implicitly and explicitly denies the principle of the separation of powers, and so it appears. The executive in Britain is a parliamentary executive, whose existence depends on the continuing confidence of Parliament. The judiciary is bound to accept law passed by Parliament. Leading members of the judiciary are still (although not perhaps for long) members of the legislature.

What parliamentary sovereignty means in practice is that, in formal terms, parliamentary authority in the United Kingdom is unlimited: Parliament can make or unmake law on any subject whatsoever. The classic statement of its omnicompetence derives from William Blackstone, the 18th-century jurist, who declared that Parliament 'can do everything that is not naturally impossible'. Statute law (law passed by Parliament) is supreme above other kinds of law.

No person may question Parliament's legislative competence and the courts must give effect to its legislation. Part of the principle is that no Parliament can bind its successors. This looks like a limitation on the power of Parliament, but clearly if an Act of Parliament contained a clause that it could not be repealed, this would in practice end parliamentary sovereignty.

It may be noted however that the constitutional principle of parliamentary sovereignty does not mean that Parliament is particularly powerful in practice. Indeed the decline in the power and effective influence of Parliament has been widely lamented (see Chapter 13). As Andrew Marr (1996: 160) has observed 'Here is the crucial conundrum for the British Parliament, which it alone can answer; if it is sovereign, indeed absolute, then why is it so weak?'

It may also be questioned whether the constitutional principle of parliamentary sovereignty remains valid in practice. For example, how far has parliamentary sovereignty been impaired by membership of the European Union (EU)? The European Communities Act (1972) gave the force of law in the United Kingdom to obligations arising under the EC treaties, and it gave EC law general and binding authority within the United Kingdom. It provided that Community law should take precedence over all inconsistent UK law; and it precluded the UK Parliament from legislating on matters within EC competence where the Community had formulated rules. Some argue that parliamentary sovereignty is not impaired, because membership of the EU has not broken the principle that Parliament cannot bind its future action. Thus, the European Communities Act could be repealed, and indeed had the 1975 referendum on continuing membership of the EC gone the other way, the United Kingdom would almost certainly have withdrawn from the Community. However, while Britain remains a member of the EU it does appear that parliamentary sovereignty has been impaired. In effect, the UK Parliament has bound itself procedurally by the 1972 European Communities Act so that in areas of EU legislative competence, EU law is supreme and the British courts will give it precedence over national UK law where the two conflict. Thus, since 1973, Britain has possessed 'dual constitutional arrangements, as an independent state and as a member of the European Community (Union)'. Since then it has had, and still has, 'a parallel constitution' (Madgwick and Woodhouse 1995: 42).

Box 10.5

The Factortame case

Britain's legal subordination to Brussels was underlined by an important legal case in 1991, R. v. Secretary of State for Transport *ex parte* Factortame Ltd no 2. (the Factortame case). The European Court of Justice in effect quashed sections of a British Act of Parliament (the Merchant Shipping Act 1988) which provided that UK-registered boats must be 75 per cent British-owned and have 75 per cent of crew resident in the UK. The Act had been designed to prevent boats from Spain and other EC countries 'quota-hopping' by registering under the British flag and using the UK's EC fishing quotas. The European Court of Justice had overturned British legislation before, but no earlier case had provoked such an outcry.

Judges are bound to accept statute law, yet they are equally bound to accept the law of the EU, which effectively overrides law passed by the Westminster Parliament. They can also now declare that British legislation 'appears incompatible' with the European Convention on Human Rights. The new Supreme Court will disentangle the judiciary from the legislature, and reinforce its independence.

It may also be questioned whether devolution may not ultimately destroy the sovereignty of the Westminster Parliament. The official answer here is clear. Devolution is not the same as federalism. Power devolved is power retained, because sovereignty or supreme power is unaffected, and thus any functions that are devolved can be called back. Devolution itself may be reversed, as the suspension of the Stormont Parliament in 1972 and the resumption of direct rule of Northern Ireland after 50 years of devolved government demonstrates. Since then the new Northern Ireland Assembly and Executive have been suspended four times, reinforcing the point.

Yet Northern Ireland is a special case. It now seems scarcely conceivable that devolution in Scotland and Wales is reversible, unless the majority of Scots and Welsh become convinced that devolution was a mistake. All the pressures seem to be the other way – to concede more powers to the Scottish Parliament and Welsh Assembly. Thus it is arguable that Britain is evolving towards a quasi-federal system of government which entails the end of UK parliamentary sovereignty. (These points are discussed further later in this chapter, and in more detail in Chapter 16.)

This may be seen as an illustration of the obvious point that the UK Parliament is subject to political constraints on what it can actually do, as opposed to what it may legally do. Government and Parliament must pay some regard to public opinion. Thus the prohibition of alcoholic liquor would be as unpopular in Britain as it was for a brief spell in the USA, and no UK government has ever tried it. Sometimes Acts of Parliament apparently embodying the full force of law can become virtually unenforceable. Trade union resistance wrecked the 1971 Trade Union Act, and widespread popular revolt helped destroy the poll tax. This suggests that parliamentary sovereignty can in practice be limited by what the people will stand (or, effectively, by democracy).

Representative democracy

Representative democracy may be considered a more fundamental principle of the British system of government than parliamentary sovereignty, even if it is a principle less discussed by constitutional lawyers. It is a mark of the evolutionary nature of the British system of government that it is difficult to pin down precisely when Britain became a democracy (and some critics would deny that it is, in some important respects, even now). Yet the extension of the vote was accompanied by a gradual acceptance of democratic principles over time, and this in turn prompted the emergence of new conventions embodying the spirit of democracy. Thus it came to be established that the peers should not frustrate the will of the democratically elected House of Commons, particularly on issues that had been submitted to the people in a manifesto by the governing party. Similarly, it became an unwritten rule that the prime minister and head of government should be a member of the House of Commons, and normally the elected leader of the majority party.

Of course, British democracy involves representative (or parliamentary) democracy rather than direct democracy (see Chapter 1). It is elected representatives of the people rather than the people themselves who decide. Thus Parliament can legislate to abolish capital punishment even when opinion polls suggest public support for it. However, British governments have made more use of popular referendums recently, on essentially constitutional issues. Thus referendums have been held on membership of the European Community (1975), devolution (1979, 1997), London government (1998), a projected elected assembly for the north-east (2004), and have been promised on other issues. It should be noted that there is an implied contradiction here between the principles of parliamentary sovereignty and popular sovereignty.

However, in Britain referendums require the passing of a specific Act of Parliament, and the result of a referendum remains theoretically advisory, thus the principle of parliamentary sovereignty is maintained. Yet it would be politically suicidal to hold a referendum and ignore the result, and increasingly it may be difficult for government and parliament to refuse a referendum where popular demand exists (or has been whipped up by a media campaign), as on the issue of the European constitution. The more referendums become a regular part of the British system of government, the further the principle of parliamentary sovereignty is eroded. The 'will of the people' will be invoked to challenge the will of Parliament.

It may of course also be questioned how far the British Parliament is truly representative of the people. MPs are representative to the extent that they are elected, yet we have already seen that the

Definitions

Parliamentary sovereignty means that parliament has supreme power.

Popular sovereignty means that supreme power rests with the people.

There is clearly potential for tension or open conflict between these two doctrines. The views of the elected representatives of the people clearly may not always coincide with the views of the people themselves.

seats political parties secured in the Westminster Parliament do not closely reflect the proportion of votes cast in general and local elections (see Chapter 6). Blair's government, like Thatcher's government, enjoys a substantial parliamentary majority secured on a minority of the votes cast (35 per cent after the 2005 election), and a much smaller proportion of the total electorate. Nor is Parliament or government a microcosm of the nation. Women, ethnic minorities and manual workers are all significantly under-represented compared with their proportions in the population. (The ways in which Parliament can be said to represent the people are explored in more detail in Chapter 13.)

The rule of law

The leading jurist A. V. Dicey (1835–1922) saw the rule of law as a fundamental characteristic of the British constitution, viewing it as of equal importance to the doctrine of parliamentary sovereignty. Although in strict constitutional terms the rule of law is subordinate to parliamentary sovereignty, which could be used to remove the rights it entails, the rule of law remains of key significance. In particular, it underpins the very important constitutional principle of the (partial) separation of powers, whereby, although executive and legislative branches are 'fused', the judicial branch is largely independent and separate and can check the executive. Second, the rule of law enshrines principles such as natural justice, fairness and reasonableness, which can be applied by the courts through the process of judicial review.

The fundamental principle is that people are subject to the rule of law, not to the arbitrary will of their governors. No one is above the law. Ministers and public authorities are bound by the law. Actions without the authority of law can be challenged in the courts. Citizens should have redress for illegal or arbitrary acts by public authorities, through the ordinary courts, administrative tribunals or other special machinery, such as complaints to the various 'ombudsmen' over what is termed 'maladministration'. (For a further discussion of the principle of the rule of law, and its application, see Chapter 14.)

The politics of the constitution and constitutional reform

It should be noted that while constitutions (written or unwritten) may be treated with great reverence, they are not 'above politics' but *about* politics and *in* politics. Constitutions are about politics because they provide the framework of rules that shape political behaviour – the main 'rules of the game'. Second, constitutions are in politics because these 'rules of the game' are subject to pressure from the competing individuals, groups and classes they affect. Constitutions at any given moment are always more or less advantageous to some and disadvantageous to others. For example, the single-member, simple majority electoral system for the Westminster Parliament benefits the major parties but operates against the Liberal Democrats (see Chapter 5). A constitution, therefore, is something that politicians and political activists are always seeking to change, radically modify, keep the same or, if they are revolutionaries, overthrow.

The process of constitutional change always consists of a kind of dialogue between (crudely) the forces of conservation and the forces of transformation, and the upshot – the constitution at any particular moment – represents in essentials a compromise between them. In that sense, the constitution represents the terms, the arrangements, on which a country can be ruled. In this quite abstract but very important sense, constitution making is about engineering consent to government. Thus, in Britain agitation by the middle and working classes and by women broke the constitutional settlements prevailing respectively in the early 19th, late 19th and early 20th centuries. At each point in time, public consent to the constitution was no longer possible on the old terms; change was a condition of political stability. In essence, the nature of constitutions is to express the conditions under which people will consent to be governed.

Britain experienced a period of intense controversy over constitutional issues in the years leading up to the First World War. After that there appeared to be a broad cross-party consensus in support of the system of government lasting up until the 1970s. Even so, this apparent agreement concealed some very different assumptions on the constitution. These different ideological assumptions help to explain the marked differences in attitude to constitutional reform that subsequently emerged between the parties in the last quarter of the 20th century.

Although Conservatives have sometimes been responsible for significant constitutional change, they have more generally been concerned to conserve the existing constitution, although not often seeking to reverse reforms carried through by their opponents. While the party came to accept 'Tory democracy' by the end of the 19th century, it was always a version of democracy that placed a continuing emphasis on the need for leadership. Conservatives see authority as flowing from above. They traditionally emphasise strong government and accord popular participation a minimal role. So government, backed by a loyal party, governs; and the electorate, through Parliament, consents to this firm leadership. Conservatives have continued to support traditional institutions, including the monarchy, the House of Lords and the established church. From the 19th century, when they strongly opposed home rule for Ireland, Conservatives have been firmly committed to the preservation of the Union. Thus the Conservatives opposed Labour's devolution proposals from 1974–9, and in the 1992 and 1997 elections John Major warned the electorate that the Union was in danger from the renewed commitment of the opposition parties to devolution.

For much of its history the Labour Party was surprisingly uninterested in radical constitutional reform, although the party intermittently pursued Lords reform, and occasionally toyed with other constitutional changes. Labour wished to capture and control the state rather than reform it. Its priorities were social and economic reform, and it was assumed that this could be achieved through the existing state apparatus. Labour, like the Conservatives, endorsed strong government, but for different reasons. Once it had achieved a parliamentary majority and a mandate from the people, Labour wanted to be able to enact its social and economic reforms. Executive control of parliament in the British system of government facilitated the passage of party programmes, while strong central control over subordinate levels of government and virtual freedom from judicial interference meant there were few checks on Labour's mandate to govern (Dunleavy, in Dunleavy *et al.* 1997: 130). Labour also benefited from an electoral system that protected the two major parties from third-party competition.

While Conservatives have strongly defended the existing constitution, and Labour was generally content to work within it, Liberals and more recently Liberal Democrats have placed more emphasis on constitutional reform. Thus in the 19th century Liberals championed parliamentary reform and, from 1886 onwards, Irish home rule (and subsequently 'home rule all round'). In the early 20th century the Liberal government took on and defeated the House of Lords. After the Second World War the Liberal Party was the first to support entry into the European Economic Community, and it continued to support devolution to Scotland and Wales as well as English regional government. It has sought to defend civil liberties and individual rights, and to strengthen the role of parliament. Unsurprisingly, it has consistently campaigned for electoral reform, as the first-past-the-post system has particularly penalised it. The Liberal Democrats under Ashdown and Kennedy have maintained this commitment to constitutional reform.

On the fringes of British politics there were always those who sought to overthrow rather than reform the state. These have included small groups on the far right or the far left of the political spectrum who rejected most of the key institutions of the British state, but also, and increasingly significantly, varieties of nationalists. It was the growing support for separatist nationalism in Ireland that led to the establishment of the Irish Free State (and later Republic). Nationalists in Scotland and Wales took longer to make an impact, and were generally committed to peaceful change, although they also sought the break-up of the British state. They only began to make an impact after nationalist pressures reignited in Northern Ireland in the late 1960s and early 1970s, and around the same time when the debate over British membership of the European Community was raising concerns over British national sovereignty.

These pressures had a particular impact on the Labour Party. The rise of nationalism threatened its own heartlands in Scotland and Wales, and converted Labour to devolution. At the same time Labour was split from top to bottom by the issue of Europe, and opted for a referendum on EC membership as a way out of its own divisions, before referendums were also held (and lost) on Labour's devolution plans for Scotland and Wales. Thus Labour became a party of constitutional reform. This mattered little while it was excluded from power at Westminster, but had immediate implications when it returned to government in 1997. By this time Labour's old state-centred collectivism no longer appeared either feasible or electorally appealing. Blair's New Labour was, initially at least, cautious on the economy, and radical on the constitution, a reversal of Labour's former priorities. Labour entered the 1997 election with an ambitious programme of constitutional change with momentous implications for the future government of Britain.

The movement for constitutional reform

Constitutional reform was a cause that had become increasingly fashionable from the late 1980s onwards. Compared with the earlier period of constitutional concern in the 1960s and 1970s, which had been limited to specific issues, this new phase was about fundamentals, and produced radical proposals for reform. An important step was the formation of the influential pressure group, Charter 88, symbolically 300 years on from the Revolution of 1688.

Box 10.6

The main demands of Charter 88

- A Bill of Rights to ensure key civil rights.
- Freedom of information and open government.
- A fair electoral system based on proportional representation.
- A reformed democratic, non-hereditary second chamber.
- The subordination of the executive to a 'democratically renewed parliament'.
- An independent, reformed judiciary.
- 'An equitable distribution of power between local, regional and national government.'
- A written constitution.

Box 10.7

Constitutional reform: the Labour–Liberal Democrat proposals, 1997

- Select committee on modernisation of House of Commons.
- Abolition of hereditary peers.
- A Scottish Parliament and Welsh Assembly elected by proportional representation.
- Referendums on creation of an elected London authority and elected English regional assemblies.
- Incorporation of European Convention of Human Rights into UK law.
- Electoral commission to recommend alternative to present voting system.
- Freedom of Information Act.

There was some support for constitutional reform on the right of the political spectrum, notably from the neo-liberal think-tank, the Institute of Economic Affairs, and individuals such as a former head of Margaret Thatcher's Political Unit, Ferdinand Mount (1992). However, much of the interest in constitutional change came from the centre and left of the political spectrum (Hutton 1995: ch. 11, Barnett 1997). In March 1997 the two centre-left parties, Labour and the Liberal Democrats, which had already been cooperating closely in the Scottish Constitutional Convention, produced an agreed raft of proposals for constitutional reform.

The reforming mood also gained some endorsement by public opinion. A 'State of the Nation' poll commissioned by the Joseph Rowntree Trust in 1995 found that the proportion of people believing the system of government works well had dropped to a mere 22 per cent. Eighty-one per cent were in favour of a Freedom of Information Act, and 79 per cent wanted a Bill of Rights and a written constitution. There was strong support also for greater use of referendums, the enforcement of the MPs' code of conduct by the courts, civil or criminal, and the investigation of ministerial misconduct by people other than politicians. The last points indicated increased concern over 'sleaze' in the final years of the Major government and diminished public confidence in the conduct of British government and politics.

Labour and the constitution: a government of radical reform?

By the end of its first term the Labour government had enacted a substantial part of its reform programme (see Box 10.8). By any standard this amounts to a formidable catalogue of constitutional reform measures, which have already had massive implications for Britain's system of government. (Further details are discussed in subsequent chapters.) In terms of achievement it compares very favourably with the efforts of previous Labour governments. Thus the Wilson government of 1964–70 was forced to abandon its plans to reform the Lords in 1969, while the Wilson/Callaghan administrations of 1974–9 failed to implement their devolution proposals. The relative ease of implementation of the Blair government reforms may partly be attributed to the size of its majority, although Labour also learned from its previous failures. Holding referendums first effectively settled the substantive issue of devolution, leaving Parliament only to decide the details. Similarly, the two-stage model adopted for reforming the Lords meant that abolition of the hereditary principle was decided and substantially implemented before Parliament became bogged down in arguments over the composition of the new second chamber.

Two 1997 manifesto pledges on the constitution were not delivered before the election in 2001. The government did not honour a commitment to hold a referendum on a reformed electoral system for the Westminster Parliament. While the government did fulfil its promise to appoint a commission to recommend a new voting system, Lord Jenkins's report was effectively shelved. However, the government's adoption of a variety of electoral systems for devolved assemblies and the European Parliament

Box 10.8

The Labour government's legislation on constitutional reform in its first term

- Referendums on devolution in Scotland (1997), Wales (1997), and Ireland (1998).
- The establishment of regional development agencies for the English regions (1998).
- A referendum on a directly elected mayor for London, with a strategic authority for governing London (1998).
- A Parliament for Scotland with legislative powers, elected by the additional member system (1998).
- An Assembly for Wales, with executive powers, elected by the additional member system (1998).
- An Assembly for Northern Ireland elected by the single transferable vote system, and a partnership executive representing both the Unionist and Nationalist communities (1998).
- A new electoral system (a regional list system) for the European Parliament (1999).
- A directly elected mayor for London, elected by the supplementary vote, and a Greater London Authority, elected by the additional member system (1999).
- A Human Rights Act (1998, implemented 2000) allowing judges to declare that legislation is incompatible with the European Convention on European Rights.
- The removal of all but 92 hereditary members from the House of Lords (1999).
- A Freedom of Information Act (1999, implemented 2005).
- Limits on election campaign spending (Elections, Political Parties and Referendums Act, 2000).
- A separate executive for local authorities, involving either a local cabinet system or a directly elected mayor (Local Government Act, 2000).

has initiated a debate and begun a process of reform which may not be easily halted (see Chapter 5). The government also did not immediately pursue plans for elected assemblies for the English regions (although it attempted to do so later). Besides these failures to deliver manifesto commitments, critics have also drawn attention to other omissions in Labour's first-term programme, including failures to strengthen the role of Parliament (beyond marginal reforms to parliamentary procedures), to strengthen significantly the role of local government, or to reform the civil service.

Labour's second term: a constitutional revolution halted?

So extensive was the programme of constitutional change in Labour's first term that the second term (2001–5) seemed almost inevitably an anticlimax. New institutions needed time to bed down. By 2005 the new arrangements for governing Scotland, Wales and London had become part of the accepted furniture of government. After an uncertain start they all had made their mark and achieved some success (see Chapter 16). Northern Ireland was another matter, but at least the ceasefire held, and some measure of normality returned to the province. Some other reforms enacted in the first term were only effectively implemented later. Thus the Human Rights Act, passed in 1998, was only implemented from 2000, and a body of precedent has taken longer to establish. Elected mayors was an initiative which depended on local referendums, under the Local Government Act 2000. Some 30 such referendums were held in 2001–2, and in just 11 the vote was in favour of directly elected mayors. The 1999 Freedom of Information Act, widely criticised for not going far enough, was only implemented in 2005.

Other 'unfinished business' from Labour's first term has been rather more troublesome, particularly Lords reform. It was always anticipated that the (partial) removal of hereditary peers from the House of Lords would be only the first stage of a more comprehensive reform of the second chamber. Here the Labour government's own proposals (for a part-elected but mainly appointed upper house) were widely rubbished, and Labour handed the issue over to a committee of both houses. However, not even the House of Commons on its own, let alone the two houses, could come up with broadly acceptable alternative proposals for the composition of a reformed Lords (see Chapter 13). Thus the Lords remain in limbo.

Tardily and cautiously, the government recommitted itself to proposals for elected assemblies for the English regions. Following consultation the government initially proposed referendums in three northern regions, reduced finally to just one, the north-east, where opinion seemed most favourable. In November 2004 the electorate delivered a decisive 'no' vote. Elected assemblies for the English regions would appear to be off the agenda for the immediate future.

The only dramatic constitutional initiative in Labour's second term also ran into problems, but may ultimately be substantially implemented. In 2003 the prime minister announced the abolition of the office of lord chancellor, the introduction of a new system for appointing judges, and proposals for a new Supreme Court to replace the judicial functions of the House of Lords. These were changes that many constitutional reformers had long called for, yet they were announced in a hurry, and provoked a strong reaction that the government seemed unprepared for. Traditionalists lamented the abolition of the centuries-old post of lord chancellor (Roberts 2004). In the event, there were unanticipated problems in implementation, so the title continues, although the responsibilities have been transformed. The law lords were divided on the proposals, and opposed to the institution of a Supreme Court without a suitable building. Other critics objected to the potential cost. Proposals for the new system for appointing judges were regarded suspiciously in some quarters, while others did not think they went far enough. (For further discussion of these reforms see Chapter 14.) Even so, the Constitutional Reform Act was passed in 2005 and the Supreme Court and the new judicial appointments system should be up and running in Labour's third term. Altogether, these reforms mark a significant stage towards a greater separation of judicial powers from executive and legislative powers in the British constitution.

Beyond specific criticisms there is a more general objection that Labour's various initiatives do not seem to be related to any overall vision (Peele, in Dunleavy *et al.* 2002: 75), that the reforms are insufficiently 'joined up' (to use New Labour terminology). Indeed, what is striking is the sheer diversity and absence of pattern in the reforms. Thus different electoral systems have been introduced for the various devolved institutions and the European Parliament. The functions and processes of the devolved bodies in Scotland, Wales and Northern Ireland are markedly different (Hazell 2000: 269–71). Lords reform has proceeded independently of other constitutional change, particularly devolution. It is as if each reform was considered in isolation. Moreover, there appears to be no clear sense of direction, nor even any realisation of the implication for established constitutional principles, such as parliamentary sovereignty and the unitary state (see Box 10.9).

One obvious consequence of devolution is increasing diversity within the 'United Kingdom' as devolved executives increasingly exercise their powers in different ways. At the moment this diversity may be relatively limited, as Labour rules at Westminster, is the dominant coalition partner in Edinburgh and now governs alone in Cardiff. However, if different parties take control of the various governments within the UK there could be increased scope for disagreements, and perhaps serious demarcation disputes between different levels of government. This may ultimately necessitate some kind of written constitution, with provision perhaps for judicial arbitration over disputes. A written constitution is part of the Charter 88 package of proposals that Labour has so far ignored or rejected, but it may prove the logical culmination of reforms already implemented. A written constitution, particularly if it contained safeguards against hasty amendment by a bare Commons majority, would effectively mean the end of parliamentary sovereignty, and in so far as it spelt out the respective functions of different levels of government, would also involve the end of the unitary state.

A federal Britain is, however, only one possible longer-term outcome of the constitutional reform process. For Irish, Scottish and Welsh nationalists, devolution and federalism are only stages on the road to separation and the break-up of Britain. Some who have opposed devolution all along (including many Conservatives and some Labour critics, like Tam Dalyell) have feared that it is a slippery slope on the road to independence, as indeed nationalists wish. By contrast, Labour and the Liberal Democrats hope that devolution will satisfy the legitimate demands of many in Scotland and Wales to have a greater say in decisions that affect them, and that devolution will ultimately strengthen rather than weaken the British state. It is impossible to know now who is right and what the eventual outcome will be.

Box 10.9

The end of parliamentary sovereignty and the unitary state?

The official orthodoxy is that parliamentary sovereignty and the unitary state remain unaffected by recent constitutional change, although some argue that it has already been eroded by UK membership of the EU. Vernon Bogdanor (in Seldon 2001) claims that it was further reduced by at least three developments:

- **The employment of referendums.** As these are advisory rather than binding, formally the sovereignty of the Parliament is unaffected. But Bogdanor argues that 'a referendum which yields a clear outcome on a reasonable turnout binds Parliament'. Thus the sovereignty of the people is substituted for the sovereignty of Parliament.
- **The Human Rights Act**, which does not give judges power to reject Westminster legislation, but 'nevertheless alters very considerably the balance between Parliament and the judiciary' so that Parliament will feel obliged to respond to a judicial decision that a statute is incompatible with the European Convention of Human Rights.
- **Devolution**, particularly Scottish devolution. While the sovereignty of the Westminster Parliament is theoretically unaffected, in practice English MPs have lost responsibility for legislation on devolved functions.

Bogdanor (Seldon 2001: 151) argues that the Human Rights Act and the Scotland Act 'have the characteristic of fundamental laws. They in practice limit the rights of Westminster as a sovereign Parliament, and provide for a constitution which is quasi-federal in nature.'

Elections in 2003 indicated some weakening in support for separatist parties in Scotland and Wales (see Chapter 16), although this may prove only temporary. The various peoples of the United Kingdom have embarked on a journey in which the final destination is unknown.

Summary

- Britain does not have a written constitution. There is no authoritative description of the British system of government in a single document.
- The British system of government has been subject to some radical changes, particularly in the last ten years. The final upshot remains unclear, but Britain could be moving towards a quasi-federal system of government. Another possibility is the break-up of Britain.
- In the absence of a written constitution, major sources of the British constitution include relevant statute law, case law, conventions and the law of the EU.
- Key constitutional principles include constitutional monarchy, parliamentary sovereignty, representative democracy and the rule of law. Compared with the USA and many other countries, there has been no clear separation of executive, legislative and judicial powers in the United Kingdom.
- There was a two-party consensus on most aspects of the constitution until relatively recently. This consensus was broken when Labour became committed to specific constitutional changes amid a growing movement for extensive constitutional reform.
- The first term of Blair's Labour government saw the introduction of a substantial programme of constitutional reform. The pace of reform has been slower in the second term, while some initiatives have failed or run into substantial difficulties.
- Parliamentary sovereignty, some claim, has been substantially eroded by recent changes.

Questions for discussion

- Is a hereditary monarchy compatible with the principle of democracy? Should Britain get rid of the monarchy and establish a republic?
- What is parliamentary sovereignty? Why is there a potential conflict between parliamentary sovereignty and popular sovereignty?
- How far have changes in Britain's system of government since 1973 eroded the principle of parliamentary sovereignty?
- How far are Labour's constitutional reforms part of a coherent vision for the future government of Britain? Why do the reforms appear 'insufficiently joined up?'
- Does Britain need a written constitution, and if so, what should be included in it?

Further reading

Britain's constitution and constitutional reform has become a difficult and fast-changing topic. A useful and reasonably up-to-date account is provided by Jowell and Oliver, *The Changing Constitution* (2004). Another recent book by a constitutional lawyer is Hilaire Barnett's *Britain Unwrapped* (2002). For academic commentary on the reforms see works by Robert Hazell and the Constitution Unit, especially *Constitutional Futures* (1999), reviewing prospects for reform after the election of the Labour government, and *The State and the Nations* (2000) and *The State of the Nations* (2001, 2003) on the early record on devolution.

There is a useful review by Vernon Bogdanor in Seldon (2001) of constitutional reform in Labour's first term, and much relevant material in chapters in *Developments in British Politics 6* (Dunleavy *et al.* 2002) and 7 (Dunleavy *et al.* 2003). Articles in journals such as *Politics Review* and *Talking Politics* provide useful updating on recent developments, but government, party, and newspaper websites are the best sources for keeping abreast of current issues.

On arguments for constitutional reform see the publications of the pressure group Charter 88 and its website www.charter88.org.uk. Holme and Elliot (1988) provide the background to its formation and programme. Some older books are still useful for a grasp of the British constitution and system of government before the Blair government's reform programme, such as Nevil Johnson, *In Search of the Constitution* (1977) and Madgwick and Woodhouse, *The Law and Politics of the Constitution of the United Kingdom* (1995). Thoughtful reflections on the principles and practice of the traditional British constitution have been provided by Ferdinand Mount, *The British Constitution Now* (1992), Andrew Marr, *Ruling Britannia* (1996), Will Hutton, *The State We're In* (chapter 11) (1996) and Anthony Barnett, *This Time* (1997). The chapter (12) on constitutions in Hague and Harrop, *Comparative Government and Politics* (2001) provides some useful comparative background against which the very unusual British constitution can be assessed.

For further reading on particular institutions and constitutional reforms, see the reading suggested for later chapters, e.g. on parliament (Chapter 13), the judiciary (Chapter 14), Europe (Chapter 15), devolution (Chapter 16), local governance (Chapter 17), quangos and regulation (Chapter 18).

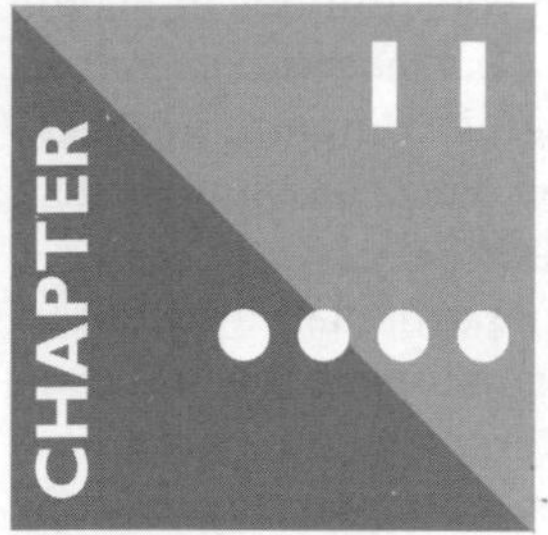

Prime Minister and Cabinet

Contents

In this chapter we consider the institutions that make up the core executive in British government. We saw in Chapter 10 that the executive in Britain is not separate from the legislature, as it is in many other countries. The British executive is a parliamentary executive. It is not separately elected (as for example is the US president). The key politicians who are members of the executive, the prime minister, Cabinet and junior ministers outside the Cabinet, are all members of the House of Commons or the Lords. Moreover the government, or executive, normally has a working majority in the House of Commons and dominates its work.

At the centre of the executive is the prime minister. We examine the various roles of the prime minister, and the sources of his or her power, and the limitations on that power. We look at the growth in size and importance of the Prime Minister's Office, and discuss the case for a Prime Minister's Department. We then consider the role of the Cabinet, Cabinet committees and the Cabinet Office in the British system of government, and explore the implications of the principle of collective Cabinet responsibility.

It has long been alleged that prime ministerial government has effectively replaced Cabinet government in the British system. More recently some saw Blair as more like a president than a traditional British prime minister (although similar observations were made about some of his predecessors). Although we review the arguments fully, we suggest that the traditional debate over prime ministerial power involves a misleading oversimplification of relations at the heart of government. The influence of individuals and institutions not only fluctuates markedly with political circumstances but is heavily constrained by all kinds of external forces. The levers of power do not always secure the effective delivery of policy. Moreover the government of Whitehall and Westminster is now only part (although still the most important part) of a complex system of multi-level governance which affects the lives of British people.

The prime minister

The prime minister is the effective head of British government. The post of prime minister emerged in the course of the 18th century, although it long remained an unofficial position, and the title only found its way into official documents in the 20th century. Sir Robert Walpole, who was the leading minister from 1721 until 1742, is generally regarded as the first prime minister. The government then was still the king's government in more than name,

Definition

Core executive: this term refers to the key institutions at the centre of government. It covers the prime minister, Cabinet and its committees, the Prime Minister's Office and the Cabinet Office, coordinating departments such as the Treasury, the government's law officers and the security and intelligence services.

Definition

The prime minister: a head of government whose power normally derives in Britain from leadership of the largest party in the legislature, more exceptionally from enjoyment of the confidence of a cross-party parliamentary majority.

but the Cabinet, consisting of senior ministers, had become the effective executive. As the king no longer chaired Cabinet meetings this crucial role fell to the leading minister. Walpole's official post was first lord of the Treasury (a title retained by modern prime ministers). This crucially put him in charge of patronage – the distribution of jobs in government – and gave him pre-eminence in the Cabinet. In the course of the 18th century, Cabinets became increasingly dependent on parliamentary support rather than royal favour, and the prime minister became the real head of government. In the process, the prime minister effectively acquired the right to exercise most of the old prerogative (or personal) powers of the Crown.

Prime ministers in the 18th and 19th centuries could come from either House of Parliament, and many sat in the Lords. (Lord Salisbury, who resigned in 1902, was the last peer to serve as prime minister.) However, the post had long required the support of a majority in the House of Commons, and increasingly democratic assumptions required a head of government who had been elected as an MP. Even so, the convention that a prime minister must sit in the House of Commons only gradually emerged in the 20th century. Modern prime ministers derive much of their authority and democratic legitimacy from their position as elected leader of the majority party in the House of Commons, although the formal election of party leaders only developed in the course of the 20th century.

The modern office of prime minister embodies a formidable concentration of power, although much of this depends on convention rather than law. In summary, the prime minister is responsible for forming a government; for directing and coordinating its work; and for general supervision of the civil service. The prime minister also has special responsibilities in the sphere of national security. Alongside these formal responsibilities the prime minister in practice can exercise a strong influence over any specific policy or service, and many recent holders of the position have taken a particular interest in defence, foreign affairs and the management of the economy. In addition the prime minister effectively decides on the date of a general election (normally after consultation with senior colleagues). Finally, the prime minister is the national leader, as evidenced by his or her role in representing the country at international conferences and meetings, signing treaties and playing host to leaders of other states.

The role of the prime minister

Patronage

The most important element of prime ministerial patronage is the power to select the 100 or so politicians – drawn mainly from the House of Commons but including some from the House of Lords – who at any given moment form the government. The prime minister appoints not just the Cabinet of normally 20–23 members but also ministers of state, under-secretaries of state, whips and law officers such as the attorney-general and solicitor-general. Between one-third and one-quarter (depending on the number of seats won) of the MPs belonging to the party victorious at a general election can realistically expect government office. By no means all politicians seek ministerial office, but most probably do. The continuing power to 'hire and fire' is a formidable source of control for the prime minister.

Ministerial changes – by forced or deliberate reshuffle – occur quite frequently. For example, only half of Tony Blair's first Cabinet of 1997 remained in the Cabinet after the 2001 election four years later. Before the 2005 election four more from that original Cabinet had departed (Cook, Short, Irvine and Blunkett, although Blunkett was briefly brought back after the election). There have been many additional shifts in posts. Gordon Brown's long tenure as Chancellor of the Exchequer is exceptional. The average tenure for a particular Cabinet post is around two years. Thus several major departments (such as Education, Health, Transport, Trade and Industry, and Northern Ireland) have had four or more different secretaries of state in charge in eight years.

The prime minister also plays a key role in the selection of individuals to fill a wide variety of other leading posts in national life. This influence extends over the creation of peers as well as over the appointment of top civil servants at the permanent secretary and deputy secretary levels, the heads of the security services and the chairmen of royal commissions. In addition, the prime minister has ultimate responsibility for recommendations of honours in the various New Year, Queen's Birthday and special honours lists.

Direction and organisation of the government

The prime minister is responsible for directing and organising the work of the government at the highest level. This involves setting broad policy objectives (within the framework of party ideology and the party manifesto) and devising short-term and long-term strategies for attaining these goals. The leadership, of course, is always in a collective context: the prime minister is not a single-person executive like the US president. Within that framework, there are clearly differences in style. Margaret Thatcher is well known for having led from the front, and the same might be said of Tony Blair. Harold Wilson and John Major both had a more consensual style. However, the prime minister expects ministerial colleagues to support government policy according to the convention of collective responsibility (see below).

The prime minister not only has overall responsibility for government, but can take a particular personal interest in key policy areas. Thus, many prime ministers (but not Blair) have taken a decisive role in the determination of economic policy in consultation with the Chancellor of the Exchequer and the Treasury. Others, notably Blair, have played a leading part in foreign and defence policy, sometimes overshadowing their foreign and defence secretaries. However, issues may arise over the whole field of government in which the prime minister either has to get involved or chooses to take a particular interest. Thus prime ministers in the 1960s and 1970s were unavoidably involved in industrial, trade union and pay policies. James Callaghan intervened in education policy, industrial relations and incomes policy. Margaret Thatcher took a direct personal interest in the management of the economy, in Europe and foreign policy generally, in trade unions and industrial relations, in changes to the civil services and NHS, and in the introduction of the poll tax in local government. Major and Blair were both centrally involved in the development of the peace process in Northern Ireland.

The prime minister draws up the Cabinet agenda, and decides the composition, terms of reference and chairs of Cabinet committees. As well as playing a key part in deciding the nature, timing and ordering of issues reaching the Cabinet agenda, the prime minister chairs Cabinet meetings. This can give the prime minister considerable influence over the direction and outcome of Cabinet discussions, by making his or her views known before and during the meeting, by determining who is called to speak and in what order, and by summing up 'the sense of the meeting'. In the process, prime ministers may deploy various manipulative 'arts' of chairmanship including delay, obfuscation of the issue, verbosity, deliberate ambiguity, adjournment (followed by 'arm-twisting'), briskness (sometimes Cabinets have complained of being 'bounced' into decisions), sheer persistence, and authority. Votes are rarely taken in Cabinet: they encourage division, dilute collective responsibility, and are vulnerable to 'leaks' and misleading reports in the media. But it is the task of the prime minister to summarise the decisions reached, taking into account the weight of opinion for or against a course of action as well as the numerical balance of opinion, and sometimes concluding against what appears to be the majority view.

The prime minister also makes decisions about the structure of the government, involving in particular the allocation of duties between the departments of state. The fluctuations in the

Box 11.1

The role of the prime minister: key aspects

- Elected by the people – the authority of the prime minister derives from being leader of the party that gains a parliamentary majority in a General Election.
- Appoints government (and others to leading roles). The prime minister 'hires and fires'.
- Steers government – the prime minister directs and coordinates government policy and strategy, chairs Cabinet, and has special interests in key policy areas.
- Organises government – including setting up, reorganising and abolishing departments of state, and overseeing the organisation of the civil service and other parts of government.
- Requests dissolution of Parliament from the monarch – effectively determines date of General Elections.
- Controls the House of Commons – through leadership of a disciplined majority party (normally).
- Gives leadership to the nation – particularly in time of national crisis (e.g. war), but has a high political profile always, and represents the country at home and abroad.

number of departments – 30 in 1951, 21 in 1983, 19 in 1993 – and the changes in their functions are evidence of considerable prime ministerial activity in this sphere. Tony Blair as premier continued this departmental restructuring, for example, establishing a new Department of International Development in 1997, and replacing the old Ministry of Agriculture, Fisheries and Food (MAFF) with a new Department of the Environment, Food and Rural Affairs in 2001 (see Chapter 12). More controversially, Blair transformed the ancient office of lord chancellor in 2003, creating a new Department of Constitutional Affairs.

Finally in this regard, the prime minister has overall responsibility for the work of the civil service (the Cabinet secretary is head of the civil service). Developments since 1979 have seen a significant strengthening of the prime minister's position in relation to Whitehall. On top appointments, prime ministers are frequently willing simply to endorse the recommendations of the Senior Appointments Selection Committee, although on occasion they have been more closely involved. However on the organisation and management of the civil service the Thatcher–Major era saw large-scale change launched and carried through, with a series of reforms initiated and supervised by advisers and personnel at the centre of government. Thus, the massive reorganisation of the civil service involved in the Next Steps programme was proposed by Thatcher's Efficiency Unit, a group within the Prime Minister's Office. Under John Major the package of reforms involving the Citizens' Charters and the market testing or contracting out of some civil service functions to the private sector was carried out by a unit within the Cabinet Office (Burch 1995a: 131). These changes have been substantially maintained, and even extended, by the Labour government from 1997 onwards (see Chapter 12).

The power of dissolution

The prime minister has the exclusive right to recommend to the monarch the timing of the dissolution of Parliament within a five-year period, leading to a General Election. (It is difficult to envisage circumstance in which such a request could be refused without dangerously involving the monarchy in party politics.) It used to be argued that the prime minister's power to call for a dissolution was a potent weapon to discipline his own government and party when faced with internal dissent. However, such a weapon could be suicidal for a prime minister calling an election in the circumstances of a divided government and party, while rebel MPs sitting for safe seats would survive. Yet while it is not an important power in relation to Cabinet and the prime minister's own party, the ability to determine the date of an election undoubtedly strengthens a prime minister's hand against the opposition parties. Prime ministers generally call an election well before the five-year limit to the term of a Parliament (commonly after four years), and can choose a date that suits the government, for example after a popular budget, or following a diplomatic triumph. Even so, it is a weapon that may backfire if a prime minister miscalculates. Edward Heath's decision to call an early General Election in February 1974, and James Callaghan's avoidance of an expected election in autumn 1978, both arguably contributed to their party's electoral defeat.

Normally, the prime minister consults with senior ministers, including the chief whip, before making a decision about an election date and then informing Cabinet of the final choice, but until a dissolution is formally requested, this date can be changed. A dramatic illustration of the prime minister's power to decide the date of the election was provided in 2001. Blair and his party had planned for an election on 3 May, and preparations were already at an advanced stage when the foot-and-mouth disease crisis intervened, and there were calls for postponement from affected areas and from sections of the media. Most of the Cabinet and party were keen to go ahead in May. However, Blair himself became increasingly convinced that a May election would appear insensitive, and on his own initiative decided on a delay until June (Rawnsley 2001: 473–9).

Some argue that the prime minister's power to determine the timing of election gives the governing party an unfair advantage, and also creates a prolonged period of political uncertainty when an election is anticipated but not called. Fixed parliaments involving predetermined election dates (perhaps every four years) would remove the unfair advantage and political uncertainty. However, there would still probably have to be some provision for an emergency earlier election, resulting for example from a government defeat on a motion of confidence in the House of Commons, and a failure to form an alternative government commanding parliamentary support.

National leadership

The prime minister occupies a special role in the life of the country which quite distinguishes the occupant of the office from other Cabinet members – as national leader. This is always the case but becomes especially apparent at times of national crisis such as war – for example, Churchill's role in 1940–5, Thatcher's in the Falklands War (1982), Major's during the Gulf War (1991), Blair's during the Kosovo (1999) Afghanistan (2001) and Iraq (2003) Wars. But the public spotlight also focuses upon the prime minister in important international meetings (such as EU and G8 meetings) and over international or domestic crises (such as the fuel crisis of September 2000, the 2001 foot-and-mouth epidemic, and the London bombings of July 2005). Prime ministers are expected to provide leadership in such circumstances and may be criticised if they fail to do so (as Blair was when he declined to end his holiday early to lead the national response to the disastrous tsunami earthquake at the end of 2004). Ultimately prime ministers are judged by their success in providing effective national leadership by opponents and neutrals as well as friends.

The prime minister's relations with party, Parliament and the media are often closely linked to the authority with which prime ministers are able to carry out their executive and national leadership roles. It is as the leader of the party that has gained a parliamentary majority in a general election that a prime minister gains office in the first place; it is the continuing regular support of that party in Parliament that maintains the prime minister's authority to govern. Relationships with the party, therefore, are of the greatest significance, and these are two-way. The prime minister seeks to maximise control of the party while the party strives for influence over the prime minister. The long-running battle between John Major and the Conservative Euro-dissidents, first over the ratification of the Maastricht Treaty and then over the European single currency, with the prime minister constantly appealing for party unity and the rebels demanding concessions, well illustrates this point.

Faced by recalcitrant backbenchers, the prime minister can appeal to personal ambition (the power of patronage is a potent weapon) and party loyalty (a general desire to do nothing to assist the 'other side'). In general, prime ministers are strongest in their relations with their parties in the months following victory in a General Election or leadership election. Such 'honeymoon' periods may be very brief indeed, as John Major's experience in 1992 showed. His unexpected election victory in April was a personal triumph, but by early November he had become the most unpopular prime minister since records began. Blair, by contrast, remained well ahead in the opinion polls from his election victory in 1997 until the unexpected fuel protests of September 2000, by which time he had enjoyed a 'honeymoon' of over three years.

Prime ministers are at their weakest when government policies seem not to be working and provoke popular hostility and opposition. It was Thatcher's mounting unpopularity as a result of high interest rates, a stagnant economy and the poll tax that led the party to revolt against her in November 1990. The Iraq War, foundation hospitals and tuition fees caused increasing problems for Blair from the Parliamentary Labour Party from 2003 onwards (leading him to contemplate stepping down in the early summer of 2004, according to some sources).

The prime minister's performance in Parliament is always the subject of close scrutiny. Every Wednesday for half an hour the premier appears in the House of Commons to answer 'Prime Minister's Questions'. (This was the result of a change introduced by Blair; formerly it was two 15-minute sessions a week.) 'Question Time' is by far the most common prime ministerial activity in Parliament. Prime ministers can expect to answer about a thousand questions per session, a large proportion of them on economic and foreign affairs. Many of the questions appear as 'supplementaries' which are more difficult to prepare for. Question Time is a testing ordeal, therefore, at which much is at stake, including personal reputation, command of party, and the authority of the government. In particular the verbal duels between the prime minister and the leader of the Opposition can attract considerable media publicity, and may affect the morale of their respective parties.

While Parliament is sitting, premiers may expect to be constantly preoccupied with it in other ways too. Their concerns include the progress of government legislation, set-piece speeches in full-dress parliamentary debates, and more generally the state of party morale. 'Parliamentary business' is always an item on Cabinet agenda. However modern prime ministers only attend the Commons for a specific purpose, and normally only for brief periods. Indeed Blair has sometimes been criticised for devoting little time and attention to Parliament (see Box 11.2).

Contemporary prime ministers need to pay particular attention to the way they and their governments are presented in the media. They inevitably spend much of their lives in public – being interviewed on television, briefing lobby correspondents, making speeches at this or that public function, responding impromptu in the street or airport lounge or on the doorstep to queries about the latest crisis, scandal or leak. If they succeed in presenting a decisive image, they will be given credit for their handling – or, more pejoratively, for their 'manipulation' – of the media. If they are tripped up, or fluff their lines, or in any way give a less than positive impression, not only their own reputation but also that of the

Box 11.2

Prime ministers and Parliament

- Answering questions at Question Time is far more common than any other prime ministerial activity, and often features on main television news. (Blair has substituted one half-hour session a week for two 15-minute sessions.)
- Statements to the House by prime ministers (less common from the Thatcher premiership onwards).
- Speeches have become much rarer – Blair 'led for the government in only three debates' in the first two sessions of the 1997 Parliament (Norton, in Seldon, 2001: 54).
- Interventions in debates in a spontaneous, unscripted way have 'completely withered and died'.
- Voting – Blair's voting record is 'the worst of any modern prime minister – voting in less than one in ten divisions in the first two sessions of the 1997 Parliament' (Norton in Seldon 2001: 54).
- Decline in prime minister's accountability to Parliament – Norton, Hennessy and others have argued that this has become particularly noticeable under Blair, although this seems just an extension of an already marked trend.

Sources: Dunleavy and Jones (1993), Hennessy (2000), Norton, in Seldon (2001), Norton (2005).

government will suffer. In other words, self-presentation through newspapers, radio and television has become another vital prime ministerial concern. Tony Blair has been rarely out of the headlines for long since 1997.

Prime ministers need also to be concerned about their personal standing in the opinion polls. The polling organisations sound public opinion on such matters as the moral qualities (toughness, integrity, truthfulness and compassion), leadership style (dictatorial/consensual) and policy achievements of the prime minister. They compare the premier's political standing with that of his or her main rivals, then often compare these ratings with party support. These relative positions – prime ministers compared with other leaders; party leaders compared with their parties – fluctuate continually during the lifetime of a Parliament.

The Prime Minister's Office

Although the prime minister wields extensive powers, and normally dominates the entire governmental system, he or she does not head a large department, but is directly served by a Prime Minister's Office of around 100 people, of whom around one-third are senior officials and advisers. It was only in 1974 that a Policy Unit was established within the Prime Minister's Office to give the prime minister an independent source of policy advice. John Major's Policy Unit had just eight special advisers, while Tony Blair initially

Box 11.3

Key posts in the Prime Minister's Office (as of August 2005)

Prime minister's chief of staff	Jonathan Powell
Prime minister's deputy chief of staff	Liz Lloyd
Prime minister's principal private secretary	Ivan Rogers
Prime minister's director of communications	David Hill
Director of events, visits and scheduling	Jo Gibbons
Director of political operations (salary paid by Labour Party)	John McTernan
Head of Policy Directorate	David Bennett
Chief adviser on strategy	Matthew Taylor
Director of government relations	Ruth Turner

Box 11.4

The 'kitchen Cabinet'

Most prime ministers have had a purely unofficial 'kitchen Cabinet' of close confidants, a circle of 'friends' to whom they can look for personal support. Some of these may be ministers, while others may hold no official position. However, following the growth of the Prime Minister's Office, many of the most important advisers to the prime minister have had official positions within Number 10. Thus Margaret Thatcher's most trusted aides came from the Prime Minister's Office. They included Charles Powell, a key foreign affairs adviser, Bernard Ingham, her chief press secretary, and – over a much shorter period of time – her parliamentary private secretary, Ian Gow. Tony Blair's close circle of trusted advisers has varied over time but in the early years included Jonathan Powell, Alastair Campbell, David Miliband, head of the Policy Unit, Charlie Falconer and Philip Gould (Hennessy 2000: 493–500). Peter Mandelson's influence seems to have fluctuated, declining after his two resignations, although he was widely reckoned still to have Blair's ear at least until his departure for the European Commission in 2004. Of the other members of the inner circle Falconer and Miliband have been promoted to the Cabinet, while Campbell has resigned as the prime minister's director of communications and strategy.

had 12 (Hennessy 2000: 487). Reflecting the importance New Labour attached to news management, the Blair government also introduced a new Strategic Communications Unit in November 1997 to coordinate press relations of the various departments and ministers, and ensure everyone was 'on message'. This led to some tension between the Labour Party's 'spin doctors' and the permanent civil servants responsible for government information. Further changes were introduced in succeeding years.

Jonathan Powell has remained in the key position of prime minister's chief of staff since 1997. Alastair Campbell was a high-profile prime minister's official spokeperson from 1997 until 2001, when he became director of communications and strategy until his resignation in 2004. Since then David Hill has been a somewhat less colourful director of communications. From 2001 a new Directorate of Government Relations was set up to deal with relations between ministers, departments and the new devolved governments (Holliday, in Dunleavy *et al.* 2002: 94–5).

A Prime Minister's Department?

It used to be argued that the prime minister was at a disadvantage compared to his leading colleagues as he lacked a department of his own, and some critics have urged the need for a larger and more powerful Prime Minister's Department at the centre of British government. However, others claim that the expansion of the Prime Minister's Office, which has continued further under Blair, makes the argument redundant. 'Do we need a Prime Minister's Department? It's largely an academic debate now because we already have one' (source close to Blair, quoted in Hennessy 2000: 485). Holliday (in Dunleavy *et al.* 2002: 94–6) has also emphasised the increased integration and coordination of the Prime Minister's Office and the Cabinet Office under Blair, which he claims 'makes them, in effect, a single executive office' (see below). By contrast, Riddell (in Seldon 2001: 31–2), while acknowledging 'that the changes introduced since June 1997 have significantly changed the scale and scope of the Downing Street operation' inclines to scepticism over a Prime Minister's Department. He points out that 'the Number 10 operation is still small by comparison with the executive offices in presidential systems, such as the United States and Germany, and even in prime ministerial systems such as Australia and Canada'.

The Cabinet

The Cabinet is the country's top executive committee. After the General Election in May 2005 the Labour Cabinet contained 23 members (Box 11.5), 21 from the House of Commons and two from the House of Lords (Lord Falconer and Baroness Amos), both with duties specifically related to the Upper House. Six Cabinet ministers were women, one fewer than before the resignation of Estelle Morris as secretary of state for education and skills in 2002. Even so, this marks a considerable advance on the recent past. Harold Wilson's 1974 Labour Cabinet included only two women. Conservative Cabinets between 1979 and 1990 generally contained just one, the prime minister, Margaret Thatcher. John Major's first Cabinet was all male. However, it may be noted that while Blair's Cabinets have contained a substantially larger female membership, none have yet occupied the most senior and prestigious posts. Status within the Cabinet is not equal, and most Cabinets divide into a small circle of ministers who may expect to be consulted frequently by the prime minister and an outer circle who count for less. The 'plum' jobs are the posts of Chancellor of the Exchequer, foreign secretary and home secretary, which a victorious party's leading few politicians may expect to occupy.

On occasion, and notably in times of war, a small inner Cabinet has been formed, as in the Falklands War, for example. Thus, although the decision to commit the Task Force in 1981 was taken by full Cabinet, Margaret Thatcher formed a small War Cabinet of five to run the war on a day-to-day basis. Blair similarly formed what was effectively a smaller War Cabinet over Kosovo in 1999, although there were regular reports to the full Cabinet (Hennessy 2000: 504–5). Some have called for a smaller Cabinet in peacetime, arguing that a Cabinet of over 20 is too large for the efficient conduct of business. However, political difficulties would arise if a major department and its associated outside interests were not seen to be

Box 11.5

The Labour Cabinet, November 2005

Prime minister, first lord of the Treasury, minister for the civil service	Tony Blair
Deputy prime minister and first secretary of state	John Prescott
Chancellor of the Exchequer	Gordon Brown
Secretary of state for foreign and commonwealth affairs	Jack Straw
Secretary of state for environment, food and rural affairs	Margaret Beckett
Secretary of state for transport (and Scottish secretary)	Alastair Darling
Secretary of state for defence	John Reid
Lord privy seal and leader of the House of Commons	Geoff Hoon
Secretary of state for health	Patricia Hewitt
Secretary of state for culture, media and sport	Tessa Jowell
Parliamentary secretary to the Treasury and chief whip	Hilary Armstrong
Secretary of state for the Home Department	Charles Clarke
Secretary of state for Northern Ireland (and Welsh secretary)	Peter Hain
Minister without portfolio (and Labour Party chair)	Ian McCartney
Leader of the House of Lords and lord president of the Council	Baroness Amos
Secretary of state for constitutional affairs and lord chancellor	Lord Falconer
Secretary of state for international development	Hilary Benn
Secretary of state for trade and industry	Alan Johnson
Secretary of state for education and skills	Ruth Kelly
Secretary of state for work and pensions	John Hutton
Chief secretary to the Treasury	Des Browne
Minister of communities and local government	David Miliband

Also attending Cabinet

Lords chief whip and captain of the Gentlemen at Arms	Lord Grocott
Attorney general	Lord Goldsmith
Minister of state for Europe in the Foreign and Commonwealth Office	Douglas Alexander

Labour Cabinet in session shortly before the 2005 election

Photograph: Reuters.

represented at the 'top table', or if particular areas of the country or sections of the population, or important strands within the party, were excluded.

Cabinet business

Cabinet meetings became more numerous throughout the 20th century up to the 1960s, but declined thereafter, slowly at first but then dramatically under Thatcher to a much lower level, which was continued by Major and Blair. The full Cabinet normally now meets once a week when Parliament is sitting, although in times of crisis it may meet more frequently. Under Blair Cabinet meetings have also noticeably shortened, commonly to an hour or less (Hennessy 2000: 481).

Very few decisions in the modern Cabinet system are actually made by the Cabinet, although virtually all the major policy issues come before it in some form. Its agenda over a period of time consists predominantly of three kinds of matter:

- Routine items such as forthcoming parliamentary business, reports on foreign affairs and major economic decisions, such as the budget and interest rate changes. From the 1980s regular slots have been found for EU matters and home affairs.
- Disagreements referred upwards for Cabinet arbitration, for example from Cabinet committees or from a departmental minister in dispute.
- Important contemporary concerns – a broad range, including national crises such as a war, issues of major controversy such as a large-scale strike and matters of considerable political sensitivity, such as the fuel protests of September 2000.

The Cabinet itself does not make many of the major policy decisions, nor does it generally initiate policy either. In the 1990s, under John Major, more extensive use was made of political Cabinets, where the Cabinet secretariat withdraws and the party chairman joins the meeting (Seldon 1994: 165). Box 11.6 summarises the role of the modern Cabinet.

Box 11.6

The role of the Cabinet

- **Formal approval** of decisions taken elsewhere.
- **Final court of appeal** for disagreements referred from below.
- **Crisis management** of emergencies and issues of major political controversy.
- **Debating forum** and sounding board for leading ministers.
- **Legitimiser** conferring full legitimate authority upon government decisions.
- **Symbol of collective executive** rather than single-person executive in Britain.

Cabinet committees

Because of the sheer volume and complexity of modern governmental business, the bulk of decisions within the Cabinet system are taken by Cabinet committees (either ministerial standing committees or ministerial ad hoc committees). Cabinet committees either take decisions themselves or prepare matters for higher-level decision, possibly at Cabinet. Official committees (of civil servants) shadow ministerial committees and prepare papers for their consideration (Burch and Holliday 1996: 44). Cabinet committee decisions have the status of Cabinet decisions, and normally a matter is referred to full Cabinet only when committees are unable to reach agreement. The prime minister and senior members of the Cabinet chair the most important Cabinet committees. The committee chairman must agree any request to take a dispute to full Cabinet, but in general such appeals are strongly discouraged. Treasury ministers however gained in 1975 the right of automatic appeal to Cabinet if defeated on public spending in committee (James 1992: 69).

The establishment, composition, terms of reference and chairmanship of Cabinet committees are the responsibility of the prime minister. Before 1992 their structure was supposedly a secret, although they did gradually come to light from the 1970s as a result of ministerial memoirs and partial statements by the prime minister. After the 1992 general election John Major decided to make public the entire system of Cabinet standing committees and the subjects they deal with.

Cabinet committees have become central to decision making in the post-war period, even though in recent years their number and frequency of meeting have fallen. Thus, Margaret Thatcher reduced the number of committees, establishing a mere 30–35 standing committees and 120 ad hoc committees in six and a half years between 1979 and 1987. She also reduced the frequency of Cabinet committee meetings, with the result that by 1990 the average annual frequency of meeting was only just over half that registered in the late 1970s. This trend continued under Major, who however tended to use ministerial standing committees more, and ministerial ad hoc committees less, than his predecessor. Under Tony Blair (see Box 11.7), some Cabinet committees reflect key long-standing functions of government (such as defence and overseas policy), while others have been established to meet current political concerns (such as anti-social behaviour, asylum and immigration). However, on some issues Blair has not used regular Cabinet committees, but relied on either ad hoc working groups, or bilateral discussions with relevant departmental ministers. The relative informality of this decision making has aroused some criticism (for instance in the Butler Report, 2004).

Box 11.7

Some important Cabinet committees in Blair's government (May 2005)

- Defence and Overseas Policy (DOP)
- Domestic Affairs (DA)
- Constitutional Affairs (CA)
- National Health Service Reform (CNR)
- Economic Affairs, Productivity and Competitiveness (EAPC)
- Public Services and Expenditure (PSX)
- Public Services Reform (PSR)
- Energy and the Environment (EE)
- Welfare Reform (WR)
- Regulation, Bureaucracy and Risk (RB)
- Anti-Social Behaviour (ASB)
- Asylum and Immigration (AM)
- The Legislative Programme (LP)

The Cabinet Office

The Cabinet Office is another institution at the heart of the core executive which has developed in response to the large growth in the volume of government business. Dating from 1916, its most important component so far as central government is concerned is the Cabinet Secretariat, a group of some 30 senior civil servants on secondment from other departments working under the direction of the Cabinet secretary. Over the years a number of new special offices and units have been brought within it, such as the Office of Public Service Reform (to oversee the implementation of the government's reform programme), the Delivery Unit (to monitor and improve policy delivery) and the Forward Strategy Unit. In addition a number of more specialised units covering policy issues which cut across departmental boundaries have been housed within the Cabinet Office from 1997 onwards. These include the Social Exclusion Unit, the Performance and Innovation Unit, the Women's Unit and the UK Anti-Drugs Coordination Unit.

The doctrine of collective responsibility, which holds that all ministers accept responsibility collectively for decisions made in Cabinet and its committees, is the main convention influencing the operation of the Cabinet. The document *A Code of Conduct and Guidance on Procedure for Ministers* (1997, previously *Questions of Procedure for Ministers*) is the first Cabinet paper a new minister

Definition

Collective responsibility: the convention of Cabinet government requires all ministers to support publicly decisions of Cabinet and its committees, or resign from the government.

is handed. This document declares, 'Decisions reached by the cabinet or ministerial committees are binding on all members of the government', that is, not just on members of the Cabinet. The argument behind the doctrine is that an openly divided government could not work together and could not command the confidence of Parliament or the wider public. Indeed there is considerable evidence that divided parties lose votes.

The doctrine of collective responsibility is clearly of value to the prime minister in the control of Cabinet colleagues. On the other hand, it does lay reciprocal obligations on the prime minister, first, not to leak decisions and, second, to run the government in a collegial way, making sure that ministers have reasonable opportunities to discuss issues. One problem for ministers is that they often play a limited part in making the decisions to which they are required to assent. This latter point has implications not only for the conduct of Cabinet itself but also for the composition of Cabinet committees which – if they are to take authoritative decisions in the name of the Cabinet – must be representative of the Cabinet as a whole (James 1992: 9).

Collective Cabinet responsibility obliges all ministers to support government policy or resign. Although such resignations are relatively uncommon, when they occur they can have serious and sometimes devastating implications for the future of the government and the prime minister in particular, especially if senior figures with a following in the party and Parliament are involved. Thus the resignations of Defence Secretary Michael Heseltine (1986), Chancellor of the Exchequer Nigel Lawson (1989) and finally Deputy Prime Minister Geoffrey Howe (1990) progressively damaged the Conservative government of Margaret Thatcher and substantially contributed to her fall (see Box 11.10). The resignation of Leader of the House Robin Cook in 2003 over the decision to invade Iraq was a serious blow to Blair's government, particularly as Cook had been foreign secretary from 1997 to 2001, and could speak with some authority on the subject. The resignation of more Cabinet ministers would have indicated a significant Cabinet split. However, Clare Short, the international development secretary, who had openly expressed disquiet over Blair's 'recklessness', was persuaded to stay on to assist in the rebuilding of post-war Iraq. She eventually resigned but the delay reduced the impact and limited the damage to the government.

Box 11.8

The practical implications of collective Cabinet responsibility

- **Cabinet solidarity.** Ministers may disagree until a decision is made, but are expected then to support it publicly, or at least not express their lack of support for it. If they feel they must dissent publicly, they are expected to resign; if they fail to resign, it falls to the prime minister to require them to do so. The underlying purpose of this is to create and maintain the authority of the government, which public squabbling between ministers could be expected to damage.
- **Cabinet secrecy.** A precondition of Cabinet solidarity is that Cabinet discussion is secret. Ministers need to feel free to speak their minds secure in the knowledge that their views will not be divulged to the media. Ministers who are known to disagree with a policy may be expected to have little commitment to it: well-publicised disagreements, therefore, have potentially damaging consequences for public confidence in government.
- **Cabinet resignation** if defeated on a Commons vote of confidence. The convention requires that the Cabinet – and therefore the entire government – should resign if defeated on a vote of confidence in the House of Commons. This aspect of the convention still operates unambiguously: when the Labour government elected in October 1974 was defeated on a vote of confidence on 28 March 1979, the prime minister James Callaghan immediately requested a dissolution. However, it rarely happens because the circumstances of a government lacking an overall majority are so infrequent.

There are only two occasions when the principle of collective responsibility has been formally suspended. In 1932 there was an 'agreement to differ' over tariffs among members of the national government. In 1975 members of Wilson's Labour government were allowed to campaign on both sides of the referendum on whether the United Kingdom should remain in the European Community. There have been other occasions when individual ministers have 'sailed close to the wind' in allowing disagreements with government policy to become public: for example Tony Benn in the 1974–9 Labour government, and Clare Short in Blair's Cabinet, before her resignation in 2003. It has also been argued that leaks of confidential information by ministers, including the prime minister, and the publication of diaries by former Cabinet ministers such as Richard Crossman, Barbara Castle and Tony Benn have breached conventions of collective responsibility and secrecy. More recently, biographies of serving Cabinet ministers whose subjects offered some cooperation with the biographer have described differences at the heart of government. Controversial examples include Stephen Pollard's (2004) biography of David Blunkett, which contributed to the problems leading to Blunkett's resignation, and Robert Peston's (2005) book on Gordon Brown, which colourfully illustrated the rift between the prime minister and his chancellor.

Cabinet minutes

Cabinet minutes are the responsibility of the Cabinet Secretariat. Like the minutes of most meetings, they involve a brief record of decisions and conclusions rather than a full account of any preceding discussion. As such they are very important as they are binding on the whole government machine. Controversy has occurred over the extent of prime ministerial involvement in the process, with certain members of Labour Cabinets suggesting that this could be considerable (Castle 1980: 252). But the then prime minister, Harold Wilson, denied it, maintaining at the time (1970) that only 'very, very occasionally' was he consulted about the minutes before issue. Wilson later provided what is now widely accepted as the correct account of routine procedure. 'The writing of the conclusions is the unique responsibility of the Secretary of the Cabinet .... The conclusions are circulated very promptly after Cabinet, and up to that that time no minister, certainly not the prime minister, sees them, asks to see them or conditions them in any way' (cited in King 1985: 40).

Prime ministerial government?

Some commentators have argued that the British system of government has evolved towards prime ministerial government (Crossman 1963; Benn 1980) or even 'presidential' government (Foley 1993, Hennessy 2000) in the post-war period. The premierships of Margaret Thatcher, and more recently Tony Blair, have been seen as validating this thesis. Briefly, these writers argue that a considerable concentration of power in the premiership has occurred, resulting in 'a system of personal rule in the very heart of our parliamentary democracy' (Benn 1980). The prime minister's powers of appointment and dismissal of ministers, control over government business, special responsibilities in key policy areas, command over government information and publicity, and constitutional capacity to request a dissolution of parliament are considered to have elevated the premiership at the expense of the Cabinet.

By making decisions through informal ministerial groups and bilateral meetings with a minister and officials, the prime minister can bypass – and downgrade – Cabinet. The prime minister has a direct relationship with all ministers and expects to be informed about all new policy initiatives, which makes it possible to kill off those he or she dislikes. While if he or she wishes a prime minister can intervene selectively over the entire field of policy making, the cabinet can deal only with the material that is put before it. Recently there have been fewer and shorter meetings of Cabinet and fewer Cabinet papers. Under Blair, meetings have 'rarely lasted more than an hour' (Hennessy 2000: 481). The prime minister's position at the centre of the Cabinet committee system enhances his or her power.

The expansion and increased status of the Prime Minister's Office since the 1970s, especially the formation of the Prime Minister's Policy Unit, has increased the prime minister's capacity 'to oversee government strategy, to monitor departmental work and to initiate policy from the centre'. Contemporary prime ministers are better informed about what is happening across the whole range of government, and there is an increased tendency for business to flow to the Prime Minister's Office and for ministers to consult Number 10 before launching policy initiatives. Some argue that the Prime Minister's Office under Blair is virtually already a Prime Minister's Department of the kind that some centralising reformers have argued for in the past (Hennessy 2000: 485–6).

The impact of British membership of the EU on top decision making has strengthened the prime minister's hand and weakened Cabinet. As the leading British negotiator in EU treaty making, the PM has to be given considerable latitude to make deals in Britain's interests, and when other ministers are involved in European policy making, to assent to any changes in negotiating positions. This point extends beyond Europe to the general enhancement of the prime minister's position by the impact of international summit meetings, such as Group of Eight (G8) meetings.

More intense media focus on the prime minister has increased the need for the prime minister constantly to demonstrate leadership, control of party, a political vision and personal charisma. The premiers' ability to do all these things is vital to the success of their parties (and to their own continuance in office); hence, their emphasis on presentation of their policies and relationships with the media. This accounts for the rise in importance of the prime minister's press officer (such as Bernard Ingham for Mrs Thatcher and Alastair Campbell for Blair) and his or her ability to put a favourable 'spin' or gloss on events. Critics argue that under Blair 'Party campaigning has been transplanted into Whitehall, with many of the same personnel and the same methods' (Scammell in Dunleavy *et al.* 2002: 180–3).

Box 11.9

President Blair? Some quotations

- 'Goodbye, Cabinet Government. Welcome the Blair Presidency.' (Peter Riddell, *The Times*, 1 August 1997)
- 'In Britain's unwritten constitution a Prime Minister is *primus inter pares*, first among equals. Tony Blair recognised no equal in his Cabinet, and only his Chancellor was sufficiently strong to challenge that supremacy. This prime minister planned to be *primus*. From the beginning it was designed to be a presidential premiership.' (Andrew Rawnsley 2001: 50)
- 'Prime Minister Blair is becoming President Blair.' (Jackie Ashley, *New Statesman*, 5 November 2001)

From 'President Blair' to 'lame duck' premier?

Some commentators proposed an extreme version of the prime ministerial power thesis to suggest that Blair was effectively Britain's president.

Yet all prime ministers seem stronger when things are going well, and often they appear more presidential in periods of war or national emergency. Significantly, it was at the end of the Balkans War in 1999 that one 'senior Whitehall figure' observed that Blair 'bestrides the world like a Colossus', while another commented, 'Because of the war, presidential government is more extreme than ever now' (reported in Hennessy 2000: 507). Yet this was a war that had broad public support, was relatively brief and appeared to achieve its objectives successfully (initially at least). By 2001 Peter Riddell, who had proclaimed the 'Blair Presidency' four years earlier, had already changed his mind:

> So far from being a dominant presidential figure, Mr Blair emerges as a more cautious leader – sharing power with his Chancellor on many issues, keen to set a broad strategic direction except when his personal involvement is needed, reluctant to take risks, and frustrated by the difficulty of achieving change.
>
> (Peter Riddell, in Seldon 2001: 37)

Two years on, in 2003, Blair was once more the dominant leader taking his country into another war, against Iraq. However, this time the war did not command all-party and public support but was bitterly controversial. Moreover, although victory appeared swift and decisive, the prolonged insurgency involving continuing graphic images of carnage meant there was no swift exit. Subsequent revelations in the Hutton and Butler enquiries further undermined trust in the prime minister, to the extent that Blair no longer appeared an electoral asset. By the 2005 election campaign he had become dependent on the support of his Chancellor, who became his heir apparent when Blair declared this would be his last election as party leader. Although Blair promised that he would serve a full term if elected, after the slashing of Labour's majority there was increased pressure for him to depart much earlier. Some observers claimed power was visibly ebbing away from a man who had become a 'lame duck' premier.

While objectively the sources of a prime minister's power may remain unchanged, their authority ebbs and flows as perceptions alter over time. Soon after the election Blair's authority appeared fully restored. This followed widespread approval of his role in securing the 2012 Olympics for Britain, his chairmanship of the G8 summit with its commitment to more aid for Africa, and most of all his conduct of affairs in the immediate aftermath of the London bombings in July. Yet in the autumn his leadership again appeared under threat, with Cabinet splits and Labour backbench rebellions over new anti-terrorism measures and further education and health reforms. In November 2005 the damaging second resignation of David Blunkett, a staunch Blair ally only recently brought back into government, appeared to bring the new mood of crisis to a head. Michael Howard (soon to depart himself as Conservative leader) referred to a haemorrhage of authority away from a 'lame duck' prime minister, who was 'in office but not in power' (echoing a jibe against John Major). A week later the government's defeat by 31 votes on an amendment to the Terror bill on which Blair had staked his authority produced the same headline in two national dailies, 'Beginning of the end?' (*The Times*, *Daily Mail*, 10 November 2005). All this demonstrates the vulnerability of political leaders to events. While the odds on Blair's departure sooner rather than later shortened, he still appeared determined to stay.

■ Constraints on prime ministerial government

However, despite the dominance of premiers Thatcher and Blair, it remains inappropriate to describe the British system as 'prime ministerial government'. In practice, prime ministerial power

Box 11.10

Comparative politics: prime ministers and presidents

- The implied comparison in the notion of 'President Blair' is with a US president. The US president is (effectively) directly elected by the American people and combines the role of head of government with head of state. He is the acknowledged head of the armed forces, and the focus of national loyalty.
- Yet as head of government the US president may often have less control of policy than a British prime minister, particularly if he does not have a majority in Congress, which is not uncommon. The main reason that a UK prime minister often appears more powerful is because of the fusion of the executive and legislature in Britain compared with the constitutionally separate executive and legislature in the USA.
- However, the US president is a rather unusual type of president. Many other 'presidents' around the world are formal heads of state, not heads of government, with little political power (for example the presidents of Germany, Italy and Ireland). Most are not subject to direct popular election.
- The French Fifth Republic comes somewhere between the US and German models. It is sometimes characterised as a 'dual executive' because it has both a directly elected president with significant powers, particularly in foreign affairs, and a prime minister (who has to command a majority in the French Assembly) largely responsible for domestic policy.
- Interestingly, the post-1997 Labour government has been compared with the French political system, with Blair as a Fifth Republic-type president dominating foreign affairs, and Brown as a French-model prime minister controlling not only the economy but large areas of domestic policy (Hennessy 2000: 513).

can vary considerably according to the disposition of the individual prime minister to exploit the capacities of the office, and political circumstances such as size of parliamentary majority and simply how 'events' fall out. Constitutional, political, administrative and personal constraints prevent the prime minister from achieving the degree of predominance suggested by the prime ministerial government thesis.

Constitutional constraints

Britain's top decision-making body remains a collective executive, and the prime minister's role therefore is to provide leadership within a Cabinet context in which collective responsibility remains the rule. In the final analysis, the 'mortal wound' to Margaret Thatcher was struck by the Cabinet, which 'rejected her' (Jones 1995: 87).

Political constraints

Appointment and dismissals: constitutionally the prime minister has a free hand in the making of government appointments but politically selection is constrained by the pool of talent within a particular party, by party standing and by the need to please sections of the party. This means in practice that Cabinets often include individuals whom the prime minister would rather be without. Cabinets also generally contain one or two politicians of the highest calibre who are actual or potential rivals for the party leadership. Political considerations also constrain the prime minister's power of dismissal and demotion. Macmillan sacked seven Cabinet ministers and nine ministers outside the Cabinet in July 1962 (the so-called 'Night of the Long Knives'), but the brutality of the sackings caused resentment in the party and gave the appearance of panic to the country. Thatcher's big Cabinet reshuffle of July 1989 which included the demotion of the reluctant Sir Geoffrey Howe from the post of foreign secretary also had very damaging consequences (Young 1990: 555–7). John Major, in an unguarded moment, revealed to an interviewer that he would not sack unfriendly Cabinet colleagues because of adverse political consequences. 'You and I can think of ex-ministers who are causing all sorts of trouble. Do we want three more of the bastards out there?' (Major 1999: 343). While Major had problems with a dwindling majority, even Blair faces significant constraints. Thus although Mowlam (2002) argued that he should remove Brown from the Exchequer because of the alleged 'poison' in their relationship at the centre of government, it was generally considered that this was politically difficult and virtually impossible.

Policy: the prime minister heads an executive whose collective task is to implement the party manifesto, in which inevitably individual ministers play key roles. Often party considerations constrain policy. A good illustration of this is policy towards Europe, which has caused a series of prime ministers from Macmillan to Blair often acute problems of party management. Wilson suspended collective responsibility and held a referendum to avoid splitting Labour, and Major resigned the party leadership in 1995 in an attempt to put to rest incessant Cabinet and party dissension over Europe. While Blair was reportedly keen to push forward entry to the euro sooner rather than later, it was clear that his chancellor wielded an effective veto on a referendum until his five economic tests had been met (see Chapter 15). Thus on a key area of policy Blair has been frustrated.

Tenure: ultimately the party may remove a sitting prime minister, but this is a rare event, having been the fate of just four of the 17 prime ministers in the 20th century. Asquith (1916), Lloyd George (1922), Chamberlain (1940) and Thatcher (1990) all resigned after losing the support of senior colleagues and a sizeable section of the majority parliamentary party (see Box 11.11).

Administrative constraints

The major institutional constraint upon a prime minister is the Cabinet. However great their powers of manipulation, prime ministers have often suffered defeats in Cabinet. Thus Wilson was defeated on trade union reform in 1969, Callaghan on his wish to declare a state of emergency during the 'Winter of Discontent' in 1979 and Thatcher on a number of issues, including the decision to enter the Exchange Rate Mechanism (ERM) in 1990, which was pushed through against her resistance. On crucial issues, prime ministers are usually

Box 11.11

The downfall of Margaret Thatcher

The downfall of Margaret Thatcher in 1990 shows that even a previously dominant prime minister, who had triumphed in three General Elections, can be brought down. The very unusual combination of circumstances that contributed to her downfall included the following:

- The resignation of Deputy Prime Minister Geoffrey Howe, who delivered a particularly wounding resignation speech, and provoked a challenge to Thatcher from a credible alternative leader, Michael Heseltine.
- The earlier resignations of Cabinet heavyweights Heseltine in 1986 and Lawson in 1989, which had highlighted divisions in the government and party.
- Public anger at the 'poll tax' for which Thatcher was generally blamed.
- An economic recession, including a marked fall in house prices after an earlier boom.
- Clear evidence of the unpopularity of the prime minister and the party she led in the disastrous results of parliamentary by-elections and local elections, and in opinion polls.
- A system of electing Conservative leaders then in force which required more than a simple majority of the votes of Conservative MPs* and excluded ordinary party members, among whom she remained popular.

* Thatcher won 204 votes against Heseltine's 152 but was four short of a total which would have given her victory on the first ballot on 20 November 1990. She was then persuaded to withdraw from the second round, for which the party rules allowed new candidates to enter the contest. John Major won with 185 votes (ironically 19 less than Thatcher on the first ballot) with 131 for Heseltine and 56 for Hurd.

careful to bind the whole Cabinet to a decision: on the sending of the Task Force to the Falklands, Thatcher asked every member of the Cabinet individually to indicate a view. John Major, especially in his first two years before acquiring a personal mandate in 1992, was careful to take decisions collectively in order to bind his colleagues to the final outcome.

The prime minister can also be restrained in a number of ways by the departments and the civil service. Government departments are 'the key policy-making institutions in British politics' and the prime minister 'does not play a decisive role in all, or even in most of, the stages of the policy process' (Smith, Marsh and Richards in Rhodes and Dunleavy 1995: 38). Characteristically, in relation to the departments, the prime minister is in 'the position of a bargainer rather than of a leader enjoying a significant power of command' (Burch 1995a: 136). Thus, policy tends to arrive at the prime minister at such a late stage that effective challenge becomes difficult. The prime minister may be able to squash ministerial policy initiatives but would find it hard to impose a policy on a minister.

Personal constraints

Finally, there are personal limits on the power of the prime minister – the limits of any single individual's ability, energy, resources and time, together with the (very considerable) extent to which decisions are shaped by circumstances beyond any individual's ability to control. Moreover, the prime minister's special concerns (foreign affairs, the economy and security) are particularly vulnerable to setbacks that rebound swiftly on the popularity and even credibility of the premier (as Blair found over the Iraq War).

To summarise: the British prime minister has very considerable powers – and these were stretched to the limit by a dynamic prime minister such as Thatcher and more recently by Blair also. But the constraints upon the premier make 'prime ministerial government' an inappropriate description. Is 'Cabinet government' a more apt one? Our earlier discussion suggested that the Cabinet itself neither originates policy nor takes more than a small proportion of major decisions. Most policy decisions in British government are taken in departments. However, the Cabinet retains what may be described as 'a residual and irreducible' authority; it has not sunk into merely 'dignified' status (Madgwick 1991: 259). It remains strong enough to help depose a dominant prime minister, and also to provide a collective shield to protect both a prime minister and his or her leading ministers when they get into political difficulties. The British system of decision making at the top has grown more complex, diffuse and extensive, but arguably it is still a collective executive in which the prime minister provides leadership within a Cabinet system.

■ Prime ministerial power – an irrelevant debate?

Although the argument over whether Britain has Cabinet or prime ministerial or perhaps even presidential government has rumbled on for at least 40 years, some modern academics consider that it is largely irrelevant to the understanding of political and governmental power in modern Britain (see e.g. Smith 1999: ch. 4 and Smith, in Dunleavy *et al.* 2003: 62–5).

- In assuming a bipolar struggle between prime minister and Cabinet the traditional debate oversimplifies the complexity of Britain's core executive, and the role of other players within that core executive, including the Treasury, departmental ministers, senior permanent civil servants, special advisers and Cabinet committees.
- It fails to distinguish sufficiently between the power of Cabinet ministers as heads of departments with real resources at their disposal and interests behind them, and the power of the Cabinet as a collective body.
- It ignores the substantial influence of the Chancellor of the Exchequer in particular over a whole range of policies. Under Brown the Treasury has gone well beyond its traditional negative role in the control of

Table 11.1 Prime ministerial power and constraints on prime ministerial power – a brief summary

Prime ministerial power	Constraints on prime ministerial power
PM's power of patronage - to 'hire and fire'	Political constraints on exercise of patronage
PM's position as majority party leader (normally)	PM faced with powerful rivals in government and potential alternative leaders
PM's position as Chair of Cabinet – heading whole machinery of government	PM can be outvoted in Cabinet
PM's control over civil service	PM has limited power over civil service, which has strong tradition of political neutrality
PM's effective control of Parliament	PM may face revolt in parliamentary party
PM's power to dissolve Parliament and choose election date	PM has limited freedom of manoeuvre in setting election date
PM's power to intervene personally in any area of government	Opportunity cost to PM's intervention in any policy area – cannot intervene everywhere
PM represents country abroad	
PM's standing in country as head of Government and party – enhanced by mass media	PM is not a President – there is a separate head of state

public spending to shape policy in areas such as social security, health, education and international development.

- It focuses too much on the traditional centre of British government in Whitehall and Westminster, ignoring the shift towards multi-level governance, in which the prime minister and Cabinet are only operating at one level.
- In focusing on the power of institutions it underestimates the importance of relationships between key players and the resources they can deploy in bargaining – resources which may shift significantly over time.
- It underestimates the importance of the context in which conflicts within government are fought out. Factors such as the size of a government's majority, the governing party's discipline and cohesion, and the poll standing of the prime minister and leading rivals are not minor incidental features, but crucial to power relationships.
- In focusing on actual and potential conflicts within the British core executive it substantially ignores the far more important external constraints on UK government policy making.

Criticism of the British core executive

Besides the debate over where power lies in practice within the British core executive, there is another argument over where ideally it ought to lie, and over the effectiveness of the executive. Before the advent of the Blair government, some political commentators lamented that a single executive capable of providing policy leadership and coherence had not emerged (Burch 1995: 33). There was 'a hole in the centre of government' (Bogdanor, *Guardian*, 4 June 1997). It was argued that policy remained largely the preserve of the departments, thereby – in default of a corrective mechanism – undermining collective decision making and accountability. One of the most frequent criticisms of the operation of modern Cabinet government was the weakness of coordination and strategic direction at the top. Many reform proposals therefore focused on strengthening the capacity of prime minister and/or Cabinet to provide improved policy-making coordination and better long-term strategic direction. Reformers argue that there is a crying need to overcome the 'short-termism' seemingly endemic in post-war British government, which has had especially damaging consequences in the fields of foreign and economic policy. Some continued to argue for a smaller inner Cabinet charged with the overall coordination and steering of government business, others for a Prime Minister's Department.

Some argued almost the opposite. The problem with the British executive, they maintained, was that it was too powerful and too secretive. Suggested reforms included limiting the premier's political and other patronage, decentralising power, making the executive more accountable to Parliament and public, and making government more open.

In some respects the Blair government seemed to respond, after some fashion, to both these diametrically opposed criticisms. As we have seen, central institutions such as the Prime Minister's Office and the Cabinet Office were overhauled and strengthened, and generally New Labour has placed considerable emphasis on coordination, or 'joined-up government' (see Chapter 12). At the same time the government has ostensibly pursued a policy of decentralisation, through national and regional devolution, modernising local government and devolving power in health and education. Some commentators have talked of a 'hollowed out' state. Thus it is suggested that the prime minister now has 'more control over less' (Rose 2001).

> While a prime minister may be increasingly powerful in the Whitehall world, policy making in the real world has increasingly shifted from that arena ...power has shifted upwards to the international arena, outwards to the private and voluntary sector, and downwards to agencies, quangos and devolved institutions.
>
> (Smith, in Dunleavy *et al.* 2003: 79)

Summary

- The executive in Britain is a parliamentary executive. The prime minister, the head of government, is not directly elected by the people, but his or her authority derives normally from being leader of a party which gains a parliamentary majority in a General Election.

- The key powers of the prime minister include appointments to government and public office, steering and organising government, determining the date of elections, and giving leadership to the nation.
- The prime minister is served directly by the Prime Minister's Office which has grown in size and importance, but is relatively small compared with the staff of many other heads of government.
- The Cabinet is chaired by the prime minister and consists of some 20–23 ministers. Most head major government departments. Most are members of the House of Commons, although a few (normally one or two) may come from the Lords.
- Outside the Cabinet are junior ministers, who mostly sit in the Commons, although a few may sit in Lords. The whole government, including Cabinet and junior ministers, numbers around 100.
- Alongside the Cabinet a complex system of Cabinet committees has grown up. Some of these are chaired by the prime minister, others by senior ministers. Junior ministers as well as Cabinet ministers may be members of Cabinet committees. Many decisions are taken in committees and not referred to Cabinet.
- All members of the government are bound by the principle of collective responsibility. They are expected to support all government policy in public (or at least refrain from public dissent). Any member of the government who wishes to make public his or her disagreement with any item of government policy is required to resign his or her ministerial post.
- Although it is widely alleged that the power of the prime minister has grown at the expense of the Cabinet, there remain important constraints on the exercise of prime ministerial power, which in any case has fluctuated markedly between and also within premierships, according to personalities and circumstances.
- The reduction of British power in the world, globalisation and the growth of multi-level governance have in any case markedly reduced the capacity of the British central executive to control events and deliver policy.

Questions for discussion

- What are the sources of the power of the British prime minister? In what respects might a British prime minister sometimes seem to have more power within his or her country's governmental system than a US president?
- Is there a case for a Prime Minister's Department, and if not, why not?
- Should the prime minister still be able to determine the date of the General Election, or should there be fixed Parliaments?
- Is the British Cabinet too large? Why is it difficult to reduce its size?
- Has the growth of the Cabinet committees involved the bypassing of Cabinet?
- Why is there an apparent need for collective Cabinet responsibility, and what are the implications in practice?
- Has Cabinet government been effectively replaced by prime ministerial government?
- Why might the debate over prime ministerial power be regarded as only marginally relevant to the real issue of power in British government?

Further reading

On the prime minister, the main source is now Peter Hennessy, *The British Prime Minister: The office and its holders since 1945* (2000). Dennis Kavanagh and Peter Riddell provide thoughtful complementary analyses of Blair as prime minister in Anthony Seldon's *The Blair Effect* (2001). Older useful sources include King (1985) and Foley (1993). Brief summaries of the continuing debate on 'prime ministerial government' are provided by Neil McNaughton in *Talking Politics* (2002) and Mark Garnett in *Politics Review* (2005).

On the Cabinet and the central executive generally see Rhodes and Dunleavy, *Prime Minister, Cabinet and the Core Executive* (1995), Burch and Holliday, *The British Cabinet System* (1996), and Smith, *The Core Executive in Britain* (1999). Useful brief discussions of developments since the 2001 election can be found in chapters by Holliday (in Dunleavy *et al.* 2002) and Smith (in Dunleavy *et al.* 2003).

Useful websites include:

10 Downing Street: www.number-10.gov.uk
Cabinet Office: www.cabinet-office.gov.uk
Office of the Deputy Prime Minister:
www.odpm.gov.uk

Ministers, Departments and the Civil Service

In the last chapter the focus was on the central direction and coordination of policy in Britain by the prime minister and Cabinet. However, relatively few government decisions are sufficiently important or controversial to be taken to Cabinet. Most are made in departments. Whenever new government responsibilities are created by legislation, Parliament confers them squarely upon ministers and departments, not on the Cabinet or the prime minister. The political and administrative importance of departments stems directly from their legal-constitutional pre-eminence. How decisions are taken within departments is consequently of vital significance in British government. Are ministers the real decision makers? How far does the real power lie with civil servants, or perhaps special advisers? Thus this chapter continues our examination of the 'core executive' by considering the major departments of state, and the respective roles of the ministers who head them and the permanent civil servants and more temporary advisers who staff them. We explore the radical changes in the civil service introduced by the Conservatives after 1979 and substantially maintained, but with some shifts in emphasis, by Labour. We consider the rise in numbers and importance of special advisers brought by ministers into the heart of government. We look at the implications of these and other developments on the traditional civil service principles of permanence, neutrality and anonymity. We examine issues of accountability and responsibility that have arisen in the relationship between elected politicians, civil servants and special advisers. We conclude with a discussion of the distribution of power and influence within government.

Contents

The organisation of British central government

The central government of the United Kingdom is organised into a number of departments of varying size and importance. Ministries or departments have emerged rather haphazardly over the last few centuries, and particularly over the last century, as the responsibilities of government have expanded. Moreover, ministries or departments have frequently been merged or subdivided in periodic reorganisations, and often renamed in the process.

Is there any coherent rationale behind these departmental reorganisations? Back in 1918 the Haldane Report into the machinery of government reckoned that there were two main principles under which the tasks of government might be grouped: by function or service (education, health, transport and so on) or by client group (children, pensioners, disabled, unemployed). Haldane came down in favour of the functional principle.

There are two other ways in which tasks might be allocated: by area, or by work process (e.g. departments of architecture or accounting).

It should be clear that the actual organisation of British central government does not completely follow any one of these principles entirely. While most departments follow Haldane's service model, there are also others that deal with particular areas of the United Kingdom – Scotland, Wales and Northern Ireland (but see below for the impact of devolution). In addition, ministers (if not departments) have sometimes been appointed for particular client groups. Thus we have had ministers for the disabled, and a minister for women. Organisation by work process has rarely been used explicitly in central government (although it was once common in local government, with departments of engineering, surveying, architecture and so on).

Administrative fashion has sometimes influenced organisational change. In the 1960s and 1970s there was a general presumption in favour of large-scale organisation in both the private and public sectors. 'Big was beautiful' because, it was argued, it could yield economies of scale and lead to better coordination of policy. Thus a number of 'giant departments' were created which merged previously separate ministries, for example the Department of Trade and Industry (DTI), the Department of Health and Social Security (DHSS) and the Department of the Environment (DoE). Subsequently there was a reaction against 'big government', and also against large departments, which were held to produce problems for effective management, and thus diseconomies rather than economies of scale. Thus the DHSS and for a time the DTI were redivided, while a separate Transport Department was hived off from the DoE. After 1988, disaggregation went further with the introduction of executive agencies (see below).

More often, organisational change seems to have reflected political factors rather than administrative theory. Thus the creation of a new department may be intended to signal the importance the government attaches to a particular responsibility. Thus Harold Wilson formed a new Ministry of Technology in 1964, and Tony Blair established

Box 12.1

Departmental reorganisation under the Blair government: transport and the environment

A mixture of administrative, political and personal factors seems to have driven some of the Blair government's departmental reorganisations. This has been particularly evident with transport and the environment.

- Part of the rationale behind the creation of the monster Department of the Environment, Transport and the Regions (DETR) in 1997 was to create an important job for the deputy prime minister, John Prescott, although it also no doubt was intended to show the importance the government attached to these responsibilities.
- Four years later, after the 2001 election, Prescott became head of the Office of the Deputy Prime Minister, based in the Cabinet Office, but retained overall responsibility for regional devolution.
- Prescott's old department was briefly replaced by the Department for Transport, Local Government and the Regions (DTLR).
- The environment was separated from transport, becoming part of a new Department of the Environment, Food and Rural Affairs (DEFRA) in 2001. This new department served a dual purpose. It replaced the old and unpopular Ministry of Agriculture, Fisheries and Food (MAFF), which had been associated with policy failures over BSE (mad cow disease) and the foot-and-mouth disease epidemic of 2001, and had been linked in the past with producer rather than consumer interests (farming rather than food). It also was an attempt to answer criticism that the Blair government was unresponsive to the countryside and rural issues.
- In May 2002, following the resignation of Stephen Byers (see below), Transport became a separate department under Alastair Darling, and the regional and local government responsibilities of the DTLR were transferred to the Office of the Deputy Prime Minister.

a separate Department of International Development in 1997. Occasionally a new department has been created to provided a senior post for a particular politician, such as the deputy leader of the Labour Party, John Prescott, for whom special responsibilities were created in 1997 and again in 2001 (see Box 12.1).

The impact of constitutional reform on the organisation of central government

Labour's constitutional reform programme has had a more fundamental impact on the organisation of UK central government. Devolution to Scotland and Wales inevitably reduced the role and importance of the secretaries of state for Scotland and Wales, and the Scottish and Welsh Office. Most of the staff were transferred to the new Scottish and Welsh executives, while the ministerial posts were effectively downgraded, becoming second jobs for Cabinet ministers whose main responsibilities lie elsewhere. Thus after the 2005 election Peter Hain, the new secretary of state for Northern Ireland, continued as secretary of state for Wales, while Alastair Darling combined the role of Scottish secretary with his main job as secretary of state for Transport. Although the titles remain, the posts of Scottish and Welsh secretaries have become virtually redundant, reduced to a liaison role. In time, the titles too may disappear.

Logically, the post of secretary of state for Northern Ireland should in time go the same way, if devolution there becomes fully and permanently operative. Yet the Northern Ireland assembly and executive have been suspended four times already, with little prospect of their imminent restoration. In these circumstances the Northern Ireland secretary retains extensive administrative responsibilities as well as a major political role in the delicate task of re-engaging the two communities in the now stalled peace process. However, if power is once more transferred to devolved institutions in Northern Ireland, and they acquire stability and legitimacy, there should be progressively less and less for the Northern Ireland secretary to do.

Far more controversial was the Blair government's attempted abolition of the lord chancellor's department, which raised a political storm. The original intention was simply to abolish the post, as part of a package of reforms which included the introduction of a new Supreme Court, and a clearer separation of executive, legislative and judicial powers. Yet although the title of lord chancellor was eventually retained, as an adjunct to the new post of secretary of state for constitutional affairs, the responsibilities of the office are much reduced (see Chapter 10 and particularly Chapter 14).

The internal organisation of government departments: politicians and civil servants

Departments are officially directed and run by politicians drawn mainly from the House of Commons, although a few come from the Lords. Today virtually all the ministers who head departments are of cabinet rank, and most of these now hold the title of secretary of state. Below the secretary of state each department frequently contains at least one minister of state and two or more parliamentary under-secretaries of state. These junior ministerial appointments are the route by which aspiring politicians gain experience of government, and often but not invariably lead in time to promotion to full ministerial rank. The Department for Education and Skills (DfES) – a large department – has a Cabinet minister at its head assisted by three ministers of state and three parliamentary under-secretaries of state. Junior ministers normally assume responsibility for specific tasks: in the DfES, for example, they cover employment and disability rights, further and higher education, school standards, life-long learning and welfare to work.

Ministers are the political and constitutional heads of departments. Departments, however, are largely composed of permanent officials. Below the ministerial 'team' there is a body of civil servants headed by the permanent secretary, the most senior official in the departmental hierarchy. In addition to acting as the minister's top policy adviser, the permanent secretary is in charge of the daily work of the department, is responsible for its staffing and organisation, and is also its accounting officer. Below the permanent secretary, in order of rank, are the deputy secretaries, under-secretaries and three other grades down to principal. Broadly speaking, each department is normally divided up, first into several areas of policy, each the responsibility of a deputy secretary, and then into a number of functional units (or branches), each with an under-secretary in charge. (Figure 12.1 brings together the points made so far about departmental structure in diagrammatic form, while Figure 12.2 provides a specific example).

The civil service, size and distribution

In 2003 total civil service staff (full-time equivalents) numbered just over 512,000 (Cabinet Office figures). Their numbers had declined from 735,000 in 1979 as a result of a deliberate policy carried out by Conservative governments between 1979 and 1997 to prune the bureaucracy. However, these figures somewhat exaggerate the reduction in bureaucracy, as some of these workers continued to be employed elsewhere in the public sector. The civil service only constitutes about 10 per cent of all public sector employees: others are employed in local government, the health service, the armed forces, and a variety of appointed agencies, often called 'quangos'.

Although the civil service is still widely associated with London, and more specifically Whitehall, it is increasingly geographically dispersed. Of the non-industrial civil servants, one-fifth (21 per cent) work in London; just under one-seventh (15 per cent) work in the rest of the south-east whilst the remaining two-thirds work in the provinces. However, it remains true that the majority of the most senior civil servants remain London-based.

Perhaps more significant than geographical decentralisation is the increasing managerial decentralisation of the modern civil service. Most executive (as opposed to policy advice) functions of the civil service are now carried out by executive agencies which have been established under the Next Steps programme (1988) to improve management in government and the delivery of services (see below). By 2002, over 73 per cent of civil servants were working in 93 Next Steps agencies or on Next Steps lines. Each agency is headed by a chief executive, who generally reports to a

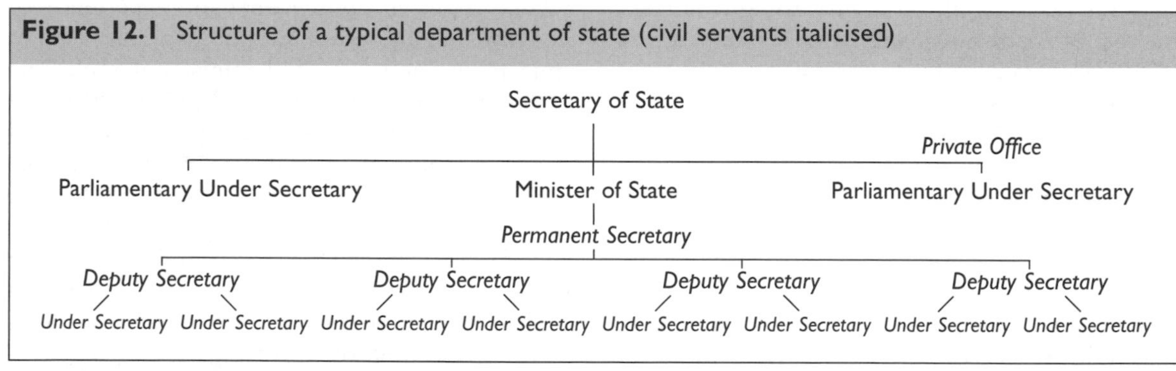
Figure 12.1 Structure of a typical department of state (civil servants italicised)

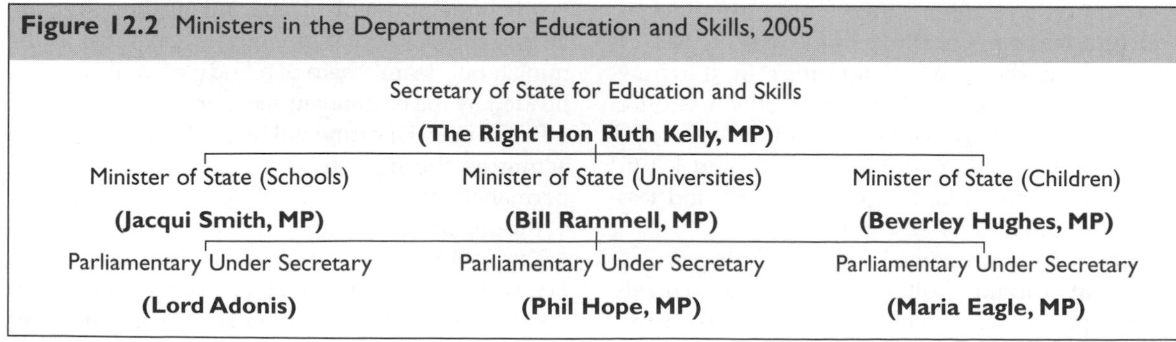
Figure 12.2 Ministers in the Department for Education and Skills, 2005

Definitions

Civil servants are 'Servants of the Crown, other than holders of political or judicial offices, who are employed in a civil capacity and whose remuneration is paid wholly and directly out of moneys voted by Parliament' (Tomlin Commission 1931). The civil service includes all those directly employed by government departments and executive agencies.

Industrial civil servants are those employed as 'blue collar' manual workers in factories and workshops. Their numbers have declined from 53 per cent of the total civil service to just 4 per cent in 2003.

Definition

Executive agencies (often referred to as 'Next Steps' agencies) are organisations with some managerial autonomy within the civil service that are responsible for the management of a specific function or service.

minister. The minister sets the chief executive output, financial and quality of service targets for each year.

However, this chapter is primarily concerned with the senior civil service (SCS) who constitute less than 1 per cent of the entire non-industrial civil service. Members of this group form the administrative elite who, in cooperation with their ministerial superiors and their special advisers, 'run the country'.

Traditional features of the British civil service

British constitutional theory has always made a clear distinction between the *political* role of ministers and the *administrative* role of civil servants. Ministers are in charge of departments and responsible to Parliament for running them, while civil servants advise ministers on policy and implement government decisions. Three features of the civil service have been traditionally linked to this distinction: permanence, political neutrality and anonymity (see Box 12.2).

Although senior civil servants are not allowed to play a formal (party) political role, as key ministerial advisers they have always been heavily involved in the politics of bargaining for influence *within* departments, *between* departments, *with* outside interests and *in their relations with* ministers. Moreover, in recent decades the traditional neutrality and anonymity of the civil service has been significantly eroded (see below and especially Box 12.7).

Box 12.2

Traditional features of the British civil service

- **Permanence.** While ministers are temporarily in post, subject to the patronage of the prime minister and electoral fortunes, civil servants are career officials enjoying security of tenure. Unlike the position in the USA (see Box 12.3), where large numbers of administrative posts change hands when the political complexion of the government changes, in Britain civil servants are expected to serve governments of any party.
- **Political neutrality.** British civil servants are required to be politically impartial, not allowing their own political opinions to influence their actions and loyally carrying out government decisions, whether they agree with them or not. Senior civil servants are not allowed to engage in any open partisan political activity.
- **Anonymity.** Because ministers are constitutionally responsible for policy, and accountable for their departments to Parliament and public, civil servants have traditionally been kept out of the public eye. It was the role of civil servants to offer confidential advice to ministers. It was argued that if civil servants became public figures, this might compromise their neutrality, since they would become associated in the public mind with a particular policy. It might also undermine the frankness of the advice offered to ministers.

Recruitment of the higher civil service: issues of expertise and bias

For much of the 19th century civil servants were recruited by a system of patronage, by *who* they knew rather than *what* they knew, which was hardly likely to promote efficient government. Following the 1854 Northcote-Trevelyan Report, competitive examinations were introduced, with the aim of recruiting the best and brightest graduates into the higher civil service. This aim was substantially achieved. In the 20th century the British higher civil servants generally had outstanding academic records, with first-class degrees from the older and more prestigious universities. However, in the latter part of the 20th century there was increasing criticism of top British civil servants on two main grounds: their lack of relevant skills and expertise, and their narrow and unrepresentative social and educational background.

While there was little doubt that the senior civil servants recruited by the rigorous selection process were in general exceedingly able, critics argued that they usually lacked relevant subject knowledge of the services they were called on to administer, and appropriate managerial skills and training. Nor were these deficiencies systematically addressed through in-service training. Moreover, as most were recruited straight from university, they had little direct experience of the outside world, particularly commerce and industry. The professional and technical expertise of British senior civil servants was compared unfavourably with their French equivalents (see Box 12.3).

The Fulton Report (1968) called for changes in civil service recruitment, promotion and training. Fulton recommended the recruitment of graduates with more relevant degrees, a considerable expansion of late entry in order to enable people from many walks of life to bring in their experience, and the widening of the social and educational base from which top civil servants were recruited. The idea of demanding 'relevance' was rejected, but although expansion of late entry had disappointing results, from the mid-1980s there was a significant programme of two-way temporary secondments between Whitehall and industry, commerce and other institutions (Hennessy

Box 12.3

Comparative politics: public bureaucracies in the USA, France and Britain

USA The US public bureaucracy is highly complex, fragmented, and at higher levels more politicised than the British. The complexity partly reflects the US federal system and division of powers. Thus bureaucracies exist at federal, state and local levels, but there is also a bewildering proliferation of departments, bureaux and agencies, often with overlapping responsibilities. Whereas British higher civil servants are expected to be politically neutral, many senior posts in the USA change hands when control of government changes (the 'spoils system'). American public officials do not generally enjoy the same prestigious status as their British or French equivalents.

France A strong, technocratic and highly prestigious bureaucracy serves the French 'one and indivisible' Republic. While senior British civil servants had the reputation of being able generalists without much specialist background or training, senior French public officials tend to be specialists with technical expertise. However, the French public service is not necessarily a career service on the lines of the British civil service. Although leading bureaucrats are recruited from the elite *Ecole Nationale d'Administration*, whose graduates are referred to as Enarques, some subsequently move into politics, and others transfer into the private sector, and sometimes back into the state service. This more specialist education combined with a greater breadth of experience may help to account for the role of French officials in modernising the economy and implementing prestigious projects.

However, changes in the British system of government (such as devolution, executive agencies and special units) have increased the complexity of the British bureaucracy. Moreover, changes in recruitment (more special advisers, short-term appointments, secondments to and from industry and so on) have reduced the permanence and uniformity of the old higher British civil service.

1990: 523–4). By 1996 there had been a dramatic increase in recruitment from the private sector, with a quarter of the 63 posts advertised in the senior civil service going to private-sector applicants. Secondments outside Whitehall had also increased, with 1500 civil servants on medium to long-term attachments in 1996. The Blair government established a new group headed by the Cabinet secretary and the president of the CBI to oversee the development of shorter, more flexible secondments from the civil service into industry, especially of junior-level civil servants from outside London.

A rather different criticism was that the senior civil service was socially and educationally unrepresentative of the public it served. It was perhaps inevitable that the aim to recruit the best brains would result in an unrepresentative civil service, but a persistent bias in favour of the recruitment of Oxbridge graduates did tend to reinforce the rather exclusive and distinctly atypical social and educational background of senior servants. Broadening the base of recruitment away from Oxbridge-educated arts graduates has occurred very gradually, although canvassing for recruits at 'redbrick' and 'new' universities intensified from 1991. Another concern has been the gender and ethnic bias. Although women make up just over half of the total number of civil servants, they are heavily concentrated at the junior levels, and only a quarter of the senior civil service are female (see Figure 12.3). Similarly, while 6 per cent of civil servants come from ethnic minorities (closely corresponding to their proportion in the economically active population), a significantly lower percentage is employed in the senior civil service (2.4 per cent) or at the senior or higher executive officer level (3.7 per cent).

As should be clear, civil service statistics have been extensively monitored and analysed, and some efforts have been made, with some success, to correct the imbalance in recruitment to, and promotion within, the civil service of women, members of ethnic minorities and those classified as disabled. The civil service is, slowly, becoming more representative of the public it serves. Yet the composition of the highest ranks in a career service almost inevitably reflects patterns of recruitment 20 or 30 years ago from a society which was different in important respects. It will take time

Figure 12.3 Women employed in the civil service by grade, 2002

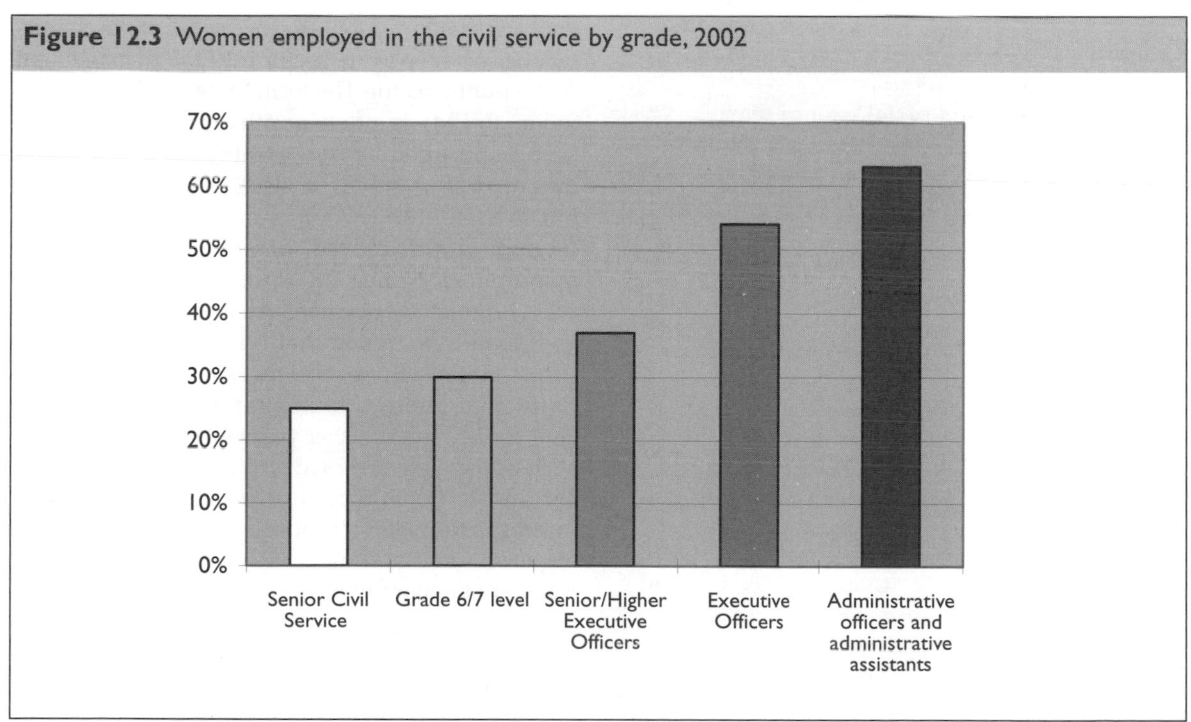

Source: civil service statistics.

before change is perceptible among the permanent secretaries, deputy secretaries and under secretaries who constitute the highest levels within the service.

As senior civil servants advise ministers and influence policy making, it is a matter of some continuing concern that important sectors of the community are under-represented in their ranks. While they may strive to give disinterested and impartial advice, their attitudes will inevitably reflect their own educational and social background, and their ignorance of very different environments. If relatively few top civil servants have had direct experience of state schools or ordinary universities they may be less competent to advise on education. If relatively few have had to juggle the demands of their professional work with the domestic work, child care or care of the elderly and infirm, which remains disproportionately a female responsibility in British society, they will have little direct insight into the problems of working women. If they have never felt at first hand the prejudice and discrimination which is the routine experience of most blacks and Asians, they can scarcely appreciate the attitudes and behaviour of ethnic minority communities and the problems of living in modern multi-cultural Britain.

Box 12.4

Possible forms of bias in the civil service

Party bias? Although some Labour sources have accused senior civil servants of a Conservative bias, past Labour prime ministers and Cabinet ministers have generally testified to the loyal support they have received from the civil service.

Establishment bias? Radical critics have argued that the atypical social and educational background of senior civil servants gives them a bias in favour of establishment (or elite) values and interests. There are continuing concerns over the unrepresentative nature of the higher civil service.

Liberal arts and social science bias? Other critics suggest that the restricted educational background from which most top civil servants are drawn means few have knowledge or understanding of business, science and technology (see also the comparison with the French civil service in Box 12.3).

Consensus bias? Both left-wing socialists and Thatcherite Conservatives have sometimes accused civil servants of a bias in favour of moderate consensus politics, and hostility towards radical policies. Civil servants who may be obliged to serve governments of different parties may prefer continuity to change, and may react negatively to radical proposals from the left or the right.

Bias towards their own interests? New Right thinkers use the assumptions of classical economics to argue that civil servants pursue primarily their own self-interest, and favour policies most likely to preserve and enhance their own pay, conditions and prospects (see also Box 12.14).

From old public administration to new public management?

The civil service has long been regarded as the core of what was described as public administration in Britain, with a distinctive public sector ethos quite different from the practice and principles of the private sector. More recently there have been persistent attempts to introduce some of the characteristics of the private sector into the management of the public sector. The term 'new public management' (NPM) is often applied to the extensive changes inspired by the private sector introduced into managing public services, not only in Britain but in many other countries, particularly in the western world. Indeed, many of the theoretical assumptions behind NPM, and many key initiatives, originated elsewhere, particularly in the USA. In Britain it is argued that NPM has increasingly displaced the values and processes associated with traditional public administration, not just in the civil service but in other parts of the public sector such as local government and the National Health Service (NHS). Although there are differences in interpretation and emphasis across varieties of organisations and services, NPM involves a number of generally recognisable features.

The new approach to managing the public sector has been pursued by both Conservative and Labour governments over the last three decades. Some of the changes are discussed in more detail below.

Box 12.5

Features of the new public management

- A managerial culture that reflects private-sector norms and practices rather than those of traditional public administration.
- The promotion of competition, markets and quasi-markets within the public sector.
- More managerial delegation, decentralisation and organisational disaggregation.
- An emphasis on economy, efficiency and effectiveness (the three 'E's).
- Performance measurement, standards and targets.
- Flexibility of pay and conditions (sometimes including performance-related pay).
- A greater emphasis on customer choice and service quality.
- The contracting out of some service provision to the private sector, with the separation of purchaser and provider (or client and contractor) roles.
- Privatisation of some former public services – with state regulation rather than state control.

The Conservative reforms: a revolution in government

The Conservative reforms between 1979 and 1997 constitute the most radical change in the civil service since the Northcote-Trevelyan reforms of 1854. Reforms initially proceeded piecemeal in line with the manifesto commitment to reduce 'waste, bureaucracy and over-government' but gathered speed after the 1988 Next Steps report which led to the introduction of executive agencies.

Reduction in size

The Conservatives achieved a very large reduction in civil service numbers (735,000 to 494,300) between April 1979 and April 1996, a drop of over 32 per cent. The lower staffing targets were attained by a combination of natural wastage, early retirement, the non-filling of vacant posts, the transfer of civil service functions to appointed public sector boards, and privatisation. Much larger cuts were achieved in the industrial civil service, which fell by 132,000 from 168,000 to 36,000 (80 per cent) in this period, than in the non-industrial civil service, where numbers dropped by 110,000 from 568,000 to 458,000 (19 per cent). Under the Labour government the numbers of the non-industrial civil service have risen slightly (491,000 in 2003), while the industrial civil service has declined further (to 21,000).

Curtailment of privileges

The Thatcher government 'de-privileged' the civil service by setting aside the settlement of pay based on the system of 'fair comparison' and then offering relatively low increases related to 'market forces' and introducing performance-related pay. The government held out successfully against the 21-week strike by civil service unions in support of their pay claim (1981) and abolished the Civil Service Department (1981), which Thatcher regarded as too much the champion of the civil service. Its responsibility for civil service pay, conditions of service and staffing was transferred to the Treasury, and the Cabinet secretary became the official head of the civil service.

Improving efficiency: the Rayner Scrutinies

The quest for greater efficiency and the elimination of 'waste' in government began in 1979 with the establishment in the Cabinet Office of a small Efficiency Unit headed by Sir Derek (later Lord) Rayner, who was then the joint managing director of Marks and Spencer. Rayner initiated a series of scrutinies of departments with the aim of reducing costs and streamlining procedure. The scrutinies led to substantial savings, amounting to £1.5 billion by 1993. Rayner also launched an attack on unnecessary paperwork, which led to the scrapping of 27,000 forms and the redesigning of 41,000 more.

Improving efficiency: the financial management initiative (FMI)

Begun in 1982, the FMI sought to improve financial management in all departments by laying down three principles. Managers at all levels were to have:

- a clear view of their objectives and the means to assess and, wherever possible measure, outputs of performance in relation to those objectives
- well-defined responsibility for making the best use of their resources, including a critical scrutiny of output and value for money
- information (particularly about costs), training and access to expert advice that they need to exercise their responsibilities effectively.

A variety of management information systems were designed to enable ministers to discover 'who does what, why and at what cost?' The overall aim was to transform the civil service culture along business lines, to enhance the role of civil servants as managers of people and resources, and to downgrade their role as policy advisers. The reforms reflected the Thatcherite ethos that the task of the civil service was to manage resources with maximum effectiveness in pursuit of policy goals set by ministers.

Improving efficiency: the 'Next Steps' programme (1988)

This programme originated in a certain disappointment at the slow progress of the FMI and other 'managerial' reforms. The Efficiency Unit, then headed by Sir Robin Ibbs, a former Imperial Chemical Industries (ICI) executive, produced a report focusing on the obstacles to further improvement in civil service management, entitled *Improving Management in Government: The next steps*. It argued that there had been insufficient focus on the delivery of services, even though the vast majority of civil servants (95 per cent) were in service delivery or executive rather than policy advice roles. The report advocated the division of the civil service into a small 'core' engaged in supporting ministers with policy advice within traditional departments, and a wide range of executive agencies responsible for the delivery of services. Departments would set the policy and budgetary objectives and monitor the work of the agencies, but within that framework, each agency, headed by a chief executive, would have considerable managerial independence, with control over the recruitment, grading, organisation and pay of its staff.

By April 1996, huge progress had been made on the Next Steps programme: altogether, with 102 agencies already established in the Home Civil Service, nearly 71 per cent of the civil service (350,000) was working in Next Steps agencies or along Next Steps lines. The Blair government has since maintained and indeed slightly expanded this proportion to over 73 per cent. Some Next Steps agencies – such as the massive Benefits Agency (71,000) – considerably reduce the size of their 'parent' departments. Most executive agencies, however, are small or medium-sized: for example, the Vehicle Inspectorate (1,471), the Royal Mint (997), the Public Record Office (455) and the Teachers' Pensions Agency (370).

It is argued that the new agencies have improved service delivery, increased cost-effectiveness and produced significant savings. Another advantage claimed for the transfer of activities to executive agencies was a reduction in ministerial overload, although critics have argued it has also further weakened ministerial accountability and effective political control, particularly in politically controversial areas such as the Prison Service and the Child Support Agency.

Box 12.6

Example of an executive agency: the Driver and Vehicle Licensing Agency (set up 1990)

- Sets itself clear targets (e.g. to reduce average waiting time for driving tests, and to reduce delays in issuing driving licences).
- Has shown considerable enthusiasm for marketing, e.g. customised number-plates.
- Has cut costs by putting provision of security and cleaning services out to private tender.

Increasing efficiency: market-testing (1991)

During the 1980s, compulsory competitive tendering (CCT) was introduced in local government and the NHS, allowing the private sector to bid for contracts to provide certain services (see Chapter 17) Following a white paper *Competing for Quality* (1991), market testing was extended to the civil service. The first part of a rolling programme of market testing (November 1992) put out nearly £1.5 billion of civil service work to competitive tender, requiring over 44,000 civil servants to compete with outsiders for their jobs. By January 1995 over £1 billion of work had been transferred to the private sector. Privatisation of some agencies had been envisaged by the Ibbs Report from the outset, although only eight small central government organisations were transferred to the private sector between 1992 and 1995.

The Citizen's Charter (1991)

The Citizen's Charter was the 'big idea' of John Major, and essentially consisted of a campaign to raise standards in the public services. It applied to public services generally and included, for example, health and education as well as services delivered by the civil service. Each service was required to publish performance targets and results against set targets, and establish well-publicised and readily available complaints and redress procedures. The aim was to improve standards of service without injecting extra resources. By 1995, nine agencies had published individual charters specifying standards that customers and clients were entitled to expect: for example, the Jobseekers' Charter published by the Employment Service Agency.

Standards in public life

The reform programme from 1980s onwards was primarily about improving the efficiency of government. The probity of government was more often taken for granted. However a series of scandals in the 1990s reawakened concerns over ethical standards among politicians and office holders. Some of the concerns were over the conduct of MPs (see Chapter 13) and several ministers were forced to resign, some for personal or sexual misconduct which had little to do with their government duties, but others in circumstances with wider implications. Beyond these scandals there were also concerns over the rules and principles covering

Box 12.7

The Nolan Report, 1995: the seven principles of public life

- **Selflessness.** Holders of public office should take decisions solely in the public interest. They should not do so in order to gain financial or other material benefits for their family or their friends.
- **Integrity.** Holders of public office should not place themselves under any financial or other obligation to outside individuals or organisations that might influence them in the performance of their official duties.
- **Objectivity.** In carrying out public business, including making public appointments, awarding contracts and recommending individuals for rewards and benefits, holders of public office should make their choices on merit.
- **Accountability.** Holders of public office are accountable for their decisions and actions to the public and must submit themselves to whatever scrutiny is appropriate to their office.
- **Openness.** Holders of public office should be as open as possible about all the decisions and actions that they take. They should give reasons for their decisions and restrict information only when the wider public interest clearly demands.
- **Honesty.** Holders of public office have a duty to declare any private interests relating to their public duties, and to take steps to resolve any conflicts arising in a way that protects the public interest.
- **Leadership.** Holders of public office should promote and support these principles by leadership and example.

those who held public office, whether as ministers or civil servants, and the relations between them. Thus Prime Minister John Major set up the Nolan Committee on Standards in Public Life in October 1994. Nolan's terms of reference were to examine current concerns about standards of conduct in public office-holders and to make recommendations as to any changes required to ensure the highest standards of propriety in public life. His brief covered Parliament (see Chapter 13), ministerial appointments to quangos (see Chapter 18) and central government. Nolan responded (Report, 1995) by laying down the 'seven principles of public life'.

The Nolan Report made a number of more specific recommendations regarding the conduct of ministers and civil servants, which were largely accepted and incorporated into a non-statutory Civil Service Code (1996) and a revised Code of Conduct for Ministers (1997).

Box 12.8

Extracts from *Cabinet Practice: A code of conduct and guidance on procedure for ministers*

This paper (Cabinet Office, July, 1997) lays down guidelines to ministers and civil servants in the operation of Cabinet government. It requires ministers:

- to uphold the practice of collective responsibility
- to account to and be held to account by Parliament for the policies, decisions and actions of their departments and Next Steps agencies
- to give accurate and truthful information to Parliament, correcting any inadvertent error at the earliest possible opportunity; ministers who knowingly mislead Parliament are expected to offer their resignations to the prime minister
- to be as open as possible with Parliament and the public, refusing to provide information only when disclosure would not be in the public interest
- to require civil servants who give evidence before parliamentary committees on their behalf or under their direction to provide accurate, truthful and full information in accordance with the duties set out in the Civil Service Code
- not to use resources for party-political purposes; to uphold the political impartiality of the civil service and not to ask civil servants to act in any way which would conflict with the Civil Service Code ...

The Blair government and the civil service: competition and coordination

Labour policy towards the civil service has largely involved the consolidation and extension of Conservative initiatives, rather than their reversal. Thus the Blair government accepted most of the Conservative reform programme, including the introduction of competition and market values into the management of the public sector, and administrative decentralisation through executive agencies. Yet there has been an important shift in emphasis towards more coordination between departments and agencies, and towards a wider cooperation between the public, private and voluntary sectors in the interests of what Labour has described as 'joined-up government'. 'Departmentalism' is a familiar difficulty of government. Problems and policies are viewed through the often narrow perspectives of individual departments. Yet specific issues (such as drugs, child poverty and care of the elderly) frequently transcend departmental and agency boundaries, and require people from different organisations to work together.

Coordination may sometimes be improved by the reorganisation of government departments, such as the replacement of the former MAFF with the new DEFRA (see Box 12.1). Yet no matter how far functions are reshuffled between different departments, there will always remain a need for cooperation across departments on specific issues (see Box 12.9). Labour has attempted to ease the problem by creating a number of special cross-departmental units (such as the Social Exclusion Unit, the Women's Unit and the UK Anti-Drugs

Box 12.9

The need for departmental and agency coordination: the case of food

Food production was long seen as the almost exclusive responsibility of the old MAFF, with its understandable concern for British farming. Yet the Department of Health clearly had an interest in the safety and quality of food, while farming practices had obvious implications for the environment. Other aspects of food production and marketing raised issues for trade and industry (for instance, the dominance of major supermarkets over food retailing), transport (for example, the long distance carriage of live animals) and international trade and development (such as 'fair trade' in agricultural produce). Each of these departments has its own associated agencies and outside interests to consider. Thus food policy in the fullest sense requires cooperation between a number of government departments and agencies, and extensive consultation with all kinds of groups and interests outside government.

Co-ordination Unit). However, to an extent the new coordinating machinery has increased the sheer complexity, and ironically even the fragmentation, of government. Responsibility and accountability are blurred.

Moreover, there is a continuing tension between the New Labour 'third way' approach to management, emphasising networks, mutual trust and cooperation, and the earlier New Right-inspired emphasis on markets, competition and consumer choice, which Labour has substantially endorsed. Thus schools and hospitals are still encouraged to compete for pupils and patients to promote more efficiency and value for money in the delivery of public service, but urged also to cooperate with their main rivals by sharing information and methods which might reduce their own competitive advantage.

The rise of special advisers

The Blair Labour government, like its Conservative predecessors, is no longer content to rely on the permanent civil service for most of its policy advice. What New Labour requires of the civil service is similar to what the Thatcher government wanted – loyal and effective implementation of government policy. All the emphasis now is on policy delivery. The Labour government prefers to draw its policy advice from party sources, independent think-tanks, and most important of all, its own special advisers, appointed on short-term contracts and brought into the centre of the government machine.

Special advisers are not new. They have been employed alongside the permanent civil service by successive governments. However their number and more particularly their influence have steadily grown. By 2002 there were 81 of these special advisers brought into assist ministers, heavily outnumbered by 3429 senior civil servants, yet by repute hugely influential on key areas of Labour government policy. Among those who have advised the prime minister are Lord Birt, Julian le Grand on health policy and Andrew Adonis on education policy. After the 2005 election Adonis was made a peer and joined the government as an education minister. Ed Balls, a key economic adviser to Gordon Brown as shadow chancellor and chancellor, was elected to the Commons in May 2005. Among the post-1997 Labour government's special advisers were a number with responsibility for government communication, who acquired a high media and public profile as New Labour's spin doctors. (The best known of these have all now left government service: Charlie Whelan, Gordon Brown's former spin doctor; Jo Moore, Stephen Byers' communication adviser; and most famous or notorious of all, the prime minister's former press secretary, Alastair Campbell; see Chapter 9.)

Some of the special advisers who served earlier governments (such as Wilson's) found themselves isolated and effectively neutralised by the permanent civil service. More recently special advisers have become some of the most influential figures at the heart of government, while top civil servants have found their traditional pre-eminence in policy advice considerably eroded. Smith (in Dunleavy *et al.* 2003) observes 'To some extent, top officials have been excluded almost completely from policy making.' Even with the qualifications this is an exaggeration. A permanent secretary's length of experience, and first-hand knowledge of past policy failures and difficulties, remain enormously valuable to his or her minister. Yet the permanent secretary is no longer substantially the voice of the department, and some have felt their role has been significantly diminished.

Some see the growing influence of special advisers as contributing to a decline in the traditional neutrality of a permanent career civil service (see Boxes 12.2 and 12.10). Yet special advisers are here to stay. Indeed, it is not unreasonable for a government to bring in some experts who share their general political philosophy to give advice on policy. In many other countries there is a far larger turnover in officials when the government changes hands (see Box 12.3). However, the rise to prominence of special advisers has caused tension with permanent civil servants in some departments, most spectacularly in the Department of Transport, culminating in the pressures which led to the resignation of two special advisers and then the minister, Stephen Byers, in 2002 (see below). Special advisers have the ear of ministers but are outside the hierarchy of permanent staff, leading to demands for more clarification of their role, particularly over how far they can issue instructions to civil servants. Their status remains unclear.

Box 12.10

The impact of reform on key attributes of the traditional civil service (see Box 12.2)

- **Permanence.** Traditionally, the civil service was a career service, characterised by security of tenure. The permanence of the civil service underpinned its public service ethos and commitment to impartial service of the government of the day. Market testing and some privatisation has eroded the traditional security of the civil service, which has become a political football of competing parties in search of efficiency savings without cuts in public services. The majority of civil servants now work for executive agencies, which have substantial responsibility for recruitment, pay (sometimes involving an element of payment by results) and conditions. Approximately one-quarter of agency chief executives and some top civil service posts were appointed from outside the service, while ministers have appointed more special advisers to provide the policy advice formerly given by senior civil servants. Today, a unified, career civil service with a single hierarchical organisation, and common pay and conditions, no longer exists.
- **Neutrality.** In traditional theory, top civil servants are politically neutral, obliged to give ministers honest and impartial advice. Yet the 1983 Armstrong Memorandum asserted that the civil service has '*no constitutional personality or responsibility separate from the duly elected government of the day*' and stressed that the duty of the civil servant was first and foremost to the ministerial head of department (rather than Parliament or the public). This over-riding duty of responsibility to a (party) government can inevitably create some problems for civil servants' political neutrality. Critics suggest that the civil service has become progressively more politicised under recent governments, Conservative and Labour. Margaret Thatcher enquired of individual senior civil servants, 'Is he one of us?' The Major and Blair governments have both been accused of involving permanent civil servants in the promotion of policies for partisan objectives.
- **Anonymity.** The anonymity of civil servants – an important corollary of ministerial responsibility – has been eroded considerably. As ministerial willingness to assume responsibility for the mistakes of officials has declined, so the practice has grown of naming and blaming individual bureaucrats. Some of the chief executives who head the more controversial Next Steps agencies have attracted considerable media attention and sometimes serious personal criticism. They are also more directly accountable to parliament. After an initial struggle, the Major government agreed to publish replies of agency chief executives to parliamentary questions in Hansard. Civil servants are increasingly summoned for interrogation by departmental select committees. It was following his appearance before the Foreign Affairs Committee, which was investigating the government's use of intelligence in the lead up to the Iraq War, that Dr David Kelly, the weapons expert, committed suicide in July 2003.

Ministerial responsibility revisited

The convention of individual ministerial responsibility governs relations between ministers, civil servants and Parliament. Ministerial responsibility means that ministers are required to inform Parliament about the conduct of their departments, and explain their own and their departments' actions. Individual ministers constantly explain and defend departmental policy before Parliament – at Question Time, during the committee stage of legislation, before select committees and privately to MPs. Ministerial answers to political questions are not always entirely full or satisfactory, and sometimes they are downright evasive. None the less, individual ministerial responsibility in its first meaning of 'answerability' or 'explanatory accountability' still applies.

Ministerial responsibility used to mean that ministers – and ministers alone – are responsible to Parliament for the actions of their departments. However, the delegation of managerial responsibility, a key aspect of executive agencies, clearly implies some reduction of direct ministerial responsibility. Chief executives of agencies have been summoned to appear before parliamentary committees, and their replies to parliamentary questions are published in Hansard. Of course, ministers remain in charge of policy, but the difficulty of dividing responsibility neatly between 'policy' and 'operations' (for which chief executives are responsible) was illustrated in the sacking of Derek Lewis, the director-general of the Prisons Agency, in 1995, following escapes from Parkhurst Prison. Lewis took the blame for failures in the Prisons Service, despite the extent to which policy and operations issues merge, and despite the extent to which intervention by the home secretary, Michael Howard, compromised Lewis's operational independence in practice (Barberis 1996: 19).

In the last resort ministerial responsibility may entail resignation, yet relatively few ministers have felt obliged to 'carry the can' for policy failure. The most celebrated example of such resignations was that of Foreign Secretary Lord Carrington and the whole Foreign Office team of ministers who resigned in 1982 for failure to foresee and prevent the Argentinian invasion of the Falklands, although the defence secretary, John Nott, survived. A more recent case involved the resignation of Estelle Morris as education secretary in October 2002, following a series of embarrassing failures in the service and department over which she presided, culminating in the A level marking scandal, in which thousands of students were given the wrong grade. It is not entirely clear how far the failings here were the fault of the minister or officials, but the minister accepted responsibility. With this doubtful exception, there is no clear case of a minister resigning for mistakes made by officials.

While there has indeed been a stream of forced ministerial resignations in recent decades, most of these have been the outcome of personal rather than policy failings, commonly sexual misconduct or financial impropriety, while some others might be ascribed to political misjudgements and mistakes (see Box 12.11). In a few instances there was a fairly clear breach of the ethical principles governing the holding of public office (and formalised by Lord Nolan in 1995: see Box 12.7). In other cases, resignation followed lurid publicity about a minister's private life and a prolonged media 'feeding frenzy' which made the minister's position untenable.

The principle of individual ministerial responsibility should be distinguished from the convention of collective Cabinet responsibility, requiring all ministers to support government policy in public (discussed in Chapter 11). Yet the distinction is by no means always clear-cut in practice. Thus a policy that was the collective responsibility of the government as a whole might be treated as a matter of individual responsibility to minimise loss of public confidence in the government. Accordingly, an individual minister might feel obliged to accept responsibility for a policy that was really a collective decision. However a matter of individual responsibility is sometimes transformed into a case

> **Definition**
>
> **Individual ministerial responsibility**: the constitutional convention by which each minister is responsible to Parliament for the activities of his or her department and 'carries the can' for failure.

Box 12.11

Examples of ministerial resignations for personal failings and political misjudgments

Leon Brittan, trade and industry secretary, resigned in 1986 after he accepted responsibility for the leaking of a confidential document on the sale of Westland Helicopters, a decision that had led to Michael Heseltine walking out of the Cabinet. (The affair briefly damaged Margaret Thatcher, who some held ultimately responsible for the leak.)

David Mellor, heritage secretary, resigned in 1992 for errors of judgement in personal conduct (an extramarital affair, and a family holiday paid for by the daughter of a senior official of the Palestine Liberation Front).

Jonathan Aitken, chief secretary to the Treasury, resigned in 1995 to fight a libel action against the *Guardian* newspaper that had alleged financial misconduct. The paper was later able to prove its allegations and Aitken was convicted for perjury and sent to prison.

Ron Davies resigned as Welsh secretary after a 'moment of madness' on Wimbledon Common in October 1998.

Peter Mandelson resigned twice, first as trade and industry secretary in December 1998 after his secret £373,000 home loan from fellow minister Geoffrey Robinson was made public, second as Northern Ireland secretary in 2001, following his failure to give a coherent account of his earlier involvement in the fast-track passport application by the Indian businessman, S. P. Hinduja.

Stephen Byers, secretary of state for transport, local government and the regions, eventually resigned in May 2002, following rows within his department. These stemmed initially from his failure to sack his special adviser, Jo Moore, for her notorious email suggesting that the attack on the Twin Towers in New York on 11 September 2001 was a good opportunity to 'bury bad news'.

David Blunkett, like Peter Mandelson, felt obliged to resign twice. In 2004 he resigned as home secretary following lurid publicity over his affair with *Spectator* publisher, Kimberly Quinn, culminating in acrimonious paternity disputes, leading to damning allegations that Blunkett had fast-tracked a visa application for his former partner's nanny. Brought back into government after the 2005 election as secretary for work and pensions, he resigned again in November after revelations that he had failed to consult the independent committee that advises outgoing ministers on business posts he had taken up before the election. Effectively he had failed to observe to the letter all the principles of public life declared by Lord Nolan in 1995 (Box 12.7) and had failed to follow specific recommendations in the revised *Code of Conduct and Guidance for Ministers* (Box 12.8). Blunkett's wounding criticisms of his Cabinet colleagues in a published biography (Pollard 2004) diluted some of the support and sympathy this blind politician who had overcome significant adversity might otherwise have received.

David Blunkett delivering his resignation speech, November 2005

Photograph: EMPICS.

of collective responsibility in order to shield a particular minister whom a prime minister is anxious to retain.

Overall, however, ministers are markedly reluctant to admit responsibility for errors. The arms to Iraq affair investigated in the Scott Report (see Box 12.12) is a particularly glaring example. More recently critics have argued that Blair should accept personal responsibility for misleading Parliament and public over Saddam Hussein's alleged weapons of mass destruction, the ostensible grounds for war with Iraq, when no such weapons were discovered. The Hutton Inquiry (see Chapter 9), however, substantially let the prime minister, and his then director of communications, Alastair Campbell, off the hook. (For a fuller discussion of the Iraq War, see Chapter 26.)

Where does power lie? Decision making within departments

The constitutional position is that ministers make policy and civil servants implement policy. Yet it has often been alleged that senior civil servants in practice have a much larger role in the making of British public policy, and indeed are the real decision makers. Ministers and civil servants, it is argued, have an adversarial relationship in which the latter have distinct advantages in terms of numbers, permanence, information, expertise and time. Ministers are not well prepared for office, lack time to learn on the job because of frequent Cabinet reshuffles, and have too many other parliamentary, party and constituency duties to concentrate fully on running their departments (see Box 12.13).

Critics on the left and the right of the political spectrum provided additional contrasting explanations for civil service power. The radical left (or Marxist) perspective suggested that the civil service was recruited from a restricted elite background, reflected establishment values, and used its expertise and permanency to thwart radical policies. The New Right, by contrast, applied neo-liberal economic assumptions to argue that the civil service had a vested interest in the expansion of the public service and public spending, as this boosted their own empires, pay and prospects. So they used their position to frustrate any attempt to prune government and cut bureaucracy. Thus many Marxists and neo-liberals, who disagreed about almost everything else, agreed that civil servants had too much power and did not serve the wider public interest.

The notion that top civil servants were the real rulers of Britain was popularised by a comedy television series of the 1980s *Yes, Minister* (and subsequently *Yes, Prime Minister*), which portrayed ministers as innocent dupes of their sophisticated and manipulative permanent secretaries. Judging

Box 12.12

The Scott Report (1996): a case study in the refusal to admit responsibility?

Controversy blew up in November 1992 over sales of British arms to Iraq in the late 1980s. The Opposition parties alleged that the government secretly relaxed its own guidelines on the sale of arms to Iraq in 1988, despite the denials of ministers and officials. The incident had come to light accidentally during the prosecution by HM Customs and Excise of three businessmen from the Matrix Churchill company for illegally exporting arms for Iraq. Denying charges of deception, Prime Minister John Major set up an inquiry into the affair under Lord Justice Scott, whose 1806-page, five-volume report was published in February 1996. The report's main findings were that the shift in arms sale policy was deliberately concealed from Parliament, that the criminal prosecution by HM Customs and Excise of the three businessmen was wrong, and that the government had wrongly used its powers to block the release of government information which would have helped their defence.

The report had serious constitutional implications. It revealed that ministers had seriously misled Parliament over government policy, and that they had been assisted by civil servants in doing so. However, the government managed to limit the political damage that might have been expected to follow such a critical report, and won the Commons vote on the report by one vote (320–319). No minister resigned.

Box 12.13

Constraints on the effective power of ministers

- **Numbers.** Ministers are outnumbered by officials: there are roughly six leading civil servants to every minister.
- **Permanence.** Civil servants are permanent while ministers are 'birds of passage' who change jobs frequently. The average tenure of ministerial office since 1945 is just over two years: there were twelve trade and industry secretaries between 1979 and 1997. It takes ministers a lengthy period to master the business of their departments (according to Crossman about 18 months), and during this time they are largely dependent on official briefing.
- **Weak preparation for office.** Few ministers have specialised knowledge of their departments on taking office, and frequent moves do not help them acquire expertise. Ministers rarely come to office with clearly defined policies, priorities or objectives. Unexpected situations which arise during their terms of office further increase their dependence on officials (James 1992: 39).
- **Ministerial workload.** Ministers face multiple demands upon their time – from Cabinet, Parliament, constituency, media and increasingly from the EU in addition to their departments; on average, they spend about two-thirds of their working week on other than departmental matters.
- **Control of information.** Top civil servants control the information going before ministers, the way in which it is presented and its timing, all of which gives them a formidable capacity to shape decisions. They can also influence public opinion by the secret briefing of known opponents of their minister's policy or by 'leaking' to the media.
- **Coordinating role.** Both formally through official committees and through informal contacts with their opposite numbers in other departments, top civil servants prepare and to a varying extent predetermine the work of ministers. Crossman (1975: 616) argued that the system of official committees was 'the key to the control by the Civil Service over the politicians'. Civil servants can also use their contacts with officials in other departments to resist the policies of their own minister.
- **Implementation.** Civil servants can employ a variety of tactics to thwart implementation of policy, including delay and finding practical difficulties.

from the surprising success of sales of the series abroad, the theme evidently struck a receptive chord in many other countries also. Yet ironically the *Yes, Minister* view of the relationship between ministers and civil servants acquired widespread acceptance in Britain at a time when the power and influence of civil servants was already under sustained attack from the Thatcher government (see above).

Indeed reality was always more complicated than the simple adversarial view of the relationship between ministers and civil servants portrayed in *Yes, Minister*. Civil servants, it has been argued, prefer strong ministers who know their own mind rather than weak ministers who can be manipulated. Strong ministers are not only more interesting to work for; they are more likely to be successful in fighting the department's battles in Cabinet and Cabinet committees. Indeed relationships between ministers and top civil servants are commonly more collaborative than competitive. They are often on the same side, battling together against ministers and civil servants from other departments over administrative territory, public spending, policy priorities and legislative time. Moreover, most senior politicians and officials come from a similar social and educational background and share many values, interests and aspirations, and belong to the same relatively small, enclosed Whitehall world (Heclo and Wildavsky 1974).

There is no simple answer to the question: who rules, ministers or top officials? One answer could be both, another might be neither, bearing in mind the constraints of powerful outside interests, and the often intractable problems with which government has to wrestle. Moreover government today

Box 12.14

Academic controversy: the bureaucratic over-supply model

The bureaucratic over-supply model came to the fore in the 1970s and is mainly but not exclusively linked with the New Right critique of government and civil service growth in previous decades. It drew on the analysis of public or rational choice theory advanced by William Niskanen and others. Niskanen applied classical liberal economic assumptions of the pursuit of individual self-interest to the public sector. In the absence of market constraints and the profit motive, public sector bureaucrats would seek to maximise the size of their own 'bureau' or department and its spending, because this would favour their own pay, promotion prospects, conditions of service and status. Such growth would involve the supply of more public services and more public spending and a bloated, inefficient and wasteful bureaucracy (bureaucratic over-supply).

Niskanen's analysis provided some theoretical support for the New Right view in the 1970s and 1980s that the civil service was wedded to the social democratic consensus and believed in interventionist government and big public spending. The Thatcherite right were as suspicious of the civil service as the Bennite left, but for very different reasons. New Right analysis was not just descriptive but prescriptive, and pointed to its own solutions: both the bureaucracy and 'big government' needed 'cutting down to size', through transferring some activities to the private sector and subjecting others to competition. Thus the bureaucratic over-supply model provided much of the theoretical underpinning for the Thatcher government's programme of civil service reform.

One influential study (Dunleavy 1991) has applied public choice assumptions to argue that bureaucrats will engage in bureau shaping rather than bureau maximising. Size (of budgets or staff) does not necessarily matter to senior bureaucrats, who do not always like managing large numbers of (sometimes difficult) junior staff. Indeed, the most prestigious departments are often among the smallest (for example, the Treasury). Cuts in public spending and institutional change have rarely affected senior bureaucrats. While competition and market testing have often adversely affected the pay and conditions of routine manual and clerical workers, it has generally involved increased opportunities and more managerial autonomy for senior officials. In pursuit of their own self-interest, they do not necessarily want or need 'big government'.

is far more complex – no longer consisting substantially of a number of great Whitehall departments, each headed by a minister and a permanent secretary, but involving a mosaic of departments, executive agencies, quangos, cross-cutting units and task forces, and sometimes operating at different levels. The key personnel may include not only elected politicians and career civil servants, but also many other appointed public officials, special advisers, as well as representatives of powerful outside interests who have the ear of ministers. Government is in a constant state of flux, so that the real movers and shakers at any one point may no longer be influential in a few months' time.

Summary

- The bulk of decisions made by central government are made in departments by ministers and civil servants rather than by the Cabinet.
- Most departments are based on the function or service principle, although there is no single coherent rational principle behind the structure of central government. Departments have been frequently reorganised for a mixture of administrative, political and personal reasons.
- Departments are headed by politicians, usually a secretary of state and several junior ministers. They are staffed by civil servants. The most senior civil servants who advise ministers are permanent secretaries and, beneath them deputy secretaries and under secretaries.
- The traditional characteristics of the British civil service include permanence, neutrality and anonymity, although changes over the last 25 years call some of this into question.
- There are around half a million civil servants, geographically dispersed around the United

Kingdom although the majority of senior civil servants continue to work in London. Although women and ethnic minorities are well represented among the civil service as a whole, they are markedly under-represented among the senior civil service, whose social and educational background remains restricted.

- The unrepresentative character of the civil service may influence its outlook. Although it is generally conceded that senior civil servants do not show a party bias, it is sometimes argued they show other forms of bias.
- The civil service has been extensively reformed over the last 25 years, along the lines of the new public management (NPM). This has involved a reduction in size, administrative decentralisation and increased competition. Senior civil servants are expected to concentrate more on the management of departments and agencies, and the delivery of services, rather than advice to ministers.
- Renewed concern over ethical standards, prompted by scandals in the 1990s, led to establishment of a Committee of Standards in Public Life, and the formalisation of principles and codes of practice for ministers and civil servants.
- The Blair government has largely maintained previous Conservative reforms but has emphasised the need for increased coordination and cooperation ('joined-up government') alongside competition.
- The rise in numbers and importance of special advisers to ministers, and the implications for the responsibilities of career civil servants, have raised some concerns.
- There is no easy answer to the question, where does power lie, ministers or civil servants? The relationship is often more collaborative than competitive. Permanent civil servants may have ceded some influence to ministers and special advisers, but government has become more complex, shifting and multi-layered, so generalisations are difficult.

Questions for discussion

- Why are government departments so frequently reorganised in Britain?
- How far is the higher civil service unrepresentative? Does it matter? How might the service be made more representative?
- In what ways, if at all, might senior civil servants show bias?
- How far are senior civil servants in Britain suitably qualified for the work they are required to do?
- In what ways have changes introduced into central government and the civil service over the last 25 years affected the traditional permanence, neutrality and anonymity of senior civil servants?
- How is the principle of individual ministerial responsibility upheld in practice? Who carries the can for policy failure? For what reasons are ministers obliged to resign?
- How far are senior civil servants the real rulers of Britain?

Further reading

For extracts from a wide range of sources, including some key public documents, see *The Whitehall Reader* ed. Barberis (1996). Among broad surveys see Pyper, *The British Civil Service* (1995). On the post-war history, the revised edition of Hennessy's *Whitehall* (1990), and Theakston's *The Civil Service since 1945* (1995) should be consulted. On relations between ministers and civil servants, see Theakston's 'Ministers and civil servants', in Pyper and Robins (1995), and Smith, Marsh and Richards, 'Central government departments and the policy process', in Rhodes and Dunleavy (1995). For analysis of the role and power of senior civil servants see Theakston, *Leadership in Whitehall* (1999).

On civil service reform since 1997 see the White Paper *Modernising Government* (1999) and subsequent Cabinet Office papers. Gavin Drewry in Blackburn and Plant (1999) and in Jowell and Oliver (2000), Andrew Massey in Savage and Atkinson (2001) and Rod Rhodes in Seldon (2001) devote rather more space to discussing New Labour's 'administrative inheritance' and speculating about the future than analysing substantive reforms. There is a very useful brief discussion of the changing relations between ministers and civil servants in Martin Smith's chapter on 'The core executive' in Dunleavy *et al.* (2003: 69–81). Tony Butcher provides a helpful review of 'The civil service under the Blair government' in *Developments in Politics* (2004).

Websites

Home Office: www.homeoffice.gov.uk
Foreign Office: www.fco.gov.uk
Department of Health: www.doh.gov.uk
Department of Education and Skills: www.des.gov.uk
Civil service: www.civil-service.gov.uk

Parliament and the Legislative Process

Contents

We now turn from government to Parliament and from the executive to the legislative process in the British political system. Britain's Parliament at Westminster is very old, dating back to 1265. It began as an English Parliament, adding Welsh, Scottish and Irish representatives with successive Acts of Union, and losing most of its Irish representatives with the establishment of a separate Irish state in 1922. The Houses of Parliament provide a visual symbol of the heart of British government, the very centre of political power. Indeed, the sovereignty of Parliament has long been regarded as the key principle of the British constitution. Yet some argue that despite its age and prestige, Britain's Parliament is no longer very powerful, but is dominated by the executive, which largely controls the legislative process. Critics dispute the effectiveness of the House of Commons, while the indefensible composition of the House of Lords has long rendered it incapable of exercising real power. Moreover, the Westminster Parliament is no longer the only representative assembly elected by British citizens, but is now just one among a number of levels of representative bodies, with considerable implications for its future.

In this chapter we explore the composition and functions of both chambers of the Westminster Parliament. We begin with the House of Commons, by far the most important. We examine how far and in what sense it represents the British people, and how effectively it fulfils its main functions, particularly its role in the legislative process and its scrutiny of the executive. We then turn to the linked issues of the composition and powers of the Upper Chamber within the context of the ongoing reform process. We conclude with a discussion of the future of the Westminster Parliament in a multi-level system of representative bodies.

The functions of the House of Commons

The House of Commons has five main functions:

- representation
- recruitment and maintenance of a government
- scrutiny of the executive
- legislation
- forum for national debate.

Representation

The representative character of the House of Commons underpins its other roles. The House of Commons has long been held to represent the common people of Britain, and this claim was strengthened by the extension of the vote to the whole adult population in the 19th and early 20th centuries. Thus it represents the people of Britain because they have chosen it.

Yet while the House of Commons represents the people it is not typical of the wider population and does not represent them in the sense of being a social microcosm of the nation, MPs still being predominantly white, male, middle-aged and middle class (see Box 13.1). Does this matter? It can be argued that electors want representatives with the skills to perform their roles effectively, and these skills are unequally distributed through the nation. It is thus perhaps no accident that occupations with an emphasis on communication skills (law, education, journalism) are well represented in the House of Commons. On the other hand, a significantly unrepresentative Parliament may lack the range of experience necessary for informed deliberation and legislation. If women are under-represented there is a risk that a woman's perspective will be insufficiently taken into account, not only on what may be traditionally thought of as 'women's issues' (such as equal rights, child care, abortion, violence against women) but on the whole range of economic and social policy. If ethnic minorities and non-Christian faiths are under-represented, the reality of racial and religious discrimination routinely experienced by minorities will not inform debate on these issues. If relatively few MPs have shared the kind of education, housing and employment of most of their constituents, there is almost bound to be some lack of understanding of their problems. Beyond that, some voters seem increasingly disenchanted with, and alienated from, the politicians who supposedly represent them.

While the House of Commons collectively represents the whole people, each individual MP represents a particular geographical area or parliamentary constituency. Groups of MPs also

Box 13.1

Unrepresentative MPs

- Women remain considerably under-represented, despite a significant advance in 1997 when 120 women were elected (compared with 60 in 1992). Since then, 118 women secured election in 2001, and 127 in 2005 (20 per cent of the total). The main reason for the rather higher numbers of women MPs in recent years has been the three successive Labour election victories, as the Labour Party in particular has made efforts to increase the proportion of women candidates. A reversal of party electoral fortunes could see a significant fall in the number of women MPs, unless the Conservative Party in particular chooses more women candidates.
- By the end of 2004 there were 11 openly gay MPs, mostly Labour. The total number of gay MPs is almost certainly considerably higher.
- Ethnic minorities are still under-represented. In 2001 the highest number ever – 12 – of black/Asian MPs was elected, but there were only nine in 2005.
- The middle-aged are over-represented: 70 per cent are aged between 40 and 59.
- MPs are better educated than the average – over two-thirds are graduates. However while 64 per cent of Conservative MPs elected in 2001 had attended an independent (or 'public') school, this was true of only 17 per cent of Labour MPs and 35 per cent of Liberal Democrats.
- Over four-fifths of MPs have a professional or business background. A large number of MPs have a background in education or law, reflecting some convergence in the composition of the main parties, although most Labour professionals come from the public sector – teaching, civil service, local government. However, while 36 per cent of Conservative MPs have a business background, this is true of only 8 per cent of Labour MPs.
- The manual working class is under-represented. Only a small and declining number (51, 12 per cent) of Labour MPs were previously manual workers, and almost none from other parties.

represent sections of the national community, most obviously political parties, but also various other organised interests. These more specific forms of representation are sufficiently important to require more detailed consideration.

The representation of constituencies

The House of Commons consists of 646 MPs, elected by single-member parliamentary constituencies. Candidates for Parliament may stand as representatives of a party, but once elected, each MP is expected to represent the interests of the constituency as a whole and to be at the service of all constituents. Through this constituency role MPs collectively may be said to represent the entire country, which would not be true of their roles as party and group representatives.

Yet if each MP represents a particular constituency, that does not necessarily mean that he or she has to represent the views of its electorate, at least according to an influential theory of representation derived from the 18th-century Whig politician and thinker Edmund Burke. 'Your representative owes you, not his industry only, but his judgement; and he betrays, instead of serving you, if he sacrifices it to your opinion' (speech to his electors at Bristol, 1774). Parliament in this view is 'a deliberative assembly of one nation rather than a congress of ambassadors'. It should lead public opinion rather than simply reflect it. This contrasts with the delegate theory of representation – part of the ideology of radical democracy – in which the elected representatives are considered to be the agents of, and directly accountable to, their constituents.

Most MPs take their constituency responsibilities seriously, and the burden of work can be considerable. MPs' constituency work falls into two main categories. First, there is the local welfare officer/social worker role, dealing with a wide variety of problems (such as housing, health and social security) on behalf of individual constituents. MPs tackle the problems at the appropriate level, conducting a voluminous correspondence with ministers, departments, local authorities and other local offices, and so on. MPs can also raise constituents' grievances through the medium of parliamentary questions and debate, and if all these means fail they can refer cases of alleged public maladministration to the Ombudsman (see Chapter 14).

Second, MPs act as promoters of local interests, working to further the interests of the constituency as a whole. Thus they may try to attract new commercial and industrial investment, to get roads built, to find solutions for local industrial disputes, and to prevent local factories, schools and hospitals closing. In a democratic society, this MP–constituency relationship serves as a barometer of public opinion for representatives and as both safety-valve and potential mechanism of grievance resolution for citizens.

The representation of parties

MPs are elected (almost always) as representatives of a party, and their party underpins their activities once in the House. Table 13.1 shows how party determines the composition of the House of Commons, structuring it decisively into a party of government (Labour) and a party of official opposition (Conservative) flanked by a sizeable third party (Liberal Democrat) and several much smaller opposition parties. However, although MPs clearly represent parties, the distribution of seats does not reflect the distribution of support for parties in General Elections (see Chapter 5.). Nor do parliamentary parties necessarily closely mirror the opinions of the party members who selected them as candidates, although MPs with markedly different views may face criticism and ultimately perhaps deselection (see Chapter 7). Alternatively, MPs who become unhappy with their party may leave it and seek to join another party.

Government is party government. All British governments since 1945 have been recruited from a single party which normally has a clear majority in the House of Commons, and it is that party which supplies a team of leading politicians to fill ministerial posts (Chapter 11). The majority party initially provides a government with a programme based on its election manifesto, which forms the basis of the legislation it puts before the Commons.

Subsequently it is crucial for governments to retain their parliamentary majority by maintaining the support of their parliamentary party (and preferably the party in the country). Discipline and cohesion are almost as important for

Table 13.1 Number of party seats in the Commons after the 1997, 2001 and 2005 elections

Party	1997	2001	2005
Labour	418	412	355
Conservative	165	166	198
Liberal Democrat	46	52	62
Scottish National Party	6	5	6
Plaid Cymru (Welsh Nationalist)	4	4	3
Ulster Unionist	10	6	1
Democratic Unionist Party	2	5	9
Sinn Fein	2	4	5
Social Democratic and Labour Party	3	3	3
Independent and others	2	1	2
Respect	–	–	1
Speaker	1	1	1
Total seats	659	659	646

opposition parties as for the government if they are to have parliamentary and electoral credibility. Thus it is vital for parties to remain united, especially in their formal activities such as voting in Parliament. Open divisions are damaging to a party and encouraging to its rivals. For a government, they may jeopardise the passing of legislation, and for an opposition, destroy any chance to embarrass or defeat the government. The worst eventuality is that a party will split and, as may happen as a result, suffer electoral defeat – as Labour did in 1983 and 1987 after splitting in 1981. Thus each parliamentary party appoints whips to maintain party discipline. However, although there are strong inducements for MPs to maintain party loyalty (see Chapter 7 and Box 13.2), the number and size of rebellions has increased (Cowley, in Dunleavy *et al.* 2002).

Party, then, dominates Parliament, but the reverse is also true. Parliament equally clearly dominates party. Thus virtually all UK parties accept the legitimacy of Parliament, and have as their major aim the winning of seats in the House of Commons. Almost inevitably, the parliamentary party assumes far greater importance than the party in the country. Parliament provides the main arena for the party battle between elections, and this parliamentary conflict, through the media, influences the shifting public support for rival parties.

The representation of interests

MPs not only represent parties, they also, less formally (and sometimes less openly) represent a range of interests. Some of this arises naturally from their past (and sometimes continuing) occupations, their membership of a range of organisations, their personal and family connections and leisure pursuits. It is only to be expected that a former teacher or miner will retain not only an interest in his or her old occupation but also useful experience and expertise to contribute to debates on the subject. Similarly, MPs who are keen church-goers, fox hunters or ramblers have an interest which they will naturally seek to defend and promote where relevant. They may indeed hold a position (honorary or otherwise) in an organisation which gives them an additional obligation to look after its interests. Much of this is relatively uncontroversial, and indeed may enrich the deliberations of Parliament. However, some representations of interests by MPs have raised rather more concern (see Box 13.3).

Box 13.2

Maintaining party cohesion and discipline in the House of Commons

- **Cabinets and Shadow Cabinets.** The Cabinet is normally drawn entirely from one party with a majority in the Commons, and thus provides a collective leadership for the party. The inclusion of ambitious potential rival leaders in the Cabinet renders a dangerous backbench revolt less likely and reinforces party unity. 'Shadow' Cabinets provide collective leadership for the official opposition party. The Conservative Shadow Cabinet is chosen by the leader. When Labour is in opposition its Shadow Cabinet is elected by the Parliamentary Labour Party, although the leader allocates Shadow Cabinet portfolios and appoints additional members of 'Shadow' teams.
- **The Whip system.** Whips play a central role in linking the party leadership with backbenchers. It is the whips who advise leaders on what the party will or will not stand; who offer ideas to leaders on how to head off backbench rebellion; and who indicate to disaffected backbenchers the likely consequences of their actions. The whips try to ensure that backbenchers support party policy in divisions (or votes) of the House of Commons. Party MPs are sent a weekly outline of parliamentary business with items underlined once, twice, or three times, depending on whether an MP's attendance is merely requested (a one-line whip), expected (a two-line whip), or regarded as essential (a three-line whip). Defiance of a three-line whip constitutes a serious breach of party rules. Yet whips are personnel managers rather than disciplinarians. They rely mainly on persuasion (which may sometimes include veiled inducements and hints of honours or promotion). The ultimate sanction against a party rebel – withdrawal of the party whip (that is, expulsion from the parliamentary party) – is rarely used, and can prove counterproductive, as the Major government discovered when the whip was withdrawn from eight Conservatives in 1994, only to be subsequently restored in 1995. (Alderman 1995: 9–10, Ludlam 1996: 118–19.)
- **Party meetings.** Meetings of the parliamentary party provide an important channel of communication between party leaders and backbenchers, allowing the airing of grievances and concerns. The Conservative Party meets weekly in the 1922 Committee when Parliament is sitting. When the party is in government, only backbenchers attend; when it is in opposition, the Committee includes all Conservative MPs except the leader. Its chairman is an important figure, and the '1922' plays a key role in the party, especially in times of controversy and crisis. When in opposition, the Parliamentary Labour Party (PLP) is attended by all Labour MPs including members of the Shadow Cabinet. When the party is in government, Labour ministers attend meetings of the PLP when the work of their departments is under discussion. Communication between the government and its backbenchers is maintained by the Parliamentary Committee, whose members include the leader and deputy leader, the chief whip, four ministers (three from the Commons) and six backbenchers.
- **Specialist party committees.** Each major party also forms a large number of specialist committees, which may enable backbenchers to influence party policy on specific subjects. These purely party committees should not be confused with all-party committees, such as the increasingly important departmental select committees (see below), which may lead to a cross-party consensus which could erode discipline and cohesion within parties.

Since 1975 Parliament has kept an annual register of interests. However, doubts remained about the adequacy of existing public information about MPs' financial interests. Public concern about the apparently declining ethical standards of MPs increased in the 1990s. Newspaper allegations that some MPs were receiving 'cash for questions' were upheld, and two Conservative backbenchers were reprimanded by the Commons, and suspended without pay for 20 and 10 days respectively. Soon afterwards, the Committee on Standards in Public Life, initially under the chairmanship of Lord Nolan, was appointed (see Chapter 12). The recommendations of the Nolan Committee (May 1995) were substantially implemented. The key moves were

Box 13.3

MPs and the representation of interests: some areas of concern

- **Sponsorship of election candidates through a particular party**, such as Labour Party candidates by trade unions. This practice ended in 1995. Unions could not instruct MPs how to speak or vote, as that would have been a breach of parliamentary privilege but they did expect MPs to watch over their interests.
- **Payment of fees to MPs to serve as advisers, consultants or directors**: the Nolan Committee (1995) found that 168 MPs (145 Conservatives, 15 Labour and 6 Liberal Democrats) shared 356 consultancies. (Publicity has led to a reduction in the number of such consultancies.)
- **Access to the Commons as MPs' research assistants and aides**: the use of House of Commons photo-identity passes by organisations as a cover for commercial lobbying activities, in return for services to the MP concerned, first became evident in the late 1980s.
- **Lobbying of MPs by professional consultancy firms**: this kind of lobbying developed into a multi-million pound industry during the 1980s.
- **Financing of all-party parliamentary groups by outside interests** (such as individual businesses, groups of companies, trade associations, lobbying firms and charities).
- **Specialised assistance on an ad hoc unpaid basis**: a wide range of groups provide information and support for MPs' parliamentary activities, such as select committees and private members' bills.
- **MPs' pursuit of outside occupations**: outside interests are represented in the House of Commons through MPs' part-time outside occupations as, for example, journalists, lawyers and company directors.

Box 13.4

Maintaining parliamentary standards: the Hamilton affair

An early task for the first parliamentary commissioner for standards, Sir Gordon Downey, was to investigate charges against Conservative MP Neil Hamilton concerning financial improprieties, including failing to declare receipt of hospitality and failing to register cash payments. Hamilton was defeated in the 1997 election by the independent candidate Martin Bell, running on an 'anti-sleaze' ticket with Labour and Liberal Democrat support. The commissioner, in a 900-page report published after the election in July 1997, found 'compelling' evidence that Hamilton had taken up to £25,000 in cash from Mohammed Al-Fayed, the owner of Harrods, to ask parliamentary questions. The Commons Standards and Privileges Committee accepted this report, criticising Hamilton for standards that 'fell seriously and persistently below' what was expected of an MP. Hamilton has continued to deny the charges. Hamilton and his formidable supportive wife have since become minor celebrities, with frequent appearances on television game shows and chat shows.

the banning of paid advocacy, the adoption of a new Code of Conduct and the appointment of a parliamentary commissioner for standards.

The Nolan restrictions on paid advocacy contributed to a 66 per cent drop in the number of consultancies declared by MPs in the 1997 Register of Members' Interests (from 240 to 80). The 2005 Register shows that some MPs continue to make substantial sums from lucrative second jobs. Former Conservative Leader William Hague topped the list with an annual income in excess of £1 million from directorships, speaking and writing. Some other former ministers and present members of the shadow cabinet derive incomes from directorships and consultancies which exceed their parliamentary salaries (*Guardian*, 22 February 2005). As the interests are transparent they raise fewer ethical issues, although extensive outside occupations inevitably reduce the time and energy devoted to the MP's role, which critics argue should be full time.

Recruitment and maintenance of a government

A key (but often insufficiently emphasised) function of the House of Commons is the recruitment and maintenance of a government. The executive in Britain is a parliamentary executive. Members of the government are drawn from Parliament, and must retain the confidence and support of a majority in the House of Commons. It might be assumed that this would render governments weak, dependent on parliamentary support that might be withdrawn at any time. Yet in practice governments normally dominate Parliament and control its business. It is virtually impossible in normal circumstances (that is, with a government in possession of a working majority) to bring a government down, and in practice it is very difficult to engineer a significant government defeat in the House of Commons. Thus executive dominance of Parliament is the general rule (see Box 13.5).

Although an opposition can make life awkward for a government in a number of ways, they normally lack the numbers to defeat the government on their own. The only time that a government has suffered defeat on a motion of confidence since the Second World War was in March 1979, when Callaghan's government, which had already lost its overall Commons majority, was defeated by one vote on a censure motion. In more normal circumstances when a government enjoys a comfortable majority it can only be defeated if some of its own backbenchers combine with the opposition. Backbench rebellions have increased in size and frequency in recent decades. Conservative rebellions seriously embarrassed John Major's 1992–7 government, whose small initial majority of 21 declined steadily as a result of by-election defeats and removal of the party whip from rebel Conservatives. Blair's government, cushioned by substantial majorities, has been able to survive sizeable Labour rebellions, most notably on Iraq, when the main opposition party supported its policy. His government came closer to defeat over university tuition fees, when Labour rebels combined with Conservatives and Liberal Democrats (Cowley 2005a).

Although in Britain it is taken for granted that ministers are drawn from Parliament, and predominantly from the House of Commons, it is not necessarily the case in other democratic states.

Box 13.5

Reasons for government control of the House of Commons

Government control of the House of Commons rests on four main factors:

- **Possession in normal circumstances of a majority, allied with the habit of loyal voting by its own supporters.** Out of 17 General Elections between 1945 and 2005, in only February 1974 did one party fail to win an overall majority of seats, although in four others (1950, 1964, October 1974, 1992) the governing party only enjoyed a small majority. Far more commonly, governments have enjoyed comfortable majorities, coupled with generally strong party discipline.
- **Power to determine the parliamentary timetable.** Although some Commons business is initiated by opposition parties and backbenchers, three-quarters of Commons time is devoted to the consideration of government business.
- **Ability to curtail debate.** The government can restrict debate by employing the closure and the guillotine. The closure – the request 'that the question be now put', stopping debate if successful – is rarely used now to restrict debate on government business. The guillotine – an 'allocation of time' motion regulating the amount of time to be spent on a bill – is normally used when the government considers that progress on a major piece of legislation is unsatisfactory at committee stage. In recent years, guillotine motions have been used more frequently.
- **Control over the drafting of legislation.** Legislation from initiation to completion is dominated by the Cabinet, Cabinet committees and the departments, and is essentially now a function of the executive (see below).

Indeed, in some countries where there is a stricter separation of executive and legislative powers, government ministers are not even allowed to serve as members of the legislative assembly. Elsewhere it is more common than in Britain for some ministers to be drawn from the worlds of business, finance or academia, without serving as elected representatives.

One consequence of the British system is that the prime minister is effectively limited in choosing ministerial colleagues by the pool of party talent available in Parliament and particularly the House of Commons. Prime ministers have sometimes sought to recruit ministers from outside Parliament, but such ministers have been obliged by convention to obtain a seat in the Commons (through a parliamentary by-election) or in the House of Lords. However, such appointments have been few, and not always successful. Businessmen and trade unionists without prior experience of Parliament have often found it difficult or frustrating to cope with parliamentary conventions and procedures.

Thus anyone seeking high office in government must normally first seek election to the House of Commons, and gain recognition there. Election to, and successful performance in, the House of Commons are the main criteria for political advancement, and promotion into government in the British political system (see Box 13.6). It is in the Commons that ambitious politicians attempt first to make, and then as ministers sustain, their reputations. Yet the skills of parliamentary debate are widely acknowledged to be no real preparation for running a department, nor are the two kinds of ability invariably present in the same person. Outstanding parliamentary orators do not necessarily make good ministers. Conversely it is possible, indeed likely, that some potentially outstanding ministers are not discovered though the British system of recruiting and training for government office.

Box 13.6

Parliament, the gateway to political power

The importance of prior entry to the House of Commons for an ambitious aspiring politician can be simply illustrated. In 1983 a young married couple both sought to become prospective Labour candidates at the forthcoming General Election, and agreed to support the political career of whoever was first successful. Both had qualified as barristers, although the wife was considered the more outstanding, and had the additional advantage of coming from a strong Labour family. However, it was the husband who, finally and rather unexpectedly, landed the nomination for a safe Labour seat at Sedgefield, and was duly elected as the (then) youngest member of the Parliamentary Labour Party. He rapidly made his mark in the much depleted Labour ranks, and was promoted to its front bench in 1984. By 1994 his reputation had risen sufficiently for him to become leader of the Labour Party, and prime minister in 1997. The story is now only too well known, but the point is that without his prior selection for a winnable Labour seat, Tony Blair would never have been able to pursue a significant political career, let alone become prime minister. If Cherie Booth had won the race for a seat, Blair would perhaps now be playing the loyal supporting role to his wife's political career.

Scrutiny of the executive

Governments are accountable to Parliament, and through Parliament to the people. Thus it is in Parliament that the government must explain and defend its actions. Major opportunities for scrutinising and influencing the government through the procedures of the House of Commons are Parliamentary Questions, general, adjournment and emergency debates, early day motions, select committees, and correspondence with ministers.

Parliamentary Questions remain the most celebrated means for calling the prime minister and ministers to account for their conduct of government. Questions for written answer enjoy less publicity, but can be a useful means of extracting information from government. Not all questions for oral answer can be dealt with in the time allotted, and ministers together with their civil servants have plenty of time to prepare answers to the pre-submitted questions, although ministers can sometimes be embarrassed by unexpected supplementary questions. Overall, the effectiveness of Question Time as a means of providing effective scrutiny of the executive is

Table 13.2 Main methods of Commons' scrutiny of the executive

Procedure	Function
Questions	◆ Backbenchers may submit oral and written questions to ministers ◆ Written questions and replies are recorded in *Hansard* ◆ Ministers reply to oral questions daily, Monday to Thursday, 2.35–3.30 pm ◆ Prime Minister's Question Time 12.00–12.30 pm Wednesday (NB: MPs may ask one (unscripted) supplementary question.)
Debates	◆ General – on Queen's Speech, no-confidence motions (rare) and motions tabled by government and opposition ◆ Adjournment debates – opportunity to raise general or constituency issues ◆ Private members' motions – 11 days per session allocated to these ◆ Emergency debates – can be demanded but rarely conceded by Speaker
Early day motions	◆ Proposing and signing early day motions enables MPs to express their views – gains publicity, but no debate follows
Select committees	◆ Able to scrutinise executive away from the floor of the Commons ◆ Powers to send for 'persons, papers and records'; can interrogate ministers ◆ Includes 16 departmental select committees and others (e.g. Public Accounts, Public Administration, European Legislation, Statutory Instruments, Standards and Privileges, Modernisation of the House of Commons) ◆ Party balance on select committees reflects that of the House as a whole (Unanimity difficult – may divide on party lines)
Letters to ministers	◆ Main way in which MPs pursue cases and issues raised by constituents

rather diminished by party point-scoring – particularly in Prime Minister's Question Time.

Further opportunities for backbenchers to raise issues are provided through general debates initiated by government and opposition, private members' motions and adjournment debates, and through the largely symbolic device of signing early day motions. However, more effective scrutiny is provided not so much by the Commons as a whole but by select committees.

An old and important select committee is the Public Accounts Committee (PAC), which has a central role in the Commons' scrutiny of government expenditure. Control of finance was once considered a crucial function of the Commons, but today, in so far as the Commons has any effective influence over government finance, it is largely through the PAC. It is composed of 15 members, and chaired by a senior member of the Opposition. It is particularly concerned to ensure the taxpayer gets value for money from public spending. Since 1983 it has been powerfully assisted by the National Audit Office, an independent body directed by the comptroller and auditor-general (CAG), with a staff of 900, which produces around fifty Value for Money reports every year. Reports of both the PAC and the National Audit Office are often extremely critical of government departments. However, PAC reports are rarely debated by the House, and when they are, they are poorly attended and receive little public attention.

Parliamentary reformers from the 1960s advocated the greater use of departmental select committees (DSCs) to improve scrutiny of the executive. A new system of select committees to provide regular scrutiny of the work of every government department was implemented in 1979. The task of these new DSCs was 'to examine the expenditure, administration and policy in the principal government departments … and associated bodies' and to make reports with recommendations. In conducting their investigations, they can send for 'persons, papers and records'.

In Focus 13.1

Prime Minister's Questions (October 2005)

The House of Commons chamber is usually full for Prime Minister's Questions. The regular exchanges between the prime minister and leader of the Opposition can be diverting, and often feature on the main television news, so are thus familiar to viewers. Whoever is perceived to be the victor may boost their party's morale. However, they have also been unflatteringly compared to a Punch and Judy show, with little relevance to the real substance of politics.

Photograph: EMPICS.

DSCs undoubtedly constitute a marked improvement on the Commons machinery to scrutinise the executive available before 1979. However, critics point out that, despite the frequent excellence of their reports and the occasional publicity achieved by their investigative sessions, they lack real clout. Thus, their occasional effectiveness is offset by their more frequent lack of impact. They are the product of 'an executive-dominated system and lack the resources or prestige to sustain the kind of inquisitorial role that US congressional committees have long enjoyed' (*Guardian*, 22 March 1995). (Some of the advantages and limitations of DSCs are listed in Table 13.3.)

Legislation

Law making is ostensibly the most important function of Parliament, which is after all a legislature. Law passed by Parliament remains supreme over other forms of British law, such as common law, even it has to accept EU law. Yet although Parliament devotes much of its time to considering legislation, it may be questioned whether Parliament effectively makes the law. Westminster legislation today is substantially an executive function. Government dominates the legislative process from start to finish. Although ordinary backbench MPs retain some limited opportunities to initiate legislation, they normally have little chance of converting their draft bills into law (see below). Most of the time devoted by Parliament to the scrutiny of legislation is spent on government bills, and it is almost entirely government bills that are ultimately successful in passing through all their stages to become Acts. Parliament's effective influence on the principles and even the details of government legislation is usually limited. Although significant amendment, and very occasionally even defeat, of a government bill remains a possibility, the government's (generally disciplined) party majority ensures that its legislation normally emerges from its passage through Parliament more or less in the form intended.

Parliament, it may be said, *legitimates* rather than *legislates.* Although it is government rather than Parliament that substantially makes law, Parliament's assent remains vital to the establishment of the *legitimacy* of that legislation. Thus the formal parliamentary stages of legislation remain important. (They are outlined in Table 13.4.) Yet they do not tell us very much about how law is really made in Britain. Where do the ideas for new laws come from? Who decides that legislation is necessary? Which interests influence the shape and content of legislation, and how? Is the formal completion of the parliamentary stages with the royal assent really the end of the process? How are Acts implemented and adjudicated upon? How far are they successful in fulfilling the intentions of the

Table 13.3 Benefits and limitations of departmental select committees

Positive benefits	Limitations
◆ Powers to send for 'persons, papers and records' improve scrutiny and accountability of executive. ◆ Coverage of proceedings aids open government. ◆ DSCs may have a pre-emptive or deterrent effect - deterring ministers and civil servants from behaviour that they might be unable to justify before the committee. ◆ Committee investigation and reports may ultimately persuade the government to change course. ◆ Committee membership helps develop specialisation and expertise – and committees can seek outside advice and assistance.	◆ Party whips' influence on membership of DSCs. compromises their independence and effectiveness. ◆ Many members of DSCs lack the necessary motivation, knowledge and skills. ◆ Most DSCs lack the staff and budgets for substantial independent research. ◆ Limited powers: ministers normally attend when requested, but are not obliged to answer questions. Civil servants may withhold information in the interests of 'good government' or national security. ◆ Lack of influence: few DSC reports are debated on the floor of the House of Commons, and ministers can (and generally do) ignore them.

Definitions of parliamentary legislation

Bill: a draft Act of Parliament. It remains a bill until it has passed all its stages.

Act: an Act of Parliament (also known as a statute) is a bill that has passed though all its stages and received the royal assent.

Public bill/Act: a bill or Act that affects the whole country. It may be introduced by the government (government bill) or an ordinary backbencher or 'private member' (private member's bill).

Private bill/Act: a bill or Act that affects only part of the country or community. (A local authority for example may seek to acquire special powers in its area through a private Act.)

Delegated legislation (sometimes referred to as secondary or subordinate legislation. The technical name is **Statutory Instruments**). Many Acts are outline in form, giving authority to ministers or to other public bodies to make necessary orders or regulations under the authority of the parent Act. Thousands of Statutory Instruments are published every year.

legislators? To answer such questions it is important to go beyond the formal parliamentary stages of legislation, to consider the crucial early formative pre-parliamentary stages of the legislative process, the extra-parliamentary influences on the formal parliamentary stages, and the all-important process of implementation, adjudication and review.

The initiation of legislation

Where does the legislative process really start? Normally, not in Parliament. The initial idea may come from a variety of sources, perhaps from a government department or an official report such as a royal commission, or possibly from a party manifesto or a pressure group or media campaign. Whatever the initial inspiration, the idea for legislation will not normally get far unless it wins government favour and eventually receives the backing of the Cabinet, and finds a place in the government's legislative programme.

Before a government decides to legislate it will consult widely across departments and other relevant public bodies, and often extensively with outside interests (see Chapter 8). This process of consultation not only provides the government with more information and expert opinion, it may also be crucial in winning the argument in Parliament and the country. If the government is able to claim it has consulted widely with affected interests and secured their support, this reduces the scope for effective opposition. In some cases the government seeks not just the acquiescence of key interests but their active cooperation. (For example, any

Table 13.4 The formal parliamentary stages of legislation

Stage	**Where taken**	**Comments**
First reading	Floor of House of Commons (unless introduced in Lords first)	Purely formal – no debate
Second reading	Floor of House of Commons	Debate on principles – very unusual for a government bill to be defeated at this stage
Committee stage	Normally in standing committee, on which government normally has majority. Some bills may be taken in committee of the whole House.	Considered in detail, clause by clause – amendments can be made, but normally only those introduced by ministers have much chance of success. Can take weeks.
Report stage	Floor of House of Commons	Report on amended bill – further amendments can be made
Third reading	Floor of House of Commons	Debate (often short) on final text and approval of bill – generally a formality
House of Lords	Bill passes through similar stages in Lords (unless introduced first in Lords). Committee stage normally taken on floor of Lords not in standing committee.	Lords may amend bill (some further amendments may be introduced by government). If bill is amended it returns to the Commons for further consideration.
Consideration of Lords amendments	Floor of House of Commons	Lords amendments may be accepted, if not the Lords usually gives way. Otherwise, the bill can be reintroduced and passed next session without the Lords assent under the Parliament Act.
Royal Assent		Purely formal (last refused by Queen Anne). Bill then becomes an Act (or Statute).

reform of the National Health Service is likely to depend on the willing support of the medical professions for successful implementation.)

Thus only after much initial consultation will the department principally concerned begin the process of drafting a bill using the services of expert parliamentary law drafters, Parliamentary counsel. Drafts are circulated to other interested departments, and consultation with outside interests will continue. It may take a year or two before the government feels ready to introduce a bill in Parliament. Thus often much activity will have taken place before Parliament gets the opportunity to consider a government bill. Debates on the Queen's Speech may provide some opportunity to comment on proposals to legislate, but unless Parliament is given the opportunity to discuss a green or white paper (see definitions), the first time Parliament has any real opportunity to debate a bill is at the second reading, as the first reading is purely formal.

Definitions

A **green paper** is a consultative document, implying the government has not finally made up its mind.

A **white paper** normally involves a firmer statement of government intention. (However, sometimes ministers may observe that a particular white paper 'has green edges', indicating a readiness to listen to arguments and make changes.)

Parliamentary scrutiny of government legislation

Bills can be first introduced into either the Commons or the Lords, although more controversial measures are normally introduced in the Commons. The first reading of a bill is purely formal, with no debate. A dummy copy of the bill is placed on the Speaker's table, and a date announced for the second reading. Only after the first reading is the bill printed and circulated. (Note, however, that draft bills are now sometimes published for Parliament's consideration.) The second reading normally involves a full debate on the principle of the bill, which can be defeated then, but this would be a most unusual fate for a government bill. If it passes its second reading the bill proceeds to the committee stage, normally taken by a standing committee, although a committee of the whole house may consider very important bills with constitutional implications, or at the other extreme, relatively simple and non-controversial bills. It is also now possible for bills to be referred to a select committee, or a special standing committee, enabling a more rigorous examination of the evidence and contributions from outside witnesses, although these procedures remain uncommon (Norton 2005: 86–7, 255).

During the committee stage the bill is considered in detail, line by line and clause by clause, and amendments may be proposed, either by the government, seeking to tidy up and improve the bill, or by government or opposition party MPs. The process of consultation with outside interests will continue throughout the committee stage. Friendly committee members may sometimes be prepared to introduce amendments drafted by such outside groups. If the governing party has a substantial majority in the Commons as a whole, it will have a commensurate majority on all committees. Thus most of the amendments passed by the committee will be the government's own amendments, although it may accept amendments proposed by its own backbenchers, and occasionally even an opposition amendment. This process may help improve the legislation, closing loopholes, removing obstacles to successful implementation, and perhaps securing the goodwill of important interests whose full cooperation may be crucial to ensure that the Act achieves its intentions.

After the committee stage comes the report stage, when the amended bill is reported back to the House of Commons as a whole. Further amendments may be considered here, before the House proceeds immediately to a debate on the third reading. If the bill passes its third reading, it proceeds to the House of Lords (assuming the bill was initiated in the Commons) and follows similar stages there, with further opportunities for consultation and amendment. After a bill has passed all its stages in both Houses it goes to the monarch for the royal assent (last refused in the reign of Queen Anne, three centuries ago). It then becomes an Act, and the law of the land.

This looks like a very thorough scrutiny, yet it is not always as effective as it appears. Governments normally seek to push through a large and complex legislative programme as quickly as possible without significant concessions. Thus MPs on the government side in standing committees often appear to have taken a vow of silence. By contrast, opposition MPs are only too voluble, speaking at length to numerous amendments – some essentially 'wrecking amendments' undermining the whole principle of the bill, to delay proceedings as long as possible. This may go on until the government loses patience and 'guillotines' debate through a timetabling measure. Often this can mean that important parts of a bill are never scrutinised in committee, although sometimes the omission is remedied in the Lords (see below). Yet governments normally get their way.

Implementation of legislation

While the royal assent may seem to mark the end of the legislative process, a new Act often requires extensive subsequent delegated legislation if it is to be successfully implemented. Thus the Act may confer on ministers or other public bodies the authority to lay detailed regulations and orders having the force of law before Parliament. Thousands of such Statutory Instruments are published annually. They are no longer regarded as a sinister threat to the power and sovereignty of Parliament, but as an essential adjunct to modern governance, allowing regulations to be amended with changing circumstances, and permitting useful experiments. Often they will involve further consultation with affected interests. For

Figure 13.1 Principal stages in the legislative process for government bills

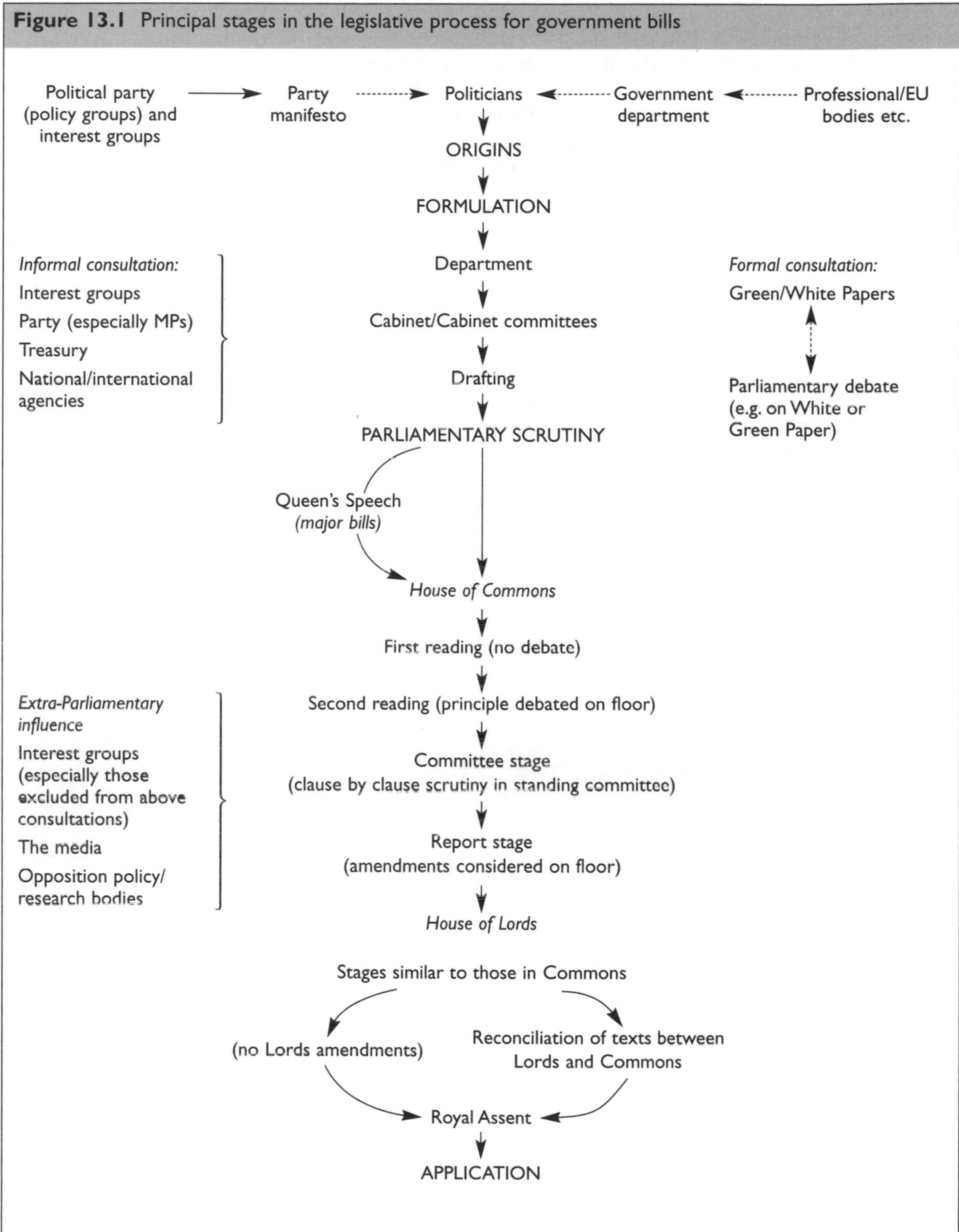

Source: Adapted from tables in Drewry, 1988: 124–5, and Adonis, 1993: 93.

example, a change in the list of dangerous substances that cannot be sold over the counter might involve discussions with chemists, doctors and the police.

With or without the addition of delegated legislation, Acts still have to be implemented. Often implementation is not the responsibility of the central government but of other agencies, such as local authorities, which may proceed slowly and reluctantly, arising from their own opposition to a particular measure. Alternatively, they may complain they have been given statutory responsibilities without adequate resources. Or there may be political problems in the way of implementation. Thus some Acts are not fully implemented, and a few have never been implemented at all. On other Acts there may be considerable discretion given over methods of implementation. Problems with implementing law may be reported to Parliament, but Parliament has no formal responsibility for overseeing implementation.

Finally, Acts are open to interpretation and adjudication in courts of law. Although judges must accept an Act of Parliament, they may sometimes interpret it very narrowly and restrictively. In such judicial interpretation only the wording of the Act will be taken into account, not the pronouncements of governments or speeches in Parliament.

Thus, the legislative process in Britain is largely executive-dominated from start to finish. Parliament has a negligible role in the origination and formulation of legislation (with the exception of private members' bills – see below), and no role in implementation beyond its generally inadequate scrutiny of delegated legislation. On the parliamentary stages of legislation, government backbenchers generally have more influence than the opposition, for the simple reason that the opposition cannot normally threaten the government's majority, while dissent in its own ranks can. Thus governments may be prepared to make some concessions to critics on its own side. Beyond that, governments can expect to carry most of their legislative proposals substantially unchanged. 'Once bills have been introduced by government, they are almost certain to be passed' (Norton 2005: 102).

Private members' legislation

The only partial exceptions to executive control of the legislative process are private members' bills.

Box 13.7

Comparative politics: the legislative role of the UK Parliament and the US Congress

The US Congress is a legislature in the full meaning of the term. It makes laws. 'All legislative powers herein granted shall be vested in a Congress of the United States' (US Constitution). Both houses of Congress, the House of Representatives and the Senate, play an important role in the legislative process, and both have to agree before legislation can go forward for presidential approval. If the president declines to approve laws passed by Congress, this veto can be overridden by a two-thirds majority of both houses of Congress. Although the president can propose laws, these may be substantially modified or rejected by Congress, which is quite often controlled by a different party from that of the president, as they are elected separately and for different terms. The system is one of 'checks and balances', deriving from the separation of powers in the US constitution.

By contrast, the executive dominates the legislative process in the UK Parliament. Virtually all government bills are passed, while most bills introduced by ordinary MPs fail, and can normally only succeed if the government does not oppose them. The subordinate role of the British Parliament stems from the fusion of executive and legislative powers in the Westminster system, compared with the separation of powers in the US constitution. Thus, the British Parliament is controlled by the government by means of its (usually) disciplined majority in the House of Commons. The British Parliament, like most in western Europe, is essentially a reactive, policy-influencing assembly that may modify or even (very exceptionally) reject government legislative proposals, but has negligible opportunities to initiate legislation. Unlike the US Congress, it is not a legislature in the full meaning of the term.

These are bills introduced by MPs who are not members of the government, including backbench members of the governing party and members of opposition parties. They can be introduced under various procedures, but the only method that normally stands any chance of success is through the annual ballot under which up to 20 backbenchers secure the right to introduce bills on a number of Friday sittings set aside for private members' measures. They then go through the same stages as government bills. Yet there are a number of practical limitations on private members' bills (see Box 13.8).

Thus only a very small proportion of private members' legislation reach the statute book. Even so, some Acts introduced by private members have been important, transformed lives and changed attitudes. Thus private members' legislation changed the law on capital punishment, homosexuality, divorce and abortion in the 1960s, outlawed video 'nasties', compelled front-seat passengers to wear seat belts, restricted advertising on cigarettes in the 1980s and banned cruelty to wild animals in the mid-1990s. Such controversial social issues with a strong moral dimension often cut across normal party lines, so both government and opposition parties find it more convenient to leave such potentially difficult questions to a free vote.

Box 13.8

Limitations on private members' bills

- They are not supposed to entail the expenditure of public money (which requires a money resolution).
- Lack of time is the crucial constraint. Ordinary backbenchers effectively lack the procedural devices used by the government to curtail debate, and thus most bills run out of time. Normally, only the first half dozen or so of the 20 bills introduced have a chance of passing all their stages and becoming law.
- Bills are unlikely to make progress if the government is opposed, because the government with its majority can use the whip system to destroy a bill. (In practice, some 'private members' bills' may be government measures in disguise, with the government offering its own facilities and benevolent support for a backbencher sponsoring a bill which the government favours but has no time for in its own legislative programme.)
- Even if the government is not opposed, a bill which arouses strong animosities among a minority of MPs may often be effectively blocked. It may be 'talked out' by opponents 'filibustering', and thus run out of time, or 'counted out' because too few MPs can be persuaded to attend on Fridays (in the absence of pressure from party whips).

Forum for national debate

In addition to the functions outlined above, the Commons is also reckoned to provide a forum for national debate. On occasions the Commons has appeared to rise above party conflict to change the course of history. A celebrated instance was when the Conservative Leo Amery famously called out to Labour's Arthur Greenwood 'Speak for England, Arthur' in the 1940 Norway debate which was to bring down Neville Chamberlain and make Churchill head of a coalition government. On this occasion a debate in Parliament had momentous consequences, which decisively transformed the conduct of the war and perhaps materially changed the course of history. Yet critics suggest that such occasions are very much the exception. More commonly, debates take the form of relatively narrow, almost ritualistic combat between rival teams of party gladiators urged on by compact stage armies of supporters. Thus the proceedings in Parliament often seem to amount to little more than episodes in a continual election campaign, rather than offering a more open and wide-ranging forum of national debate.

Indeed, Parliament is not always even given the opportunity to debate issues of national importance. Parliament is not in session for substantial periods of the year, including some three months in the summer. While events may lead to demands for a recall of Parliament, this is rarely conceded. Even when Parliament is in session it is not easy to organise an extensive debate on some unanticipated development. Much of the parliamentary timetable is determined well in advance. While emergency debates may be demanded, they are rarely conceded by the Speaker. Explicit parliamentary approval is not required for some of the most momentous decisions that a government can take. The British prime minister has inherited most of the old prerogative powers of the Crown, and does not need express parliamentary sanction for such crucial and potentially far-reaching acts as signing treaties and even declaring war (see Chapter 11). As Hennessy (2000: 89) has observed, 'here, the royal prerogative is all. Unless primary legislation is required, Parliament does not have to be routinely involved at all.'

In practice, a wise prime minister will normally try to involve Parliament as much as possible over national crises and war. Churchill during his wartime premiership treated the Commons with 'high respect', addressing numerous 'secret sessions' which gave MPs 'a sense of being privy to special knowledge' (Jenkins 2001: 622). Eden, by contrast, failed to carry Parliament with him over Suez in 1956, refused a request for the recall of Parliament from the leader of the Opposition (Hennessy 2000: 245), and (it is now clear) lied to the House of Commons on the crucial issue of foreknowledge of Israeli plans. Mrs Thatcher wisely agreed to an exceptional Commons debate on a Saturday over the Falklands crisis, and this perhaps helped her to maintain a level of bipartisan support for the subsequent task force. Blair, often criticised for his neglect of Parliament, took the precaution of seeking explicit parliamentary sanction for military operations against Iraq in 1998 (Hennessy 2000: 503). After some apparent initial reluctance, he also agreed to an emergency recall of Parliament in September 2002, and addressed the House of Commons in a debate on the Iraq crisis. There were major Commons debates on the eve of war on 26 February and 18 March 2003, when Blair secured a parliamentary majority despite the opposition of 139 Labour rebels. According to one impressed witness, Anthony Sampson (2005: 18) 'The House had surprised itself with the seriousness and impact of its speeches; it could still assert itself as the cornerstone of democracy, connecting up the opinions of ordinary people with its government.'

However, Parliament does not always provide an effective forum for national debate. Even if Parliament is generally given the opportunity to debate issues of national importance, it no longer appears to be at the centre of national debate. The proceedings of Parliament are now much less reported, even in the quality press. Although the Commons reluctantly let in the television cameras after a long delay, and it is now possible for members of the public to follow parliamentary proceedings on minority channels, the main BBC and commercial news and current affairs programmes devote only cursory treatment to Parliament. Indeed, much of the real national debate now seems to take place through the media.

Reform of the House of Commons

While the House of Commons in theory is the centre of democracy in Britain, it has often seemed to operate more as a private club determined to keep the public at arms' length. When the television cameras were finally allowed in, and the public could hear and see their representatives, they were unimpressed by MPs' behaviour and the quality of debate in an often near-empty chamber. The House remains cramped and ill equipped, and its procedures antiquated. Thus while town halls have long used push-button voting, votes in the Commons are decided first by acclamation (shouting) and then by queuing in the division lobbies to be counted manually by tellers, a process which can take 20 minutes or more. For long periods, particularly over the summer, the House does not meet, and until 2003 its daily timetable began at 2.30 pm and continued without an official break until 10.30 pm, and sometimes on into all night sittings. Although some of its more meaningless mumbo-jumbo has been simplified, quaint language and rituals continue to bewilder outsiders.

Reform of the Commons has been long debated, and indeed some important reforms have been carried through in recent decades. Thus departmental select committees were introduced in the 1980s, and so was a Standards Committee to provide more effective safeguards against corruption and 'sleaze' (both described above). Improved office and secretarial facilities have been provided to help MPs to work more effectively. Recent reforms have focused on the Commons timetable and methods of working. The Blair government was committed by its election manifesto to a reform of Prime Minister's Questions and the appointment of a Commons select committee to review its own procedures.

Blair swiftly changed Prime Minister's Question Time from a twice-a-week quarter of an hour event on Tuesdays and Thursdays to one taking place once a week for half an hour on Wednesdays. The aim of the reform was ostensibly to move away from the traditional mutual slanging match towards more considered and constructive exchanges between the prime minister and leader of the Opposition, although it has not been noticeably effective in this respect. The confrontations between Blair and successive leaders of the Opposition remained markedly adversarial. Some critics considered the reduction in the number of sessions weakened the prime minister's accountability to Parliament (even though the time devoted to them remained the same), and Blair has been more generally criticised for devoting 'less time to parliamentary activity than his predecessors' (Norton, in Seldon 2001: 54). Partly in answer to such criticisms, Blair inaugurated in 2002 regular prime ministerial appearances before the Liaison Committee of the House of Commons, mainly composed of chairs of select committees. This has proved a more successful innovation.

The promised Select Committee on the Modernisation of the House of Commons was appointed in 1997, and proceeded to recommend, in a series of reports, a number of proposed reforms, mostly to be tried initially on an experimental basis. Some of these have been implemented. Thus Westminster Hall has been utilised as a 'parallel chamber' for debates not involving votes, enabling more MPs to participate in Commons debates. Some changes in the scrutiny of legislation were introduced, for example, enabling the scrutiny of legislation to be carried over between parliamentary sessions, and improvements were made to the scrutiny of European business (Cowley, in Dunleavy *et al.* 2002; Norton, in Seldon 2001).

When the reform-minded Robin Cook became leader of the House after the 2001 election, there was some further impetus for change. In October 2002 the Commons finally voted for a revised parliamentary day, starting in the morning and finishing in the early evening, and for a shorter summer recess. These changes were expected to make the House more amenable to the increased number of women MPs as well as some of their more family-minded male colleagues. However, many opposed the new timetable on both sides of the House, and in 2005 a fresh vote led to a compromise which seems unlikely to satisfy either side.

Philip Norton (in Seldon 2001: 48) observed that the Blair reforms 'appeared limited and failed to change significantly the relationship between the legislature and the executive'. He concluded that Parliament had 'if anything, been further marginalised'. Thus the government rejected 'modest' proposals for the reform of the appointment and scrutiny of select committees. However, this was perhaps unsurprising. Few governments would readily acquiesce in reforms which might significantly increase Parliament's effective scrutiny of their work, or impede their own ability to get their business through. It seems unlikely that any major transformation of executive dominance of Parliament will be achieved while governments retain secure parliamentary majorities backed by party discipline.

Philip Cowley (in Dunleavy *et al.* 2000: 120) argues that 'the greatest of the reforms to the UK Parliament ... will be the indirect reforms, those that occur as a result of Labour's other constitutional policies'. Cowley goes on to cite the Human Rights Act (see Chapter 14) and devolution (see Chapter 16). However, the most significant development of all could be an extension of the new voting systems introduced for the European Parliament and devolved assemblies. Although Blair's government has deferred reform of elections for the Westminster Parliament, voting reform is now on the political agenda. A change in the voting system in the direction of more proportional representation (see Chapter 5) is perhaps the only reform that might fundamentally alter executive–legislative relations in Britain.

The House of Lords

If reform of the lower chamber under the Blair government has so far been relatively modest and (for some) disappointing, major changes have been made already to the composition of the House of Lords, although they remain highly controversial and as yet incomplete.

The British Parliament, like most legislatures around the world, is bicameral: in other words it has two chambers or houses. In many other countries the second chamber has a significant role. The US Senate is actually rather more powerful and prestigious than the US lower house, the House of Representatives. However, the British Upper House, the House of Lords, because of its bizarre composition (until recently composed largely of hereditary peers), has long been of marginal significance to British government and politics. One indication of its declining role is that while in the 19th century many prime ministers and other leading ministers came from the House of Lords, since 1902 there have been no prime ministers who have sat in the Lords, and very few senior ministers besides the lord chancellor. The powers of the Lords are relatively marginal. Although it can delay legislation for up to a year, its undemocratic composition has generally inhibited their lordships from exercising even this limited power too often.

Powers and functions of the Lords

The main functions of the House of Lords are as follows:

- **Legislation:** revision of House of Commons bills, giving ministers the opportunity for second thoughts; initiation of non-controversial legislation, including government bills, bills by individual peers, private bills (promoted by bodies outside Parliament, such as local authorities), and consideration of delegated legislation.
- **Deliberation**: the provision of a forum for debates on matters of current interest.
- **Scrutiny**: the Lords subjects government policy and administration to scrutiny through questions and through the work of its select committees (such as European Communities and Science and Technology).
- **Supreme court of appeal**: the Lords has long been the ultimate court of appeal in the United Kingdom, although the government is engaged in transferring this function to a new Supreme Court (see below and Chapter 14).

Legislation

Constitutionally, despite its reduced powers, the Upper House remains an essential part of the legislative process, and spends rather over half its time on legislation. By the Parliament Act of 1911, the Lords completely lost its power to delay or amend money bills, which receive the royal assent one month after leaving the House of Commons, whether approved by the Lords or not. But it retained the power to delay non-money bills for up to two successive sessions (reduced to one session only by the Parliament Act of 1949). The present powers of the House of Lords – as defined by the Parliament Acts of 1911 and 1949 – are as follows:

- To delay non-money bills for up to one year.
- To veto (a) bills to prolong the life of Parliament beyond the statutory five-year period; (b) private bills (not to be confused with private members' bills); and (c) delegated legislation.

In practice the Lords has accepted further limitations on its own power of delay. The main guiding rule – firmly established by Conservative opposition peers in the immediate post-war period – is that the Upper House does not oppose measures included in the governing party's manifesto at the previous election (the Salisbury/Addison doctrine). In addition, the Lords rarely press an amendment or delay a measure to the point where the Parliament Acts have to be invoked (although the partially reformed House has proved more difficult – see below).

The House of Lords can cause political embarrassment to the government of the day, but no more. The Upper House has on numerous occasions impeded government legislation and forced concessions, although generally on minor issues. But it is far from being a severe constitutional obstacle to the party in power. Nor can it be said to treat the legislation of both parties impartially, being much more severe on Labour than on Conservative legislation. Yet during recent periods of substantial government majorities and weak oppositions in the House of Commons, the Lords have sometimes offered more substantial if ultimately ineffective resistance to government.

Another significant trend in recent decades has been the greater use made of the Lords by governments to revise and generally tidy up their legislation. Because much of this tidying-up process has to be done hurriedly at the end of sessions, one peer has described the Upper Chamber as 'a gilded dustpan and brush'. Suggested causes for this development include inadequate consultation, government indecisiveness and poor drafting in the early stages of legislation, but whatever the reasons, it has made the House of Lords an increasingly attractive target for pressure groups (Shell, in Jones and Robins 1992: 165–6).

Deliberation and scrutiny

The House of Lords – which devotes approximately one day per week to general debate – is often praised for the overall quality of its debates, but their overall impact is questionable. Its exercise of its scrutiny functions (through questions and select committees) is of greater consequence. The House of Lords Select Committee on the European Communities, which considers initiatives proposed by the EU Commission, is well staffed, able to consider EU proposals on their merits, and expert. It produces over 20 reports a year which, like other Lords select committee reports but unlike their equivalents in the Commons, are all debated. Overall, however, the House of Lords has made no attempt to establish through its select committees a mechanism for consistent, comprehensive scrutiny of government, but has rather used them to fill gaps left by the Commons select committee system.

Supreme Court of Appeal

The House of Lords not only contributes to making the law, but has long adjudicated on the law in its role as the UK's supreme court of appeal, which in most other countries would be considered a dangerous confusion of functions which should be constitutionally separate. Specialist law lords were appointed from the 19th century to assist the Lords to fulfil its function as a supreme court, and by convention only those suitably qualified take an active part in this judicial role. However, critics have long argued that the dual role of the Upper Chamber in making and adjudicating on laws is indefensible. In 2003 the government proposed to transfer the Lords judicial function to a new Supreme Court (see Chapter 14 for further discussion). Although there has been substantial controversy over both the principle and details of the government's proposals, this major reform is now well under way, and the Lords judicial function will soon disappear (Ryan 2004).

Composition of the House of Lords

If the powers of the Lords have been controversial, the traditional composition of the Upper Chamber has come to be regarded as unsustainable in a modern democratic era. The House of Lords long consisted of lords temporal (holders of hereditary titles) and lords spiritual (the archbishops and senior bishops of the Church of England). In the 19th century specialist law lords, appointed for life, were added to assist the Upper Chamber in its judicial capacity as the highest court in the land (see above). The composition of the House of Lords was more significantly affected by the Life Peerages Act 1958, which empowered the Crown (effectively the prime minister) to create life peers and peeresses. The Peerages Act 1963 allowed hereditary peers to disclaim their titles, and admitted hereditary peeresses into the House of Lords in their own right. These two Acts had the incidental effect of introducing a small proportion of women (7.0 per cent) to what had been an all-male chamber. Rather more significantly, the Upper Chamber was transformed over a period from an almost entirely hereditary chamber to a chamber in which appointed life peers commonly outnumbered hereditary peers in the work of the Lords. This occurred because whereas most of the hereditary peers did not attend regularly, many of the life peers were 'working peers', and these constituted the bulk of the active membership. However, the hereditary peers retained a nominal majority, which could become effective when a subject dear to their hearts (such as hunting) was debated.

Figure 13.2 Composition of unreformed House of Lords (pre 1999)

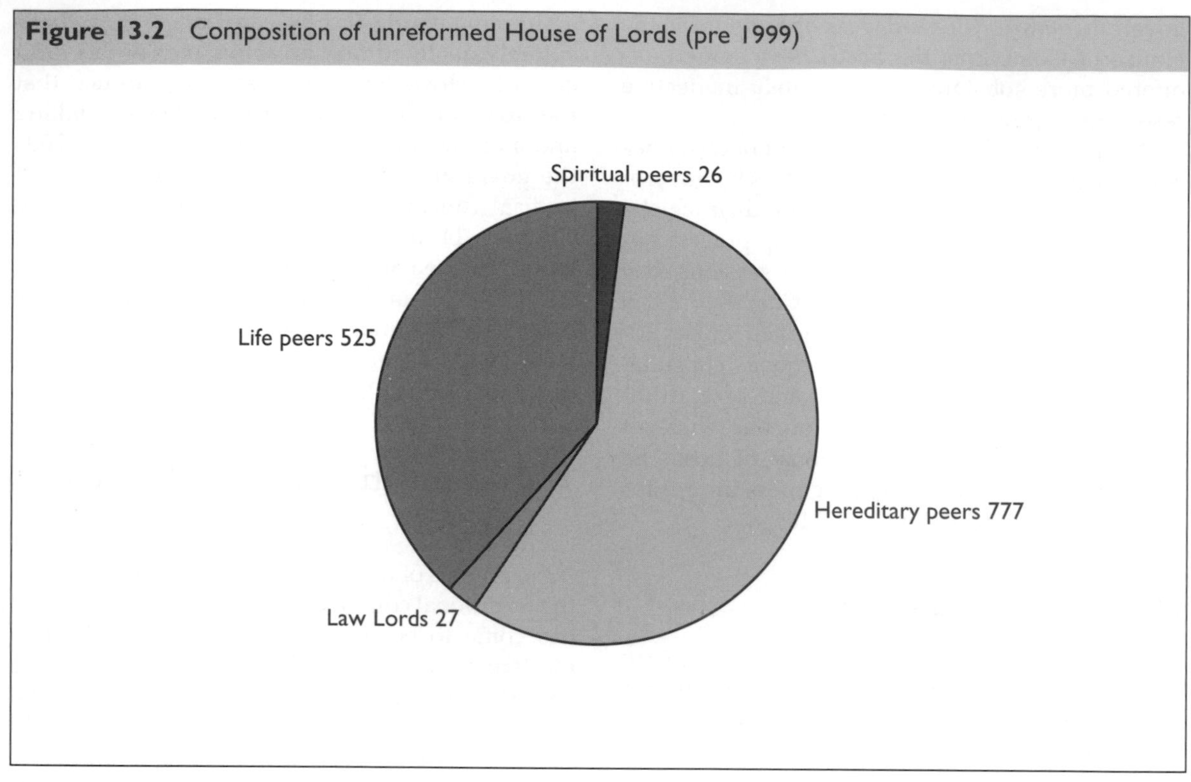

However, the composition remained bizarre, and not only because the majority of members still claimed their seats from an accident of birth. The only religion represented as of right is the established Church of England, which hardly seems appropriate in what has become a multi-faith Britain. Moreover, while appointment may constitute an advance on heredity as a qualification for membership, the life peers owe their appointments to prime ministerial patronage (although the prime minister normally accepts recommendations from the leaders of opposition parties), which hardly seems much more democratic. In practice, retired ministers and long-serving MPs are among those who are commonly offered peerages. Thus debates in the Lords often feature elderly politicians, who were once household names but are now largely forgotten, giving substance to a quip of the former Liberal leader, Jo Grimond, that the House of Lords proves there is life after death.

A final objection to the composition of the unreformed Upper Chamber was its unbalanced representation of political parties. Although a substantial minority of peers are crossbenchers who are independent of party allegiance, among those who took a party whip Conservative peers outnumbered Labour peers by 300, before the Labour government reform process started. Although the built-in Conservative advantage was less than these figures imply because Conservative peers were less regular attenders than Labour or Liberal Democrat peers, even in the 'working house' the Conservatives remained by far the largest party. Moreover, this built-in Conservative advantage has had a marked effect on the Lords' function as revising chamber. On average, whereas the Lords inflicted 70 defeats a year on Labour governments between 1974 and 1979, it defeated Conservative administrations only 13 times a year between 1979 and 1997.

■ Reform of the House of Lords

While it has long been recognised that the hereditary second chamber is indefensible in a democratic era, reform of the Lords has proved difficult. As Robert Hazell (1999: 114) has observed, 'it is impossible to decide a satisfactory system for

Lords' membership without first deciding what interests peers are there to represent'. This is not easy in Britain. The key function a second chamber performs in a federal state is to represent the interests of the states, as the Senate does in the USA or the Bundesrat in Germany. It is more difficult to establish such a clear function in a unitary state, as the UK remains, at least in theory.

The government's proposals for reforming the Lords have sometimes been criticised for being insufficiently related to other ongoing constitutional changes, particularly devolution. However, the final outcome of the devolution process as yet remains unclear. It might be easier to devise a logical role for a second chamber if British government continues to evolve towards a quasi-federal or ultimately perhaps a fully federal system. In one sense Lords reform is long overdue, and some would argue that it has come a century late, but in the immediate context it is perhaps a little premature.

One solution to the Lords reform dilemma is simply abolition. Unicameral legislatures have become more common (112 of the world's 178 parliaments), as some mature democracies have abolished their second chamber while many new and post-Communist states only have one chamber (Hague and Harrop 2001: 219). Yet this solution has never found much favour in Britain, although Labour proposed it for a time. It is commonly argued that a second chamber provides an opportunity for second thoughts on over-hasty legislation from the lower house. If it is accepted that some kind of revising chamber is necessary or desirable, it is then a question of deciding how that chamber should be composed. While many favour a wholly or largely elected second chamber, a problem here is that such a democratically elected chamber could challenge the legitimacy and primacy of the House of Commons.

Because previous reform proposals had foundered on the failure to agree on the composition and powers of the second chamber, Blair's Labour government opted for a two-stage model of reform. Stage one was to involve simply removing the hereditary peers, stage two a more long-term and comprehensive reform. The government moved quickly towards the abolition of the right of hereditary peers to sit in the Lords, but faced with the prospects of a prolonged battle with the Upper House, instead reached a compromise. This allowed the hereditary peers to elect 92 of their number to remain as members of the transitional House pending a more fundamental final reform. After the 92 peers were chosen, the rest of the hereditary peers lost their powers to speak and vote in the Lords. (The interim composition of the half-reformed House of Lords, compared with its former composition, is indicated in Table 13.5 and Figures 13.2 and 13.3)

The projected second stage of Lords reform has proved far more difficult. The government adopted a time-honoured device for dealing with politically awkward questions, appointing an independent Royal Commission chaired by Lord Wakeham, a former Conservative minister. Wakeham's Commission reported in January 2000, and recommended no radical change in the functions of the Upper Chamber; the Commons was to remain the dominant body and the Lords judicial role was to continue. On composition, the report argued that at least 30 per cent of members should be female (a substantially higher proportion than the 16 per cent in the present Lords, or 20 per cent in the Commons), while ethnic minorities and different

Table 13.5 Old and interim composition of the Lords, after House of Lords Act 1999

	Old composition	Interim new House
Spiritual peers (archbishops and senior bishops of Church of England)	26	26
Hereditary peers	777	92
Law Lords	27	7
Life peers	525	525
Total	1355	670

faiths should be represented fairly. No political party should have an overall majority and at least 20 per cent of the whole house should be cross-benchers. However, the crucial proposal was the chamber would be largely appointed, with only a minority of peers elected. The government largely endorsed the Wakeham Report. Lord Irvine, then lord chancellor, drafted a white paper in November, 2001, which proposed a small elected element (20 per cent), with a further 20 per cent appointed by an independent Appointments Commission and 60 per cent appointed by party patronage.

These government proposals met with very wide-ranging opposition. The Liberal Democrats (like the constitutional pressure group Charter 88) wanted a fully elected second chamber. The Conservatives, who had defended the hereditary element, switched to support an 80 per cent elected chamber. Many Labour backbenchers also wanted a larger elected element, while others favoured Lords abolition (*Guardian*, 14 May 2002). The Commons all-party select committee, chaired by Labour MP Tony Wright, reported in favour of a 60 per cent elected house, with law lords and spiritual peers abolished. Responses to the Government's white paper indicated a strong preference for a mainly elected chamber. The government thus accepted there was no consensus in support of its own proposals and established an independent joint committee of both houses to undertake widespread consultation and issue a report on options for reform.

The Joint Committee reported in December 2002. The report identified five desirable qualities in a revising chamber: legitimacy, representativeness, independence, expertise, and the absence of domination by any one party. They considered some 600 members should sit for a 12-year term. Yet they did not propose a clear recommendation on the detailed composition of the revised Upper Chamber, instead presenting seven options, ranging from a wholly appointed to a wholly elected house. When both houses were given the chance to vote on the options in 2003 there was no clear majority for any of them. In the absence of agreement the government has proposed simply to remove the remaining hereditary peers without a more comprehensive modernisation of the composition of the second chamber.

Figure 13.3 Composition of interim House of Lords 1999

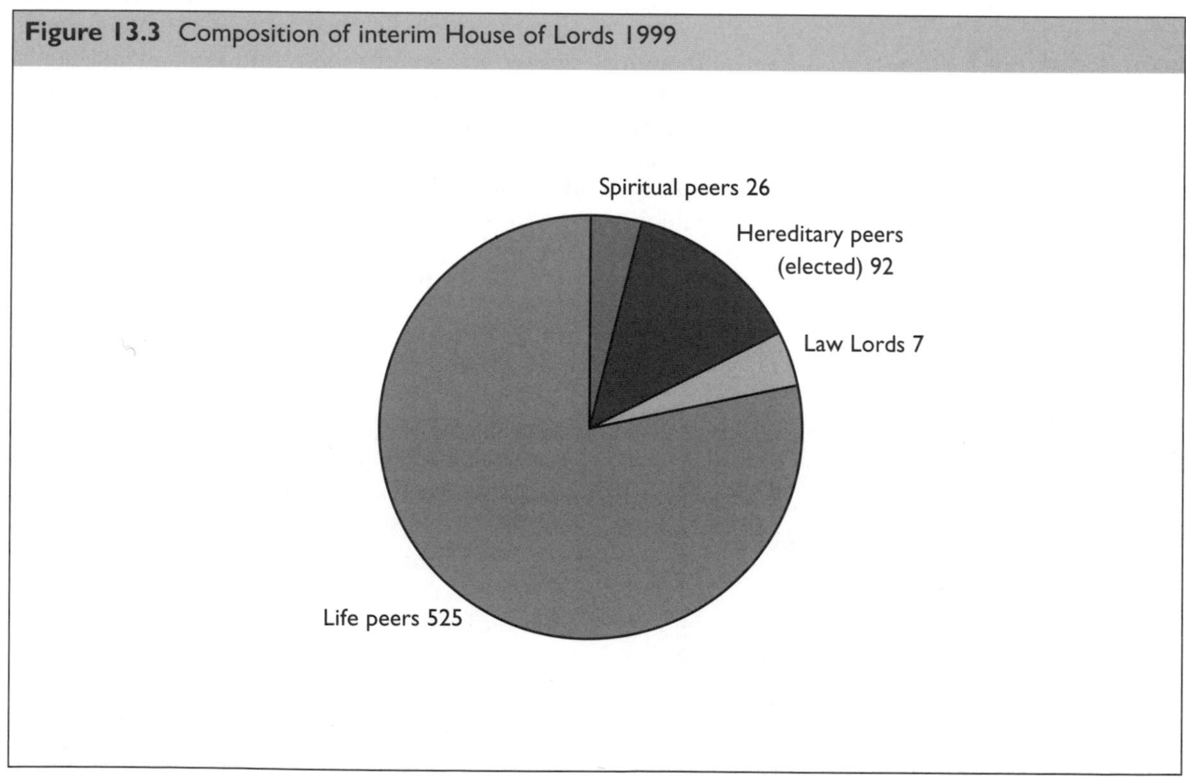

Figure 13.4 Party affiliations of members of Upper House, 2005

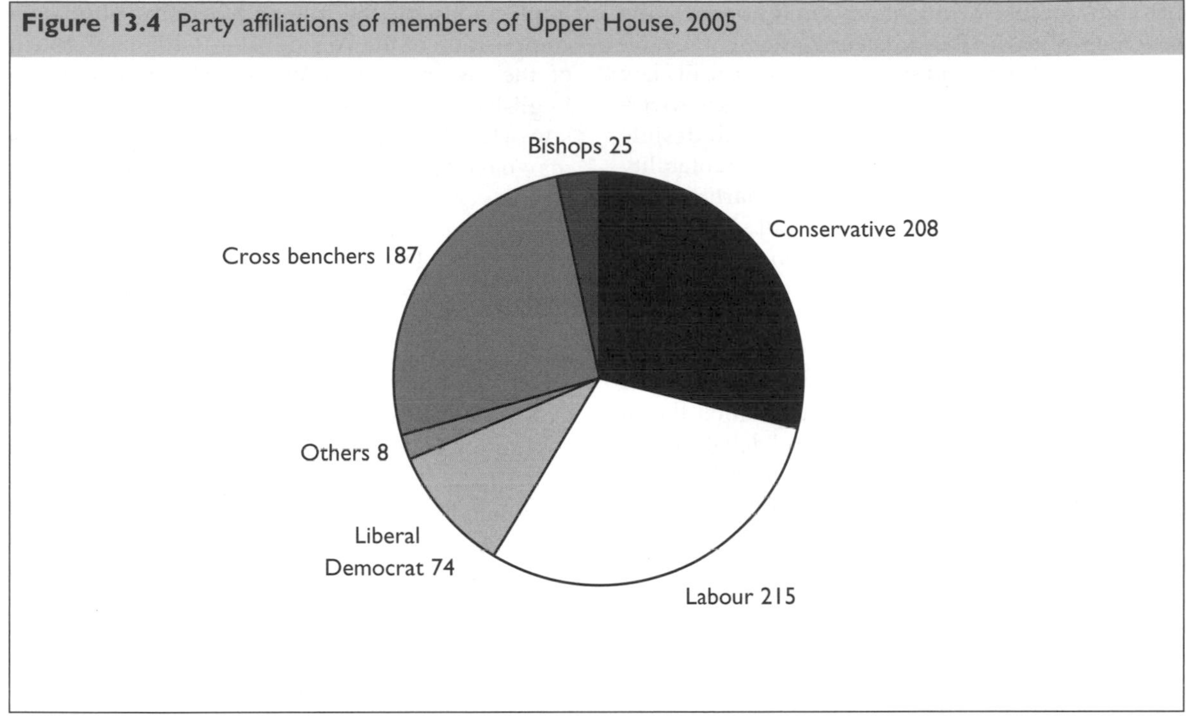

Source: www.parliament.uk

However in 2004, following opposition in the Lords, the government decided not to proceed with this limited measure. The second stage of Lords reform thus remains in limbo.

By 2005 the party affiliations of the still only partially reformed Upper Chamber were as indicated in Figure 13.4, with 208 Conservatives, 215 Labour, 74 Liberal Democrat and 187 crossbenchers, plus 25 bishops (excluding eight peers on leave of absence). Ironically, however, although Labour is now better represented in the Lords than formerly, this partially reformed Upper Chamber has caused rather more problems for the Labour government than the old House of Lords.

The Westminster Parliament and other parliaments

Although the Westminster Parliament remains at the centre of British politics, formally at least, in the sense that its sovereignty remains a key principle of the unwritten (or uncodified) British constitution, it is no longer the only parliament with which British politics is concerned. UK membership of the European Union has meant that representatives are also elected to the European Parliament. While this used to be dismissed as a mere talking shop, its influence on EU decision making, and hence on decisions that affect Britain, has grown steadily in recent years (see Chapter 15). Indeed, some would argue that it has become a more effective policy-influencing body than the Westminster Parliament. Additionally, since 1999 the Westminster Parliament now coexists with a Scottish Parliament with legislative powers, and assemblies for Wales and (when not suspended) Northern Ireland (see Chapter 16) There is also a new Greater London Assembly, although the additional prospect of elected English regional assemblies has receded. Thus the Westminster Parliament may increasingly appear one of many representative assemblies in the evolving British system of governance. The existence of these other parliaments and assemblies has considerable and potentially increasing implications for the role and functions of the Westminster Parliament, and they require considerable liaison and coordination.

UK membership of the European Union already

has considerable if contentious implications for the sovereignty of the Westminster Parliament. Under the Treaty of Rome and subsequent treaties, EU law is binding on member states. Parliamentary sovereignty seems increasingly circumscribed, despite attempts to improve the legislative accountability of the European Union to national parliaments. With an increasing proportion of legislation emanating from the European Union, Westminster surveillance of European directives and regulations is a matter of some importance. The task involves both Houses of Parliament. In the Commons the Select Committee on European Legislation (the 'Scrutiny Committee') refers EU legislation that it sees as requiring further scrutiny and debate to one of the two standing committees. These have the power (1) to question ministers and officials; (2) to debate the merits of the issues at stake on a substantive motion; and (3) to refer documents for debate on the floor of the House, subject to the agreement of the leader of the House. However, debate by the House as a whole can lead not to amendment but only to a 'take note' motion, in the hope that the government will modify its position. The House of Lords also has a scrutiny committee, the Select Committee on the European Communities (1974), whose task is to decide which of the hundreds of EU documents deposited with it each month require scrutiny because they raise important questions of policy or principle or for other reasons. Six sub-committees, whose reports are normally debated by the House, undertake this scrutiny.

While the EU remains a hybrid political system in which institutions representing member states continue to play a major or preponderant role, the scrutiny of European legislation seems likely to remain a dual function of the European Parliament and the parliaments of member states. That being so, there is clearly a need for improved cooperation between national parliaments and the European Parliament. In the case of the UK, this may be facilitated by formal and informal party links between MPs and MEPs. From a party perspective there is however a possibility of some divergence of interests between a party's national and European representatives, especially as the latter are part of wider European parties (see Chapter 15).

The longer-term implications of the devolution of power to the Scottish Parliament and Welsh and Northern Ireland Assemblies also have profound implications for the role and perhaps ultimately composition of the Westminster Parliament. Much of the law passed at Westminster will now be English (or English and Welsh) law rather than UK law, while law passed in the devolved assemblies may have knock-on implications for Westminster. At the very least there is a need for considerable liaison between the various parliaments and assemblies. Initially the potential for serious conflict between parliaments was somewhat lessened by Labour or Labour-dominated governments at Westminster, Edinburgh and Cardiff. More problems are predicted if a future Conservative majority at Westminster faces Labour-controlled bodies in Scotland and Wales, or if a Labour UK government confronts an SNP-dominated Scottish Parliament. Some of the implications of these developments for long-established British constitutional principles, particularly the sovereignty of the Westminster Parliament and the unity of the United Kingdom are discussed in Chapters 14 and 16.

Summary

- Although the Westminster Parliament is very old, prestigious, and constitutionally sovereign, critics allege it is not in practice very powerful, or particularly effective.
- MPs represent electoral areas called constituencies. They are not socially representative of those who elect them, nor are they expected to reflect their views. Almost all represent parties, and all of them also reflect a range of outside interests. While this can be very useful, some outside interests raise ethical questions.
- Government is recruited from and maintained by Parliament (essentially the House of Commons). There has long been a close interdependence between the executive and legislature in British politics. In practice the government dominates the Commons.
- Traditional means of parliamentary scrutiny of the executive have been supplemented by the development of departmental select committees which oversee all ministerial departments.

- Most of the legislation examined in the Commons and almost all the laws that are passed are government measures. Legislation is in practice substantially an executive function.
- The Upper House has only powers of delay over legislation. Its undemocratic composition restricts its legitimacy and authority.
- Although most hereditary peers have been removed, detailed proposals for further reform of the Upper House have failed to secure broad support, and it remains a mainly appointed chamber.
- The Labour government is currently transferring the judicial functions of the House of Lords to a new Supreme Court.
- The Westminster Parliament is no longer the only representative assembly elected by UK voters. There is a need for more liaison with the European Parliament and with the new devolved Scottish Parliament and Welsh and Northern Ireland Assemblies.

Questions for discussion

- Should MPs vote according to their constituents' wishes?
- Should MPs be full-time? What restrictions (if any) should be placed on MPs' pursuit of outside interests?
- How might MPs be given a more effective role in the legislative process?
- How might the House of Commons be given more effective influence over the executive?
- Why does Britain need an Upper House? Should the House of Lords simply be abolished?
- If members of the second chamber should be wholly or mainly elected, how should they be elected, and who should they represent?
- Is there any case for keeping Britain's most important members of the judiciary in a legislative assembly?

Further reading

Philip Norton's *Parliament in British Politics* (2005) can be recommended as an up-to-date introduction to the subject. Older, but still useful is Griffith and Ryle, *Parliament* (1989). Ridley and Rush, *British Government and Politics since 1945* (1995) contains valuable essays on aspects of Parliament, whilst Rush, *Parliament and Pressure Politics* (1990) considers the relationship between Parliament and pressure groups. For developments under the Blair government see the chapters by Blackburn and Ryle in Blackburn and Plant (1999), by Cowley in Dunleavy *et al.* (2000), by Oliver in Jowell and Oliver (2004) and by Norton in Seldon (2001). The first stages of Lords reform are discussed in Richard and Welfare, *Unfinished Business: Reforming the House of Lords* (1999).

As on many other topics there is a problem in keeping up with recent developments. Gamble in Dunleavy *et al.* (2003) has a few pages on Commons and Lords reform. Recent issues of *Politics Review* and *Talking Politics* are a useful source for ongoing changes. For current developments on Lords reform and the Supreme Court consult weekly political journals, such as the *New Statesman* and *Spectator*, as well as quality newspapers and their websites. Some institutional websites are listed separately below.

Websites

Parliament (links to House of Commons and House of Lords):
www.parliament.uk
Committee on Standards in Public Life:
www.public-standards.gov.uk
Department for Constitutional Affairs:
www.dca.gov.uk

The Law, Politics and the Judicial Process

Contents

The state is involved in law making (Chapter 13), executing the law through its ministers and public officials (Chapters 11 and 12), and adjudicating on the law, which is the subject of this chapter. Some political theorists have long argued that these functions should be kept strictly separate. While this separation of powers has been enforced as far as practicable in some constitutions (notably the US Constitution), this has not previously been the case in Britain. Yet constitutional reforms first announced in 2003, involving the establishment of a separate Supreme Court, changes in the system for appointing judges and the reform of the office of lord chancellor are intended to emphasise the independence of the judiciary from both the executive and legislature. These reforms remain politically contentious and incomplete, yet involve a significant shift in constitutional theory and practice.

These reforms may appear to separate the administration of the law further from government and politics. However, in this chapter we argue that inevitably (and particularly in Britain) the law and politics are closely intertwined. The language of the law, and legal concepts and precepts, permeate the theory and practice of politics. Lawyers still play a leading role in government and Parliament, and figure prominently in public bureaucracies and business. Court judgements can have significant political consequences, affecting both governments and the lives of ordinary people. Judges themselves continue to wield massive power and influence, not just through the courts but in politics and government generally, and questions can and should be asked about their social and educational background, and their personal and political views. These are among the issues that we seek to address in this chapter.

Questions can be also asked about the efficiency and effectiveness of the judicial system in Britain. Does it deliver justice fairly, quickly and reasonably economically? How might it be improved? There are also important issues surrounding the enforcement of law and the pursuit of prosecutions by the police. Finally there are other vital questions about the protection of human rights and civil liberties in Britain, and the effectiveness of the various channels for securing redress of grievances against the state and public authorities.

The rule of law

The rule of law has long been considered one of the fundamental principles of the unwritten (or uncodified) British constitution. It has, however, been variously interpreted from the time of the 19th century jurist, Dicey. Today the

> **Definition**
>
> **The rule of law**: the framework of legal rules guiding and restraining political behaviour in a liberal democratic society.

rule of law involves a number of assumptions, although each of these involves some qualification or raises some questions.

- **Everyone is bound by the law.** No one is above the law. Ministers and public officials are subject to the law and have no authority to act beyond the powers conferred on them by law (the *ultra vires* principle). *However*, British ministers are usually in a strong position to change the law because of executive dominance of the parliamentary legislative process, coupled with the doctrine of parliamentary sovereignty and the supremacy of statute law.
- **All persons are equal before the law.** All citizens have legal rights and can have recourse to the law, and the law is supposed to treat all citizens on an equal basis. *However*, there are some doubts over equality before the law in practice. 'The law, like the Ritz Hotel is open to all.' Legal proceedings can be expensive, and although there is legal aid for those with limited means, it is restricted (for example, it is not available for libel cases). Some would argue that the law in practice has systematically favoured property owners and established interests.
- **Law and order must be maintained** through the officials and institutional machinery of the state, which has a monopoly of the legitimate use of force within the state's borders. Citizens should be protected from violence and disorder, but should be forcibly restrained from taking the law into their own hands. *However*, the maintenance of law and order may lead to restrictions on individual liberty, such as restrictions on freedom of movement, and detention of suspects without trial. The war against terror has been used to justify restrictions on civil liberties by the Blair government, particularly after the London bombings of July 2005.
- **Legal redress is provided for those with complaints** against other individuals, organisations or the state. *However*, doubts are still expressed over the effectiveness of some of these remedies (see below).
- **The law and legal processes and personnel should be independent and free from political interference.** The courts are generally reckoned to be free from political pressures in practice, despite the fact that judges have been appointed by politicians. Labour's Constitutional Reform Act (2005, see below) was supposed to establish more formally the separation of powers and the independence of the judiciary. *However*, judges still complain about the interference of politicians, for example criticism of judicial sentencing by David Blunkett, the former home secretary.

Law in England, Scotland and Europe

It is difficult to summarise briefly the legal and judicial system in the United Kingdom, because there are marked differences within the state, particularly between English and Scottish law and their respective judicial systems.

Scottish law, by contrast with that of England, is influenced by Roman law, like continental European law, and involves distinctive principles and practice and a separate system of administration. Although Scottish law, like English law, remains bound by the theoretical sovereignty of the Westminster Parliament, the devolution of legislative powers to the new Scottish Parliament has already led to some further significant divergences between English and Scottish law, and these differences seem likely to become more marked over time.

Besides these differences between legal principles and practice within Britain, law in Britain is subject to growing supranational influence and control. Thus the British government ratified the European Convention on Human Rights in 1951, and allowed individual petitions from 1966, permitting British citizens to take their case to the court at Strasbourg. The Human Rights Act (1998) enabled judges to declare that legislation appeared incompatible with the European

Box 14.1

Types of law

Law is conventionally subdivided into a number of categories, such as criminal, civil and administrative.

Criminal law provides standards of conduct as well as machinery (police, the courts system) for dealing with those who commit crimes. Crimes are normally classified as (1) against the state (treason, public order), (2) against the person (murder, assault, rape), and (3) against property (robbery, malicious damage). A successful prosecution in a criminal case leads to a sentence (e.g. fine, imprisonment, community service, probation).

Civil law is concerned with the legal relations between persons. Normally, proceedings in a civil court depend upon a plaintiff pursuing an action against a defendant, and they generally result in some remedy, such as damages, specific performance (where the defendant has to keep his or her side of the bargain), or a 'declaration' of the plaintiff's legal rights. Cases in criminal law have to be proved 'beyond reasonable doubt'; actions in civil law are decided on the 'balance of probabilities'.

Administrative law is 'the body of general principles which govern the exercise of powers and duties by public authorities' (Wade 1988). Administrative law is more systematically developed on the European continent than in Britain. However, this sphere of law has grown considerably in Britain over the last century, as the state has intervened through legislation in aspects of social life hitherto untouched. Administrative law is concerned with the legal restraints which surround the activities of those who apply policy decisions. It is a key example of the interconnectedness of politics and law, with a variety of judicial and quasi-judicial institutions (the ordinary courts, tribunals, the ombudsman) supplying and applying a framework of rules within which public authorities act. It is centrally involved in the question of citizen rights and redress of grievances (see below).

Box 14.2

Comparative politics: English law and law in other European countries

The English legal and judicial system differs markedly from that prevailing over most of the European continent.

While continental law is generally based on written codes deriving ultimately from Roman law, English law is based on common law, assumed to be the immemorial but uncodified law of the English people, and declared by judges in court cases. Thus the law is essentially contained in decisions on past cases, which are binding on subsequent cases of a similar nature. Although judges are theoretically only declaring the law, particularly when new circumstances arise, they are in effect making new law. However, statute law is supreme over common law, so the law made by Parliament (and effectively by the government) overrides judge-made case law.

Convention on Human Rights (see below). From 1973 the United Kingdom has also been a member of the European Community (now Union). Thus the UK is subject to EU law, and to the decisions of the European Court of Justice at Luxembourg (not to be confused with the European Court of Human Rights at Strasbourg, which formally is nothing to do with the European Union). Naturally EU law is strongly influenced by the mainstream European continental legal tradition, and this in turn has had some impact on English law, particularly perhaps in the growth of judicial review (see below). It seems likely that over a period of time there will be more convergence between legal principles and systems within Europe.

On top of this, the United Kingdom is increasingly influenced by international law and international conventions. Thus critics of the Iraq War argued that it was illegal under international law without clear United Nations authorisation. The attorney general, a member of the government and its official legal adviser, eventually declared that the war was legal, although it was alleged that the short published version of his advice omitted qualifications and reservations indicated

Figure 14.1 The system of courts in England and Wales

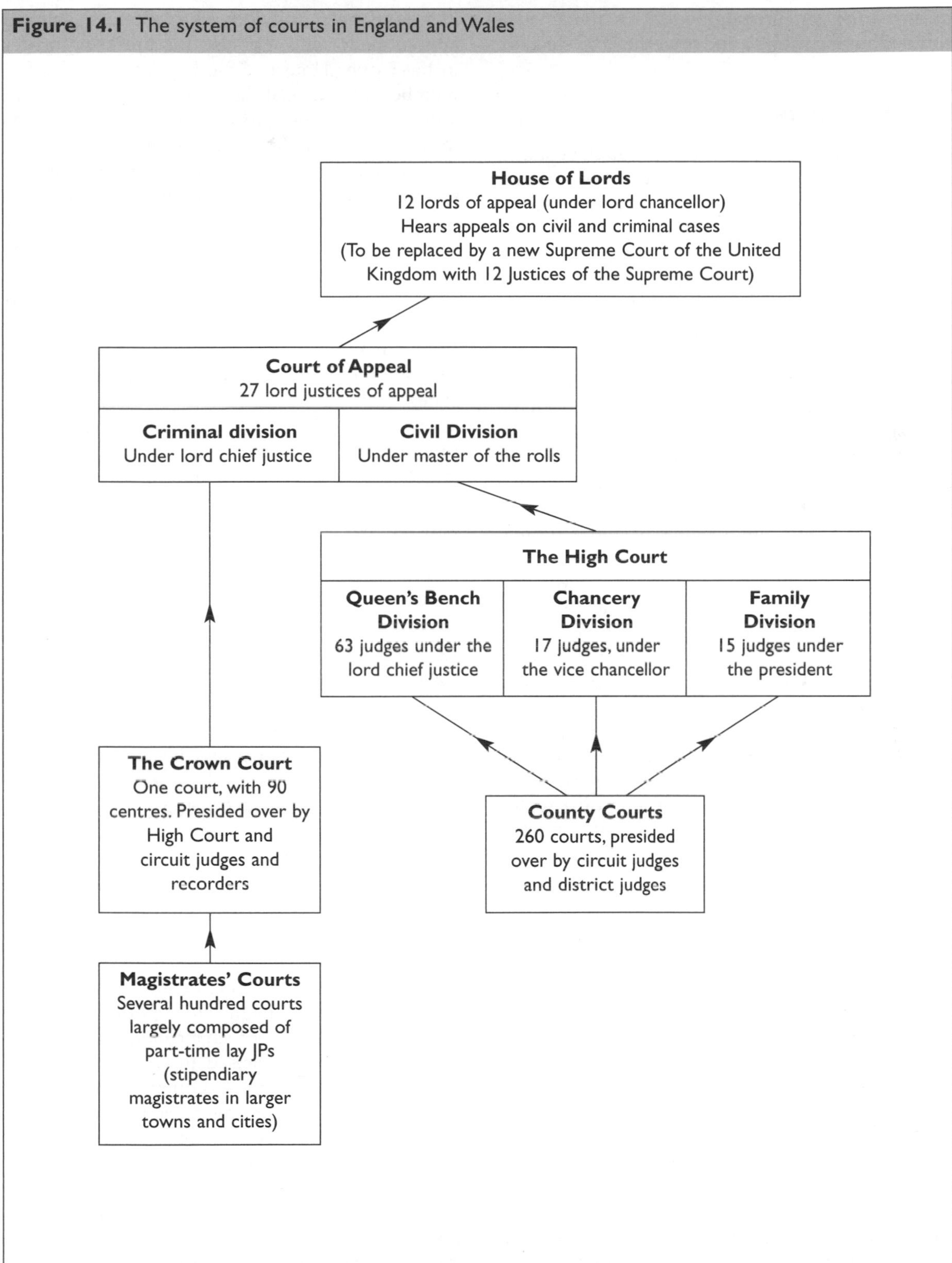

in an earlier longer judgment. This remained a contentious issue up to and after the 2005 election.

The courts

The UK system of courts is complicated. Scotland and Northern Ireland have their own rather different court systems. Most of what follows applies particularly to England and Wales (see Figure 14.1).

Minor criminal cases are tried without a jury in magistrates courts: by legally qualified, full-time stipendiary (paid) magistrates in the cities and by part-time lay magistrates advised by a legally qualified clerk elsewhere. More serious criminal cases for 'indictable' offences and appeals from the magistrates court are heard in the Crown Court before a judge and jury (unless the defendant pleads guilty, which is commonly the case, when a jury is not required). Appeals from conviction in the Crown Court are usually to the Criminal Division of the Court of Appeal. The Court of Appeal consists of lords justices of appeal and other judges who are members *ex officio*. A further appeal on a point of law may be allowed to the House of Lords, sitting as a court composed of the lord chancellor and law lords (soon to be replaced by the new Supreme Court).

A few minor civil cases are heard in magistrates courts but most minor cases are heard by county courts, presided over by circuit judges. More important cases are heard in the High Court, which is split into three divisions – Queen's Bench Division, dealing with common law, Chancery Division, dealing with equity, and the Family Division (dealing with domestic cases). Appeals from lower courts are heard in the appropriate division of the High Court. Appeals from the High Court can be made to the Civil Division of the Court of Appeal, and from there to the House of Lords, whose appellate functions are to be transferred to the new Supreme Court (see below).

Labour's constitutional reform programme: towards a new Supreme Court

Until the Labour government's Constitutional Reform Act (2005), the head of the judicial system had long been the lord chancellor, a political appointment, who was also the presiding officer in the Upper House of the legislature and a full member of the Cabinet. The most important judges besides the lord chancellor, the law lords (or lords of appeal in ordinary) were appointed by the Crown on the advice of the prime minister specifically to exercise the judicial functions of the House of Lords. Other judges were appointed by the Crown, on the advice of the lord chancellor. This entanglement of the judicial functions of the state with its executive and legislative functions appeared thoroughly confusing and even downright dangerous to critics familiar with the stricter separation of powers in the constitutions of other states such as the USA and France. Although many commentators in the UK conceded that in practice the judiciary was independent and largely free from political interference, constitutional principles and practice did not guarantee judicial independence. Critics, including a few senior judges, had long urged reform, and some had urged the establishment of a Supreme Court.

Even so, this did not figure in Labour's initial constitutional reform programme, nor in its 2001 election manifesto. Suddenly, and linked with a Cabinet reshuffle that saw the departure of Lord Irvine, the lord chancellor, the Blair government announced three major reforms in June 2003. The post of lord chancellor was to be abolished, a new system for appointing judges was to be introduced, and the appellate functions of the House of Lords were to be transferred to a new Supreme Court. The law lords would no longer sit in the House of Lords but would become the first justices of the Supreme Court. There was no prior warning or consultation and, it appears, little preparation.

The proposals were highly contentious. Some questioned the government's motives – Home Secretary David Blunkett had reportedly clashed with the outgoing lord chancellor, Lord Irvine, and had publicly criticised judges and attacked recent judicial decisions. Others lamented the projected abolition of the ancient post of lord chancellor, while critics suggested the government's proposals did not go far enough. The law lords were divided. Some welcomed the proposed Supreme Court, while others were unhappy with their removal from the Lords. They insisted that the Supreme Court should not be established before a suitably prestigious building was found and thoroughly modernised to meet their needs.

The government described the new body as the Supreme Court 'of the United Kingdom', but it will not receive appeals on criminal cases from Scotland, as the law lords did not hear such cases in the past. As Lord Falconer, the new secretary of state for constitutional affairs and lord chancellor, acknowledged, there is no single United Kingdom judicial system, nor was it the government's intention to create one. The only new powers to be transferred to the Supreme Court not previously exercised by the law lords were over appeals on jurisdiction under the Devolution Acts, previously given to the Judicial Committee of the Privy Council. It is only on such devolution issues that 'decisions of the Supreme Court will be binding in all legal proceedings throughout the United Kingdom' (Le Sueur, in Jowell and Oliver, 2004: 332).

The UK Supreme Court will not closely resemble some other supreme courts. It will not, like the US Supreme Court, be able to invalidate legislation for contravening the constitution, for this would undermine the principle of parliamentary sovereignty to which the government is still officially committed. The Supreme Court will not be the guardian of the constitution.

Judges are to be recommended through new processes. When a vacancy occurs in the Supreme Court, the secretary of state for constitutional affairs will select from a recommended short list for new justices. For other new judges in England and Wales, a new Judicial Appointments Commissions will nominate individuals, with the secretary of state retaining only veto powers (which it is anticipated would be rarely used), and not an effective choice. While they retain the final say, the role of politicians in the appointment of judges should be much reduced, and the independence of the judiciary further emphasised.

> **Definition**
>
> **Judicial independence**: the constitutional principle that in order to protect individual freedom the judiciary should be independent from the other branches of government, the executive and the legislature.

Lawyers, judges and politics

The reforms described above have important constitutional implications, but will not have much impact on the nature and character of the British legal profession. This is divided between some 4000 or so barristers, who alone can plead cases in the higher courts, and around 50,000 solicitors who deal directly with the public, and among their other duties prepare the cases for barristers to plead. This division of labour is relatively unusual in other countries, and some critics suggest that it is, in effect, a restrictive practice that benefits lawyers rather than their clients. The cost and length of training for barristers in particular, and the uncertain rewards in the early years in the profession, have tended to restrict entry into the legal profession predominantly to those from well-to-do family backgrounds. Yet if they do become successful, the rewards for a sought-after barrister can be huge. Thus while lawyers may frequently have to defend the interests of the poor and marginalised in British society, very few successful barristers share the social background of many of their clients.

It is from the ranks of senior barristers that judges are mainly drawn. Once appointed, they are virtually irremovable before the obligatory retirement age, which was reduced from 75 to 70 in 1993, with the proviso that the lord chancellor could authorise continuation in office until 75 if it was in the public interest. Unsurprisingly, senior judges are drawn almost exclusively from the ranks of the white, male upper middle class. There are no lords of appeal, heads of division or lord justices of appeal, and only 1 per cent of High Court and circuit judges from ethnic minorities. Rather more women are now being appointed as judges, but few to the higher ranks of the judiciary (see Table 14.1). As judges are normally only recruited after a long career at the bar, and are not obliged to retire at the same age as most of the working population, they are also predominantly elderly.

Judges are powerful and often controversial figures. They may become celebrated or notorious public figures because of their sentences in criminal cases, their comments during the course of a trial and their observations in summing up (for which they cannot be sued). Politicians and the media have sometimes criticised judges for

In Focus 14.1

Cherie Booth (Blair)

Tony Blair's wife has pursued a successful career as a barrister. She has preferred to keep her maiden name in her profession, where she specialises in human rights cases (involving some potential for embarrassing the government). She has had to balance the conflicting demands of her semi-official position as the prime minister's wife, her role as mother of four, and her professional career, where she reportedly has ambitions to be a High Court judge, a position relatively few women have achieved (see Table 14.1). Her ambitions have been hindered rather than helped by her political prominence, for which she has been targeted by sections of the press.

Photograph: EMPICS.

passing sentences that are considered too light. Judges in their turn have deplored mandatory sentences for certain categories of crime, which reduce judicial discretion, and have roundly criticised interference by politicians such as former home secretary David Blunkett. As law and order is an emotive political issue, it is perhaps unsurprising that politicians and judges are drawn into conflict. Because of their role in declaring (and effectively making) the law, they are inevitably helping to shape public policy and influence public attitudes. In addition to their judicial activities, judges because of their public standing and legal expertise are often invited to conduct or chair major enquiries into controversial political areas. Examples include the Scott Inquiry on the arms to Iraq scandal in 1996 (see Box 12.12) and the 2003 Hutton Inquiry into the circumstances surrounding the death of the weapons inspector David Kelly, and government and media handling of communications leading up to the Iraq War (see Box 9.2).

The orthodox view is that the judicial system is impartial, symbolised by the blindfold figure

Table 14.1 Senior judges by gender, 2005

Level of judiciary	Men	Women	Percentage women
Lords of appeal in ordinary	11	1	8
Heads of division	5	0	0
Lords justices of appeal	35	2	5
High Court judges	97	10	9
Circuit judges	561	67	11
Recorders	1214	195	14

Source: Department of Constitutional Affairs.

of Justice above the Central Criminal Court. Judges balance the scales of justice fairly, without fear or favour. The acknowledged impartiality of the judiciary legitimises the whole administration of justice in the United Kingdom. Judges are moreover sometimes seen also as stout defenders of the rights and freedoms of citizens against arbitrary and unjustified acts by governments and public authorities. The growth of judicial review over the last 30 or 40 years (see below) provides some support for this perspective. The 1998 Human Rights Act seems likely to provide further opportunities for judicial intervention against government.

Yet critics argue that judges are almost inevitably biased in their attitudes and decisions because of the kind of people they are. While they may strive earnestly to appear impartial, their own highly restricted and exclusive social background is almost bound to affect their assumptions and outlook, which is inevitably conservative with a small 'c' and, critics allege, generally with a large 'C' also (Griffith 1997). Indeed, some judges almost seem to pride themselves on their ignorance of mass culture and common language. More disquietingly, they sometimes appear more sympathetic to 'white collar' criminals than their working-class counterparts, show marked leniency to men in rape cases, and send more blacks than whites to prison for longer periods for equivalent offences.

Blair's Labour government is committed to more diversity within the judiciary, although this was not made explicit in the 2005 Constitutional Reform Act. By contrast, the Scottish and Northern Ireland commissions for appointing judges were required to bring about a judiciary more reflective and representative of the community, and less overwhelmingly male and white (Le Sueur, in Jowell and Oliver 2004: 329). Yet given the type and length of legal experience required of a judge, and the relatively restricted social background of senior barristers, it will be difficult to achieve significant changes in the short to medium term. Although it could be argued that juries composed of ordinary citizens provide protection against the (perhaps largely unconscious) bias of an unrepresentative judiciary, jury trials are only used in a minority of cases, and there are proposals to restrict their use still further (see Box 14.3).

Box 14.3

Trial by jury under threat?

Trial by jury was enshrined as a principle in Magna Carta (1215) and is still widely regarded as an important right, and the essence of a 'fair trial'. Yet most trials no longer involve a jury, while jury trials are expensive and time-consuming, not least for those summoned for jury service. Indeed, it is sometimes alleged that juries no longer represent a fair cross-section of the community because some sections of the population successfully plead to be excused. In criminal cases many police believe jury trials lead to more acquittals of defendants they 'know' are guilty. There are also cases where jurors have been threatened or intimidated. It is also suggested that juries are not competent to decide on complex legal issues, such as fraud cases. Anecdotal evidence suggests that the deliberations of some juries may involve a muddled compromise between the diametrically opposed gut reactions of individual jurors, even if most of the time they seem to follow the guidance of the judge. Yet juries can sometimes show an obstinate independence.

The police and policing

All states require police to enforce the criminal law and prevent disorder. It is the most vulnerable members of society, such as the old, the young, women and minorities facing discrimination and prejudice, who most need the protection of an efficient and impartial police force. Yet even more than judges, police appear to represent the coercive role of the state. Although a good police force is a requirement for any civilised nation, the police in many countries are feared and hated, while the chief of police has become a familiar figure of demonology. It says something for the British police that they long avoided this unenviable reputation. While fictional portrayals in novels, music hall, and early films and television occasionally showed police officers as bumbling, they were almost never portrayed as harsh or corrupt. If this image of the friendly 'British bobby' was always somewhat idealised, it was not altogether a myth. Unusually, the ordinary police did not (and still do not) carry guns, indicating an uncommon degree of mutual trust between the police and the communities they serve. This trust still survives in many parts of the country. However, confidence in the impartiality and efficiency of the police in Britain was never universal, and now appears lower than it used to be.

Just as there are issues over the possible bias of the judiciary, there are similar concerns over the police. This is not because the police are recruited from a very restricted social and educational elite (as could be said of judges). On the contrary, most police are recruited from lower white-collar and working-class family backgrounds. In spite or perhaps even because of this, it is widely alleged that the police behave in a more deferential manner towards 'respectable' people. Many senior police officers are members of the secretive Freemasons, and socialise with the local elite. Moreover, it is suggested that they are less concerned, or less well equipped, to pursue 'white collar' crime.

However, possible class bias has received rather less scrutiny of late than the alleged sexist, homophobic and racist attitudes of sections of the police. Women police officers (roughly one in six of the total force) do not fit easily into the rather 'macho' police culture, and have found it difficult to secure promotion to the highest levels. This macho culture sometimes led in the past to the unsympathetic treatment of female victims of rape and male violence, with the police particularly reticent over intervention in 'domestic' issues. This was one factor in the reluctance of women to report rape and other crimes of violence, although more recently many police forces have made strenuous efforts to treat such crimes sympathetically and pursue them seriously. The same macho culture has sometimes contributed to a marked lack of sympathy and sometimes hostility towards homosexuals – with some forces energetically pursuing prosecutions of homosexuals, involving police spying on activities in public lavatories and even acting as agents provocateurs in clubs. Again, attitudes are changing, perhaps more slowly, but sufficiently to allow a few police themselves to 'come out'.

Allegations of police racism have received considerable publicity in recent years. It has to be said that racism in the police largely reflects racism in wider society, although the problems have perhaps been more pronounced in some forces. Relatively few blacks and Asians have been recruited into the police (less than 2 per cent), and they have often found it difficult to obtain acceptance from their white colleagues and secure promotion. This has tended to reinforce the mutual suspicions, amounting sometimes to marked antipathy, between the police and minority communities. Members of ethnic minorities have long maintained that they are far more likely to be stopped and searched than members of the majority white community, and there is substantial evidence in support of the allegation. There is also evidence of routine racist abuse of blacks and Asians, and some cases of violent maltreatment of black suspects. Tragically there have also been high-profile police failures to secure convictions of those responsible for black victims of crimes of violence, most notably Stephen Lawrence and Damiola Taylor. It was the Macpherson Inquiry into the handling of the murder of Stephen Lawrence that led to acknowledgement that there was institutional racism in the Metropolitan Police and other police forces. (See chapter 24 for a discussion of institutional racism and policies to combat racism.)

The efficiency and effectiveness of the police have also been called into question by some high-profile miscarriages of justice and failures to solve crimes. Some miscarriages of justice were perhaps the consequence of intense media and public pressure on the police to secure convictions, leading to hasty and ill-prepared prosecutions, but a few cases involved the extraction of dubious confessions from suspects and even the fabrication of evidence. Some former police officers have been jailed for corruption, undermining faith in the integrity of the police.

All this raises important concerns over the accountability and control of the police, an issue in many countries. It is considered important on the one hand that the police should be independent from direct control by party politicians, but on the other that they should be fully accountable to the public or their representatives. Squaring that circle is difficult, and in Britain police accountability and responsibility are somewhat blurred. The police used to be a local authority responsibility, but control by elected councillors, never very effective particularly on operational issues, has progressively been weakened as a consequence of police force amalgamations and a reduced councillor element on police authorities. Today these are virtually quasi-autonomous local public bodies, often covering several local authorities, headed by chief constables with substantial operational control.

If local accountability is not particularly effective, what of accountability at the centre? Nationally, the minister in charge of crime and the police is the home secretary, but he or she has only ever had direct responsibility for London's Metropolitan Police, and even this was transferred to the Metropolitan Police Authority in 2000. Thus the home secretary is not answerable in the Commons for the conduct of police authorities and local police forces. Despite having overall responsibility for the police, successive home secretaries have found it difficult to pursue reorganisation and modernisation of the police. Thus most of the recommendations of the 1993 Sheehy Report have successfully been resisted by the police.

The machinery for handling complaints against the police has improved but remains controversial. Formerly, the investigation of complaints was wholly in the hands of the police themselves (although officers from another force might be brought it for serious cases). A Police Complaints Board was introduced to supervise the process in 1976. Following the 1984 Police and Criminal Evidence Act this was replaced by a beefed-up Police Complaints Authority, which supervises the investigation of serious complaints, although the actual investigation is still carried out by police officers, so it is still questioned whether this amounts to a genuinely independent inquiry.

Policing, together with law and order generally, can hardly be taken out of politics. Indeed it remains a hotly contested political issue, particularly under Blair's Labour government, which has tried to counter the accusation that the party was 'soft on crime'. Blair first came to national prominence as shadow home secretary, with his soundbite that Labour would be 'tough on crime and tough on the causes of crime'. New Labour's first two home secretaries – Jack Straw from 1997 and David Blunkett from 2001 – have been notably 'tough', and the prime minister has also made periodic interventions on law and order issues. Labour's claims of increased police recruitment and reduced crime rates have been criticised by the Conservative opposition, notably in the 2005 election campaign. Statistics in such areas require careful interpretation. Increased reports of certain crimes may follow media publicity, yet there may also be substantial 'unreported crime' for a variety of reasons. Increases or decreases in police convictions may reflect changes in police activity. People's fears of some kinds of crime may be intensified by media campaigns or scaremongering, creating a 'moral panic'. Yet the fear of crime, and indeed the reality of crime, is sufficiently serious to blight lives. An impartial, efficient, well-organised and accountable police service, trusted by the communities it seeks to protect, remains an obviously important objective for governments of any party.

Human rights and civil liberties

The hallmark of a liberal democratic state, it is often said, is the effectiveness with which a range of basic citizen rights or civil liberties is guaranteed. These rights or liberties have long been enthusiastically extolled by British people, and it is vital, therefore, to examine to what extent this confidence in the security of such rights is justified. Three points provide a context for this discussion:

- Virtually all British civil liberties stem from a fundamental principle: that people may do what they like so long as no law prevents them.
- Legal protections against infringements of this fundamental freedom in specific instances (such as freedom of expression, meeting and association) have been established gradually throughout history and were not enshrined in any particular statute until the Human Rights Act, which came into force in 2000.
- The question of citizen rights or liberties has both a positive and negative aspect: the right to do certain things and the right not to have certain things done to you.

Box 14.4 is concerned with the civil rights enshrined in the principle of classical liberal theory, rights which have achieved gradual realisation in Britain, some from as far ago as Magna Carta (1215) but largely over the past two centuries. (They were given further protection in the Human Rights Act of 1998: see below.)

Box 14.4

Civil rights in the United Kingdom (and some limitations)

- **Political rights**, including the right to vote, guaranteed by Representation of the People Acts (1918, 1928, 1948, 1969).
- **Freedom of movement**, which includes the right to move freely within, and the right to leave, Britain (but note powers to detain suspected terrorists, and police powers to stop and search on suspicion).
- **Personal freedom**, including freedom from detention without charge (Magna Carta 1215, habeas corpus legislation in the 18th century – but note exceptions, especially detention without charge in Northern Ireland, and more recently for suspected terrorists in Britain).
- **Freedom of conscience**, which includes the right to practise any religion, the right of parents to withdraw children from religious instruction in state schools, and the right of conscientious objection to conscription into the armed forces.
- **Freedom of expression**, which includes the right of individuals and the media to communicate information and express opinions, but note freedom of expression is limited by laws on treason, sedition, blasphemy, obscenity, libel, incitement to racial hatred, defamation, contempt of court and the Official Secrets Act.
- **Freedom of association and meeting**, which includes the right to meet, march and protest freely, but note some restrictions by police and other bodies on public order grounds, and restrictions on 'secondary picketing' in industrial disputes.
- **The right to property**, which includes the right to own property and to use it, and not be deprived of it without due process, but note compulsory purchase orders, planning restrictions and the like.
- **The right to privacy**; a general right to privacy is contained in article 8 of the European Convention of Human Rights, now incorporated into English law through the 1998 Human Rights Act, but note exceptions in the interests of state security, which are used to justify political surveillance, phone tapping and the like.
- **Rights at work**, including protection against unfair dismissal, the right to a satisfactory working environment, and freedom from racial and sexual discrimination (all embodied in a series of Acts of Parliament).
- **Social freedoms**, including the freedom to marry and divorce, to practise contraception and seek abortions, and to practise homosexual relations between consenting adults (contained in several post-war Acts of Parliament).

Administrative law: protecting civil liberties and redressing grievances

How are the rights and freedoms set out in Box 14.4 protected in practice? What channels of redress do citizens, groups and organisations have if they feel they have been illegally, unfairly, unreasonably or arbitrarily treated by a public official or public authority? Of course, aggrieved citizens will commonly first pursue a complaint with the organisation directly concerned. They may ask to see the manager, or follow a publicised complaints procedure within the organisation. However there are a number of other recognised channels which may be taken to achieve a remedy. While the first of these is a political channel, the others are judicial or quasi-judicial.

- Contact an elected representative – a Member of Parliament or local councillor.
- Appeal to the ordinary courts for judicial review and remedy.

> **Definition**
>
> **Redress of grievances**: the legitimate expectation by a citizen in a democratic society that complaints against public officials will be considered fairly and impartially, and that legal remedies for wrongs will be available should malpractice be found.

- Appeal to an administrative tribunal.
- Provide evidence to a public inquiry.
- Complain to an ombudsman.
- Invoke the European Convention on Human Rights.

Judicial review

Recourse to the courts can often be expensive and time-consuming, and is normally only effective where a clear breach of the law is involved. Often citizens complain about the merits of a particular decision rather than a breach of the law. However, the ordinary courts have been interpreting more administrative behaviour as involving a breach of the law, and providing more effective remedies. While critics have often accused the judiciary of having a pro-establishment or pro-government bias, over the last 30 or 40 years the political role of the courts in scrutinising the actions of government and public officials has become steadily more important.

The grounds on which an application for review can be made were summarised by Lord Diplock in the GCHQ case as illegality, procedural impropriety and irrationality, to which proportionality can now be added (Box 14.5).

There are however some significant limitations to judicial review in Britain.

> **Definition**
>
> **Judicial review**: the constitutional function exercised by the courts to review the legislation, regulations and acts of the legislative and executive branches of government.

- Judges work within the framework of parliamentary sovereignty. Because Parliament is sovereign, judges cannot strike down legislation as unconstitutional. Thus, in the UK judicial review means preventing public authorities from doing anything that the ordinary law forbids or for which they have no statutory authority. By contrast, in codified constitutions such as the USA, the Supreme Court from the early days of the Republic assumed the role of striking down legislation deemed unconstitutional.
- Judges in Britain cannot pronounce on the merits of legislation – that is, they are not justified in substituting what they would have done for what Parliament enacted on a given occasion. Judges distinguish clearly between matters of policy, on which Parliament is the only authority, and matters concerning lawfulness, on which the courts may legitimately intervene. (However, judges can now declare that legislation appears incompatible with the European Convention on Human Rights: see below.)
- Judicial review can be subject to statutory exclusion.
- The courts themselves in particular types of case have imposed strict limitations on their own power to scrutinise executive action. These types of case relate to executive decisions made under the royal prerogative. They were defined by Lord Roskill in the GCHQ case (1985) to include the making of treaties, the defence of the realm, the prerogative of mercy, the grant of honours, the dissolution of Parliament and the appointment of ministers (Madgwick and Woodhouse 1995: 88).

Administrative tribunals

Appeal by an aggrieved citizen to an administrative tribunal may be more appropriate where a particular decision is involved that does not involve a clear breach in the law – for example the refusal of a grant, or a pension or a licence. Tribunals are a very important part of the British system of administrative justice. They are normally established by legislation and cover a

Box 14.5

Grounds for judicial review

- **Illegality.** The principle here is that exercises of power by public authorities must have specific legal authority. The fundamental doctrine invoked by the courts is *ultra vires* (beyond their powers), which prevents public servants taking actions for which they have no statutory authority (in effect, from acting illegally). When courts investigate an administrative action under an enabling statute, they consider whether the power in question was directly authorised by the statute or whether it may be construed as reasonably incidental to it. They can also consider whether a minister or other public authority abused his, her or its powers by using them for a purpose not intended by statute, or whether, in exercising power, a decision maker took irrelevant factors into account or ignored relevant factors.
- **Procedural impropriety.** The courts also allow executive decisions to be challenged on the grounds that the procedures laid down by statute have not been followed. In reviewing administrative actions, the courts may also invoke the common law principles of natural justice. These are twofold: first, the rule against bias (no one to be a judge in his own cause); and second, the right to a fair hearing (the judge must hear the other side). Under the first rule, administrators must not have any direct (including financial) interest in the outcome of proceedings, nor must they be reasonably suspected of being biased or of being likely to be biased. Justice must not only be done but should be seen to be done. The right to a fair hearing requires that no one should be penalised in any way without receiving notice of the case to be met and being given a fair chance to answer that case and put his or her own case.
- **Irrationality.** This ground for review dates back to a case in 1948 when the judge held that a decision made by an authority would be unreasonable if 'it were so unreasonable that no reasonable authority could have come to it'. Although the test of unreasonableness has been used since then to strike down local authority actions, its use is rare.
- **Proportionality.** The use of proportionality as a ground for judicial review in the 1990s reflects the increasing influence of EU law on British judges, especially the European Court of Justice. Thus the Treaty of Maastricht declares, 'Any action by the Community shall not go beyond what is necessary to achieve the objectives of the Treaty'.

wide range of functions, many of them in the field of welfare. Thus there are tribunals for national insurance, pensions, housing, education, the National Health Service (NHS) and immigration. Claims arising out of injuries at work, industrial disputes, unfair dismissal and redundancy are dealt with by industrial tribunals.

Tribunals are usually composed of a chairman with legal qualifications (often a solicitor) and two lay members representing interests related to the concerns of the particular tribunal. They are independent and not subject to political or administrative interference from the departments under whose aegis they usually work. Their functions may be described as quasi-judicial: to hear appeals against initial decisions of government agencies, or sometimes disputes between individuals and organisations. Their role is to establish the facts of each case and then apply the relevant legal rules to it: that is, in the majority of instances to decide what the statutory rights and entitlements of the aggrieved actually are. Except where the parties request privacy, tribunals hear cases in public. They provide simpler, cheaper, speedier, more expert and more accessible justice than the ordinary courts in their specific sphere of responsibility. It is possible to appeal against their decisions – normally to a superior court, tribunal or a minister. For a small number of tribunals however, including the NHS Tribunal, the Social Security Commissioners and the Immigration Appeal Tribunal, no appeal is available.

Back in 1957 the Franks Committee on Administrative Tribunals and Inquiries recommended that tribunals move towards 'greater openness, fairness and impartiality'. Proceedings should be held in public and reasons for decisions should be given. The parties before tribunals should know in advance the case they have to meet, should have the chance to put their own case either personally or through representatives, and should be able to appeal against decisions. Finally proceedings should not only be impartial, through stronger safeguards regulating their composition, but also be seen to be impartial by no longer being held on the premises of government departments. The general trend of the last quarter of a century has been towards making the procedure of tribunals more judicial, but without forfeiting the advantages of tribunals over ordinary courts. These are greater informality, specialisation, capacity to conduct their own investigations and flexibility in terms of the formulation of reasonable standards in their own spheres.

Public inquiries

Often aggrieved citizens are concerned with some proposed, rather than past, action of a public authority – such as a planned new road, housing development or airport runway. The standard method for giving a hearing to objectors to a government proposal is the public inquiry. Proposals have to be adequately publicised, and third parties have to be afforded the opportunity to state their cases before decisions are taken. Decisions of inquiries may be challenged, on the grounds of either procedure or the substance of the decision, in the High Court within six weeks of the decision.

Courts hearing appeals from inquiry decisions have sought to safeguard the rights of the public. For example, they have ruled that objectors at an inquiry should be able to take 'an active, intelligent and informed part in the decision-making process' (1977) and that they must be given 'a fair crack of the whip' (1976) in putting their case. From the point of view of public authorities, major inquiries have often been unduly expensive and time-consuming. From the perspective of objectors to planning proposals, the dice are heavily weighted against them. They lack the expertise, time and resources available to government and developers. Often objectors claim the terms of reference are too narrow. Thus they may permitted to raise objections to a particular route for a road, but normally not to the need for a road. Yet they do provide a forum where objectors can make their case, and oblige planners to defend their proposals with evidence.

The ombudsman system

As well as legal rights, citizens have a more general right to a good standard of administration. In 1967 the office of the parliamentary commissioner for administration (PCA) was established (commonly referred to as the 'ombudsman', the term long used in Sweden from where the idea came). The ombudsman's brief is to investigate, and if possible remedy, complaints by individuals and corporate bodies who feel that they have experienced 'injustice in consequence of maladministration' at the hands of central government. Maladministration relates to the way in which decisions are made, and can include:

> corruption, bias, unfair discrimination, harshness, misleading a member of the public as to his rights, failing to notify him properly of his rights or to explain the reasons for a decision, general high-handedness, using powers for a wrong purpose, failing to consider relevant materials, taking irrelevant material into account, losing or failing to reply to correspondence, delaying unreasonably before making a tax refund or presenting a tax demand or dealing with an application for a grant or license, and so on.
>
> (de Smith and Brazier 1998)

Appointed by the Crown on the advice of the lord chancellor, the PCA enjoys an independent status similar to that of a High Court judge, and a staff of about 55, largely drawn from the civil service. During investigations, which are conducted in private, the ombudsman can call for the relevant files of the department concerned, and can compel the attendance of witnesses and the production of documents.

Complaints must be referred to the ombudsman through MPs. This was because MPs were concerned that the ombudsman should supplement rather than supplant their own historic role in securing redress of constituents' grievances. Normally only a small proportion of complaints are accepted for investigation – complaints are rejected if they do not involve maladministration, or if there is a right of appeal to a tribunal. The ombudsman issues a report on each investigation to the referring MP, with a copy to the department involved. Where maladministration is found, a department is expected to correct it – for example. by issuing an apology or financial recompense to the aggrieved person – but the ombudsman has no power to compel it to do so. If the department refuses to act, the ombudsman may first bring pressure to bear on it by means of the Commons Select Committee on the PCA, and if this fails, can lay a special report before both Houses of Parliament.

Initially limited to the investigation of maladministration in central government, the ombudsman system was later enlarged by the addition of ombudsmen for Northern Ireland (1969), the National Health Service (1973), and local government in England and Wales (1974) and Scotland (1976). Unlike the position with regard to the PCA, direct access to these ombudsmen is allowed (in the case of local government, only since 1988), and both the health and the local government commissioners receive a much larger volume of complaints than the PCA. As with the PCA, however, neither local government nor health commissioners have any enforcement powers. If a local authority in mainland Britain chooses not to comply with an adverse report by a local ombudsman after various efforts have been made to persuade it, the ombudsman can however require it to publicise the reasons for non-compliance.

Ombudsmen have made a less dramatic impact on British public administration than their early advocates hoped, partly because of lack of public awareness of the system and inadequate powers of enforcement. The only powers of the ombudsmen against a recalcitrant public authority are those of publicity. However, most of their recommendations are accepted and implemented by the departments and authorities concerned, and on occasion they have secured substantial compensation for victims of maladministration. More usually, small-scale payments in compensation follow a report, and sometimes just an apology.

The European Convention on Human Rights and the Human Rights Act

The European Court of Human Rights has long played a part in upholding and enlarging civil liberties in Britain although between 1966 and 1997 it did so in a somewhat roundabout way. The United Kingdom ratified the European Convention on Human Rights in 1951 and allowed individuals to petition the Court from 1966. Although these were not legal rights in Britain and therefore not enforceable in British law, they turned out to be an important influence on civil rights. British courts could take note of the convention and presume Parliament did not intend to legislate inconsistently with it. Moreover, the UK government normally complied with judgements of the European Court. However, these rights were not enforceable in British law because although Britain renewed its ratification of the Convention every year, unlike the other countries who have signed the document it did not incorporate the Convention into British law until 1998. Hence, British citizens were not able to use the Convention to appeal to British courts when their rights were infringed. They were able to appeal to the European Court at Strasbourg, but only after they had tried and failed to find remedies in the British courts. No legal aid was available, and the Court took a long time to reach its judgements – an average of five years for a case to move through the entire process. In all, down to 1997, the Court pronounced on 98 British cases and found violations of human rights in 50 of them. (The United Kingdom has lost more cases before the European Court than any other signatory state.) The decisions of the European Court were not, strictly speaking, enforceable in the United Kingdom. But the UK government agreed to respect the decisions made by the Court, and in practice its verdicts were observed, normally by changing British law accordingly. (Box 14.6 lists the rights available under the European Convention on Human Rights and its Protocols.)

Following its 1997 manifesto promise to incorporate the European Convention on Human Rights into British law, the Labour government passed a Human Rights Act in 1998, which came into force in 2000 (Wadham, in Blackburn and Plant 1999; Wadham and Mountfield 2000; Lester and Clapinska, in Jowell and Oliver 2004). This means that British citizens who consider that their rights have been infringed are now able to take their cases to British courts rather than to the European Court of Human Rights in Strasbourg. The Act makes it illegal for public authorities, including the government, the courts and public bodies discharging public functions, to act in a way incompatible with the European Convention on Human Rights (Box 14.6).

In theory, the Human Rights Act preserves parliamentary sovereignty. Judges do not have the power to strike down Acts of Parliament (as they do in Canada, for example). Instead, they are able to declare a law 'incompatible with the Convention', which should prompt the government and Parliament to change the law through new fast-track procedures. However, Bogdanor (in Seldon 2001: 146–8) argues that the Act 'alters considerably the balance between Parliament and the judiciary' and enables judges 'to interpret parliamentary legislation in terms of a higher law, the European Convention'. Thus 'the Human Rights Act in effect makes the European Convention the fundamental law of the land'. The argument is contentious. Morris (also in Seldon 2001: 378) seems sceptical of the argument that 'major social and political change will be driven by judges rather than legislators', pointing out that 'there is little evidence of this in those countries in which the Convention has long been domestically incorporated'.

While it is perhaps too early to assess the longer-term impact of the Human Rights Act on the British constitution and the relations between the judiciary and the legislature, it has certainly had some significant immediate implications for British politics and law. Thus the European Court of Human Rights declared in 1998 that some provisions in the Representation of the People Act limiting election expenditure violated the Convention, requiring the rewriting of UK legislation on political funding. In 2001 the Court upheld an action by residents in the Heathrow area which claimed that night flights involved an infringement of a basic human right (to sleep). Yet ironically the Human Rights Act has not prevented some British citizens from being deprived of what is generally regarded as a far more basic and important right. Following the attack on the twin

Box 14.6

Rights under the European Convention on Human Rights, and its Protocols (summarised)

Convention

2 Right to life.
3 Freedom from torture or inhuman or degrading treatment or punishment.
4 Freedom from slavery or forced labour.
5 Right to liberty and security of person.
6 Right to a fair trial by an impartial tribunal.
7 Freedom from punishment for an act which did not constitute a criminal offence under law when it was committed.
8 Right to respect for family and private life, home and correspondence.
9 Freedom of thought, conscience and religion.
10 Freedom of expression.
11 Freedom of peaceful assembly and association, including the right to join a trade union.
12 Right to marry and found a family.
13 Right to an effective remedy before a national authority (not included in Human Rights Act 1998).
14 Freedom from discrimination on grounds of sex, race, colour, language, religion, etc.

Protocol No 1

1 Right to peaceful enjoyment of possessions.
2 Right to education. Parental right to the education of their children in conformity with their own religious and philosophical convictions.
3 Right to free elections with a secret ballot.

Protocol No 4 (not ratified by UK, or in the Human Rights Act 1998)

1 Freedom from imprisonment for debt.
2 Freedom of movement for persons.
3 Right to enter and remain in one's own country.
4 Freedom from collective expulsion.

There are other protocols which are yet to be ratified by the UK and are not included in the Human Rights Act (Wadham and Mountfield 2000: 142–8). However, Protocol 6 (abolition of the death penalty except in time of war) is included in the Human Rights Act 1998.

towers on 11 September 2001, the British government introduced emergency legislation to deal with terrorism, including powers to hold terrorist suspects without trial, which would normally infringe article 5 of the Convention – the right to liberty. However article 15 allows the suspension of rights in an emergency. Further measures to counter terrorism followed, and after the bomb attacks on London in July 2005 more proposals were brought forward. How long the courts will be prepared to countenance increasing restrictions on civil liberties to combat the very real threat of terrorism remains to be seen.

Summary

- Britain has not in the past accepted the need for a strict separation of powers. Although the judiciary may be generally free from political interference, leading judges are appointed by politicians, and the head of the judiciary has long been a member of the executive and the presiding officer in the Upper House of the legislature, which combines judicial with legislative functions.
- Reforms initiated in 2003 involve the transformation of the role of the lord chancellor, the introduction of a new and independent Judicial Appointments Commission and the transfer of the House of Lords judicial functions to a new Supreme Court.
- Judges remain unrepresentative of the communities they serve. They are predominantly elderly, white, male and come from an upper-middle-class background.
- While the image of the police in Britain has generally been positive, parts of the police force have been accused of racist, sexist and homophobic attitudes and behaviour, although efforts have been made to remedy this.
- There is no clear coherent system of administrative law in Britain, although there are a number of channels for citizens wishing to make a complaint against government and public authorities.
- Although Britain was an early signatory to the European Convention on Human Rights (ECHR), it was only incorporated into British law in 1998. This has implications for the constitutional principle of parliamentary sovereignty, even though this is formally maintained, as judges have not been given the power to strike out laws incompatible with ECHR.

Questions for discussion

- Why should the judicial functions of the House of Lords be transferred to a new Supreme Court?
- How far and in what respects might judges be considered to be biased?
- How far can the police be trusted to act impartially towards all sections of the community? Are procedures for complaints against the police adequate?
- Should trial by jury be retained?
- Are human rights adequately protected in Britain?
- Has the Human Rights Act effectively destroyed the sovereignty of Parliament?
- How far is it possible to reconcile requirements to protect the community from terrorism with full respect for individual human rights and freedoms?

Further reading

On key themes covered by this chapter, including the rule of law, the executive and the courts and redress of grievances, see Madgwick and Woodhouse, *The Law and Politics of the Constitution* (1995), de Smith and Brazier, *Constitutional and Administrative Law*, 8th edn (1998), Hood-Phillips, Jackson and Leopard, *Constitutional and Administrative Law*, 8th edn (2001) and Barnett, *Constitutional and Administrative Law*, 5th edn (2004).

On the judiciary, see Griffith, *The Politics of the Judiciary* (1997).

On rights, and the debate leading up to the Human Rights Act 1998, see Klug, Starmer and Weir, *The Three Pillars of Liberty* (1996), a special issue of *Political Quarterly* (68:2, April–June 1997), and an article by M. Freeman 'Why rights matter' (1997). Contrasting views of the Human Rights Act can be found in the comments of Bogdanor and Morris in Seldon's *The Blair Effect* (2001). Further background and critical analysis is provided by the director of Liberty, J. Wadham, in Blackburn and Plant, *Constitutional Reform* (1999) and by Lester and Clapinska in Jowell and Oliver, *The Changing Constitution* (2004). A more detailed account, including key texts, is provided in Wadham and Mountfield, *Human Rights Act 1998* (2000).

For the UK Supreme Court and associated constitutional reforms, see Ryan, 'A Supreme Court for the United Kingdom' (2004). For more depth refer to Le Sueur in Jowell and Oliver (2004). See the Department for Constitutional Affairs website www.dca.gov.uk for key documents and latest developments.

Britain and the European Union

Contents

Among the other levels of government beyond Whitehall and Westminster which are now affecting the everyday lives of people living in Britain the most important is the European Union (EU). This is an organisation which did not exist even in embryo at the end of the Second World War, and which the United Kingdom only joined in 1973. Yet it should already be clear from the discussion of many topics in earlier chapters that the European Union has already had massive implications for British politics. It is now necessary to provide in this chapter some more detailed analysis of the European Union, its development, institutions and processes, in order to understand more fully the often problematic relationship between Britain and Europe. We explore the implications of UK membership of the EU for the British state, its politics and its policies. We conclude with a brief examination of the future of the EU, and UK's role within it.

The European ideal 1945–58

The new Europe that emerged in the second half of the 20th century was driven by both politics and economics, but political considerations were paramount. Centuries of division and conflict within Europe, culminating in the death and destruction of the Second World War, had convinced many of the need to end old antagonisms and promote instead a new era of cooperation, peace and prosperity. The wastes of war were all too apparent in 1945. Most of Europe had suffered massively from a conflict that affected civilians as much as, or more than, the armed forces. Many countries had endured the humiliation and privations of defeat and occupation. A substantial part of the industrial capacity and social fabric of Europe had been physically destroyed. Millions of refugees were left homeless and starving. Both those countries that were technically victors in 1945 and those that had clearly been vanquished faced an uncertain economic and political future.

The prospects for democracy in the new and restored states emerging from the ashes of war seemed precarious, particularly in the two countries that had been at the centre of the conflict. Although France had been accorded the status of a partner in the final victory, this hardly obscured the reality of the military and political collapse of France in 1940, or the enduring problems of the French economy, or the continuing depth and bitterness of political and social divisions. Indeed many of these problems remained only too apparent throughout the brief and troubled existence of the Fourth French Republic, which was established in the aftermath of war but never managed to secure legitimacy. Germany seemed in far worse shape, after 12 years of Nazi dictatorship, followed by military defeat and the destruction of its economy. The war's end involved occupation and division of a much reduced Germany, which was additionally burdened by millions of German refugees from Poland, the Baltic states and Czechoslovakia.

It was partly because of the scale of the problems faced by Europe in general, and France and Germany in particular, that many sought Franco-German reconciliation and closer European integration, to prevent any recurrence of the scale of the disasters that had overwhelmed Europe twice in 30 years. Thus the prime motive of the architects of what is now the European Union was the prevention of war. While it was certainly hoped that closer European integration would help rebuild agricultural and industrial production, a principal objective was to lock the economies of France and Germany so closely together as to render another war between them impossible, as Robert Schuman argued in introducing the Schuman Plan in 1950. This was a strong motive also for other European states (such as Belgium) which had suffered from Franco-German conflict.

Robert Schuman and Jean Monnet, the founding fathers of the new Europe, did not imagine that a closer European union could be established quickly or easily. Rather, they envisaged that an ongoing process of integration of key policy areas would lead over time to closer union, as states and peoples experienced the practical benefits of cooperation. Thus the European Coal and Steel Community (ECSC) of 1952 established a supranational body, the High Authority (forerunner of the European Commission), with extensive powers to regulate the coal and steel industries in the member states. The same countries as formed the ECSC, France, Germany, Italy and the Benelux states, went on sign the Treaty of Rome in 1957, inaugurating the European Economic Community (EEC), which established a customs union with internal free trade and a common external tariff, and the European Atomic Energy Authority (Euratom). The most important common policy established in the early years was the Common Agricultural Policy (CAP), which initially absorbed three-quarters of the EEC budget, although subsequently increasing funds were devoted to social and regional policies.

Britain and Europe 1945–73

British governments initially took no part in these developments. Geography and history have combined to keep Britain both part of, and apart from, Europe. While the channel has continued to provide a physical and symbolic barrier, Britain has remained closely linked with western Europe in terms of its religion, culture, trade and politics. Despite growing global interests from the 16th century onwards, concerns over the balance of power on the continent and rivalry with other European states over trade and colonisation involved Britain periodically in coalitions and wars with its continental neighbours, culminating in the World Wars of the 20th century.

At the end of the Second World War, however, British concerns and interests appeared different from those of the rest of Europe. Britain retained the illusion of great power status, one of the 'big three' that had defeated Nazi Germany, with a still-extensive overseas empire. Its political system was stable, its economic and financial interests remained worldwide. Not having experienced the miseries of defeat and occupation, British politicians and the British public generally saw no imperative need for closer economic and political integration with other European states. British politicians were certainly concerned about the future of Europe. However, Britain's Empire and Commonwealth, coupled with the transatlantic 'special relationship' with the USA, provided strong conflicting influences on Britain in the period immediately after the Second World War (see Chapter 2). Although Winston Churchill called for 'a kind of United States of Europe' in a speech at Zurich in 1946, he went on to make plain that Britain would be among the 'friends and sponsors of the new Europe' rather than an integral part of it. Thus although British governments took a generally benevolent interest in the moves towards closer European integration by their continental neighbours, they remained aloof from the establishment of the European Coal and Steel Community in 1952 and the European Economic Community in 1958 by France, Germany, Italy and the Benelux countries. Indeed, the UK government took the lead in establishing a rival trading block, the European Free Trade Association.

Political and economic developments combined to provoke a rapid reassessment of

Britain's relations with Europe from the mid-1950s onwards. The swift liquidation of the British Empire was one factor. The opposition of the USA and even some Commonwealth countries to the disastrous 1956 Anglo-French Suez expedition was a defining moment, which destroyed lingering illusions of Britain's world power status. Continuing economic problems evidenced by low growth, adverse trade balances and recurring sterling crises contrasted with the strong economic performance of the EEC countries. Thus Harold Macmillan's Conservative government sought entry in 1961. Diplomatic negotiations dragged on into 1963, when they were abruptly terminated with the veto of the French president, General de Gaulle. Wilson's Labour government met a similar rebuff when it tried to enter the EEC in 1967, and it was only the removal of de Gaulle from power which finally enabled Heath's Conservative government to join the EC, along with Ireland and Denmark, in 1973.

Box 15.1

Europe: What's in a name?

European Coal and Steel Community (ECSC) Precursor of EC/EU established in 1952 following Treaty of Paris.

European Economic Community (EEC) Established 1958, along with Euratom (European Atomic Energy Community) after 1957 Treaty of Rome.

Common Market Term used in Britain to describe the EEC in its early years. The Rome Treaty did involve a Common Market, but promised more.

European Community (or the **European Communities**) Technically resulted from the merger of ECSC, EEC and Euratom in 1965.

European Union Term adopted after the Treaty of the European Union (TEU or Maastricht Treaty), 1992.

The development of the European ideal: integration and enlargement

The history of the EU can be presented as a triumphal process towards ever-deeper European integration and a steady expansion in membership, population and boundaries. Yet the progress has often been slow and uneven, while there has been some increasing tension between enlargement and integration, between widening and deepening the European Community/Union.

One indication of the success of any club is the enthusiasm of new members to join it. By that token the EU has been very successful. There has been a progressive enlargement of what began as the European Economic Community in 1958. The original six members were joined in 1973 by three more, the United Kingdom, Ireland and Denmark. Greece joined in 1981 and Spain and Portugal in 1986. German reunion following the fall of the Berlin Wall led to a significant increase in the size of the German state and the population of the EU. In 1995 Austria, Finland and Sweden joined, bringing the number of member states to 15. In 2004 a further ten states, mainly from former communist eastern Europe, became part of the EU, following the enthusiastic endorsement of membership by their citizens in referendums. Bulgaria and Rumania are negotiating for membership in 2007. Rather more controversially, in October 2005 accession talks began with Turkey, despite strong reservations from some EU states, particularly Austria. The issue is by no means decided, and major obstacles remain (including a still divided Cyprus). The earliest date Turkey could join the EU is 2014.

The EU remains popular not only with the original six founding states, but among a substantial majority of the peoples of the states that joined from 1973 onwards. Ireland has prospered economically. For Greece, Spain and Portugal, which had only recently escaped from dictatorial government, membership of the European club brought both political and economic benefits. Many of the former eastern European states, and new states established following the collapse of the USSR, similarly hope for increased political stability and economic growth from being locked into the western European political and economic system.

Alongside the continuing enlargement of the EC/EU there have also been some uneven but significant steps towards closer integration among

Table 15.1 Enlargement of the European Community/Union

Dates	Countries
1952, 1957 (original members of ECSC and EEC)	Belgium, France, Germany, Italy, Luxembourg, Netherlands
1973 (first enlargement)	Denmark, Ireland, United Kingdom
1981	Greece
1986	Portugal, Spain
1995	Austria, Finland, Sweden
2004	Cyprus, Czech Republic, Estonia, Hungary, Latvia, Lithuania, Malta, Poland, Slovakia, Slovenia
2007 (projected)	Bulgaria, Rumania

Figure 15.1 Enlargement of the European Community/Union 1952–2007

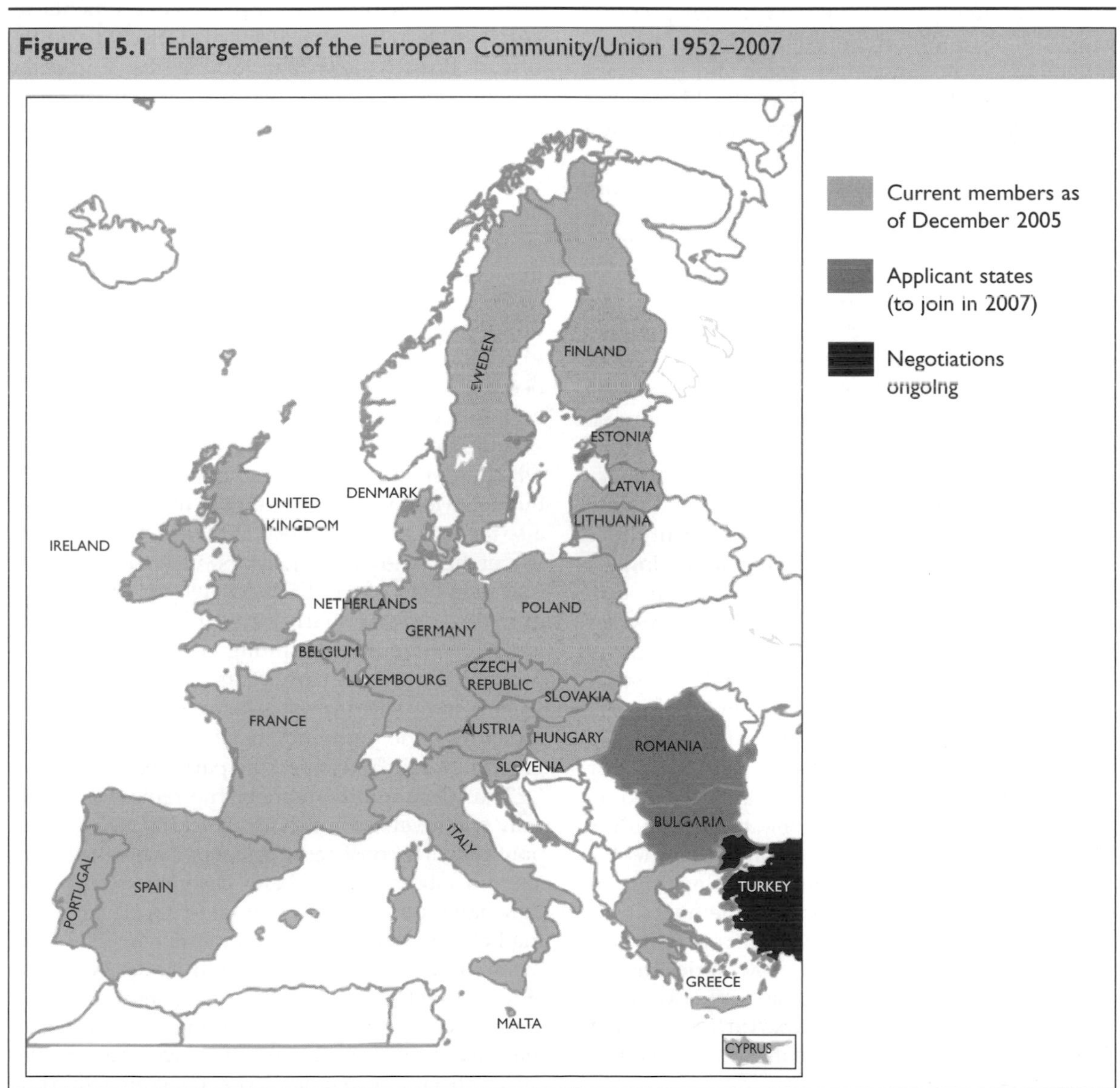

Source: adapted from Nugent, 2002.

its existing member states. This was initially rendered more difficult by the unanimity rule, as common policies required the full consent of all member states and could be prevented by the veto of any member. Thus after the early progress of the EC, the pace of European integration slowed in the 1970s and early 1980s. Crucially, non-tariff barriers to trade still impeded the development of a full European internal market. It was only in 1986, with agreement on the Single European Act, that a timetable was finally agreed for the elimination of non-tariff barriers to trade and competition by 1992.

The 1992 Maastricht Treaty, or Treaty of the European Union (TEU), marked further progress towards closer integration, particularly a timetable towards monetary union and the adoption of a Social Chapter by 11 of the 12 member states. It also involved agreement on a common foreign and security policy, and cooperation on justice and home affairs. The new momentum towards closer integration was maintained with the Treaties of Amsterdam (1997) and Nice (2000), and particularly with the formal inauguration of the common currency, the euro, in 1999 and the introduction of notes and coins to replace national currencies in 12 member states in 2002.

Yet there are some doubts on the capacity of the EU to absorb so many new states without impeding further progress towards closer integration. Each of the past enlargements shifted the balance of power and interests within the EC/EU, and each has put some strain on existing institutions and policies. The 2004 enlargement, involving ten new member states, required an extensive modification of existing institutions and procedures (see below), and some fundamental adjustments to existing policies, particularly the CAP. A massive redirection of social and regional funds is needed to reduce the increased disparities between regions following enlargement. This inevitably involves reductions in regional aid directed to poorer regions of older member states, including Britain. Moreover, the euro cannot become the single European currency for the whole of the EU for the foreseeable future, as new member states are not ready, and some older member states (the UK, Denmark and Sweden) have so far declined to participate. The entry of Bulgaria and Rumania (expected in 2007), and perhaps Turkey also at a later date, may further impede the development of more common policies.

Britain and Europe

British entry into the European club failed to settle the issue of UK relations with Europe, for the British conversion to the EC was never wholehearted, at either elite or mass level. In so far as Community membership was sold to the British public it was on the basis of presumed economic benefits – higher growth and living standards. The EC's political implications, evident from the pronouncements of its leading founding figures and in the Treaty of Rome, were largely ignored. This was not (as has sometimes been suggested) a deliberate conspiracy by British governments to keep people in the dark. It simply reflected a widespread British view that joining the European 'Common Market' (as it was then widely called in Britain) was essentially a 'bread and butter' issue – quite literally in the case of some opponents, who made much of the projected effect of entry on the price of a standard loaf and a pound of butter.

Yet the economic benefits of UK entry were not immediately obvious. Partly this was because the UK joined too late to influence the shape and early development of the EC. Thus the UK had to sign up to rules designed by others to meet the economic needs of the original six member states. The British economy with its relatively tiny agricultural sector was unlikely to benefit significantly from the CAP, which then absorbed three-quarters of the EC budget. Moreover 1973, the year of UK entry, was also the year of the energy crisis which signalled the end of the post-war economic boom. While the original members of the EC had enjoyed substantial growth rates and sharply rising living standards which ensured the continuing popularity of European integration, the early years of UK membership were accompanied by 'stagflation' (see Chapter 2) rather than the promised sustained higher rates of growth. Britain had joined the party too late.

Thus Community membership remained politically controversial in Britain. The only mainstream political party consistently in favour were the Liberals, and subsequently Liberal Democrats (and even they have contained a few dissidents). The bulk of the Labour Party had opposed entry in 1973, and the return of a Labour government under Wilson in 1974 entailed a renegotiation of the terms of entry and a referendum in 1975, resulting in a two-thirds majority for staying in. Yet although the government officially recommended a Yes vote, a third of the Cabinet campaigned on the opposite side, and Labour remained deeply divided on the issue. On the British left the EC was widely perceived as a rich man's capitalist club, providing the economic underpinning for NATO. By 1983, and back in opposition, Labour was pledged to withdrawal from the EC without even a prior referendum.

Most Conservatives were then far more enthusiastic about Europe. After all, Britain's membership of the EC was a Conservative achievement, supported in her early years by Margaret Thatcher who, although she had belligerently demanded and obtained a rebate from the EC budget, went on to sign and endorse the 1986 Single European Act. It was only towards the end of her premiership that Thatcher's own reservations on European integration and the threat it presented to Britain's national sovereignty became clearer:

> To try to suppress nationhood and concentrate power at the centre of the European conglomerate would be highly damaging...We have not successfully rolled back the frontiers of the state in Britain only to see them reimposed at a European level with a European superstate exercising a new dominance from Brussels.
>
> (Margaret Thatcher, speech at Bruges, 1988)

Even so, Thatcher (rather reluctantly) agreed to UK entry to the Exchange Rate Mechanism (ERM) in October 1990, and it was only after her fall from power soon afterwards that her opposition to the whole European project intensified. John Major, her successor, seemed more enthusiastic about Europe:

> My aim for Britain in the Community can be simply stated. I want us to be where we belong. At the very heart of Europe. Working with our partners in building the future.
>
> (John Major, speech, 1991)

However, the Maastricht Treaty was to mark further divisions with Britain's European partners, as John Major's government negotiated an opt-out from the 'Social Chapter' and monetary union (see below). Indeed, the problems that Major's government encountered over Britain's brief membership of the ERM and the ensuing catastrophe of 'Black Wednesday' in 1992 (see Chapter 2) fuelled increasing Euro-scepticism on the Conservative benches. At the same time the Labour Party was becoming more favourable to the European Union, and, in principle, towards European monetary integration. Thus the two major parties had almost reversed their positions compared with 20 years previously.

Blair came to power in 1997 with an apparently much more positive attitude to the EU, and his government quickly signed up to the Social Chapter. Yet after two full terms of Labour in power the divisions between Britain and much of continental Europe appear as strong or stronger than ever, particularly on the key issues of monetary union, economic policy and foreign policy.

Monetary union is perhaps the most significant step towards European integration that has been taken since the establishment of the EC, yet Britain remains on the sidelines. While the prime minister continued to insist that the government was committed to joining the euro in principle, his chancellor, Gordon Brown, sounded a more cautious note, laying down five economic tests which must be met first (see Box 15.3). Following the second landslide election victory in 2001, over a Conservative Party fighting to 'Save the pound', there were predictions that Labour would seek entry early in the new Parliament. Yet this did not happen. The real obstacle was perhaps less Brown's economic conditions than Labour's commitment, made in opposition, to hold a referendum should the government seek to join the euro. Opinion polls continued to suggest that the government would have great difficulty in winning such a referendum. In 2004 Blair did commit his government to a referendum, planned for 2006, but on the issue of the proposed new European constitution rather than the single currency. The rejection of that constitution by French and Dutch voters appeared to render a British referendum pointless (see below). The new crisis over the constitution means there is little immediate prospect of Britain joining the euro.

However it was not simply the euro that has continued to divide the UK from Europe. Despite acceptance of the Social Chapter, the Blair government continued to champion flexible labour markets in the face of the more corporatist approach of the European Union and most other member states. It is sometimes suggested that New Labour prefers what has come to be called the Anglo-Saxon or American free market model

Box 15.2

Gordon Brown's five economic conditions for British membership of the euro

1. A sustainable convergence between the economies of Britain and Euroland.
2. Sufficient flexibility to cope with economic change.
3. New opportunities for investment.
4. A positive effect on the UK financial services industry.
5. A beneficial impact on UK employment, growth and trade.

of capitalism rather than the more interventionist Rhineland or European alternative.

More significant perhaps are the differences that have emerged over foreign policy since 11 September 2001, with Blair's Britain emerging as the closest ally of US President Bush's global campaign against terrorism. This was in marked contrast to increasing French and German reservations over US policy in general, and towards Iraq and Israel in particular, and has reawakened doubts over Britain's European credentials. The old tensions between Britain's relationship with Europe and its 'special relationship' with the USA that have plagued previous governments have re-emerged.

Thus the UK is still widely perceived as an 'awkward partner' (George 1998), at a time when the European Union was taking decisive steps towards closer integration and substantial enlargement. Yet other European countries have sometimes shared British reservations over the pace and extent of European integration. France has at times also appeared an 'awkward partner', particularly under President de Gaulle, who feared that French national sovereignty and interests might be subordinated in a federal Europe. Since then France has often been slow to implement EU regulations. Voters in Denmark initially rejected the Maastricht Treaty. Both Denmark and Sweden, along with the UK, initially declined to join the euro, and even the Germans had considerable reservations over exchanging the strong and successful deutschmark for the new and untried European currency. Germany and France are both currently resisting long-overdue reforms of the CAP, which must be completed. Even the Irish threatened to derail the Nice Treaty (together with EU enlargement) by voting to reject it in a referendum, a decision reversed by a second referendum in 2002. The rejection of the EU constitution in 2005 by voters in two of the original six member states, France and the Netherlands, was a bigger shock. However, it is the British who are still largely perceived as the most reluctant Europeans. In the aftermath of the rejection of the new constitution, the British government is under strong pressure to give up the rebate negotiated by Thatcher, which is considered unjustifiable in the changed circumstances of a much enlarged EU. On this issue, Britain appears to be isolated.

The European Union: superstate or intergovernmental organisation?

From its beginning there has been controversy over the nature of the EC/EU and the direction in which it is going. Some talked from the start of a United States of Europe, a 'USE', whose political and economic clout would match that of the USA. They had no reservations in proposing a federal system on US lines, in which supreme power or sovereignty would be effectively divided between two or more levels of government. Others envisaged a weaker form of association, sometimes termed a confederation rather than a federation. General de Gaulle, the former French president, talked of a *Europe des Patries*, essentially an intergovernmental association of sovereign nation states. Fifty years after its original establishment, the nature and scope of Europe's political union remains both unclear and extremely contentious.

Much of continental Europe is untroubled by talk of federalism. Countries such as Germany, Belgium and Spain, already federal or quasi-federal countries, see the EU as just another tier in a system of multi-level governance. Sovereignty is not lost, but pooled. For a substantial body of opinion in Britain, federalism is the dreaded 'f word'. Euroscepticism and euro-phobia have been fed by fears of the EU's political agenda and the threat to the

Table 15.2 Time chart: key dates in the development of the EC/EU and in UK involvement

1950	The Schuman Declaration (or Schuman Plan)
1951	Treaty of Paris to establish the European Coal and Steel Community
1952	European Coal and Steel Community instituted
1957	Treaty of Rome to establish European Economic Community (EEC) and Euratom
1958	EEC and Euratom initiated (France, Germany, Italy, Benelux countries)
1960	Rival European Free Trade Area (EFTA) established
1961	UK (Macmillan, Conservative government), Ireland and Denmark apply to join EEC
1963	French veto (President De Gaulle) terminates UK entry negotiations
1967	Second UK attempt to join EEC by Labour government under Harold Wilson leads to renewed French veto
1970	Conservative government under Heath initiates third attempt to join EEC
1973	UK, Ireland and Denmark join the EEC. Membership enlarged from six to nine states
1974	Labour government (Wilson) begins renegotiation of terms of entry
1975	Labour government recommends 'Yes' vote in referendum on whether UK should stay in EC. Two-thirds of voters vote 'Yes'.
1979	First direct elections for European Parliament
1981	Greece joins the European Community
1983	Labour Party pledged to UK withdrawal from EC without a referendum
1986	Spain and Portugal join the EC. Single European Act signed.
1990	UK (Thatcher government) joins European Exchange Rate Mechanism (ERM)
1992	Maastricht Treaty (TEU). John Major secures opt out from 'Social Charter' and monetary integration. 'Black Wednesday': UK forced out of ERM.
1995	Austria, Finland, Sweden join European Union
1997	Amsterdam Treaty (in force 1999). Labour government signs up to Social Chapter.
1999	The euro becomes the official currency for 11 EU member states. European Commission resigns following fraud and corruption allegations.
2000	Nice Treaty
2001	Conservatives (under Hague) fight election campaign to 'Save the Pound'
2002	Euro notes and coins replace national currencies in 12 EU member states
2004	Ten more countries join the European Union, increasing the number of member states to 25. Blair promises a referendum on the new constitution for the EU. EU leaders agree start date (October 2005) for accession talks for Turkey.
2005	Voters in France and the Netherlands reject the proposed new European constitution. Blair scraps plans for a referendum in Britain. Britain faces new pressure over the rebate negotiated by Margaret Thatcher.

sovereignty of the Westminster Parliament and British independence. Indeed, as EU law is supreme over the law of member states, the constitutional principle of parliamentary sovereignty is now questionable (see Chapters 10 and 14).

It was fears of the growing power of EU institutions that led to the formal declaration at the Maastricht Treaty of the clumsily-named 'principle of subsidiarity' (see Box 15.3). Thus the Treaty requires the Community 'to take action … only if and insofar as the objective of the proposed action cannot be sufficiently achieved by the Member States' and can 'by reason of its scale and effects be better achieved by the Community'. This may be seen as an application of a wider principle that decisions ought to be taken at the lowest level consistent with efficiency. The implication here is that decisions might be devolved below the nation-state level to devolved regional government or local government. Indeed, the Maastricht Treaty gave some encouragement to such devolution of power, establishing a new Committee of the Regions to represent such sub-national interests. The devolution of power to national executives and assemblies in the UK, and variable pressure for English regional government, fit into this agenda.

European monetary union has appeared the most serious and immediate threat to those concerned over a potential loss of British national sovereignty and British (or English) national identity. Euro-sceptics see the national currency as a crucial symbol of national independence and a key element of national economic policy. The challenge has been further emphasised by the introduction of euro notes and coins among 12 member states in 2002. Yet others fear that if Britain remains outside 'Euroland' the country will lose influence in Europe, 'left in the slow lane' in a 'two-speed' EU.

British Euro-sceptics also raised alarms over the proposed new European Constitution. Much of this simply codified past treaties and confirmed principles already accepted, such as the supremacy of European law over the law of member states, although it also involves some changes in institutions and procedures made necessary because of enlargement. The emphatic 'no' votes in France and the Netherlands on this constitution in 2005 enabled Blair to abandon plans for a referendum in Britain which increasingly looked unwinnable.

Box 15.3

The principle of subsidiarity

The Community shall act within the limits of the powers conferred on it by this Treaty and of the objectives assigned to it therein.

In areas which do not fall within its exclusive competence, the Community shall take action, in accordance with the principle of subsidiarity, only if and in so far as the objectives of the proposed action cannot be sufficiently achieved by the Member States and can therefore, by reason of the scale or effects of the proposed action, be better achieved by the Community.

Any action by the Community shall not go beyond what is necessary to achieve the objectives of this Treaty.

Article 3b of the Treaty Establishing the European Union.

The institutions and processes of the European Union

The controversy over the very nature of the EU discussed in the last section is an essential preliminary to any appreciation of the issues surrounding its very complex institutions and processes. From the start there was a tension between the interests of the EC/EU as a whole, and the interests of the separate member states, and this tension is fully reflected in EC/EU institutions. Those who wish to see and those who fear the development of a European 'superstate' or a federal United States of Europe can find in the supranational institutions all the elements of a sovereign state. There is a kind of executive in the form of the European Commission, a legislature (at least potentially) in the shape of the European Parliament, and a judiciary in the European Court of Justice (see Table 15.3). (Other supranational bodies include the Economic and Social Committee, the Court of Auditors, the European Central Bank and the European Investment Bank.)

Yet alongside these institutions which are all supposed to serve the interests of the EC/EU as a whole there are others that look after the interests of member states. These include the Council of Ministers, consisting of national politicians served by their own national civil servants in the

Table 15.3 The location, composition and functions of key European Union institutions

Institution	Location	Composition	Functions	Comments
European Commission	Brussels	1 Commissioner for each member state. Serves for 4 years	Propose laws Draft budget Administer laws and policies	Commissioners swear allegiance to EU, head Directorates
European Court of Justice	Luxembourg	26 judges, 1 from each member state plus 1 additional	Rules on EU law, adjudicates in disputes	EU law supreme over state law
European Parliament	Strasbourg – committees may meet in Brussels	MEPs directly elected by voters in member states (by regional list system)	Largely consultative, but increasing role in legislation, and budget	MEPs sit in European parties, not in national blocks
Economic and Social Committee	Brussels	Representatives of interests	Purely consultative	Marginalised in modern EU
Committee of the Regions	Brussels	Representatives of regions of EU	Consultative role, particularly on regional policy	Established after Maastricht Treaty
Council of Ministers	Largely in Brussels	Relevant ministers of member states	Defends member state interests	Unanimity still needed on major issues
COREPER (Committee of Permanent Representatives)	Brussels	Civil servants on secondment from member states	Bureaucracy serving Council of Ministers	Do initial work for Council of Ministers
European Council	Peripatetic	Heads of government	Forum for resolving key issues	From 1974, now crucial

Committee of Permanent Representatives (COREPER), but increasingly more important than either, the European Council, involving regular meetings of the heads of government of member states (see Table 15.3). Each member state currently holds the presidency of the European Union for a six-month period in rotation, and initial meetings are held at locations in the country holding the presidency (although if the new constitution is ever ratified, this will involve a more settled longer-term EU presidency).

Even in the early days when there were only six member states, decision making was not made easy in the Council of Ministers by the unanimity rule, which meant that the government of any single member state could prevent action by using its veto. In 1965 French ministers refused to attend the Council of Ministers, effectively preventing any decisions. The 'empty chair' crisis was eventually resolved by the 'Luxembourg compromise' under which the veto was retained for issues of great importance to member states, but a system of qualified majority voting (QMV) is used for other issues. Progressive enlargement of the EC/EU has made it more necessary to streamline decision making. Today some matters are decided by simple majority, others by qualified majority, but the veto is still jealously guarded by member states, particularly the UK, for some key policy areas.

While some of these procedural issues are of mind-boggling complexity, the crucial point is not too difficult to grasp. The EU involves a curious constitutional hybrid, part embryo state, part intergovernmental organisation. Throughout its history there has been a built-in tension between its quasi-federal and intergovernmental institutions and interests. Where the balance of power really lies is partly a matter of perception, but partly also may vary over time and particularly over policy areas. It is difficult to be definite over longer-term trends. Increased EU regulation and common policies fuel the fears of Euro-sceptics, but the obstinate and often successful defence of national interests particularly by the larger member states can make Euro-enthusiasts despair.

The European Commission

It is the European Commission that is commonly perceived as the essence and centre of the supranational authority of the European Union. Although it has not become the effective executive for the federal Europe envisaged by Jean Monnet, it retains a key role in the initiation of legislation and new regulations, and has detailed responsibility for the administration of the EU. While commissioners are nominated by member states, the commissioners are not supposed to look after the interests of their own country, but have to swear an undertaking to serve the union as a whole. They each take charge of at least one of the Commission's directorates (or departments), which are each responsible for a particular policy area or service. Until the 2004 enlargement the larger member states nominated two commissioners each, while the smaller countries nominated one. Now each country regardless of size nominates one commissioner. The president of the Commission is a key political figure. Past presidents include Britain's Roy Jenkins and the controversial French politician, Jacques Delors.

While Euro-sceptics lament the power of the European Commission, it is often suggested that this supra-national body has progressively lost its leadership role (Nugent 2002: 148–9, Cram, Dinan and Nugent 1999: 44–61). From the start the Commission was relatively less dominant than the equivalent High Authority in the European Coal and Steel Community, and the Commission by itself proved unable to lead and develop further European integration in the face of French opposition under de Gaulle. It was only intergovernmental conferences that finally succeeded in breaking the deadlock, and restoring some forward momentum to the European project. This reflected the reality of the power of the member states. Since then the Council of Ministers and the European Council (effectively a new supreme intergovernmental institution not envisaged by the Founding Fathers) have gained at the expense of the Commission. In 1984 the secretary general of the European Commission complained of the 'institutional drift away from the spirit, and indeed the letter, of the Treaties of Rome'. He argued that 'the Community system is gradually degenerating into intergovernmental negotiation', which he blamed on the unanimity rule and 'the constant intervention of the European Council'. The prestige of the Commission was further damaged by revelations of fraud and corruption. These led to the resignation of the entire Commission in 1999 and the initiation of a reform programme. These developments obliged the Commission to take more notice of the European Parliament, which in 2004 declined to accept the proposed new Commission until changes were made in key posts.

The European Court of Justice

The European Court of Justice (ECJ)is the supreme judicial body in the EU. One judge is nominated by each member state for a six-year period. The Court interprets and rules on EU law, and adjudicates in disputes between EU institutions and member states. European law overrides the national law of member states, and has to be implemented, although implementation has sometimes been delayed. The increasing workload of the ECJ led to long delays in obtaining judgements, so a subsidiary Court of First Instance was introduced to speed up the judicial process. However, national courts are also required to apply European law and existing case law of the European Court of Justice. This principle has already been accepted by the House of Lords (Craig, in Jowell and Oliver 2004, ch. 4)

The European Parliament

The European Parliament gained some additional authority and legitimacy following the introduction of direct elections in 1979, although consistently low turnouts by voters in Britain and increasingly in other countries (see below) suggest some lack of interest in democracy at the European level. Part of the problem is that these elections do not appear to decide very much. National elections in Britain, France, Germany and other countries may lead to the fall of governments, and sometimes significant changes in policy. However, elections for the European Parliament have little if any immediate impact on the government and decision making of the EU, even though the European Parliament has gained additional powers from the Single European Act and Maastricht Treaty.

Each member state elects a number of members of the European Parliament (MEPs) roughly in proportion to the size of population, but allowing some over-representation of the smaller states. Germany has 99 MEPs, France, the UK and Italy 78 each, other countries fewer, down to Malta with just five. There are currently 732 MEPs in all. Until 1999 elections for the European Parliament in Britain were conducted under the first-past-the-post system, leading to wildly fluctuating party representation at Strasbourg. Other member states used some version of proportional representation, mostly a regional party list system, which Britain adopted in 1999.

In practice, elections for the European Parliament involve large remote electoral areas, generally little-known candidates, and predominantly national rather than European issues, which may help to explain the low and declining turnout figures that have caused concern. Until 2004 the turnout in Britain was invariably the lowest by far in the European Union – only one in four bothered to vote in 1999. In 2004 UK elections for the European Parliament were held on the same day as local elections, while trials of postal ballots also raised turnout levels to 38 per cent. Meanwhile turnout levels fell markedly from previously higher figures in France and Germany (both 43 per cent) and Sweden (37 per cent). Surprisingly, some of the new member states recorded even lower voting figures (for instance, Poland 20 per cent, Slovakia 17 per cent) despite the enthusiasm their citizens has earlier shown for joining the EU. Only those countries where voting is compulsory have high turnouts (such as Belgium, 91 per cent).

Once elected, MEPs do not sit in national blocks but in European party groups. Thus British Labour MEPs form part of the European Socialists Group, Conservative MEPs currently belong to the European Peoples Party and European Democrats

In Focus 15.1

The European Parliament

Often dismissed as a talking shop, the European Parliament has acquired more real power in recent years. The multi-lingual slogans on the EU Parliament building at Strasbourg underline the practical problems involved in the large and growing number of official languages in which EU institutions have to conduct their business. Members of the European Parliament can address the Parliament in their own language. An army of translators almost instantaneously converts the speech into all the official EU languages, so that MEPs, officials and visitors can listen to it in their own language through headphones. This generally works well, although words in translation can have political connotations absent in the original. Another problem is multi-site working. Main sessions are at Strasbourg, while much committee work is undertaken at Brussels, and administrative support is provided from Luxembourg.

Photograph: EMPICS.

(although David Cameron is pledged to take Conservative MEPs out of this pro-Europe party group), while the Liberal Democrats belong to the Alliance of Liberals and Democrats for Europe. No party has an overall majority. The 2004 elections are difficult to compare with 1999 because of the additional MEPs elected for new member states. Overall, parties responsible for national governments tended to be punished by voters, and there was some increase in support for Euro-sceptic or anti-European parties. Thus in Britain the UK Independence Party won 12 seats, compared with just three in 1999. Whether this turns out to be a significant long-term political breakthrough or a flash in the pan remains to be seen.

Much criticism has been directed at an alleged 'democratic deficit' – the apparent weakness of democratic control and accountability within Europe. Yet while the European Parliament is often denounced as a mere talking shop with little real power, the same is widely alleged of many national parliaments, including the Westminster Parliament (see Chapter 13). Indeed, recent reforms have given the European Parliament more involvement in legislation and the budget. The Commission has become more accountable to the European Parliament following the scandal over corruption in 1999 and the refusal of Parliament to accept the proposed new Commission in 2004. In some respects MEPs arguably now have rather more influence over the Commission than backbench MPs at Westminster have over the British Cabinet.

The real problem for the European Parliament is the hybrid nature of the EU and the power of intergovernmental bodies such as the Council of Ministers and the European Council. In so far as the governments of member states, accountable to national parliaments, often seem to take the crucial decisions, the influence of the European Parliament is likely to remain peripheral. Nor is it likely in these circumstances that voters will perceive European Parliament elections as important or meaningful. Yet there is an element of hypocrisy in some of the criticisms. Thus Euro-sceptics routinely condemn the 'democratic deficit' at Strasbourg and Brussels but generally resist proposals to give the European Parliament more powers, because this would encroach on the sovereignty of nation states and national parliaments.

Bureaucracy in the European Union

The EU is also widely criticised for its bureaucracy. In so far as bureaucracy implies regulation and 'red tape', that is the essence of modern government and indeed modern organisation. If bureaucracy is taken to mean officialdom, there are obvious reasons why the bureaucracy of the EU should appear cumbersome. The institutional complexity of the EU requires a similarly complicated bureaucracy. Besides the bureaucracy serving the Commission (which is small by the standards of member state administrations), there are the officials of COREPER on whom the Council of Ministers and European Council is dependent, and the administrative support services for the European Parliament and

Table 15.4 Party representation in the European Parliament following the 2004 elections

Party	Seats	UK MEPs
European United Left/Nordic Green Left	41	
Party of European Socialists	200	19 (Lab)
Greens European Free Alliance	48	5 (Greens, SNP, PC)
Independence and Democracy	37	11 (UKIP)
Alliance of Liberals and Democrats for Europe	88	12 (Liberal Democrats)
European People's Party and European Democrats	268	28 (27 Con, 1 UUP)
Union for Europe of Nations	27	
Non-aligned	29	2 (DUP, SF)

other EU organisations. Operating in three principal sites hardly helps. While MEPs attend plenary sessions of the European Parliament at Strasbourg and committee meetings in Brussels, their officials are based in Luxembourg. More important still, the number of languages now involved in the EU requires a veritable army of translators and interpreters. Procedures are undoubtedly complex, as anyone can testify who has struggled to interpret the convoluted flow diagrams that are sometimes helpfully supplied to provide a 'simplified' summary of the various procedures for approving new legislation or the annual budget. Some of this complexity arises from the necessity of consulting and winning the approval of member states, key institutions and major interests within the EU.

The impact of the European Union on the British state and government

The impact of membership of the EU on the British state and system of government can be considered at various levels: first, its effect on the British constitution and long-established constitutional principles, second, its effect on the machinery of government, and third, its impact on the day-to-day process of governing.

Some initial discussion of the impact of EU membership on the British constitution has already been provided (for example in Chapter 10). Needless to say, the issue remains highly contentious. For Euro-sceptics, the EU presents a continuing and increasing threat to British national sovereignty and the sovereignty of the Westminster Parliament. Those more well disposed toward the EU emphasise the gains resulting from pooled sovereignty (e.g. Cope, in Savage and Atkinson 2001). Indeed, it can be argued that even if the UK was outside the EU, the freedom of action of the British government would be constrained by the EU and its influence on world trade and investment, without it being able to influence EU policy. The European treaties signed by British governments are not so very different from other treaties: benefits are secured in exchange for undertakings that constrain future freedom of action.

Yet obligations arising from membership of the EU do differ from the obligations imposed and freely accepted in other treaties and international associations, in both scope and kind, particularly because of their major implications for a wide range of domestic policies. More specifically, the British government and the Westminster Parliament have had to accept the supremacy of EU law over UK law. It is true that the British government can influence the framing of EU law, and that there are procedures for consultation with the parliaments of member states as part of the EU, but it is difficult to deny that parliamentary sovereignty has been affected. However, it is not just membership of the EU that has undermined the principle of parliamentary sovereignty. The use of referendums, the devolution Acts and the incorporation of the European Convention on Human Rights (incidentally, unconnected with the EU) have all had damaging implications for parliamentary sovereignty, even if the principle has been theoretically but tortuously upheld (see Bogdanor, in Seldon 2001, and the discussion in Chapters 10, 14 and 16 of this book). Moreover some modern critics of the British constitution would argue that parliamentary sovereignty is not a principle worth defending anyway (Mount 1992, Hutton 1995, 1996).

Membership of the EU has had an impact on other aspects of the British system of government. The referendum was first introduced into Britain for a vote on whether the country should remain in the EC, and has since become an accepted if irregular mechanism for settling controversial issues of a constitutional nature (such as devolution). EU membership contributed significantly to the pressures for electoral reform in the UK. Britain's first-past-the-post electoral system produced even more disproportionate results in elections for the European Parliament than it did for Westminster, and the UK system was markedly out of line with that used by other member states. Thus in 1999 the regional list system was used for British elections to the European Parliament, while the system of election used for the Scottish Parliament and Welsh Assembly (the additional member system) followed another model familiar on the European continent. Although pressures for electoral reform existed prior to EU membership, they were strengthened by European precedents. Much the same could be said of demands for devolution and regional government. These demands predated membership of the EC, but were reinforced by the parallel pressures for more national and regional autonomy in other member states, and by the development of European regional policy and the establishment of the Committee of the Regions. European legal principles and procedures have also begun to influence British law.

The machinery of government has been less affected than might have been expected by EU membership – the British state has adjusted its institutions and procedures incrementally rather than radically (Bulmer and Burch, in Rhodes 2000). Departmental organisation has been scarcely affected. There is no separate department for Europe nor a secretary of state for Europe in the Cabinet. As a consequence, there is also no Departmental Select Committee for Europe in the House of Commons, although there is a European Legislation Committee to examine (mainly) proposals for European legislation. There is now a European section of the Cabinet Secretariat, which signals the importance of Europe at the heart of British government. Even so, anyone studying the changing formal structures of the Cabinet, departments and Parliament over the last 30 years or so would hardly conclude that they had been much affected by EU membership.

Yet if the formal structure of British government at the centre appears little altered, the change in the working practices of ministers and civil servants, and in the business content of British government, has been marked:

> On an administrative level, most senior British ministers and many senior civil servants spend many days each month commuting to Brussels for EU meetings. Much of the rest of their time back in Westminster and Whitehall is spent tackling questions relating to the EU agenda.
> (Hix, in Dunleavy *et al.* 2002: 48)

This reflects the extensive consequences of EU membership for so many areas of policy (see below).

The impact of EU membership on British parties

Membership of the EU has had considerable implications for British parties and the party system. Both major parties have been split over Europe, which has been a cross-party issue regularly threatening party realignment. Labour was manifestly deeply divided on the issue from the 1960s onwards. It was the European issue that was a major factor in the 1981 SDP split from Labour, which nearly 'broke the mould' of British party politics, but in any event helped ensure Conservative dominance for 18 years. Conservative divisions over Europe date back at least as far as Labour's, but were initially less disastrous for the party, although it was on Europe that Powell broke from the Conservatives and recommended a vote for Labour in 1974, perhaps tipping a close election in Wilson's favour. Conflicting attitudes towards Europe caused tension within Thatcher's last administration, but became far more damaging under John Major, threatening the survival of his government. These divisions helped undermine any immediate prospects of a Conservative Party recovery after the landslide defeat of 1997.

The Liberals and their Liberal Democrat successors perhaps profited from the divisions among their opponents, but otherwise their more consistent and united support for Europe has hardly profited them electorally, particularly in elections for the European Parliament, where the voting system gave them negligible representation until 1999 (see Table 15.5).

The European issue has also spawned new parties with some impact on the British political scene. Thus the single issue Referendum Party appeared a threat to the Conservatives in 1997, while the UK Independence Party managed to pick up three seats on the new voting system introduced for elections for the European Parliament in 1999, and dramatically secured 12 seats in 2003. (However, its performance in the 2005 General Election suggests it does not pose a serious threat to the major parties.)

The need to organise for European elections, and subsequently the need to become part of European parties in the European Parliament, has had some knock-on effects for the major British parties. For Labour this was perhaps less of a problem as the party was a member of the Socialist International, and leading Labour politicians were used to fraternising with European socialists and social democrats. Thus they have been consistent members of the European Socialist party. The Conservatives find the search for acceptable ideologically sympathetic partners in Europe rather more difficult. The ideas of Christian Democracy

Table 15.5 Votes and seats for UK parties in European Parliament elections 1979–2004

Party	1979		1984		1989		1994		1999		2004	
	votes	seats	votes	seats	votes	seats	votes	seats	votes	seats	votes	seats
Con	48%	60	39%	45	33%	32	27%	18	36%	36	27%	27
Lab	32%	17	35%	32	39%	45	43%	62	28%	29	23%	19
Lib/LD	13%	1	19%	0	6%	0	16%	2	13%	10	15%	12
SNP	2%	1	2%	1	3%	1	3%	2	3%	2	1%	2
Plaid C	1%	0	1%	0	1%	0	1%	0	2%	2	1%	1
UKIP									7%	3	16%	12
Greens			1%	0	15%	0	3%	0	6%	2	6%	2

Note: elections from 1979–94 under first-past-the-post system, from 1999 by regional party list system. (Northern Ireland elects three MEPs by single transferable vote.)

which were influential on the centre-right on the continent involved too much state intervention and social partnership for a Conservative Party convinced of the virtues of the free market, while Christian Democrats found British Conservatives rather too right-wing. Thus for a time the Conservative MEPs were linked with a few Spanish and Danish MPs in the European Democratic Group, but they then joined the main centre-right European People's Party, which they now plan to leave.

There is always the potential for tension and perhaps open conflict between the parties focused on Westminster and Strasbourg. One danger, particularly for the now more Euro-sceptic Conservatives, is that their MEPs might 'go native', becoming markedly more sympathetic to European institutions, processes and policies than the parent party back home. Indeed, the 1999 European Parliament elections did provoke an open split in the Conservative Party, although in the event the pro-European Conservatives did not secure much support. There is now a similar problem with the Scottish Parliament and Welsh Assembly, so the parties will simply have to learn to accommodate multi-level governance, and adjust their organisations accordingly.

How far closer involvement with other parties in Europe has influenced the political thinking of British parties is perhaps less clear. German and Swedish social democracy, and to a lesser extent perhaps French socialism, certainly helped influence the transformation of the Labour Party in the 1980s and 1990s. Labour's red rose symbol was borrowed from François Mitterrand's French socialists. Germany's Gerhard Schroeder was for a time closely linked with Tony Blair over the Third Way or 'Middle Way'. Some of this might have happened outside the EU anyway, although it does seem that involvement with European socialists has contributed to the softening of Labour attitudes to Europe. British Conservatism seems much less susceptible to influence from its continental neighbours, although this may be changing as the party desperately seeks new ideas for running public services.

The impact of the European Union on pressure group politics

As the impact of the European Union on UK public policy has grown, Brussels has become increasingly a natural target for pressure group activity (Mazey and Richardson 1993). Some of this has just involved British groups like the Confederation of British Industry (CBI), the National Farmers' Union (NFU) or British-based firms extending their range, acquiring their own offices in Brussels or employing professional lobbyists. However, many groups have sought to combine with comparable interests in other member states to establish Europe-wide groups, with potentially more muscle to influence EU policy. It is estimated that there are some 700 of these Europe-wide groups, of which over 65 per cent represent business, 20 per cent public interest groups, 10 per cent the professions and 6 per cent trade unions, consumers, environmentalists and other interests (Nugent 2002: 281–2).

The European Commission is the main target of most groups, partly because of its powers and its readiness to consult with interests, especially Eurogroups. It is more difficult to lobby directly either the European Council or the Council of Ministers, so groups tend to seek to influence these bodies indirectly through national governments (Grant, in Mazey and Richardson 1993). The increase in the influence of the European Parliament on the legislative process and the EU budget has led to more intensive lobbying at Strasbourg. There is also the Economic and Social Committee (ESC), which is the EU's own institution for representing group interests – yet most groups prefer to target more influential bodies directly rather than through the ESC (Nugent 2002: 284).

Box 15.4

Examples of Europe-wide interest groups

Committee of Professional Agricultural Organisations in the EU (COPA)

Union of Industrial and Employers Confederation of Europe (UNICE)

European Trade Union Confederation (ETUC)

Association of European Automobile Constructors (ACEA)

European Chemical Industry Council (CEFIC)

European Association of Manufacturers of Business Machines and Information Technology (EUROBIT)

Council of European Municipalities and Regions (CEMR)

European Citizen Action Service (ECAS) (represents and lobbies for the voluntary and community sector)

The impact of the European Union on the British public

It has proved much more difficult to persuade the British people to engage with Europe. There is continued evidence of widespread ignorance and confusion about the EU and over specific institutions and issues. Turnout levels for elections to the European Parliament have generally been the lowest in Europe since the first elections in 1979 (see above). Although the only referendum held on Europe resulted in a substantial majority in favour of remaining in the EC in 1975, opinion surveys since then have indicated a pervasive if ill-informed Euro-scepticism, and more recently opposition to the single currency (Hix, in Dunleavy *et al.* 2002: 53–8).

Curiously however, parties that have aligned themselves with Euro-sceptic public opinion have signally failed to profit electorally. Labour in 1983 and the Conservatives in 2001 both campaigned on a manifesto hostile or unsympathetic to Europe, and both managed to lose disastrously, indicating that it was not a priority issue for voters. However, while Labour has proved it can win General Elections despite being out of step with voters on Europe, the problems of winning a referendum on the single issue of the EU constitution or joining the euro have proved too daunting to risk.

The impact of the European Union on UK policies

The actual impact of the EC/EU on UK policy has been increasingly significant but highly variable, depending on the policy area concerned. Fiscal policy has clearly been affected. UK entry to the EC involved the introduction of value added tax, and there are EU rules that constrain taxation and expenditure. Even so, pressures to harmonise taxation have been generally resisted. In so far as there are factors favouring greater convergence on, for example, duties on alcohol, these have more to do with the loss of revenue from smuggling than from EU regulations.

Yet Simon Hix argues that while:

> The British Government is still sovereign in deciding most of the main areas of public expenditure ... this is only one aspect of policy making. In the area of regulation, over 80 per cent of rules governing the production, distribution and exchange of goods, services and capital in the British market are decided by the EU.
>
> (Hix, in Dunleavy *et al.* 2002: 48)

Hix goes on to argue that this severely constrains British economic policy, preventing the adoption of either neo-Keynesian demand-management and pump-priming or a Thatcherite deregulatory supply-side policy.

As far as specific policy areas are concerned, agriculture and fisheries policies have been most dramatically affected, as EC entry required a shift from farm income support policies (with low prices) towards price support policies. Both systems involved agricultural subsidy, although the CAP notoriously led to periodic over-production, with 'butter mountains' and 'wine lakes'. Britain, with its relatively small agricultural sector, was always likely to be a net loser from the CAP. British farmers have, however, benefited substantially from EU subsidies. Persistent efforts to reform the CAP have been partly frustrated by the strength of farming interests in some member states. However, some British criticism of continental agriculture seems exaggerated or misplaced. The BSE and foot-and-mouth disease crises were substantially the consequence of British farming practices and British policy, and cannot be attributed to the EU.

The UK has gained rather more from the EC/EU regional and social policy. The net benefits to deprived regions has sometimes been less than they might have been, as British governments have sometimes seen EU funding as an alternative rather than addition to UK spending on economic regeneration, contrary to the intentions and sometimes the regulations of the European Commission.

Many other policy areas have been much less affected. The management and funding of health services differs markedly between the member states of the EU. Educational policy and social security payments and social services have been only relatively marginally affected by membership of the EU, although member states increasingly face common problems (for example, over funding pensions) which may ultimately lead to increased convergence. Foreign and defence policy was until recently also only marginally affected. Early attempts by the original six members to develop a European Defence Community foundered in the 1950s, and defence and foreign policy has been shaped by the requirements of NATO. Attempts to develop a common foreign policy after Maastricht have not been conspicuously successful. It remains to be seen whether the European Rapid Reaction Force proves significant. The UK however has been accused of being more subject to US influence than working with its European partners.

A new crisis for the European Union?

The relatively smooth introduction of the single European currency in 2002 followed by the substantial enlargement of the European Union in 2004 appeared a triumphant culmination of the original European vision of the Founding Fathers, Jean Monnet and Robert Schuman. Closer European integration had taken a decisive step forward. Many of the countries of eastern Europe, long divided from the west by the 'iron curtain', were now full members of the European club, with further enlargement in prospect. European unity had triumphed over old national rivalries and ideological divisions. The new European Constitution was expected to put the seal on the new Europe.

The unexpected rejection of the proposed new European Constitution by voters in two original member states, France and the Netherlands, has not only caused an immediate crisis for the institutions and processes of the EU, but has thrown a long shadow over the earlier triumphs. The verdict of the voters has been variously interpreted, but it seems to have involved not just a rejection of the Constitution, which few seem to have read or understood, but a wider rejection of the whole current direction of the EU. Thus some voters seemed to be opposed to EU enlargement (both recent and proposed), while others were registering their objection to the single currency. Behind these grievances lie more fundamental economic concerns over growth and living standards, unemployment and prospects. The old EC was popular with the original member states because it had apparently delivered economic prosperity and steadily rising living standards. These countries have experienced low growth and increased economic difficulties in the new larger EU, in which they are proportionally less politically influential.

The 'no' vote may also be attributed to the impact of globalisation, and the EU's response to it. While the British government has pressed for market reforms to make the EU more competitive, many French critics seek to maintain protection for European producers, and labour regulation to look after the interests of workers. The European Constitution which British Eurosceptics condemned for being too federalist and interventionist was attacked in France for being too neo-liberal and pro-market, and British.

The French 'no' made things easier for Blair in Britain by enabling him to avoid a referendum which had looked increasingly unwinnable. Yet it also made the government's position in Europe more difficult. One by-product of the apparent breakdown of the ratification of the Constitution has been the revival of attacks on the British rebate. This now appears less defensible, both because of enlargement and because of the relative success of the British economy. Thus poor new member states from eastern Europe appear to be subsidising rich Britain. Blair has countered with demands for a comprehensive reform of the EU budget, particularly the CAP, from which French farmers remain the most conspicuous beneficiaries, and on which no French government can afford to make concessions. In the event Blair sacrificed part of the rebate to secure agreement on the EU budget.

The European project is thus stalled, temporarily at least. Some fundamental rethink seems required to re-engage the peoples of Europe with the EU. Enlargement is now seen by some of the older member states as part of the problem rather than the solution. Absorbing so many more new and poorer nations is already placing a strain on EU resources, with some adverse effects for older member states. Bulgaria and Rumania should still join in 2007, but

Box 15.5

What is Europe?

Geographical Europe? Europe is commonly regarded as a continent, bounded by the Atlantic ocean to the west, the Arctic ocean to the north, and the Mediterranean to the south. The eastern border is more contentious, but is sometimes marked by the Black Sea and the Ural mountains. This would include the Ukraine and other countries west of the Urals which were once part of the USSR, including western Russia. It would exclude Turkey and the southern and eastern shores of the Mediterranean.

Christian Europe? Some EU member states wanted to include a specific reference to Christianity in the proposed new EU constitution. This would exclude not only Turkey, but other Muslim countries such as Albania, the Muslim populations of Bosnia and Kosovo, and send a negative message to the increasing Muslim minorities in Britain, France, the Netherlands and other countries, as well as other non-Christian minorities. ('Christian Europe' also remains divided between Catholic, Protestant and Orthodox variants, and numerous other sub-divisions.)

Ethnic Europe? Geographical Europe is inhabited by a range of ethnic types. The Holocaust provides a grim reminder of the dangers of any attempt to define Europe in terms of race or ethnicity. If Europe is perceived as 'white', this risks the alienation of a substantial and growing non-white minority.

Historical and cultural Europe? This definition is inevitably more subjective. Yet Turkey was commonly regarded as part of Europe in the 19th century, and was substantially westernised in the 20th century. Most Turks regards themselves as European, and Turkey is also a long-standing NATO member. Israel is also sometimes regarded as a European state (for what it is worth, it participates in the Eurovision Song Contest and European football competitions). Russia was generally seen as a European power, particularly from the reign of Peter the Great to the Russian revolution, which divided it from the west.

(For a brief discussion see the *Guardian* G2 section, 17 December 2004. For more extended analysis see the introduction to Norman Davies, *Europe: A history* (1996).)

there is increased resistance to the accession of Turkey and other hopeful applicant states (such as Serbia and the Ukraine). The initial enthusiasm of the ten new member states that joined in 2004 could easily turn to disillusion if the hoped-for economic and political benefits do not soon materialise. Ironically, the culmination of the European dream with the reunion of Europe's east and west has reopened old debates on the very nature of Europe, its culture and civilisation (see Box 15.5).

EU policy towards the rest of the world, particularly the developing world, will also come under scrutiny. The continuation of high levels of agricultural protection could effectively cancel out efforts towards debt cancellation and improved aid. A large question mark remains over the potential for developing a coherent and distinctive European foreign and defence policy, particularly following differences over the Iraq War, but such a policy may appear increasingly necessary if European and US aims and priorities diverge significantly in the future.

The British role in Europe remains problematic. Partly this is because of conflicting pulls on policy, particularly the 'special relationship' with the USA which has markedly influenced both Conservative and Labour governments, and has often appeared to damage the country's European credentials with its EU partners (Gamble 2003). Many Britons seem to lack or positively reject a European identity, and may feel a closer affinity with the USA, because of a common language and a substantially shared culture. Yet the possibility that is sometimes canvassed of the UK exchanging EU membership for membership of the North American Free Trade Agreement (NAFTA), even if feasible, would substitute for a partnership between equals an unequal dependent relationship with a superpower inevitably preoccupied first and foremost with the interests of the Americas. Isolation appears dangerous in an era of intensifying globalisation, and there seems little realistic alternative to continued if troubled engagement with the rest of Europe.

Summary

- Britain initially failed to engage with the movement for European integration because of the continuing illusion of world power status and interests, the special relationship with the USA, and continuing ties with the Commonwealth.
- Britain eventually joined in 1973, too late to help shape early institutions and policies, and did not seem to secure the same economic benefits as founder members and some later members enjoyed.
- UK membership of the EC/EU has long been a divisive issue in British politics, leading to splits in old parties and the establishment of new ones. While enthusiasts have welcomed Britain's closer engagement with Europe, Euro-sceptics have been critical of the impact on national independence and parliamentary sovereignty.
- UK membership has contested implications for the British constitution and the principle of parliamentary sovereignty. While it has had only minor implications for the institutional machinery of British government, it has had a major impact on the process of government and on key areas of policy.
- The EU is a complex organisation. Some institutions represent the EU as a whole (European Commission, European Parliament, European Court of Justice) while others represent the interests of member states (European Council, Council of Ministers, COREPER).
- There has been some tension between the promotion of further integration of policies within the EU (deepening) and enlarging the EU to include new members (widening). Recent and proposed further enlargements cause some problems for EU institutions and policies, and raise questions over the nature of Europe itself.
- Britain's role in Europe remains a central issue in British politics. The single European currency and the proposed new European constitution seemed to pose new challenges for the British government and people, but decisions on these have been avoided or indefinitely postponed.
- Particularly following the war on terror and the Iraq War, a key question is how far Britain

can engage fully with Europe and maintain its 'special relationship' with the USA.

Questions for discussion

- Why did European statesmen seek to promote European integration? Were the motives economic or political?
- Why did the UK government not seek to join the European Coal and Steel Community and the European Economic Community from the beginning?
- Account for the generally lukewarm or hostile attitude to the EU shown by much of the British public compared with the apparent enthusiasm of the citizens of other member states.
- How far has Britain been a significantly more 'awkward partner' than other EU member states?
- Is the EU a federal superstate, or an intergovernmental association of sovereign states? How far do specific EU institutions meet either description?
- Where does real power lie today within the EU: with the governments of member states or with the European Commission and other pan-European institutions?
- How far is there a 'democratic deficit' within the EU?
- How far is there a tension between further enlargement and closer integration of the EU?
- How would you define Europe? Should the following states in due course be admitted to the EU if their governments and peoples so wish: Turkey, Ukraine, Russia, Israel?
- Can Britain play a full part in the European Union if it remains outside the single European currency (the euro)? What are the arguments for and against British membership of the euro?
- How far has membership of the EU transformed British government and politics?
- How far does Britain's future lie in Europe? Are there realistic alternatives?

Further reading

Pinder provides a useful introduction in *The European Union* (2001). Nugent, *The Government and Politics of the European Union* (2002) remains the best guide to European institutions and procedures. See also Cram, Dinan and Nugent, *Developments in the European Union* (1999) and Cowles and Dinan, *Developments in the European Union 2* (2004). On enlargement see Nugent, *European Union Enlargement* (2004). Detailed up-to-date information on all current developments can be obtained from the EU website www.europa.eu.int

On the troubled history of the UK's relationship with the EU, Young's *This Blessed Plot* (1998) provides a full and lively account from the perspective of a Euro-enthusiast. See also George, *An Awkward Partner: Britain in the European Community* (1998). For a more recent interpretation see Geddes, *The European Union and British Politics* (2003). Andrew Gamble's *Between Europe and America* (2003) provides a stimulating analysis of the impact of these conflicting pulls on British politics. The accounts of key protagonists such as Heath, Thatcher and Major can be consulted in their memoirs. There is a useful chapter on Blair's approach to Europe in J. Rentoul's biography (2001). S. Bulmer and M. Burch examine 'The Europeanisation of British central government' in Rhodes (2000). Simon Hix reviews the impact of the EU and the euro on British politics in Dunleavy *et al.* (2002), while Ben Rosamond has a chapter on 'The Europeanization of British politics' in Dunleavy *et al.* (2003). Some of the constitutional issues arising from Britain's membership of the EU are discussed by Paul Craig in Jowell and Oliver (2004).

Devolution: a disunited kingdom?

Contents

The British state appears to be under pressure from both above and below. While some fear British national sovereignty is threatened by the growth of a European superstate (see Chapter 15), others suggest that it could disintegrate into smaller component parts in response to demands from separatist nationalists in Scotland, Wales and Northern Ireland. It cannot be simply assumed that the British state will go on for ever, in its present form with its current boundaries. At the heart of the problem are confused and conflicting national identities and interests within the United Kingdom.

In this chapter we explore briefly the ideology of nationalism and its implications for British government and politics. We examine the growth and possible decline of British nationalism, as well as the variously expressed nationalist pressures in Northern Ireland, Scotland and Wales. We go on to discuss the political background to the development of different forms of devolved government within the United Kingdom, and some of the unresolved problems remaining, including the substantial problem of England, and the now stalled prospects for English regional devolution. We conclude with a brief analysis of alternative scenarios.

Nationalism

Nationalism has been a remarkably potent political force in the modern world, from at least the French revolution onwards. Men and women have been prepared to die for their nation, or to kill for it. Nationalism has been defined as 'a political principle which holds that the political and the national unit should be congruent' (Gellner 1983). In other words nations should form independent sovereign states, and states should consist of nations. This simple principle had dangerous implications for old dynastic states that included various national or ethnic groups, such as 19th-century Austria and Russia. Nationalists demanded political unification for Germany and Italy, and independence for nations then subject to foreign rule, such as Greece, Poland, Hungary and Norway. In the 20th century nationalist movements demanded and secured independence for former colonies from imperial powers, including Britain and France. Following the destruction of the Berlin Wall in 1989, nationalist movements led to the creation of new or revived states in the former Soviet Union.

However, national self-determination was never an easy doctrine to apply. What precisely is a nation? There are no easy definitions or clear criteria. Language, ethnicity, religion, culture and history may all contribute to a sense

Definitions

A **nation** is a community of people bound together by some common characteristics (real or imagined).

A **nation state** is an independent sovereign state whose inhabitants belong to a single national community.

Nationalism is a political doctrine that holds that nations should form independent sovereign states.

National self-determination requires that a nation should be able to pursue its own future, normally involving a free and independent sovereign state.

of nationhood, but ultimately a nation exists in the minds of its members; it is an 'imagined community' (Anderson 1991), although it is also clear that a sense of national identity can evolve and change over time. US President Woodrow Wilson sought to apply the principle of national self-determination at the end of the First World War, in the hope that it would lead to a new world of nation states at peace with each other. Yet rival and inconsistent nationalist demands fuelled further bitter conflicts. Many nationalists were less concerned with nationalism as a universal principle than the advance of their own specific nation, which might involve the rejection of other nationalist claims. Indeed, for Breuilly (1993: 2), a basic assertion of nationalism is that the interests and values of the nation take priority over all other interests and loyalties, although some forms of nationalism seem more prepared to accommodate multiple identities and allegiances. More exclusive variants of nationalism have posed problems for minorities, sometimes involving the denial of full rights of citizenship, and occasionally persecution or even genocide for those not perceived as part of the nation.

Nationalism and the British state

For a long time it appeared that nationalism and the doctrine of national self-determination had little immediate relevance to Britain. It was a principle to be applied to others – to Greeks, Belgians, Italians and Poles – whose demands for national freedom were regarded sympathetically by many British politicians in the 19th century. It was assumed that Britain was already a kind of nation state, although a 'British' state only really emerged after the Act of Union between England and Scotland in 1707 (following the 'union of crowns' from 1603). A new sense of British national identity was substantially forged in the 18th and early 19th centuries, symbolised by the figure of Britannia on coins and in the anthem *Rule, Britannia*. Pride and loyalty in Britain were strengthened by successful industrial development, imperial expansion and the visible evidence of great power status (Colley 2003).

Mainstream accounts of British history imply that the growth of the British state was a beneficial and largely voluntary process from which all Britain's peoples ultimately benefited. Thus, it could be claimed, Wales and Scotland prospered from being partners with England in a profitable commercial and imperial enterprise. There is something in the claim, particularly as far as Scotland is concerned. Scottish and Welsh nationalists of course tend to interpret history rather differently, arguing that their culture, and perhaps their economy, suffered as a consequence of English dominance.

Indeed British nationalism overlaid rather than replaced older Scottish and Welsh identities, while in Ireland the incompatible claims of Irish and British nationalism led ultimately to the establishment of an independent Irish Republic in the south of the island. The now reduced United Kingdom of Britain and Northern Ireland was a more awkward and less satisfactory focus for national loyalty. The historian Norman Davies (2000: 870) has asserted categorically, 'The United Kingdom is not, and never has been, a nation state'. The Scottish nationalist Tom Nairn (2001) has coined the term 'Ukania' to describe what he regards as an outdated and artificial multinational state (like the old Austro-Hungarian empire), ripe for disintegration into its separate nations.

The establishment of the Irish Free State (later the Irish Republic) was one stimulus to some revived stirrings of separatist nationalism in Scotland and Wales. Plaid Cymru, the Welsh nationalist party, was founded in 1925, while the Scottish National Party dates back to 1928. Yet these did not initially achieve much political impact. Sir Ivor

Jennings still felt able to claim in 1941, in the midst of the Second World War, that 'Great Britain is a small island with a very homogeneous population. Few think of themselves as primarily English, Scots or Welsh' (Jennings 1966: 8).

Today the population of Britain appears less homogeneous, and the cultural identities and political allegiances of the varied peoples living within the borders of the UK state have become particularly complex and confused. Most of the Catholic community in Northern Ireland has long continued to regard itself as Irish rather than British, owing political allegiance to the Irish Republic, although the Unionist majority passionately insist on their British identity. Opinion polls indicate that an increasing proportion of those living in Scotland and Wales regard themselves as Scots or Welsh rather than British (see Chapter 3), which is one factor that helps to explain rising support for the Scottish and Welsh nationalist parties from the early 1970s onwards. England remains by far the largest part of this complex mosaic of nations and communities. Many of its inhabitants still refer to themselves as interchangeably 'English' or 'British' (to the annoyance of Scots and Welsh), although there has been some recent debate over 'Englishness' and its potential political implications (e.g. Paxman 1998)

Post-war immigration has intensified and complicated ethnic divisions that cut across these old national communities and identities. Some of the ethnic minorities in many of Britain's large cities maintain a complex pattern of allegiances, often retaining strong cultural or religious links with other countries and communities, alongside a sometimes strong sense of British identity, unless they have become alienated by rejection and discrimination. In some respects it seems easier to be 'black and British' than to be black and English, Scottish, Welsh or European.

Conflicting cultural influences resulting from the pressures of globalisation have added additional dimensions to these confusions over identity and allegiance. Membership of the European Union (as well as the growth of package tour holidays to European destinations and increased sporting and cultural ties) should have helped to reinforce a sense of a common European cultural heritage. Yet the media reflect more the influence of the US and English-speaking world, and weaken a sense of a pan-European identity. Not all citizens of the UK would, however, freely identify with Anglo-American, western or liberal capitalism, as the anti-globalisation movements indicate (see Chapter 8). Nor clearly would they all any longer identify with Christian values and civilisation. A multi-faith and multilingual Britain has created new tensions and divisions within the state.

For the future much depends on how far these various identities are felt to be exclusive and overriding. Norman Davies (2000: 874) argues that 'multiple identities are a natural feature of the human condition', as 'everyone feels a sense of belonging to a complex network of communities, and there is no necessary tension between them'. Indeed, multiple identities fit comfortably with the notion of multi-level governance (see Chapter 18), suggesting that it is unnecessary to choose between being Glaswegian, Scottish, British or European. Yet many nationalists remain unwilling to settle for anything less than full national sovereignty. In the end the British state is likely to last as long as the various peoples who live within its borders want it to last, and this will depend on issues of political identity and allegiance.

Northern Ireland and Irish nationalism

If Britain does break up as a political unit, 'John Bull's other island' – Ireland – began the process. It was the demand for Irish 'home rule' in the 19th century which provided the stimulus for the policy which the Gladstonian Liberal Party adopted of 'home rule all round' – the forerunner of devolution. Irish nationalism and Irish separatism subsequently provided a precedent for Scottish and Welsh nationalism.

Ireland was always the least integrated part of the 'United' Kingdom. Its people had remained predominantly and obstinately Catholic while those in Great Britain were largely converted to varieties of Protestantism. What has come to be called the 'Irish problem' was really an 'Ulster' or 'British problem' resulting from 'the English, and their self-serving strategies of plantation and subordination begun in the seventeenth century' (Judd 1996: 49). Protestants were deliberately settled in Northern Ireland. Hatreds stirred then remain alive today. Union with Ireland only came

Box 16.1

The British state: core and periphery

Some political scientists have attempted to explain the inter-relationships between Britain's nations and regions in terms of 'core–periphery' theory. The 'core' of the British state is south-east Britain, with an 'outer core' comprising East Anglia, the Midlands and 'Wessex'. Beyond the core is an 'inner periphery' made up of the north of England, Wales and the south-west, and an 'outer periphery' – Scotland. These areas correspond with arcs drawn around London at 80, 200 and 300 miles. The core–periphery idea has been developed in terms of the colonial domination of the Celtic periphery by the English core. Michael Hechter (1975) advanced a persuasive theory of internal colonialism, whereby the advanced core areas dominate and exploit the less advanced peripheral areas. In other words, just as Britain colonised much of the wider world, so the area making up Britain's core colonised the areas on its periphery. Historically this process was marked by the statutes of 1536, 1707 and 1800 which brought Wales, Scotland and Ireland respectively into the English-dominated Union.

Relations between the core and periphery are complex and vary over time. The Second World War had an integrative effect on the whole of the United Kingdom; even the communities in Northern Ireland were drawn closer together in the face of the common German enemy. However, the rapid liquidation of the British Empire after the war and Britain's relative economic decline increased the strains between the periphery and the core within the United Kingdom.

about in 1801 following the crushing of the revolt of the United Irishmen in 1798, and was never a success. The growth of British power and prosperity hardly impacted on the bulk of the Irish, who earned a bare subsistence from land rented from absentee landlords. The 1845 Irish potato famine and the failure of land reform fed a growing nationalist movement which eventually convinced the Liberal leader, William Gladstone, that home rule was the only solution to 'the Irish problem'. This led to a crisis in British politics, split the Liberal Party and resulted in a 20-year period of dominance by the Conservatives, who supported the Union. The failure to concede home rule to moderate nationalists before the First World War led to the Easter Rising of 1916 and its bitter aftermath, with the dominance of a new breed of nationalists who demanded full independence and were prepared to fight for it. The failure of repression led to the Irish Treaty of 1921 and the emergence of the 26-county Irish Free State, leaving the remaining six counties as a Northern Ireland statelet within the United Kingdom.

It is often said that Northern Ireland is 'a place apart'. The people of Northern Ireland live in a distinctive political culture, support different political parties (see Table 16.1), and face a unique constitutional problem yet to be resolved. The partition of Ireland in 1922 did not solve the 'Irish problem', since a sizable Catholic and substantially Republican minority, now amounting to 40 per cent of the population, still lived in the north. In a sense, two minorities live side by side in Ireland: the Catholic minority in Northern Ireland which feels threatened by the Protestant majority, and the Protestant minority in the island as a whole which feels threatened by the Irish nationalism and Catholicism of a united Ireland. The troubles in Northern Ireland arise from centuries of divisive historical experiences that have embittered relations between the communities to an extent that it is difficult to comprehend outside the province. Rulers and politicians long forgotten in Britain are celebrated in exotic murals. Quaint ceremonies, ritual marches, rival flags and symbols have become central to Northern Irish politics. Anyone seeking a solution to the Irish problem would prefer 'not to start from here'.

The troubles in Northern Ireland

However, although the roots of the Irish troubles lie in the distant past it is only comparatively recently that they re-erupted. The years following the end of the Second World War were relatively peaceful ones in Northern Ireland. It appeared that differences between the two communities might be progressively eroded by their shared interest in increasing affluence. Although Catholics remained discriminated against in terms of employment, welfare and political rights, they appeared better off than their counterparts to the south. The Irish Republican Army (IRA) waged an unsuccessful campaign in the late 1950s, and this too was taken as evidence that Catholics now accepted the political status quo in return for improved living standards. The emergence of moderate Unionists, such as Terence O'Neill, who became Northern Ireland's prime minister in 1963, offered the prospect of further improvements in community relations. However, O'Neill's brand of progressive Unionism was opposed by many Ulster loyalists determined to resist change, and he was forced out of office. Serious rioting led to British troops being sent to restore order. Initially Catholics welcomed these troops, but inevitably their strong-arm role became identified with supporting the Protestant state rather than defending the Catholic minority. The political condition of Northern Ireland moved close to a state of revolution.

Violence against Catholics led many into accepting the more militant provisional wing of the IRA as their defence force. Support for the IRA was strengthened by the policy of internment, a practice sometimes referred to as the 'recruiting officer for the IRA', as it involved the imprisonment of suspected terrorists without trial. The troubles were to become yet more intense in January 1972 when, in controversial circumstances, British paratroopers appeared to overreact on the streets and killed 13 unarmed individuals participating in a civil rights march, a tragedy which came to be known as 'Bloody Sunday'. British Prime Minister Edward Heath announced that the Parliament at Stormont was suspended. From April 1972 Northern Ireland came under direct rule from Westminster. A referendum on the future of the province in 1973 did little to clarify the position because of Catholic abstention. Some 57.5 per cent of Northern Ireland's electorate wanted to remain part of the United Kingdom, 0.6 per cent wanted Northern Ireland to unite with the Republic of Ireland outside the United Kingdom, but 41.9 per cent abstained.

Northern Ireland experienced a grim cycle of violence. Discrimination and repression won recruits to the Provisional IRA, who regarded British soldiers and members of the (largely Protestant) Royal Ulster Constabulary as representatives of an alien occupying power and thus legitimate targets. Loyalist paramilitaries attacked Catholics, particularly those suspected of IRA sympathies, and there were well-grounded nationalist suspicions of collusion between loyalist paramilitaries and the security forces. Much of the killing seemed more random: sometimes just the religious affiliation of the victim seemed to provide sufficient excuse for murder. The escalation of violence led to a rising cumulative total of death and serious injury in the province, besides the economic damage caused by the destruction of businesses and the deterrent to new investment. Social segregation was intensified as Catholics living in mainly Protestant areas, and Protestants in mainly Catholic areas, were forced out of their homes. In some parts of Belfast and Derry (or Londonderry to Unionists) virtual no-go areas were established, 'policed' by paramilitaries using punishment beatings and shootings to maintain internal discipline.

Periodically, violence was exported to the British mainland. Thus the Conservative MP Airey Neave, who had played a leading role in securing the Tory leadership for Margaret Thatcher, was murdered in 1979. In 1984 Margaret Thatcher herself narrowly escaped when an IRA bomb exploded at the Conservative Party conference, killing five and seriously injuring two senior ministers, Norman Tebbitt and John Wakeham. John Major's Cabinet survived a mortar attack on Downing Street in 1991. There were other more random victims of IRA violence following pub bombings in Guildford and Birmingham. To the British government and the bulk of British public opinion the perpetrators were despicable terrorists and murderers. However, IRA volunteers who died in the course of the 'armed struggle' were treated as heroes and martyrs within their own community. Such divergent perspectives are not uncommon in similar conflicts where particular communities totally reject the legitimacy of the state and its agents. (Examples include the Basque extremists in Spain, Tamil Tigers in Sri Lanka and Kashmir separatists in India.) However, it became increasingly clear over time that neither side could win by the use of force. The British government could not defeat the IRA, and the IRA could not achieve its goal of a united Republican Ireland by armed struggle.

Whatever the root cause of the conflict between the two communities (see Box 16.2), further divisions have developed within both, leading to a complex and confused party system. Northern Ireland parties were always distinctive. The main British parties refrained from contesting Northern Ireland elections. In the old Stormont Parliament and in representation at Westminster until the 1970s the dominant (almost the only) party was the Ulster Unionists, who were linked with the Conservatives. Sinn Fein commonly won a couple of mainly Catholic constituencies, but the victors refused to take their seats.

The troubles from the late 1960s onwards led to a split in Unionism. Ian Paisley was elected as an independent Unionist against the official Unionist in 1970, and founded the Democratic Unionist Party (DUP) in 1971. In 2003 the DUP finally overtook their Ulster Unionist rivals, who have suffered from periodic splits and have become deeply divided over the ongoing 'peace process'. There are also smaller parties linked with loyalist paramilitaries. On the Catholic or nationalist side the most obvious division is between the peaceful constitutional nationalism of the Social Democratic and Labour Party (SDLP) and Sinn Fein (linked with the IRA). However, the peace process also opened up fissures in the republican ranks, reportedly between the military leadership of the IRA and the political leadership of Sinn Fein, but more obviously between the main provisional IRA and splinter movements such as 'Continuity IRA' and the 'Real IRA' opposed to the Republican ceasefire. Attempting to bridge the community divide is the small Alliance Party.

Box 16.2

The roots of conflict in Northern Ireland: different perspectives

Religious struggle? Some see religion as central rather than incidental to the conflict. The struggle between Protestantism and Roman Catholicism, which began in 16th-century Europe as a life and death contest between rival ideologies, has survived in Ulster when antagonism has long softened elsewhere. Religious differences still keep the two communities apart. Church attendance remains high (contrary to trends on mainland Britain). Other institutions preserve a link between religion and politics, including the Orange Order, a semi-secret fraternal organisation which has the support of around two-thirds of Protestant males, and segregated schooling, which provides the children of the Catholic community with an Irish identity.

Internal colonial struggle? Alternatively, the conflict in Northern Ireland might be understood as an internal colonial struggle between periphery and core, similar to the struggle of Algeria for independence from France in the 1950s. The argument runs as follows. Although the native populations enjoyed rising living standards under minority colonial rule, they still demanded full equality with the more privileged settlers (in the case of Northern Ireland, the descendants of the Scots Presbyterians settled in Ulster from the 17th century). The beleaguered settler population includes fundamentalists ('loyalists' in Ulster terminology) unwilling to compromise. There is a struggle, often bloody, between the native majority who have discovered nationalism and want independence, and a settler minority who want to maintain the power and privileges enjoyed under the colonial system of exploitation.

Class struggle? Finally, the conflict may be viewed as essentially a class struggle distorted by the labels of Ulster Protestantism and Irish Catholicism. This perspective suggests the dominant class has maintained its position of power by pursuing a policy of 'divide and rule', manipulating members of the working class into fighting each other. According to this analysis the Protestant working class 'have been duped into thinking they enjoy (economic) advantage' over Catholics (Bruce 1986: 254). The advantage may be more illusory than real: the economic gap between members of the Protestant and Catholic working class in employment has diminished, and a common culture of poverty afflicts Protestants and Catholics alike who are without work and rely on welfare. However, because they believed that they were better off than Catholics, the Protestant working class remained loyal to the state and were unwilling to unite with the Catholic working class in order to advance their common class interests.

The search for peace in Northern Ireland

A series of attempts to find a peaceful settlement were made in the 1970s and 1980s, although in all these attempts Sinn Fein was regarded as beyond the pale, while Paisley's DUP was effectively excluded also, for they regarded every new initiative as a sell-out. Instead, British governments tried to secure agreement between the moderate nationalist SDLP and moderate Unionists.

The Sunningdale Agreement (1973–4)

Direct Rule from Westminster was not seen as a long-term future for Northern Ireland by Heath's Conservative government, which sought the re-establishment of a new form of devolved government acceptable to both communities. Following an agreement at Sunningdale in 1973 a new assembly was elected by proportional representation, leading to the establishment of a power-sharing executive with Unionist and SDLP representatives which would gradually assume greater policy responsibilities. This early attempt at power sharing split the Unionists and was effectively ended in 1974 by a general strike organised by the Ulster Workers Council which brought the province to a standstill. The 'Orange card' had been played to great effect, and left some commentators asking whether Ulster militants or the British state now governed Northern Ireland.

The Prior plan (1981–5)

James Prior, secretary of state for Northern Ireland in Margaret Thatcher's Conservative government, conducted a rather similar experiment with 'rolling devolution'. Once again an assembly was elected which (it was hoped) would assume greater responsibility for policy making over time. As before, there was relatively little support for the idea, which was made unworkable in practice, and the assembly was dissolved after four years. Yet again the devolution experiment ended in failure.

The Anglo-Irish Agreement (1985)

A new agreement was signed by Mrs Thatcher and the Irish premier. This involved provision

Table 16.1 Some of the political parties in Northern Ireland

Party	Support and aims	Politicians
Ulster Unionist Party (UUP)	Protestant, supports union with Britain, has supported the peace process, but is increasingly divided.	David Trimble, Rev Martin Smyth, Sir Reginald Empey
Democratic Unionist Party (DUP)	Protestant, supports union with Britain, opposed peace process and power sharing.	Ian Paisley, Peter Robinson, Jeffrey Donaldson
Social Democratic and Labour Party (SDLP)	Catholic, republican and nationalist, but committed to constitutional methods. Supports peace process.	Seamus Mallon, John Hume, Mark Durkhan
Sinn Fein (SF)	Catholic, republican and nationalist, linked with IRA and 'armed struggle' but signed up to peace process.	Gerry Adams, Martin McGuinness
Alliance Party of Northern Ireland (APNI)	Non-sectarian – seeks to bridge gap between two communities.	John Alderdice, Sean Neeson

for more cooperation between Britain and Ireland, including greater cross-border cooperation to defeat terrorism, with Dublin consulted routinely on Northern Ireland affairs. Unionists were outraged by this provision to give a foreign government power to influence domestic policy in a part of the United Kingdom. Sinn Fein also opposed the agreement, but for different reasons. The SDLP was in favour, as were the front benches of all Britain's major parties, although there was fierce opposition from some Conservative backbenchers.

The Downing Street Declaration (1993) and the peace process

What differentiated the peace process that began in 1993 from earlier initiatives was that for the first time Sinn Fein (and effectively the IRA also) was party to the negotiations. The SDLP could support successive plans for peace but could not end the violence. Only the IRA and Sinn Fein could do that. After 20 years of armed struggle it was clear that the IRA could neither be defeated nor achieve victory by force. A series of both public and secret communications broke the deadlock. Talks between the SDLP's John Hume and the Sinn Fein leader Gerry Adams, secret messages from the Republican leadership to the British government, and finally talks between British Prime Minister John Major and Albert Reynolds (the Irish taoiseach) led to the Downing Street Declaration. This renounced any long-term British strategic interest in Northern Ireland and accepted the right of the peoples of north and south to unite at some time in the future. Sinn Fein would be able to join negotiations for a settlement if they renounced violence.

The Official Unionists responded to the Declaration in a cautious but positive way, while Ian Paisley's DUP condemned it as a 'sell-out'. Dramatic progress was made in August 1994 when the IRA announced a 'complete cessation of military operations'. This led in turn to agreement on Joint Framework Documents by the British and Irish governments in 1995, which foreshadowed most of the details of the later Belfast Agreement of 1998. However, further progress in the peace process was put on hold by Unionist demands for prior IRA decommissioning of its weapons. John Major opted for pre-talks elections to a Northern Ireland forum, which Sinn Fein and the IRA regarded as a delaying tactic, and in February 1996 the IRA ended its ceasefire. In April 1996 elections went ahead, in which both the Unionists and Sinn Fein did better than anticipated. Negotiations between the parties began in June, but could make little progress before the UK General Election of 1997.

The Good Friday Agreement

The Labour election victory in 1997 effectively restarted the Northern Ireland peace process. The IRA announced a restoration of a ceasefire in July 1997, and after six weeks of non-violence the new Northern Ireland secretary, Mo Mowlam, invited Sinn Fein to join the peace talks on the long-term future for Northern Ireland. Ian Paisley's Democratic Unionists had already pulled out, but David Trimble's Ulster Unionists continued to participate. After a period of intense negotiations in which Mo Mowlam wooed the Republicans while Tony Blair reassured the fearful Unionists, a formal agreement was eventually reached on Good Friday 1998. Most of the ideas in the Belfast Agreement 'were articulated or prefigured before Labour took office' (O'Leary, in Seldon, 2001: 449). Key elements included:

- parallel referendums to be held on the Agreement in both parts of Ireland
- a devolved assembly in Northern Ireland, elected by the single transferable vote system of proportional representation, with legislative and executive functions
- a first minister and deputy first minister to be elected together by parallel consent of parties representing a majority of unionists and of nationalists
- an executive consisting of ten ministers to be allocated by the D'Hondt procedures (to ensure proportionate power sharing)
- a North-South Ministerial Council
- an inter-governmental 'British-Irish Council' (to provide an east–west forum to balance the north–south body).

The agreement was popularly endorsed in May by a referendum majority of 94 per cent in the Republic of Ireland and 71 per cent in the north, where nearly all Catholics and a more narrow majority of Unionists voted in favour. There was also important backing not only from the UK and Irish governments but also from the US government, and the terms were incorporated in an international treaty, the British-Irish Agreement. However, the key issue of arms decommissioning remained unresolved. Here Blair gave assurances to Trimble which were to be a source of trouble later.

The peace process from 1998 onwards

Implementation of the Agreement has been predictably difficult, and its future still seems precarious. While the nationalists have been broadly supportive of the peace process, the unionists remain deeply divided. The first elections to the new Northern Ireland Assembly in June 1998 produced a delicate balance on both the nationalist and unionist sides. Sinn Fein came closer to parity with the more constitutional and peaceful SDLP among the nationalists, while the Ulster Unionists and their pro-agreement unionist allies only just won more seats (and fewer first preference votes) than Paisley's DUP and other anti-agreement parties. This, however, led to the election of Ulster Unionist David Trimble and the SDLP's Seamus Mallon as first and deputy first ministers in July. Further progress was stalled by wrangling over the north–south bodies, arms decommissioning and Chris Patten's report on the police body to replace the Royal Ulster Constabulary. Unionists feared they were making all the concessions without any guarantee that violence was over.

In November 1999 Trimble secured 58 per cent support from his party's Ulster Unionist Council for entry into government, promising to resign if there was no progress on arms decommissioning. The Assembly proceeded to choose the ministers for the new Northern Ireland Executive – three UUP, three SDLP, two Sinn Fein (including Martin McGuinness, as minister of education) and two DUP (who were nominated but refused to participate in the Executive). In December the Republic of Ireland modified its constitutional claim to Northern Ireland to reassure Northern Ireland's Unionists, and in the same month the first meetings of the North–South Ministerial Council and the British–Irish Council were held.

It appeared that the main elements in the agreement were all in place, but arms decommissioning remained a ticking time bomb under the peace process. In February 2000 the Assembly was suspended to stave off the resignation of Trimble on the decommissioning issue, to the fury of nationalists. After further prolonged negotiations between the British and Irish governments and the main parties the IRA made a statement promising that it would eventually 'place its arms beyond use' in May 2000, and the Assembly and Executive were temporarily restored. IRA arms dumps were inspected by international commissioners in June, and subsequently small quantities of arms were reported to have been put beyond use. However, the future of the agreement remained precarious. In Autumn 2002 Trimble and the Unionists withdrew from the Executive, and devolved institutions were suspended for a fourth time. Further attempts were made to restore the Assembly in autumn 2003, but progress on arms decommissioning by the IRA failed to satisfy the Unionists, and fresh elections eventually went ahead while the devolved institutions remained suspended.

The results of the elections in November 2003 intensified the deadlock between the nationalists and unionists, and prevented any early restoration of the Assembly and Executive. The DUP, opposed to the 1998 agreement, emerged as the largest party, while Trimble's Ulster Unionists were weakened further when three of their elected members, led by Jeffrey Donaldson, defected to the DUP. On the nationalist side Sinn Fein similarly overtook the more constitutional SDLP. The single transferable vote system enabled the small cross-denominational Alliance Party to retain six seats despite losing first preference votes, while other fringe parties lost votes and seats (see Table 16.2).

These gains for the more extreme nationalist and unionist parties seemed most unlikely to assist any early resumption of the peace process and the return of devolved government. Yet in December 2004 further talks sponsored by the British and Irish governments reportedly came close to a remarkable agreement between the DUP leader Ian Paisley and Sinn Fein's Gerry Adams.

This apparently broke down once again on the issue of arms decommissioning by the IRA, on which Paisley insisted on photographic evidence, which Sinn Fein rejected as tantamount to the appearance of surrender. Any further prospects for an early compromise were destroyed by two subsequent events: a raid on the Northern Bank (in which the IRA was implicated) and the murder of Catholic Robert McCartney, apparently by known members of the IRA. The stalemate thus continues, reinforced by the results of the 2005 General Election in which only one Ulster Unionist MP was elected and Trimble lost his own seat, resigning immediately as party leader. The Ulster Unionists who had long dominated Ulster politics have been reduced to a fringe party, while Paisley's DUP, with nine seats, has emerged as the only Protestant party that now counts. On the republican side Sinn Fein won five seats and the constitutional nationalist party, the SDLP, three.

On 28 July 2005 the IRA issued a statement in which they 'formally ordered an end to the armed campaign' and instructed volunteers to 'assist the development of purely political and democratic programmes through exclusively peaceful means'. This was hailed as an historic breakthrough, particularly by the British and Irish governments, but greeted with suspicious hostility by Paisley and many unionists. Had it happened in December of the previous year at the time when negotiations were proceeding between the DUP and Sinn Fein it might have made a difference. As it is, the IRA commitment to disarm has not transformed Ulster politics. Young Protestants in particular seem more alienated than ever, and the re-routing of an Orange march in September 2005 led to the worst rioting and violence in Belfast for more than a decade, with 'loyalists' firing at the police (see Figure 16.1). The apparent decommissioning of the IRA's entire arsenal of weapons, witnessed by the head of the international decommissioning body, John de Chastelain and two clergymen (one Catholic, one Protestant) on 26 September, failed to satisfy the DUP, and it seems unionists generally. Another 'historic landmark' may fail to have much immediate effect.

Yet peace of a kind survives in Northern Ireland. It may be flawed but it has already brought economic and political benefits to both communities. The Omagh bombing in 1998, in which six men, 13 women and nine children were killed, served to marginalise extremism, while 9/11 and the war against terror have transformed attitudes to Northern Ireland politics in the United States. While not all nationalists have been prepared to renounce violence, both Sinn Fein and the IRA are now committed to 'exclusively peaceful means' to achieve their long-term objectives, and have taken the bulk of the IRA sometimes grudgingly with them. Sinn Fein has tasted a share of power, and its politicians are keen for devolved institutions to be restored. Moreover, now that the DUP is the largest party, Paisley or another DUP leader is placed to become first minister if the assembly and executive are re-established. The problem for the DUP leadership is the problem faced by previous unionist politicians who were themselves prepared to accept power-sharing selling the deal to their supporters. In the wake of increased 'loyalist' violence this seems more difficult than ever.

Table 16.2 Results of the November Northern Ireland 2003 elections (1998 figures in brackets)

Party	% first preference votes		Number of seats	
Democratic Unionist Party	25.7	(18.1)	30	(20)
Ulster Unionist Party	22.7	(21.3)	27	(28)
Sinn Fein	23.5	(17.6)	24	(18)
Social Democratic and Labour Party	17.0	(22.0)	18	(24)
Alliance Party of Northern Ireland	3.7	(6.4)	6	(6)
Other parties	5.6	(19.4)	2	(10)

Sources: derived and adapted from various sources including O'Leary, in Seldon (2001: 458), Hopkins, (2001), *Guardian* 29 November 2003, Norris (2004).

Figure 16.1 Riots in Northern Ireland, September 2005

Recent riots (this time by 'loyalists') in September 2005 indicate that Northern Ireland's troubles are far from over.

Photograph: EMPICS.

It has been argued that ultimately, demographic trends will produce a nationalist majority in Northern Ireland and Irish unification, although this prospect now seems distant and uncertain. Meanwhile the Republic appears less threatening to unionists. Its constitution has been changed. The Catholic Church has lost some of its former dominance. Ireland moreover has prospered economically as a member of the European Union, and no longer appears a poor relation. Thus the two Irelands may draw closer together over time. Altogether it seems improbable that Northern Ireland will remain part of the United Kingdom in the long term, although there could be interim arrangements for joint sovereignty, and almost certainly some political framework for continuing Anglo-Irish cooperation on matters of mutual interest.

Scottish nationalism and the pressure for devolution

Scotland could ultimately go the same way as Ireland, although that seems unlikely at present. Scotland had been an independent state for centuries when its King, James VI, succeeded to the English throne in 1603 as James I. This union of crowns became a full union of the two states and parliaments in 1707, but the inequalities in population, wealth and power ensured that England dominated. However, Scotland retained its distinctive national identity which, in the 20th century, was reflected in a separate legal system, education system and established church. Scottish affairs were handled by the Scottish Office, with a 'mini-parliament' of Scottish MPs meeting in the form of the Scottish Grand Committee.

Many Scots shared a wider British nationalism. Scots peopled the empire, including the settlement of Scottish Presbyterians in Northern Ireland in the early years of the 17th century. Even as late as the 1945 General Election, Scottish nationalist sentiment was weakly expressed, with the Scottish National Party winning only 1.3 per cent of the Scottish vote. The decline of Britain's Empire and world role, along with industrial decline which adversely affected the Scottish mining, shipbuilding and textile industries, gave renewed significance to Scottish nationalism. The SNP began to win significant votes and seats in the 1970s. These successes worried the Labour Party which had come to dominate Scottish politics, and helped commit the 1974–9 Labour government to Scottish devolution.

The 1979 devolution referendum was lost because of a requirement of support from at least 40 per cent of the Scottish electorate (not just those who voted). In the event, although 32.5 per cent of the Scottish electorate voted 'yes', compared with

Definitions

A **unitary state** is a state in which sovereignty or supreme power is retained at the centre, and there is no significant delegation of authority to any regional institutions. All citizens are subject to the same laws, and taxes and services are administered on the basis of equal treatment for all in the same circumstances.

Devolution involves the transfer of some power to nations or regions within the state from the central government and parliament, although the latter retains sovereignty or supreme power.

Rolling devolution involves the transfer of various powers over a period.

Asymmetrical devolution suggests that there is no common pattern to the devolution of powers within the state. Different nations or regions within the state involve very different size ranges, and involve different institutions, powers and processes.

Federalism is a system of government in which sovereignty is divided between two or more levels, with each level supreme in its own sphere.

30.7 per cent who voted 'no', the largest proportion of the electorate (37.1 per cent) abstained. The failure of the referendum effectively brought down Callaghan's Labour government, and ushered in 18 years of Conservative rule, ending any immediate prospects for devolution. The SNP initially lost votes and seats, although nationalist feelings were aroused by Margaret Thatcher's strident expression of English nationalism, and by policies such as the poll tax (introduced in 1989 in Scotland, a year earlier than in England). One consequence was that the number of Conservative MPs returned for Scottish seats declined with each successive election, until none at all were elected in 1997.

Labour became strongly recommitted to devolution in the 1980s, and from 1988 to 1995 joined with the Liberal Democrats, Scottish trade unions, local authorities and other organisations in a Scottish Constitutional Convention. This hammered out an agreed programme for devolution, which was to provide the basis for the 1998 Scotland Act. The SNP, committed to full independence, declined to join the convention, while the Conservative government under John Major and the Conservative Party in Scotland maintained its opposition to devolution and its support for the Union. Tony Blair upset some Scottish Labour supporters by announcing that there would be a referendum prior to any devolution, in which Scottish voters would be asked, first, whether they wanted a Scottish parliament and, second, whether it should have tax-varying powers. However, when the referendum was held in September 1997, after Labour's election victory, it gave an overwhelming backing to a Scottish parliament (74.3 per cent) and a 63.5 per cent support for tax-varying powers. This conclusively settled the issue, rendering further Conservative opposition to the parliament and what they had described as a 'tartan tax' fruitless. The party of the Union was obliged to accept a major constitutional change that they had previously argued would lead to the break-up of Britain.

The Scottish Parliament and government

The first elections for the new Scottish Parliament were held in May 1999. The results were expected to be much closer than in Wales, as the SNP appeared to be making substantial inroads into Labour's vote. In the event, Labour maintained its position as the largest party in Scotland but under the additional member voting system predictably failed to secure an overall majority. The electoral system benefited both the nationalists and (ironically) the Conservatives, who had always opposed proportional representation.

Labour moved immediately towards a coalition administration with the Liberal Democrats, with whom they had worked closely in the Constitutional Convention. A key sticking point in the negotiations between the two parties was student fees, which the Liberal Democrats had opposed, but a compromise was eventually agreed and the new coalition executive was formed with Labour's Donald Dewar as first minister and the Liberal Democrat Jim Wallace as deputy first minister. Donald Dewar, widely respected and regarded as the 'father of the nation' and its new parliament, did not live long to enjoy his new position. He died on 11 October 2000, and after a Labour Party election, was

In Focus 16.1

The Scottish Parliament

The debating chamber of the new Scottish Parliament in Edinburgh. The Scottish Parliament began its work in a temporary home in the Mound, Edinburgh, but a firm of Barcelona architects won an international competition to design a new parliament building for a site at Holyrood adjoining Queensbury House. The spiralling cost of this new building was an embarrassing political issue for the devolved Scottish government. However, although the exterior of the completed building remains controversial, its interior design has won widespread approval. Members of the Scottish Parliament now enjoy much more room and much better facilities than MPs at Westminster.

Photograph: Robert Leach.

Table 16.3 Elections for the Scottish Parliament, May 2003 (1999 in brackets)

Party	% constituency votes		Constituency seats		% regional list votes		Regional list seats		Total seats	
Labour	34.6	(38.8)	46	(53)	29.3	(33.6)	4	(3)	50	(56)
SNP	23.9	(28.7)	9	(7)	20.9	(27.3)	18	(28)	27	(35)
Conservative	16.6	(15.5)	3	(0)	15.5	(15.4)	15	(18)	18	(18)
Lib Dem	15.4	(14.2)	13	(12)	11.8	(12.4)	4	(5)	17	(17)
Greens	0	(0)	0	(0)	6.9	(3.6)	7	(1)	7	(1)
Scottish Socialist	6.2	(1.0)	0	(0)	6.7	(2.0)	6	(1)	6	(1)
Others	3.4.		2		9.0		2		4	(1)

succeeded by Henry MacLeish, who himself was obliged to resign following accusations over the funding of his private office, to be replaced by his rival in the earlier party election, Jack McConnell.

A second round of elections in 2003 (see Table 16.3) left the Conservatives and Liberal Democrats with the same number of seats as before. Labour (down to 50 from 56) and more particularly the SNP (down from 35 to 27) lost ground to the Greens, Scottish Socialist Party and a handful of minority political groups. However, the Labour-Liberal Democrat coalition headed by Jack McConnell survived, albeit with a smaller overall majority. Moreover, it seemed unlikely that the very diverse opposition parties (SNP, Conservatives, Greens and Socialists) could mount a coherent challenge.

There has been some disappointment with the record to date of Scottish devolution, although it has been relatively successful compared with the Welsh and Northern Ireland assemblies. Major political difficulties were caused by the early intra-coalition differences over student fees and proportional representation in local elections, and rows with pressure groups over the abolition of hunting and the scrapping of the notorious 'Section 28' of the Local Government Act prohibiting local authorities from 'promoting' homosexuality. A

Box 16.3

The Scottish Executive 2005

First minister:	Jack McConnell, MSP (Labour)
Deputy first minister and minister for enterprise and lifelong learning:	Jim Wallace, MSP (Lib Dem)
Deputy minister for enterprise and lifelong learning:	Allan Wilson, MSP (Labour)
Minister for justice:	Cathy Jamieson, MSP (Labour)
Deputy minister for justice:	Hugh Henry MSP (Labour)
Minister for health and community care:	Andy Kerr, MSP (Labour)
Deputy minister for health and community care:	Rhona Brankin, MSP (Labour)
Minister for education and young people:	Peter Peacock, MSP (Labour)
Deputy minister for education and young people:	Euan Robson, MSP (Lib Dem)
Minister for finance and public service reform:	Tom McCabe, MSP (Labour)
Deputy minister for finance and public service reform:	Tavish Scott, MSP (Lib Dem)
Minister for environment and rural development:	Ross Finnie, MSP (Lib Dem)
Deputy minister for environment and rural development:	Lewis Macdonald, MSP (Labour)
Minister for communities:	Malcolm Chisholm, MSP (Labour)
Deputy minister for communities:	Johann Lamont, MSP (Labour)
Minister for parliamentary business:	Margaret Curran, MSP (Labour)
Deputy minister for parliamentary business:	Tavish Scott, MSP (Lib Dem)
Minister for tourism, culture and sport:	Patricia Ferguson, MSP (Labour)
Minister for transport:	Nicol Stephen, MSP (Liberal Democrat)
Lord advocate:	Colin Boyd, QC
Solicitor general:	Elish Angliolini, QC

particular scandal has been the escalating cost of the new Scottish Parliament building, but now that this is up and running, to general approval, the issue appears to be of diminishing political significance.

As far as the parties are concerned, Labour has been troubled by internal differences and allegations of sleaze, while the Liberal Democrats have struggled to assert their separate identity in the Labour-dominated coalition. However, the opposition parties seem in no better shape. The SNP has found it difficult to come to terms with the 'half-way house' of devolution, and has made less impact than might have been expected, which was perhaps a factor in their charismatic leader Alex Salmond surrendering the leadership to John Swinney, only for Salmond to return in 2004. The Conservatives, obliged to accept both Scottish devolution and PR as an accomplished fact, have ironically been rescued from political oblivion north of the border by developments they had previously strenuously opposed. Yet they have made little or no further progress. They narrowly won back just one seat in the 2001 General Election in Scotland after their wipe-out in 1997, failed to make any gains in 2003 in the Scottish Parliament elections of 2003, and only emerged once more with a single seat in the 2005 General Election.

After two elections to the Scottish Parliament, the opening of the new Parliament building and several years of stable devolved government, Scottish devolution appears here to stay.

Differences in the funding of higher education and the care of the elderly have caused some political problems for the Labour Party which controls the UK government and is the major partner in the Scottish Executive. Yet such differences are the inescapable consequence of devolution, although more difficulties might arise if and when a Scottish government confronts a UK government of a markedly different party complexion. Over time it is possible, even likely, that the Scottish government and Parliament will demand and acquire further powers, and the United Kingdom as a whole could move to a fully federal system of government. Independence is another possibility. Should the SNP ultimately succeed in displacing Labour as the leading party in Scotland, the future of the current devolutionary settlement would appear fragile, particularly if the nationalists secured an overall majority. Scottish independence could hardly be denied if it was clearly the settled wish of the majority of the Scottish people.

Devolution in Wales

Early support for Welsh nationalism had more to do with preserving the Welsh culture and language from extinction than with Welsh self-government. By the early 20th century, English was taught as the language of advancement, and the use of Welsh was 'actively discouraged' (Madgwick and Rawkins 1982: 67). Support for Plaid Cymru, the Welsh nationalist party, remained negligible until the late 1960s, and, even after that, was substantially confined to the Welsh-speaking areas of north and central Wales. In the 1979 devolution referendum only 11.8 per cent of

Box 16.4

Comparative politics – The future of Scotland: the Quebec scenario or the Slovak scenario?

The nationalist Tom Nairn (1981, 2000, 2001) has gleefully described the break-up of Britain as virtually accomplished, assuming it is only a question of time before Scotland becomes an independent state. Iain McLean (in Seldon 2001: 444–6) has suggested two alternative future scenarios, based on comparisons with Quebec and Slovakia.

Quebec is a French-speaking province of Canada where there has been persistent pressure from nationalists for an independent Quebec state. Yet voters, perhaps fearful of adverse economic consequences, have narrowly rejected the independence option in referendums. Thus Quebec for now remains part of Canada, in contrast with Slovakia, which having threatened separation from the former Czechoslovakia, suddenly found itself 'unexpectedly independent, to its short run disadvantage' (McLean, in Seldon 2001: 444). Both the Czech Republic and Slovakia however have gone on to join the European Union in 2004 .

Will Scotland's future resemble the Quebec scenario (substantial home rule within a federal state) or the Slovak scenario of independence? Either seems possible, but two major linked issues may decide the outcome – the future of the Scottish economy, and the funding of Scottish public spending. The discovery of North Sea oil in the 1970s enabled the SNP to claim that an independent oil-rich Scotland would be better off. Declining revenues from the North Sea have damaged this argument, although Scottish nationalists now point to Ireland as an example of the economic growth which could follow independence. However, the Scots could be worse off if they lose the very generous funding they receive within the United Kingdom. Under the so-called Barnett formula, public spending per capita in Scotland is now reckoned to be 31 per cent above the British average, while Scottish income is now close to the UK average, so that Scotland no longer appears particularly disadvantaged.

McLean argues that the 'Slovak scenario' could result if the UK government attempts to reduce Scottish funding, perhaps in the face of political pressure from hard-pressed English regions. A UK government squeeze on Scottish funding would create a strong reaction from opposition parties and voters in Scotland. The resulting political crisis could lead to separation on the Slovak model. McLean (in Seldon 2001: 445–6) concludes that if the Quebec scenario unfolds, Blair 'will be hailed as the saviour of a new flexible union', whereas if the Slovak alternative scenario comes about, devolution will be seen as his 'biggest mistake'.

the Welsh electorate voted 'yes' to devolution, heavily crushed by the 46.5 per cent who voted 'no' and the complacent 41.7 per cent who did not bother to vote one way or the other. An even lower turnout marked the 1997 devolution referendum, and although the percentage voting 'yes' more than doubled and secured a wafer-thin majority for devolution, it still only represented one in four of the Welsh electorate.

Welsh devolution was the product of the demand for Scottish devolution rather than the result of Welsh pressure. The relatively limited demands from the Welsh for autonomy were reflected in the relatively weak powers of the proposed new Welsh Assembly (especially when compared with those of the Scottish Parliament) with no tax-raising powers and no right to pass primary legislation.

However, the bare majority for devolution on a low poll was enough to trigger the introduction of a Government of Wales Bill in November 1997, which became an Act in July 1998. The executive powers of the Welsh Office were transferred to the Assembly, which however had only secondary legislative powers. The first elections took place in May 1999, and surprised expectations by failing to produce an overall Labour majority (only 28 seats out of 60). While support for Plaid Cymru had been boosted by the devolution process, Labour had been weakened, first by the bizarre resignation of the secretary of state for Wales and Welsh Labour leader Ron Davies, after he was robbed on Wimbledon Common, and second by the manipulation of the party's internal electoral processes to secure the new leadership for the Blairite Alun Michael, who was 'widely perceived to be the choice of London rather than Wales' (Osmond, in Hazell 2000: 39) instead of the more popular Rhodri Morgan.

The Welsh Labour group initially formed a minority Cabinet with its leader Alun Michael as first secretary. A minority administration seemed feasible as Labour remained much the largest party, and it appeared unlikely that the Conservatives would be able to combine with other opposition parties to provide a viable alternative. Yet Labour suffered some embarrassing defeats, culminating in a successful opposition vote of no confidence in Alun Michael in February 2000. Rhodri Morgan succeeded him, and governed initially by an informal understanding with Plaid Cymru, and subsequently in a full coalition with the Liberal Democrats. In fresh elections in May 2003 both Labour and the Conservatives made gains at the expense of Plaid Cymru, with the Liberal Democrats maintaining their share of the votes and seats. With half the seats Rhodri Morgan's Labour Party went on to form a single-party administration.

Welsh devolution has so far hardly been an unqualified success. Labour's internal dissension got the Assembly off to a bad start, and there were rows over EU regional funding, free eye tests, teachers' pay, and particularly agriculture. Hazell (2001: 46) declares that the part of Labour's constitutional settlement 'which is clearly not working is the National Assembly for Wales'. Even so, it appears that support for devolution in Wales has

Table 16.4 Welsh National Assembly: election results, May 2003 (1999 results in brackets)

Party	% constituency votes		Constituency seats		% regional list votes		Regional list seats		Total seats	
Labour	40.0	(37.6)	30	(27)	36.6	(35.4)	0	(1)	30	(28)
Plaid Cymru	21.2	(28.4)	5	(9)	19.7	(30.3)	7	(8)	12	(17)
Conservative	19.9	(15.9)	1	(1)	19.2	(16.3)	10	(8)	11	(9)
Lib Dem	14.1	(13.5)	3	(3)	12.7	(12.4)	3	(3)	6	(6)
Others	4.8	(4.7)	1*	(0)	11.8	(5.6)	0	(0)	1	(0)

*Former Labour Assembly Member John Marek, who held Wrexham as an Independent

Sources include *Guardian*, 3 May 2003, and Bradbury (2003).

strengthened rather than weakened (Osmond, in Hazell 2000: 63–6). The Richard Commission (2004) found increased support for a Welsh Parliament, more on the Scottish model, while the number wanting no elected body at all had dropped from 40 per cent to 21 per cent. There is a widespread view that the present Assembly has been given too few powers to be effective, and it seems likely that there will increased pressure from all parties for primary legislative powers and more budgetary discretion. This indeed was the conclusion of the Richard Commission (www.richard.commission.gov.uk), which also recommended a slightly larger assembly of 80 members, to be elected by single transferable vote (STV) rather than the additional member system. Whatever happens, it seems unlikely that the current model of Welsh devolution will survive long without further changes.

Rhodri Morgan has notably departed from the timid approach of his predecessor, Alun Michael, citing the Welsh national hero Owain Glyndwr.

> Owen Glyndwr wanted a country united in properly organised society with representation from all parts of Wales. He envisaged a Welsh future in a European context...Six centuries later we are starting to think in those terms again.
>
> (Rhodri Morgan, *Western Mail*, 17 April 2000, quoted by Osmond, in Hazell 2000: 41)

As Osmond notes, this is strikingly different language from that used by Alun Michael, but what is equally striking is that Welsh politicians are only just 'starting to think in those terms again' after the institution of the National Assembly.

Asymmetrical devolution

Although the devolution process in Wales, Scotland and Northern Ireland has run in parallel, with new assemblies and devolved governments established in each within a few months, what is striking is how different the pattern of devolution in each country has been. 'One's overall impression of Labour's constitutional design is its incoherence' to the extent that it must be 'incomprehensible to most citizens' (Ward, in Jowell and Oliver 2000: 135). 'Each of the assemblies has a different size and composition, a different system of government, and a very different set of powers' (Hazell 2000: 3). The divergence is more striking still if the new London government and (very limited) progress towards English regional governance are included in the overall assessment of devolution, as they commonly are (Hazell 2000: chs 5 and 9).

Does this administrative untidiness matter? On the one hand it provides supporting evidence for the view that Labour's constitutional reforms lack any coherent overall vision; each initiative has been seemingly pursued in isolation, and

Box 16.5

The Welsh Cabinet, 2005

First minister:	Rhodri Morgan (Labour)
Minister for finance, local government and public services:	Sue Essex (Labour)
Business minister:	Jane Hutt (Labour)
Minister for social justice and regeneration:	Edwina Hart (Labour)
Minister for health and social services:	Brian Gibbons (Labour)
Minister for economic development and transport:	Andrew Davies (Labour)
Minister for education and lifelong learning:	Jane Davidson (Labour)
Minister for environment, planning and the countryside:	Carwyn Jones (Labour)
Minster for culture and Welsh language:	Alun Pugh (Labour)

some of the differences appear arbitrary. On the other hand it could be argued that most of the more obvious differences reflect very different histories, cultures and political problems. The legacy of inter-communal strife and hatred in Northern Ireland, and the entire history of the British engagement with Ireland as a whole and its contentious partition, mark off the province from the generally peaceful nationalist politics of Scotland and Wales. Thus an awkward collection of unique institutions with clumsy checks and balances designed to protect minorities and assuage the fears and suspicions of the majority was the minimum requirement for progress.

Scotland and Wales are more superficially similar. Yet whereas Wales was effectively colonised by England, the political union of England and Scotland (whatever Scottish nationalists may now claim) began as a more equal partnership, with the willing assent and even some enthusiasm from the Scottish establishment. Scotland retained its own distinctive church, legal and education systems, and substantially separate administration, which could be readily transferred to a new Scottish government. Moreover, the demand for a Scottish Parliament was based on a distant historical precedent and a more recently established but fairly clear consensus in favour of devolution. Detailed plans had been drawn up in the Scottish Constitutional Convention, backed by a broad swathe of Scottish opinion, and only required implementation.

The situation was very different in Wales, where devolution had been decisively rejected only 20 years before, and where popular backing remained in doubt until the last minute. It is often argued that Welsh nationalism is more commonly expressed in terms of culture and language than political institutions. Welsh law and administration were closely integrated with that of England, there were fewer functions that could readily be transferred, and the case for legislative devolution appeared more questionable. It could be claimed that the Welsh voted uncertainly for devolution first, and only then began to consider what powers their new devolved institutions should have. Thus Osmond (in Hazell 2000: 37) argues that the Welsh Assembly became in its first year 'a constitutional convention by other means'. It may be that Welsh devolution over time comes to resemble the Scottish pattern, as more powers are demanded in imitation of Scottish precedents, but it is unsurprising that the Welsh Assembly began so markedly inferior in powers to its Scottish equivalent.

How far this administrative untidiness really matters is perhaps questionable. Most federal systems involve a considerable range in state populations, reflecting specific historical and cultural factors. Other countries that have pursued devolved government, such as Spain, have like the UK tackled the process incrementally, with considerable variations in powers and levels of autonomy for different areas. Yet it seems likely in such situations that regions with fewer powers will, over time, demand functions and resources comparable to those where devolution has been extended further. Thus Welsh politicians

Table 16.5 Devolution in Scotland and Wales compared

Powers	Scotland	Wales
Executive functions	Health, education, local government, social services, housing, economic development, agriculture, fisheries, food, transport, tourism, environment, sport, arts, legal system, penal policy, policing	Health, education, local government, social services, housing, economic development, agriculture, fisheries, food, transport, tourism, environment, sport, arts, Welsh language
Legislative functions	Primary legislative powers devolved for above functions	No devolution of primary legislative powers
Finance and taxation	Funded by block grant from UK. Scottish Parliament can vary level of income tax by 3p in £1 (but has not so far used these powers)	Funded by block grant from UK

are already demanding similar powers to those exercised in Scotland (Goodlad 2005).

For all these reasons, devolution in its current form does not appear a final settlement. Ron Davies, the Welsh politician and former secretary of state for Wales, who led the devolution campaign until his abrupt political demise in October 1998, has declared that devolution was 'a process not an event'. This was particularly true in Wales, where the case for and extent of devolution continues to be debated, but it is also manifestly the case for the UK as a whole. The referendums of 1997 and 1998, the Acts establishing devolved parliaments and assemblies in 1998 and 1999, and the elections for those devolved bodies in 1999 and 2003 have not marked the achievement of devolution, but are stages in the devolution process which remains unfinished. Where it will eventually lead is unclear, and may be so for decades.

Box 16.6

The 'West Lothian question'

The so-called 'West Lothian question', named after the old constituency of the dissident Labour MP Tam Dalyell who asked it, has yet to be answered (Dorey 2002). As Tam Dalyell has pointed out, Scottish MPs cannot vote on, for example, Scottish education because that has been devolved to the Scottish Parliament, yet they can vote on education in England. This seems illogical. Thus Dalyell himself declared that he would not vote on English matters. The Conservative Party under William Hague's leadership demanded 'English votes on English laws', restricting involvement on legislation affecting only England, or England and Wales, to those MPs representing English, or English and Welsh, constituencies. This could involve the development of a two-tier House of Commons, with some MPs with considerably restricted responsibilities. It could also profoundly affect executive–legislative relations. A future UK government with an overall Commons majority could find itself in a minority on English matters, which might constitute the bulk of its work, particularly if further powers are devolved, in Wales as well as Scotland.

The English question

An obvious problem with devolution to date is that it is asymmetrical in another sense to that described in the section above. Devolution to Scotland, Wales and Northern Ireland together only involves a small minority of the population of the United Kingdom. Of the 'four nations in one', England is much the largest in area and even more in population (see Chapter 3). Thus England remains a massive cuckoo in the devolution nest. The growth of nationalist politics and changing national identities and allegiances pose questions for members of the majority nation, accustomed to consider themselves interchangeably English and British. Some fear a narrow and racist English nationalist backlash, while others more optimistically believe that devolution, and perhaps the ultimate break-up of Britain could help the English rediscover their own national culture and identity. There has been a spate of books on what it means to be English (e.g. Paxman 1998).

There are more pressing political and constitutional concerns arising out of devolution. One issue concerns the number and role of Scottish MPs in the Commons following devolution. Scotland has been over-represented at Westminster, which was always difficult to justify, but became more anomalous once Scotland had its own Parliament. The implementation of the Scottish Boundary Commission recommendations has largely removed this anomaly. Scotland has lost 13 (mainly Labour) seats in the Commons, and Scottish and English constituencies now have a similar average electorate. This does not, however, resolve the issue of the post-devolution role of Scottish MPs at Westminster (see Box 16.6).

One apparently logical solution is the creation of a separate English Parliament in addition to the Westminster Parliament representing the whole of the United Kingdom. If the Scots, Welsh, and Northern Irish are entitled to home rule, why not the English also? Thus each 'nation' within the union would acquire its own devolved assembly (which could also provide the basis for the development of a federal Britain). This solution, however, has not yet attracted much support. One problem is the sheer preponderance of the population of England within the UK. An English Parliament would represent 83 per cent of the UK population. There would be damaging scope for duplication and conflict between the UK and English Parliaments.

English regional government

Another solution is the development of English regional government, particularly if the main aim of devolution is seen as bringing government closer to people, decentralising power and promoting regional economic development rather than satisfying nationalist aspirations. This would match initiatives in several other member states of the European Union, which itself established a Committee of the Regions as part of the Maastricht Treaty.

Under John Major's Conservative government some efforts were made to rationalise the untidy pattern of existing regional administration, bringing together previously separate regional offices of central departments into new integrated government offices for the regions (GORs). The Labour government went further with the introduction of appointed regional development agencies (RDAs: see Box 16.7) with very limited budgets and powers. Labour also promised referendums on elected regional assemblies, a promise not implemented in its first term but reaffirmed in a white paper published by the Department of Transport, Local Government and the Regions in May 2002 (Cabinet Office/DTLR 2002). However referendums were initially planned in just three northern regions, and this was subsequently reduced to one, the north-east, considered the most likely region to support devolution. Yet the outcome in 2004 was a massive vote against a regional assembly, which has pushed plans for further regional devolution onto the back burner for the foreseeable future (Rathbone 2005a).

Devolution, federalism or separation?

Some alternative future scenarios have already been touched upon. One possibility is that the process will not go much further. The present pattern of sub-UK national devolution will more or less continue within the current complex system of multi-level governance. Extensive further powers may not be conceded to existing devolved bodies, and the sovereignty of the Westminster Parliament may appear unaffected (as indeed Blair's Labour government always insisted). However, for different reasons it seems unlikely that the present arrangements for governing Wales and Northern Ireland can persist for long in their current form.

Even this minimalist scenario will involve (and to a degree has already involved) considerable problems of liaison and coordination between the Westminster government and the various devolved administrations. As we have seen (Chapter 11), the Prime Minister's Office has already been reorganised to create a Directorate of Government Relations, with a particular concern for relations with the new devolved forms of government within the United Kingdom. Beyond the issue of the relations between central government and the devolved administrations there is the issue of the relationship of the latter with each other. This is particularly important for unionists in Northern Ireland. They hope that the British–Irish Council promised in the Belfast Agreement will strengthen east–west links within the British Isles and balance the developing north–south links within Ireland of which they are

Box 16.7

The regional development agencies

Eastern	East of England Development Agency (EEDA)
East Midlands	East Midlands Development Agency (EMDA)
North East	One North East (ONE)
North West	Northwest Development Agency (NWDA)
South East	South East England Development Agency (SEEDA)
South West	South West of England Regional Development Agency (SWERDA)
West Midlands	Advantage West Midlands (AWM)
Yorkshire & Humber	Yorkshire Forward (YF)

apprehensive. Apart from this, however, the devolved administrations may learn from each other. Members of the Welsh Assembly looking for increased powers will certainly take a strong interest in Scottish institutions and processes. The devolved governments are hardly in competition with each other, and indeed may sometimes find it advantageous to combine together to extract concessions from the centre.

Intergovernmental relations ultimately may have to be more formalised. It is possible that the devolution process will be extended to create, over time, a quasi-federal or fully federal Britain (with, or more probably without, Northern Ireland). This, Ward (in Jowell and Oliver 2000: 130) argues, is the only logical way out of what he describes as the representation dilemma (or what has been termed the 'West Lothian' question). This would end the unitary status of the United Kingdom and the sovereignty of the Westminster Parliament. The Scottish and Welsh levels of government would appear no longer conditional and subordinate, but sovereign in their own sphere. This would almost certainly require a written constitution, if only to regulate the functions and interrelationships of the various levels of government.

How far the British system of government has already progressed in this direction is contentious. Bogdanor (in Seldon 2001: 148–51) argues that parliamentary sovereignty has already been virtually destroyed and a quasi-federal system established. O'Leary (in Seldon 2001:. 468–71) by contrast cites Mandelson's suspension of the Northern Ireland assembly in February 2000 as evidence of the maintenance of Westminster sovereignty. He argues that it 'spells a blunt warning to the Scottish Parliament and Welsh Assembly .... Sovereignty remains indivisibly in Westminster's possession'.

A third possibility is that Northern Ireland could eventually unite with the south, and Scotland and perhaps Wales also could become independent sovereign states within the European Union. These areas of the present United Kingdom would cease to send representatives to the Westminster Parliament, which would become an English rather than a UK or British Parliament. The 'break-up of Britain' predicted and advocated by nationalists like Tom Nairn would become an accomplished fact.

The eventual separation of Northern Ireland from Britain seems quite likely, although some joint sovereignty or consociation arrangements could survive as a viable alternative. The political circumstances that could lead to Scotland's separation have already been lightly indicated. It is certainly a highly plausible future scenario, although certainly not the only one (see Box 16.4 on the Quebec and Slovak scenarios). A sizeable minority of Scots (from a quarter to a third in recent years – see Curtis, in Hazell 2000: 228) support independence, but it would need the settled support of a majority to succeed. Religious differences are a major factor inhibiting further nationalist advance, as the large Catholic minority which has been the bedrock of the Scottish Labour vote has shown little interest to date in the SNP. Support for independence in Wales is currently much lower than in Scotland – around 10 per cent (Curtis, in Hazell 2000: 238).

Whatever eventually happens will no doubt appear in retrospect 'inevitable'. Yet at present the future seems uncertain, to be influenced by events, the successes and failures of politicians, and ultimately the decisions of peoples. States in a democratic era require popular legitimacy. The British state will survive as long as enough people in its constituent parts want it to survive. It will break up if national communities seek independence. Ultimately what matters are the political consciousness and identities of peoples rather than institutional machinery, although of course the perceived effectiveness of institutions may influence political attitudes.

Summary

- Nationalism, the doctrine that states should consist of nations (nation states), has been one of the most successful ideologies of the modern world, and a threat to the survival of non-nation states.
- To many Britons in the 19th century, nationalism was a doctrine to be applied in other countries, as it was widely assumed that there was a British nation, and Britain was therefore a nation state.
- Yet British nationalism confronted Irish nationalism in Ireland, and never fully

replaced older Welsh, Scottish and English identities and allegiances.

- Independence for 26 Irish counties, and divided allegiances in Northern Ireland, coupled with the rise of Scottish and Welsh nationalism, have contributed to the erosion of a sense of British national identity and posed problems for the long-run survival of the British state.
- In Northern Ireland 30 years of bitter conflict between republicans on the one hand, and the British state and 'loyalists' on the other, have resulted in deadlock. The British government was unable to defeat the IRA, yet the armed struggle of the IRA was no nearer its goal of a united Ireland. The Anglo-Irish agreement (1998) led to new devolved institutions with power sharing, but these have been suspended several times, largely over the issues of arms decommissioning. However, the fragile ceasefire has substantially held.
- The growth of nationalism in Scotland and Wales converted the Labour Party to a policy of devolving some powers to representative bodies in those countries. After the first attempt at devolution failed in 1979, Blair's Labour government established a Scottish Parliament and Welsh Assembly (with fewer powers), and new executives responsible to them.
- Liberal Democrats were consistent supporters of devolution, while Conservatives opposed it until referendums in favour made further resistance unprofitable. Nationalists were at best lukewarm about devolution, but were prepared to accept it as a stage towards their final goal of independence.
- Devolution is asymmetrical in that it involves different institutions, functions and electoral systems in Northern Ireland, Scotland and Wales. It is also asymmetrical in that it does not cover England (with 83 per cent of the UK population).
- One possible solution, a separate English Parliament, would involve too much duplication with Westminster. Another, devolution to the English regions, is only weakly supported: an elected regional assembly was decisively rejected in the north-east.
- Outside England devolution is unlikely to be reversed. It is more likely that more powers will be devolved over time. Possible future scenarios could be a fully federal Britain, or the break-up of Britain into separate nation states.

Questions for discussion

- What is nationalism, and why might it appear as a threat to some existing states?
- In what sense does a British nation exist? Why are national identities in Britain confused?
- What is the real problem in Northern Ireland? Why has a solution appeared so difficult?
- Account for the growth of Scottish nationalism. Why has this growth been halted (for the present at least)?
- Why has Welsh support for an elected assembly been lukewarm? How far does Welsh nationalism differ from Scottish nationalism?
- How does devolution differ from federalism?
- Account for the apparent lack of support for elected assemblies in the English regions.
- What political conflicts have arisen and could arise between the Westminster government and devolved governments?
- Is devolution likely to satisfy demands in the peripheral regions of the United Kingdom for more say in their own affairs? How far might devolution be a stage on the road to federal Britain or the break-up of Britain?

Further reading

The ideology of nationalism is discussed very briefly in Chapter 6 of this book, and rather more in Chapter 5 of Leach, *Political Ideology in Britain* (2002). There is an extensive literature on nationalism in general; rather less on nationalism in Britain. Davies' *The Isles* (2000) provides a stimulating history of the British Isles, which is a corrective to

Anglo-centric accounts. Marr (1992) and Harvie (1994) both offer readable accounts of modern Scottish politics and the growth of nationalism, while Nairn (1981, 2000, 2001) provides a provocative nationalist perspective. Hall (2004) provides a brief general survey of nationalism in the UK. There is rather more theoretical substance in Hechter (1975) and Bulpitt (1983). Paxman (1998) provides an engaging perspective on *The English*.

Jeffery (2003) has written a useful overview, 'Devolution: What's it all for?'. The early stages of implementation of devolution are explored by various authors in Blackburn and Plant (1999), by A. J. Ward in Jowell and Oliver (2000), and in Hazell (2000, 2001, 2003). There is now also *Devolution and British Politics*, a volume edited by M. O'Neill (2004). There are chapters by Iain Maclean on 'The national question' and Brendan O'Leary on 'The Belfast Agreement and the Labour government' in Seldon (2001). See also Jonathan Tonge (in Dunleavy *et al.* 2003), and Tonge's own book *The New Northern Ireland Politics* (2004). Dorey (2002) discusses 'The West Lothian question.' There are useful articles by Jonathan Bradbury on the 2003 Welsh Assembly elections and by David Denver on the Scottish Parliament elections (both in *Politics Review*, November 2003) while Paul Norris (2004) analyses the 2003 Northern Ireland Assembly elections. Graham Goodlad (2005) compares devolution in Scotland and Wales. On the debate over devolution to the English regions there is a special issue of *Regional Studies* (volume 36, no. 7, October 2002). Mark Rathbone discusses the north-east referendum of 2004 (2005a).

Journal articles, newspapers and websites are essential for further updating – e.g.:

www.wales.gov.uk

www.scotland.gov.uk

The Richard Commission report can be consulted on www.richardcommission.gov.uk

Local Governance and Politics

Contents

Local governance clearly fits into the framework of multi-level governance under which the European and devolved dimensions of British government have already been discussed (Chapters 15 and 16). Some features of local government and politics are fairly old and familiar. A comprehensive system of local councils was in place before the end of the 19th century. Yet democratic local institutions have been subject to almost continuous change over the last half-century, as their structure, functions, finance and internal workings have been radically and sometimes repeatedly reformed. Moreover, this chapter is not just concerned with elected local authorities, but with the whole range of (largely appointed) local public bodies that have grown up in recent years. These form part of a local public sector that works extensively with the private and voluntary sectors in formal and informal partnerships and policy networks.

From local government to local governance

Although the old local councils never ran all local public services, they controlled most of them, and were thus effectively the local government for their areas. This is no longer the case. Whole functions have been transferred, while effective control of others has been significantly eroded, so that, as Blair (1998: 10) himself has observed, 'There are all sorts of players on the local pitch jostling for position where previously the local council was the main game in town'. Here the term 'governance' is particularly apt. What is involved is not just the formal institutions of local government but the whole process of delivering local services and governing communities through complex inter-relationships of public, private and voluntary bodies. Much of this fits with the changed emphasis on government 'steering' rather than 'rowing' (Osborne and Gaebler 1992), or 'enabling' rather than 'providing' (Clarke and Stewart 1988, Brooke 1989). It echoes much of the language of the new public management (see Chapter 12) on the one hand, and New Labour's 'third way' on the other (see Chapters 6 and 7).

To most people local public services are important, and some sections of the community – the young, the old, and those who are disabled, sick or poor – are very heavily dependent on them. Services that are locally delivered include:

- schools
- health services

Definitions

Local government: is conventionally understood to mean the government provided by elected local authorities (or local councils).

Local governance includes appointed agencies and other local governing bodies besides elected local authorities, but also emphasises the process of governing, rather than the institutions of government, and relations between organisations and sectors, and with the local community.

- social services
- public or social housing
- land use and planning
- roads and public transport
- environmental health (including refuse collection and disposal)
- vocational training
- local amenities (such as parks, libraries and sports facilities)
- public protection (police and fire services).

At one time nearly all these services were the responsibility of elected local councils, but this is no longer true. The provision of local health services is now the responsibility mainly of hospital trusts, the new foundation hospitals and primary care trusts (responsible for health care in the community). Police services are controlled by essentially independent police authorities (although these still contain some indirectly elected local authority members). Vocational training is controlled by learning and skills councils. Local public transport is operated by private bus and train companies, although they are partly regulated and often subsidised by local councils. Much remaining public or social housing is provided by voluntary housing associations.

Even where elected local authorities retain statutory responsibility for a service, it may be actually provided by another organisation – by a voluntary body largely funded by the council, by a private company under contract, or by another public agency. Working with voluntary bodies, such as the Women's Royal Voluntary Service, goes back a long way, and is generally cheaper and often more effective than direct public provision. The voluntary or 'third' sector is popular with both the New Right who are critical of public bureaucracies, and with much of the centre and left, keen to encourage more public participation in service provision. Partnership with the private sector has also always existed, particularly in urban redevelopment schemes and other major capital building projects. The recent increased involvement of the private sector in public service provision is however more controversial. It reflects New Right faith in competition and market forces as an antidote to the perceived

Table 17.1 Some of the appointed councils, authorities and trusts operating at local level

Organisation	Number
Learning and skills councils (replaced TECs, 2000)	47
Local enterprise and careers service councils (Scotland)	39
Registered social landlords (housing associations)	2421
Housing action trusts	4
Police authorities	49
Health authorities/boards	114
Hospital trusts	387
Primary care trusts	488

Source: House of Commons Select Committee on Public Administration (2001).

waste and inefficiency of monopoly public providers, and a New Labour commitment to partnership with business.

Thus the Thatcher government first encouraged and then obliged Health authorities and local authorities to put certain services out to tender (compulsory competitive tendering, CCT). As a consequence some refuse collection, cleaning, ground maintenance, vehicle maintenance, catering and laundry services, and subsequently leisure services, are now provided by private firms under contract, although still publicly funded and regulated (Wilson and Game 2002: 327–36). Even where such services are retained 'in-house' by councils, they are commonly run on commercial lines as quasi-autonomous units.

Another important development by the Thatcher government, substantially implemented under the Major government, was the introduction of more managerial delegation and competition within the public sector. Thus under the local management of schools (LMS) the bulk of local education authority spending was delegated to school governing bodies, which henceforth had to manage their own budgets. Schools could also apply to 'opt out' of local authority control altogether and become 'grant maintained schools' with more power, and receiving funds direct from central government. In a similar move, hospitals could apply to become 'trusts' independent of the district health authority, and GP practices could apply to be fundholders, controlling their own budget. These developments encouraged more competition between schools and between hospitals in 'internal markets'. School budgets were 'pupil related'. The more pupils attracted by successful schools, the more money they obtained. Similarly, in the health service 'money followed patients' and hospitals could attract more finance by offering better services in a competitive environment. (However, lack of capacity often inevitably limited the scope for expansion.)

These extensive changes have resulted in the appearance of 'all sorts of players on the local pitch', to the extent that the provision of local public services seems increasingly fragmented. The proliferation of agencies presents particular problems for the 'wicked issues' which cut across agency and service boundaries and require a more coordinated approach (Leach and Percy-Smith 2001, ch. 8). Governments have had to place increased emphasis on inter-agency collaboration. Thus the Conservative government promoted Care in the Community, involving the cooperation of health authorities, local authority social service departments and voluntary organisations. The Labour government has introduced a whole raft of new cross-agency initiatives in the interests of 'joined-up government'.

In this new world of local governance, elected local authorities increasingly were expected to play the role of 'enablers' rather than 'providers'. Once, as 'the major game in town', they provided nearly all the local public services themselves. Some of those functions they have lost entirely, while for others they retain the ultimate responsibility, but they no longer provide them directly, rather they 'enable' others to provide them. The new enabling role requires new skills, in drawing up and monitoring contracts, in inspecting and regulating. Where local councils are working with other agencies and the private and voluntary sectors in partnerships and networks, diplomatic cooperation is required, rather than the line management local government officials were used to in large hierarchical organisations. This is sometimes referred to as 'third-way management'. Instead of the command and control management of old large and hierarchically structured public sector organisations, or the competition and profit maximisation which drives the private sector, third-way management emphasises leadership, diplomacy and collaborative joint working.

However, local councils retain some advantages in this fragmented jumble of local agencies and networks. They still have extensive statutory powers, control many key resources, remain multi-purpose bodies, and crucially are the only directly elected bodies that can claim to represent their local community. This gives them a legitimacy lacking in other public agencies, and in the business and voluntary sector, however public spirited they may claim to be. As the only bodies with some claim to represent the whole of their local communities, local authorities remain well placed to take the lead on major local issues and projects which concern the community.

Blair's Labour government has not sought to reverse the fragmentation in the delivery of local public services brought about by its Conservative predecessors. It has, however, introduced some significant further changes, converting grant-maintained schools into foundation schools, bringing fundholding GPs within its new primary care trusts, and replacing training and enterprise councils by local learning and skills councils. In general it has emphasised cooperation rather than competition, while retaining some aspects of the competitive regime. Thus in the interests of 'joined-up government' it has set up a number of inter-agency partnerships and policy networks to address issues such as drugs, social exclusion, crime and community safety.

However, as far as contracting out is concerned, Labour has relaxed the element of compulsion but still insists councils should seek 'best value', but not necessarily the lowest price, through competition. Labour has sought to encourage improved service provision under the Beacon Council scheme, through which local authorities can apply to become Beacon Councils for particular services, and undertake to share best practice with other authorities (Leach and Percy-Smith 2001: 206, Wilson and Game 2002: 342–3). More recently, the Labour government has agreed local public service agreements (PSAs) with individual local authorities, under which the government provides additional grant in return for progress on agreed local objectives. The government has also promised a relaxation of central controls over high-performing councils (Wilson and Game 2002: 344–9).

Representing communities and securing accountability

For many, local governance is not just about the efficient delivery of local public services, as the last section perhaps implied, but about local democracy and community self-government. The 19th-century French writer Alexis de Tocqueville declared that without local self-government people lacked the spirit of liberty. John Stuart Mill considered local representative bodies provided a crucial education in democracy. For these theorists, representative democratic institutions at local and national level were mutually dependent. This assumption has been shared by many of those who have written on local government in Britain since their day. A recurrent lament in recent books has been the erosion or

Box 17.1

Some examples of 'joined-up' policy initiatives

Education action zones to encourage innovation and flexible approaches to learning in areas of high deprivation – involving clusters of schools, the local authority, learning and skills councils, local business and community interests.

Employment zones to improve employment opportunities for the long-term unemployed in the poorest areas.

Health action zones to tackle ill-health and health inequalities to improve the health of local people – involving the NHS, local authorities, community groups, the voluntary sector and business.

Quality Protects to improve the health and education of children being looked after by social services, and to improve opportunities for them when leaving care.

Sure Start – local partnerships to bring together health, education and child care services to help young children and families in deprived areas to prepare for schooling and to prevent subsequent social problems (such as truancy, youth crime and drug abuse).

New Deal for Communities – local partnerships to develop and implement community-based plans to address the problems of 'the worst housing estates', including crime, drugs, unemployment, failing schools and community breakdown.

National Strategy for Neighbourhood Renewal to deliver policies for poor neighbourhoods across a wide range of issues, including housing, education, jobs, skills, community development and shops.

Local Government Association's New Commitment to Regeneration involving 22 pathfinder local authorities working in partnership with the public, private, voluntary and community sectors to develop strategies for the long-term regeneration of the area.

Source: adapted from Leach and Percy-Smith (2001: 202–3).

Box 17.2

The case for local democratic institutions

- **Choice**: elected local authorities offer local communities a degree of choice over local decisions and service levels, allowing them to satisfy different needs and preferences within a diverse United Kingdom.
- **Experimentation and variety**: a degree of autonomy for elected local authorities allows experimentation and the development of policies, which may be copied elsewhere or become national policy.
- **Public participation**: elected local authorities provide more opportunities for participation in the political process, and a training ground for national politicians.
- **Dispersal of power**: local councils help to avoid central government wielding too much power.

bypassing of democratic local government by appointed agencies, or the 'new magistracy' or 'local quangocracy' (Cochrane 1993, Skelcher 1998, Wilson and Game 2002).

There is much in the criticism of the 'democratic deficit' in current local governance. However, it should be acknowledged that not all is well with what remains of democratic local government in Britain.

- Turnout in local elections is very low, 30–40 per cent on average, but much lower in some inner-city areas.
- The first-past-the post system, still used in local elections as in Westminster elections, distorts the representation of parties and interests in the community, and creates many virtually one-party councils, where there is no effective opposition and no prospect of a change in control.
- Those who do vote in local elections vote overwhelmingly on national trends and issues, almost regardless of the record of the local council, thus undermining effective accountability.
- Very few participate in local government in any way beyond voting (for example by attending council or party meetings, inspecting accounts, involvement in school governing bodies, or council tenant bodies).
- Surveys reveal low public interest in, and extensive public ignorance of, the functions, personnel and issues of local government (which goes some way to explaining some points above).
- Elected members are not socially representative of those they serve (being predominantly elderly, white, male and middle class).
- There has been some criticism of the calibre of councillors, and the reluctance of people with relevant experience and expertise to stand for election to the council.
- There have been some scandals that have undermined public trust in local government (as in Doncaster).

Some of these points may be exaggerated – scandals are rare, and the general standard of conduct is reckoned to be high. There are elements of contradiction in other criticisms. Higher-calibre councillors would almost certainly mean councillors who were less socially representative. Thus although it is sometimes lamented that not enough businessmen become councillors, businessmen are commonly over-represented compared with their numbers in the community. Moreover, it is still the case that elected multi-purpose bodies remain the simplest and most effective means of representing local communities. If local democratic institutions are not working as well as they might, this suggests a need for reform rather than their further erosion. A number of changes have been tried or canvassed.

- Making voting easier, for example by holding elections on Sundays or public holidays, improving the location of polling stations, making more use of postal votes, or using telephone or internet voting.

- Reforming the electoral system, to make councils more representative, and make votes count more.
- Reorganising local government by relating local authorities to meaningful communities.
- Rendering local authority decision making more effective and transparent, for instance by scrapping the committee system for a strong executive such as a local cabinet system or directly elected mayor.
- Taking local government to the people, decentralising power through area committees and neighbourhood councils, and improving opportunities for citizen participation.

Some of these changes have already been tried, with varying success. Thus limited experiments in easier postal voting, telephone and electronic voting did increase turnout in 2002 (Lynch 2002). Blair's Labour government has also legislated to force through stronger executive leadership on councils. So far, there have been mixed results on referendums to introduce directly elected mayors, and whether this experiment will increase interest in local government remains to be seen (Wilson and Game 2002: 360–6). While some are enthusiastic, the local government world and many academics are sceptical. Relating local authorities to meaningful communities was one of the objectives of the 1992–6 Banham Commission on local government reorganisation set up by John Major, which was generally accounted a failure (Leach 1998). Reforming the local electoral system has yet to be tried, although it is on the agenda in Scotland. This might reduce the number of 'wasted' votes (and thus increase the incentive to vote), and also reduce one-party councils. However, the introduction of more proportional representation in other elections (such as to the European Parliament, Scottish Parliament and Welsh Assembly) has not had a marked effect on turnout. Decentralising power and increasing participation have been recurrent themes in experiments from the 1960s onwards, often with some immediate effect but with generally little longer-term impact. While it may be argued that much of the participation on offer is more token rather than real, it is also the case that active participation requires interest, time, energy and long-term commitment, commodities that are generally in short supply.

The difficulties of local democracy cannot be divorced from the general problems of public apathy and alienation, as shown by declining turnout in other UK elections (see Chapter 4), by declining participation in political parties (see Chapter 7), and by declining interest in traditional forms of political communication (see Chapter 9). If democracy is to be meaningful, new ways of engaging with people may have to be developed.

If elected local authorities are imperfectly democratic, most of the other agencies involved in the delivery of local public services are hardly democratic at all. Some however contain directly or indirectly elected elements. Thus parent and staff governors of schools are elected. School governors also include members (commonly elected councillors themselves) nominated by the council, and such indirect representation is found on some other bodies. More commonly members are appointed, and research shows that such appointed members are generally much less socially representative of the local community than councillors. Many of these other local agencies are less open in their procedures than elected local authorities. Yet although more could be done to make some of this 'other local government' more open and accountable, there is more to be said for it than is admitted by critics.

- Some bodies enable service users and community representatives to become directly involved in service management and provision, aiding citizen participation (sometimes among the 'socially excluded') and arguably a more direct form of democracy. The ballot box is not the only way to give people a voice in decisions that affect them.
- Some more specialist agencies are able to tap community resources (such as voluntary labour, specialist expertise and money) that might be less easily available to large multi-purpose organisations.
- More complex partnerships and networks may be essential to accommodate multi-agency and cross sector working.

The politics of local governance: local interests and parties

Politics is about power. Just as decisions by national governments create winners and losers, so do the processes of local governance. A decision to redevelop a city centre, close a school or hospital, build a new sports centre or high-speed tram system, give a grant to a youth club, transfer housing stock to a housing association, will inevitably impact on the local community, benefiting some and upsetting others. Rightly or wrongly decisions may be perceived to benefit particular groups at the expense of others – middle-class suburban dwellers, or ethnic minorities, or unmarried mothers. Those living in 'sink estates' may feel that 'they' never do anything for 'us'. Those concerned by their rising national and council taxes may feel too much money is 'squandered' on people who trash the expensive services and facilities lavished on them by 'do-gooders'. Some of those in authority may be seen as acting in a systematically biased way, destroying trust in institutions such as the police, social services departments or schools. Such perceptions can even raise inter-community tensions to such an extent as to provoke riots and serious disorder. Even where such violent manifestations of conflicting interests are fortunately absent, there may be a host of cross-cutting political differences – between motorists and public transport users, between inner-city dwellers and suburbanites, between commercial and residential interests, between second-home owners and rural workers, between those who favour developments which offer employment opportunities (such as a new airport, supermarket or factory) and those who wish to conserve the local environment.

Some of these conflicts are manifested in local party politics. Most local authorities and virtually all of the major urban councils are run on party political lines, contested by the same parties that contest national elections (although independents still predominate in some more rural areas). While some critics suggest that party politics is unnecessary or positively harmful in local government, the same issues and interests that divide parties nationally are largely replicated at local level, so party involvement is inevitable and assists the democratic process for the same reasons as in national politics. In practice party politics involves more contested elections and voter choice, and party campaigning tends to increase interest and turnout.

Traditionally, Labour dominates in the cities, particularly in the inner urban areas, while the Conservatives have controlled the more rural and suburban authorities. Liberal Democrats, like lightning, can strike anywhere, including northern cities such as Liverpool, Sheffield and Newcastle, prosperous commuter territory (such as some of the outer London boroughs, and Harrogate in Yorkshire), and the Celtic fringe – the south-west of England, rural Wales and Scotland.

By and large, Labour-controlled authorities are more likely to favour spending on core public services, while Conservatives are keener to keep council tax low, although there are some important differences within both parties as well as between them. The Liberal Democrats in particular may be associated with different interests in different areas, championing inner-city interests sometimes taken for granted by Labour, and competing with the Conservatives for suburban votes elsewhere.

The relatively recent success of first Liberals and now Liberal Democrats in local government has led to more 'hung' or 'balanced' councils where no single party has overall control. This has led in many cases to informal and often formal coalitions, most usually between Labour and the Liberal Democrats (as in the Scottish Parliament), but sometimes between Conservatives and Liberal Democrats. Such coalition politics would undoubtedly increase further were proportional representation ever to be introduced into local elections. As it is, some councils are virtually one-party.

Decision making within organisations: local politicians, managers and professionals

Just as in national politics there is some debate over the relative power of elected politicians and appointed bureaucrats (see Chapter 12), there is a similar debate over the influence of councillors and senior local government officers in local government. Officers have their own professional and departmental interests to defend, and have familiar advantages in terms of permanence, expertise and control over information. Some have concluded that it is officers who effectively rule rather than elected members. Yet it is members who have formal authority and thus legitimacy, and a party organisation behind them. Increasingly also, leading members of larger authorities are virtually full-time rather than part-time amateurs. Members can take effective control if they have the will, as is demonstrated by the record of both some left-wing Labour councils and New Right-inspired Conservative councils. Moreover, as with ministers and civil servants, the relationship between members and officers may often be collaborative rather than competitive, sharing an interest in a particular department or service, and often supporting similar policies. There is a wide range of authorities in which senior local government officers can choose to make their careers, and officers may gravitate towards councils in which they will feel politically comfortable. Yet the local government professions also have their own interests to advance and defend.

The internal decision-making processes of local councils aroused much criticism in the past, particularly the delays involved in the traditional and often very complex committee system. Moreover, the committee system obscured the realities of power in many councils, for the real debates and decisions took place behind closed doors in prior meetings of officers and in party group meetings. Thus the all-party committee meetings, which were open to the press and public, commonly involved little more than the formal registering of officers' recommendations or decisions already taken by the ruling party group. All this, it was argued, was confusing to the public and hardly helped the cause of increased accountability, democratic governance and local participation.

One fashionable remedy, advocated by the Conservative politician Michael Heseltine among others, was directly elected mayors with real power, an idea borrowed from local government in France and some US cities. The incoming Labour government also saw merit in elected mayors. In 1998 the government issued a consultation paper *Modernising Local Government*, which argued for a stronger executive, followed by a white paper in the same year, with a strong steer towards elected mayors, although a local cabinet system was another recommended option. Legislation followed in 2000, which obliged every council to consult the local community on plans for reform. It was hoped that prominent local figures outside conventional local party politics might be tempted to stand.

From a Labour perspective the promotion of elected mayors got off to a bad start with the voters' choice of Ken Livingstone (then standing as an independent) as Mayor of London over the Conservative and official Labour candidates (see Box 17.3). Things have hardly improved since. Most local referendums held to date have rejected elected mayors. There have been some surprising results in the few local authorities where mayoral elections have already taken place. Thus 'H'Angus the Monkey' (Stuart Drummond) was elected as Mayor of Hartlepool on a platform which included free bananas for school children, a pledge apparently unfulfilled (Rathbone 2002, Wilson, *New Statesman* 13 January 2003). It is too early to tell whether the introduction of directly elected mayors will transform local government decision making, or increase interest and involvement in local government, but the record to date is not very encouraging (Wilson and Game 2002: 100–7, 360–6).

Needless to say, there is politics involved also in the internal decision making of appointed bodies, although this may not involve overt party conflict (even if the parties may exert considerable influence on appointments to some bodies). Thus there are conflicts between different professions and different specialisms in the health service, with some prestigious areas (like surgery) often claiming a large share of scarce resources. These conflicts may mirror the differing priorities of national and local politicians. There is also sometimes a conflict between the appointed and largely part-time lay members of authorities and the full-time professional officers and managers, similar in some respects to the conflict between elected members and officers in local government. In hospital trusts there are often tensions between medical practitioners who insist on their professional autonomy, and general managers or accountants seeking to reduce costs. The wider public may be less aware of these conflicts than those within elected local government, as there is less accountability and publicity, but the conflicts

Box 17.3

Comparative politics: running US cities, mayors and city managers

US city government has provided some of the models for proposed reforms of UK local government, and particularly the introduction of elected mayors. There are four principal systems used in the USA.

- **Strong mayor and council**: there is a directly elected mayor who is the most powerful person in the city, and appoints all departmental heads, although an elected council debates and endorses local policy and legislation.
- **Weak mayor and council**: the mayor is directly elected but so are many departmental heads, so the power of the mayor is less (although it may be strengthened by a disciplined party organisation).
- **City commission**: a small number of commissioners are elected to run the city on a citywide ballot. (This system was introduced in the early 20th century to counteract corruption in city politics.)
- **Council-manager systems**: councillors (or commissioners) are elected by the city, but appoint a city manager to execute their policy. The city manager appoints heads of department and other employees. Although city managers effectively run cities, they are not elected, but are employees of the council and can be (and often are) sacked.

may be just as sharp, with significant consequences for service users.

Both elected and appointed local agencies are subject to a wide range of pressure group interests (see Chapter 8). These include groups of local residents or council tenants, parent-teacher associations (PTAs), groups concerned with particular diseases or medical conditions (such as epilepsy or Alzheimer's), leisure groups (such as allotment associations and sports clubs), producer interests (chambers of commerce representing business interests and trades federations representing workers and trade unions). These are generally engaged in the political process not entirely for altruistic reasons, but to secure benefits for their members – policy decisions in their favour, new equipment or facilities, often financial support of some kind. Some groups however have something to offer local public bodies – information, expertise, even voluntary labour in the case of some established third sector groups. Gerry Stoker (1991) concluded that the willingness of councils to respond to various types of pressure groups depended closely on their prevailing politics. Labour councils may be more prepared to listen to trade unions, tenants groups, women's groups and ethnic minority associations, while Conservative councils may pay more attention to the local chamber of commerce and business interests generally, as well as professional interests and local residents' associations. Other groups may be relatively ignored.

Box 17.4

Academic controversy: the community power debate

There has been a long academic debate among scholars in Britain, to an extent echoing similar debates in other countries such as the USA and France, over power in the local community. Pluralists who argue that power is widely distributed have often used urban politics to demonstrate this. They have cited evidence from urban decision making to demonstrate that there is no single local elite dominating the town and its policy processes. Others have cited different kinds of evidence to demonstrate the existence of urban elites. American radicals and French Marxists have argued that urban decision making systematically favours business interests.

Much of this community power debate has been replicated in Britain, although it has been similarly inconclusive. Older case studies found evidence for a quasi-pluralist policy process in Birmingham (Newton 1976), elite decision-making in Kensington and Chelsea (Dearlove1973), and strong business influence in Lambeth (Cockburn 1977) and Croydon (Saunders 1980). Perhaps these merely confirmed the initial perspectives of some of the academics involved, although they do all illustrate the complexity of the conflicting interests involved in the governance of urban areas, and dramatise some of the issues involved in the distribution of power locally.

Territory and community: the reorganisation of local governance

Local governance, by definition, is about locality, but what kind of locality? How are the areas for the local governmental bodies drawn up? How large can they be (in area or population) and still be termed local? How small can they be and still fulfil their functions effectively? How far do they match the pattern of life and work in modern Britain, and how far do they match the local communities with which people actually identify? The reform of local government and governance has been obsessed with these questions for 40 years or more, and they are no nearer a resolution than at the start.

Behind theoretical discussions over efficiency and community there are often more covert concerns over power and influence. New boundaries may transform the balance between parties and interests. Most debate has taken place over the structure of Britain's elected local authorities, but there has also been a long-running argument over the optimum areas for administering health, and more recently bodies concerned with specific functions such as the police and vocational training. Needless to say, different areas and boundaries for different agencies increase the problems of collaboration between them.

A common perception was that many of the ills of local government stemmed from a defective structure. Thus from the early 1960s onwards there have been a series of real and projected reorganisations of the size, boundaries and functions of elected authorities. Some of these reorganisations have been widespread, covering all or most of the country, such as the major upheavals of 1972–4, and the more recent reorganisations of Scottish and Welsh local authorities (1996) and English shire counties and districts (1992–6) under John Major's government. There have also been other changes restricted to particular parts of the country. Thus a London-wide strategic authority was established by one Conservative government (Macmillan's) in 1963, abolished by another (Thatcher's) in 1986, to be reestablished in rather different form by Blair's Labour government in 2000 (see Box 17.5).

In retrospect, many of these reforms reflected prevailing fashion or current academic and political wisdom. In the 1960s it was argued that larger local authorities would result in economies of scale and improve efficiency. In the 1980s and 1990s there was a subsequent reaction against 'big government' in favour of more flexible units 'closer to the people'. Particular models drifted in and out of fashion – the notion of 'city regions', based on cities and their hinterland (which partially inspired Scottish reorganisation in 1974), or 'estuarine authorities', straddling both banks of river estuaries (Humberside, Teesside). Reorganisation commonly stirred up a hornet's nest. Although relatively few people know much about local government or can be sufficiently bothered to vote in local elections, a minority seem to care passionately about particular names, areas and boundaries, fervently campaigning to save or restore Rutland, abolish Humberside, reinstitute the Yorkshire Ridings.

One theme has dominated much of the recurrent debate over local government reorganisation and remains influential – the principle of unitary local authorities, involving one level of local government for all local government services. Such unitary authorities, it is argued, make it easier for the public to understand who does what, and improve the coordination of services. Cities and larger towns in the old pre-1974 system were substantially all-purpose unitary authorities, and this ideal was the inspiration behind the abortive Redcliffe-Maud Report of 1969. These recommendations were largely endorsed by the then Labour government but rejected by the incoming Conservatives in favour of a revised and two-tier system of counties and districts in the reorganisation implemented in 1974. However, a subsequent Conservative government under Thatcher removed a tier of elected government in London and other major conurbations in 1986.

Major's government proceeded to impose unitary authorities in a fresh reorganisation of Scottish and Welsh local government, and gave a strong steer in favour of unitary authorities to a Local Government Commission appointed to make recommendations for England. In the event, the outcome of the Banham Commission's proceedings was an unsatisfactory modification of the two-tier status quo (Leach, S. 1998). Overall, the resulting structure of elected local authorities in Britain is more complicated and confusing than ever (see Figures 17.1, 17.2, 17.3 and 17.4). The

Box 17.5

The Government of London: the London mayor and Greater London Authority

The earlier Greater London Council, established by a Conservative government in 1963, was abolished in 1986 by the Thatcher government, which detested its left-wing Labour council and leader, Ken Livingstone (dubbed 'Red Ken'). The 1997 Labour government was pledged to restore a strategic authority for London. It proposed a new Greater London Authority (GLA) with a directly elected mayor and a 25-member Assembly, elected by the additional member system. These proposals were endorsed by 72 per cent of voters (on a turnout of 34 per cent) in a referendum of Londoners in 1998. The GLA was given strategic (but not operational) responsibilities for transport, policing, fire and emergency planning, economic development and planning, and is now housed close to Tower Bridge in a new building designed by Lord Foster.

The Labour Party was confident of winning the election in 2000 for the high-prestige post of mayor, but the Labour leadership was determined to block the candidacy of the old GLC leader, Ken Livingstone, who had sat as a maverick Labour MP from 1987. The former health secretary Frank Dobson very narrowly and controversially defeated Livingstone for the Labour nomination. The final outcome was a severe embarrassment for Labour. Livingstone stood as an independent, defeating Steve Norris (who had replaced the disgraced Jeffrey Archer as Conservative candidate) under the supplementary vote system, with Dobson a distant and eliminated third. The first elections for the 25-strong Assembly resulted in nine Labour members, nine Conservatives, four Liberal Democrats and three Greens.

The position of London Mayor combines a high profile with relatively weak powers. Livingstone initially tried to run an all-party administration, although he and Steve Norris subsequently parted company, and he has relied largely on Labour within the GLA. He was engaged in a long-running battle with the Labour government over its public-private partnership for the modernisation of the London tube, which did little to heal his rift with the party. A bold but controversial initiative was the introduction of congestion charges to alleviate London's traffic jams. This has generally been regarded as successful, and is being copied by other cities.

Livingstone was subsequently readmitted to the Labour Party and chosen as the official party candidate in time for the second mayoral election in 2004, which he won fairly comfortably under Labour colours. In the elections for the GLA Labour did less well, losing two seats to win just seven. The Conservatives retained nine seats, with five for the Liberal Democrats and two each for the UK Independence Party and the Greens.

Ken Livingstone

Photograph: EMPICS.

view of many of those who had followed the twists and turns of the reorganisation saga up to then was that future governments would be well advised to think twice before embarking on another attempt (e.g. Leach, R. 1998).

However, further local government reorganisation cannot be ruled out. It did once seem likely as a by-product of the introduction of elected English regional assemblies, to which both Labour and the Liberal Democrats were committed before the 1997 election. Both Labour and the Liberal Democrats were conscious that the introduction of an extra tier of government would be contentious, and proposed a simplification of local government involving

Figure 17.1 The structure of elected local government in Britain

England				Scotland	Wales
London	Provincial Conurbations	Rest of England			
Two tier	Unitary	Mixed		Unitary	Unitary
Greater London Authority & Mayor (1)	Metropolitan Districts (36)	Unitary authorities (46)	County Councils (34)	Unitary authorities (32)	Unitary authorities (22)
London Boroughs (32)			District Councils (238)		
(Parish or Neighbourhood councils)					

unitary authorities as a corollary of English regional devolution. When the Blair government cautiously tried to introduce elected regional assemblies piecemeal in its second term (see Chapter 16), their proposals were linked with the elimination of two-tier local government in the regions involved. The resounding rejection of a regional assembly in a referendum (November 2004) in the one part of the country, the north-east, where opinion had appeared favourable, seemed to put both further regional devolution, and with it local government reorganisation, off the agenda for the foreseeable future. Yet in 2005 there were renewed media reports that the government was contemplating the introduction of unitary local authorities, not as a casual by-product of regional devolution, but on the grounds of presumed benefits to democratic local government.

The delivery of services

The division of the main functions between English county and district councils is shown in Table 17.2. By and large, the most important and expensive services are run by the counties. As we have seen, London also now has two elected tiers (London boroughs and the GLA), but here it is the boroughs that have most effective control of the delivery of local services. Unitary authorities (all those in Scotland and Wales, and in the metropolitan areas of England, plus a few new unitaries established by the 1992–6 reorganisation in England) combine county and district functions. To complicate matters further, some areas (mainly more rural areas) have flourishing small parish councils with few powers, and others have introduced largely consultative lower-tier neighbourhood or community councils.

The areas for administering local health services have generally been determined by the perceived functional requirements of the service rather than notions of community. Thus local health management has generally been based on hospital catchment areas, although in the 1974 reorganisation area health authorities were devised to match the boundaries of local authority authorities responsible for social services. This never worked quite as intended, as the main operational tier consisted of smaller health districts, and in 1982 the Thatcher government abolished the area tier. Under the Blair government, hospital trusts (including the proposed new foundation hospitals) and the primary care trusts do not generally cover the same areas as elected local authorities.

The same has been true of other single-purpose local agencies. Training, once a function of elected local authorities, was transferred first to training and enterprise councils, which have been abolished by the Blair government to make way for

Figure 17.2 The local authority map in England from 1998

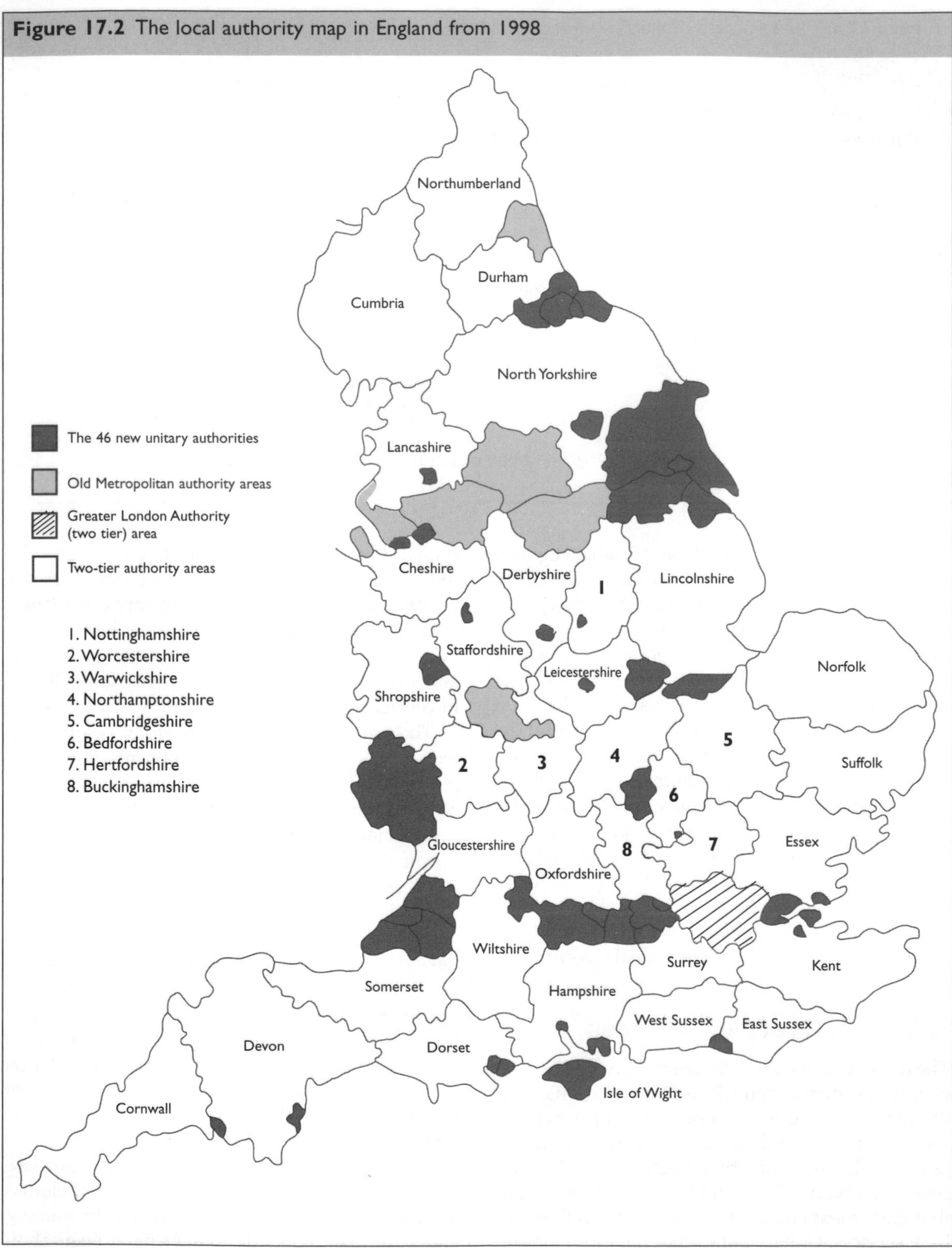

Source: Based on Wilson and Game, 2002.

Table 17.2 Who does what? Principal functions of English county and district councils

County council	District council
Education (most of budget now delegated to schools)	
Social services (largely community social workers, but councils also regulate privately provided institutional care)	
	Housing (regulation and some provision, but much former council housing sold to tenants and transferred to other landlords, especially housing associations)
Planning (structure plans, environment and conservation, economic and tourism development)	**Planning** (local plans, development control, environment and conservation, economic development)
Highways and transportation (transportation planning, county road building & maintenance)	**Street cleansing and lighting**
Public protection (waste disposal, trading standards, fire services)	**Public protection** (refuse collection, food safety, pollution control)
Leisure and amenities (libraries, county parks, grants to village and community projects)	**Leisure and amenities** (allotments, museums, local parks, playing fields, swimming pools, sports centres)

fewer and larger learning and skills councils. Police authorities have become increasingly autonomous from elected councils, and the operational requirements of the police force are generally held to require larger areas than those of many local councils. While economic regeneration remains a major concern of elected local authorities, a plethora of initiatives from central government have involved the establishment of some more localised agencies. These have covered both relatively small and relatively limited inner-city areas (for example, the now defunct urban development corporations), as well as wider regional bodies (such as the new regional development agencies – see Chapter 16). For some functions, such as transport, there are ongoing debates over the most appropriate level, regional or local, for sub-national planning and administration.

Many of these developments take local governance further away from the local communities with which people identify, but which are generally deemed too small for the efficient delivery of some local services. This tension between community self-government and functional efficiency has been a key theme of the debate over areas and structures for 40 years or more. The debate is no nearer resolution, although the general trend is still towards larger areas, despite the reaction against 'big government' (see above), and large authorities which appear more remote and less comprehensible to many people.

Reforming the finance of local governance

On the finance of local governance (as of the finance of government nationally), an initial distinction should be drawn between capital spending and current or revenue spending. Capital spending includes long-term projects like hospitals or schools, and very expensive equipment expected to have a long life. Current or revenue spending includes money needed for wages and salaries of staff, fuel, materials, interest payments on borrowing and so on. Public bodies usually finance their capital spending by borrowing (similar to the way most individuals finance their purchase of houses and cars). Formerly most of this money came from the issuing of government or local authority bonds. As this was part of public-sector borrowing, which successive governments have tried to keep under

Figure 17.3 The 32 unitary authorities in Scotland operational from April 1996

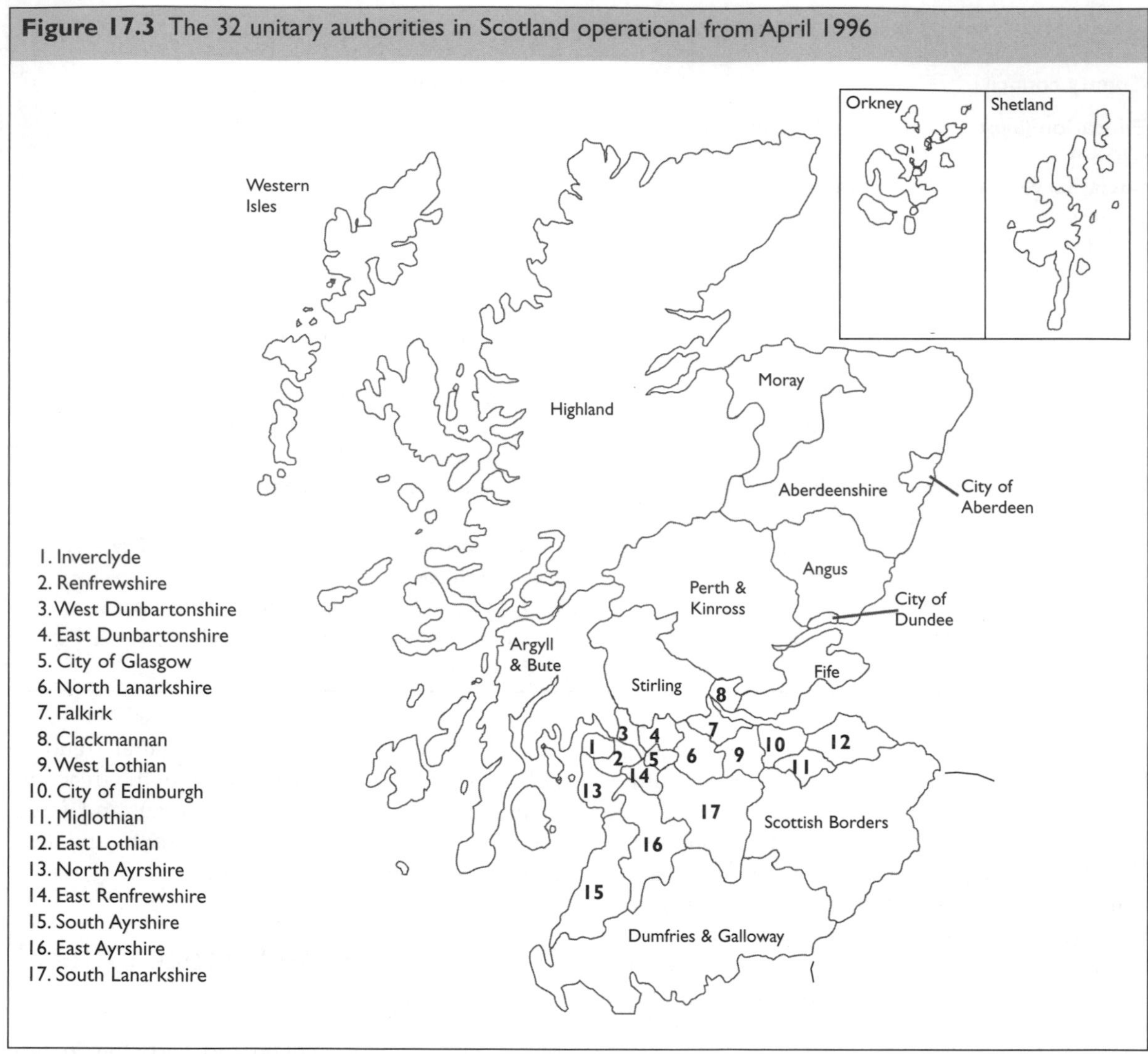

Source: Based on Wilson and Game, 2002.

control to comply with the dictates of prudence and international rules, public services have often been starved of capital investment. As a consequence, both the Major Conservative government and the Blair Labour government have sought new sources of capital investment from the private sector under the private finance initiative (PFI). The private sector provides the up-front capital finance, supposedly bears the risk, and undertakes responsibility for completion of projects on time (with penalties for under-performance). The cost to the public sector is transferred to the revenue budget. Generally, critics argue, this is a more expensive way of raising capital investment in the long run. The advantage for government is that the investment does not show up as part of public-sector borrowing, while hospital trusts and local authorities may obtain new purpose-built hospitals and schools sooner rather than later.

As for current expenditure, the chancellor's recent budgets involve substantial increased spending on health and education, and more money for a range of other services. Most of this money, although raised centrally through national taxation, will be spent locally, by schools, hospitals, primary care trusts, police

Figure 17.4 The 22 unitary authorities in Wales operational from April 1996

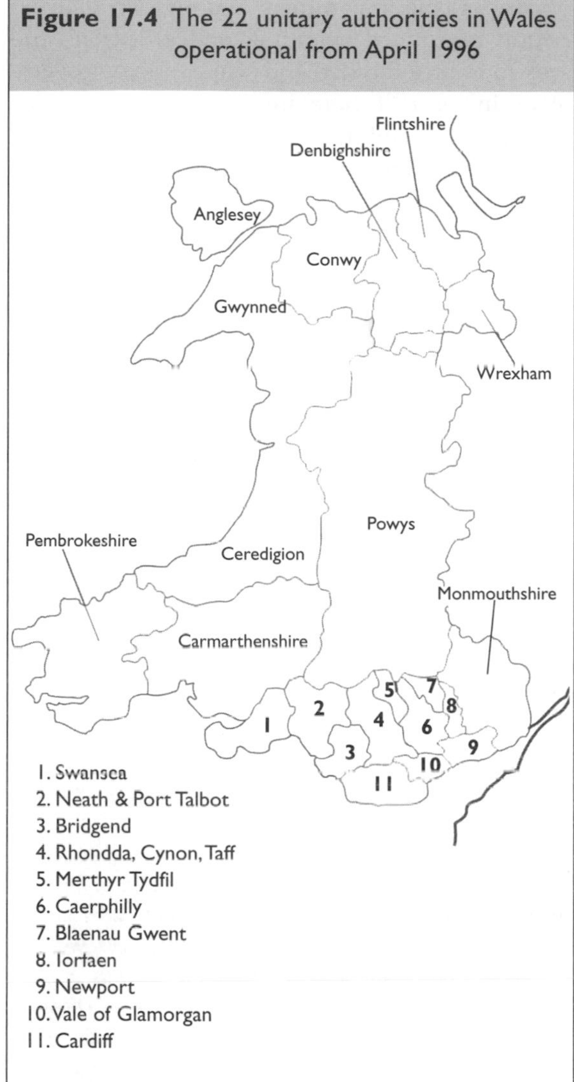

Source: Based on Wilson and Game, 2002.

authorities and other bodies. Local governance is thus big business, involving major spending. There is a delicate balance between central direction and local discretion over how this money is spent. All central governments tend to employ the rhetoric of decentralisation – of devolving more autonomy to those responsible for the actual delivery of services. Yet all governments are aware that they will be judged on the effectiveness of their spending and service delivery, so money is given with strings attached – including an increasing number of centrally determined targets which have to be met. Otherwise, it is feared, increased spending might disappear into a 'black hole', with no perceptible improvement in public services. At the same time, governments are also aware that meeting their targets depends on the active cooperation of front-line agencies and workers on the ground, who have knowledge of specific local conditions and problems, and need to be given some discretion over management and spending.

There is no easy answer to this tension between central direction and local autonomy, which is particularly evident over spending, because for many services local bodies rely substantially or almost entirely on income that they do not raise themselves. Hospital trusts may raise some money from voluntary sources and from marginal activities like car parking fees, but this is an insignificant part of their income. The introduction of internal markets in health and education by the Conservative governments of Thatcher and Major gave hospital trusts, GP fundholders and school governing bodies some financial incentives to increase their activities. If money follows patients or pupils, hospitals and schools can increase their income by increasing the numbers of patients treated and pupils admitted. Yet of course additional patients and pupils also involve additional costs, so careful calculations of income and spending are required. In addition, the rules governing internal markets are determined by government and can be changed. The same goes for rewards for meeting government targets. Local institutions may distort their own priorities to secure additional funding, and then discover that the government's priorities and funding regime have changed.

Conceivably it would be better if local agencies had to raise money locally and justify their spending to the local community, but one obvious problem here is that some local communities are much better off than others. If the quality of local services depended largely or exclusively on the money that could be raised locally, the poorest areas with the greatest needs would have the least income for spending on public services. That is one reason why even elected local authorities that do have their own tax-raising powers still rely on grants from the national exchequer for the bulk of their spending. The same goes for other services and agencies. If police authorities, hospital trusts or learning and skills councils had to rely mainly on some form of local taxation, the areas with the most acute law and order problems, health needs and training requirements would receive the least money. Thus almost inevitably local governance is substantially dependent on central funding in some form or other, and the old adage 'he who pays the piper calls the tune' applies.

This is not to deny that there may be more scope for local funding and increased local accountability. This is an argument that has been particularly applied to elected local authorities. Commonly, the local council is the largest single employer in its area, and local authorities are responsible for more than a quarter of all public spending. Unsurprisingly, local government expenditure is politically controversial. Those opposed to big government and high taxation are critical of council spending and efficiency, and seek to reduce the size and scope of local government. In contrast there are strong pressures from public-sector unions, client groups and other specialised interests to improve service levels and raise spending.

Besides controversy over the size and scope of local spending, there are arguments over the sources of revenue to meet that expenditure. The bulk of the money spent by councils comes from sources over which they have little or no control, from central government grant (which governments of both parties have often manipulated to favour areas where their own party predominates) and from the now centrally determined business

Box 17.6

The poll tax: a policy disaster

The poll tax was a local government tax which was only levied for three years, 1990–3 in England and Wales and for four years in Scotland (1989–93). It was introduced to replace domestic rates, an ancient tax on property, unpopular for a variety of reasons. Rates were a highly visible form of taxation, unlike, for example, value-added tax (VAT) which is 'hidden' within the price of goods. It was a regressive tax, as poorer households paid a larger proportion of their income in rates than affluent households. It was not directly related to the use made of local authority services. Only householders paid rates, so other residents used local services without contributing directly to their cost. The rates were based on old rental values that few understood. However rates also had advantages from a local government perspective. They were easy to collect, cheap to administer, and difficult to avoid. They could be easily adjusted from year to year to meet a council's spending needs, and their yield could be predicted very accurately. The regressive element in rates was substantially compensated for by the introduction of up to 100 per cent rate rebates for poorer householders.

The Conservative government decided to replace rates with a 'community charge'. The name was significant. It was to be supposed to be a *charge* on *consumers* for local government services, rather than a *tax* on local *citizens*. Yet it became universally known as the 'poll tax', a per capita tax (similar to the poll tax which provoked the Peasants' Revolt back in 1381!). Almost all adult residents rather than just householders would pay, restoring the link between taxation and representation. The government hoped that this would deter high spending by local councils, who would be punished by voters through the ballot box for their higher poll tax.

Critics argued that the new tax was regressive and unfair because it was not linked to ability to pay. Most local voters found they were paying more, sometimes much more. It proved a bureaucratic nightmare, three times as expensive to collect as the old rates and subject to widespread evasion. (Many councils were still chasing up defaulters years after the tax was abolished.) It was also widely seen as a tax on voting. Those seeking to evade the new tax (including many students) avoided registering to vote. This also affected population figures used as a basis for government grant calculations. Poorer councils thus suffered twice over – from loss of revenue from defaulters, and loss of income from grants based on an assessment of needs from low population estimates.

Public reaction was very hostile. The tax provoked serious riots and led to major reverses for the Conservatives in parliamentary by-elections and local elections, and contributed significantly to Margaret Thatcher's departure from Number Ten. The new Conservative government, under John Major, moved to scrap the poll tax, replacing it with a new council tax in 1993: a tax on domestic properties, like the old rates, but based on capital values rather than rental values, and with a simpler method of evaluation.

rates (national non-domestic rates, or NNDR). Additionally councils derive some income from fees and charges, many of which are discretionary, and from their own council tax. Critics argue that this financial dependence on the national exchequer reflects excessive central dominance of local government, and also reduces effective local accountability, as councils are not responsible for raising most of the revenue they spend.

The council tax was introduced in 1993 (following the disaster of the poll tax: see Box 17.6). It is a tax on the capital value of domestic properties (houses or flats) divided into eight property bands, but with a 25 per cent rebate for one-person households. The actual tax levied will depend not only on the property band (and whether or not a rebate applies) but on the money needed by each local authority for its expenditure after all other receipts are taken into account (including business rates, central government grant and income derived from fees and charges). Thus levels of council tax depend on the spending of local councils where householders live, the value of their property and the number of people in the household. The proportion of total revenue that councils derive from the council tax can vary considerably between authority and authority, as well as over time, but the average council in recent years has met around a quarter of its spending needs from the tax. Because income from other sources can fluctuate considerably from year to year, it does not necessarily follow that an above-inflation increase in council tax is the result of some commensurate increase in a council's spending, nor does a reduction in tax necessarily mean spending cuts. Because changes in council tax levels often bear little relation to changes in spending, effective accountability to the local electorate is reduced. It is difficult even for the tolerably well-informed local taxpayer to know who to blame (or to reward) for a council tax bill.

Local government taxation remains acutely controversial. The council tax introduced in 1993 initially provoked surprisingly little criticism, largely because many were happy to see the poll tax abolished (see Box 17.7), while across the political spectrum there was little appetite for further change after recent upheavals. However considerable opposition has grown, particularly in those parts of the country where large numbers of retired people live, often in highly rated properties (such as Cornwall). The Liberal Democrats have long advocated a local income tax, and their pledge to abolish the council tax has played well in local elections, and was an issue in the 2005 General Election. Local income tax however would pose considerable administrative problems, and would inevitably create losers as well as winners. Even the Liberal Democrats are reported to be having second thoughts about the proposal. Meanwhile Labour announced in September 2005 that it was postponing revaluation of council tax until after the next election. Local government tax remains a political hot potato.

Central–local and inter-authority relations under 'multi-level governance'

There has been a long academic debate over what used to be called 'central–local relations', perceived as the relationship between the government at Westminster and elected local authorities. Central–local relations implies that there are only two levels of government which matter, and is now a rather inadequate term to describe the still developing system of multi-level governance in Britain.

Among the various levels of government with which English local authorities have to relate, the most important by far remains the government at Westminster, but it is no longer the only level which counts. Thus the European Union has a large and growing impact on British local governance, for example as a source of additional funding, chiefly through the European Regional Development Fund and the Social Fund, as well as specific funding for problems such as the decline of coal mining. EU legislation also affects local responsibilities for the environment, waste management, transport and planning. Local councils are now amongst the most vigorous lobbyists in Brussels.

Similarly, local authorities in Scotland and Wales now have devolved national as well as the more remote UK government to cope with. Even in England government offices for the regions, regional development agencies and regional chambers constitute together a growing regional administrative tier with which local councils have to deal. Moreover, decentralisation of decision making to institutions like schools means that councils have to relate to an increasingly important level of government below them. The position is further complicated by the fragmentation of local governance. Local agencies have to deal 'horizontally' with each other, and the private and voluntary sectors locally, as well as 'vertically' with other levels of governance.

Central–local relations have commonly been illustrated in terms of various analogies or models. Thus some saw local government as the 'partner' of central government, which implies a degree of equality, while others perceived local government in a position of impotent dependence as the 'agent' of the centre. A third view uses the term 'steward', which emphasises the subordinate position of local government but suggests rather more discretion than the agent model. Finally, the 'power dependence' model suggests that both central and local government have resources that they can use in relationship with each other (Rhodes 1981, 1988).

These models can be adapted (if somewhat awkwardly) to meet the more complex relationships arising within multi-level and inter-authority governance. If elected local authorities are too dependent on central government for their powers and finance to be regarded as 'partners', the same is even more true of other public agencies which do not have the legitimacy of election, or their own taxes. Yet knowledge of local conditions and responsibility for implementation of central policies can give local agencies of all kinds considerable leverage over decisions locally and policy outcomes. In practice there are significant differences between policies and service levels between local authorities, and similar differences between individual learning and skills councils, hospital trusts and primary care trusts. Thus the chances of patients receiving certain forms of treatment, their waiting times, and their survival rates from difficult operations depend to a significant degree on where they live. If such bodies were simply agents implementing national policy, these substantial differences would not exist.

It is the 'power dependence' model that can be most usefully adapted to inter-authority relations, and relations between the public, private and voluntary sectors (Rhodes 1997). In partnerships and policy networks, for example, each participating organisation may bring in certain strengths or resources which will help to determine its influence in decision making. Thus in a public–private partnership, a local council may contribute significant statutory powers, finance, information, and legitimacy arising from its election, while a private firm may offer additional finance, commercial enterprise and experience, and specific expertise. In a collaborative relationship between public agencies, such as between a local authority and health authorities over Care in the Community, each participant brings something that is useful to the other, and both may benefit from a fruitful cooperation (in a positive-sum rather than zero-sum game). Health authorities benefit from the transfer of some patients from expensive institutional care to cheaper community care, while cash-starved local authorities obtain some health service finance to improve levels of care. If the policy operates properly, patients should benefit also, as many prefer to stay in their own homes or in sheltered accommodation rather than have to enter a long-stay hospital or local-authority-regulated care home to obtain the level of personal and nursing service they need. (However, in practice some of the burden of care is often transferred not to professional staff but to largely female relatives.)

Optimists see the new world of local governance as offering many opportunities for the development of cooperative policy networks, in which organisations from the public, private and voluntary sectors work together, drawing on a wide range of resources, and encouraging the inclusion and participation of people from across the whole local community. Both the command and control relationships typical of old-fashioned public bureaucracies, and the competitive zero-sum relationships of the free market are rejected. Instead, a true 'third way' of managing and delivering services to people is envisaged, involving collaborative networks of organisations and individuals working together as equals, employing more diplomatic and less authoritative forms of leadership (Rhodes 1997).

Pessimists by contrast emphasise the fragmentation of government, the potential waste, duplication and inefficiency resulting from too many agencies with overlapping responsibilities. They are more cynical over the prospects for mutual cooperation between organisations in policy networks, assuming that each will follow its own self-interest, guided by its own organisational culture. Some formal partners will be only token participants and will offer few if any useful resources. The bulk of the local community will be bemused by the more complex and fast-changing institutional environment, and will become apathetic and alienated rather than engaged participants. No one will be effectively in charge, and accountability will be weaker. Decisions will take longer and less will be achieved.

Summary

- Local governance is a term widely used to cover all local community decision making and the delivery of local public services. It includes both traditional local government, involving elected local authorities, and other local public bodies, which are generally appointed.
- Elected local authorities are increasingly expected to enable others, including the voluntary and private sectors, to provide local services rather than provide those services directly themselves.
- Other local public bodies may sometimes find it easier to involve local business, the voluntary sector, excluded sections of the community and service users, although such bodies are commonly less socially representative and less accountable than elected local authorities.
- While there is a strong case for democratic local institutions, there are problems with the practice of local democracy, including public ignorance and apathy and relatively weak local accountability.
- Suggested remedies include local government reorganisation to reflect real communities, changes in voting, the introduction of elected mayors, more direct citizen participation, and reform of local government finance and taxation.
- Repeated reorganisations over half a century have failed to produce a structure that satisfactorily reflects community identities and ensures efficient and effective local service provision. Local government remains varied and confusing, particularly in England.
- All local public bodies are heavily dependent on central government for finance, although they might be able to increase their resources by meeting government targets or attracting new consumers in internal markets or quasi-markets established by the government (particularly in education and health).
- Local councils can raise some of their own resources through local government taxes (now the council tax). Local government taxation has long been controversial. Liberal Democrats seek to replace the council tax with a local income tax.
- Local public bodies of all kinds now work within a framework of multi-level governance. They have to work with other public bodies, the private and voluntary sectors within their own area, but also need to relate upwards not only to UK central government, but also to the European Union, devolved national and regional government, and downwards to particular institutions, community and parish councils.

Questions for discussion

- Why are there 'all sorts of many players on the local pitch'? Should all local public services be run by elected local councils? Why are there so many appointed local bodies?
- How far are modern elected local authorities more enablers than providers? What are the implications in practice?
- In what ways are the private and voluntary sectors involved in the provision of local services? What advantages and disadvantages might there be in their involvement?
- Why is public knowledge and interest in local government apparently so low?
- Should local authorities be headed by directly elected mayors?
- Why has it proved so difficult to reorganise local government so as to provide for both local democratic accountability and efficient and cost-effective local services?

- Should the present council tax be replaced by a local income tax?
- Who holds real power in local communities: local politicians, officials or business interests? Is power concentrated in the hands of the few (elitism) or relatively widely dispersed (pluralism)? What evidence could be cited in support of either view?
- What are the obstacles to devolving more power to local councils and other local agencies?

Further reading

The relevant chapters (mainly 5, 6 and 7) of Greenwood, Pyper and Wilson, *New Public Administration in Britain* (2001) offer a very useful introduction. Wilson and Game, *Local Government in the United Kingdom* (2002) provides a more thorough account of contemporary local government which focuses largely on elected local authorities, although it provides some coverage of non-elected local government. The most recent edition of an older textbook, Byrne, *Local Government in Britain* (2000) can also still be recommended. Leach and Percy-Smith, *Local Governance in Britain* (2001) focuses on governance (including other public bodies, the private and voluntary sector) as well as traditional local government. Stoker (2003) analyses the changes that have taken place. Rhodes, *Understanding Governance* (1997) does not focus exclusively on local governance, but his analysis of policy networks is useful for understanding much of the governance literature. Stoker and Wilson (2004) have edited an excellent survey of recent developments in local governance and services.

Books covering more specific aspects of local governance include Gyford, *Citizens, Consumers and Councils: Local government and the public* (1991), Stoker, *The Politics of Local Government* (1991) and Skelcher, *The Appointed State* (1998). Butler, Adonis and Travers, *Failure in British Government: The politics of the poll tax* (1994) provides a detailed analysis of the poll tax story. Travers (2003) can be consulted on the government of London.

As always, websites provide important sources on recent and current developments, such as www.local.gov.uk and the Local Government Association's website www.lga.gov.uk. Most local authorities have their own websites. Newspapers and specialist academic journals (such as *Local Government Studies*) and professional journals (such as *Municipal Journal*) are other useful sources.

The New British State: Towards Multi-Level Governance

In this chapter we seek to bring together some of the strands identified in previous chapters, as well as some additional material, in an attempt to characterise the newly emerging British state. While it is clear that the British state has changed and will almost certainly be subject to further transformation, there is less agreement on the nature of the British state today. Here we outline and evaluate some of the contrasting verdicts on modern British government. We re-examine the New Right criticism of government and the public sector, and its impact on the British state, and we explore New Labour's approach to governing, which has emphasised partnership with the private and voluntary sectors, policy networks, and 'joined-up government'. We review the role of non-elected government (quangos), the growth of regulation, and the impact of freedom of information on the traditional secrecy of British government. We conclude with a discussion of the role of the fast-changing British state within a system of multi-level governance.

Contents

Characterising the modern British state

There have always been conflicting characterisations of the British state. For much of the 20th century admirers saw in Britain a free modern democratic state, while critics abroad and at home saw a repressive, secretive, tradition-ridden imperialist state. Although Marxists regarded the British state as a capitalist state dominated by business interests, those in the centre of the political spectrum saw a welfare state with a mixed economy, while neo-liberal critics dubbed Britain a collectivist state. All this serves to emphasise the contentious and essentially subjective nature of such descriptions. How the British state is viewed, both in the past and today, inevitably reflects ideological assumptions.

While it is widely agreed that the British state and the processes of British government have changed massively over the last 30 to 40 years, there is less agreement over how that change should be characterised. Some would emphasise the extent to which reforms of institutions and processes have, over a period, transformed traditional constitutional principles such as parliamentary sovereignty and the unity of the United Kingdom (see Chapter 10). Yet from another perspective the real changes seem to have more to do with the functions of the state than its constitution. Thus it was the Thatcher government's privatisation and contracting-out programme, in reaction against 'big government', which has led to the 'rolling back' or 'hollowing out' of the state (Rhodes 1997, 2000).

By contrast, for some commentators, Thatcherism involved a strong state rather than the minimal state lauded by neo-liberals (Gamble 1994), and centralisation rather than the decentralisation to consumers and service users claimed in government rhetoric. The apparent contradiction was sometimes resolved by the suggestion that the government was seeking 'more control over less' (Rhodes 2000: 156). While some largely sympathetic politicians and commentators emphasised the new enabling role of the state, under which government sought to enable others, including the private and voluntary sectors, to deliver public services, critics pointed to a massive increase in state regulation, and the creation of a regulatory rather than the old 'welfare' or 'control' state (Moran 2000, 2001). Yet the Thatcher government claimed to be in the business of deregulation – relaxing planning controls and deregulating bus transport, as well as criticising the 'excessive regulation' emanating from Brussels.

Today the state appears more complex. The fashionable term 'governance' emphasises the process of governing rather than the institutions of government, and blurs the distinction between government and governed. Governance does not just include those who are part of 'government' as ministers, civil servants or elected councillors, but business and the voluntary sector, as well as parties and pressure groups in so far as they contribute to the process of governance and the delivery of services to the community.

Governance necessarily involves collaboration between agencies and sectors, and partnership working rather than the clear lines of authority and responsibility found in more traditional management hierarchies (Rhodes 1997, Pierre and Stoker. in Dunleavy *et al.* 2002). It draws on the agenda of the Americans Osborne and Gaebler in *Reinventing Government* (1992), some of the ideas of the new public management (see Chapter 12), together with strands of New Labour and third way thinking (Giddens 1998, Newman 2001).

Another prominent theme has focused on the extent to which the British state has become more or less democratic. One trend, commonly lamented, has been the growth of appointed bodies or quangos, apparently at the expense of control by democratically elected politicians. Thus critics talk of the 'appointed state', 'quangocracy' or the 'new magistracy', and lament a 'democratic deficit' as more decisions are apparently made by unaccountable appointed agencies or bureaucrats (Skelcher 1998). The most obvious manifestation of this trend has been the erosion of powers and responsibilities of elected local authorities (see Chapter 17). Yet there are also now many more opportunities for citizens to cast votes than 30 or 40 years ago – for the European Parliament, for devolved assemblies, in national and local referendums, for school governing bodies and user councils. Indeed declining electoral turnout and apathy is sometimes blamed on 'voter fatigue' or overload.

Table 18.1 From old government to new governance: the shifting focus

Old government	**New governance**
The state	The state and civil society
The public sector	Public, private and voluntary (or third) sectors
Institutions of government	Processes of governing
Organisational structures	Policies, outputs, outcomes
Providing ('rowing')	Enabling ('steering')
Commanding, controlling, directing	Leading, facilitating, collaborating, bargaining
Hierarchy and authority	Partnerships and networks

Source: adapted from Leach and Percy-Smith (2001: 5).

Definition

Quango is an acronym for (originally) quasi-autonomous non-governmental organisation. Quangos are, however, normally funded, appointed and ultimately controlled by the state (so they are part of government). They are appointed rather than elected, and not directly accountable to elected politicians. National quangos are officially described as 'non-departmental public bodies' (NDPBs) and are thus distinguished from executive agencies (see Chapter 12) which have some managerial autonomy but are attached to departments.

While democracy has long been linked with more open government, the British state in the past often appeared highly secretive. Indeed, the term 'the secret state' was often ascribed not simply to the cloak and dagger activities of Britain's security and intelligence services, but to the internal workings of much of British government. Some tentative steps towards more open government were taken by the Thatcher and Major governments, while the Labour government eventually honoured a manifesto commitment to a Freedom of Information Act, albeit one with too many restrictions and exceptions according to critics. Whether it marks the end of the 'secret state' remains to be seen.

Finally, and fundamentally, there is now considerable debate over how far the state is or can remain British. Doubts on the survival of a British state are relatively recent. Although there has sometimes been considerable controversy over the direction in which British government and politics was going, it is only in the last 40 years, and more particularly the last ten years, that serious doubts have grown over the extent to which the state would remain British. Today it is sometimes argued that the independence and sovereignty of the British state have been substantially eroded from above by the European Union and other supra-national bodies, as well as by the more intangible power of global capitalism, and from below by devolution, decentralisation and fragmentation. Perhaps more important than the institutional changes associated with these trends are issues of identity and allegiance. Thus devolution can be seen as a consequence rather than a cause of a declining British identity, and the fragmentation of personal allegiance. Yet at the same time it is also possible that UK citizens will be able to embrace multiple allegiances and identities within an evolving system of multi-level governance.

The attack on government

The last two centuries have seen a massive and unprecedented growth in the activities of the British state and the size of public spending. The growth has not been steady and continuous. Wars in general, and both 20th-century world wars in particular, have provided a strong stimulus to increased government intervention and regulation while accustoming people to higher levels of taxation. Thus while peace involved a fall from previously high wartime expenditure, it did not involve a return to pre-war levels. After the Second World War, following an initial fall, public spending rose steadily, partly in response to demographic trends (including longer life expectancy), but more especially as a consequence of deliberate public policy. All parties were apparently committed to the welfare state and Keynesian demand-management policies. This meant the state accepted extensive responsibilities for the provision of health, housing and full employment, on top of a new system of social security from the 'cradle to the grave'.

By the mid-1970s there was a marked reaction against 'big government'. Partly this reflected opposition to rising levels of taxes to meet the bill for rising public spending, but it also reflected some disillusion with the results of state welfare provision and full employment policies. Thus it appeared that the welfare state had not succeeded in abolishing poverty, as the rediscovery of child poverty had made apparent. State housing and planning policies had produced some conspicuous disasters in the form of uninhabitable tower blocks and 'sink' estates. Keynesian demand management no longer appeared able to deliver full employment, growth and tolerable levels of inflation: instead Conservative and Labour governments alike presided over 'stagflation' – economic stagnation with rising unemployment on the one hand and accelerating inflation on the other – a combination which orthodox Keynesian economists had previously considered impossible.

Critics, particularly on the right of the political spectrum, but not just from the right, argued that the problem was not this or that specific government policy, but government in general. Government had grown too big. Public spending was absorbing dangerously high levels of total national income, crowding out private sector enterprise and investment. High marginal levels of taxation were destroying incentives to hard work and risk taking. Government organisations, it was argued, were inherently inefficient, as they were not subject to effective competition and the profit motive. The remedy was thus to cut public spending and roll back the state (Kavanagh 1990). The attack on big government became the new orthodoxy, pursued with some reluctance by Callaghan's Labour government (1976–9), and then more enthusiastically by Thatcher's Conservative government.

Restructuring the state – quangos and agencies

The Thatcher government, as we have seen (Chapter 6), was ideologically committed to a revival of free market thinking which favoured a substantial reduction in the public sector coupled with policies to encourage competition and the private sector. Some of the cuts in public spending were real and painful enough to those who felt their effects, but the overall reduction in state expenditure was no more than marginal. That was because cuts in some services were matched by increases in others, sometimes as a result of deliberate policy (increased spending initially on defence and law and order) but more substantially because of the steep rise in unemployment, with inevitable consequences for the social security budget. Moreover, some areas of the welfare state, such as the National Health Service (NHS), remained too popular to touch; thus Thatcher herself declared that the NHS was safe in her hands. Thus the rhetoric of Thatcherism outran its performance. The state and public spending were restructured rather than drastically cut back. There were certainly cuts in some parts of the public sector, in the number of civil servants, and, later, in the size and spending of elected local authorities. However, many of the activities involved were not simply abolished or transferred to the private sector, but reorganised within the public sector.

One aspect of this restructuring was the growth in number of quangos, appointed public bodies not directly controlled by elected politicians. There were always persuasive reasons for putting some government-sponsored or funded activities in the hands of an appointed body rather than party politicians. In some cases it was particularly important that certain bodies were seen to be independent of the government of the day – older examples include the BBC and ITA, the Equal Opportunities Commission and the Commission for Racial Equality. In other cases a key motive was to attract the services of relevant experts. While some quangos have important executive responsibilities, employ numerous staff and manage multi-million pound budgets, many others are purely advisory, and experts provide part-time services for little or nothing. Indeed, it may often be much cheaper to establish a quango than run an activity as part of a government department.

The main criticisms of quangos are over the issues of patronage and accountability. Many positions on appointed bodies are effectively in the gift of ministers, and there has been considerable criticism of the criteria by which appointments are made. Under both Labour and Conservative administrations the partners and other relations of politicians have not infrequently been appointed. This may be more innocent than it sounds – there is pressure to appoint more women to such bodies, and the wives of politicians are a known quantity, and often intelligent and well qualified to fill relevant posts – yet inevitably it appears they are chosen for their connections rather than themselves. In the past, Labour governments appointed leading trade unionists to many quangos, partly because of their expertise, and partly because some organisations needed representatives of 'labour' to balance business representatives. Conservative governments were sometimes accused of stuffing health authorities, training and enterprise councils and urban development corporations with businessmen (often Conservative supporters), although they too could respond that such people brought essential management expertise to running these organisations. It is difficult to evade accusations of political partisanship in appointments, as sometimes a particular organisation is seen as inherently party political. Even more clearly, many quangos are not very accountable to the public. Not only are they unelected, their proceedings are often held in secret, and even if reports and accounts are published, they receive little effective public scrutiny (although the Freedom of Information Act has already made an impact here).

It would be inaccurate and unfair to link the growth of quangos too closely with Thatcherism. Quangos had been identified and criticised well before the advent of the Thatcher government. Indeed, initially quangos were part of the over-mighty state that New Right Conservatives railed against, and Mrs Thatcher promised a bonfire of quangos. Some indeed were abolished as the result of a report into 'non-departmental bodies' (Pliatzky Report 1980). However, Conservative governments proceeded to establish a wide range of new appointed bodies, although they generally refused to accept that these were 'quangos' because of the term's pejorative associations. Many new quangos were created as the consequence of the government's determination to 'hive off' activities from the civil service and traditional local government. Indeed, some argued that the proliferation of quangos was part of a deliberate strategy to make the centre appear smaller – a somewhat cosmetic attack on 'big government'.

Yet the creation of some new 'regulatory' quangos may be seen as a direct consequence of a shift away from the old welfare state which provided and controlled services directly towards a 'regulatory state' where other public, private and voluntary bodies provided services subject to state regulation (see below). Naturally regulatory bodies or 'watchdogs' must inspire confidence in their neutrality and independence of direct government control, so almost inevitably they are controlled by appointed qualified experts rather than elected politicians. However, it has also been argued that the proliferation of appointed bodies reflected a purposeful bypassing of democratic institutions, particularly elected local government, in favour of a 'new magistracy' (after the appointed local magistrates who administered much of county government until 1888).

The transformation of most of the old unified civil service into a diverse collection of executive agencies with substantial managerial autonomy (following the introduction of the Next Steps programme from 1988 – see Chapter 12) has made British government more complex and diverse. Although distinctions can be drawn between older non-departmental public bodies (or quangos) and the new executive agencies (see Box 18.1), variations within both types of organisation seem rather more significant than the differences between them. Indeed, even some leading participants appear confused over the formal status of their own organisation. In effect, the Next Steps programme has created many more public bodies with variable autonomy from direct ministerial control.

The Blair government has not significantly challenged the trend towards the proliferation of agencies and fragmentation of government. It has continued Next Steps agencies, and replaced some

Table 18.2 Types and examples of quangos

Type	Examples
Executive	Arts Council, regional development agencies
Advisory	White Fish Authority, Advisory Committee on Hazardous Substances
Quasi-judicial	Pensions Tribunal, Employment Tribunal, Disability Appeal Tribunals
Regulatory	Audit Commission, National Audit Office, OFCOM, OFWAT, OFGEM, OFSTED, QAA, Food Standards Agency
Cross-cutting	Social Exclusion Unit, Better Regulation Taskforce, New Deal Taskforce

older quangos with newer quangos of its own. It has, however, placed rather more emphasis on collaboration and cooperation between agencies and sectors, and the creation of public–private partnerships (PPPs) and policy networks. To counteract some of the problems of coordination arising from increased institutional fragmentation, it has established a number of cross-cutting units or task forces in the interests of 'joined-up government', such as the Social Exclusion Unit. Taylor (2000) has argued strongly that such developments do not involve the 'hollowing out' of the state, but rather 'filling in' the gaps between agencies in the interests of more effective government control over policy delivery. This is consistent with other characterisations of the Blair premiership, as involving a stronger executive with increased control over the government machine (see Chapter 11).

Whether or not quangos, agencies and cross-cutting units involve more or less government and central control, they remain an area of legitimate concern. Once the only government bodies that seemed to count in the UK were government departments, staffed by civil servants, and (a long way behind) elected local authorities. Both old central departments and local councils have increasingly lost out to these other public bodies.

Box 18.1

Executive agencies and quangos

Executive agencies are still part of the civil service, subject to civil service conditions and codes of practice. They are organised within government departments, and are subject to ministerially imposed policy objectives, budgets and performance targets. Yet they are headed by chief executives and operate within framework documents that give them considerable operational autonomy. Examples include the Child Support Agency and the UK Passports Agency.

Quangos may be sponsored and financed by government departments but they are non-departmental public bodies, and are not staffed by civil servants. They have rather more autonomy, and are normally less accountable to ministers and Parliament, and less subject to ministerial control and policy directives.

Government has become more complex, and less subject to direct control by elected politicians. It seems unlikely that the trend can now be reversed.

Privatisation, contracting out and competition

If the Thatcher and Major governments involved extensive restructuring to the state, they also saw a significant transfer of assets and activities from the public sector to the private sector. Most significant here was the privatisation of nearly all the former nationalised industries, the industries that the 1945–51 Labour government had transferred to state control (although some had previously been municipally owned and run). After a few relatively minor privatisations, gas, steel, telecommunications, water, electricity, coal and railways were sold off between 1984 and 1995 (see Chapter 2, Box 2.6). Most of the early share issues were over-subscribed, following a massive public advertising campaign, so that shares rose immediately, well above the launch price, enabling many subscribers to take an immediate and substantial profit, but also provoking accusations that assets had been underpriced and sold off too cheaply. Subsequently shareholders in British Telecom, and more conspicuously Railtrack, found that shares could go down as well as up. The most obvious beneficiary of the sale of assets, however, was the Treasury, which was able to reduce British public borrowing substantially as a consequence. However, the impact on current expenditure and taxation was less than might be expected. Some former nationalised industries broke even, and those that required massive exchequer subsidies, such as the former British Rail, still needed similar injections of cash following privatisation.

Of course, the New Right argued that transfer to the private sector would also secure substantial gains in efficiency as a result of a more competitive environment. One problem here was that several of the former nationalised industries appeared to be natural monopolies with little scope for the injection of much competition. However elements of competition were introduced into electricity generation and supply, and British Telecom also faced competitive suppliers. In practice consumers were protected from the exploitation of monopoly power not so much by competition as by regulation, and new regulatory bodies were introduced for each of the major privatised industries (see below).

Perhaps the privatisation with the most profound and far-reaching effects was none of those described briefly above, but the sale of council houses. This had been Conservative policy since the early 1950s, but the Thatcher government turned a vague aspiration into reality by passing legislation that obliged local authorities to sell houses to sitting tenants (with substantial discounts for long occupancy). The policy was undoubtedly popular, enabling many former council house tenants to become home owners, and 1.3 million houses were sold in this way in ten years, involving a massive cumulative transfer in assets. Many of the buyers gained handsomely, sometimes selling on their houses at a substantial profit, although others who bought houses on large estates in more economically deprived areas sometimes found that the purchase was not a good investment. More recently, some critics have suggested that the sale of council houses, particularly in the prosperous south-east, has removed a substantial pool of cheap housing for relatively poorly paid workers. This has intensified problems in recruiting nurses and teachers in such areas.

Besides such massive transfers of assets, the Conservative governments from 1979–97 also attempted to introduce more competition into the provision of public services. One mechanism was the introduction of compulsory competitive tendering (CCT – already briefly described in Chapter 17) into parts of the NHS and local government. The deregulation of bus transport led to a substantial shift from publicly owned and controlled bus companies into the hands of private operators. Thus many services previously provided exclusively by public organisations are now undertaken by private firms for profit, although they remain the statutory responsibility of local or health authorities who lay down the terms of the contract and monitor its implementation (Walsh 1995). In addition, in the last years of the Thatcher government and under the Major government further competition was introduced through the introduction of internal markets (or quasi-markets) into health, and to a lesser extent education. As a consequence, health providers such as hospitals were competing to some extent for patients, and schools for pupils.

As we have seen (Chapter 12), more financial delegation and commercial practices were also introduced into the civil service in the 1980s. From 1988 the introduction of executive agencies involved more managerial autonomy but also obliged civil servants to reach prescribed targets and operate in a more commercial manner. A few of these executive agencies have since been privatised. In 1991 market testing was introduced into the civil service, and certain government activities put out to tender, and some privatised. The introduction of the Citizen's Charter in the same year emphasised higher standards in public service provision but also reaffirmed the importance of competition to achieve this goal.

New Labour, and partnership with the business and voluntary sectors

The Labour Party in opposition strenuously opposed most of the Conservative privatisation programme, and initially promised renationalisation of some public undertakings. It also opposed CCT and many of the changes introduced into the health and education services, including internal markets. However, the Blair government has generally proved unable or unwilling to put the clock back. The major Conservative privatisations have not been reversed (with the partial exception of the collapse of Railtrack in the autumn of 2001: see Box 18.2), and Labour has proceeded with the part privatisation of air traffic control. Although CCT has been replaced by the more flexible 'best value' regime, the provision of key local government services is still subject to competition, and many remain privately provided. The Labour government has effectively endorsed greater managerial delegation and autonomy by continuing Next Steps agencies and proceeding to further significant decentralisation and delegation within the NHS.

New Labour has enthusiastically embraced partnership with the private sector, through PPPs under which government departments, local authorities and other public bodies enter into partnership agreements with private firms on key developments and initiatives. Perhaps the most politically controversial of these schemes have been the partnership agreements funding an extensive programme of new investment in the London Underground railway system, despite the strong opposition of the London Mayor, Ken Livingstone (see Chapter 17).

Increased private sector investment in the public sector is provided through a particular form of PPP, the private finance initiative (PFI). Many new PFI hospitals, schools and prisons have already been built, using the money and expertise of the private sector, paid for by the relevant public authority over a period, commonly 25 years. While PFIs were introduced by Major's Conservative government they have been endorsed and extensively utilised by Blair's Labour government. Under a PFI the ownership and maintenance of the building (such as a school or hospital) commonly remains the responsibility of the private consortium, while the relevant public authority retains responsibility for running the service, employing and paying for professional staff, and meeting other day-to-day service costs. Some PFI prisons however are both built and run by the private sector.

The main attraction for government of PFIs is that they increase the funds available for public-sector capital investment (chronically under-funded in the past) without requiring public sector borrowing. Some argue that there are also efficiency gains arising from private sector involvement. Critics contend that PFIs are more expensive than traditional public sector borrowing, because of the pursuit of profit and the need to provide a return to shareholders. They also argue that there is little effective transfer of risk to the private sector, as the state cannot afford to allow the projects to fail. The long record of PFI hospitals, schools and prisons remains contentious, and includes some claimed successes and failures. Perhaps a more balanced verdict on the costs and benefits of PFIs will only be obtainable as projects reach the end of their 25-year agreements, and the ownership and maintenance of the buildings reverts to the public sector.

Although much of the ideological debate has been over the relative merits of public provision on the one hand, and private provision for profit on the other, there has been some focus also on a third way – provision by mutually owned or voluntary organisations. The most important example of 'mutuals' used to be the building societies, which were owned by their members and

Box 18.2

From Railtrack to Network Rail

The Labour government took a politically controversial decision in 2001 to put Railtrack into receivership, and introduce a new not-for-profit body, Network Rail, to administer Britain's rail infrastructure. Critics in the Conservative opposition and the city accused the government of back-door renationalisation. They argued that the decision to pull the plug on Railtrack would undermine private-sector investors' faith in PPPs, and make it far more expensive for the government to borrow, because of the extra element of risk and uncertainty.

By contrast the government argued that Railtrack was a failed and effectively bankrupt company which required huge additional public funds to bail it out. It was unreasonable to expect taxpayers to foot the bill. Shareholders should realise that shares can go down as well as up. In the event a compromise deal was reached which involved some compensation for shareholders, although this did not prevent legal proceedings by angry former Railtrack shareholders. They were still challenging the government's decision in 2005, seeking more compensation through the courts. While Network Rail has performed more satisfactorily than its predecessor, there have been continuing tensions with the train operating companies.

Definitions

Public–private partnerships (PPPs) involve formal partnerships between government bodies (such as local councils), private firms and sometimes voluntary organisations to manage a specific initiative or deliver a policy.

The **private finance initiative (PFI)** is a specific and controversial form of partnership, under which the private sector funds, builds and maintains public sector investment in, for example, hospitals, schools, prisons and roads. The relevant sponsoring public authority (such as a local council or hospital trust) makes annual payments, typically for a period of 25 years, after which the assets become its property.

not run for profit. However, most of the largest building societies have become public limited companies with shareholders instead of members, who were generally happy to vote for the legal transfer of assets and pocket (often substantial) sums in recompense. The most significant example of voluntary provision of public services is now the housing associations which were favoured as a 'third force' in the supply of rented accommodation by the Conservative government (the other two being the council and private landlords). While most Labour councils opposed the sale of council houses in the 1980s, many voluntarily cooperated in the transfer of much of their remaining housing stock to housing associations which over time have become major providers of rented 'social housing'.

Voluntary provision of public services is far from new in the UK. Indeed in the 19th century it was generally the preferred method of provision. Thus schools were provided by voluntary religious organisations, with increasing state subsidy, and many hospitals were initially established on a voluntary basis. This suited Victorian opinion which was suspicious of state intervention, and it remains more ideologically acceptable today to both free market advocates hostile to direct state provision and many within the Labour party who retain an aversion to private provision of public services for profit.

Voluntary organisations conjure up images of small-scale operations by well-meaning but inexpert amateurs. However, many voluntary associations today are big businesses, employing substantial numbers of well-paid professional staff. Although they are 'not for profit' they are run on commercial lines, and while they are not part of government, they rely substantially on state financial support. They thus inhabit a 'grey area' between the public and private sectors. Although they lack some of the disadvantages of each, they may also lack some of their advantages. They may be less susceptible to the private sector discipline of market competition and less publicly accountable than mainstream government organisations. However, they remain attractive to those seeking a third or middle way between the state and the market.

'Steering, not rowing' – the enabling state

The cumulative impact of all these changes has transformed the character of the British state. While many services are still publicly funded, they are often no longer controlled and provided by centralised public sector organisations, but by the private sector, the voluntary sector or by decentralised quasi-autonomous public sector bodies. This has been described as a 'hollowing out' of the state. Yet it also suggests the state is performing an essentially different role – an enabling role, to borrow a term first used in Britain to describe the new role of local government (see Chapter 17), but which could equally well be applied to the role of the state as a whole. The key point is that the state is no longer necessarily providing services directly but 'enabling' others to do so – business, PPPs, the voluntary sector, the community itself. An analogous term employed by the Americans Osborne and Gaebler (1992) is the notion of the state 'steering' rather 'rowing'. Governments should facilitate and coordinate rather than attempt to do everything themselves.

Yet there are some obvious problems, including potentially serious difficulties of coordination. The new governance, with its myriad forms of organisation and its emphasis on partnership and networks, involves considerable institutional fragmentation. Responsibility and accountability are blurred. Leading and coordinating require different and more demanding skills than those required of business managers or public officials in old hierarchical public sector organisations. It may seem more difficult to get things done. In devolving and decentralising, governments may lose effective control of service delivery, which is a major problem, if it is on successful service delivery that they are judged. Thus to achieve the goals they have proclaimed, governments may fall back on increased regulation.

The regulatory state

There is nothing essentially new in regulation. Governments have always been in the business of regulating, although the extent of regulatory activity and regulatory bodies seems to have increased dramatically over the last 30 years of so, sufficiently to justify the term 'regulatory state' which some writers have used (e.g. Loughlin and Scott 1997, Moran 2000, 2001). Three kinds of state regulatory activity have attracted the attention of commentators:

- Regulation of private-sector bodies. The private sector has long been subject to some regulation, but this has increased substantially of late because of specific problems, particularly in the financial sector.
- Regulation of recently privatised industries. This may seem particularly important where these privatised industries retained substantial monopoly elements.
- Regulation of the public sector. While the public sector was accustomed to regulation, this has intensified as a consequence of increased managerial delegation and decentralisation.

Important older bodies to regulate the private sector include the Monopolies and Mergers Commission (now the Competition Commission), and various planning, licensing and public health bodies which have an essentially regulatory role. The European Community/Union introduced further elements of regulation into British life, particularly with regard to health and safety, the workplace, and the environment. For a long time the private sector chafed against state regulation, and the Conservative Party in particular stressed the importance of relaxing regulation to reduce the burden of bureaucracy on business enterprise and agriculture (Loughlin and Scott, in Dunleavy *et al.* 1997: 210–11). Thus Michael Heseltine promised a 'bonfire of red tape' while planning regulations were progressively relaxed in the 1980s, and some of the closer regulation of farming was reduced. In general, internal voluntary self-regulation was reckoned to be preferable to the heavy hand of the state. More recently a succession of scandals and disasters have led to fresh demands for more regulation to protect the public. Moran (2000) links this with the decline of deference towards authority in general and of trust in professions.

Despite repeated criticisms of the 'nanny state', 'red tape' and 'over-regulation', problems in the private sector regularly provoke a media and popular outcry for the government to 'do something', leading to the creation of new watchdog bodies. Thus the BSE and foot-and-mouth disease crises, coupled with more general concerns over food safety, additives and quality have led to more rigorous inspection and regulation of food production and retailing through such bodies as the Food Standards Agency. The mis-selling of insurance, endowment mortgages and pension schemes provoked new demands for the regulation of the financial sector to protect the public. Accordingly, the Blair government created a new super-regulator, the Financial Services Authority, to take over regulatory functions previously performed (not too effectively, many would allege) by nine separate agencies, including the Bank of England, which had until then had responsibility for regulating the commercial banks (Sinclair, in Seldon 2001).

Privatisation of the former nationalised industries created a new raft of regulatory bodies, so that state ownership and control was effectively replaced by state regulation. This would perhaps not have been necessary had competition and market forces been reckoned sufficient to protect consumer interests. Yet in most cases a state monopoly was replaced by a privatised monopoly, or at best very imperfect competition. The unrestrained pursuit of profit in such circumstances would have led to considerable exploitation of consumers. Thus a series of regulatory bodies were established, primarily to control prices, but also to monitor service standards and investment, and deal with public complaints. These bodies have become known memorably by their new shorthand descriptions – such as Ofgas to regulate the gas industry, Oftel to regulate telecommunications, Offer to regulate electricity supply and Ofwat to regulate water. (Gas and electricity are now jointly regulated by Ofgem, the Office of Gas and Electricity Markets, and communications by Ofcom.) Views of the effectiveness of the new regulatory regimes vary. Predictably, the left think the new regulators are only cosmetic, while the industries themselves complain of over-regulation. Yet clearly regulation of these privatised industries is here to stay – and the pressures are for more rather than less state regulation.

One of the interesting aspects of privatisation is that the transfer of assets from the public to the private sector has not removed these industries from the sphere of public policy, or even significantly reduced pressures on government to remedy perceived problems. Thus government is still held to account for the problems and deficiencies of rail transport despite the removal of the industry from state ownership and control. This is hardly surprising, as whether state-owned, privatised or controlled by a not-for-profit organisation, the rail network still requires massive injections of public money which ultimately come from taxpayers. Rail crashes provoke legitimate public concerns over rail safety, and demands for government action and tougher safety regimes. The state may divest itself of the ownership of troublesome industries, but not, it seems, of their problems.

However, the most substantial recent growth in state regulation has not been over the private or recently privatised sectors but over the activities of the state itself. Again, this is hardly new. In the 19th century central government departments established inspectorates to monitor services delivered by local government. More recently, from 1967 onwards a system of ombudsmen (as they are popularly known) was set up to cover complaints from the public against central government departments (the Parliamentary Commissioner for Administration), local government and the health service (see Chapter 14). Yet it is only in the last 20 years or so that the number of bodies to regulate the public sector has really exploded. Paradoxically pressures for decentralisation and delegation have increased the pressures on the centre to closely regulate and monitor service delivery. Managers of schools, hospitals and a whole range of devolved executive agencies have been given more autonomy and 'freedom to manage'. Yet demands for improved services – for reduced class sizes or hospital waiting lists, for better exam results or improved treatment – lead to the setting of targets and the establishment of new regulatory bodies to measure performance. Thus schools, universities, hospitals, local authorities and other bodies not only have their performance measured against a wide range of criteria, but these performances are published and ranked in league tables.

In Focus 18.1

The Hatfield rail crash, 17 October 2000

Although rail remains much safer than road transport, train crashes attract huge media publicity and public concern. The Hatfield crash in which four people were killed and 35 injured after a train derailment, caused by a known fault, proved the catalyst for further upheavals in the management and regulation of British railways. Revelations of poor track maintenance reflected badly on Railtrack, while speed restrictions in the interests of safety created further problems for the privatised company, contributing to the government decision to declare the company bankrupt and replace it with a new body, Network Rail (see Box 18.2). In July 2005 Network Rail and Balfour Beatty, the track maintenance company, and some of their executives, were acquitted of manslaughter charges over Hatfield, but the companies were subsequently found guilty of breaches in health and safety laws and fined £13.5 million.

Photograph: EMPICS.

Table 18.3 Some important regulatory bodies

Office of Fair Trading (OFT)	Regulator charged with making markets work for consumers
Competition Commission (formerly Monopolies and Mergers Commission)	Promotes competition in the private sector, may declare that mergers are not in the public interest
Health and Safety Executive	Responsible for whole range of health and safety (e.g. on railways)
Audit Commission	Audits local authorities and health authorities
National Audit Office	Audits central government
Office of Water Services (OFWAT)	Regulates privatised water industry
Office for Standards in Education (OFSTED)	Responsible for inspecting and raising standards in schools
Financial Services Authority (FSA)	Regulates banks, building societies, insurance companies, stock exchange etc. Absorbed functions of nine former regulatory bodies.
Food Standards Agency	Independent regulator to monitor the food production and supply industry – set up by Blair government in the wake of the BSE scandal
Office of Gas and Electricity Markets (OFGEM) (formerly OFGAS and OFFER)	Regulates gas and electricity industry
Office of the Rail Regulator (ORR)	Regulation of train operators and rail network (prices, services etc.)
Strategic Rail Authority	Responsible for longer-term rail investment

Much of this is laudable. The measurement of performance enables comparisons to be made between institutions, authorities and areas. It leads to investigations into the reasons for variations in performance. It enables others to imitate the successful methods of the best providers. It puts pressure on poor performers to improve. Moreover, it is urged that the public have a right to know about service and performance levels, particularly where there is an element of public choice of service providers, as for example where parents are choosing a school for their children. It serves the interests of public accountability and open government. From a government perspective it is crucial to be able to demonstrate that the money it is putting into a service, particularly if it is extra money, is achieving measurable improvements in standards. Otherwise critics will allege that the money has been wasted and swallowed up by more bureaucracy.

Yet measurement brings some problems. Some measures may be misleading. It does not necessarily follow that a school with better exam results than another has really performed better. To make a fair comparison it would be necessary to know much more about the two schools – for example their catchment areas, and the respective achievements of pupils when they entered the two schools, the support and facilities made available by their families, and any extra private coaching they received. Other measures may be manipulated. Moreover, league tables may not measure what is most important. Performance yardsticks tend to focus on the easily quantifiable – class sizes, hospital waiting lists, offences notified to the police – rather than issues of service quality that are not so easily measured. Thus measurement may distort priorities.

Unsurprisingly, those who are regulated complain of increased pressure, and of the costs in time and money of compliance with the numerous controls and yardsticks. Compliance costs may become a serious drain on resources that might have been better employed. More resources may go into satisfying the regulators than serving consumers or users. This is hardly surprising, as the stakes are high. Poor scores reflect badly on a service or institution, which is competing for resources and clients. Thus a university department which scores badly on the Research Assessment Exercise loses money for research, and will find it more difficult to recruit students and staff. It may lead to staff contracts not being renewed, or even the closure of a department. Considerable ingenuity will be devoted to impressing the assessors. Cheating is not unknown.

If regulation can be excessive and counterproductive, it can also be ineffective. 'Regulatory capture' is a term long used by the observers of regulatory agencies in the USA. A particular agency established to regulate a profession or industry may become effectively captured by the interests it is supposed to regulate, instead of looking after the interests of consumers or the wider public. Some observers would argue that some British regulatory bodies have similarly 'gone native', adopting the perspective of those whose activities they were expected to police. Indeed, some regulatory agencies have proved singularly ineffective in detecting and publicising dubious practices and preventing major scandals (Loughlin and Scott, in Dunleavy *et al.* 1997; Moran 2001).

■ A secret state?

The British state has sometimes been described as a secret state. The term is perhaps most often used to describe the British secret services and other clandestine aspects of British government. There are certainly serious questions to ask about the power, accountability and performance of these services. However, the term can also be employed to characterise British government generally, as secretiveness has often appeared to be one of the trademarks of the practice of government in the United Kingdom. The more recent commitment to 'open government' indeed reflects a recognition that government has been less than open in the past.

To begin with the narrower but important issue of the British intelligence and security services, it would perhaps be generally conceded that all states may have to resort to clandestine operations in the interests of defence and internal security. Intelligence gathering on potential threats may save lives and prevent or deter serious threats. For example, better intelligence could have led the Thatcher government to anticipate and perhaps prevent an Argentine invasion of the Falkland Islands, and conceivably rendered the task force to recover the islands unnecessary. More recently, better intelligence in the west might have detected and prevented the terrorist attacks of 11 September 2001 or conceivably 7 July 2005.

When the stakes are high, particularly in times of war, it would also be conceded that secret operations, including 'dirty tricks' to destabilise the enemy, are to be commended, particularly if they are shown to materially affect the outcome. Thus Churchill established the SOE in the Second World War, and British agents who operated behind enemy lines are celebrated as heroes (although of course enemy agents are more commonly considered despicable). There is a continuing fascination with, and some admiration for, the whole world of espionage. Yet there are also important civil liberties issues surrounding the activities of the security services. There is a delicate balance to be struck between protecting British citizens against internal and external threats to their well-being and safety, and violations of the fundamental human rights and freedoms of those same citizens.

However, although the British secret services are often viewed as glamorous, some hard questions may be asked about their record, overall effectiveness and value for money.

- ◆ The discovery in the 1950s and 1960s that some high-ranking members of the security services were double agents working for the

Soviet Union undermined faith in the reliability of the services, and their recruitment and internal vetting. Doubts resurfaced in the 1970s and 1980s with further prosecutions and damaging (but unproved) allegations against senior figures.

- Ostensibly far-fetched allegations that some elements of MI5 were plotting against Prime Minister Harold Wilson and attempting to destabilise his government were shown to have an element of truth and raised questions about the judgement, loyalty and political bias of the security services (Hennessy 2000: 372–5).
- The alleged use of the security services for partisan purposes, including intelligence gathering on trade unions and industrial disputes in the 1980s, renewed allegations of inappropriate targeting of those with left-wing politics. Ironically, some senior members of Blair's government were themselves earlier subjects of surveillance by the security services (Jack Straw, Harriet Harman and Peter Mandelson, according to former MI5 officer David Shayler).
- The failure of western intelligence services generally, including the British intelligence services, to anticipate and prevent the events of 11 September 2001 and of 7 July 2005 suggests that they are ill-equipped to counter the new global terrorism, and are too much locked into activities and methods of the Cold War.
- The additional powers acquired by the government to counter terrorism and the detention without trial of suspects have provoked concerns over civil liberties in general and Islamophobia in particular.
- The serious deficiencies in the evidence gathered by the intelligence services on Saddam Hussein's 'weapons of mass destruction' which was used to justify the Iraq War in 2003.

By their very nature there are bound to be problems with the accountability and control of secret services. Full accountability would require detailed publicity for activities that would no longer be secret. Information on the activities of the security services is thus confined to as few politicians as possible, on a 'need to know basis', and overall responsibility lies with the prime minister alone. The most delicate secret operations have to be cleared with the prime minister personally (Hennessey 2000: 83). Even so, the secret services have not been immune from the trend towards more open government. Stella Rimmington, whose appointment to take charge

Table 18.4 Britain's security services

Security and intelligence agency	Functions
MI5 (Security Service)	Concerned with domestic security, primarily with internal threats to British state, and countering 'serious crime'
Special Branch (Note a 2005 proposal that this should become part of a larger national force to counter terrorism etc.)	Internal security arm of police. Works with MI5 to counter terrorism, protect VIPs, conduct surveillance etc.
MI6 (Secret Intelligence Service)	Gathering political, military and economic intelligence in foreign countries. Combating serious crime, e.g. money laundering, drug smuggling, illicit arms deals, illegal immigration.
Government Communications Headquarters (GCHQ)	Intercepting and decoding of international communications

of MI5 was announced by the Major government, has since published her own (rather unrevealing) memoirs. MI5 and GCHQ now have their own websites. Yet all present and former employees of the security services are bound by the Official Secrets Act which they are obliged to sign, and can be prosecuted for breaches, as former MI5 officer David Shayler discovered.

Beyond the fascinating world of the secret services proper there are however much wider questions about secrecy in British government. It is sometimes argued that the lack of open government and fuller accountability to Parliament and the public is the consequence of particular features of the unwritten British constitution. Thus British ministers and public servants formally serve the crown rather than 'the people' or 'the public interest'. As ministers, and particularly the prime minister, have inherited most of the old prerogative powers of the crown, in practice civil servants, and public officials generally, are expected to serve the government of the day. Advice to ministers is confidential. Civil servants are obliged to sign the Official Secrets Act, and can be prosecuted for unauthorised disclosure of classified information. No public interest defence is allowable.

Towards more open government?

Once our knowledge of the internal workings of British government depended substantially on gossip, leaks and politicians' memoirs rather than more authoritative sources. Some progress towards greater openness was made under recent governments. The comprehensive system of departmental select committees set up under the Thatcher government led to some more effective parliamentary scrutiny of the executive (see Chapter 13). The Major government published details of Cabinet committees, their membership and terms of reference (see Chapter 11), provided a legal right of access to non-computerised personal files, and published a new 'Open Government Code of Practice' on information to be provided by government departments and agencies. The Citizen's Charter initiative led to the publication of much useful information on standards of service the public could expect, with procedures for complaint and redress. Yet despite this apparent commitment to greater openness, the veil of secrecy on government decision making is commonly only lifted when something has gone badly wrong, leading to an independent investigation and report. Examples include the Scott Report (on arms to Iraq, 1996), the Phillips Enquiry on BSE (2000), and the Hutton and Butler Reports in 2004 on the use made of intelligence leading to the Iraq War.

Two pressure groups, the Campaign for Freedom of Information and Charter 88, have led demands for more open government, including a Freedom of Information Act. Blair as opposition leader in 1996 proclaimed 'We want to end the obsessive and unnecessary secrecy which surrounds government activity and make government information available to the public unless there are good reasons not to do so'. His government eventually honoured its manifesto pledge to pass a Freedom of Information Act in 2000, although critics argued that the initial proposals had been substantially watered down. Thus Austin (in Jowell and Oliver 2000: 371) claimed that the Act involved such an 'extraordinary list of exemptions' that it was 'a regime for open government only by consent of government ministers' and 'a denial of democracy' (see also Rathbone 2001). Yet the Act contributed to the changing of attitudes and procedures within government even before it finally became operative in 2005. Since then a mass of information has been made available (some of it for partisan political purposes in the run-up to the election). As anticipated, some other requests for information have been refused. Only time will tell whether the Act will usher in the new era of open government that campaigners have long sought.

Meanwhile, some still question how far openness is practical or desirable. All governments retain an interest in maintaining some confidentiality for their internal deliberations. Many ideas which are tentatively floated by ministers or their advisers never come to fruition, and some are abandoned at an early stage, but the knowledge that they had even been contemplated, however briefly, could have damaging political repercussions. If all deliberations and all advice to ministers were made public, this might inhibit the range of debate. Ministers would no longer dare to 'think the unthinkable' or come up with unpopular but perhaps necessary policy proposals because of the potential political damage. Governments might even become wary of making contingency plans to cope with threats or disasters, from fear of creating public alarm and perhaps panic.

The disintegration of the British state – or towards multi-level governance?

Although writers may not fully agree over exactly how and why the British state has changed, there is widespread agreement that it has changed, and profoundly. Instead of a unified, highly centralised state with its traditional core institutions in Westminster and Whitehall, there is a complex, fragmented and multi-layered system of government of politics that is still evolving. This more complex pattern of governance operates at an increasing range of levels – international, European, UK, devolved national, regional, local and institutional (see Table 18.5). While some levels remain more important than others, the balance is clearly shifting over time. Key decisions affecting the lives of British citizens are made not just in London but in Brussels or Edinburgh. or within hospital trusts, primary care trusts and leaning and skills councils around Britain, and within a range of other devolved agencies, units and networks. The unitary state associated with the old 'Westminster model' of British government has been replaced by a 'differentiated polity' in which a variety of agencies and interests are involved in the framing and delivery of policy at a number of different but interdependent levels.

For some this trend towards multi-level governance is natural and inevitable in the modern world. It is the old nation-state that is obsolete (Giddens 1998, Pierre and Peters 2000, Pierre and Stoker, in Dunleavy *et al.* 2002). For others who cherish the traditional British state, British national independence and the sovereignty of the UK Westminster Parliament, the changes are deeply unsettling. From their perspective the growing importance of the European Union on the one hand (see Chapter 15), and the devolution of power to sub-UK nations and regions on the other (see Chapter 16) represents a danger to the British state which could prove terminal.

Partly the issue is what is the most appropriate level of government for functional efficiency and effectiveness. It might seem appropriate to decentralise some decision making down from the UK

Table 18.5 The new multi-level governance, as applied to Britain

Level	Institutions
Global	United Nations, IMF, WTO, G8, transnational organisations and companies
Trans-Atlantic	North Atlantic Treaty Organisation
European	European Union, European Commission, European Parliament, European Court of Justice, Council of Europe, European Court of Human Rights
UK	Cabinet and core executive, Westminster Parliament, 'Whitehall'
Devolved national	Scottish Parliament and Executive, Welsh Assembly and Executive, Northern Ireland Assembly and Executive
Regional	Government offices, regional development agencies, regional chambers
Local	County, district, unitary and parish councils, non-elected local government (learning and skills councils, police authorities etc.)
Institutional	Hospital trusts, universities and colleges, foundation schools etc.

government level to local communities or even institutions in the interest of improved delivery of (for example) education and health services. There are other issues, such as international trade, disarmament, global pollution and conservation, which can only be tackled effectively at a supranational and global level. Yet for many services and functions there are many levels at which decisions may be appropriately taken, and multi-level governance appears almost inescapable.

However, issues of functional efficiency are bound up closely with the politics of identity and allegiance. The demands for closer European union, for a Scottish Parliament, and even for successive UK local government reorganisations were driven not just by expectations of more efficient government and service provision, but by political ideals and loyalties. Much of the debate over Europe, on devolution, or local authority boundaries, is ultimately about how people feel about who they are, and the communities they identify with. Do they feel part of Europe or the English-speaking world? Are they Scots or British? Do they identify with their city or county? Other identities – ethnic, religious, class – may cut across spatial boundaries. Some are comfortable with multiple overlapping identities and allegiances, but to others a particular identity may appear exclusive and all-important. For them we are either British or European, either Scots or British; we have to choose between UK national sovereignty or a European super-state, between allegiance to the United Kingdom or an independent Scotland. The whole notion of multi-level governance is hardly compatible with more exclusive identities and allegiances.

There is much that seems confusing and contradictory about this emerging system of multi-level governance, which explains some of the range of competing terms that have been employed to describe it (see Table 18.6). Is the new British politics all about devolution and decentralisation, or does it more plausibly involve a new concentration of power by a bunch of control freaks? Has the state been 'hollowed out' or 'joined up'? Has the welfare state been replaced by a regulatory state? Has representative democracy effectively been replaced by a new magistracy or quangocracy? Does the rhetoric about open government merely conceal the maintenance of secrecy? In part different answers reflect different assumptions and partisan viewpoints, yet they also reflect genuine uncertainty. Clearer answers to such questions may be subsequently available to historians with the benefit of hindsight but it is difficult to spot the truly significant trends in an era of extensive political and institutional upheaval.

Summary

- British government is still in the process of extensive transformation. It is not yet clear how the newly emerging British state should be characterised.
- The boundaries of the state have become blurred. In academic literature there has been some switch in emphasis from considering

Table 18.6 From the old Westminster model to the new British governance

The Westminster model	The new British governance
The unitary state	The 'differentiated polity'
Parliamentary sovereignty	The devolution of power
Ministerial responsibility	Delegation of management
Central–local relations	Multi-level governance
Homogeneity, uniformity, 'Fordism'	Diversity, fragmentation, 'post-Fordism'

Source: adapted from Leach and Percy-Smith (2001: 7).

the institutions of government to the process of governing (or 'governance'), which can involve the private and voluntary sectors.

- Under Conservative governments from 1979–97 the rhetoric was about reining back the state. Some state assets and activities were privatised and others subjected to competition either from the private sector or through the introduction of internal markets.
- New Labour has emphasised partnership with the private and voluntary sectors and 'joined-up government'. Much new capital investment for the public sector has been financed through the controversial private finance initiative (PFI).
- Under all governments there has been a growth in importance of appointed public bodies (quangos), for a variety of reasons.
- Under both recent Conservative and Labour governments the state's role has changed from providing to 'enabling'. A centralised and largely uniform welfare state has been replaced by more diversity of provision, and this is supervised by what has been described as a regulatory state.
- Despite moves towards more open government, culminating in the passage and implementation of the Freedom of Information Act, critics argue that British government is still too secretive.
- The old British state centred on Westminster and Whitehall has ceded some authority upwards to the European Union and other international bodies and devolved some power downwards. Multi-level governance has replaced the old centralised unitary state, with uncertain implications for the future.

Questions for further discussion

- In what ways has the state been 'hollowed out'?
- How far does the growth of appointed public bodies threaten the principle and practice of representative democracy?
- How far and how successfully have the free market principles of competition and choice been introduced into the running of public services?
- Has the old welfare state been replaced by a new regulatory state? Why has regulation grown? What are the difficulties associated with regulation?
- Has the Freedom of Information Act created a new climate of open government in Britain?
- How far has multi-level governance replaced parliamentary sovereignty and the unitary state?

Further reading

On the attack on the post-war consensus and 'big government' see Kavanagh's *Thatcherism and British Politics* (1990). On quangos and the 'democratic deficit' see Weir and Hall (1994), Weir (1995), Skelcher (1998) and Weir and Beetham (1999). On privatisation and marketisation see Ascher, *The Politics of Privatisation* (1987), Self, *Governing by the Market? The politics of public choice* (1993), and Walsh, *Public Services and Market Mechanisms* (1995).

On regulation and the regulatory state see Loughlin and Scott, 'The regulatory state', in Dunleavy *et al.* (1997), and Moran, 'From command state to regulatory state' (2000) and 'Not steering but drowning: policy catastrophes and the regulatory state (2001).

On freedom of information see Rodney Austin in Jowell and Oliver (2000), and Rathbone (2001). The Freedom of Information Act was the responsibility of the Home Office (website: www.homeoffice.uk). The Campaign for Freedom of Information's website can be consulted: www.cfoi.org.uk. On the security services it is possible to access the official MI5 website (www.mi5.gov.uk) and the GCHQ website (www.gchq.gov.uk). The Butler Report (2004) can be consulted on the uses (and misuses) of secret intelligence leading up to the Iraq War.

On governance, see Rod Rhodes's *Understanding Governance* (1997), Pierre and Stoker, 'Towards multi-level governance' in Dunleavy *et al.* (2002), Pierre and Peters, *Politics, Governance and the State* (2000), Leach and Percy-Smith, *Local Governance in Britain* (2001), Newman, *Modernising Governance* (2001), Flinders, 'Governance in Whitehall'(2002), and Moran, *Politics and Governance in the UK* (2005).

Issues and Policies

Issues, Problems and the Policy Process

So far this book has focused on political and governmental institutions and processes, and only incidentally on issues, problems, policies, and outcomes. In this chapter we examine how issues and problems get on to the political agenda, how they are analysed, decided and approved, how policies are implemented (or in some cases not implemented), monitored and reviewed. We shall see that issues and problems are regularly addressed, but seldom solved. Indeed policy making is an iterative process. The 'end' of one policy cycle is frequently the beginning of the next. While the chapter draws on the analysis in earlier chapters of key political and governmental institutions and processes, it also serves as an introduction to subsequent chapters on particular issues and policies. These chapters are not purely illustrative. On the contrary, they focus on problems that are at the very heart of British politics. In considering the outcomes of the policy process, they address the crucial questions asked by Lasswell, 'Who gets what, when, how?' (see Chapter 1).

Contents

Policy making and decision taking

Governments at all levels make policy and take decisions. Policy is about aims, objectives or ends, while decisions are means to an end. Policy provides a framework within which particular decisions can be taken. Thus a transport policy should provide a framework for decisions on particular road proposals. In practice the distinction between policy and decision making is not clear cut, but one of interpretation and degree.

Both governing parties and opposition parties are expected to have a range of policies on, for example taxation, health, education, transport, the environment, defence and foreign affairs, and often on more specific issues such as the euro, local government finance and student fees. Yet there is an obvious difference between the policies declared by governing parties and by opposition parties. Government policies are designed to be implemented. Indeed, any problems in the policy may soon be apparent as it is implemented, and any inconsistency between particular decisions and the broad policy will also be noticed. Yet governments can hardly avoid having policies (declared or inferred) for virtually all the functions and services for which they are responsible.

Opposition policies involve pledges that will only have to be implemented should the party gain power. They may never have to find the money to implement them, or discover the potential snags. Moreover, opposition parties lack the resources of government for a full investigation of possible

Definitions

Policy making involves taking up a clear position on a function, service or issue that will prove a framework for decision making (for example, an integrated transport policy or an ethical foreign policy).

Decision taking involves making particular decisions, often within an overall policy framework. Thus an ethical foreign policy may provide a framework for decisions on arms exports to particular countries. Decisions often involve selecting from a range of options (the site of a new hospital, the route of a bypass).

Figure 19.1 The policy cycle

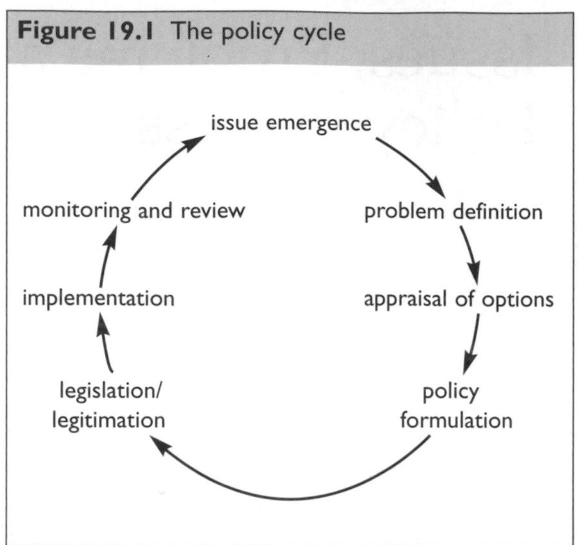

costs and consequences. Thus many opposition policies may be a 'wish list' of hopeful aspirations. Yet if their policy proposals are not costed and potential difficulties not considered, the governing party will happily do it for them. Policies are hostages to fortune. Oppositions may prefer to play it safe with as few policy pledges as possible, but there are dangers here also. If a party does not have a declared policy on an issue that is deemed important, its opponents will soon invent a damaging one for them, and challenge them to deny it!

The policy cycle

Policies may be declared in a speech, government document or party election manifesto, but they commonly emerge over a period. Policy making is best thought of as a process or cycle, involving a number of stages (see Figure 19.1). This may suggest a more rational process than often occurs in reality. Governments facing a sudden unexpected crisis (such as the 2000 fuel protests) may have to respond quickly and 'make up' policy as they go along. Some of the stages in the policy process may be brief or perfunctory. There may not be time to appraise all the options. Implementation can be problematic, and on occasion may not even happen. Monitoring and review may be thorough, superficial or almost non-existent. Even so, the stages of the policy cycle provide a useful conceptual framework for examining policy making both in theory and reality. It may help to identify shortcomings. Above all, it serves to emphasise that policy making is an iterative process. Problems are rarely solved. The 'end' of one policy cycle is commonly the beginning of the next, as difficulties in implementation, revealed by monitoring and review, or exposed by critics, lead to attempts to modify or transform established policy.

At any one time there appears to be a limited number of issues that the political system can address. A useful analogy is with the agenda for any formal meeting. The agenda consists of a list of items to be considered. The agenda determines not only what is to be discussed but the order in which the items will be discussed. A common experience is that very long agendas result in some items being discussed very briefly or not at all. Often only the items that are high on the agenda are really considered. Some other items might be hastily approved without discussion, and the rest postponed for consideration at a subsequent meeting, if at all.

While there is a formal agenda for meetings of particular political institutions such as the Cabinet or Parliament, and their numerous committees, there is not literally an agenda for the whole British political process. Yet at any moment there are a number of issues on that political agenda that seem to have a high profile with politicians, the media and the wider public.

This is particularly obvious at elections. Take the British General Election of 2005. The issues that seemed to dominate political debate included crime, immigration, health, education, the economy and taxation. Items that were relatively ignored include Europe and the pound, transport, agriculture and the environment (key issues in 2001), and devolution and the minimum wage, important issues in 1997. Some big issues from previous decades have disappeared almost completely from the electoral radar screen – unemployment, inflation, the balance of payments, trade union power, nationalisation, nuclear disarmament. Between elections particular issues come to the fore, and frequently subsequently fade from view – pit closures, new roads, food safety, football hooliganism, fuel costs, paedophiles, the triple vaccine (for measles, mumps and rubella), live animal exports. All these have aroused political passions in the recent past. A few of the issues have perhaps been resolved satisfactorily. In other cases the problem still exists, but the media and public have lost interest. They are low on the political agenda, until something happens to make them news again.

Of course, one reason that an item may be high on the political agenda is that leading politicians have put it there, in manifestos, speeches and photo opportunities. Competing parties will seek to emphasise those issues they feel are to their advantage, and try to ignore other more awkward issues that might be potential vote losers. They may be successful in shaping the agenda, although sometimes they find that the media and the public are not particularly interested in the issues they want to focus on, but are concerned about something else. Events such as the fuel protests of 2000, the foot-and-mouth disease outbreak of 2001, and the race riots in northern towns in the same year can take politicians by surprise and force new issues onto the agenda (or, more commonly, old issues back onto the agenda). It may take a food scare or a rail crash to push food or rail safety up the agenda. Groups or individuals outside mainstream politics may sometimes command attention. Shortly before the 2005 election a celebrity chef managed to put school meals briefly near the top of the political agenda, obliging leading politicians to respond. An issue long neglected suddenly seemed to strike a chord with the public. The mass media may reflect public concerns, but often may effectively stimulate them (see Chapter 9).

In Focus 19.1

Jamie Oliver serving up school meals in Leicester Square, February 2005

There were growing concerns about the effect of junk food on children's health, but it took a one-man campaign by the celebrity chef Jamie Oliver over the poor nutritional standards of school meals to provide the catalyst for policy change. After a series of television programmes and a petition with over 270,000 signatures, the Labour government announced it was providing another £280 million to tackle the crisis in school meals, a figure the Conservatives agreed to match. It was a remarkable victory for the chef, who welcomed the extra money. Yet there were some unanticipated and unwelcome side-effects. The bad publicity for school dinners led to a marked drop in their take-up. They were commonly replaced by packed lunches 'mostly high in fat, sugar and salt'. Where efforts were made to introduce healthier school meals, some children stopped taking them because they did not like the new food, which they were not used to at home (BBC Radio Five Live Report, 14 September 2005).

Photograph: EMPICS.

At any one time there are myriad issues and interests competing for the attention of politicians and other decision makers. Getting an issue onto the agenda is the crucial first step. Maintaining it there may be more difficult. After a time it is no longer news. The problem may appear more difficult than first realised. It may be too expensive to make an appreciable impact. There may be conflicting interests to take into account. Proposed remedies may even seem worse than the disease. (see Anthony Downs' five-stage model for environmental issues, Chapter 25).

Defining the problem

An issue may be raised by a particular event, but it is often far from self-evident what the problem really is. A major riot takes place in a British city. People are seriously injured or killed. Property worth billions of pounds is destroyed. It is an issue that must be addressed, but what really is the problem? Why did the riot take place? Only if the causes are understood can the real problem be addressed. Yet there are often competing explanations, implying very different remedies. Was it essentially a 'race riot' arising from ethnic tensions? Was it more the consequence of urban deprivation and unemployment? Was the physical environment a contributory factor? Did it reflect a breakdown in community, or the collapse of family life? Was it provoked by outside agitators or political extremists? Was it the consequence of poor or inadequate policing, or too lenient sentencing? Upon the definition of the problem depends the policy response.

Different interests may try to 'capture' the problem, defining it in such a way to suggest more resources for the police, urban planners, inner city schools, social workers, local authorities or learning and skills councils. They are not necessarily cynically pushing their own interests. Different professionals – police officers, economists, planners, teachers, social workers – naturally view the world through the prism of the assumptions involved in their own professional training and experience. They will be sincerely convinced that the 'real answer' is more trees, more jobs, better educational resources, more police and increased police powers, improved community resources, or whatever.

The riot itself is a form of political behaviour that commands political attention, but political values and interests also help shape how the problem is defined and addressed. Some interests may seek to play down or marginalise potential contributory factors, such as alcohol or drugs, ethnic tensions or discriminatory policing, while others may want to exaggerate them. Commonly there will be an investigation, involving the collection of evidence and the publication of a report with recommendations for action, some of which may lead to a response. The report may be thorough and its analysis sensible, but it is not holy writ, and can never be the whole truth. Different interests will emphasise different parts of the report and put their own interpretation on the conclusions. Then the riot and its possible causes may be largely forgotten until another riot happens, perhaps somewhere else in rather different circumstances, and the whole anguished debate will start up again.

A similar process will follow any significant political crisis – a major rail crash like Hatfield, a foot-and-mouth disease outbreak as in 2001, the collapse of a company, like Rover in 2005. The 'real issue' will be defined according to underlying ideological assumptions and political interests. There is no objective interpretation, and normally no easily identifiable villain and no single ideal solution.

Appraising options

Nevertheless, attempts may be made to analyse a range of options more thoroughly: at least when governments enjoy the luxury of time, for sometimes an immediate decision is required. In such circumstances governments have to act fast, and work out some rational justification for their actions afterwards. On other occasions governments may be able to explore a range of options or appoint a commission to do it for them (see Box 19.1).

A variety of techniques may be used in an ostensibly rational appraisal of options. Economists have sometimes used cost–benefit analysis (CBA) to assess particular projects or alternative possibilities. This involves putting a monetary value on all the identifiable costs and benefits to the community (not just the direct

Box 19.1

Government by commission?

Faced with a particular problem, a government may decide to appoint an independent commission or committee of experts to examine the issues, collect opinions, commission research and make recommendations in a final report. Most of this can be done anyway, using the normal resources and contacts of government, but there may be political advantages to an independent royal commission or committee of inquiry.

- The government may be genuinely undecided, or internally divided, on a particular issue, and a commission may be a useful way of trying to resolve the issue.
- On controversial issues likely to cause political trouble, the conclusions of a prestigious royal commission, backed by extensive research, may add authority and legitimacy to a difficult decision that the government needs to make.
- Although the commission may be independent, the government can influence or substantially determine the outcome by the choice of chair and members, and by setting the terms of reference. Thus the final report may come up with what the government thinks is the 'right' answer.
- Alternatively, the government is not obliged to accept the recommendations (particularly if they lead to a political outcry). It can 'pick and mix', accepting some recommendations and rejecting others. Critics of the report may be relieved if the government decides not to implement the most objectionable proposals.
- Appointing a commission may sometimes be a way of avoiding the need to declare a policy. Thus the government can fairly say it is awaiting the outcome of a report that it would be unreasonable to prejudge.
- Finally, appointing a commission may be a way of burying a difficult or politically damaging issue. With any luck, media and public attention will be transferred elsewhere when it finally reports.

Even so, it can be embarrassing if an independent commission or committee comes up with the 'wrong' or politically unacceptable answer. There are numerous examples of recommendations by high-profile commissions or committees being rejected, including the Roskill Commission on the site of the third London airport, the Layfield Committee on local government finance, the Banham Commission on local government reorganisation, and the Jenkins Commission on electoral reform. The conclusions of Roskill and Layfield were ignored, while the Jenkins Report was effectively 'kicked into the long grass' by the Blair government. Some of the Banham Commission recommendations were implemented, others modified or ignored, until John Major's government lost patience, and the chair and members were sacked and replaced by a new slimmed-down commission.

financial costs and benefits) to decide whether a project should go ahead, or which of several options is the best buy. Accountants have argued in favour of more overtly rational techniques for managing and controlling the budgetary process, such as planned programmed budgetary systems (PPBS), very fashionable in the 1970s, or more recently zero-base budgeting (ZBB). These rational systems have been advocated, however, precisely because much policy making in practice has not always appeared particularly rational, but commonly involves relatively small shifts (or increments) from past policy, without any real analysis of how far various options meet clear aims and objectives. Yet some argue that what has come to be called 'incrementalism' is not just the way in which most policy is made in practice, but is actually preferable to more ostensibly rational approaches (see Box 19.2).

It has been claimed that the budgetary process is almost inevitably incremental. Commenting on the UK budgetary process, observers suggest that the next budget can only involve a shift of around 2.5 per cent at most from the previous budget. The Chancellor of the Exchequer does not start with a blank sheet, but with past revenue and expenditure involving continuing programmes, with commitments and expectations that can only be ignored at considerable political cost. Yet understandably, successive governments have sought to make the process more rational, by linking spending to clear objectives, and planning

Box 19.2

Academic debate: rationalism and incrementalism

Rationalism: one common version of the rational model (the **ends–means model**) emphasises the importance of first determining the **ends** or **objectives** of policy and then exploring all possible means to secure those ends, and choosing the best.

Herbert Simon (1947), the leading theorist of rationalism, has argued that ideally, a decision maker should start from the **situation**, trace through all possible courses of action and their consequences, and choose the one with the greatest net benefits. However he recognised that in practice administrators are limited by time, information and skills, so that they cannot find the optimum solution, and search until they find a tolerably satisfactory solution. Thus they '**satisfice**' rather than **optimise**. This approach was described by Simon as involving '**bounded rationality**'.

Incrementalism: Charles Lindblom (1959) argued that in practice policy makers choose between relatively few options. Most policy making involves small-scale extensions of past policy. It does not commonly involve a single decision maker impartially sifting options, but requires accommodation and compromise between different interests, a process Lindblom described as '**partisan mutual adjustment**'. He also argued that much policy making does not follow any coherent plan, but proceeds rather disjointedly ('**disjointed incrementalism**'). Lindblom argued that his model better fitted the reality of policy making, so was the better descriptive model. He also argued that it led to better results than attempts at rationalism. It was thus also a prescriptive model. Incremental policy making, building on the past, was more likely to be successful than radical shifts. It was also more likely to be acceptable because it was based on consultation and compromise. Provocatively, Lindblom (1959) referred to his model as the '**science of muddling through**'.

The debate begun by Simon and Lindblom continues. Critics of Lindblom argue that we should aspire to more than 'muddling through'. They also argue that there is an in-built conservative bias in incrementalism. Sometimes radical change is necessary. Lindblom has responded that a series of incremental shifts can achieve a radical change in policy over a period, although he has conceded the case for some forward planning and 'strategic analysis' in later versions of his model. There have also been attempts to construct a model incorporating elements of rationalism and incrementalism, such as Etzioni's (1967) 'mixed scanning.'

spending over a longer period than the budgetary year. However, inevitably plans are blown off course by unanticipated developments and political pressures. Spending and taxation were central to the 2005 election campaign, as they were central to previous campaigns. Yet the differences in planned expenditure and taxation between the major parties were relatively tiny, as commentators observed.

Many other areas of policy are inevitably substantially incremental. Health policy and education policy depend on past decisions on training and investment. Staffing, buildings and equipment cannot be transformed overnight. Yet radical shifts can and do take place in British government. Whatever might be said about the privatisation programme of the Thatcher government or the constitutional changes of the Blair government, neither could be characterised as incremental.

Policy formulation

Sooner or later a policy emerges or a key decision is taken. Once a policy has been declared it is difficult to retreat, at least until the policy has been tried and perhaps found wanting. It is, however, not always easy to determine exactly when a new policy is established. It may be announced in a speech, or a government circular or sometimes a white paper. This provides a convenient firm date, although of course a decision will normally have been made inside government, sometimes well ahead of any public announcement. Although the policy will be associated with the appropriate departmental minister and, under the assumption of collective Cabinet responsibility, with the government as a whole, its real instigator may be someone else, perhaps the prime minister or chancellor, possibly a civil servant or a government adviser. More commonly, many prominent and less prominent individuals will have contributed over time to a new policy.

Some policies, however, emerge almost by default, as other options are rejected or become discredited, and it gradually becomes clear that there is no realistic alternative. There may be no formal announcement, and indeed the policy may only become clear in retrospect. Thus after a long debate over the location of London's proposed third airport from the 1970s onwards, a number of proposed sites were rejected. As a consequence Stansted, an initially small airport rejected at an early stage by the official Roskill Commission, gradually grew to become in effect London's third airport as a result of the failure of successive governments to reach a decision. Luton has since developed as a fourth airport, while both Heathrow and Gatwick have expanded to cope with increased traffic. Faced with strong local political opposition to any new airport in the 'home counties', governments have tended to prevaricate, and in practice have preferred the rather less politically contentious expansion of existing airports (although the proposed new runway for Heathrow has already encountered strenuous objections).

After an issue has aroused strong public emotions and demands for action, a government may eventually decide to take no action, because of the economic or political costs. Some analysts suggest that non-decision making may tell us more about the exercise of power in western society than decision making (see Box 19.3).

Legislation and legitimation

Government may decide what it wants to do, the policy may have been determined, but policy generally requires some form of official ratification if it is to be widely accepted as legitimate. This may involve legislation. Government policy may have been announced in a speech or white paper, but it still may need to become the law of the land for it to be accepted by the courts, media and public. Thus the transfer of the judicial functions of the House of Lords to a new Supreme Court was established as government policy in 2003, but it took until 2005 for it to become law. A policy of that importance clearly required legislation, and indeed there is always the possibility that a policy may be substantially modified or even abandoned as a bill proceeds through Parliament.

Box 19.3

Academic debate: the politics of non-decision making

Much of the debate on power and decision making has been conducted by American academics using US examples, although the analysis has also been applied to British politics. Robert Dahl (1961) concluded from his own studies of decision making in New Haven, Connecticut, that power was dispersed rather than concentrated in the hands of the few. Bachrach and Baratz (1970) argued that there were 'two faces of power'. One involved overt conflicts of interest on key political issues, of the kind analysed by Dahl. Yet a second face of power involved the suppression of conflict and the effective prevention of decisions through 'the mobilisation of bias' against interests effectively excluded from the decision-making process (such as black people in many American cities).

Stephen Lukes (1974) argued that there was a 'third dimension of power' involving the shaping of people's preferences so that neither overt nor covert conflicts of interests exist. People are so conditioned by the prevailing economic and social system that they cannot imagine alternatives. Thus potential political issues do not even get on to the political agenda. Lukes drew particularly on the work of Crenson (1971), who had shown that the issue of pollution control had not even come up for debate in some American cities whose economies were dominated by a major industry with a pollution problem. This was not because of the use of direct power and influence by employers, but because the bulk of the community had become conditioned to think that pollution was a natural and inescapable by-product of the employment and prosperity created by the industry.

There are some obvious problems in analysing 'non-decisions'. Moreover, Lukes and others assume that people's 'real' interests may differ markedly from their 'felt' interests. While this is plausible, it does conflict with the assumption of liberal democracy that individuals are the best judge of their own self-interest.

Other forms of legitimation may effectively derail a policy. Thus the Labour government instituted what has been described as a rolling programme of devolution for the English regions, involving directly elected regional assemblies, but gave voters an effective veto with the commitment to referendums in the regions concerned. Referendums initially announced for three regions were reduced to one, the north-east, where there was a well-established lobby for regional government. The overwhelming rejection of an assembly by voters in the north-east has seemingly buried the policy for the foreseeable future. The commitment to a referendum before Britain joins the euro, a referendum that polls indicate would be difficult to win, has been a strong factor deterring the government from pursuing a policy Blair was known to favour.

By no means all important government decisions require legislation, and only major constitutional issues are thought to require a referendum. Other decisions do normally depend on some kind of formal authorisation or ratification, perhaps in the form of a Cabinet minute or a circular, order or regulation issued by a departmental minister under delegated authority. Important decisions in local government require formal council approval. On planning decisions there is normally a right of appeal, followed by a public inquiry. This can be a very important part of the legitimation process, although some argue that the whole inquiry system is weighted against objectors.

Constitutionally, some of the most important powers of government, including making war, are part of the prerogative powers of the Crown, and strictly speaking do not require special authorisation. Yet a prime minister who took a country to war without the support of Cabinet and Parliament would not survive. On Iraq the Cabinet did back Blair (with initially one and eventually two dissenters), and so did Parliament. The legality of the war was later challenged, partly because it was alleged that Blair had misled Parliament, but rather more because it seemed questionable under international law. Much has since hinged on the advice given by the attorney general.

Implementation

Implementation is perhaps the most under-regarded part of the policy-making process, but the most important. The passing of a law in Parliament, or a policy pronouncement by a minister, is often regarded as the end of the policy process when it may be just the beginning. Cabinet decisions may be taken, laws may be passed, but the policy is not necessarily implemented as intended. There is often a considerable 'implementation gap' when it comes to applying policy (Hogwood and Gunn 1984, ch. 11). Why?

A policy may break down because of significant strong opposition from the public or a section of the public (as some examples in Box 19.4 indicate). Yet the explanation for imperfect implementation can often be rather less dramatic. One reason is

Box 19.4

Some examples of failed or imperfect policy implementation in Britain

- The 1970 Chronically Sick and Disabled Persons Act, an ambitious policy imperfectly administered because of lack of resources.
- Heath's industrial relations policy, effectively destroyed by the 1974 miners' strike.
- The incomes policy of Callaghan's government, which eventually broke down in the 'winter of discontent' because of opposition from trade unions and some employers.
- The introduction of identity cards for football supporters, enacted by the Thatcher government, but never implemented, partly because of administrative problems.
- The poll tax introduced by the Thatcher government in 1989 and 1990 was evaded by a substantial minority, and eventually abandoned after riots in the streets and the replacement of Margaret Thatcher by John Major.
- The ban on hunting with dogs, which became law in 2005, with only marginal changes to hunting in practice, partly because of the determination of influential people to defy the law, partly because of alleged difficulties in policing the act.

that ministers often rely on individuals or organisations outside central government to implement policy. Much government policy is implemented not by civil servants, but by local authorities, hospital trusts and primary care trusts, and a range of quangos. In health and education successive governments have made a virtue of devolving control to local professionals and to the community. Competition and choice require some autonomy for local producers and consumers. Local councils in particular are elected bodies, retaining some significant discretion over priorities and spending. Their priorities may not be the same as the governments – they are often controlled by different parties. Even where the law seems clear, councils may 'drag their feet' on policies to which they or local communities are opposed.

Public officials may often have significant discretion in administering policies. Terms such as 'street-level bureaucracy' (see extracts from Lipsky and Hudson in Hill 1997b) or 'street-level policy making' express the notion that often quite low-level staff who deal with the public at the sharp end of policy may have considerable powers to interpret regulations to grant or withhold benefits or services. Such people may be 'gatekeepers', effectively policing public access to resources.

The problem is clearer still in areas where central government is reliant on organisations and interests outside government altogether for implementation. This was one of the difficulties with incomes policy, sometimes backed by the authority of the law, pursued by both Labour and Conservative governments in the 1960s and 1970s. Yet whether the policy was 'voluntary' or 'statutory' it still depended on the cooperation of employers and unions for implementation, and this was not always forthcoming. Much industrial, agricultural and environmental policy relies on private sector firms if it is to succeed. Much social policy depends heavily on the local community and the voluntary sector. While much can be done by central government through the stick of regulation and the carrot of grants, ultimately the implementation of policy is often in the hands of people who are outside the line management control of central departments.

However, the biggest obstacle to effective policy implementation is generally resources. Governments will specify the ends, but do not always provide adequate means. There may be lack of finance, lack of skilled staff, lack of usable land, lack of sufficient powers. Even where government is prepared to provide additional resources, it takes time for these to be converted into usable resources on the ground. It takes many years to train new teachers, doctors, nurses, police officers; often longer still to plan, build and equip new hospitals and schools. There is no tap that can be turned to provide an instant supply of additional resources.

Over and above all this there are problems with coordination of policy and its implementation. Many programmes require cooperation between different levels of government, between different agencies and departments, between the public, private and voluntary sectors. Issues such as drugs, vandalism, school truancy and drink-fuelled violent disturbances require cooperation between the police, schools, social workers and community organisations. Frequently there are difficulties in achieving coordination, arising from the different organisations, processes and cultures of the services and agencies involved.

The problem of coordination is not new. In the 1960s and 1970s there was an extensive literature on corporate management in local government, which was essentially about overcoming narrow service, departmental and professional attitudes. Today the concerns are much the same, although the jargon is slightly different. A New Labour mantra is 'joined-up government'. It is easier to proclaim than achieve.

Yet without effective implementation, or 'delivery' in the language of New Labour, policy will fail to achieve its goals. The Blair government has discovered, like its predecessors, there is no shortage of policy advice inside and outside government. What it requires of its civil servants, and others involved at different levels and across sectors, is the effective delivery of policy. Thus a special Delivery Unit was established inside the Cabinet Office to monitor the implementation of government policy.

Finally, it is important to acknowledge that policy can have unintended as well as intended effects. A distinction can be drawn between policy *outputs*, the direct and intended result of inputs of resources and policy *outcomes*, including the unintended consequences of policy. Thus some welfare payments, intended to help the low paid and unemployed, involved a perverse disincentive against seeking work or higher-paid employment, in so far as it would entail the loss of means tested benefits, and in some cases even leave people worse off. The tax and benefit system created a 'poverty trap' from which it was difficult to escape, although the politicians and civil servants who had designed the policy had certainly not expected or intended this outcome.

Monitoring and review

To judge whether a particular policy is working it is important that its implementation is thoroughly monitored and reviewed. This appears common sense, but it did not always happen in the past, nor is it necessarily practised effectively today.

Many organisations ostensibly build internal monitoring and review into their own processes, to check that they are meeting their own aims and targets. Thus many local councils established performance review committees to monitor their own policies. Other public sector organisations formally review their own performance. This is very much in their own interest as there are all kinds of external reviews that will draw attention to problems, and it is better to identify weaknesses internally and seek to remedy them to forestall more damaging criticism.

From the 19th century onwards various inspectorates were established by central government to measure performance. More recently, central government's performance review has been reformed and extended. (For some of the regulatory bodies involved, see Chapter 18.) The auditing of public spending used to be concerned primarily with the legality of expenditure – was money being spent as voted by Parliament? It is now much more concerned with achieving value for money, and the three 'E's – economy, efficiency and effectiveness (see Box 19.5). The National Audit Office reviews performance in government departments and associated quangos, while the Audit Commission reviews the performance of local authorities and health authorities.

In addition, the government may set up inquiries or commissions to review a particular service and recommend reforms. Parliament now has its own comprehensive system for monitoring the performance of all government departments and services through departmental select committees. Professional bodies such as the Chartered Institute of Public Finance and Accountancy (CIPFA) have also long published their own performance statistics.

There is no doubt that all this performance review has had a massive impact on government at every level. There are sanctions on poor performance. Pay, prospects and sometimes jobs are on the line. Comparative performance indicators can throw up some substantial variations in costs and standards, the money spent on school meals for example, or death rates arising from particular medical conditions in different hospitals or areas of the country. Poor performance can be addressed and remedied. Good practice can be analysed and copied. Some object that the publication of comparative league tables can distort priorities, concentrating on the easily measurable at the expense of more important but less easily

Box 19.5

The three 'E's – economy, efficiency and effectiveness

Economy – minimising the cost of resources, or inputs (e.g. land, labour, capital) involved in producing a certain level of service (e.g. reducing the cost of providing a hospital bed for a patient).

Efficiency – securing maximum quantity and quality of outputs for a given quantity of inputs (e.g. treating more patients in the NHS without an increase in resources).

Effectiveness – securing effective outcomes (e.g. improved health in the community).

While economy is about reducing costs, and efficiency about increased productivity, effectiveness is about realising objectives – but this is the most difficult to measure. If a school teaches more pupils without any increase in resources, this implies increased economy (reduced costs per pupil) and increased efficiency, if exam results appear unaffected. Yet both teachers and parents assume that larger classes in some way involve less effective education, which is plausible but difficult to measure and prove. Similarly the quantity of patients treated in the NHS may increase, perhaps at the expense of quality of care.

quantified outcomes. While there is some truth in the argument, the answer lies not in less performance review but better and more sensitive performance review. Government, service users and voters can hardly assess whether the large sums devoted to public services are efficient and effective without it.

Finally, performance review can throw up evidence that existing policy is not working, and new thinking is required. Thus the end of one policy cycle can provide the stimulus for the beginning of the next.

Summary

- Policy making may be analysed as a cycle involving a number of stages, including issue emergence, problem definition, option appraisal, policy formulation, legislation and legitimation, implementation, monitoring and review.
- The crucial first stage is for an issue to get onto the political agenda, and to be identified as a priority.
- Once an issue is on the agenda, it is not necessarily self-evident what the 'real problem' is. Some familiar and recurring problems have been defined very differently. The problem may be 'captured' and defined by a particular interest in its own terms.
- Various options or proposed solutions may be appraised using a variety of ostensibly rational techniques. However, much policy making in practice appears incremental rather than rational, and some argue that the incremental approach may be preferable.
- A policy may be clearly announced, or emerge over time. Some analysts suggest that non-decision making explains more about the nature and distribution of power than decision making.
- A policy is normally decided well in advance of legislation or some other form of legitimation. However, legitimation is crucial for public acceptance and democratic accountability. Sometimes problems with legitimation may effectively derail a policy.
- Policies may not always be effectively implemented, for a variety of reasons, including inherent problems, lack of resources, dependence on other agencies or interests for implementation, and political difficulties.
- There is extensive machinery for the monitoring and review of policy. This may not always work as well as it might and can be counterproductive, but is essential in measuring efficiency and effectiveness. It can reveal that existing policies are not working, and thus inaugurate a new policy cycle.

Questions for discussion

- How and why do issues get onto the policy agenda? What kind of issues might be relatively neglected?
- Why are some familiar issues, such as crime and inner-city poverty, so variously defined and explained? How important are the different definitions for policy?
- Why does it often appear that past policy is the most important factor influencing future policy? What radical shifts in policy have occurred in recent years and why?
- Do the issues that are not debated tell us more about power in Britain than those issues that are debated?
- In what ways are policies legitimated? How might problems in legitimation derail a policy?
- Why are some policies not implemented effectively (and sometimes not implemented at all)? How might governments secure fuller implementation?
- Why has the monitoring and review of policy become politically controversial?

Further reading

There is an extensive literature on policy making and policy analysis. Hill (1997a) provides a good overview of the policy process, while the same author (1997b) has edited an excellent reader, which contains extracts from some of the sources referred to here, and many others besides. Wayne Parsons (1995) provides more extensive and detailed analysis of specific aspects.

Some of this chapter refers back to analysis in earlier chapters, most notably the discussion of power and democracy in Chapter 1, the chapters on pressure group politics and the media, and chapters on particular institutions and processes. There are a few illustrative examples of policy making in this chapter, and some in earlier chapters. However, the following chapters which look at particular policy areas and services provide a number of examples, many of which could have been included in this chapter to illustrate specific points about the policy process.

Managing the Economy

Contents

Successful management of the economy is vital for the living standards and well-being of the members of any country, and thus central to government and politics. In the USA, Bill Clinton's Democrats coined the slogan 'It's the economy, stupid!' underlining the crucial importance of the state of the economy to electoral support. Some have argued that in Britain there is a very close correlation between economic performance and the poll ratings of the governing party (see Chapter 5). Normally, management of the economy is central to British election campaigns and their outcome. Inflation, unemployment, interest rates, and most of all perhaps taxation and expenditure have a direct impact on living standards and confidence. Moreover, a flourishing economy makes it much easier for a government to do other things, such as improve public services, or increase public investment in hospitals, schools and transport, or reduce poverty, or increase international aid.

How the economy is run reflects political as well as economic assumptions. What should be the main aim of economic policy: high growth, full employment, stable prices or greater equality? How far, and in what ways, should governments intervene to secure their economic goals? Should governments interfere as little as possible with private enterprise and free market forces? These are questions to which economic theory can certainly contribute, but they have long also been central to the debate between mainstream political ideologies (see Chapter 6). Key issues over Britain's place in Europe and the global economy are as much about politics as economics.

This chapter reviews Britain's economic performance since the war, but particularly under New Labour, the tools of economic management, and the economic choices facing Britain today, together with their implications for government and politics.

Britain's relative economic decline in the 20th century

There have long been some fundamental questions over the health of the British economy. Britain was the first country to industrialise, and was once the world's leading economic power. Yet although the British economy has continued to grow over the last century or more, other countries have grown faster, and Britain has thus suffered a relative economic decline. This relative economic decline began in the late 19th century, was manifest between the two world wars, and became the subject of heated economic and political argument in the post-war period (see 'the under-performing economy',

Chapter 2). Productivity, growth and living standards were higher not only in north America but in Japan and among Britain's main competitors in Europe. Successive governments sought to diagnose and address Britain's economic problems, but largely failed. Economic failure was perhaps the main explanation for the defeat of Attlee's Labour government, of the Conservative government in 1964, of Wilson's defeat in 1970, Heath's in 1974, and Callaghan's in 1979. No government had managed to achieve steady economic growth, and none had ultimately had been able to escape from the 'stop–go' boom and bust cycle of the post-war years (see Figure 2.1, 'The stop-go cycle', Chapter 2).

The Conservative record from 1979 to 1997 remains rather more contentious. Admirers credit the Thatcher government with addressing long-standing problems with the British economy: poor industrial relations reflecting trade union power, inflation, escalating public spending, lack of incentives for enterprise, and over-reliance on subsidies. Critics argue that the economic, social and political costs of Conservative remedies were worse than the disease. High interest rates led to two recessions that virtually destroyed British manufacturing industry, and led to over three million unemployed. Boom and bust in the housing market led to repossessions and ruin. The defeat of union power, symbolised by the bitter miners' strike of 1984/5, coupled with divisive tax and welfare policies, split the country and intensified social and political opposition to Thatcherism. This, more than the immediate political circumstances, explains the fall of Thatcher from power in 1990.

Major's more emollient style enabled him to win a narrow election victory in 1992, despite continuing economic problems which culminated in Britain's forced expulsion from the European monetary system on 'Black Wednesday' later in the same year (see Box 20.1). With this, the Conservatives lost their reputation for economic competence, a reputation they have never managed to recover, even though the economy subsequently improved under the chancellorship of Kenneth Clarke.

Labour for once inherited a sound economy. New Labour's economic management is reviewed at greater length below. However, in public perception they have captured the record of economic competence previously enjoyed by the Conservatives, with a record of low inflation and relatively low unemployment over two terms of government. Chancellor Gordon Brown has claimed he has broken the cycle of boom and bust of earlier years, achieving unbroken, steady economic growth. In marked contrast to earlier decades, Britain's economic performance has been better than most of its leading competitors.

Yet critics allege that the real structural weaknesses of the British economy have not been addressed. Productivity (as measured in output per employee per hour) remains poor compared with Britain's main competitors. Manufacturing industry continues to decline. Britain's economic prosperity seems to depend on a consumer boom, fuelled by mounting debt. It is thus too early to claim that Blair and Brown's Labour government has halted or even reversed Britain's long economic decline.

Who makes and shapes economic policy in Britain?

The Chancellor of the Exchequer and the Treasury are more important today than ever in the framing of economic policy. From time to time there have been attempts to separate longer-term economic policy from immediate decisions on budgets and public finance (as with Wilson's creation of a separate Department of Economic Affairs in 1964). Other departments, such as Trade and Industry, have sometimes briefly appeared to have a major proactive role in various aspects of economic policy. Some prime ministers, particularly those with some claim to economic expertise (Wilson), strongly held economic assumptions (Heath, Thatcher), or who have previously served as chancellor (Churchill, Macmillan, Callaghan, Major) have taken a particular interest in economic policy. Some chancellors have been effectively subservient to dominant prime ministers (Selwyn Lloyd to Macmillan, Callaghan to Wilson, Barber to Heath, Howe to Thatcher) while others have been forced out because their economic policies diverged from those of Number 10 (Thorneycroft, Lawson). Among post-war premiers only Attlee, Eden, Home and, most recently Blair have been content to leave economic management to others. In the case of Blair, this self-denying ordinance

Box 20.1

The legacy of 'Black Wednesday' 16 September 1992

Margaret Thatcher was reluctantly persuaded by her Cabinet colleagues in 1990 that Britain should enter the European Community's Exchange Rate Mechanism (ERM), under which the government undertook to maintain the exchange value of sterling against the currencies of other member states of the European Community. It was recognised that this might cause some economic hardship in the short term, particularly if inflation made British goods uncompetitive abroad, but the longer-term benefits of ERM membership would be low inflation and low interest rates. However, the depth and length of the recession that began in the late 1980s surprised the government. At first it was described as a 'blip' in the economy; later it was clear that Britain was in the middle of the deepest recession since the 1930s. From December 1990 chancellor Norman Lamont began observing the 'green shoots of recovery' and reassured the public that the recession would be 'relatively short-lived and relatively shallow'. Yet the persistent poor performance of the British economy, coupled with a growing conviction in world money markets that the pound appeared over-valued, led to increased pressure on sterling. The crisis came to a head with massive selling of the pound in mid-September 1992. The government tried to defend the pound by using almost all its reserves of foreign currency to buy sterling in a desperate attempt to maintain the exchange rate, and by raising interest rates on 16 September to an unprecedented 15 per cent. It all proved fruitless, and Lamont had to announce the withdrawal of sterling from the ERM, and a consequent devaluation of the pound.

This may appear to be increasingly remote past history, but it proved a pivotal moment in people's confidence in the economic competence of the major parties. Previous economic disasters, such as the 1931 crisis, the devaluations of 1949 and 1967, and the 1976 IMF crisis had been associated with Labour (although arguably Labour was not only to blame for the underlying problems). By contrast, the Conservatives were credited with understanding the economy. 'Black Wednesday' destroyed the Conservative party's reputation for economic competence almost overnight, and since then Labour has become the party most trusted to manage the economy. It is a remarkable transformation.

In some ways the Conservatives, like Labour earlier, were unfairly blamed alone for 'Black Wednesday'. The Labour opposition had supported ERM entry in 1990. Had they won the 1992 election they would have encountered the same problems with almost certainly a similar outcome. Labour would have been confirmed once more as the party that could not manage the economy. It was instead Major's government that carried the can for failure. Nor did the government benefit from the subsequent economic recovery. Labour inherited a healthy economy, and went on to establish a reputation for prudent economic management under chancellor Gordon Brown.

In February 2005 Treasury documents relating to 'Black Wednesday' were published under the Freedom of Information Act, conveniently reminding voters of this Conservative government crisis in the run-up to the election in May 2005.

allegedly goes back to a secret pact with Brown in 1994, under which Brown agreed not to challenge for the Labour leadership in return for assurances from Blair that included a free hand for him in economic policy and related areas. Even without such a pact it would have been difficult for Blair to challenge Brown in the economic sphere. Blair was a lawyer, with no great claims to economic expertise, while Brown had not only studied economics but had been shadow chancellor since 1992, with five years to prepare for office.

The Treasury's power has sometimes been perceived as largely negative, responsible for cutting down the creative policies and spending plans of other departments. This has particularly been the case during recurrent periods of economic crisis in Britain. Brown's role has been much more proactive, extending over welfare, labour and industrial policy, Europe and international development. Indeed, critics complained that 'the Treasury had become the Department of Social Policy' (Sampson 2005: 130). At times also the Department of Trade and Industry appeared virtually redundant. Thus Brown has dominated much of the Labour government's domestic policy making, and has increasingly appeared Blair's co-equal.

Within the Treasury chancellors have often become the mouthpiece for their officials, the formidable Treasury mandarins. Yet Brown dominated the Treasury from the start. Although the Treasury's authority extended across Whitehall, 'it was exercised by the chancellor rather than by the institution'. Indeed 'Officials accustomed to a culture in which policy decisions were debated from first principles found the new chancellor less than receptive. He had already taken the decisions that would set the new government's economic course' (Stephens, in Seldon 2001: 187–8). Instead, Brown relied on his own personal advisers, such as Ed Balls and Ed Miliband, marginalising some of his junior ministers, and even showing scant regard for his Cabinet colleagues.

Among other institutions the Bank of England, formally nationalised by Labour in 1946, but operating as an independent body, has long loomed large in economic policy. Under John Major the discussions between chancellor Ken Clarke and the Bank's Governor Eddie George were dubbed 'the Ken and Eddie show'. On the surface, the power of the Bank of England was enlarged still further by Brown's decision to hand over decisions on interest rates to the Bank's monetary policy committee. However, as the chancellor still sets the economic framework for the committee's decisions and appoints more than half its members, he retains effective control over monetary policy. Moreover, the Bank of England soon lost most of its former regulatory power over the financial sector to the Financial Services Authority.

Economy policy making, although dominated by the chancellor, is still strongly influenced and constrained by outside forces. Influence is sometimes attributed to important or colourful individuals such as Richard Branson, Alan Sugar or Rupert Murdoch, although rather more significant are impersonal institutions, interests and markets, many of these transcending national boundaries. Among these are business interests in general and financial interests in particular. The power of pension funds has become more obvious. Major firms, including transnational corporations, may exert a direct influence on government, and various sectors of the economy are represented by their own organisations (such as the Society of Motor Manufacturers and Traders). Powerful groups such as the CBI and the Institute of Directors have both a high public profile and also exert influence behind the scenes. Prestigious think tanks, professional associations and some academic institutions are also listened to. There are powerful health and education lobbies to which any government would be advised to pay some attention. Trades unions have recovered some of their former influence with Labour in government, but they remain much less powerful than in the immediate post-war decades. 'One of the things that struck most visitors to 11 Downing Street during the first Blair Parliament was that they were as likely to meet a departing venture capitalist as a trade unionist' (Stephens, in Seldon 2001: 198).

Beyond the ranks of organised business and labour, more specialist interests can be amplified considerably if they secure significant media publicity and public support, as was the case with the truckers' protest in the fuel crisis of September 2000, which led to some modification of fuel taxation. Behind these particular institutions and interests are the wider public as voters, taxpayers and consumers of goods and services, including public services. Governments that ultimately must seek re-election ignore wider public concerns at their peril.

International obligations as represented through such bodies as the G8, the World Trade Organisation (WTO), the International Monetary Fund (IMF) and of course the European Union inevitably constrain British economic policy and effectively rule out some options. Beyond all this, impersonal global markets can have a massive impact on national economies, particularly the British economy, which is so locked in to the global economy. Wyn Grant (2002: 8–9) recalls a seminar of international economic decision makers. Someone asked, 'Who calls the shots?' 'Not us', say the international financial institutions, 'it's the G7 finance ministers'. 'Not us', say the finance ministers, 'it's really the markets'.

The tools of economic management: direct intervention, fiscal policy and monetary policy

Political fortunes rest substantially on successful economic management. How then do governments try to manage the economy? They can intervene directly to control key aspects of the economy. They can use fiscal policy (taxation and government spending). They can use monetary policy (control of the money supply and interest rates). They may emphasise the need for less government intervention and regulation, and seek to actively encourage free-market forces and business enterprise. More commonly, governments have employed a mix of economic management tools.

Direct intervention

Governments can manage the economy through direct controls and intervention. In Britain such direct control of the economy has been most evident in wartime. In directing the wartime economy, the coalition government led by Winston Churchill assumed massive powers of intervention in controlling the labour force, deciding on the location of industry, requisitioning economic assets, rationing the supply of raw materials to factories and so on. Some of these controls were briefly retained in the immediate aftermath of war, but they largely disappeared during the 1950s. Nevertheless peacetime governments have attempted since to control aspects of the economy through direct intervention.

Most contentious was Labour's policy of nationalisation, involving the compulsory acquisition by the state of a number of key industries. Had Labour pursued a policy of wholesale nationalisation of industry, as implied in clause 4 of its constitution (see Chapter 6), this might have involved the kind of direct state management of the economy long advocated by many socialists. Yet in practice Labour only nationalised what they described as 'the commanding heights of the economy', and industries that were either already substantially municipally owned (gas, electricity, water) or that appeared to be declining or in trouble (coal, gas again, railways, iron and steel). Moreover the government did not seek to manage these industries directly, nor were they owned and run by workers, as some socialists had demanded. Instead they were placed in the hands of 'arms' length' public corporations. While governments could and did sometimes lean on the chairs of boards to influence decisions on pricing or investment, they never sought to use state-owned industries to manage the economy.

With the exception of steel, the maintenance of a mixed economy with a substantial state sector remained a bipartisan policy from the 1950s through to the 1970s, when governments of both parties were prepared to take failing industries into public ownership. This policy was sharply reversed by the Thatcher government (see below).

Both major parties pursued other policies involving direct intervention in the economy. For example, in the fight against inflation Labour and Conservative governments implemented prices and incomes policies (see Box 20.2). Both Labour and Conservative governments from 1945 through to 1979 pursued an industrial policy involving incentives to encourage investment and growth. Impressed by the success of economic planning in France, a Conservative government set up the National Economic Development Council (NEDC) – familiarly known as 'Neddy' – in 1962 as a forum in which governments and both sides of industry discussed plans to improve Britain's industrial efficiency and international competitiveness. Later Labour governments set up other interventionist bodies – the Industrial Reorganisation Corporation (IRC) in 1966 and the National Enterprise Board (NEB) in 1975 – with a view to restructuring and strengthening Britain's industrial base. Labour and Conservative governments also strove to help economically depressed areas of Britain with an interventionist regional policy to attract new investment though grants and other financial incentives. During Thatcher's years in office her governments pursued a more free market and less interventionist approach to the problems of the British economy, privatising the former state industries, abandoning incomes policy, cutting regional aid, scrapping interventionist bodies and allowing unemployment to rise, and manufacturing industry to contract. (Urban policy however remained interventionist.)

New Labour has not sought a return to traditional interventionist policies. The government has not attempted to reverse the Conservative privatisation programme (with the arguable exception of Railtrack) and indeed has even extended it (for example with the part-privatisation of air traffic control). Nor has it rescued declining industries (such as Rover), or returned to the days of subsidies and ambitious regional aid policies. (Indeed, the European Union and international bodies such as GATT would rule out such

Box 20.2

Incomes policies in the 1960s and 1970s

In 1961 a Conservative chancellor, Selwyn Lloyd, introduced the 'pay pause', a nine-month-long incomes policy designed to hold down pay awards. It was hoped that this direct attack on wage increases would help restrain price inflation. Between 1965 and 1969 Labour pursued a prices and incomes policy, and the Conservative government which followed converted an informal incomes policy into a statutory policy which controlled all incomes between 1972 and 1974. The Labour government returned to office in 1974 developed a voluntary incomes policy – known as the 'social contract' – under which trades unions accepted wage restraint in return for welfare benefits (the 'social wage'). Yet neither voluntary nor statutory incomes policy proved effective in holding down wages for long. The social contract finally broke down in the 'Winter of Discontent' of 1978–9. This was an important factor in the 1979 Conservative election victory which saw Margaret Thatcher enter Number Ten promising economic management which would rely much more on market forces and far less on government intervention. Since then governments of both parties have avoided any formal incomes policy (either statutory or voluntary).

intervention as involving unfair competition.) There has been no return to a general incomes policy, although Labour has introduced a national minimum wage. Labour's direct economic intervention, if it can be so called, has involved incentives for investment and training, the micro-management of the delivery of public services (see Chapter 21) and tax and welfare policies designed to increase incentives to work and reduce child poverty (see Chapter 22).

Fiscal policy

Governments have to raise taxes to pay for their expenditure. Gladstonian public finance (named after William Gladstone, the great 19th-century Liberal chancellor and prime minister) involved 'balancing the books' in the annual budget, ensuring that planned government expenditure over

Definition

Fiscal policy is about the management of public finances through taxation and government spending. Thus all governments use fiscal policy to finance their spending plans. Governments may also use fiscal policy to achieve other objectives, to influence the behaviour of individuals and businesses by providing financial incentives or disincentives, and/or influence aggregate (or total) demand in the economy.

the coming year was met by planned government revenue from taxation and other sources. The budgetary process has always involved awkward choices between the calls on the public purse from different departments with spending needs, and between different ways of raising taxation, with varying implications for individual taxpayers and businesses.

Government spending, now around two-fifths of national income, inevitably has a major impact on the wider national economy, while taxation can have a major impact on the economic behaviour of individuals and firms. Thus changes in taxation may encourage or discourage saving, investing and spending by households or firms, and may increase or decrease incentives for work and enterprise. Tax changes may be used for more specific purposes – for example, to discourage consumption of harmful goods (alcohol and tobacco) or encourage 'green' energy saving.

More broadly, fiscal policy may be used to stimulate or deflate the national economy. From the 1940s through to the 1970s, governments of both parties used fiscal policy as a key tool of Keynesian demand management policies (see Chapter 2). The theories of Keynes provoked a revolution in economic thinking. Keynes was never a socialist, but a progressive liberal who believed in capitalism and free enterprise. He sought not direct state intervention and detailed control of the economy but a system of managed capitalism. Under this, the state would seek to influence the aggregate (or total) demand for goods and services in the economy as a whole through the use of both fiscal and monetary policy, to secure the economic goals of full employment, stable prices and steady growth. This involved a crucial distinction between what economists call micro-economics and macro-economics. The government would leave micro-economics, the behaviour of individual households and firms, substantially to free market forces. It would seek instead to influence and control macro-economics and aggregate (or total) demand in the economy. Keynesian theory suggested governments could and should act to pursue full employment and economic growth.

The basic assumption behind Keynes's theory is that economic depressions are caused by a lack of sufficient demand in the economy to purchase all goods and services when all economic resources (and particularly labour) are fully utilised. Total demand is insufficient to meet total supply under conditions of full employment. There is too little money chasing too many goods. Cuts in wages and/or employment will reduce demand still further, leading to a vicious economic circle and a deepening recession. The Keynesian remedy is to increase demand using both fiscal and monetary policy. Inflation, on the other hand, is caused by excessive demand in the economy – too much money chasing too few goods. If the economy is already operating at full employment it is not possible to increase supply to meet excess demand, and the consequence will be higher prices. Here, the Keynesian remedy is to reduce aggregate demand by taking purchasing power out of the economy through fiscal and monetary policy.

Keynesian macro-economic theory is most commonly associated with fiscal policy, although Keynes himself emphasised the need to combine fiscal policy with monetary policy. Keynesian fiscal policy is also often equated with 'tax and spend' policies and deficit finance. This is not just an over-simplification but a distortion of the ideas of Keynes. Keynes' theory was an equilibrium theory – how to secure a balance between desirable economic objectives which might involve contrasting policy solutions. Although his theory was developed in a period of depression for both the British and wider world economy, with policy implications for achieving economic expansion, it also involved remedies for inflation. Deficit finance, a deliberate surplus of government expenditure over income, was only supposed to be applied for a specific purpose for a limited period. However, politicians used the ideas of Keynes to justify government borrowing in general.

Moreover, haunted by the memories of depression in the 1930s, governments of both parties in the post-war period tended to respond to any rise in unemployment with measures to increase demand. They were also tempted to use 'Keynesian' remedies for political purposes, to engineer a boom before an election, which commonly required deflation afterwards, with cuts in spending, and higher taxation and interest rates. Thus the way governments interpreted Keynes, long after the economist's death, led to the association of Keynesianism with inflationary consequences. When 'Keynesian' remedies appeared to lead to both steeply rising inflation and unemployment (or 'stagflation', as it was termed), as well as a mounting deficit in public finances, a Labour government under James Callaghan effectively abandoned Keynes (see Chapter 2).

Definitions

Micro-economics involves theories about the behaviour of individual consumers, households and firms in the economy. Basic micro-economic theory assumes free markets, although it goes on examine the effects of imperfect competition and government intervention on market forces.

Macro-economics is concerned mainly with the performance of the national economy, including levels of inflation, employment, growth and the balance of payments, and techniques for influencing or controlling these. It focuses on aggregate (or total) demand and supply in the economy. Basic macro-theory assumes initially a closed economy, without foreign trade, but goes on to build in imports and exports and international trade. Macro-economic theory assumes that governments have considerable potential influence on inflation, employment, foreign trade and growth.

Monetary policy

Just as all governments inevitably use fiscal policy, they also can hardly avoid having a monetary policy. The issue and control of money have long been government functions, with substantial implications for the economy. In the early 16th century

King Henry VIII expanded the money supply by debasing the coinage, with serious inflationary consequences. In 1923 the German government provoked hyper-inflation by issuing too many banknotes, which were ultimately not worth the paper they were printed on. Today it is rather more difficult to define, let alone control, the money supply, but it is still the case that a failure in monetary policy can have dire consequences.

British governments in the immediate post-war period often tried to restrict the availability of credit, for example requiring a substantial down-payment as a condition of a bank loan or 'hire purchase'. More generally, governments have sought to influence the cost of borrowing by influencing or determining interest rates. Higher interest rates may deter borrowing and encourage saving, thus damping demand in the economy, while lower interest rates may encourage spending and investment, stimulating an economy in recession. British governments have also sometimes felt obliged to increase interest rates to encourage foreigners to hold sterling when there is pressure on the currency in international money markets. Yet governments can only normally alter interest rates within fairly narrow limits set by market forces. Moreover, as a major borrower, government is not above the market but part of it. If the government seeks to increase its own borrowing by issuing more bonds, it will normally have to offer higher rates of interest to attract savers.

Overall, however, there are limits to the effect of changes in interest rates on behaviour. Very low interest rates will not encourage consumption and investment if households and businesses remain pessimistic about the future. Very high interest rates may similarly be ineffective. As we have seen, a 15 per cent interest rate did not discourage the selling of sterling on 'Black Wednesday', and indeed it had almost the opposite effect. Currency speculators saw it as a panic measure, confirming that devaluation was inevitable, and sold pounds in the expectation of being able to buy them back later at a lower price.

The discrediting of Keynesianism, deficit finance and 'tax and spend' policies led to more emphasis on monetary policy as a means to manage the economy, and in particular to restrain inflation, which had appeared 'out of control' in the early and mid-1970s. The economic policy of the Thatcher government was described as 'monetarism'. In narrow terms, monetarism meant controlling the money supply as the means to control inflation. Yet it also entailed a return to Gladstonian public finance, and the need to 'balance the books', in part because persistent government borrowing to finance current spending leads to inflationary pressures. Thus monetarism involved cuts in public spending, firstly because these were demanded by the International Monetary Fund as a condition of its massive loan to tackle Britain's economic crisis, and later because the Thatcher government saw the control of inflation rather than unemployment as the paramount aim of economic policy.

To control the money supply, interest rates were kept high, which pushed up the value of the pound against other currencies. High interest rates and a high pound depressed investment and exports, with disastrous consequences for British manufacturing industry. Monetarism in the narrow sense proved unsuccessful. Whatever definition of the money supply was used, it did not seem to have much direct impact on the performance of the economy. If the Thatcher government achieved any success in the economic sphere it was in spite of its failure to control the money supply or secure significant cuts in overall public spending.

Interest rates began to come down after 'Black Wednesday', in the latter years of Major's government, and have remained historically low under Labour. Labour appeared to abandon any control of monetary policy with its surprise decision to

Definition

Monetary policy is about influencing the money supply and the cost and/or availability of credit. Other things being equal, high interest rates may deter individuals from buying houses, cars and consumer goods, and businesses from new investment. Low interest rates may encourage both consumption and investment. Thus monetary policy, like fiscal policy, can also be used to reduce or stimulate aggregate demand in the economy, although it was subsequently advocated as an alternative to Keynesian demand management. Some economists argued that effective control of the money supply was the key to the control of inflation.

hand over control of the minimum lending rate (MLR) to the Monetary Policy Committee of the Bank of England. This was a clever political move which gained the all-important confidence of business and the markets. Yet the government retains influence over monetary policy through its appointments, and more importantly through its broader economic policy which provides the background to the decisions of the Monetary Policy Committee.

Encouraging market forces

Behind the debates over Keynesianism and monetarism lies an older and wider argument over the whole role of government and the state in the economy. In the immediate post-war decades there was a presumption in favour of state intervention to provide work, welfare 'from the cradle to the grave' and social justice. This presumption was shared by many 'one nation' Conservatives, as well as Labour. Yet from the 1970s it was increasingly challenged by many on the 'New Right' who argued that the state had grown too big, that high taxation destroyed incentives and enterprise, and that state welfare encouraged a 'dependency culture'. A radical remedy was needed which went beyond tinkering with fiscal and monetary policy. The state must be 'reined back' and market forces allowed to work.

Advocacy of the free market by the Thatcher government never involved a wholesale rejection of state intervention, public spending and public services. To this extent her economic policies disappointed the more enthusiastic apostles of the free market in the Institute of Economic Affairs. Thatcher's free market policies involved, first, a freer labour market, through a reduction in the power and influence of trades unions; second, the privatisation of state-owned assets, involving wider share ownership and 'popular capitalism'; and third, the introduction of elements of competition and 'quasi markets' into the management of public services, particularly health and education (see Chapter 21). The intellectual climate was transformed. A presumption in favour of state intervention and state provision which had dominated the politics of the post-war decades was replaced by a presumption in favour of the free market and private enterprise. Even the Labour Party was partially converted. Although it had opposed the Thatcher government's trade union reforms, the privatisation of public utilities, the sale of council houses and the marketisation of public services, it did not subsequently seek to reverse them, and indeed embraced the language of competition and choice. Under Blair's leadership, Labour increasingly courted business, at a time when business support for the Conservatives was eroding (see Box 20.3).

Box 20.3

The pro-business party loses the support of business

In the months leading up to the 1997 general election newspapers carried reports of increasing disillusion in the business community with the performance of the Conservative government. The image of New Labour was no longer seen as a threat by business people who, a decade earlier, would have feared the election of a Labour government. Labour neutralised a potential Conservative attack by accepting Conservative public spending limits for two years and promising no income tax rises for five years. Labour also worked hard on what journalists called the 'prawn cocktail circuit', attending business lunches and other meetings, in order to convince the business community that New Labour was both 'business-friendly' and more competent than the Conservatives. The chairmen of top companies, such as Granada and Great Universal Stores, openly declared their support for Tony Blair. A poll of business people revealed that 80 per cent were not at all worried by the prospects of a Labour government being elected, while 15 per cent actually believed that their businesses would do better under Labour. Another poll of business managers found that support for the Conservatives had dropped from 62 to 40 per cent over a five-year period.

It was not just the positive image of New Labour that won the support of many business people, but also concerns over mounting Euro-scepticism within the Conservative Party. For British business European markets were increasingly important. Their old political nightmare of a nationalising Labour government was replaced by the new nightmare of a right-wing Conservative government hostile towards the European Union.

Economic management under New Labour: Brown's prudence

In 1997, for the first time an incoming Labour government inherited an economy that was performing relatively well. Trends in inflation, growth, exports and unemployment were all moving in a favourable direction in 1997. Labour's new chancellor, Gordon Brown, soon established a reputation for prudence. He was determined to keep Labour's pre-election pledge to stay within Conservative taxing and spending plans for two years, and did so. He immediately and unexpectedly announced the transfer of decisions on interest rates to the Monetary Policy Committee of the Band of England. He also signalled his determination to keep inflation low by announcing a 2.5 per cent target rate, and further announced his 'golden rule' of only borrowing to finance investment, and keeping public debt at a stable and prudent proportion of national income over the economic cycle. These measures were generally well received, particularly in the City. By establishing Labour's credibility in managing the economy the chancellor improved the prospects for long-term stability and growth.

Two further Labour pre-election pledges had caused some anxiety in the business community. One was the commitment to sign up to the Social Chapter of the Maastricht Treaty (Treaty of the European Union) from which Major had secured an opt-out. The other was to introduce a national minimum wage. Both pledges were honoured, but neither proved as damaging to business as critics had feared. Labour's trade union allies were disappointed with the relatively low level at which the national minimum wage was set, and it had little if any measurable impact on inflation and unemployment. Indeed, the Conservative Party, which had vigorously denounced Labour's proposals for a minimum wage when in government, changed its stance in opposition, and declared its support.

The commitment to keep within Tory spending plans and not increase income tax constrained Labour's policies in the first two years. However, Brown did raise some additional revenue from a windfall tax on the privatised utilities to finance his 'New Deal' (see below), raising national insurance contributions and removing some forms of tax relief. These 'stealth taxes', as the opposition called them, enabled him to pursue some (very limited) redistribution of income, and inject some additional money into public services.

Beyond this the chancellor emphasised 'supply-side' reforms to improve the performance of the economy, and stimulate investment and employment. Most important of all was the 'New

In Focus 20.1

Gordon Brown on budget day, April 2005

Gordon Brown felt obliged to stand aside for Tony Blair in the contest to succeed John Smith as Labour leader in 1994, but reportedly remains ambitious for the top job. As Chancellor of the Exchequer for a record period from 1997 he has shown a remarkable dominance of not only economic policy but much social and European policy as well. His economic record made him Blair's heir apparent, well before the prime minister's surprise announcement in the midst of the 2005 election campaign that he would not fight another election as party leader. However, Brown's prospects of succeeding Blair and winning a fourth successive election for Labour may still depend on the performance of the British economy, and his skill in tackling a widely predicted 'black hole' in the nation's finances.

Photograph: EMPICS.

Deal' to move the young unemployed 'from welfare to work': £3 billion was earmarked to get them into jobs or training. There were additional tax and benefit incentives to make work financially worthwhile to single parents and poor families (for instance, through the working families tax credit). Investment was encouraged through the establishment of regional development agencies (with limited budgets, however) and, more controversially for Labour Party members and the trade unions, enthusiastic encouragement of the private finance initiative (PFI) developed under the previous government. A major attraction was that the use of PFIs enabled substantial additional much-needed investment in the public services without increasing public sector borrowing. Critics argued that PFIs were more expensive than traditional public borrowing to finance investment in new hospitals, schools and prisons (see Chapter 21).

One very important issue was, however, ducked. All major parties had pledged a referendum before any final decision was taken on whether Britain should join the single European currency, for which plans were far advanced when Labour came to power. In the 1970s and early 1980s the Conservatives had been much more pro-Europe than Labour. By 1997 the position was substantially reversed, and the Conservatives were more Euro-sceptic (see Chapter 15). The new government was more favourable to the single currency than its predecessor, but there were reservations over its possible implications for the British economy, and political doubts over whether a referendum was winnable (see Box 20.4).

Box 20.4

Labour and the euro

From January 1999 11 members of the EU, but not including Britain, fixed their national currencies against the euro. These 11 were later joined by Greece, adjudged to meet the criteria for membership. From January 2002 the first euro notes and coins started replacing national currencies in these 12 countries. A combined total of 290 million people inhabited 'Euroland' using the new single currency. Blair seemed keen that Britain should join. Brown was more cautious, supporting entry only if five economic tests could be met (see Box 15.3). The Treasury has responsibility for assessing whether the tests have been passed. However, the main problem was perhaps always political: winning a referendum in the face of public opinion that remained hostile to the euro.

The growth of public spending: prudence abandoned?

Towards the end of Labour's first term the self-imposed shackles on public spending were partially removed, and substantial new money was made available for public services, particularly health and education. In Labour's second term, following the election victory of 2001, spending on public services was increased still further, particularly in the 2002 budget. Some argued that Brown was abandoning prudence and that Labour was returning to its traditional 'tax and spend' policies. Increased spending was achieved partly through economic growth (resulting in a higher tax take) and expectation of further growth, although some extra revenue was raised through 'stealth taxes' (taxes with a less immediately visible impact on most people). Thus while the standard of rate of income tax was actually reduced, along with some business taxes, national insurance contributions and indirect taxes were increased. Yet although the Conservative opposition attacked the increases in 'stealth taxes', they promised to match Labour's increased spending on health and education. By the time of the 2005 election they could only promise minor cuts in taxation, financed largely by claimed 'efficiency savings'. For all the political heat generated by rival claims on taxation and expenditure, some detached observers could detect little difference between the parties. While Labour had earlier been accused of adopting Conservative policies, the Conservatives were increasingly accepting Labour's agenda.

By the end of Labour's second term some admirers were hailing Gordon Brown as Britain's most successful chancellor for a century or more. Through his long period at the Treasury the British economy experienced low inflation, low interest rates, relatively high employment and continuous economic growth higher than most of Britain's major competitors, a combination many previous chancellors of any party would have died for. Moreover, Brown had also appealed to Labour and progressive opinion by achieving some modest redistribution to benefit poor families and mothers, and by taking a lead in cancelling third-world debt and supporting international trade and development. Labour's record on the economy was central to the party's 2005 election campaign, and perhaps the main reason why the party secured another fairly comfortable (although much reduced) majority, and a third term.

The contrast with previous Labour governments is marked. Without Brown, and the successful economic record over which he had presided, Labour would have lost in 2005, at least according to many commentators. Brown's position in the Labour government has become unassailable. He was virtually anointed as Blair's successor, a change his numerous supporters wanted to see earlier rather than later. Even before any formal transfer of authority, he appeared to many observers to be at least co-equal with Blair in the government, and increasingly perhaps, the power behind the throne.

Yet Brown has his critics. Ken Clarke, his Conservative predecessor at the Treasury, has claimed that Brown's 'success' is attributable largely to the favourable economic conditions he inherited, an inheritance that Clarke alleges Brown largely wasted. 'I left Gordon Brown a strong economy. He squandered it' (*Guardian*, 26 April 2005). Business interests have become increasingly critical of the rise in public spending and the economic consequences in terms of higher taxation. Moreover, Brown has not managed to halt, let alone reverse, the decline in manufacturing industry. Pro-Europeans have blamed Brown for preventing any moves towards British membership of the European single currency. Greens have deplored his uncritical pursuit of economic growth, his concessions to the road lobby on fuel taxes, and his refusal to make the aircraft industry bear the full cost of the energy it consumes and the damage it causes to the environment (see Chapter 25). Some left-of-centre critics have argued that he has not significantly increased equality in general, and has only tinkered with the substantial inequality among pensioners. The growing pensions crisis has yet to be addressed (see Chapter 22).

A more immediate concern is the alleged 'black hole' in Britain's public finances. Many independent critics suggest that Brown's economic forecasts are over-optimistic, and that he will have to increase taxation (or conceivably cut spending) if he is to maintain his 'golden rule' of balancing taxation and expenditure over the economic cycle and only borrowing to fund new investment. In September 2005 Brown conceded that his growth forecasts had been over-optimistic, with damaging implications for tax revenue. Some fear that Britain's apparent economic success is based on a long consumer boom that may be coming to an end.

Overall, it is too early to provide a definitive assessment of Brown's handling of the economy. Budgets that are praised at the time are often subsequently criticised in the light of subsequent developments. Chancellors who win high marks in office may see their reputations tumble later. It has been said that there are only two kinds of chancellor – those who fail and those who get out in time. It remains to be seen whether Gordon Brown will upset this cynical judgment. It could be ten or 20 years, or perhaps more, before it is possible to pass a reasoned verdict on Labour's economic record (see Box 20.5).

■ Britain's open economy

While Brown has claimed to have ended 'boom and bust', the British economy cannot escape the effects of the global economic cycle which plainly still exists. Moreover, it is questionable how far many of the old problems in the British economy have been addressed. There is still a balance of payments problem resulting from Britain's heavy dependence on imports. There remain a lack of skills and lack of investment in manufacturing industry and a persistent productivity gap with Britain's main competitors.

Over and above the short-term performance of particular governments and chancellors there are broader questions about the British economy and its relationship with the world economy, which affect any British government. Substantial increases in the price of oil in 2005, reflecting

Box 20.5

Academic controversy: depoliticising economic policy?

Some commentators claim that economic policy has been substantially 'depoliticised', partly as the consequence of globalisation, but partly as a result of Brown's own economic management – the transfer of decisions on interest rates to the Bank of England, and his 'rule-governed' approach to public finance (Grant 2002, and in Dunleavy *et al.* 2003). Others argue that Brown had effectively converted the Treasury from a ministry of finance into more of a department of economic affairs. Thus the reach of the Treasury has grown to include welfare policy, industrial policy, training and investment, and international trade and development. Much of this has involved proactive intervention rather than depoliticisation. He has ambitiously sought to address long-standing weaknesses in both the private and public sectors of the economy. In terms of ideology, Brown has combined a (Thatcherite or New Labour) emphasis on markets, deregulation and public–private partnerships with a more traditional Labour commitment to public services, fairness and social justice, both at home and abroad. He is thus 'hard to place' on any conventional left–right political spectrum (Coates 2005: 56–61).

increased demand and shortages in supply (as a result of both natural disasters and the continuing chaos in Iraq) have increased inflationary pressures, added to the costs of industry and dented consumer confidence. This illustrates the vulnerability of the British economy to external developments. A prolonged downturn in the global economy would inevitably impact on Britain, reduce prospects for exports and growth, and result in reduced tax revenue.

Although the City of London remains one of the world's most important banking and finance centres, the health of Britain's economy depends in large part on attracting inward investment from large overseas companies and transnationals. Large and frequent capital flows, along with the internationalisation of credit, make it increasingly difficult for national governments to control aspects of economic policy making. For example, globalisation:

> makes it more difficult for governments and central banks to clearly identify, let alone control, the domestic money supply. These developments transform the capacity of governments to control effectively the money supply and interest rates, as well as the impact of both on output and inflation.
>
> (Held *et al.* 1999: 229)

Many of Britain's biggest industries, including some recently privatised public utilities, are foreign owned. Many established British companies have moved their manufacturing to lower-wage economies in the developing world. Taking all these factors into account, Andrew Baker observed that 'Britain is now more heavily integrated into a global circuit of capital than any other country in the world' (Baker, in Stubbs and Underhill 2000: 364). Furthermore, other policies of liberalising and deregulating initiated by the Thatcher governments and continued by their successors have resulted in complex changes to the political economy. 'Not only is the state less involved in the economy and the provision and distribution of material resources, the British economy is also increasingly internationalised' (ibid: 365). In other words, seemingly domestic policies such as the privatisation of public sector assets deepen globalisation 'since they involve the increasing interweaving of the domestic economy and the global economy' (Cerny 1996: 134).

The so-called 'Washington consensus' has been constructed around the needs of international capital: free markets, low inflation, prudent government finances resulting in balanced budgets, and a preference for distancing economic policy making from electoral pressures. The decision to give the Bank of England autonomy on deciding base rates, and the move to balanced budgets, reflected such needs. The degree to which the British economy is absorbed into an extensive global economy also presents a potential barrier to Britain's entry to the euro, for the economies of 'Euroland' are far less integrated into the global economy than is Britain's. Where a 'one size fits all' interest rate might arguably work for the relatively insulated economies of France, Germany and other European states, it exposes Britain's economy to wider fluctuations, since the health of Britain's economy is more dependent on global trends.

Summary

- The economic policies of successive governments in the post-war period have had to tackle deep-seated problems in a British economy that has suffered relative decline.
- Although both the Thatcher governments and more recently the Blair government have been credited with halting and reversing Britain's relative economic decline, it is still too early to tell whether improvements will prove more than transitory.
- The Treasury and the Chancellor of the Exchequer remain at the heart of British economic policy making, but this is increasingly constrained by domestic, European and global pressures.
- The main tools of economic management are direct intervention, fiscal policy and monetary policy. The balance between them has changed over the years, with less direct intervention, less reliance on fiscal policy to manage the economy, and rather more emphasis on monetary policy, although this has become more depoliticised through the transfer of decisions on interest rates to the Bank of England.
- Under both Conservative governments after 1979 and New Labour there has been increased emphasis on markets, competition and choice in the public sector, through contracting out, internal markets and the private finance initiative.
- New Labour's economic policy was characterised initially by prudence and a restraint on public spending and taxation, and subsequently by substantial increased spending and investment particularly on health and education, financed from economic growth and 'stealth taxes'.
- New Labour has succeeded in achieving low inflation, low interest rates, relatively high employment and steady growth, although it is not yet clear how far deep-seated problems in the British economy (under-investment, poor training, low productivity) have been addressed successfully.
- Britain's open economy remains substantially dependent on developments in the global economy, so there are inevitably limits on what any British government can achieve through its management of domestic policy.

Questions for discussion

- Why has the British economy suffered relative decline? What are the enduring problems of the British economy?
- Who 'calls the shots' on decisions over the British economy?
- Why has Labour abandoned nationalisation?
- Why has Keynesian demand management become less fashionable?
- How far was the monetarism pursued by the Thatcher government a failure?
- How far and with what success has New Labour embraced markets, competition and choice?
- Has Labour succeeded in ending 'boom and bust', and, if so, how?
- Are there any significant differences in the economic policies of the major British parties today?

Further reading

Grant's *Economic Policy in Britain* (2002) examines economic policy and policy making in the post-war years. The economic management of earlier Labour governments is usefully discussed by Thomas, *Government and the Economy Today* (1992). Gamble's *The Free Economy and the Strong State* (1994) examines the political context of Thatcherism.

There is a useful analysis of economic management of New Labour's first term by Philip Stevens, and a complementary discussion of industry policy by Geoffrey Owen, both in Seldon (2001). Good surveys which also cover some of the second term include that by Wyn Grant, in Dunleavy *et al.* (2003) and Claire Annesley and Andrew Gamble in Ludlam and Smith (2004). Anthony Sampson (2005, ch. 9) includes a perceptive discussion of the Treasury under Labour. Much of David Coates's (2005) book on new Labour involves a simulating analysis of economic policy (see especially ch. 4).

British economic policy within a global context has been usefully and briefly examined by Baker, 'Globalization and the British "residual" state' in Stubbs and Underhill (2000).

Useful official websites on economic policy include the Treasury, www.hm-treasury.gov.uk, Downing Street, www.number-10.gov.uk, the Cabinet Office, www.cabinet-office.gov.uk, and the Bank of England, www.bankofengland.co.uk. Further analysis can be derived from the websites of think-tanks, the financial press, business and trade unions.

Delivering Public Services

Contents

Most people in Britain depend substantially on public services, such as the National Health Service (NHS) and state education, to provide for the needs of themselves and their families. The welfare state requires the delivery of major public services, free at the point of use, and paid for through taxation.

Particularly from the 1970s onwards the cost and efficiency of these public services has been central to political debate in Britain. Conservative governments from 1979 to 1997 sought to improve the efficiency of public services by exposing them to increased competition and market forces. Labour governments since 1997 have continued to reform the management of public services, while increasing substantially spending on health and education in particular.

How far has this extra cash, paid for by taxpayers, led to real improvements in service delivery? In an attempt to demonstrate real progress Labour has imposed tough performance targets, and compared the records of the country's schools, hospitals and social services in comprehensive league tables, designed to improve public accountability and performance. Those that succeed are held up as examples or 'beacons' for others to imitate, while 'failures' are named and shamed. New priorities, performance indicators and targets are determined to guide each service towards achieving greater quality in delivery. The targets and league tables have become politically controversial. Some argue that the whole process involves increased central control and diminished discretion for local areas and front-line workers. Others suggest that targets can distort priorities and provide perverse incentives that may be counter-productive.

This chapter reviews the debate on the management and reform of public services, with particular reference to health and education.

The welfare state: consensus and controversy

The welfare state was very much part of the post-war consensus (see Chapter 2). Some of its foundations were laid by the coalition wartime government (1942 Beveridge Report, 1944 Education Act, family allowances), although the post-war Labour government was responsible for the establishment of the NHS and the implementation of education and welfare reforms. The cost of extending public services was under-estimated. For example, it was assumed that NHS costs would fall in the long run as a consequence of the nation's improved health, after an initial backlog of untreated conditions had been cleared. In reality an ageing population (in part the consequence of improved health care) coupled with medical advances and rising public expectations increased demand for health services. Demographic change fuelled an ever-expanding demand for welfare services for the elderly. While school-age children were a declining proportion of the population, increased demand for nursery education, post-16 and (particularly) higher education led to increases in education spending.

As the rising cost of public services became increasingly burdensome to taxpayers, it was also questioned whether particular services were really delivering the anticipated benefits. In the 1960s and early 1970s problems such as child poverty, inner city deprivation, homelessness and failing schools indicated that the welfare state was not providing effective security 'from the cradle to the grave'. Some critics went on to claim that welfare provision actually made the problem worse, by encouraging a 'culture of dependency' and stifling initiative. Neo-liberal economists argued services free at the point of use were bound to stimulate an excess of demand, while what they termed 'bureaucratic over-supply' was in the interests of pay and careers of public service workers. Thus an alliance of welfare-dependent service users and public service professionals would provoke an ever-expanding growth of public spending and taxation.

Conservative reforms to public services 1979–97

The Conservative response was to restructure rather than abolish the welfare state. Some public services (notably public housing) were cut. The management of others was reformed through the introduction of more competition and increased private provision. Thus the provision of residential care for the elderly was substantially privatised, with local authorities providing regulation and much of the funding. Ancillary services in health and education (such as cleaning, catering, laundry and ground maintenance) were subjected to compulsory competitive tendering (CCT), leading to increased private-sector provision, at lower cost, but with poorer conditions of service for the workers involved (see Chapter 17). For core teaching and medical services, 'internal markets' or 'quasi-markets' were introduced to provide more consumer choice (in theory at least), and promote more efficiency and drive down costs through the stimulus of competition between rival contractors or providers. This involved a new and more private-sector approach to the management of public services, termed the 'new public management' (see Chapter 12 and Box 12.4) in place of traditional public administration (see Table 21.1).

Market reforms reduced some costs and improved efficiency. However, competition between service providers inevitably also involved some reduction in effective cooperation. Moreover, the introduction of financial costs and benefit calculations by accountants and business managers into decisions on health care and education conflicted with the notion of the provision of public services on the basis of need, almost irrespective of cost, particularly in the health service. While it could be argued that escalating demands

Table 21.1 Contrasting administrative cultures

Traditional public administration	New public management
Informed by a 'public service ethos'	Informed by private sector management principles
Services delivered according to written rules, minimum managerial discretion	Services delivered more flexibly with more managerial autonomy
All citizens in the same circumstances receive the same service – equity and uniformity	Services tailored to the requirements of consumers – variations in services
Service delivery audited to ensure strict legality – the spending of money as authorised	Service delivery audited to measure economy, efficiency and effectiveness (the 3 'E's)

on public services compel some form of rationing in the public sector, doctors and teachers feared their professional judgement was eroded by such financial decision making. Thus in the NHS patients might not be given the best treatment where there were cheaper if less effective alternatives, while the elderly, with low life expectancy, might find they could not receive certain forms of treatment at all.

The overall cost of the NHS and spending on education per pupil continued to rise, although at a slower rate. Margaret Thatcher famously declared the NHS was safe in her hands. Her successor, John Major, promoted more competition within public services, but also introduced the Citizen's Charter and specific charters for particular services which published standards for provision and clear procedures for complainants to secure remedies where promised performance fell short. More positively, Charter Mark awards were given for those demonstrating 'excellence and innovation in delivering services in line with Charter principles' (Chandler 1996: 4).

Labour and the public services: a third way?

The Labour Party has long seen itself as the creator and champion of the welfare state and public service provision. Health and education in particular were very much Labour issues, and a source of support for the party. They were signalled as priorities for the new government in 1997. Yet it was always going to be difficult for Labour to satisfy the hopes and demands of voters, taxpayers, service users and particularly public service workers. Their unions looked to Labour to reverse the market-oriented reforms introduced by the Conservatives and substantially to improve public service pay and conditions. Labour's opponents had long criticised the party for extravagant 'tax and spend' policies, and for a readiness to make damaging concessions to pressure from their public-service union allies. Labour needed to rebut such criticisms, deliver improved public services without a substantial hike in taxation to satisfy its new middle-class voters, while keeping its core supporters reasonably happy. In practice, New Labour has combined the provision of substantial additional resources for public services with maintaining much of the thrust of Conservative management reforms.

The language of a 'third way' (see Chapter 6) has been used less of late, but around the time that Labour came to power in 1997 it was used extensively, and applied particularly to the management of public services, most notably health. Thus Labour's white paper *The New NHS* (Department of Health 1997) declared, 'There will be no return to the old centralised command and control system of the 1970s .... But nor will there be continuation of the divisive internal markets of the 1990s.' After rejecting both old Labour and New Right approaches to managing health, New Labour promised a 'third way of running the NHS based on partnership and driven by performance' (Department of Health 1997).The new buzzwords were partnership, cooperation and networks, implying collaboration rather than competition. The Labour government wanted to maintain elements of competition between providers both as a spur to efficiency, and to provide more choice for consumers.

Thus although Labour claimed that it had scrapped the Conservatives' internal market in the health service, this was 'more superseded than abolished' (Denham, in Dunleavy 2003: 288). The hospital trusts established by the Conservative government continued, and subsequently the best performers were allowed to apply for foundation hospital status (see below). The Conservatives had also encouraged groups of doctors in general practice to apply for fundholder status, to control their own budgets. Labour technically abolished GP fundholders, but effectively made all GPs and other 'primary care' health workers (such as community nurses, midwives and chiropodists) join new primary care trusts (PCTs) with control of their own budgets as both suppliers and purchasers of health care. These PCTs contract with hospitals of their choice for the supply of further health care, although some work previously performed in hospitals, including some simple operations, can now be performed in PCT clinics. A new central body, the National Institute for Clinical Excellence (NICE), was established to advise on common standards of health treatment and best medical practice. Another body, the Commission for Health Improvement, advises on the quality of local services. These new arrangements were designed to reduce some of the differences and inequalities in health care provision, although inevitably they also reduced somewhat the autonomy of the medical profession.

Some observers now detect very little difference between the parties over the management of Britain's public services. Thus the Conservative opposition has pledged itself to maintain Labour's spending plans on health and education. While there are undoubtedly some Conservatives who would like to cut public spending much more drastically, so as to facilitate significant tax cuts, this is far from being current party policy. Indeed one MP who suggested to a private meeting that a Conservative government might be able to find more cuts than the party had indicated was promptly disowned by Michael Howard and prevented from standing as a Conservative in the 2005 election. If Labour has accepted some of the policies of its Conservative predecessors, more recently the Conservatives have felt obliged to follow Labour's public spending agenda.

Partnership with the private sector

It was over the delivery of public services that New Labour parted company from its union allies and 'old Labour' critics, for whom public services have to be delivered by the public sector. For New Labour (including Brown as well as Blair), 'a sharp distinction is drawn between how services are funded and how they are delivered' (Denham, in Dunleavy *et al.* 2003: 282). While still committed to state funding of public services, delivered free at the point of use, the government also sought more private-sector involvement in the delivery of public services, breaking up the old public-sector monopoly. It particularly sought funding from the private sector through the private finance initiative (PFI) for a massive programme of public sector investment to remedy decades of underinvestment (see below).

In part this was simple pragmatism – 'what matters is what works'. If there was unsatisfied demand for health services – for example for the removal of cataracts from eyes or for hip replacement – and this demand could not be met within the public sector, it made sense to buy in resources from the private sector to meet demand and reduce waiting times. NHS patients want free and effective treatment as soon as possible, and it hardly matters to them who provides it. Much the same goes for the provision of state education. School pupils and their parents want good facilities and good teaching, without having to pay for private education, but precisely how this is provided is a secondary consideration. From New Labour's ideological perspective, private sector involvement in the delivery of public services stimulated competition and choice, but also exemplified the principle of partnership between the public and private sectors.

To critics, private-sector involvement in the provision of state services is a Trojan horse, threatening the future of the welfare state through the creation of a two-tier system. Public service providers fear that the private sector will 'cream off' the most potentially profitable parts of the system, leaving them with the most difficult and expensive patients and consumers. Thus the private sector will perform routine uncomplicated surgery, leaving NHS staff and facilities to cope with the more problematic cases, incidentally involving a much lower potential 'success rate'. Similarly, it was feared the new city academies would not take their share of pupils with special needs or with marked behaviour problems, who would be left in 'bog-standard comprehensives'. Those who defend Labour's reforms point out there has always been a 'two-tier' or indeed a 'multi-tier' NHS and state education system, with marked differences in performance between schools and health treatments across the country, the quality of service depending on a 'postcode lottery'. Additional resources, wherever they come from, public, private or voluntary sector, can only raise standards of provision.

Public services free at the point of use, paid for by taxpayers, inevitably involve some elements of redistribution, a point much emphasised by past Labour governments and both socialist and social democratic thinkers. New Labour has rather played down the role of public services in redistribution (see Chapter 22), partly perhaps to satisfy middle-class supporters that it is delivering value for taxpayers' money. Some of the middle classes had already deserted state education and the NHS for the private sector. If this flight continued, middle-class voters would no longer have a vested interest in improvements in the NHS or state education, and would be less prepared to pay a rising tax bill for their provision. As a result these could become underfunded rump services for the poorer classes rather than genuine national services. Thus improved services with more flexibility and choice to meet the demands of discriminating users who might otherwise vote with their feet were a necessity for Labour.

Spending on public services

Initially there was not even much extra money for public services. Labour's first priority was to establish its credentials for sound management of the national economy, by honouring its commitments not to raise personal taxation and to keep within Conservative spending limits for the first two years (see Chapter 20). The government rather exaggerated the relatively small increases in health and education spending it did manage to introduce, and some over-claiming and double-counting unfortunately contributed to a climate of media and public scepticism when very substantial additional sums were later promised and delivered.

There can indeed be no doubt that the Labour government did eventually make available extensive new money for public services, particularly health and education. In 2004 Gordon Brown claimed, 'Over the whole ten year period to 2008 … overall expenditure on education will have risen in real terms by an average of 5.2% a year, transport by 5% a year and health by 6.% a year' (statement to Commons, 12 July 2004, quoted in Coates 2005: 65). In health it was necessary to make up for decades of under-funding and under-investment, to the extent that Britain's health expenditure was well below the European average. Blair pledged to raise health spending from 6.8 per cent of GDP to the EU average (then 8 per cent) by 2006. This has been reached, and Gordon Brown's three-year spending plan for 2005 involved a further rise to 9 per cent of GDP. It does not sound much, but the sums involved were huge. Indeed there was some doubt that the additional money could be spent effectively (Toynbee and Walker 2005: 15).

Targets and league tables

Increased spending simply involves additional inputs into a service. It does not guarantee a commensurate improvement in outputs and outcomes, in service quality. Indeed, critics of high public spending had long argued that problems cannot be solved simply by 'throwing money at them'. Thus it was important and politically necessary for the government to be able to demonstrate that the additional money raised from taxpayers involved real improvements in public services, rather than being simply squandered in additional waste and bureaucracy. This meant that the government had to publish clear targets, and measures for achieving those targets. Moreover, in so far as the government sought to widen patient and parent choice, it was important to provide more facts about hospitals and schools to enable service users to make an informed choice. Thus 'league tables' of performance against various criteria were published. Those hospitals that met government targets were given star ratings, and those that did not were 'named and shamed'.

There can be little doubt that some clear targets were necessary and that improved audit of performance was essential. Critics, however, argued that there were far too many targets. The government sometimes appeared to be bent on 'micro-managing' detailed aspects of service provision better left to the discretion of front-line staff. Moreover, too much emphasis on meeting government targets could be dysfunctional, involving disproportionate energies devoted to satisfying quantifiable targets at the cost of the quality of service provision. Some measures were misleading and unfair, it was suggested. Some hospitals appeared to have poorer success rates in surgical operations because they were treating patients with more serious and difficult conditions. Some schools had poorer exam results because their pupils came from more disadvantaged backgrounds, with fewer skills on entry. It was thus necessary to measure instead the 'added value' that schools had provided to their pupil intake. To an extent the government tried to respond to some of these criticisms by providing more sophisticated measures of performance, and attempts were made to provide measures for 'added value' in school league tables.

For public-sector managers and staff the stakes could be very high indeed. Failure to reach government targets and performance indicators could lead to the sack for individuals deemed responsible, and sometimes even for the takeover or closure of failing institutions. By contrast, success might be rewarded not only with additional resources for the institution, but also with more discretion over their use. Thus institutions could 'earn autonomy' by their own successful performance. Yet all this has increased the strains and pressures on public-sector staff.

Control and autonomy

There is some tension at the heart of Labour's management of the public services. On the one hand the government genuinely believes its own rhetoric about the need for greater flexibility, choice and the delegation of more responsibility and discretion to institutions and front-line staff. On the other hand it is politically essential for it to be able to demonstrate successful service delivery and year-on-year improvements in performance, which means it cannot afford to give up detailed regulation and control.

Delegation of real responsibility and discretion to front-line staff is politically appealing (see Box 21.1). Doctors, nurses and teachers command more respect and trust than politicians, civil servants and 'faceless' bureaucrats. Yet it is not that simple. There are conflicts of interest within any organisation or service. The interests of service providers do not necessarily coincide with those of consumers. Teachers do not necessarily have the same priorities as pupils or their parents. Various specialists and professionals in the NHS have their own interests to advance and defend. More money for surgery may mean less for geriatric care. Hospitals may be effectively competing for resources not only with each other but with PCTs and health care in the community. Consultants, general practitioners, nurses and auxiliary medical services all have their own concerns, interests and priorities, and these may conflict. Accountants tend to be unpopular with medical and educational professionals who resent any interference with their clinical autonomy or professional judgement, yet financial considerations can not be taken out of educational or medical decision making. Politicians are even less

Box 21.1

'Bringing back matron'

'I mean, how hard is it to keep a hospital clean?' asked the Conservatives in the 2005 General Election campaign, responding to public concerns over hospital-acquired infections, particularly from the MRSA 'super-bug', widely blamed on poor hygiene and inadequate cleaning. Michael Howard's Conservatives claimed the NHS was 'too impersonal, too inflexible, too centralised and too bureaucratic to respond to the needs of patients'. Instead, 'We should trust local professionals – doctors and nurses'. Dirty hospitals, it was suggested, were the indirect consequence of centrally set targets for the NHS, which the Conservatives would abolish. Staff did not dare close wards because they would be unable to reach government targets. The Conservatives promised, 'We will bring back matron, who will have the power to close wards for cleaning' (Conservative Election Manifesto 2005). Labour, however, claimed it had 'already reintroduced hospital matrons and given them unprecedented powers to deal with cleanliness and infections in their wards' (Labour Party Manifesto 2005). Thus 'bringing back matron' had bipartisan support.

One problem with this appealing solution is that matron normally has no direct responsibility for cleaning staff. The Conservatives compelled the contracting out of 'ancillary' services such as hospital cleaning from 1983. More recently, under the terms of PFI schemes favoured by Labour for financing, building and maintaining new hospitals, cleaning is part of building maintenance. Either way, most cleaning staff are employed by private companies, not the NHS. As cleanliness is a health issue, with damaging potential consequences for hospital hygiene, it may make sense to bring cleaning staff under a ward matron's overall control. However, this could require a change in the law and the abolition of the internal market for ancillary health services that the Conservatives established, as well as the redrafting of thousands of existing cleaning contracts. Even if this were done and over-zealous matrons subsequently closed wards up and down the country, leading to cancelled operations and the premature discharge of thousands of patients, the public would no doubt demand immediate government intervention to deal with the new crisis.

popular, particularly when they seem to be 'interfering' with decisions that should be left to 'front-line staff', but if they do not take action in response to public concerns they will 'carry the can' for perceived failures. Thus politicians are damned if they intervene, and are also damned when they do not.

Labour has developed the idea of 'earned autonomy' through the introduction of new 'foundation hospitals' for successful 'three-star' hospital trusts. Foundation hospitals will be freed from detailed control by the Department of Health, and will be able to own and manage their own assets, and raise private funds for investment purposes (Coates 2005: 125). In education there are similar proposals to devolve more power to successful schools, particularly for 'beacon schools' and the new private-sector-backed city academies (Coates 2005: 136).

Box 21.2

Some major PFI contracts in health and education

Health
University College London Hospitals £404 million
Edinburgh Royal Infirmary £180 million
Norfolk and Norwich NHS Trust £158 million

Education
Stoke on Trent LEA £93 million
Liverpool City Council £72 million
London Borough of Haringey £62 million

Partnership in investment in the public services: the private finance initiative

Private and voluntary sector involvement in the delivery of health and education services has been encouraged by Labour. However, the private sector contribution to the day-to-day delivery of state education and the NHS remains essentially peripheral. The bulk of current spending on both services is still financed out of taxation, and services remain free at the point of use (with a few long-standing exceptions, such as prescription charges and the more recent innovation of tuition fees for higher education). The private sector has become much more heavily involved in new capital investment in public services, particularly through the PFI launched by a Conservative chancellor, Norman Lamont, but eagerly adopted by Blair's Labour government (see also Chapter 18).

It is important not to exaggerate the novelty of private-sector involvement in public-sector building projects. Private architects and private building firms have long designed and constructed new hospitals and schools. Yet in the past, while the private sector built new schools, hospitals and prisons, it was the public sector that had to raise the loans (for example through the issue of government bonds) and the public sector that owned and maintained the new buildings once they were completed. Today, hospitals and schools built under the PFI involve a private consortium raising capital, designing and constructing the buildings, and commonly subsequently maintaining them. The public sector does not have to provide finance up front, and leases the buildings for a period of years (commonly 25 or 30 years), after which ownership is transferred to it.

The big attraction for the government was that PFIs allowed a massive and much-needed increase in public sector investment without this showing as part of public borrowing. It was also argued that the private sector brought new expertise to public-sector investment, with potential efficiency savings, and the transfer of risk to the private sector. However, critics argued that PFIs were in the long run more expensive than traditional public-sector finance of capital investment, that risk was not transferred, as schemes were effectively underwritten by government, and that many PFI schemes were badly designed and did not provide value for money. The jury is still out. A full assessment of costs and benefits may not be available until the terms of leases expire and ownership is transferred. In the meantime, nearly all new hospitals and many schools have been financed and built through PFIs.

Has Labour delivered?

As we have seen the Labour government has committed substantial extra resources to public services. There is no doubt that considerably more money has been spent on health, education and public services generally, whether it is measured in terms of increases in year-on-year total expenditure in real terms, or as a proportion of national income, or spending per head of population or service users. This money has not simply been swallowed up by increasing bureaucracy, as opposition politicians have sometimes alleged. Thus by 2005 there were already 27,000 more doctors in post or in training, 79,000 new nurses, 28,000 more teachers and 105,000 more teaching support staff. There has also been substantial additional investment in new buildings and equipment.

However, all these statistics, impressive though they appear, are only measures of the inputs into public services, not the outputs in terms of performance and service quality, nor outcomes in terms of a healthier and better-educated people. Measures of such outputs and outcomes are notoriously more difficult. Yet it is politically crucial for a government spending substantially more of taxpayers' money on public services to be able to demonstrate that these have led to measurable improvements in service quality. Hence much of the obsession with targets and league tables.

Thus in the health service a major aim has been reducing waiting times, from ordinary GP appointments to the diagnosis and treatment of serious medical conditions, sometimes requiring major operations. Waiting times are not a peripheral concern, but central to the NHS. Delays in seeing GPs and consultants prolong patient anxieties and often also lead to real pain and suffering which could be alleviated by earlier treatment. In some circumstances delays may also involve a significant reduction in the chances of a full recovery, or even survival. Yet resource constraints in the past have compelled rationing by queuing. It is to escape queues and avoidable suffering in the NHS that many who can afford to pay have 'gone private'. Sometimes a consultant has been able to offer an immediate operation for a patient prepared to pay, compared with a wait of many months or years for NHS treatment. Labour thus set new ambitious targets for reducing waiting times. Labour promised to cut waiting times for an operation from an 18-month maximum under the previous government to initially six months, already substantially met, and to 18 weeks from the first GP referral to the day of operation by 2008 (Toynbee and Walker 2005:12–13, 45–6). There were also targets for reducing waiting times for primary care, with access to a nurse promised within 24 hours and a GP in 48 hours. Such targets can have unintended consequences. The prime minister was startled to discover, in the 2005 election campaign, that some patients were being denied preferred later appointments because this would involve breaching the 48-hour pledge.

In education there has been a substantial increase in the availability of nursery schools, a major benefit for all parents in paid work. Infant school classes above 30 have been abolished. There were initial marked improvements in literacy and numeracy by age 11. By 2000 75 per cent of all pupils reached level 4 or above in Key Stage 2 tests in English compared with 57 per cent in 1996, and 72 per cent reached level 4 or above in mathematics, compared to 54 per cent in 1996. However ambitious targets to increase performance to 85 per cent were missed by a wide margin. GSE and A level results showed steady incremental improvements, although there was some media scepticism over standards.

Labour has sought improvements in skills for work through its learning and skills councils (replacing the old training and enterprise councils), and has put money into IT courses and new apprenticeship schemes, although further education and training remains 'the Cinderella in Labour's education kitchen' (Toynbee and Walker 2005: 118–20). Numbers in higher education continued to rise, and the government has set a target that half the age group should receive a university education by 2010. Labour sought not only to get more young people into higher education, but to raise particularly the number going to university from manual working-class families. However, there was persistent evidence of major class-based differences in access to higher education. Thus 'the top social class sent 80 per cent of its sons and daughters to university while the bottom sent only 7 per cent' (Toynbee and Walker 2005: 122).

Overall, Labour has delivered much of what it has promised on health and education. It has put significantly more money into these public services. This money has been translated into more staff, better buildings and equipment. It has produced some real improvements in performance, although significant problems remain in both health and education. In the health service,

Box 21.3

Financing higher education: the row over top-up fees

Labour's changes to the finance of higher education have proved hugely controversial. In their 2001 election manifesto the party declared, 'We will not introduce top-up fees and have legislated to prevent them'. On this issue the government did a U-turn, legislating to introduce top-up fees. In January 2004 the government's majority was reduced to just five on the issue. In May 2005 the unpopularity of top-up fees with students was reflected in substantial anti-Labour swings in parliamentary constituencies with a large student population.

The problem for the government is that higher education has continued to expand over decades, while spending on higher education has not grown commensurably. Thus funding per student has decreased significantly and university finance has been in crisis. It seemed unfair to expect taxpayers, including those from the manual working class, of whose children relatively few benefited from university education, to bear the escalating costs.

Labour initially introduced flat-rate tuition fees, covering only a small proportion of course costs, and abolished maintenance grants, leading to an accumulation of student debt. Elite universities, disturbed at their increasing difficulty in competing internationally, wanted to be able to charge more for degrees that enabled their graduates to earn higher salaries. As part of a package of reforms, Labour allowed variable fees, with interest-free loans repayable by students after graduation, and reintroduced non-repayable maintenance grants for students from poorer families. The package was actually more generous for low-income students, and compared favourably with state support for higher education in other countries. Yet the government's U-turn on top-up fees involved reneging on a manifesto pledge, and has caused the government and the party huge political difficulties. There are no easy answers. A graduate tax might be easier to 'sell' but would have similar financial implications ultimately for students.

Student demonstration against top-up fees, January 2004

Photograph: EMPICS.

care of the elderly continues to be the major concern, while the scarcity of NHS dentists is a national scandal. In education a substantial minority of children are under-achieving in schools that are under-performing. Significant numbers of children are still leaving school without useful skills and qualifications. Yet real progress has been made. One indication of the relative success of government policy in health and education has been a halt in the flight of the middle classes from state provision. Fewer now pay for private operations, as they can now obtain them on the NHS for free within a few months. The numbers opting for expensive private education have scarcely increased – only 7.1 per cent of pupils were in private schools in 2004, although the numbers were much higher in some London boroughs (Toynbee and Walker 2005).

Yet the media and the wider public view government claims of significant improvement in health and education with considerable scepticism. This may partly be the government's own fault in over-claiming and double-counting increases in spending in its first years in power.

It may also partly reflect the time it takes for additional resources to show through in terms of performance. New buildings take years to complete; new staff, particularly doctors and consultants, take years to train. Beyond that, individual case histories, however atypical, often have more impact than volumes of statistics, and scandals and scare stories sell more papers than good news. There is some evidence that while most people are happy with their local schools and hospitals, they assume from the media coverage that their own local experience is untypical.

Summary

- A consensus over Britain's welfare state in the post-war decades gave way to increased questioning of the efficiency of public services, and attempts to introduce more competition and private-sector methods into their management.
- New Labour has continued much of the reform process, while increasing substantially spending on public services such as health and education.
- Labour has set numerous targets for public services, and extensively monitored performance, publishing 'league tables' on the record of schools and hospitals and other institutions. Some argue that targets and league tables are dysfunctional and distort priorities.
- There is a continuing tension between the government's own emphasis on decentralisation and delegation and its intervention in specific areas of public service management.
- Although statistics indicate significant improvements in some aspects of health and education, there remains considerable media and public scepticism over government claims of better provision.

Questions for discussion

- How far does Britain still have a welfare state providing security from the cradle to the grave?
- How far are there significant differences between the parties in the delivery and management of public services?
- What are the objections to the proliferation of targets and league tables in health and education?
- Why is it apparently so difficult for governments to devolve the management of services to local communities and front line staff?
- How should higher education be funded?
- Overall, has new Labour delivered improved public services?

Further reading

It is difficult to keep up with this fast-changing subject. For the performance of the Labour government in its first term see the chapters by Glennester (on social policy) and Smithers (on education) in Seldon (2001), and the chapter by McCaig (on education) in Ludlam and Smith (2001). Andrew Denham in Dunleavy *et al.* (2003) has a good review of public services going into Labour's second term. David Coates (2005) provides a critical but balanced assessment of Labour in power, including some very useful analysis of both health and education policies. Toynbee and Walker (2005) have produced an extensive audit of Labour's record up to the 2005 election, with good chapters on health and education, including masses of statistics and useful graphs.

Relevant government websites: the Department of Health, www.doh.gov.uk, the Department for Education and Skills, www.des.gov.uk

Equality and Social Justice

Contents

Inequality in the distribution of income and wealth, it is often assumed, tells us much about the real distribution of power and influence in society. The pursuit of greater equality and social justice has long been the aim of socialists everywhere, as well as the British Labour Party, while Conservatives have generally sought to maintain the established order, and Liberals have championed individual liberty and equality of opportunity rather than outcome. The case for and against some redistribution of income and wealth has thus long been central to ideological debate in Britain (see Chapter 6).

Yet today, the case for greater equality and social justice has largely dropped out of public political discourse. Concerns are expressed instead over the poverty or exclusion of particular sections of the population. Thus Labour has pledged to end child poverty, and tackle pensioner poverty as well as the 'social exclusion' of such groups as the largely unemployed communities on 'sink' housing estates, or disaffected teenagers, or alienated minorities. It is tacitly assumed that these are regrettable exceptions to the general pattern of prosperity, contentment and inclusion.

This chapter explores the extent of poverty and inequality in Britain, the more recent changes that have take place in the distribution of income and wealth, and the impact of government policy, both intended and unintended, on poverty and inequality. Is Britain becoming a more or less equal society? Who are the new poor in Blair's Britain?

Rich Britain: poor Britain

In the 1940s Sir William Beveridge set out a blueprint for the government, which would banish the 'giant evils' of want, disease, squalor, ignorance and idleness from Britain. The purpose of the Beveridge Report was to combat poverty and the social ills that accompanied it. It received all-party support. Yet well over half a century later, and despite the creation of a welfare state, Britain remains a society plagued by social inequalities. Britain has the fourth largest economy in the world and yet some of its people in both town and country live impoverished lives. Even with some of the trappings of affluence, they feel economically, socially and politically excluded from mainstream British society.

Post-war governments of the 1950s, 1960s and 1970s accepted in general terms that a redistribution of resources from the better-off to the poor should be a key principle of social policy. Although governments, and the electorate, accepted that there would inevitably be rich and poor people, it was also accepted that reducing these inequalities was politically and socially beneficial. Taxation was progressive, with the better-off paying much greater percentages of their incomes in tax than the less well-off. Tax revenues were used by governments to provide a 'social wage', including free education, free health care, pensions and subsidised housing for all who needed them, and who would not otherwise have been able to afford them. Thus an intelligent observer like Sir Ivor Jennings reckoned that social divisions were 'tending to disappear through heavy taxation at the one end and high wage rates at the other' (see quotation in Chapter 3). Similarly a social democrat like Anthony Crosland assumed that a progressive tax system that paid for welfare benefits largely drawn by the less well-off would inexorably produce a more equal society. 'One nation' Conservatives like Butler and Macmillan also both expected and accepted this apparent trend towards greater equality.

New Right ideas began to challenge this progressive consensus on the possibility and desirability of greater social and economic equality from the 1970s onwards. The result was that the assumptions shared by earlier Conservative and Labour governments – that poverty was an evil which should be tackled by government – were no longer held with such certainty. Indeed it was argued that the high levels of taxation that were needed to finance the welfare state actually reduced people's incentive to be enterprising and to work hard. Furthermore, it was argued that a high level of welfare had a negative impact on the poor, for it produced a 'dependency culture' which sapped their determination and ability to lead independent lives. Cutting taxes and reducing welfare would, it was argued, increase incentives and release enterprise and energy that would result in the creation of more wealth. The fear of poverty, no longer cushioned by generous welfare benefits, would encourage many poor people to 'get on their bikes' in search of work. Yet even those in poverty who, for whatever reason, could not redirect their lives, would benefit from the 'trickle down' of prosperity from the richest to the poorest. In other words, the New Right argued that the creation of wealth was more socially beneficial than the redistribution of wealth.

Definitions

Poverty: a distinction is commonly made between absolute and relative poverty.

Absolute poverty involves the lack of basic necessities of life: food, clothing, shelter and so on. There are millions of people around the world who experience absolute poverty, but virtually no one does so in advanced western economies like Britain.

Relative poverty rather than absolute poverty exists in Britain. Relative poverty means not being able to afford those things that most people in society take for granted, such as annual holidays. Relative poverty changes over time. In the 1950s most Britons did not own a television, refrigerator or telephone, but were not as a consequence considered poor, although they would be today. In a society where most adults have the use of a car, those who do not feel deprived, and may suffer real disadvantage in communities based around car ownership and use.

Some critics on the right argue that relative poverty is a term invented by the left to describe inequality, which they claim is inevitable and essentially desirable as an incentive to labour and enterprise.

A change in attitudes to economic and social inequality involved changes in public policy and society. Inequalities in income and wealth, which had been declining somewhat in the post-war decades, began to increase again in the 1980s and 1990s. Partly this was the consequence of deliberate changes in the tax and benefit system. There were a shift from direct to indirect taxation and cuts in the higher rates of income tax. At the same time most welfare benefits did not keep pace with rises in wage rates. Many more people, however, were dependent on welfare benefits because of the rise in unemployment. Previously well-paid jobs in mining and manufacturing became more precarious as both international competition and technological change reduced the demand for labour. Miners, print workers, dockers and car workers, part of the old aristocracy of labour, faced an uncertain future. Some of those in the relatively booming service sector prospered and became homeowners and shareowners. The term 'yuppie' ('young urban professional' or 'young upwardly mobile professional') entered the language. The comedian Harry Enfield invented the brash young cockney product of Thatcherism, 'Loadsamoney', with his catch phrase 'Feel my wad', as well as his layabout unemployed feckless counterparts 'the slobs', dramatising perceptions of a widening gulf between the new rich and the new poor (see Box 22.1).

New Labour, equality and social justice

John Smith died before the Commission on Social Justice reported (see Box 22.1), to be succeeded by Tony Blair and 'New Labour'. Some argued that the changes Blair introduced into the party marked a significant shift of emphasis away from the pursuit of greater equality and social justice. Labour's new Clause Four, adopted in 1995 (see Box 6.7) still aspired to create 'a community in which power, wealth and opportunity are in the hands of the many not the few'. Yet the key word here is perhaps 'opportunity'. Coates (2005: 39-40) argues that 'New Labour came to power preferring policies that privileged equality of opportunity over equality of outcome', a criticism also made by some social democrats associated with the old Labour right, like Roy Hattersley. 'Equality of opportunity' was more a slogan of 'One Nation' Conservatism than the old Labour Party. Coates (2005: 198–9) quotes from an interview of Blair in 2001 where Jeremy Paxman asks whether 'it is acceptable for the gap to widen between rich and poor?' Blair replies with an awkward double negative, 'It is not acceptable for poor people not to be given the chances they need in life', but declines to answer the question that Paxman actually asked.

One problem for Blair and the modernisers within the party was that they had concluded that an open commitment to redistribution was a potential vote loser. Some considered that it was shadow chancellor John Smith's very mildly redistributive 'alternative budget' that had cost Labour the election in 1992. Labour could not win by appealing to the have-nots, who were no longer in the majority (and were also less inclined to vote). It had to win over a substantial proportion of 'middle England', who would be frightened off by the prospect of tax rises to help the poor. Yet both Blair and Brown were also convinced by some of the economic arguments of their opponents in favour of free market enterprise. Wealth creation was more important than wealth distribution. Better economic performance would create the resources to do the kind of things Labour traditionally favoured – better public services, and a better life for the most vulnerable in society, including the young and the elderly. Labour governments in the past failed to deliver the economic modernisation and prosperity that was the condition for effective social reform.

Yet this was not so very new. Indeed, New Labour's rhetoric was markedly similar to the classless appeal of an earlier Labour moderniser, Harold Wilson, who also hoped to finance social reform from economic growth (Coates 2005: 30–1). Moreover, as Denham has

Box 22.1

The Commission on Social Justice (1992–4)

In 1992, 50 years after the Beveridge Report, the new leader of the Labour Party, John Smith, who had succeeded Neil Kinnock after Labour's election defeat, set up the Commission on Social Justice to provide an analysis of the problems of contemporary Britain and some policy proposals. It was, of course, a partisan document, yet it provides a well-documented account of inequality and social division in Britain following three terms of Conservative government.

The Commission's report concluded that 'the gap between the earnings of the highest paid and those of the lowest paid is greater than at any time since records were first kept in 1886'. Between 1979 and the early 1990s the share of national income received by the bottom half of the population had dropped from a third to a quarter. The poorest tenth of the population were significantly worse off, while the richest tenth were over 60 per cent better off. One in three children, the Commission estimated, grew up in poverty. Pensioner inequality was rising. Poverty significantly affected life chances and life expectancy. While home ownership had risen to over 70 per cent, higher than in most of Europe, a third of a million people were still registered as homeless, including 150,000 young people, making Britain 'nearly top of the homelessness league' (Commission on Social Justice, 1994, Part 1).

observed (in Dunleavy *et al.* 2003: 285–6), much of New Labour's 'approach to social policy was anticipated by the analysis of the Commission on Social Justice' (1994, ch. 3). This explicitly rejected 'a strategy for social justice based on redistribution of wealth and incomes', involving 'a kinder, poorer Britain'. Instead, it emphasised investment through a market economy, arguing that 'the extension of economic opportunity is not only the source of economic prosperity but also the source of social justice'. The difference between 'old' and 'new' Labour approaches to equality and social justice has been exaggerated, while the actual record of the Blair government might be considered stronger than its predecessors (Fielding 2003, ch. 7).

In place of an overt commitment to a general redistribution of income and wealth in pursuit of social justice, New Labour instead promised to tackle 'social exclusion', and made more specific commitments to reduce 'child poverty' and 'pensioner poverty', while Gordon Brown's budgets involved some limited 'redistribution by stealth'. There were political advantages to explicitly targeting children and the elderly, who appeared 'deserving' and less responsible for their own deprivation. However, helping children out of poverty meant in practice helping their families, including not just the 'hard-working families' favoured by politicians of all parties, but some who might appear less deserving. Brown's targeted tax and welfare reforms were, however, designed to provide positive incentives for work as a way out of poverty and dependence on welfare.

From welfare to work

At the heart of New Labour's thinking is the belief that employment, or paid work, is crucial in combating poverty and social exclusion. 'The best way to tackle poverty is to help people into jobs, real jobs' (Labour Election Manifesto 1997: 15). A key part of Labour's strategy (following US precedents) was to get people off welfare and into work, which involved both the provision of training for skills to improve employability, and tax and welfare changes to make work pay. Gordon Brown's welfare to work programme was initially funded by a £5.2 billion windfall tax on the profits of the privatised utilities. Key elements of Labour's policy included:

- The New Deal, which was allocated £3 billion, initially to get the young unemployed into training or work. The programme was subsequently extended to the long-term unemployed, single parents and the disabled. Behind the carrot of subsidised work experience or training lay the stick of the loss or reduction of benefits, such as the jobseeker's allowance. It is difficult to assess how much of the reduction in unemployment and the rise in paid employment under the Labour government was due specifically to the New Deal, and how much to the general improvement of the economy.
- The government also poured money into adult learning, focused particularly on developing basic literacy and numeracy to help those held back by low skills. The DfeS made lifelong learning a priority, providing subsidies for training courses through individual learning accounts, a programme which proved rather too attractive and open to abuse, involving dubious claims for dubious courses, and was eventually closed down. Another initiative, the University for Industry, is however up and running, with more than half a million learners enrolled (Coates 2005: 100–1).
- The national minimum wage was designed to reduce the extent and impact of low pay, and increase the incentive to work. Although it is fixed at a level substantially below that sought by the Trades Union Congress (TUC), it is reckoned that it has increased the wages of around 1.5 million low-paid workers, the majority of whom are women.
- A national child care strategy was launched in 1997, providing a massive increase in subsidised child care.
- To help further those raising families on low and inadequate pay, Gordon Brown increased child benefit, and then in 1999 introduced a new working families tax credit, guaranteeing a tax-free minimum income, and a children's tax credit (replacing the old married person's

allowance). In 2003 these tax credits were consolidated and replaced by the child's tax credit.

All this has helped erode the 'poverty trap' or 'benefit trap' under which the poor were often better off on benefits than in work (Annesley, in Ludlam and Smith 2001: 209). It also particularly helped women who wanted paid work to enter the labour market. Coates (2005: 76) remarks, 'To an unprecedented degree, Gordon Brown has been a chancellor sensitive to the problems of combining child care and paid work, and to those of raising children on low and inadequate pay'. He was also aware of the problems 'faced by working women in a society that was still deeply patriarchal in its private division of labour'.

Ending child poverty

Child poverty had risen up the policy agenda in the 1960s, when alarm over its extent had led to the founding of the Child Poverty Action Group. Then it was reckoned that some 10 per cent of Britain's children were poor. One response was the introduction of more generous child benefit in 1976, paid to the mother, which consolidated the old family allowance and former child allowances on taxation (the latter largely payable to fathers). Yet increased unemployment drastically reduced family income in some communities in the 1980s, with adverse effects on child welfare. Child poverty was also increased by the growth of one-parent families, nine out of ten of which were headed by women. Absent fathers were often paying little or nothing at all towards the upbringing of their children. A well-intentioned solution to remedy this situation was the introduction of the Child Support Agency, although this, while hugely contentious, largely failed to make an appreciable difference to family income (see Box 22.2). Thus by 1997 the proportion of British children classified as poor by the European Union had trebled. When Labour came to power in 1997 Britain had the highest rates of child poverty among the (then) 15 member states of the European Union.

Many of the measures designed to assist the transition 'from welfare to work' (discussed above) also contributed to tackling child poverty.

Box 22.2

The Child Support Agency

The Child Support Agency (CSA) was set up by the Conservatives with the laudable aim of making absent parents (largely fathers) contribute to the cost of bringing up children. In theory, this should have helped children in the now substantial number of one-parent families (mostly headed by women). In practice, tracing absent fathers and assessing their contributions proved an administrative nightmare. The agency naturally focused on those who were easiest to trace and assess, mainly those already making financial contributions, some of whom were supporting second families. A sense of outrage among some absent fathers at the sums demanded was aggravated where they were denied access to their children, leading to the establishment of the pressure group 'Fathers 4 Justice' which proceeded to use high-profile stunts to obtain media publicity. Labour proved no more successful than its Conservative predecessors in making the Child Support Agency work (Toynbee and Walker 2005: 59–60).

A good proportion of those assisted through incentives in cash and kind had children who benefited from the additional family income and from improved services such as nursery care and homework clubs. According to Toynbee and Walker (2005: 56), Brown's complicated child tax credit schemes were 'the lift carrying a quarter of children out of poverty'. In addition 'baby bonds' were introduced for each newborn child, which might mature into a 'life changing' amount in later adult life, for example helping with education costs or a deposit on a first home. Older school pupils from poorer families could receive cash payments to enable them to remain at school after 16.

Both the chancellor and prime minister are committed to halving child poverty by 2010 and abolishing it by 2020. There is still a long way to go if these ambitious targets are to be reached, but already by 2005, over a million poor children have been taken out of poverty, enabling the UK to rise from fifteenth to eleventh place in the EU child poverty table. Labour's measures to tackle child poverty have drawn substantial approval from both the anti-poverty lobby and other commentators (Toynbee and Walker 2005: 53, Coates 2005: 79).

Pensioner poverty

The government also aims to end pensioner poverty, but no date has been attached to this aspiration, which could be far more difficult to achieve. Earlier retirement coupled with increased longevity has dramatically increased the scale of the problem not just in Britain but in many other western countries. The problem has been considerably aggravated by several additional factors – the long erosion over time of the value of the basic state pension, the more recent move away from private-sector pension schemes linked to final salary, and the collapse of some pension funds on which some people were relying for a comfortable retirement. Most of those who have to rely largely on their own savings to supplement the state pension do not save nearly enough for their old age. For the young it is difficult to imagine being old, let alone planning for it, and there always seem to be more pressing financial demands.

As a consequence, there is marked inequality among pensioners. Some of those who have retired with good inflation-proof occupational pensions enjoy a high standard of active and rewarding life, sometimes including several holidays abroad a year, or a second home in a warmer climate. Others, relying on the state pension topped up by means-tested benefits, experience real poverty in their old age, finding it difficult to meet the costs of housing, heating, food and clothing. If they are too ill or disabled to live on in their own houses, these may have to be sold to meet the high cost of nursing care in residential homes.

The plight of pensioners arouses humanitarian concerns as well as some self-interest, as everyone whose life is not cut short can expect to have to cope with old age, even if it may appear a long way off. Moreover, as the increasing numbers of elderly are more inclined to use their votes than the young, politicians are bound to take some notice of 'grey power'. Apart from that, governments, and particularly chancellors, are inevitably exercised by the huge cost to the Exchequer of pensions, welfare benefits, health and social care for the elderly, and the implications for taxation.

The Labour government was made painfully aware of 'grey power' when Brown put up the basic state pension by just 75p (in line with inflation figures) in 2000. The political backlash obliged rather more generosity in future budgets, so that the basic state pension has increased by 7 per cent in real terms from 2000 to 2004. Yet it is universally recognised that the basic state pension alone remains totally inadequate for survival. Its value has been eroded since the Thatcher government broke the previous link between rises in the state pension and rises in average earnings, and tied it instead to prices. Labour has declined to restore the earnings link. Brown has argued that more can be done for poor pensioners through targeted benefits rather than raising the universal state pension. The pension credit, its value linked with earnings, supplements the state pension for the poorest third of pensioners. Yet the pension credit does not reach all who need it, a familiar problem with selective means-tested benefits.

'Stakeholder pensions', another Labour initiative targeting those in work who are not covered by adequate occupational schemes, has had relatively low take-up among those for whom it was designed. Labour has also given a pensioners a mix of other benefits, including winter fuel payments, free local public transport off-peak, free television licences for the over-75s, and help with council tax bills. All these are useful benefits, but hardly compensate for inadequate pensions.

Labour has done something to alleviate pensioner poverty, but has hardly addressed the

Figure 22.1 Pensioner poverty: huddling for warmth over an electric fire

Photograph: Photofusion.

scale of the problem considered by the Pensions Commission chaired by the former CBI director Adair Turner. There is no easy magic solution. Among the various politically unpalatable options are increasing the age of retirement to 70, abolishing or limiting state pensions for particular categories of the population, such as graduates, and compulsory saving for retirement among those not covered by adequate occupational pensions. The government is hoping to build a political consensus for change, but it seems unlikely that opposition parties would willingly sign up to the tough and almost inevitably unpopular decisions that may be required.

■ Social exclusion

Social exclusion is a rather broad and woolly term. In opposition, Blair declared:

> We have what amounts to a new "underclass", cut off and alienated from society. Part of our job is to ensure that the people frozen out of Tory Britain are brought in from the cold, their talents used, their potential developed.
>
> (quoted in Coates 2005: 143)

In government a Social Exclusion Unit was established in Number Ten, charged with finding ways of bring the excluded into mainstream society. Thus the Exclusion Unit identified 1400 poor housing estates, with high unemployment, poor housing, high mortality and morbidity, low educational performance, excessive under-age pregnancies and high crime rates. Those living in such estates were surrounded by apathy and failure, and cut off from the rising prosperity of communities only a short distance away. Prospects of escape from such blighted areas were poor.

> **Definition**
>
> **Social exclusion** is the experience of people who suffer from a combination of connected problems such as unemployment, poor education and poor skills, low incomes, poor housing in high-crime areas, bad health and family breakdown. Social exclusion includes poverty, but is a broader concept.

The government introduced its 'New Deals for Communities' programme, the latest in a long string of initiatives by successive governments to tackle 'depressed urban areas' or break 'the cycle of deprivation'. Social exclusion was thus a new label for an old and familiar problem. While the Social Exclusion Unit continued to produce useful analysis and reports, it became progressively sidelined, particularly after its transfer to the Office of the Deputy Prime Minister. According to some critics it was never given the powers and resources needed to tackle the scale of the problem.

There were other groups who were apparently excluded from the rising prosperity of mainstream British society, including some of the ethnic minorities. While 20 per cent of the white population was classified as poor, the figure for Pakistanis and Bangladeshis was 69 per cent. Unemployment was significantly higher among all non-whites. There were other telling indications that many among the ethnic minorities were effectively second-class citizens. Thus:

> Three times more Pakistanis and Bangladeshis lived in unfit housing. Black students were three times more likely to be excluded from school. Some 16 per cent of the African Caribbean men were in jail, when they formed only 2 per cent of the population.
>
> (Toynbee and Walker, 2005: 72)

Inequality in British society had a marked gender as well as ethnic dimension. Women still on average had poorer pay, and suffered from lower pensions (although as we have seen, New Labour did give considerable assistance to mothers). The homosexual community was, however, substantially brought in from the cold and given equal rights with heterosexuals. The Civil Partnership Act 2004 gave gay and lesbian couples the same tax and legal rights as married couples.

Over time, however, New Labour's response to the problems of those living in deprived communities became more punitive than supportive, as drugs, drink, crime, vandalism and anti-social behaviour of all kinds were targeted, and the 'work-shy' pressurised into jobs or training. Increasingly many of the people living in run-down neighbourhoods were not seen as victims of deep-seated inequality in British society, and of lack of facilities and opportunities. Instead they were perceived as irresponsible, feckless and sometimes criminal people who failed to take advantage of the assistance given them, and refused to accept responsibility for their own lives and those of their children.

Overall, it did not seem that many of those who felt alienated and excluded from mainstream British society became more socially included. In the 2005 election the poor turnout among working-class communities generally, the disaffected whites who voted for the BNP and the alienated younger Muslims who deserted Labour for Respect or the Liberal Democrats indicated that if anything a sense of social exclusion was on the rise.

A fairer society?

New Labour has made considerable progress in reducing child poverty, has alleviated pensioner poverty somewhat, and grappled rather less successfully with the more amorphous problem of social exclusion. The significant increase in spending on health and education (see Chapter 21) has also brought substantial benefits to the poor. Has Labour overall managed to reverse the increasing gulf in income and wealth between rich and poor and establish a fairer more equal society? The answer to that question is rather more contentious, but it seems that so far at least, New Labour has not significantly reduced the considerable gap between rich and poor. Indeed, the rich continue to grow richer. Thus 'inequality in disposable income (after tax and benefits) appears to have slightly increased since 1997' (IPPR Report 2004, quoted in Coates 2005: 200). Similarly 'the percentage of wealth held by the wealthiest 10% has increased from 47% to 54%' (IPPR press release, quoted in Coates 2005: 201). Top salaries and associated perks continue to rise much faster than average wages, sometimes, it appears, regardless of success or failure.

Some of the poorest have benefited significantly also, particularly single parents and couples in low-paid employment bringing up children. However, not all the poor have gained: 'adults without children who were not in jobs … were left behind', leading to an increase in the number of childless adults below the poverty line from 3.3 million in 1995 to 3.8 million in 2003 (Toynbee and Walker 2005: 67). These of course would be widely regarded (by government, society and the media) as the 'undeserving poor' as opposed to the 'hard-working families' extolled by politicians. Yet they included many whose lives had been blighted by industrial decline, poor environment and prospects.

Summary

- The British welfare state, largely instituted at the end of the Second World War, was supposed to take people out of poverty. Welfare benefits free at the point of use, combined with a progressive system of taxation, were expected to create a more equal society. There was a cross-party consensus supporting the assumption that the government had a responsibility to reduce poverty and inequality.
- This progressive consensus was increasingly challenged by New Right (or neo-liberal) analysis that suggested that welfare benefits encouraged a dependency culture which reduced incentives to work. Government intervention to reduce poverty and inequality harmed initiative and enterprise, and ultimately also harmed the poor it was supposed to help.
- Under Conservative governments after 1979, top-rate taxes were reduced and unemployment increased, leading to a wider inequality in income and wealth.
- New Labour from 1997 has sought to reduce poverty primarily by measures to encourage the transition from welfare to work. It has significantly reduced child poverty through a package of reforms and has introduced some measures to alleviate pensioner poverty. However, it has so far not effectively tackled the growing pensions crisis, and has largely failed to reduce inequality.

Questions for discussion

- How far should it be the business of government to reduce inequality and promote greater social justice?

- Is British society substantially more unequal than that in other leading western countries?
- Why is there so much child poverty in Britain? How has the government sought to tackle it, and how effective have Labour's policies been in reducing child poverty?
- Why is there so much inequality among the elderly? How far has New Labour managed to alleviate pensioner poverty? What is needed to tackle the pensions crisis?
- What is social exclusion and who does it affect? How successfully has Labour managed to promote social inclusion?
- How far is Britain a fairer society than it was?

Further reading

There are some references to inequality in Britain in earlier chapters of this book, including Chapters 1–4. For a lucid analysis of political ideas on the linked concepts of equality, social justice and welfare, see Heywood (2000). For contrasting ideological perspectives on equality and social justice see chapters on mainstream ideologies in Leach (2002) and Heywood (2003). Ellison and Pearson have edited a very useful volume *Developments in British Social Policy* (2003). On New Labour's approach to social justice and redistribution, see chapters by Stephens and Glennerster in Seldon (2001), by Clift, Gamble and Kelly, and Annesley in Ludlam and Smith (2001), by Alcock in Dunleavy *et al.* (2002), and by Annesley and Gamble in Ludlam and Smith (2004). For an overview of New Labour's record see chapter 7 in Fielding (2003), chapter 2 in Toynbee and Walker (2005), and for more detailed analysis Coates (2005). The report of the Commission on Social Justice (1994) and Hutton (1995), particularly chapters 7 and 8, provide useful analyses of inequality in Britain in the early 1990s.

The Politics of Sex and Gender

Until the 20th century women were excluded from the political process almost everywhere, reflecting their inferior status in society. The 'rights of man' demanded by 19th-century revolutionaries did not generally extend to women. The demand 'Votes for women' went hand in hand with demands for women's equality more generally. Women's rights have been formally conceded, but women remain unequal in many crucial respects in Britain.

This chapter examines the changing position of women in Britain's society and politics, and discusses the contribution of feminist ideas and the women's movement to the struggle for women's liberation and greater gender equality. It goes on to explore the extent of continuing discrimination against women in Britain today, and the demands of modern feminists. It concludes with a brief discussion of attitudes to alternative life styles and different sexual orientations, and the overall impact on the position of women today.

Contents

The changing condition of women in post-war Britain

Many thought that the battle for women's equality had been substantially won in the first half of the 20th century. Following agitation by the suffragettes, women had secured the vote on the same terms as men by 1928, had acquired legal rights to own and dispose of property, and gained (in practice very limited) access to the professions and higher education. In the Second World War many jobs that had previously been almost monopolised by men were of necessity opened to women, who were enabled to work by the provision of child nurseries. Yet these advances in opportunities for women were halted and reversed with the end of war. Women were expected to surrender their wartime jobs to returning servicemen, and the wartime nurseries were closed.

In the 1950s life seemed to revolve around the small nuclear family, of husband (and 'breadwinner'), housewife, son and daughter in advertisers' stereotypes. Women who had 'failed' to find a husband were pitied for being 'left on the shelf'. Unmarried men, however, were often referred to as 'gay bachelors', 'gay' meaning simply happy or merry, the term not having acquired the later meaning 'homosexual'. Indeed homosexuality, even between consenting adults, remained a crime until 1967. Whatever the tensions behind the lace curtains, the overt breakdown of marriage was relatively uncommon, and divorce rare, outside the upper reaches of society. Abortion was illegal, while contraception largely involved furtive purchases of condoms by men at

Figure 23.1 Votes for Women! The suffragettes, 1910

Photograph: EMPICS.

hairdressers, who tactfully asked their customers whether they wanted 'anything for the weekend, sir?' Illegitimacy, involving birth outside wedlock, was still stigmatised. Some older women who had given birth to illegitimate children remained locked up in mental institutions as 'moral defectives'.

> **Definition**
>
> **Suffragettes** campaigned for women's suffrage (the vote) and other issues affecting women in the period up to the First World War. Leading suffragettes included Emmeline Pankhurst and her daughters Christabel and Sylvia. Votes for women, secured in 1918 and 1928, did not achieve a dramatic shift in gender relations in politics and society generally.

More commonly, unmarried pregnant women were persuaded to conceal their 'disgrace' by going into a home for their confinement, and surrendering their babies immediately and permanently for adoption, a source of much subsequent anguish for both mothers and children.

What changed all this was not just the 'permissive sixties' but also wider economic and social change. The 1960s were something of watershed, however. The widespread availability of new forms of contraception (principally the pill), controlled by women rather than men, made it easier for both married and unmarried women to avoid pregnancy. Many 'career women' sought to delay motherhood, and some chose to avoid it altogether. The legalisation of homosexuality and abortion, and the reform of divorce laws in the late 1960s, both reflected changes in social attitudes and assisted further change (see Box 23.1).

Women did not always gain from the new social and legal climate. Men were arguably the main beneficiaries of sexual liberation and increased marital breakdown. Despite easier birth control, some women were left literally holding the baby. Women who had not worked since marriage and found themselves divorced in middle age often found it difficult to make a new life for themselves. Yet most women did have more choice in relationships and work, particularly as traditional male employment in mining and heavy manufacturing declined and opportunities for employment for women grew in the services and professions. Increasingly many women were no longer financially dependent on men, but had means and purchasing power of their own.

However, despite these social and economic advances the condition of women remained profoundly unequal in what was still a man's world. Thus women did not compete on equal terms in the labour market. They were commonly paid less than men for the same work. Part-time and lower-paid jobs were filled overwhelmingly by women. Hidden barriers and social conditioning effectively excluded them from better-paid skilled manual work (as train drivers, plumbers or builders). Opportunities for career advancement remained far more limited. Women seeking promotion to the higher levels in their chosen careers frequently encountered a 'glass ceiling'. Although some women had entered the prestigious and well-paid professions of law and medicine, they were conspicuous by their relative rarity, and very few progressed to the highest ranks.

Sexist attitudes also prevailed within the family. Women in paid employment were still commonly responsible for virtually all the unpaid domestic work and child care in the home. They had not exchanged housework for the world of paid work, but were widely expected to perform a dual role as paid employee and housewife. While many women had been socialised to accept that this was their role in life, others increasingly felt they were shouldering a grossly unfair burden.

There were numerous other indications of women's subordinate and unequal role in British society. Thus married women who wished to open their own bank account were commonly required to obtain their husband's signature, and effectively his permission, although of course a husband was never expected to secure his wife's signature before he could open an account.

> **Definition**
>
> **Sexism** involves attitudes and behaviour that discriminate against women or demean them. Unequal pay and prospects for women, demeaning images of women in the media or pornography, and the use of language that neglects or diminishes women are all examples of sexism.

The women's movement

The women's movement that grew in the 1960s and 1970s was swelled by the continuing evidence of the injustice and inequality of women's role. The women's movement was the archetypal new social movement (see Chapter 8). It lacked formal organisation, identifiable leaders or even members. It involved, at most, a very loose network of groups (some well-established and national, others more ephemeral and local) and individual sympathisers and supporters. It contained many different shades of opinion and attitude (see below). Its broad aim has not unfairly been described as women's liberation (or, more dismissively 'women's lib'). This aim implicitly acknowledged that women's formal legal and political equality had not secured their liberation. The women's movement involved other implicit premises: that only women could really understand the problems of women, and that women would have to rely substantially on themselves for their liberation.

The women's movement was perhaps more about securing changes in attitude and behaviour (both of men and women) than changes in the law, institutions and public policy. Yet it did provide substantial pressure for further reforms in these areas. An Equal Pay Act was passed in 1970 and an Equal Opportunities Act in 1975, the latter also establishing the Equal Opportunities Commission to monitor the implementation of both Acts (see Box 23.1). Over a period this has opened up more employment opportunities for women, and led to a significant reduction in the gap between average male and female earnings, although figures from the Equal Opportunities Commission show that much remains to be done. Thus average hourly earnings for full-time women workers even today lag 18 per cent behind those of men, while part-time women earn 40 per cent less than part-time male workers. At the highest level of employment in the professions and management, the differences remain stark. Very few senior judges are women (see Chapter 14) and few surgeons. According to the Fawcett Society only 2 per cent of executive directors in the FTSE top hundred companies are women.

Another significant reform of considerable benefit to mothers, steered through by Labour's Barbara Castle, was the merging of child tax allowances (paid to men) with family allowances to create a more substantial child benefit (paid to mothers). The woman's movement also agitated for better child care and nursery provision, with some eventual success. It has become a major plank in New Labour's attempt to move women and poor families from welfare into work (see Chapter 22). While one motivation was clearly to reduce the social security bill, the increased provision of child care and nursery education, coupled with changes in the tax system, have enlarged choices for many relatively poor women, and enabled them to escape the poverty trap.

The women's movement drew attention to a long-standing evil that had long been virtually ignored, the evidence of persistent violence against women, and the sexual abuse of women. This has led to more serious and sympathetic police investigations into allegations of violence and rape, and some change in public attitudes, although it remains very difficult to persuade women to pursue prosecutions, and even more difficult to prove them. Women's groups have however been active in the establishment of refuges and other forms of support for abused women.

Most of all, perhaps, the women's movement has helped achieve a substantial change in the portrayal of women, in both the visual images and the language used by the mass media and people in public life. While sexist attitudes undoubtedly remain, sexist vocabulary and sexist advertisements are much less in evidence. Indeed some television commercials have gone almost to the opposite extreme, portraying powerful women bosses or househusbands in mini soap operas, implying that such a reversal of traditional roles has gone much further than it has in reality. Even so, for aspirational women this was an improvement on their previous almost invariable media depiction in subordinate roles.

Not all feminists were interested in conventional politics, but specific women's pressure groups drew attention to the continuing under-representation of women in Parliament and local councils, and pressed for changes. The Labour Party in particular responded, by the introduction of all-women short lists in winnable parliamentary seats. Although this increased the number of women candidates and MPs it was declared illegal, ironically under the Equal Opportunities Act, as it denied the rights of aspiring male candidates in the constituencies involved. (The law has since been modified.) There is a continuing debate on the rights and wrongs of positive discrimination to reverse inequality. However, despite the relatively recent increase in the representation of

Box 23.1

The law and women: some measures affecting the position of women in the UK society and economy

1945 The introduction of family allowances, paid to mothers

1967 The Abortion Act, legalising abortion

1969 The Divorce Reform Act made divorce simpler and cheaper, allowing divorce by mutual consent

1970 The Equal Pay Act, intended to ensure equal pay for equal work, and outlaw explicit discrimination against women

1975 The Sex Discrimination Act banned sexual discrimination against women and established the Equal Opportunities Commission to monitor implementation

1976 Child Benefit Act consolidating family allowances (paid to mothers) with child tax allowances (formerly paid to men) in a new child benefit paid to mothers – a transfer from the man's wallet to the woman's purse, and a significant contribution to alleviating family and child poverty

women in Parliament and the Cabinet, women remain substantially under-represented in politics at almost every level (see Box 23.2).

Has the increased presence of women in Parliament made a difference to the style and content of politics? The impact of a more diverse Parliament in which one in five MPs is female has been disputed. Some of Labour's new female MPs entered Parliament in 1997 thinking that they would challenge the traditional, male-dominated confrontational style of politics in preference for a politics of 'partnership'. Many quickly became disillusioned, with MPs continuing to indulge in 'yah-boo nonsense, point scoring and silly games' which had little bearing on constituents' problems in the real world (*Guardian*, 20 June 2001). They felt that they had no impact, and some stood down. Some felt that women MPs had 'feminised' the Commons but in subtle ways. Certainly they were influential in changing the hours of the Commons, partly with the aim of making Parliament more accommodating to women and men with family responsibilities (see Chapter 13), although this has provoked a substantial backlash among traditionalists and a partial retreat. Others disparaged the New Labour women as 'Blair's babes', docile loyalists, unwilling to criticise or vote against the government, although some Labour women MPs, such as Clare Short or Diane Abbott, are conspicuous exceptions.

While women's organisations take some satisfaction in the increased representation of women at various levels of mainstream government and politics, although wanting it go much further, the

Box 23.2

Women in UK politics

- **Voting**: women outnumber men in the population, and women voters outnumber male voters. This is the only level at which women predominate in representative politics.
- **MPs at Westminster**: less than 5 per cent of MPs were women for the whole period from 1945 to 1987, when 41 women MPs were elected (6 per cent). Sixty women were elected in 1992 (9 per cent) and 121 in 1997 (18 per cent), of whom 101 were Labour. The number slightly declined in 2001, but rose again to 128 in 2005 (20 per cent).
- **Lords and ladies**: until the introduction of life peers there were no women in the Upper House, and even after that very few. In the semi-reformed House of Lords following the 1999 Act, 16 per cent of all peers are women.
- **Women in the Cabinet**: for most of the post-war period there was rarely more than one woman Cabinet minister and sometimes not that. Margaret Thatcher, Britain's first woman prime minister, was generally the only woman in her Cabinet (although wags who admired her macho style claimed she was the only man in the Cabinet!). John Major's first Cabinet was all-male. Blair's Cabinet has included up to seven women, although none have occupied the most senior posts. Indeed there has never been a female chancellor of the Exchequer, foreign secretary, home secretary or lord chancellor.
- **Women in local government**: although the proportion of women councillors has doubled over the last 30 years, they still constitute only 27 per cent of all councillors in England and Wales.
- **Women in devolved assemblies**: here women have fared rather better. Following the 2003 elections exactly half the representatives in the Welsh Assembly (30 out of 60) were women, including 19 out of 30 Labour members
- **Prominent women politicians in Britain**: these include Barbara Castle, a controversial Labour MP and Cabinet minister in Wilson's governments from 1964–70 and 1974–6, Shirley Williams, Labour Cabinet minister and later SDP MP and president and leader of the Liberal Democrat peers, Margaret Thatcher, Conservative leader from 1975 and the first and so far only woman to become prime minister (1979–90, the longest-serving prime minister for 150 years), Clare Short, a controversial secretary of state for overseas development from 1997 who resigned over Iraq in 2003, and Margaret Beckett, Labour's deputy leader under John Smith, and a senior member of Blair's Cabinets from 1997 onwards.

women's movement is only partly about politics as it has been traditionally understood. Overall, it has succeeded in substantially redefining what politics is about. Many of the issues discussed above – the division of labour within households, sexual relations between men and women, ill-treatment of women – were not previously seen as political issues, but part of the 'private sphere' of life in which politics should play no part. Political parties and conventional politics had little or nothing to say about them. Yet for many women it was these private or interpersonal issues that were a fundamental cause of the injustices they were trying to remedy. They were not thus outside politics, but the very stuff of politics. As radical feminists argued, 'The personal is political'.

Yet if the women's movement has been extremely successful in some respects, it is no longer perhaps quite as influential or united as it was. There has been some reaction against feminism or specific interpretations of feminism, not only among men but among some women. There are others who think women's liberation has been substantially achieved and there is no longer a need for the women's movement. Finally there are clear differences among feminists, not only on specific issues like abortion, but over analysis and strategy. It is to these that we now turn.

■ Varieties of feminism

Conventionally, three principal strands of modern feminism are distinguished – liberal feminism, socialist or Marxist feminism, and radical feminism (see Table 23.1), although there is in practice considerable overlap between these categories, while some feminists are difficult to pigeonhole.

Liberal feminism goes back a long way. Early feminists like Mary Wollstonecraft sought to extend the rights liberals demanded for men to women. They built on liberal assumptions and principles, including the freedom of the individual, rationalism, political and legal equality (see Chapter 6) but sought to apply them to both sexes. Liberal feminists sought equal rights for women, on the implicit and sometimes explicit assumption that apart from the obvious physical differences, women were much the same as men in terms of their nature and capacities. Liberals assumed that they could persuade both men and women of the justice of the demand for equal rights by rational argument. It may be claimed that liberal feminism was largely responsible for the formal establishment of women's legal and political equality, and other advances such as the expansion of education opportunities for females. Modern liberal feminists have continued to press for further changes in the law and increased political representation for women. Yet they have had some difficulty in explaining why formal legal and political equality has fallen well short of achieving actual equality for women.

Socialist or Marxist feminists explain women's inequality in terms of social pressures and in the context of wider inequality in a capitalist society. Low wages in what was once still a predominantly male full-time paid workforce could only be sustained through the unpaid domestic and childcare labour provided by women. Many women had a dual role as paid workers and unpaid mothers and housewives, and this prevented them from competing on equal terms with men. Women in the workforce, many part-time and not members of trade unions, constituted an 'industrial reserve army', particularly important when there were labour shortages, but always useful to employers in keeping wages down. Working-class women were doubly exploited, both as members of a subordinate class, and because of their gender. However, even the lifestyle of some women married to middle-class professionals or businessmen had more in common with working-class women, eating baked beans with their children while their husbands drove prestigious company cars and enjoyed expense-account meals and corporate hospitality.

Socialist feminists have sought to raise the political consciousness of women, get them to join trade unions and secure more effective protection for part-time and casual work. One contentious suggested remedy for women's exploitation at home was wages for housework, probably never practical, but opposed by many feminists because it appeared to legitimise the unfair domestic burden placed on women. Thus many socialist feminists saw the solution in terms of a dramatic extension of paid maternity leave and nursery and workplace creche provision. While Marxism provided a body of theory that could explain some of women's subordinate role in modern western

Table 23.1 Varieties of feminism

Varieties of feminism	Liberal feminism	Socialist or Marxist feminism	Radical feminism
Who?	('first wave')Mary Wollstonecraft John Stuart Mill Harriet Taylor The suffragettes ('second wave') Betty Friedan	('first wave')W.Thompson Friedrich Engels ('second wave') Juliet Mitchell Michelle Barrett	Germaine Greer Kate Millett Shulamith Firestone Eva Figes Susan Brownmiller Angela Dworkin 'Ecofeminists'
Key ideas and terms	Application of liberal principles to women, gender equality, freedom of opportunity	Economic exploitation of women as 'industrial reserve army', women's role in reproduction of labour	Patriarchy and male dominance. 'The personal is political.' Sexual politics. Celebration of women's difference.
Aims	Extension of rights of man to women, legal and political rights, women's education, equal opportunities, equal pay	Politicisation and unionisation of women. Nurseries and workplace creches. Wages for housework?	Alternatives to nuclear family. A woman's right to choose (on abortion). End of violence against women. End of pornography. lesbian rights, green issues. Peace.

society, it could not explain all of it. Thus left-wing women who became involved in the 1968 student revolts and the peace movement often found they were still expected to make the tea.

Radical feminists concluded that the real problem was not the lack of formal political and legal rights for women, nor inequality in society generally, but simply men and men's power over women, patriarchy, in the family and society more generally. Male power was exercised sometimes through crude physical force and violence against women (including rape), often through more subtle social and educational conditioning to accept subordinate roles. One target was the images of women in the media and pornography, another the subliminal messages conveyed by everyday language (chair*man*, business*man*, *his*tory), and by literature from Jane Austen onwards, suggesting that women's ultimate fulfilment lay in love and marriage to a man.

While liberal feminists (and subsequently most socialist feminists) had sought equality and partnership with men and were only too happy to campaign alongside sympathetic men, such as John Stuart Mill, radical feminists argued that women had to achieve their own liberation. While liberal and socialist feminists assumed there were no fundamental differences between the minds and mental capacities of men and women, some radical feminists preferred to emphasise and celebrate the differences between the sexes. Women thought and behaved differently. While men were inherently competitive and prone to violence, women were more cooperative and pacific. Thus men were largely excluded from the women's movement and from some women's political initiatives (such as the Greenham Common peace camp). Some radical feminists even sought to exclude men from their lives altogether, as heterosexual relations involved 'sleeping with the enemy'.

Radical feminism has perhaps contributed most to changing attitudes towards women, yet it has provoked some divisions within the women's

Definition

Patriarchy means literally rule of the father. The term is used by feminists to mean the habitual domination of men over women in the family and wider society, even in states where equal rights are enshrined in law.

movement and a broader backlash against what were perceived as the excesses of 'women's lib', not least among many women. The vituperative opposition of some radicals to men, to heterosexual relations, to marriage, motherhood and family, and to any manifestation of femininity, upset many women who supported the broad aims of the women's movement but did not want 'to throw out the baby with the bathwater'. Thus some feminists have reasserted the value of motherhood (Freely 1995). Eco-feminists, who combine feminism with environmental concerns, and emphasise the nurturing role of women, often reject abortion, in marked contrast to earlier feminists who strongly proclaimed women's right to control their own bodies. Other 'new feminists', dismissed by Germaine Greer as 'lipstick feminists', have defended feminine clothes and make-up as empowering women, enabling them to feel good, while asserting the continued importance of the women's movement in the struggle for equality (Walter 1999).

Some critics have suggested most modern feminists belong to the white middle class, and their concerns are not necessarily those of working class women, black or Asian women, or women in the third world, who have different and more fundamental concerns than, for example, gay and lesbian rights. Today the voice of black feminism is being heard rather more however. In some respects these differences and even conflicts within the women's movement testify to its richness and diversity, although they also raise a question mark over the direction of feminism.

Box 23.3

Lesbian and gay rights

The lesbian and gay lobby group Stonewall has traditionally looked to Labour to promote and defend gays' political rights, and the post-1997 Labour governments have been responsive to their interests. However, polls indicate that Conservative supporters can be more tolerant of gay relationships than Labour supporters, that women are more tolerant than men, and that the skilled working class can be more tolerant than the middle classes. Certainly public attitudes have changed, enabling more politicians and others prominent in national life to 'come out' without damaging their career and public standing. There is increased recognition of gay and lesbian rights.

- The Law Lords have ruled that a homosexual couple living in a stable relationship could be defined as a family. This conferred new legal rights for gays and lesbians, such as the right of one partner to claim damages if dependent on the other partner who died through a third party's negligence. Also, one partner now has the right to inherit a tenancy in the name of a dead partner.
- The Children's Society has lifted its ban on gay and lesbian couples adopting children.
- The European Court of Human Rights ruled that the Ministry of Defence's policy of sacking gay members of the armed forces was 'inhuman and degrading'.
- A voluntary code on sexual orientation and discrimination in the workplace has been agreed.
- Section 28 of the Local Government Act (1988), which banned the 'promotion' of homosexuality in schools and colleges, has been repealed.
- The age of consent is now the same (16) as in different-sex relationships.

Diversity in families and lifestyles

The woman's movement has certainly contributed to the growing diversity of families and lifestyles in modern Britain, which reflects increased choice, particularly for women. What used to be called 'living in sin', heterosexual partnerships outside wedlock, have become far more common, and the stigma of illegitimacy has been so far removed that partners no longer feel obliged to marry if and when children arrive. Many more women than formerly seem content to remain single, pursuing careers unencumbered by family ties. There are many more single-parent families, either as a consequence of deliberate choice, or more commonly as the consequence of the breakdown of marriage and long-term relationships, or simply a casual fling. There are also same-sex couples bringing up children. Indeed, same-sex relationships between gay men and lesbian women have achieved a degree of tolerance and social acceptance unthinkable only a few years ago (see Box 23.3). However, 'coming out' can still be very difficult, while in some communities and occupations gays and lesbians still experience substantial prejudice and oppression.

Overall however, there is far more diversity and real choice for both women and men. Parliament and government have increasingly felt a need to legislate to accommodate new relationships and new kinds of families. There is now also a variety of role models for both sexes, which opens up possibilities for a better relationship between them. If women are divided by class, ethnicity and sexual orientation, so are men. Masculinity, like femininity, is socially constructed, and dominant forms of masculinity 'may be experienced as oppressive by some men'. Gay men may have something to teach 'real' men in that respect. Thus feminists should 'welcome and strengthen non-oppressive forms of masculinity' and 'attempt to move beyond the binary divisions of a gendered society' (Bryson 1999: 203). This is a hopeful vision, offering the prospect of a more equal partnership between the sexes, in which both might find more fulfilment. Yet it has to be said that many feminists do not believe in 'new man', but still see the 'old Adam' in much male behaviour. Thus surveys continue to show that women remain largely responsible for the care of children and elderly relatives, and most household chores.

Summary

- The achievement of formal legal and political equality for women has not succeeded in securing substantive equality in the world of work, at home or in politics.
- The women's movement, an archetypal 'new social movement', has raised consciousness of the continuing injustice and discrimination suffered by women, and has achieved some changes in attitude and behaviour.
- Various strands of feminism have contributed substantially to the understanding of the causes and nature of women's continuing inequality and oppression, and its remedies, although they have also highlighted differences among women over analysis, strategy and specific issues.
- There is evidence that women are benefiting from wider career opportunities and more equal pay, but statistics from the Equal Opportunities Commission suggest there is still a substantial gender gap.
- There are more women than formerly involved in politics at every level, although they are still substantially under-represented. It is unclear whether increased female representation has led to a significant change in the style and content of politics.
- Women have been substantially affected by changes in families and lifestyles and by more tolerant attitudes to different sexual orientations. This has enlarged choice for women and men, and may, over time, contribute to new models of masculinity and femininity, and to a shift in gender relations.

Questions for discussion

- Why are women still unequal despite the achievement of formal legal and political equality?
- Why are women so under-represented in Parliament and local government, especially when there are more female voters than male?
- Are women interested in a different kind of politics, a different political style and different issues?
- What differences have women made in Parliament and politics generally?
- How significant are divisions among feminists and women generally over women's aspirations and interests?

- Have women generally benefited from greater sexual permissiveness and the increased variety in families and lifestyles?
- How far are women's problems really the problems of men?
- Is the new man a myth?

Further reading

On feminism see chapters in textbooks on ideologies, such as Heywood (2003), Leach (2002) and Eccleshall *et al.* (2004). An excellent much fuller account is Bryson's *Feminist Political Theory* (2003). Celebrated classical feminist texts include Wollstonecraft (1792, 1995 edn) and Mill (1869, 1988 edn). Modern classics include Greer (1970), Millet (1977) and Figes (1978). More recent contributions to debates within feminism are Freely (1995) and Walter (1999). Good accounts of women in politics and the women's movement are provided by Randall (1987), Carter (1988) and Lovenduski and Randall (1993). Two more recent books are Sarah Childs, *New Labour's Women MPs* (2004) and Wendy Stokes, *Women in Contemporary Politics* (2005). Statistics can be found in recent editions of *Social Trends* and the publications of the Equal Opportunities Commission, www.eoc.org.uk. A long established campaigning organisation for equal rights is the Fawcett Society, www.fawcettsociety.org.uk.

The Politics of Race and Multiculturalism

Contents

Fifty years ago British society appeared relatively homogeneous, with social class being the only politically significant division. With the partial exception of the Jewish community, ethnic minorities were so small as to be politically insignificant, and religious differences were declining sharply in political significance. In sharp contrast, contemporary Britain is characterised by ethnic diversity and multi-faith politics, particularly in most major cities. Britain's new multi-cultural society arguably offers a rich variety of experience and opportunity to the general benefit, although it has also brought some tension within and between communities which place complex demands on the system of governance and politics.

This chapter explores aspects of cultural diversity, and their impact on political life in general and policy making in particular.

Black and British

Britain has a long history of immigration and emigration. Some who came to settle in Britain in the more distant past might now be described as 'economic migrants', attracted by opportunities for a better life. Others were more like today's 'asylum seekers', victims of persecution elsewhere, such as the Protestant Huguenots from Catholic France, or Jews from Russia and eastern Europe, who sought a safe haven in Britain. Some of those who left Britain were also asylum seekers, victims of religious persecution at home, such as the Pilgrim Fathers or Quakers, who settled in north America to practise their faith undisturbed. Many others were Britain's own economic migrants, seeking their fortunes in the territories of the once-extensive British Empire, commonly appropriating the land of the native inhabitants in the process.

After the Second World War, when Britain's former colonies sought and secured their independence, the empire 'came home'. The British Nationality Act 1948 allowed citizens of the 'new Commonwealth' and former Empire to settle in Britain. Most of the immigrants were not former white settlers from the 'old Commonwealth' but blacks or Asians from the 'new Commonwealth': the Caribbean, the Indian subcontinent and East Africa. Many were economic migrants, attracted by the prospect of jobs in Britain's textile industry, London transport or the National Health Service (NHS). For others there were significant 'push factors'. Thus many Anglo-Indians felt they were not wanted in the new independent India. Kenya's and Uganda's substantial and formerly prosperous Asian communities were expelled. Later

Definitions

Asylum seekers are migrants escaping persecution in their country of origin. They might otherwise face death, like the Jews fleeing Nazi Germany. They might face other forms of persecution, including restrictions on their personal freedom. These are 'push factors' behind emigration.

Economic migrants seek better prospects and a higher standard of living elsewhere. These are 'pull factors' behind immigration.

still, several thousand Hong Kong Chinese sought a new home in Britain on the eve of the former colony's transfer to China.

This new post-war immigration into Britain created a substantial minority, over four million people by the year 2000, who were both black and British. The term 'black' is often used to cover all who are 'non-white', although 'black' and 'white' do not even describe skin colours accurately, and say nothing about other physical differences, let alone profound diversities in origins, language, religion, traditions and economic circumstances. Yet skin colour, coupled in some cases with distinctive dress, does make Britain's black and Asian communities readily identifiable as 'different' by the native 'white' population. It hinders their acceptance, facilitates discrimination, and often panders to prejudice and racism (see below). Apart from the unhelpful colour symbolism (white is good, as in 'white knight'; black is bad, as in 'the black sheep of the family'), there is also the legacy of colonial attitudes towards 'lesser breeds without the law' and peoples 'half devil and half child' (in the poet Rudyard Kipling's words).

Some of the language employed about blacks and Asians suggests they belong to a different race. Thus there have been 'race riots', after which efforts were made to improve 'race relations' by, among other things, establishing a Commission for Racial Equality. Yet it has long been recognised that the concept of 'race' has no scientific validity, and some critics argue that continued use of the term only lends a spurious legitimacy to a bogus concept that should be abandoned (Miles 1989). In the 1960s and 1970s 'immigrant' was often used as a euphemism for blacks and Asian, ignoring the obvious points that some immigrants are white (many recent immigrants have come from eastern Europe), and that many blacks and Asians were born in Britain, and thus are not immigrants at all. Skin colour has, however, hindered the integration of the children of black and Asian immigrants, compared with the children of Polish immigrants, for example. 'Ethnic minorities' is a term that can be applied to white minority groups, such as Jews, Irish or Poles, although it too is largely employed as a euphemism for blacks and Asian.

There is considerable diversity both within and between communities. In Leicester, for example, one resident in five is a member of what is popularly known as the 'Asian community'. Yet this community is actually made up of numerous groups based on seven main languages further divided into numerous dialects. Some groups have to resort to a second language, such as English, in order to communicate at anything more than the most basic level with other groups.

Definitions

Race is a term sometimes loosely used to mean any group of people with common characteristics. In the 19th century and into the 20th century there were attempt to categorise humankind into distinctive racial groups, with their own measurable distinctive features, of which skin colour was one. This 'scientific' racism was employed to justify Nazi racial theories. Today it is acknowledged that 'race' has no scientific validity. It would be preferable to drop the term altogether, not least because it is employed to justify or excuse racist discrimination and prejudice. Yet it is still commonly used, for example in the term 'race relations'.

Ethnicity is a more acceptable term, usually taken to involve any group of people conscious of their own distinctive shared origins, identity and traditions. This implies cultural rather than biological differences between ethnic groups. Yet it is a notoriously imprecise term. Are communities of Polish or Italian origin living in Britain ethnic groups? Commonly the term is associated with minorities, as in 'ethnic minorities', and frequently applied in Britain to 'non-white' blacks and Asians. **'Ethnic cleansing'** has become a chillingly familiar term to describe the forced expulsion or murder of particular ethnic groups around the world.

The Asian community is further fragmented by different religions, values, cultural practices and castes, as well as by the political tensions found in the politics of the Indian subcontinent.

Racism, prejudice and discrimination

It is a sad fact that many individuals have negative attitudes towards others purely on the grounds of perceived racial or ethnic difference. Racial prejudice can be expressed by whites against blacks, blacks against whites, or indeed between other ethnic groups, as in the case of Asian prejudice against West Indians (Mohapatra 1999: 79). Clearly, however, the most politically significant prejudice in Britain is that expressed by the white majority against the black minority.

Up to 1965 prejudice and discrimination could be displayed openly. Job advertisements might state 'no blacks need apply', while landlords could prescribe 'no coloureds' ('coloured' was a term frequently used in the 1950s and 1960s to cover blacks and Asians). In 1964 a Conservative candidate won a parliamentary seat from Labour against the general trend, using the offensive slogan, 'If you want a nigger neighbour, vote Labour'.

Governments at first did nothing to combat the problem. They were only forced to act when prejudice involved civil disorder. In the late 1950s Britain experienced its first major 'race riots' – as opposed to gang skirmishes – when whites attacked blacks in Notting Hill and Nottingham. These riots came as an unexpected shock, and the government adopted both 'tough' and 'tender' responses. The former, involving restrictions on immigration, represented a response to public anxiety about black immigration to Britain, while the latter was an attempt to promote racial harmony within Britain.

The Commonwealth Immigrants Act 1962 was the first of a number of Acts which restricted the entry of black first-time immigrants and their families to Britain. A second Commonwealth Immigrants Act was rushed through Parliament in 1968 to tighten up the 1962 Act, which did not apply to East African Asians. The Immigration Act 1971 tightened controls still further, although its restrictions were waived on humanitarian grounds to allow Asians expelled from Uganda to enter Britain freely. A new Nationality Act in 1981 represented even tighter restrictions. All this legislation, passed by both Conservative and Labour governments, has been criticised for being founded on racist principles. The prime goal has been not the restriction of immigrants who have claims to be British, but the restriction of black immigrants who have claims to British status. Fringe fascist groups and some mainstream politicians sought a virtual halt to black immigration and the 'repatriation' of those already in Britain (see Box 24.1).

Illiberal immigration policies have generally been accompanied by more liberal policies towards ethnic minorities already resident within Britain. The Race Relations Acts of 1965, 1968 and 1976 outlawed direct and indirect discrimination in widening areas of public life and provision such as housing, employment and education. What is sometimes called the 'race relations industry' was established, with complaints taken to the Race Relations Board, later replaced by the Commission for Racial Equality, with community relations councils operating at local level. The view expressed by many liberal-minded individuals of the time was that the 'race' problem would eventually wither away. It was hoped that the children of immigrants would not suffer from the cultural problems and disadvantages of their parents, and would over time integrate successfully into British society.

Positive discrimination?

It was hoped that procedures to ensure as far as possible that all individuals were treated fairly and equally regardless of their ethnic origin would successfully reduce discrimination against minorities over time. Yet, as with the case of women, anti-discrimination legislation has not ensured the equal treatment of ethnic minorities, who continue to be under-represented in many occupations and professions as well as in the political arena (see Box 24.2). Similarly most black and Asian minorities are much more likely to be unemployed or employed in low-paid work with poor conditions than their white counterparts. Ethnic minorities are conspicuous by their absence from most company boardrooms, and in the

Box 24.1

Fascism and racism in Britain

Before the Second World War Oswald Mosley's British Union of Fascists was subsidised by Mussolini and Hitler and attracted some initial media support (notably from the *Daily Mail*). Fascism offered a middle way between capitalism and communism, it was claimed, but its main appeal was to xenophobia and anti-Semitism. After the war Mosley periodically attempted a political comeback, exploiting concerns over 'coloured' immigration rather than anti-Semitism. However, it was new openly fascist or quasi-fascist and racist parties like the National Front and the British National Party that attracted more publicity and support. Yet although advances in by-elections and local elections have sometimes raised alarm, neither has come remotely closely to winning a seat at Westminster. (Yet the BNP secured 17 per cent of the vote in Barking in 2005, beating the Liberal Democrats into fourth place.)

The electoral failure of racist parties may reflect a determined rejection by British voters not of racism, but rather of politicians and parties linked with Britain's wartime enemies. In that respect the Anti-Nazi League slogan 'The National Front is a Nazi front' was highly effective. Nick Griffin, the leader of the British National Party, has given his party a more outwardly respectable image. Nazi-type uniforms have been replaced by smart suits, and the tone of public pronouncements has been moderated, leaving racist language for more private meetings.

Mainstream politicians have also sometimes 'played the race card'. Most controversially, Enoch Powell in 1968 called for a halt to black immigration and for moves to repatriate blacks already settled in Britain. He declared, 'Like the Roman I seem to see the River Tiber foaming with much blood'. He was immediately sacked from the Shadow Cabinet by the Conservative leader, Edward Heath. Powell was never a fascist, nor even really a racist in the crude sense, but a distinctive kind of nationalist, who emphasised national and parliamentary sovereignty along with British culture and traditions, and vehemently opposed British membership of the European Community. Black immigrants, he thought, could never become British as they had not shared Britain's past culture and traditions and could not become part of its future. He thus rejected the whole notion of a multi-cultural society. However, if he was not a racist himself, he contributed to the legitimising of racist attitudes and behaviour. Other mainstream politicians have sometimes seemed to exploit fears of immigrants, and more recently asylum seekers (for example in the 2005 election campaign).

higher ranks of the civil service, judiciary and police (see Chapter 3).

A more radical approach to equal opportunities involves a fair distribution of resources and not simply fair procedures. Employers may proclaim their equal opportunities credentials, and establish what appear to be tight procedures to eliminate any bias, yet still not employ many (or even any) blacks and Asians. Yet discrimination is difficult to prove, even where it may be suspected. Moreover, anecdotal evidence of discrimination, coupled with a virtual absence of positive role models, may deter members of ethnic minorities from applying for certain jobs. It is unlikely that young Asians will consider joining the police force if they have never seen Asian police officers in their own area. Thus targets or quotas may be established for the recruitment and promotion of those from ethnic minorities to ensure they obtain a similar proportion of posts to their numbers in the local community. If 10 per cent of those living within a particular police authority are Asian, it may appear reasonable that 10 per cent of the police and 10 per cent of its higher ranks should also be Asian.

Such a policy has been pursued for a time in the USA, where it is called 'affirmative action'. In the United Kingdom it is more usually described as 'positive discrimination'. It could help to reduce much faster the marked under-representation of blacks and Asians in certain occupations, and particularly at higher levels. The objection is that it could mean appointing someone who is apparently less well qualified than a white applicant, in order to meet the requirements of the target quota. Such positive discrimination to favour certain categories is actually illegal under equal opportunities legislation. Even if the law could be changed it might worsen rather than improve race relations.

Box 24.2

Ethnic minorities and political representation

- **Voting**: one consequence of the Iraq War has been to shake up the political allegiances of British Muslims. Previously the Muslim vote had been overwhelmingly a Labour vote. Iraq alienated many former Labour supporters within the Muslim community, and increased support for parties that opposed the war, such as the Liberal Democrats and Respect. The former Labour MP George Galloway won a seat for Respect in 2005, defeating the sitting black Labour MP for Bethnal Green and Bow in a constituency with a large Bangladeshi population. Yet in some constituencies the Muslim vote largely stayed Labour.
- **Parties**: although blacks and Asians overwhelmingly supported Labour, their voice was formerly marginalised within the party, leading to strong demands that were not conceded for separate black sections. More recently Labour has selected more ethnic-minority candidates for both local and national elections, and other parties have begun to follow suit.
- **Representation at Westminster**: while there has been some increase recently in the number of black and Asian MPs, to 12 in 2001, this is still less than 2 per cent of the House of Commons. After the 2005 election there were four Muslim MPs (all Labour) and five black MPs, four Labour and the first black Conservative MP (elected for Windsor). MPs such as Bernie Grant, Diane Abbott and Paul Boateng have done something to raise the profile of ethnic minorities.
- **Government**: ethnic minorities have been conspicuous by their absence at the higher levels of British government, at least until recently. Paul Boateng became the first black Cabinet minister in 2001, soon followed by Baroness Amos, the first black leader of the Lords. Yet in a poll of ethnic minorities 71 per cent did not expect to see an ethnic minority prime minister in their lifetime (ICM research, reported in *Guardian* 21 March 2005).

There is already a persistent myth that governments unduly favour ethnic minorities and asylum seekers (against much available evidence to the contrary), and the open adoption of positive discrimination might only serve to inflame racist sentiments. Yet it is important that employers monitor the ethnic composition of their workforce, because the under-representation of certain minorities may suggest there could be something wrong with the way posts are advertised, or there may be some hidden bias in selection procedures. Interviewers may often be unconscious of their own prejudices, or they may worry about the prejudices of prospective colleagues, and conclude that the applicant may not be able to fit in with other members of the team. It is generally not too difficult to find some plausible reason other than ethnic origins for the rejection of an applicant.

Institutional racism?

The concept of institutional racism suggests that racist assumptions are so embedded in organisations and society generally that discrimination can persist even in the absence of overt racist intentions and behaviour on the part of individuals. The concept was developed by race theorists in the USA, who suggested that racism was deeply ingrained in US society as a consequence of the historical experience of slavery and racial segregation. Thus the dominant majority white group continued to unconsciously exclude and disadvantage the black subordinate group.

British scholars have used the term 'institutional racism' in a sense broadly derived from the American use of the concept, but have often applied it more specifically to particular institutions such as the police, whose practices may be 'unwittingly discriminatory' against black people. The term became more familiar in Britain as a result of the Macpherson Inquiry into the murder of the black teenager Stephen Lawrence (see Box 24.2).

Allegations of a racist bias in the police were often made by ethnic minorities well before the Macpherson Inquiry. Blacks and Asians were more likely than whites to be stopped on suspicion and searched. Surveys and anecdotal evidence

Box 24.3

Institutional racism in the police? The Macpherson Inquiry, 1999

This was set up to inquire into the response of the Metropolitan Police to the murder of the black teenager Stephen Lawrence, almost certainly by a racist white gang whose members were identified and accused, but not convicted, because of alleged delays and errors in the police investigation. An internal police inquiry found no evidence to support the allegation of racist conduct by police officers who 'roundly denied racism or racist conduct'. The Macpherson Inquiry agreed that it had 'not heard evidence of overt racism and discrimination', but even so concluded that the Metropolitan Police Service was 'institutionally racist' according to the Inquiry's own definition:

> The collective failure of an organisation to provide an appropriate and professional service to people because of their colour, culture, or ethnic origin. It can be seen or detected in processes, attitudes and behaviour which amount to discrimination through unwitting prejudice, ignorance, thoughtlessness and racist stereotyping which disadvantage minority ethnic people.
>
> (Macpherson 1999: 28)

Other evidence to the Inquiry accepted that institutional racism was a feature of police forces in other parts of Britain and reflected 'racism which is inherent in wider society which shapes our attitudes and behaviour'. Thus racism in the police was not the fault of a few 'bad apples' – individual police officers who were racist in thought and behaviour. However, the Inquiry's conclusion that the Metropolitan Police were 'institutionally racist' was widely interpreted by the police and the media to mean that all police officers were personally racist, when the Inquiry suggested the opposite. (Indeed, a criticism of the concept of institutional racism is that it too readily excuses individuals for their own racist attitudes and behaviour.)

suggested the existence of a 'canteen culture' in the police that was both sexist and racist. Some police forces have made strenuous efforts to counter racism, and recruit more officers from ethnic minorities. However, such officers have sometimes found it difficult to secure acceptance from colleagues and promotion within the force.

Institutional racism has also sometimes been blamed for the under-performance of black pupils in schools. The Commission for Racial Equality noted that young black males were more than three times as likely to be excluded from schools as their white counterparts. Predominantly white teachers may unconsciously have low expectations of black pupils, and these low expectations and negative stereotypes contribute to low self-esteem and poor behaviour among the students themselves, who lack positive role models to inspire them. Yet this does not seem to affect all ethnic minorities equally; Indian and Chinese children perform better, indicating that the causes of poor performance among some groups may be more complex.

Multi-cultural Britain?

Ethnic minorities have contributed hugely to the British economy, and many would argue that they have also enormously enriched British culture. The arts, the media, sport, fashion and cuisine would be immeasurably poorer without the variety and vitality of the contributions of Britain's ethnic minorities. Britain has become a multi-ethnic, multi-faith and multi-cultural country, yet this is far from being universally welcomed. Some see it as threat to the traditional British way of life and national identity. Norman Tebbit, the Conservative politician, claimed 'most people in Britain did not want to live in a multicultural, multiracial society, but it has been foisted on them' (quoted in Solomos 2003: 218). Moreover, although there are areas where different communities freely intermingle in a genuinely multi-cultural society, residential segregation and mutual misunderstanding and suspicion are rather more common.

A fresh outbreak of race riots in 2001 in a number of northern towns, including Bradford, Burnley and Oldham, dramatised some of the inter-community tensions. Subsequent inquiries, such as those by Cantle (2001) and Denham (2002), confirmed much that was already evident to many observers. The populations of these towns (and several others where riots had not occurred) appeared to be fragmented and polarised in terms of ethnicity. People from different ethnic backgrounds were effectively segregated in housing and schooling, and were leading 'parallel lives' with little interaction between the communities. In these towns multi-culturalism was little more than a consenting form of apartheid. The lack of contact between different groups fuelled mutual fear and suspicion, which was then exploited by extremist political groups like the BNP. What was needed, the reports advocated, was the development of more 'cohesive communities'.

Racial tensions and racial prejudice in Britain have been complicated and reinforced by religious prejudice. While blacks from the Caribbean are overwhelmingly Christian, Asian communities built Islamic, Hindu and Sikh temples in British cities. The religious observances, dress codes and diet of these new faith communities caused some problems over school uniform requirements and school and hospital meals, but these have largely been accommodated without too much difficulty. Rather more serious conflict arose from the publication of Salman Rushdie's *The Satanic Verses*, a book that Muslims regarded as offensive to their faith, leading to death threats against the author, who was obliged to go into hiding with police protection. For western liberals the principle of freedom of speech was at stake. For many Muslims the Rushdie affair symbolised a wider lack of respect for their religion and their community.

Thus there is a continuing debate over the extent to which Britain has become a multicultural society in reality. There is also another debate over multi-culturalism both as a principle and its practical implications for policy (see Box 24.4). A common assumption in many modern nation states is the existence of a national culture that all citizens should share. Thus the USA in the past welcomed immigrants but insisted they should be formally instructed and thoroughly assimilated into the American way of life and become loyal US citizens. The British approach was less formal but still assumed a process of naturalisation and assimilation. The ideal was integration.

Figure 24.1 A positive aspect of multi-cultural Britain? The Notting Hill Carnival, August 2005

Photograph: EMPICS.

Multi-culturalism, in both the USA and Britain, involved an alternative approach to assimilation and integration. Rather, differences among immigrant communities should be accepted and respected. Children from minority ethnic communities should have pride in their own language, religion and culture, which should be part not only of their own school curriculum, but also that of the wider community, to promote mutual understanding. Such an approach provoked something of a backlash from those who claimed that English culture and Christian values were being sacrificed on the altar of 'political correctness'. Others argued that the new multi-cultural education involved the neglect of vital skills which young blacks and Asians needed if they were to prosper in the British labour market and British society: 'Unfortunately the right to be different can all too readily be conceded without allowing for equality of opportunity and perhaps positively reinforcing inequality of opportunity' (Rex 1986: 120). Others again have claimed that multiculturalism has encouraged the development of separate faith schools and separate community facilities for ethnic groups, which have impeded the development of cohesive communities in which minorities might interrelate with each other. Some have suggested that important individual rights and freedoms could be sacrificed in attempts to satisfy the cultural or religious convictions of some ethnic or religious minorities (see Box 24.4).

The war on terror and Islamophobia

The attack on the twin towers of 9/11 followed by the 'war on terror' and the London bombings of July 2005 drove a potentially far more dangerous wedge between British Muslims and the rest of the population. To some in the west 9/11 and subsequent atrocities in Bali, Madrid and London chillingly confirmed the predictions of Samuel Huntington (1996). He had argued that the old Cold War ideological conflict between two superpowers would be replaced by broader struggles between rival cultures, such as between Islam and the West.

Box 24.4

Academic controversy: Bhikhu Parekh and Brian Barry on multi-culturalism

The political theorist Bhikhu Parekh (2000a) chaired a group established by the Runnymede Trust which produced a controversial report, *The Future of Multi-Ethnic Britain*. In the same year his book *Rethinking Multiculturalism* (2000b) argued that western liberals wrongly assume that their ideas have universal validity, and thus accord insufficient respect to cultures that involve different beliefs and practices. Thus liberal western ideas and values embodied in declarations of rights may conflict with other communities' cultures, involving values of 'social harmony, respect for authority, orderly society, a united and extended family and a sense of filial piety'. Human beings, he argues, are not the same everywhere, but 'culturally embedded in the sense that they are born into, raised in and deeply shaped by their cultural communities'.

Brian Barry (2001: 58) argued that this approach 'is liable to be harmful to women and children in minority communities and to those within them who deviate from prevailing norms'. Respecting the values of other cultures might entail accepting discrimination on grounds of gender or caste, and legitimising prejudices against different sexual orientations. Thus cultural values may restrict women's rights, gay rights and even the rights to free speech (as with the Rushdie affair, discussed above). Barry goes on to argue that it was the appeal to universal principles and rights that helped to abolish slavery and transform the status of women, whereas hitherto prevailing cultural norms had justified discrimination on grounds of race and gender.

Parekh (2000b: 196) does however acknowledge that there are inevitable tensions between the norms of majority and minority communities. Any society 'should foster a strong sense of unity and common belonging among its citizens'. The problem is how to reconcile unity with diversity. Parekh explores sensibly and sensitively a number of controversial issues, including female circumcision, polygamy, Muslim and Jewish methods of slaughtering animals, arranged marriages, initiation ceremonies, and exemption from legal or school requirements on dress.

Although Bush and Blair insisted that the wars in Afghanistan and Iraq involved a 'war against terrorism' not 'a war against Islam', to many in the Muslim community it appeared that the west was indeed involved in a war against Islam. Inevitably the conflict provoked divided loyalties for British Muslims, and for some it further weakened their British allegiance and identity. At the same time fears aroused by al Qaida atrocities inflamed popular prejudice and suspicion against British Muslims, even though leading British Muslim organisations had roundly condemned the terrorists. Extremists groups and parties exploited popular fears, suggesting that Muslims were a potential 'enemy within'. There were some 'revenge attacks' against Muslims and their mosques, and even attacks on some non-Muslim Asians. Needless to say, this indiscriminate Islamophobia has further damaged inter-community relations.

Asylum and immigration

Another problem damaging community relations is the continuing political row over asylum and immigration. Concerns over immigration are hardly new. Hysteria over the influx of (principally) Jews from Russia and eastern Europe before the First World War led to the introduction of the rather sinisterly titled Aliens Act (1905). Immigration from the new Commonwealth became a hot political issue again in the 1960s and 1970s. Today the general issue of immigration has become confused with the more specific issue of asylum, and particularly 'bogus' asylum seekers. This in turn has been linked with the terror threat, creating a climate of fear.

It is worth pointing out that half the ethnic minority population was born in Britain, so they are not immigrants. Most of the others are not recent immigrants but long-resident British citizens. Relatively few of these or more recent immigrants claimed asylum. The issue of asylum should not be confused with the issue of immigration, although there is some overlap. Britain has long granted a safe haven to those suffering persecution in their country of origin, and now additionally has international obligations to fulfil in considering applicants for asylum. Britain takes 3 per cent of the total worldwide number of refugees. Some of the countries shouldering the largest burden are relatively poor countries unfortunate enough to border war torn-territories from which families have fled in real danger of their lives.

Many of those claiming asylum in Britain in recent decades are part of the legacy of empire, for which the state has a moral responsibility – east-African Asians for example, and Chinese from Hong Kong. Inevitably, some of those claiming asylum might more realistically be considered economic migrants. However, immigrants may be motivated by a mix of push and pull factors, and some are effectively driven out of their country of origin by being prevented from practising their occupation, or the confiscation of their property.

Immigration into Britain has been permitted and often encouraged to fill vacancies in employment. Thus doctors and nurses are recruited from elsewhere in Europe and the rest of the world. The NHS would collapse without its foreign workers, often trained at the expense of other countries who cannot easily afford the loss of medical skills. Other sectors of the economy, such as catering, retailing and transport, are heavily dependent on immigrant workers. Poorer immigrants often take low-paid casual jobs with unsocial hours which native British workers reject.

There was a brief panic over enlargement of the European Union in 2004, with the prospect of hordes of foreign workers from eastern Europe coming to Britain. In practice this has been little more than a trickle (and of course many from Britain have taken advantage of the free movement of labour within the EU to live and work abroad).

At the bottom of the heap are illegal immigrants, who have often paid vast sums and taken huge risks to enter Britain. Outside the law and official recognition, they are exploited by unscrupulous bosses, who ignore minimum wage and health and safety legislation. A dramatic example was the drowning by the incoming tides of 21 Chinese cocklepickers in February 2004, in Morecambe Bay, for which the 'gang masters' in charge of them later faced prosecution.

Over the last ten years asylum and immigration have become political issues once more. William Hague raised the issue in 2001, arguing that Britain should be a safe haven for genuine asylum seekers and not a 'soft touch' for economic migrants. In 2005 Michael Howard made immigration a central plank in the Conservative election campaign, with the slogan 'It's not racist to want firm limits to immigration'. He accused the government of rewarding asylum seekers who 'trick their way into the country'. The *Daily Mail* (15 April 2005) raised the temperature further, publishing pictures of long queues of asylum seekers in Calais waiting to come to Britain under the heading, 'Queue here for open-door UK', claiming that the pictures proved Howard's allegation that immigration was 'out of control'. (Subsequent investigations by other papers could find very few of these asylum seekers.) In a climate of hysteria whipped up by politicians and the media it is difficult to have a rational debate on the subject of immigration. Howard's successor David Cameron has, however, shown a much more positive approach.

Identity and allegiance

Experiences of routine discrimination and prejudice have hardly encouraged some of Britain's ethnic minorities to identify wholeheartedly with Britain. A survey for the *Guardian* (21 March 2005) by ICM found that 56 per cent of all minorities had been subjected to name-calling or other verbal abuse, 30 per cent considered they had been denied a job or promotion because of their ethnic background, and 18 per cent had suffered physical attack or harassment. However, 35 per cent thought society had become less racist in the last ten years, although an equal proportion thought there was no change and 26 per cent thought society had become more racist. Unsurprisingly in view of these experiences, only 39 per cent of those from ethnic minorities saw themselves as 'fully British', although a clear majority considered themselves either mainly or fully British. More surprisingly perhaps, it was blacks rather than Asians who were most resistant to a British identity: 22 per cent considered themselves 'not at all British'. Interviews with some successful members of ethnic communities reveal a richer and more complex mixture of identities and allegiances in practice (see Box 24.5).

The real problem is not those from ethnic minorities who have prospered in British society, but those who feel excluded and alienated from it, such as the children of Asian immigrants tempted by jobs in the British textile industry that have since disappeared. This new generation of British-born Asians is still facing prejudice and discrimination, competing for jobs against local working-class whites who resent them and blame them for their own poor economic prospects. It is hardly surprising that they fall back on their own ethnic and religious identity, and some reject the country that rejects them. Nor is it surprising that some feel more solidarity with their co-religionists in other countries than the white neighbours who do not mix with them. It is also hardly surprising that a few turn to an extremism that their elders rejected.

Britain's ethnic minorities are numerically fewer than the minority nations within the United Kingdom, yet in some respects pose a potentially bigger problem for British politics than nationalism. If it becomes the settled wish of the majority of Scots and Welsh to belong to independent nation states, it will happen, probably peacefully, without much animosity, and without substantial difficulty – there are after all well-established borders and institutions for Scottish and Welsh states. The union of the United Kingdom could be dissolved with a mutually agreed divorce. However, if Britain's ethnic minorities feel alienated and rejected by British society and politics there is no possibility of a clean break. They are unlikely to benefit from the break-up of Britain, should it happen. Indeed it may be more difficult for them to feel and be accepted as English, Scots or Welsh than British. Yet most of them cannot 'go home' because there is no home for them to go to. They are here to stay, and have to be accepted on equal terms, or Enoch Powell's dismal prophecy will be fulfilled.

Summary

- Immigration in Britain has a long history. What was distinctive about many of the post-war immigrants into Britain was their skin colour. This made them identifiable and hindered their integration.
- This immigration has created a multi-ethnic, multi-faith Britain, particularly evident in Britain's major cities.
- Ethnic minorities continue to face discrimination and prejudice in Britain. This is clear from employment statistics and from their under-representation in British politics.
- Institutional racism is blamed for some of the discrimination still faced by ethnic minorities.

Box 24.5

Identities of individuals from ethnic minorities

David Yip, actor. When I was a kid I was just a Liverpudlian. It was only when I got older that I began to think of myself as a British-born Chinese.

Les Isaac, Pentecostal church minister. Race is an important part of my identity. I think people need to know who they are, where they came from and what they are part of. After being here for 40 years, there are times when I feel I am a foreigner and times when I feel I am British.

Benjamin Zephaniah, poet. Race is an important part of my identity, but I wish it wasn't. I'd like to identify myself as a martial artist, an Aston Villa supporter, or a hip-hop reggae person; but when a policeman stops me on the street it has nothing to do with that.

Uani Seshmi, independent school director. I see myself as African and British.

Michelle Forbes, vice-chair of Mothers Against Guns. I am British in terms of what I contribute, but I don't always feel accepted as such.

Kwame Kwei-Armah, playwright and actor. I define myself as black British, but most importantly as tri-cultural: Ghanaian, Grenadian and English.

Mike Phillips, author. Race is much less important to me than it was .... Too many black people have embraced a racialist definition of themselves and can't let go. I don't accept other people's outline of Britishness. I have my own and I'm in the centre of it.

Tommy Nagra, television producer. I see myself as Brummie Punjabi British – I am comfortable being all three and don't feel it compromises whatever is meant by 'Britishness'.

Sunder Katwala, general secretary, Fabian Society. I am British and mixed race, with Indian and Irish parents. I can be proud of that. But forms asking me to identify my ethnic group never quite seem to offer the right box.

Sham Sandhu, television controller. For me being a British East-African Asian is as important as being a thirty-something, single, gay Londoner.

Lord Ahmed, Labour peer. I am a Muslim Kashmiri but also a Yorkshire lad who loves his fish and chips and his curry and chapati. One of the most important parts of my identity is the values I share with my fellow Britons.

Sources: derived from the *Guardian*, 21 March 2005.

- The 'war on terror' and the attack on Iraq have created problems for the Muslim community in particular, stimulating Islamophobia.
- Many whites refuse to accept a multi-cultural Britain, while a significant minority of blacks and Asians reject a British identity. This could pose considerable problems for British politics in the future.

Questions for discussion

- Why is the term 'race' still used when it has no scientific validity? Is the term 'ethnicity' any clearer?
- How far and why are ethnic minorities under-represented in British politics?
- Why has fascism never attracted the support in Britain that it secured in some other European countries?
- How far do religious differences pose more problems than racial or ethnic differences for modern British politics?
- How useful is the concept of institutional racism?
- Why do some of Britain's ethnic minorities reject a British identity? Does this matter? What could be the consequences for British politics?

Further reading

Saggar (1992), Solomos (2003) and Skellington (1996) provide broad surveys of race and politics in contemporary Britain. Key texts which focus on theory from different perspectives include Rex (1986), Miles (1989), Solomos and Back (1996) and Mac an Ghaill (1999). Bulmer and Solomos (1999) and Back and Solomos (2000) have edited readers on racism, with extracts from many key writers. Celebrated reports on racism in Britain include Scarman (1981), Macpherson (1999), Parekh (2000a), Cantle (2001) and Denham (2002). Parekh (2000b) is also responsible for an extended discussion of multi-culturalism. His work has been subjected to criticism by Brian Barry (2001).

Politics and the Environment

Green ideas may go back a long way but they have only moved up the political agenda in the last few decades, in both Britain and the rest of the world. Initially raised by a handful of thinkers, they were taken up and popularised by influential pressure groups such as Greenpeace and Friends of the Earth. These groups are international. Green concerns have always been global, transcending the narrow boundaries of British politics. Indeed, some of the most serious environmental problems can only be addressed through international cooperation. Yet if green politics are essentially international, they still require action at other levels, including action by national governments, such as the British government. Moreover, green thinking has permeated British politics.

This chapter examines the rise of environmental politics in Britain and explores briefly green ideas, issues and concerns. It evaluates the contribution of pressure groups, mainstream political parties and the Green Party to the debate on the environment. It considers the response of British governments, particularly the post-1997 Labour government, to those issues and concerns, and explores briefly the increasing role of the European Union and other levels of governance in pollution control and environmental conservation. Finally the chapter address some of the particular problems with the politics of the environment.

Contents

Green ideas

Green thinking is often referred to as 'environmentalism' or (now more rarely) as 'ecologism'. Yet as the name and colour 'green' has become almost universally identified with concern for the environment, there seems little point in using less familiar terms for what has become an important and distinctive political ideology. Other ideologies focus on the interests and needs of humankind in general or a particular section of humanity – a class, a nation, a race or gender. The green slogan 'Earth First!' subordinates the future of humankind to the future of the planet, although of course greens would argue that the futures of both planet and people are bound up together.

While mainstream ideologies and parties from left to right welcome economic growth as a means of satisfying conflicting human interests and demands without necessarily making anyone worse off, greens insist there are limits to growth. Many of the resources on which our current standard of living depends are non-renewable and thus finite. Unless renewable energy resources are utilised to replace the dwindling stocks of fossil fuels, humans will ultimately exhaust those supplies. Pollution is also causing irreversible damage to the environment, destroying flora and fauna and threatening climate changes which could prove catastrophic. The relentless pursuit of growth to satisfy the needs of a still fast-expanding human population threatens not only other species but future generations of humanity. (See Box 25.1 for key green ideas.)

Green predictions for the future are contentious. Some scientists, as well as some politicians, are more optimistic about the prospects for technological solutions to resource depletion and pollution. Some greens have also perhaps exaggerated the more immediate threats, and thus damaged their case by crying 'Wolf!' too soon. Most people would prefer to believe the more optimistic scenarios (or ignore the problem altogether), particularly if the recommended solution to the darker predictions involves sacrifices of current living standards, particularly in advanced western societies like Britain.

Box 25.1

Green ideas: key points

- **'Earth first!'** The needs of the planet should have priority over the needs and wishes of humankind. This is sometimes called an eco-centric approach rather than an anthropocentric approach, putting ecology ahead of humankind, men and women.
- **Limits to growth.** Greens argue that there are limits to the increases in productivity that can be derived from the exploitation of finite natural resources (an argument distantly derived from the economist Thomas Malthus). Greens have also identified significant costs to the pursuit of growth in terms of damage to the environment and to humanity.
- **Sustainability.** Humans should only pursue policies that can in the long run be sustained without irreversible damage to the resources on which the human species and other species depend. Any growth has to be sustainable.
- **Protect future generations.** Those alive today may not pay the price for unsustainable policies, but our descendants will. Greens argue we need to consider the interests of future generations, and we should leave the earth in no worse shape than we found it.
- **Animal rights.** Many greens are strong supporters of animal rights, and refuse to eat or wear dead animals. (Greens also argue that the production of meat consumes too many resources compared with the production of cereals and vegetables.)
- **'Think global, act local.'** While greens believe that environmental issues and problems are global, they stress the need for action at the local level. Many greens are suspicious of central government and the state, and believe (with the economist Schumacher, 1973) that 'small is beautiful'. They favour decentralisation and increased self-sufficiency of local communities.

Green strategy: light and dark greens

Perhaps the biggest challenge greens face is over strategy – how to achieve their objectives. How far, for example, should they engage in the conventional political arena? There is an obvious problem. Unlike mainstream political parties greens advocate many interests that have no vote or voice in state politics, such as people in the third world, future human generations and animals. Thus some greens prefer to opt out altogether from conventional politics and pursue a green lifestyle, or work with other greens to look after the local environment. Yet such personal and local activity can only have a minimal effect on the scale of the problem. Alternatively, greens can campaign on particular issues through single-issue pressure groups or broader environmental groups like Greenpeace and Friends of the Earth. However, the occasional victory that halts a proposed development, or reduces pollution in a limited area, is not going to save the planet.

Many people show some concern for the environment and green ideas without necessarily adopting the whole green philosophy. Some who accept that philosophy nevertheless are prepared to work for more immediate limited political goals. A distinction is sometimes made between light and dark (or deep) greens, or between realists and fundamentalists. Light greens are commonly concerned with specific environmental causes – live calf exports, or roads, or nuclear power – while dark greens have a 'holistic' concern for the global environment, of which specific interests are at best only a part. At worst, limited objectives may appear a dangerous diversion from more fundamental goals, as in the case of lead-free petrol, with its promise of 'greener motoring' (see case study in Box 25.2). Green realists, however, counter that greens have to engage with the political process, and pursue more immediate and limited objectives if they are to have any chance of influencing policy on the environment. This will often necessitate compromise with mainstream parties and concessions to other interests.

The rise of green politics in Britain

Much of the post-war consensus in British politics (see Chapters 2 and 4) was built on the assumption common to both Labour and the Conservatives that economic growth would provide the extra resources for higher living standards and an expanding welfare state, without the need for higher taxation. Maximising growth and promoting affluence were seen as the key to economic and political success. The Conservative Prime Minister Harold Macmillan boasted in 1957, 'You've never had it so good'. Labour's Harold Wilson argued that Britain's growth rate was too low, and fought and won the 1964 election on a programme based around a projected 4 per cent annual growth.

The modern environmental debate began, in a modest, undramatic way, with the publication of Rachel Carson's book *Silent Spring* in 1962, which drew attention to the deadly impact of pollution on the natural environment. In 1972 the Club of Rome report *The Limits to Growth* (Meadows *et al.* 1972) showed that current rates of economic growth were unsustainable. Their projections showed that non-renewable resource depletion, population growth and environmental pollution would lead to a collapse of the world system (how soon depending on a number of variables, although the most optimistic projection suggested catastrophe by 2100, and others much earlier).

The new concerns over the environment spurred by these and other warnings led to the establishment of the major international radical pressure groups Friends of the Earth in the USA in 1969 and Greenpeace in Canada in 1972. Membership expanded rapidly in Britain, where the new groups became part of a growing environmental lobby. This included some traditional well-established

Box 25.2

Green motoring? The campaign for lead-free petrol

Petrol contained lead long after it was known that lead pollution could have a serious impact on children's health as well as the environment. Des Wilson, who had gained a reputation for campaigning on homelessness and freedom of information, set up the Campaign for Lead-free Air (CLEAR) in 1982, and in a textbook pressure group campaign helped persuade the public, Parliament and ultimately the government that action was necessary. Wilson claimed that CLEAR secured a change in government policy in 15 months, although the decision was helped by a report of the Royal Commission on Environmental Pollution, and parallel German pressure to cut vehicle pollution to protect forests. The British government encouraged the switch away from leaded petrol with a tax cut for lead-free petrol. Similar pressure for more environmentally friendly petrol in other European states, helped by a changed directive from the European Union, meant that lead was taken out of petrol over most of western Europe. The pumps at filling stations were given green labels. Pollution had been reduced. It appeared a substantial victory for the environmental lobby (Wilson 1984, McCormick 1991: 136–40).

Yet it was at best a limited victory from a green perspective. At worst, it could be seen as ecologically counter-productive by encouraging the notion of green fuels and green motoring. Greens would argue that the rapidly escalating use of cars remains one of the main causes of non-renewable resource depletion and environmental pollution in the world. Thus the only longer-term solution is to reduce humanity's dependence on the motor car, through for example higher taxation, congestion charges, and much stricter controls on car travel and perhaps travel in general.

organisations such as the National Trust, the Council for the Protection of Rural England and the Royal Society for the Protection of Birds, and some newer, more radical groups such as Transport 2000 and the Centre for Alternative Technology. These groups over the years helped draw the attention of the British public and politicians to a number of important environmental issues in British politics (see Box 25.3).

However, as some of these issues indicate, it is easier to raise the alarm than find politically acceptable remedies. Anthony Downs (1973) argued that political concern about the environment would pass through a five-stage process (Box 25.4). Downs's model has often proved to be broadly accurate in terms of a range of environmental issues (such as oil pollution, carbon dioxide emissions and nuclear waste), although some clear progress has been made on others (such as lead in petrol, salmonella and BSE). Part of the

Box 25.3

Some important environmental issues in British politics

Nuclear energy. In the 1960s nuclear power ('atoms for peace') was seen as a clean solution to Britain's energy needs. Concerns however grew over environment pollution from nuclear waste, and the risks of leaks or more serious disasters, dramatised by the Chernobyl disaster in 1986. The costs of nuclear energy and the risks led to the halting of the construction on new nuclear power stations, although the depletion and high cost of alternative energy sources have led to some rethinking on the nuclear option.

Acid rain. Pollution from coal-fired power stations endangers plant and animal life both in Britain and in neighbouring countries. It has been a factor leading to the running down and replacement of coal-fired power stations.

Food scares. A succession of food scares (such as salmonella in eggs, BSE and contaminated beef, pesticides on fruit and vegetables, foods with genetically modified (GM) ingredients) has raised public concerns over farming practices and food safety. Such concerns led to the establishment of the Food Standards Agency and the Department of the Environment, Food and Rural Affairs (DEFRA). More recently there have been concerns over the impact of 'junk food' on obesity and health in general, particularly for children.

The environmental costs of transport. Pressure groups have highlighted the serious resource depletion and pollution consequences arising from the growth of road and air transport in particular. Yet although new roads and airports arouse furious protests from local residents (combining with environmentalists), restrictions on car use and cheap air flights are seen as extremely unpopular and electorally damaging. Planned increases in petrol tax to help deter car use were scrapped, following the fuel protests of September 2000.

Global warming, climate change and floods. Freak weather and flooding in Britain have been widely blamed on global warming, leading to more pressure on government to address the perceived cause by cutting greenhouse gas emissions, and the perceived consequences through, for example, flood control measures.

Box 25.4

Downs's five-stage model for environmental issues

Stage 1: the pre-problem stage. The problem exists, is recognised by experts, but the public is unaware, the media are uninterested and only interest groups are alarmed.

Stage 2: alarmed discovery and euphoric enthusiasm. The public are alerted to the issue, often by a dramatic event (such as the Chernobyl disaster). The public demand solutions and politicians promise action.

Stage 3: realising the cost of significant progress. Over time public and politicians come to realise that the cost of proposed solutions is likely to be high and involve sacrifices.

Stage 4: gradual decline of public interest. Public and media interest declines, either from boredom or from a realisation of the scale of changes necessary and costs involved.

Stage 5: post-problem stage. The issue has lost its previously high position and receives only spasmodic attention.

Sources: derived from Downs (1973), Richardson and Jordan (1979) and Savage and Robins (1990).

problem is that there are often marked conflicts of interest between sections of the public on environmental issues (for example bypasses, wind farms and flood management).

The greening of British political parties?

As environmental concerns rose on the issue agenda, mainstream parties sought to address them. Each party developed its own green organisations – Labour the Socialist Environment and Resources Association (SERA), the Liberal Democrats the Green Democrats (replacing the old Liberal Ecology Group) and the Conservatives the Tory Green Initiative. Such groups tried to push green issues higher on each party's policy agenda, although with rather limited success. The most apparently dramatic conversion was of Margaret Thatcher, who startled the 1988 Conservative Party Conference with a speech in which she proclaimed:

> We Conservatives are not merely friends of the Earth – we are its guardians and trustees for generations to come. The core of Tory philosophy and the case for protecting the environment are the same. No generation has a freehold on this Earth. All we have is a life tenancy – with a full repairing lease. And this Government intends to meet the terms of the lease in full.

Thatcher was a science graduate, and appears to have been convinced of the scientific arguments on the dangers of population growth, global warming and environmental pollution. To that extent her conversion was genuine. Coming from such a source it brought environmental concerns into the British political mainstream.

Yet while all mainstream parties began to show more concern for environmental issues, there were conflicts of interest and ideas within each of them that prevented a wholehearted commitment to a green philosophy. For example, while it was true that Conservatism involved conservation, and within the party there were strong interests committed to the preservation of the countryside, Thatcherism had emphasised the free market and deregulation, whereas many environmental issues appeared to require more regulation. In practice, in Britain as elsewhere, greens are more likely to be found on the left than the right, and Labour contains some radical environmentalists. Yet Labour was historically committed to economic expansion, high growth and full employment. Both Labour and its trade union allies were more concerned to defend jobs than the environment. The Liberal Democrats have often appeared more sensitive to environmental issues than the other major parties, but even they have felt obliged to make concessions to conflicting interests, for example concerns in rural areas over fuel costs. All mainstream parties are wary of offending motorists, and thus are wary of advocating higher car taxes or restrictions on car use.

The problem is that parties have generally competed by promising to make people better off, whereas a more thorough green philosophy might entail making them worse off, at least in material terms, and this is an intrinsically difficult message to sell to voters. Thus the parties prefer to express a generalised concern for the environment, particularly the global environment, and only emphasise some relatively easy voter-friendly environmental issues that will not cost too much or upset significant vested interests.

The Green Party

The Green Party would claim that it is the only party wholeheartedly committed to a green agenda. So far it has not made the same progress as some green parties in other countries (notably Germany, see Box 25.5). The British Green Party can trace its origins back further than the more successful German Greens. The party began as the People Party in 1973, changed its name to the Ecology Party in 1975, and finally to the Green Party in 1985. In the early years it only secured between 1 per cent and 1.5 per cent of the vote in General Elections, although rather more in local elections. Then in 1989 it appeared to make a decisive breakthrough in electoral politics, winning 15 per cent of the vote in the elections for the European Parliament, although no seats under the first-past-the-post system then used in Britain for European elections. It proved a false dawn. The circumstances in 1989 were unusual. The centre was in disarray, as the old Liberal Party and its recent electoral partner the SDP had proceeded to a clumsy and hotly contested merger after the 1987 election, and the greens attracted protest votes from those who did not want to support either of the two main parties.

The greens have never approached their 1989 performance in any subsequent election. However, they have benefited modestly from the introduction of more proportional representation into elections for Europe and devolved assemblies. Thus in 1999 and again in 2004 they won two seats in the European Parliament on 6 per cent of the vote (a much smaller share than in 1989), seven seats in the Scottish Parliament in 2003 (on 6.9 per cent of the regional list vote), and two seats in the London Assembly in 2004 (down one on 2000). This representation has given the Green Party a rather higher profile, but they have come nowhere near winning a seat at Westminster under first past the post. They are penalised not only by the electoral system, but also by a lack of financial resources.

However, the greens have perhaps not helped their cause by refusing to behave like a normal political party, reflecting some ambivalence towards conventional parliamentary politics. Thus they have generally declined to choose a single party leader, preferring to nominate several spokespersons. All this is reminiscent of the behaviour of the early German Greens as an 'anti-party party' (see Box 25.5). Yet it is worth noting that their level of support (over 6 per cent) in recent elections held under proportional representation is very close to that of the German Greens who were in the German government from 1998 to 2005. Even so, the Green Party remains marginal to British politics, and much less influential than the green lobby and the major pressure groups, Greenpeace and Friends of the Earth.

Box 25.5

Comparative politics: the German Greens (*die Grünen*)

The green movement developed in Germany in the late 1970s. Green candidates won election to state parliaments and in 1983 the Green Party won 5.6 per cent of the vote and 28 seats in the German federal parliament (the Bundestag). The new green representatives caused a stir by turning up in jeans and T-shirts and placing potted plants on their desks in the chamber. Their best-known early leader, Petra Kelly, proclaimed they were an 'anti-party party'. However the greens were soon split between *realos* (realists, who were prepared to make compromises and form alliances with other parties) and *fundis* (fundamentalists), who were not. Some greens joined the Social Democrats in 'red–green' coalitions in state parliaments. Party fortunes subsequently fluctuated at national level, until in 1998 they won 6.7 per cent of the vote and joined in a coalition government with the Social Democrats under Gerhard Schröder. The green leader Joschka Fischer became foreign minister, and three other greens entered the Cabinet. Against predictions the red–green coalition remained in power until 2005.

The German Greens show what could be achieved by the British Green Party, particularly if a more proportional electoral system was introduced at Westminster. However, the internal tensions and splits among German Greens show the problems in moving from an anti-party of protest to a party of government.

New Labour and the environment

Blair and New Labour came to power in 1997 committed to placing the environment at the heart of their policy making. Labour embraced sustainability and announced a number of targets – to meet 10 per cent of UK energy needs from renewable resources by 2010, to cut the 1990 level of greenhouse gas emissions by 23 per cent by 2010, to recycle 35 per cent of all household waste by 2015. Moreover, Labour was also pro-active in the international arena, and tried (but failed) to persuade the Bush administration not to withdraw from the Kyoto agreement (see Box 25.6).

Energy

The Labour government took over at a time when the decline of coal-fired power stations and the 'rush for gas' to replace them was already far advanced. Labour sought to arrest the decline in the coal industry and maintain competition in energy supply. Even so, the energy white paper

Box 25.6

The Kyoto Agreement

Negotiated in 1997, the Kyoto Agreement sets targets for 186 states (including 38 developed states) to bind them to reduce their emissions of carbon dioxide and other greenhouse gases by 2012. The European Union has committed all member states to keep to their targets by law. However, the USA has unilaterally withdrawn from the Kyoto Agreement. While President Clinton was supportive, the Senate rejected the Agreement. The election of George Bush was the final nail in the coffin for US participation in climate change. Tony Blair has criticised the USA for its non-participation, but on matters of global environmental protection, Blair and Bush stand far apart.

published in 1998 predicted that on current trends coal would meet just 10 per cent of the electricity industry's needs by 2003 (compared with 70 per cent in 1990) while gas would supply 50–60 per cent. The switch might help the UK to meet its emission targets, but at the cost of making the country dangerously dependent on gas, and increasingly imported gas, as Britain's own supply of gas from the North Sea was rapidly declining.

The government has sought on the one hand to cut energy consumption, by the encouragement of more efficient use of energy both by industry and households, and on the other hand to seek new renewable energy resources. Neither has yet made an appreciable impact. Initially, in the first few years of the Labour government energy prices fell, as a result of increased competition between suppliers, among other factors. While this helped the government to keep inflation low and to satisfy consumers, it scarcely helped the cause of energy conservation. It remains to be seen whether a change in attitudes will result from more recent rises in energy prices.

Wind farms, it was hoped, would help the government meet its target of meeting 10 per cent of energy needs from renewable resources. Yet electricity produced by wind farms is irregular and expensive, and can meet only a tiny proportion of the UK's energy needs. Moreover, the location of large numbers of giant windmills on attractive countryside has aroused increasing opposition from local pressure groups demanding a shift to offshore windmills, which would be more expensive (see Box 25.7). Other bold schemes to generate electricity through the use of wave power (such as the proposed Morecambe Bay barrage) have yet to get off the ground.

In the circumstances, some, including the CBI, the Royal Society and (it seems) the prime minister have begun to 'think the unthinkable' and urge reconsideration of the nuclear option. Nuclear power (or 'atoms for peace') once appeared the fuel of the future. Yet the high costs of nuclear energy coupled with increasing concerns over safety and security led to a moratorium on the building of new atomic power stations. Sizewell B, completed in 1994, was the last. The remaining nuclear power stations currently deliver around 20 per cent of Britain's electricity, but this will decline sharply as more are decommissioned, leaving the country dangerously dependent on electricity generated by gas-fired power stations. Thus the government announced a new review of energy policy in November 2005, with nuclear power apparently back on the agenda. Nuclear power has some advantages over its competitors. It generates electricity around the clock and is 'relatively greenhouse friendly' (Jordan, in Dunleavy *et al.* 2002: 273). Yet it remains much more expensive than electricity generated by gas because of massive initial building costs and subsequent decommissioning costs. Greenpeace and Friends of the Earth argue that no solution has been found to the problem of radioactive waste, and that there can be no guarantees on safety. The Liberal Democrats and many in the Labour Party are implacably opposed, while public opinion remains hostile. A massive political battle looms if the nuclear option is reopened (*Guardian*, 30 November 2005).

Transport

Transport is of course a major contributor to Britain's energy requirements, but affects the environment in many other ways. Thus transport infrastructure – roads, airports, railways – has an obvious major impact on the physical environment, and almost all new developments are politically contentious. Noise pollution is an important factor here, with massive effects on the quality of

Box 25.7

The politics of energy: wind farms split the green lobby

A public inquiry began in April 2005 on proposals by Chalmerston Wind Power (CWP) to build 27 wind turbines at Whinash on the edge of the Lake District. Wind power was seen as the green answer to Britain's energy needs – a renewable, clean, non-polluting source of electricity. Yet turbines have to be sited where there will be sufficient wind to drive them, normally on hilltops, where they can ruin familiar landscapes and local beauty spots. The projected Whinash wind farm is just outside the Lake District national park and close to the borders of the Yorkshire Dales national park, It is opposed by the Council for National Parks, the Council for the Protection of Rural England and the Countryside Agency, as well as local residents groups, but supported by the Friends of the Earth and Greenpeace. All these organisations are part of the green lobby, which is deeply split on the issue of inland wind farms in general, and this proposal in particular. One well-known environmentalist, David Bellamy, has threatened to chain himself to a turbine if the wind farm is built. The CWP project manager argued that they had to find sites where the wind blew, and Whinash was the most appropriate site in the north-west. 'A quarter of England is covered by national parks or areas of outstanding national beauty. We have to pick up the scraps that are left.'

Opponents of inland wind farms argue that offshore wind farms are viable alternatives. Two offshore wind farms are fully commissioned, and a further nine were due to be completed by the end of 2006. Another round of larger wind farms is expected from 2008. Offshore wind farms are more expensive to build and run, but have more reliable wind. They do not arouse strong local opposition, and public attitudes are favourable, although there are some problems with shipping and fishing interests, and there are concerns over migrating birds (*Guardian*, 20 April 2005).

life and both physical and mental health, but there are also invariably concerns also over the impact on the landscape and flora and fauna. So transport and the environment have become closely linked.

In 1997 the environment, transport and the regions were combined in a single large department under the deputy prime minister, John Prescott. It was hoped that this high-profile integrated department would aid 'joined-up' policy making, place environmental concerns at the centre of government, and aid Labour's traditional aspiration to build an integrated transport system in which public transport would no longer suffer neglect and under-investment. It did not work out quite like that. The new department proved too large for effective control, although in another sense its influence was too limited, as it seemed unable to prevent producer interests from dominating in other departments with an impact on the environment. After the 2001 election the department was broken up, and the environment was combined with food and rural affairs in a new ministry (DEFRA) to replace the old Ministry of Agriculture, Fisheries and Food, while transport re-emerged as a separate department.

Labour's integrated transport policy had soon run into trouble, compelling a U-turn. John Prescott had boldly announced in 1997, 'I will have failed if, in five years time, there are not many more people using public transport and far fewer journeys by car'. Yet it was clear that Labour was reluctant to upset motorists for electoral reasons. After the September 2000 fuel protests the government abandoned higher motoring taxes as a policy instrument, and the chancellor has since fought shy of increasing petrol taxes. The Labour government was not directly responsible for the only significant curb on car use. Congestion charges, introduced in London in 2003 by the then-independent mayor, have proved reasonably successful in reducing congestion and raising revenue, and have led to interest in other cities (although Edinburgh residents voted in 2005 against following London's example). Meanwhile, Labour's hopes of boosting rail transport were dealt a major blow by the emergence of serious problems in the rail management system it had inherited. The Hatfield crash forced a rethinking of priorities, led to substantial delays because of new safety restrictions, and contributed to the collapse of Railtrack. Labour has effectively abandoned any prospect of reducing car use, and indeed expects road traffic to increase by 17 per cent by 2010.

Food, agriculture and the countryside

Agriculture and food production in Britain have become big business. Small farms have become increasingly uneconomic as farming has become more mechanised and capital-intensive. An already small agricultural workforce has become smaller – only around 1 per cent of the working population. Most of those who live in the more rural parts of Britain no longer work there, although the countryside has increasingly attracted refugees from the pressures of urban life. While farmers and landowners might claim to be the custodians of the natural environment, they are, like those engaged in other kinds of business, also and primarily intent on securing the maximum return on their investment, regardless of the environmental consequences, unless it is feared these may affect future profits.

Major supermarkets increasingly dominate food production, because of their purchasing power and marketing. Thus most British agricultural produce is not consumed locally but transported, sometimes hundreds of miles, to be processed, packaged and promoted. Consumers predominantly want cheap and convenient food, and most are not concerned where it comes from,

Box 25.8

Frankenstein foods? The controversy over genetically modified (GM) crops

Genetically modified (GM) crops were a familiar feature of American agriculture throughout the late 1980s and 1990s, and it was anticipated they would become equally familiar in Europe. The British government had initially been a strong supporter of the biotechnology industry, as Britain was a world leader in GM research. GM foods appeared to offer the prospect of increased agricultural productivity, and thus more food for all. But in 1998 the British public became aware of alleged risks from GM food, while environmental groups were particularly concerned about the threat to wildlife.

In 1998, a decision by the transnational Monsanto sparked public concern in Britain over GM food. Monsanto planned to cease separating GM and non-GM soya beans, meaning consumers could no longer choose between the two in food products that used Monsanto beans. Environmental groups such as Greenpeace helped alert public opinion, turning it against GM crops and the companies that created and sold them. Major supermarkets capitalised on the public concern and offered GM-free products.

The events of 1998 forced the government to backtrack on its full support of GM food, and rather than rely on original, mainly favourable, scientific research the government opted for a neutral position, claiming more research was needed. The biotechnology industry announced a moratorium on the introduction of commercial crops until 2002. This did not ease public concern, as the trials of new GM crops across the British countryside led to fears that GM crops could cross-pollinate other species of plant. Greenpeace activists participated in the destruction of GM crops around Britain, claiming they had a moral duty to do so. The hysteria over what were described as 'Frankenstein foods' scarcely helped any rational scientific assessment of the costs and benefits of genetically modified seeds, although the outcome of trials suggests that both the claimed advantages and the dangers have been exaggerated.

A Friends of the Earth protestor against GM foods, March 2005

Photograph: EMPICS.

although there are periodic food scares which cause alarm and lead to consumer boycotts.

British governments, including the Labour government, have not generally sought radical change. Cheap food helps keep inflation low. Beyond that, much of the regulation of British agriculture now lies primarily with the European Union, whose subsidies largely reward the big 'agri-businesses', for all the proclaimed interest in small farms, although more recently some financial assistance has been directed towards environmental conservation and organic farming. The Labour government has sought to give rather more priority to these areas, although like its predecessor it has necessarily become involved with periodic food scares and crisis management, particularly over GM foods (see Box 25.8) and the foot-and-mouth disease outbreak in 2001. The government's handling of the latter, involving the mass slaughter of animals, was widely criticised, although the policy broadly followed expert advice and the wishes of the leadership of the National Farmer's Union. The crisis helped to precipitate the replacement of MAFF by DEFRA (see above). Since then the government has announced that vaccination would be used to help contain any future outbreak.

In 2004–5 concerns over obesity, particularly child obesity, linked with concerns over diets and 'junk food' with high sugar and salt content, and numerous additives for colour and flavouring, have increased pressure for more regulation of the food industry, and healthier school meals. In September 2005 the education secretary announced that junk food was to be banned in schools, including a ban on slot machines selling chocolate bars and fizzy drinks (see In Focus 19.1).

Labour has had a troubled and disputatious relationship with rural interests, who accuse the party of urban bias. The government's most significant achievement has involved opening up the countryside to walkers under the Countryside and Rights of Way Act. This had the support not only of the Ramblers Association but of the green lobby, whose environmental concerns were largely met, although the measure was resisted by most farmers and landowners. Increased access to the countryside largely serves the leisure needs of urban dwellers, although it can be argued that it is they who pay through their taxes for substantial subsidies to agriculture, and the countryside should be for the benefit of all. It was, however, the hunting issue that stoked up rural resentment and led to the creation of the Countryside Alliance, covering a number of rural grievances (although hunting always remained the chief motivating force). The Countryside Alliance was defending traditional rights and a traditional way of life, and they would argue, the countryside itself. Yet most of the environmental lobby was on the other side. Hunting itself is a highly emotive but essentially peripheral concern. The real political issues are why and how to preserve the countryside, and who for.

Multi-level governance and the environment

The most important environmental issues clearly transcend national boundaries. Britain may suffer from sudden or creeping disasters far away – Chernobyl, the destruction of the Amazonian rain forest, the failure of the US government and people to restrain their own energy consumption and greenhouse gas emissions. Equally, other countries may suffer from practices and policies in Britain – the impact of acid rain from British power stations on Scandinavia, for example, or our trade policies on third-world agriculture. Many problems can only be dealt with through international action, as Blair has acknowledged: 'It is time to accept firm limits for global warming. We are all in this together. No country can opt out of global warming or fence in its own private climate' (Blair, quoted in Kegley and Wittkopf 1999: 311). Thus there have been a series of international summits on the environment, starting from the 'earth summit' held in Rio de Janeiro in 1992. It is, however, one thing to commit states to targets, quite another to secure their effective implementation.

The European Union has also been increasingly active on the environmental front, partly because of the importance of environmental conservation and sustainability, but also because of the need to ensure a level playing field in the single market. Effective pollution control and recycling are expensive, and the countries and their industries that avoided these costs would have an unfair competitive advantage over those countries that pursued more environmentally friendly policies.

Thus the European Union has issued a series of directives with fairly tight timescales for all member states to comply with (see Box 25.9). Fisheries policy is another area requiring European cooperation, for if the fishing fleets of member states continued to fish unrestrained and unregulated, fish stocks would rapidly be exhausted and the fishing industry destroyed. EU fisheries policy has, however, often been politically contentious in Britain because of its immediate impact on the livelihood of fishermen.

Environmental issues are tackled not only at supranational level above the level of the British state, but at other levels. Within the United Kingdom much environmental policy is the responsibility of devolved government in Scotland and Wales. Local councils have extensive environmental responsibilities for regulating pollution and for waste collection and disposal. Here council policy on, for example, recycling waste can have a significant impact. Beyond that local voluntary groups and individuals can take appropriate action themselves. The green slogan 'Think global, act local' has some relevance here. In some cases the actions of councils and individuals may reflect pressure from above, from the British government or EU directives. In others, local action may be innovative, an example to be followed elsewhere, and perhaps adopted as national policy.

The politics of the environment

However, environmental policy frequently conflicts with other policy objectives. This is true of all policy making. Different departments and the policy areas for which they are responsible are frequently in competition with each other for government priority and resources. Environmental policy frequently cuts across a government's broad economic objectives for growth, high employment and low inflation, and the aim of business to maximise profits in a free market, with minimum regulation. Thus the now substantial environmental lobby frequently comes up against a well-organised, influential and highly resourced business lobby, which can

Box 25.9

The European Union, the UK and the environment

It has been estimated that 'over 80 per cent of British environment policy originates in the EU' (Jordan, in Dunleavy *et al.* 2002: 262). Of course, the British government has often played a proactive role in the shaping of EU environmental policy, notably over Kyoto and emission targets. However, on other occasions the British government has been caught out by its failure to take steps to implement EU directives, notably on the disposal of old refrigerators and the disposal and recycling of old cars.

On refrigerators, an EU directive prevents their disposal before the removal of all chlorofluorocarbons (CFCs), but there was no plant in Britain capable of this when the directive took effect in 2002, so millions of old fridges piled up in council dumps. Similarly, the government seems ill prepared to meet the EU End of Life Vehicle Directive, requiring that 85 per cent of the elements of a car be recycled by 2006, rising to 95 per cent by 2015. (Currently the UK manages around 74 per cent.) The issue is, who should pay for the recycling costs, estimated at between £40 and £125 per vehicle? If the cost falls substantially on the last owner, generally the least affluent and least able to pay, there is a likelihood that more vehicles will be dumped and burned out (to prevent identification of the vehicle and its last owner). Yet there is considerable resistance to bearing the cost from the motoring industry.

While the British government is prepared to set ambitious targets for recycling waste, it frequently seems unable to deal with the detailed problems of implementing EU directives which should contribute to meeting their broad targets. As a consequence of this failure, crises arise (fridge mountains, indiscriminate car dumping, fly tipping) that the media tend to blame on the EU directives rather than the UK government (Humphrey, in Dunleavy *et al.* 2003: 314–16).

While the green lobby generally approves of the EU approach to recycling, there are other aspects of EU policy that appear less environmentally friendly, including much of the Common Agricultural Policy (protection, intensive farming, draining of wetlands) and some environmentally damaging major civil engineering schemes.

often argue that particular restrictions and regulations will damage competitiveness in world markets. This is an argument that can be highly persuasive with politicians and governments, and also with workers and ultimately consumers and voters. Politicians may be quite sincere in the concerns they express for the environment, but in the real world they have to balance these concerns against other desirable objectives over jobs, services and living standards.

There is another particular problem with environmental issues and policies. Their impact is frequently long-term and sometimes contentious, while politicians deal primarily with the short term and the immediate impact on the economy and political prospects. Many of the presumed beneficiaries of environmental conservation are not voters and have little weight in the political marketplace. There often appears to be an urgent need to satisfy present demands. 'What do we want? More pay! When do we want it? Now!' The horizons of us all, not just politicians, tend to be short-term. It is often difficult to persuade people, in their own interests, to forgo current consumption for some benefit, such as a comfortable retirement. It is much more difficult to persuade them to forgo current consumption for the benefit of unknown peoples in distant continents, still less for future generations yet unborn. Thus the green lobby has its work cut out. The political process, not just in Britain but more generally, has an inbuilt bias against their concerns.

Summary

- Green thinking or environmentalism is a relatively recent but distinctive ideology, marked off from mainstream political ideologies by its concerns for future generations and non-human interests.
- Its main impact on British politics has been through pressure groups rather than mainstream parties, although all these have increasingly sought to address environmental concerns.
- The British Green Party has had negligible political influence until very recently, partly because it has been under-represented under the British electoral system. The introduction of more proportional voting systems has led to its representation in the European Parliament, Scottish Parliament and London Assembly.
- New Labour has claimed that the environment is central to its programme, yet its record on energy, transport and agriculture has been mixed and contentious, reflecting other political pressures.
- Longer-term green issues and problems are not well served in a democratic political system that (inevitably?) reflects the immediate concerns and demands of current voters.

Questions for discussion

- How far is sustainability compatible with a real increase in living standards in countries like Britain?
- How far should greens engage in traditional politics? What else can they do?
- Why is it difficult for mainstream British parties to pursue environmental policies wholeheartedly?
- Why has the German Green Party apparently been so much more successful than the British Green Party?
- How might Britain's dependence on imported fossil fuels be reduced?
- What might a green transport policy look like, and what would be the problems in achieving it?
- Is there a case for further trials of GM crops?
- Who or what is the British countryside for? Who can be best trusted to look after it?
- How far is the democratic political process ill-equipped for addressing environmental concerns?

Further reading

There are useful short chapters on green thinking or environmentalism in several general books on contemporary ideologies, including Heywood

(2003), Leach (2002), Adams (1998) and Eccleshall *et al.* (2004). Green thinking is explored further in Goodin (1992), Eckersley (1993) and Dobson (1995). Some older accounts are still useful for the growth of green politics in Britain and more generally, including Porritt and Winner (1988), McCormick (1991), Robinson (1992) and Garner (2000). Useful accounts of recent environmental policy in Britain are provided by Jordan in Dunleavy *et al.* (2002) and by Humphrey in Dunleavy *et al.* (2003). Foster discusses the Blair government's transport policy in Seldon (2001).

Britain and the World: Making Foreign Policy

Contents

Foreign policy often seems different from the essentially domestic policy making described in earlier chapters, part of a closed secretive world, substantially insulated from the routine political pressures affecting other parts of government, yet with potentially massive consequences for the British people and the wider world. British foreign policy since 1945 has had to adapt painfully to the loss of empire and world power status (see Chapter 2). Until the collapse of the Soviet empire, British foreign and defence policy was conditioned by the Cold War between the two superpowers, the USA and USSR and their allies in NATO and the Warsaw Pact, with Britain claiming a 'special relationship' with the USA. However, the contraction of Britain's world role and its closer engagement with Europe provided another focus for British policy.

The tension between Europe and America in British politics has intensified following the end of the Cold War, which failed to produce the hoped for 'peace dividend', but instead posed new threats from revived ethnic and religious conflicts around the globe. While British governments hoped to preserve both the special relationship with the USA and its ties with Europe, in practice, and particularly since 9/11 and the growth of the terrorist threat, they have drawn closer to the USA.

This chapter examines the making of British foreign policy in the context of international relations in which independent sovereign states are no longer the main or even necessarily the most important players. It explores the tensions between the pursuit of national interest and the acknowledgement of wider obligations to the international community and international law. It concludes with an examination of the contentious foreign policy associated with Blair's Labour government.

Making foreign policy

Foreign policy differs from internal or domestic policies in three important respects. First, foreign policy tends to be reactive rather than proactive. The government has far greater control over areas such as education or health, where it can direct policy through legislation and financial support. Foreign policy by contrast commonly involves reacting to the behaviour of other governments and international organisations. Second, public opinion tends to divide less on foreign policy than on domestic policy. Government economic, education and health policies tend to create 'winners' and 'losers', where some gain at the direct expense of others. This is rarely the case when the government faces a foreign crisis or perceived external threat, when it can usually count on widespread cross-party public support. Third, foreign policy has generally tended to interest only a relatively small minority of the population. It receives very little coverage in the media, and is particularly ignored by the popular press. It is seldom a major election issue. Partly as a consequence, pressure groups, parties and the media play a lesser role compared with their influence in shaping domestic policy. Indeed, much foreign policy seems to be made not through any pluralist process but by a small bipartisan specialist elite.

Even so, foreign policy has on occasion been acutely divisive, spawning massive popular demonstrations. Examples include the 'Ban the bomb' marches, the anti-Vietnam War demonstrations, and most recently, the protests against the Iraq War. Public opinion may not always appear decisive (as these examples demonstrate), although it can constrain foreign policy. Thus although popular opposition to the Vietnam War in Britain did not lead to any official condemnation of US policy by the British government, it was perhaps one reason why Wilson's Labour government declined to send any troops in support. While Blair committed Britain to war on Iraq despite considerable public opposition, the decision appreciably weakened his position, and was a major factor in Labour's reduced electoral support in 2005. The prospect of further public and party opposition may inhibit any similar initiatives in the future. War in the absence of broad public support is a very risky undertaking.

In constitutional terms, responsibility for foreign policy lies with the secretary of state for foreign affairs, and is implemented both directly by the Foreign and Commonwealth Office (FCO), and through British embassies and missions abroad. Defence, trade and aid (the responsibilities of the Ministry of Defence, the Department of Trade and Industry and the Department of International Development) are closely linked with foreign policy. and require careful coordination. Other departments, such as the Department of the Environment, Food and Rural Affairs (DEFRA), whose responsibilities are primarily domestic, may be frequently involved in international or EU negotiations.

Most prime ministers have had a major role in foreign policy, and some have overshadowed their foreign secretaries. A few prime ministers, such as Churchill, Eden and Macmillan, could claim some special prior experience or expertise to justify their dominant role in foreign policy. However, neither Margaret Thatcher nor Tony Blair, who both substantially controlled Britain's foreign policy from 10 Downing Street, had any special preparation for that role. Yet it is difficult for prime ministers to avoid involvement in foreign affairs. In the modern world any head of government is expected to represent his or her country abroad. The relationships he or she can establish with other national leaders may be crucial in shaping informal alliances and agreements, as well as more formal treaties

At times prime ministers with strong convictions on foreign affairs may be in conflict with the prevailing view among senior officials and career diplomats in the FCO. As prime minister, Margaret Thatcher was noted for her long-running hostility towards the FCO and occasional bitter battles with her own foreign secretary. There were complex reasons for this antagonism, but of central importance amongst them was the clash between Thatcher's Atlanticist foreign policy outlook and the Europeanism of the FCO. Similarly, Blair's foreign policy, particularly his close alliance with George W. Bush, has not always had the full support of senior officials in the FCO and the Ministry of Defence, as became clear from some of the evidence to the Hutton Inquiry.

Nor should the influence of the Chancellor of the Exchequer on foreign policy be underrated. Part of this influence is essentially negative. It is the Treasury that has to fund foreign policy as well as domestic policy. Thus the implicit support of the chancellor is essential for international commitments, defence spending, and above all war. Financial constraints have played a key role in shaping and limiting Britain's diplomatic and defence commitments, for example leading to the closure of bases 'east of Suez', and the abandonment of specific weapons programmes. Moreover, the strength or weakness of the British economy substantially determines the extent of British influence in Europe and the world. The responsibility of the chancellor for the health of the national economy, coupled with his (or her) role in European and international economic decision making, necessarily involves him in foreign policy at the highest level. Gordon Brown as chancellor has effectively vetoed any moves to early UK membership of the

Figure 26.1 The British foreign policy making process

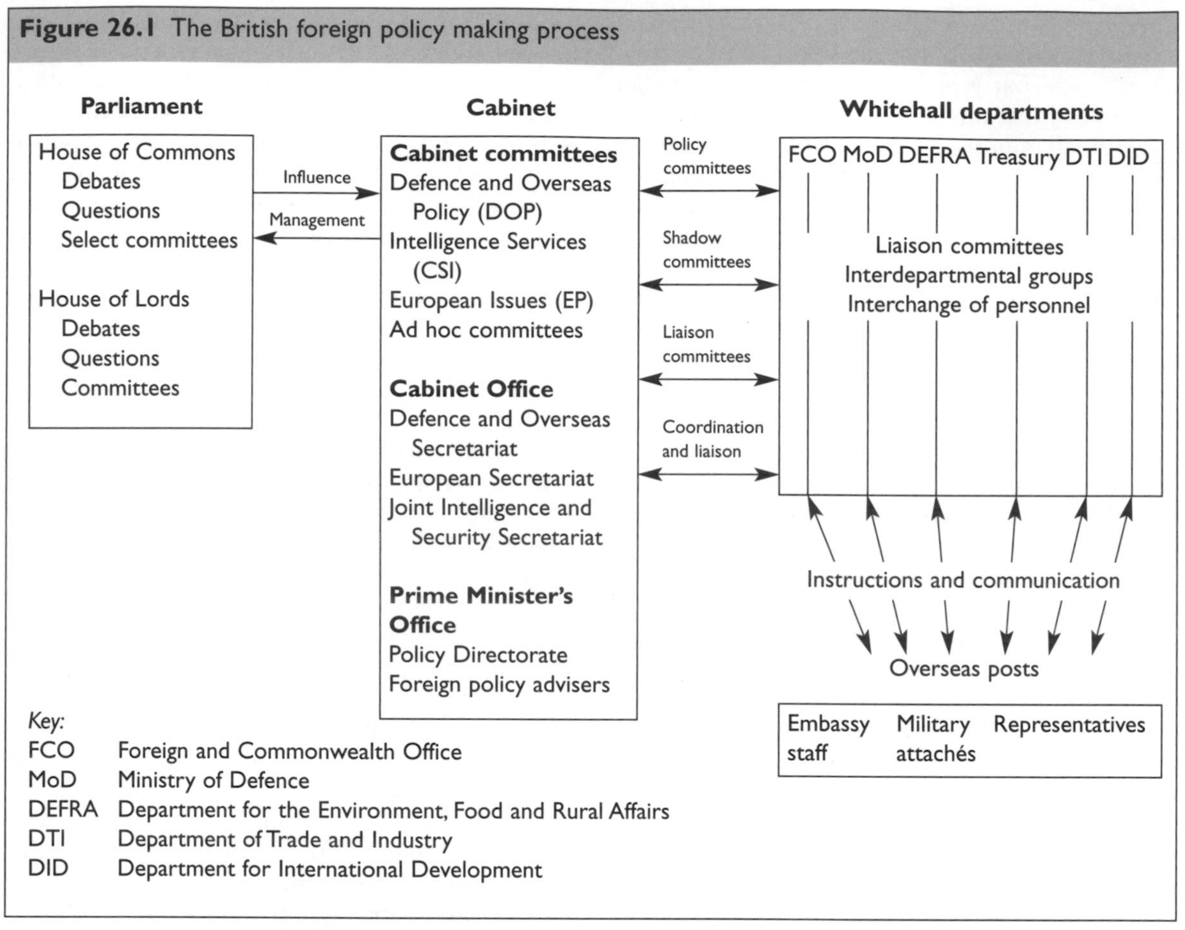

Source: adapted from Sanders, 1990 and Clarke, 1988.

euro, has played a leading role in advocating more competitive labour markets within the EU, and has taken the lead in cancelling third-world debt and promoting international development to help the African continent. Before the 2005 election there was some speculation that Blair might shift Brown from the Treasury to the FCO. Among the other reasons for rejecting such a move was perhaps the consideration that Brown had more effective influence on foreign policy as chancellor than he might have secured as foreign secretary.

National interests and international obligations

There has long appeared an inherent conflict in foreign policy between the pursuit of national interest and the honouring of international obligations. A realist interpretation of international relations suggests that state power and state interests determine foreign policy. From this perspective, international obligations are only accepted when they appear to be in the national interest, and are freely broken when this no longer seems to be the case. Might is right, a concept sometimes described by the German words *Machtpolitik* (power politics) or *Realpolitik* (the politics of the real, of the world as it is, as opposed to the world as one might prefer it to be). Alliances should depend on advantages to the national interest rather than ethical considerations or ideological sympathies. Such an approach has often seemed to guide the foreign policies of states. Thus republican France forged an alliance with Tsarist Russia in the lead-up to the First World War, while Nazi Germany signed a non-aggression pact with the Communist Soviet Union in 1939. Both the Nazi-Soviet pact and its subsequent violation with the German invasion of Russia apparently confirmed *Realpolitik*.

National interest, however, is a rather nebulous concept. It appears to suggest that nations or states have a single exclusive objective interest that can be determined. This national interest is not the same as the public interest. It cannot be simply identified with the expressed interests of the majority of the population of a state. It may indeed be the case that among the citizens that belong to a state there are diametrically opposed views over what is in the national interest. As far as Britain is concerned, some are convinced that it is in Britain's national interest to engage fully with the European Union, while others argue that it is in Britain's interest to disengage from Europe and pursue a close alliance with the USA (see Chapter 15). In practice the national interest is what leading politicians and officials with responsibility for foreign policy declare it to be. Whatever foreign policy is pursued by ministers or their civil servants, it will inevitably be accompanied by claims that this decision or that treaty is 'in the national interest'.

Others argue that the recognition of international law and obligations is in the interests of states and peoples, in the same way as acceptance of the rule of law and freely entered agreements are in the interests of individuals within states. Just as rational individual self-interest and the wider public interest may coincide within communities, so state interests and international interests may coincide in the global community. A rising number of multinational and international institutions has arisen to regulate inter-state relations – the International Court of Justice, the United Nations, the International Monetary Fund (IMF), the World Bank, the World Trade Organisation (WTO), the International Criminal Court, G8 (the Group of Eight advanced industrial states). The jurisdiction of these international institutions has been recognised by increasing numbers of states including the United Kingdom, although not always by their peoples. Thus the World Bank, the WTO and G8 have increasingly been targeted by demonstrators opposed to global capitalism (see Box 26.1).

Such international institutions may offer opportunities to national governments to wield influence in the wider world on issues of concern, such as security, trade, development and the global environment, but may also limit or control their relations with other states and even aspects of their domestic policy. The British government, as a permanent member of the United Nations Security Council and a founder member of G8, has considerable influence on the decisions of these bodies. Yet these and other international institutions such as the WTO and IMF have also from time to time acted as significant constraints on British policy.

Nation states pursuing national interests are not the only, nor perhaps even the main, actors in the global economy and the international political system. Powerful transnational corporations operating across state boundaries can move capital across frontiers, and manipulate transfer prices and costs between their subsidiaries and thus minimise the effects of particular countries' business taxation and regulation. Indeed they can be far more powerful than the states that have the theoretical authority to control them. The turnover of some of these transnationals exceeds the national income of many of the supposedly independent sovereign states represented at the United Nations, and they have far more influence on the operation of global capitalism.

Alongside the transnational corporations there is the growing influence of non-governmental organisations (NGOs), global pressure groups representing a range of interests and causes that also transcend national boundaries. NGOs are defined by the United Nations as 'any international organisation which is not established by a government entity or international agreement'.

Definitions

Transnational corporations (TNCs) are business firms that operate in many countries, and across national boundaries. They can shift their operations between countries to maximise profits.

Non-governmental organisations (NGOs) are international organisations or pressure groups not established by governments or international agreements.

Box 26.1

International organisations

The **International Court of Justice** (1946) was established under the auspices of the United Nations as the successor body to the Permanent Court of International Justice, at The Hague (Netherlands) in 1922. Using international law, it adjudicates on disputes between states.

The United Nations (UN) is a voluntary association of states who have signed the UN Charter (1945), committed to the maintenance of international peace and security, the solution of problems through international cooperation, and the promotion of human rights. Based in New York, it is headed by a secretary general, with a Security Council of five permanent members (each of whom can use a veto on decisions) and ten further members elected by the General Assembly representing all states. UN peacekeeping is dependent on troops and finance from member states. Its reputation for effective peacekeeping was blighted by the failure of UN troops to prevent the massacre in Srebinica, Bosnia. The US government has become critical of the UN.

The **International Monetary Fund (IMF)** was set up following the Bretton Woods agreement, 1944, to oversee currency exchange rates and the international payments system. Governments could borrow from the IMF to defend their currencies, but often with onerous conditions attached on state finance and economic policy (as was the case with the UK loan from the IMF in 1976). As a promoter of sound finance and economic liberalisation (often with harsh consequences for particular economies), the IMF has attracted criticism and protest.

The **World Bank** (strictly speaking the International Bank for Reconstruction and Development, IBRD, along with affiliated organisations) was established in 1945. It is owned by the governments of member states, and makes loans to developing countries, although the conditions have made the bank a target for anti-globalisation protestors.

The **World Trade Organisation (WTO)** emerged from the former **General Agreement on Tariffs and Trade** (GATT, established 1947). WTO regulates world trade, promoting free trade and adjudicating on disputes between countries involving restrictions on trade, and over 'dumping' surplus goods on world markets. Anti-globalisation protestors argue that free trade does not always benefit developing countries.

G8 is a group of eight advanced industrialised states that meet every year to discuss important economic and political issues. The present G8 began in 1975 as a group of five states (the USA, UK, Germany, France and Japan), joined by Italy and Canada to make the G7, and subsequently Russia, to make G8 in 1998. It has attracted criticism from anti-globalisation protestors as a rich man's club. At Gleneagles in 2005 representatives of African states attended the meeting of G8 that discussed aid, trade and debt cancellation in Africa.

The **International Criminal Court** was created following an agreement in Rome in 1998, and formally established in 2002 in The Hague, the Netherlands. Whereas the International Court of Justice is concerned with disputes between states, the International Criminal Court will be able to bring to justice individuals, including former heads of state, accused of war crimes or atrocities. The government of the USA has not recognised it.

The UN already recognises around 2000 NGOs, many of which have also established relationships with other international governance institutions, such as the WTO and IMF. Although there are inevitably some problems with the democratic accountability and legitimacy of NGOs, they can all the same put pressure on states, transnational corporations and international institutions to consider the moral and humanitarian implications of their decisions and behaviour.

Besides these recognised international organisations there are today many more amorphous and loosely organised interests and causes. Some of these freely indulge in the politics of protest, while generally avoiding violence (such as most of the campaigners against global capitalism). Other more clandestine organisations pursue violence and terrorism as a means to often ill-defined ends which allow no compromise. The most infamous of these is al Qaida, responsible for a string of atrocities across the world in New York, Bali, Istanbul, Madrid and (almost certainly) London. Individually and collectively, states increasingly have to take into account the threats such terrorist organisations with a global reach represent to their own peoples, as much as or more than the potential threats from hostile states. Global terrorism provides a new and potent challenge to the conduct of foreign policy.

In the context of a more complex and interdependent world involving layers of governance and a variety of NGOs transcending national boundaries, the pursuit of national interest, even if it can be discerned, inevitably involves compromise and negotiation. This is particularly the case when the 'national interest' of any state, such as the UK, runs counter to the interest of other states, or major transnational corporations, or the wider international community. There are, moreover, political costs if the authority of international bodies is flouted or the views of influential NGOs are ignored. A state, or a transnational, or even an international institution loses moral and political credibility when it appears to reject the consensus of the global community. Thus a more 'ethical' foreign policy (see below) may be in the national interest.

Definition

MAD, the acronym for **mutually assured destruction**, was the basis of nuclear deterrence throughout the Cold War. It rested on the premise that if both the USA and USSR had nuclear parity (that is, they each posed an identical risk to the other) then neither would risk a first strike as this would guarantee destruction of the attacking side. MAD demanded a second-strike capacity, which accounted for the thousands of warheads stockpiled by the superpowers during the Cold War.

British foreign policy – between Europe and America?

In the past British national interest often appeared to require a 'balance of power' in Europe to prevent the emergence of a dominant continental state that might threaten Britain's commerce and industry. Thus British governments sought allies to resist French dominance of Europe in the 18th and early 19th centuries, German dominance in the first half of the 20th century, and Soviet Russia's dominance after the Second World War. The relative decline of Britain's economic and military strength in the post-war era obliged Britain (as well as other western European states) to accept US leadership in NATO, an alliance founded to contain the perceived threat of Soviet expansion.

The Soviet threat appeared to require the development and retention of nuclear weapons to deter aggression through the prospect of 'mutually assured destruction' (MAD). It could be argued that this 'balance of terror' worked, and kept the two great powers out of direct military conflict with each other. Although the USSR armed and encouraged resistance to the USA in Korea and Vietnam, while the USA similarly armed and financed opposition to the USSR in Afghanistan, both superpowers avoided steps that might have engaged them directly with each other in a war neither could win.

For those responsible for Britain's foreign policy there initially appeared to be no realistic alternative to the US alliance – certainly not the new Commonwealth, replacing the fast vanishing British Empire, which was little more than a loose association of independent states with different interests. Nor initially did closer European cooperation seem the solution. Early attempts to build a European Defence Community had failed. Not just Britain but Western Europe generally depended on US arms and NATO for its defence. The one occasion when Britain and France risked independent military action in defiance of American opinion, over Suez in 1956, ended in a humiliating withdrawal. British membership of the European Community when it was sought and eventually obtained in 1973 was not perceived as an alternative to Britain's 'special relationship' with the USA, which then welcomed closer European integration as another bulwark against Communism.

The abrupt end of the Cold War following the destruction of the Berlin Wall, the reunification of Germany and the re-establishment of independence for states in eastern Europe removed the perceived Soviet threat that had dominated British and western European foreign policy for more than three decades. There was no longer a single clear enemy, a single obvious threat to prepare against. The democratic revolutions that swept through Eastern Europe ended the ideological division of Europe which had existed since the

Box 26.2

Britain's 'special relationship' with the USA

Britain's 'special relationship' with the USA involved the leaders of both countries working together closely. It developed out of the close cooperation between the two states during the Second World War. Subsequently, Labour Foreign Secretary Ernest Bevin helped draw the USA into a post-war European defence commitment with the establishment of the North Atlantic Treaty Organisation (NATO, see Box 26.4). The USA continued to contribute directly to Britain's defence when, after the failure of Britain's own nuclear weapons system, it provided Britain with the most modern systems in the shape of Polaris and Trident, advanced submarine-launched inter-continental ballistic missiles. This underlines the point that the relationship was always unequal, reflecting the unequal military and economic strength of the two countries, and meant more to the British as the weaker, dependent partner. Indeed the former German Chancellor Helmut Schmidt once dryly observed that the relationship was 'so special that only one side knows it exists' (quoted by Ash 2005: 199).

Yet the special relationship was never altogether a myth. It was facilitated by a common language and the notion of an 'English-speaking union'. It was sometimes further strengthened by the ideological and party affinities of particular national leaders, and the development of close personal friendships. Thus Margaret Thatcher's brand of Conservatism found an ideological soulmate in the republicanism of Ronald Reagan, in both domestic and foreign policy. Similarly New Labour drew early inspiration from Bill Clinton's new Democrats, while Blair forged a strong personal relationship with the US president. More surprisingly, Blair developed an equally close bond with Clinton's successor, George W. Bush, particularly after 9/11, despite the apparently wider ideological gulf between Blair's brand of social democracy and Bush's neo-conservative Republicanism. Indeed the 'special relationship' appeared stronger than ever before, with significant implications for British foreign policy. Thus while seeking to provide a bridge between Europe and the USA, Blair in practice chose the US alliance over working more closely with Britain's European partners, notably over Iraq.

A special relationship? Blair and Bush at the G8 summit, July 2005

Photograph: EMPICS.

end of the Second World War. The old bipolar certainties of the Cold War disappeared very rapidly; Germany reunited, the communist Warsaw Treaty dissolved, and President Yeltsin announced that he wanted Russia to join NATO. Some optimistically predicted a 'peace dividend' as defence spending was diverted to more productive purposes. In practice the Cold War was replaced by a series of more localised but brutal conflicts in outlying parts of the former Communist bloc, the Middle East and Africa. This increasingly looked not so much like the 'end of history' celebrated by Fukuyama (1992) as a return to the petty nationalist and ethnic conflicts of the era before the First World War in place of the ideological conflict between liberal capitalism and communism.

The end of the Cold War also increased the potential for conflict between the USA and an enlarged European Union pursuing further ambitious policies involving closer European integration in economic and monetary policy and a revival of aspirations for a distinctive European foreign and defence policy. The old European Community had appeared to some as the economic underpinning for NATO. The new European Union seemed to aspire to become an alternative to NATO, whose whole role and purpose appeared problematic following the end of the Cold War (see Box 26.3).

During the 1990s the European Union itself sought to develop more effective common foreign and defence policies. Thus the Maastricht Treaty incorporated the objective of a common foreign policy. The Treaties of Amsterdam and Nice involved the development of a Common Foreign and Security Policy (CFSP) and as essentially a part of this a common European security and defence policy (ESDP). The European Council has determined that 'The Union must have the capacity for autonomous action, backed by credible military forces, the means to decide to use them, and a readiness to do so, in order to respond to international crises without prejudice to actions by NATO'.

Part of the rationale for the capacity for EU military action was the experience of the problems in former Yugoslavia, and the inability of the European Union to deal with a crisis on its own doorstep. These plans received some criticism from the Conservative Party and sections of the media in Britain, who argued that this new EU initiative could lead to differences with NATO. To an extent it reflected a realisation that the USA could not be expected to sort out all Europe's problems, and a fear, prior to 9/11, that the USA might retreat into isolationism, as it has done previously between the wars.

Box 26.3

Academic controversy: three influential American views on the end of the Cold War

Francis Fukuyama (1989, 1992) provocatively announced the end of history. The end of the Cold War marked the decisive victory of economic and political liberalism over its ideological rivals, and the end of the contests that had dominated the history of the 20th century.

Samuel Huntington argued in *The Clash of Civilisations* (1996) that ideological conflicts between superpowers would be replaced by broader struggles between cultures, such as between Islam and the West. His analysis acquired greater resonance with the growth of the threat of Islamic fundamentalism and al Qaida terror.

Robert Kagan asserts in *Paradise and Power* (2004) that 'on major strategic and international questions today, Americans are from Mars and Europeans are from Venus'. Europeans prefer to rely on international law and diplomacy to deal with crises because of their military weakness, while Americans are prepared to use force, if necessary unilaterally, because they have the military resources. Yet, Kagan argues, European peace and security continues to depend on the USA's readiness to use force to defend western values and democracy from real threats.

Box 26.4

A new role for NATO?

The North Atlantic Treaty Organisation (NATO) was founded in 1949. The original member states included the USA, Canada and 12 European countries, including the United Kingdom. Greece and Turkey also joined in 1952. Members of the alliance were obliged to assist each other if attacked.

NATO was established in the face of what appeared to be a threat from the Soviet Union and its allies or satellites. These in 1955 established the rival Warsaw Pact. Following the end of the Cold War and the dissolution of the Warsaw Pact in 1991, it was not immediately clear whether NATO still had a role. Yet NATO has grown. The former Communist states of Poland, Hungary and the Czech Republic joined in 1999, five years before they joined the European Union. Since then seven other former Communist states have joined, bringing the total membership to 26 states. Talks with the Ukraine are proceeding, with a view to membership.

Russia is no longer perceived as the enemy, and has indeed combined with NATO on joint manoeuvres. NATO today is a US-led coalition of countries prepared to intervene if deemed necessary in trouble spots around the world. Thus the war on Serbia in 1999 to assist the Muslim majority in Kosovo was a NATO operation. NATO countries also supplied most of the coalition military force in the First Gulf War in 1991, and the Afghanistan War.

However it has to be said that the European Union has never played a large role in British foreign and defence policy. This is, perhaps, also because Britain, along with most other EU members, is a member of NATO. Many strategic thinkers do not believe that the EU structures have the potential for being the basis of Britain's foreign or defence policy. The EU has been described as an 'economic giant but a military worm' (Kegley and Wittkopf 1999: 168). The massive spending gap between the USA and its western European NATO allies sets the two apart. Others have commented that a common security and defence policy, including Britain, remains impractical for the European Union because it is too diverse an organisation, unable to take on a robust defensive military role for the foreseeable future. Thus Britain's foreign and defence policies continue to be developed within an Atlanticist framework.

Even so, most leading British politicians had never wanted or expected to make a choice between Europe and the USA. They thought they could and should preserve the special relationship with the USA along with involvement in Europe. Even Margaret Thatcher, the most pro-American prime minister since Churchill, signed the Single European Act and agreed to British entry to the Exchange Rate Mechanism while she was in office. Major announced he wanted Britain to be at the heart of Europe, while wholeheartedly supporting the US-led First Gulf War in 1991. Yet Major felt increasingly constrained by the growing Euro-scepticism in his party.

Box 26.5

An ethical foreign policy for Britain?

When Blair's government took office in 1997, Labour's new foreign secretary, Robin Cook, declared that he wanted to put 'an ethical dimension' into international politics by putting human rights at the heart of Britain's foreign policy (Rawnsley 2001: 169). The centrepiece of this approach was the promise not to sell arms to repressive regimes that might use them to suppress their own civilian population or aggressively against neighbouring countries.

An early illustration of New Labour's more ethically focused foreign policy was the signing and ratifying of the 1998 Ottawa Convention, which banned the use, production, stockpiling and export of anti-personnel landmines (APLs). However, the wider arms trade remained 'big business' for Britain, the second largest supplier of arms in the world behind the USA. Export earnings and jobs were at stake. The international arms industry is highly competitive, with arguably little room for ethics. Thus arms continued to be exported to Indonesia, then engaged in the brutal suppression of a revolt in East Timor. Indeed Buller (in Ludlam and Smith 2001: 231) concludes, 'Labour's record shows a rather depressing continuity with the activities of previous governments'.

New Labour's foreign policy

Labour's return to power in 1997 might have been expected to herald a marked change in direction in the conduct of foreign affairs. Indeed, Labour's new foreign secretary, Robin Cook, proclaimed in a mission statement that Britain would 'once again be a force for good in the world'. No longer 'could the national interest be defined by realpolitik'. Instead there would be a new 'ethical dimension' to Britain's foreign policy (Rawnsley 2001: 169). In the event this commitment proved a damaging hostage to fortune (see Box 26.5).

In practice, New Labour's foreign policy showed much more continuity with the past than might have been anticipated. Neither Robin Cook nor his successor at the Foreign Office, Jack Straw, proved able to put their own personal stamp on their government's foreign policy, which was substantially dominated by Blair himself. It was soon apparent that the prime minister was as committed to the US alliance as his Conservative predecessors, developing a strong relationship with US Presidents Clinton and Bush. Yet at the same time Blair also initially appeared to be the most enthusiastically pro-European premier since Heath, prepared to sign up to the Social Chapter and eventually (or so it seemed) the single European currency, as soon as the time was ripe. To Blair there was no contradiction between his Atlanticist and European commitments. In a favourite metaphor he saw Britain as a bridge between Europe and America.

There is little reason to doubt the sincerity of Blair's commitment to the European Union in general and the single European currency in particular, yet he faced significant obstacles. First, the Euro-scepticism of the British press and public rendered any attempt to promote a promised referendum over Britain's entry into the euro a very hazardous political enterprise. Second, Blair had to overcome the reservations of his own chancellor, who had effectively appointed himself judge and jury over the economic conditions for joining the euro. Thus a decision was repeatedly pushed back until it was conveniently overtaken by the new issue of the European Constitution. Yet third, by that time a major rift had developed between the British government and some of the leading members of the European Union, particularly France and Germany, over the Iraq War. To them it appeared that the British government had once more chosen to ally with the USA rather than Europe.

The rejection of the new European Constitution by first French and then Dutch voters in May and June 2005 intensified a mood of crisis and mutual recriminations in the European Union, culminating in a row over the British budget rebate, and a renewed British counter-assault on the Common Agricultural Policy. Once more, despite having a self-proclaimed passionate European as prime minister, Britain appears an awkward partner in Europe.

The enduring close alliance between the Blair government and the US government has surprised many, not least inside the Labour Party. The early good relationship between Blair and Clinton was not so surprising. New Labour had copied some of the campaigning techniques of the Clinton Democrats, with whom they shared some ideological inspiration. The Republican Party of George W. Bush however was never a natural ally of the British Labour Party. Yet Blair, apparently encouraged by Clinton, sought to establish good relations with Bush, and these were cemented by the events of 9/11 that led to British forces joining the US-led invasions of Afghanistan in 2001 and Iraq in 2003. One argument advanced for the strong support Blair has given to the government of George W. Bush is that it has given Britain a restraining influence on US policy. Thus Blair was able to persuade his ally to seek a second UN resolution (unsuccessfully as it turned out) before invading Iraq. Critics, however, have suggested there is little other evidence that Blair has had much influence on the Us administration (for instance, on the Palestinian question or the issue of global warming).

Even before 9/11, however, Blair's Labour government had been prepared to resort to arms. In December 1998 it had supported US airstrikes against Iraq in December 1998 (Operation Desert Fox). From March 1999 British planes had joined with the USA and other NATO allies in bombing Serbia in response to its treatment of Albanian Muslims in Kosovo. Finally, after a prolonged civil war in Sierra Leone, the British government took unilateral action in 2000, sending a small force, initially to protect British citizens, but ultimately and in effect to support the elected government against rebel forces. While the latter two wars could both be criticised as involving unwarranted outside interference in the internal affairs of independent sovereign states, they were substantially justified both in Britain and the wider world in terms of humanitarian intervention to prevent further atrocities and ethnic cleansing (see arguments below). As a consequence, the Kosovan refugees were able to return home and the Serbian leader Milosevic was toppled and put on trial for war crimes, while an elected government and a measure of peace was restored in Sierra Leone. Many would argue that in these two cases, the ends justified the means.

The attack by al Qaida terrorists on New York's Twin Towers on 11 September 2001 had a dramatic impact on the foreign and defence policy of both the USA and Britain, its closest ally. It led directly to the invasion of Afghanistan in the same year, and the overthrow of the Taliban government, which had been providing shelter and training facilities for Bin Laden's terrorists. Less directly, it led to the far more controversial invasion of Iraq in 2003, and the removal from power of Saddam Hussein's regime.

While British involvement in the Afghanistan War had substantial cross-party and public support, the subsequent Iraq War divided Parliament and public. The former foreign secretary Robin Cook resigned from the government immediately, along with two junior ministers, while Clare Short, the development secretary, resigned subsequently. 139 Labour MPs broke ranks and rebelled on an anti-war motion in the Commons. They were joined by the Liberal Democrats and a small number of Conservatives, including Kenneth Clarke. (The main body of the official opposition sided with the government.) A majority of the public was initially against war (although this briefly changed once British troops were in action) and the Stop the War coalition organised another massive demonstration in London. Perhaps the most damaging consequence was the impact that the two wars had on some of Britain's Muslim population, who saw them as an attack on Islam. The controversy over British involvement in Iraq has persisted, kept alive by the continued bloody insurgency in Iraq. It was a significant issue in the 2005 election, and some were quick to link the terrorist attacks on London in July 2005 with the Iraq War.

■ The case for and against Blair's wars

It is difficult to summarise briefly and dispassionately events and policies that have proved so divisive. Few would have anticipated that a Labour government would have involved Britain in series of wars: five, if the airstrikes on Iraq and the intervention in Sierra Leone are included (Kampfner 2004). Some have argued that the Iraq war, and perhaps others, were illegal under international law. According to the UN Charter the use of force against another sovereign state is illegal, except in self-defence. The Clinton administration argued that some rogue states justified pre-emptive action as they were developing weapons of mass destruction which threatened their neighbours and the wider international community. Both before and increasingly after 9/11 it was maintained that these states were also harbouring and exporting terrorism.

The case for pre-emptive self-defence could be argued most convincingly in the case of Afghanistan, where the link with al Qaida terrorism was clear. In the case of Iraq there was no clear evidence of a link with al Qaida. There were however reasonable grounds for suspecting that Saddam Hussein had dangerous weapons: some had been earlier sold to him by the west, and he had used them both against neighbouring Iran and Kuwait and against his own people. Moreover, the Iraq government's failure to cooperate with the UN weapons inspectors gave grounds for suspicion that there were continuing programmes to develop weapons of mass destruction. The threat posed by these weapons was the main justification for war. Yet after Saddam Hussein's regime was overthrown no such weapons were discovered.

While the case for armed intervention and even for 'regime change', was partly advanced on the grounds of a real or potential threat to peace, it was also argued on humanitarian grounds. In the 1990s the failure of the international community to prevent a series of massacres, sometimes amounting to systematic ethnic cleansing, in Rwanda, Bosnia, the Congo and Chechnya had led to much agonised soul-searching, not least in Britain and elsewhere in Europe. Thus 'most Europeans at the time and ever since have insisted that the Kosovo war was legitimate. They believed Europe in particular had a moral responsibility to avert another genocide on the European continent' (Kagan 2004: 124).

Blair's government also justified intervention in Sierra Leone on humanitarian grounds (see above) and used some similar arguments in both Afghanistan and Iraq. Thus the Taliban government had breached human rights, most notably in their denial of the rights of women, while Saddam Hussein had massacred many thousands of opponents of his regime, particularly Kurds and Shia Muslims. While some would still insist that Afghanistan is a better place for the removal of the Taliban, the benefits of the removal of Saddam Hussein's brutal dictatorship in Iraq still appear far more questionable, not least to many Iraqis who have suffered from the continued anarchy there. Needless to say, the humanitarian argument for regime change (passionately argued by the Labour left-winger Ann Clwyd in the case of Iraq) remains highly contentious. It could justify further intervention against numerous other repressive governments around the world.

The British and US governments interpret these recent conflicts in the context of an ongoing war against terrorism. The global reach of the new terrorism, threatening states and peoples across continents, is a new phenomenon (see Box 26.6) requiring new kinds of responses by governments. Yet critics suggest that western actions have intensified rather than diminished the threat of terrorism, not least because many Muslims interpret the wars with Afghanistan and Iraq as part of a western war against Islam. This perception is hardly justifiable. In Kosovo the US-led NATO intervention was in support of Muslims. Afghanistan was attacked not because it was Muslim but because it was harbouring terrorists, while Saddam Hussein's regime was essentially a secular dictatorship opposed by many Muslims. Even so, the long-running saga of Palestine, coupled with US support for repressive regimes in the Middle East, lends some support to the grievances of Muslims against the west. These and other grievances have been fed by the continuing insurgency against the western occupation of Iraq (although most of the victims of this insurgency have been other Muslims).

While much British foreign policy often appears to be conducted by a small number of specialists in relative secrecy, with minimal impact on the wider public, some decisions clearly can have dramatic and long-running repercussions for the British people, most obviously when they involve war. Yet dire consequences may follow from government inaction as well as action. Much British and western foreign policy since 1945 has been conditioned by the failure of appeasement in the 1930s, as politicians and diplomats learned the lessons of the last world war. Thus the reaction to perceived threats (whether from the Soviet Union or most recently from international terrorism) has

Box 26.6

How real is the threat of terror?

Some critics have argued that the threat of terrorism has been deliberately exaggerated by the USA and Britain to justify repressive measures at home and aggressive action abroad. A few conspiracy theorists have even alleged that the US and UK governments have colluded in, or actively promoted, acts of terror like 9/11 and the London bombing for their own ends. Yet the history of terrorist atrocities around the world over four continents suggests the threat of terrorism is only too real. Attacks credibly linked to the terrorist organisation al Qaida, associated with Osama bin Laden, include:

New York, 26 February 1993 Bomb at the World Trade Center. Six killed, more than a thousand injured.

East Africa, 7 August 1998 Bombs at three US embassies killed 224 and injured 5,000 (largely Africans).

New York, 11 September 2001 Planes flown into the World Trade Center kill 2948 and injure thousands more.

Bali, Indonesia, 12 October 2002 Bombs in beach resort kill 202 and injure many others.

Mombasa, Kenya, 28 November 2002 Bomb in Israeli-owned hotel kills 16.

Riyadh, Saudi Arabia, 12 May 2003 Suicide bombers kill 34 in attack on housing compounds for expatriates.

Istanbul, 15 and 20 November 2003 Bombs outside synagogue and at bank and British Consulate kill 55.

Madrid, 11 March 2004 Bomb attacks at stations kill 191, and leave 1463 injured.

London, 7 July 2005 Bombs on three underground trains and a bus kill over 50 and injure hundreds. (A second similar attack on 21 July caused further disruption but no deaths when bombs failed to explode.)

Sharm el-Sheikh, Egypt July 2005 Three car bombs in holiday resort kill over 60 (mainly Egyptians rather than western tourists) and injure many hundreds.

The terrorists appear to regard anyone who does not adhere to their own extreme and fanatical version of Islam as a legitimate target, regardless of ethnicity or religion (indeed many of their victims have been Muslims). The terrorist threat is more potent because of its indiscriminate nature and the abundance of 'soft' targets that are difficult to protect. The knowledge and technology to kill hundreds is now relatively widespread and fairly simple. The terrorists are as careless of their own lives as those of their victims, willingly embracing what they see as martyrdom. While some states like Afghanistan may have given active assistance to terrorists, they are quite capable of acting without such help. al Qaida terrorists have been compared with the IRA. However, IRA acts of terror, although devastating in their consequences, were generally more targeted, often involved a coded warning, and did not involve suicide bombers.

been confrontation rather compromise. A readiness to use force may sometimes have saved lives. Thus the invasion of Afghanistan may have prevented the planning and execution of further acts of terrorism. Yet equally the invasion and occupation of Iraq has stimulated the recruitment of more terrorists and the loss of innocent lives. In foreign policy the stakes can be very high. Recent British foreign policy has inevitably had far-reaching consequences for British society as well as the British economy and political system.

Summary

- Although foreign policy is often perceived as a relatively specialist and elitist field, it can have massive consequences for the wider public, with considerable potential implications for British politics.
- British prime ministers have often appeared more important in shaping foreign policy than their foreign secretaries. Under Blair in particular the influence of the Chancellor of the Exchequer has also been significant.
- There is persistent tension in foreign policy between the pursuit of national interests, and the acceptance of international obligations and international law.
- Increasingly international institutions, transnational corporations and NGOs have become influential players alongside state governments in global politics.
- In the period of the Cold War between the two superpowers of the USA and USSR, British foreign policy was shaped by NATO and the special relationship with the USA. The European Community was perceived as complementary to (rather than competing against) the US alliance.
- The end of the Cold War posed new and different threats, with implications for the role of an enlarged NATO and European Union, with some potential tensions between the two, and for British foreign policy, caught 'between Europe and America'.
- International terrorism, particularly after 9/11, strengthened the Atlanticist tendencies in British foreign policy, involving the Blair government, as America's closest ally in the invasions of Afghanistan and Iraq, with potentially far-reaching consequences for British politics and British society.

Questions for discussion

- Is foreign policy inherently more elitist and less subject to effective democratic control than other areas of policy?
- Why is it that prime ministers often appear more important in making and shaping British foreign policy than foreign secretaries?
- How far do international institutions and a body of accepted international law effectively restrain state governments from pursuing their national interest? Are international relations essentially determined by *Realpolitik*?
- Consider the perspectives of Fukuyama, Huntington and Kagan on the end of the Cold War and the post Cold War world. Which, if any, is the most persuasive and illuminating?
- For what purposes is there still a role for NATO following the end of the Cold War?
- Why does there appear to be a growing rift between Europe and the USA, particularly following the end of the Cold War? How far can Britain be a 'bridge' between the two?
- How far has Britain's 'special relationship' with the USA imposed obligations on both sides?
- Account for the growth of international terrorism, particularly that associated with al Qaida. Why has it proved so difficult to combat? How far have British and American policies contributed to a diminution or increase of the terrorist threat?
- How far is there a case for humanitarian intervention, involving armed intervention if necessary, to prevent atrocities or genocide?

Further reading

A thought-provoking overview that is illuminating on the foreign policy dilemmas facing Britain (although it covers far more than foreign policy) is Andrew Gamble's *Between Europe and America* (2003). Useful surveys of the foreign policy of the Blair government are provided by Caroline Kennedy-Pipe and Rhiannon Vickers in Dunleavy *et al.* (2003) and by Jim Buller in Ludlam and Smith (2004). A more detailed critical account of *Blair's Wars* is provided by John Kampfner (2004). Events in foreign policy and the war on terrorism are however so fast-moving that even the most recent book sources may appear dated. Analysis of more recent developments can be found in newspapers and their websites, and from a variety of perspectives on the internet. (Some useful sites are indicated below.)

Some of the wider issues of international relations are rather beyond the scope of a book on British politics, although some might wish to consult some of the texts that have been influential and widely quoted, such as Francis Fukuyama, *The End of History and the Last Man* (1992), Samuel P. Huntington, *The Clash of Civilizations and the Remaking of World Order* (1996) and Robert Kagan, *Paradise and Power* (2004). Timothy Garton Ash's *Free World* (2005) is a thought-provoking British contribution to the debate on modern global politics and Britain's role within it.

Useful websites include the government departments the Foreign and Commonwealth Office (www.fco.gov.uk), the Ministry of Defence (www.mod.gov.uk) and the Department for International Development (www.dfid.gov.uk), and various international organisations such as NATO (www.nato.int), the European Union (www.europa.eu.int) and the United Nations (www.un.int).

Who Rules This Place? Power and the New British Politics

Contents

In the opening chapter of this book it was argued that politics was about power. At the conclusion, are we any nearer to an answer to the question 'Who rules this place?'? (It was asked by the journalist Anthony Sampson (2005) in the final title of a succession of books stretching over 40 years of intelligent inquiry into the distribution of power in Britain.) Anyone who has read this far should at least have learned how difficult it is to provide an easy answer to this apparently simple question. In this final chapter we try to draw together some of the principal themes of the book, to recapitulate on some of the major questions surrounding British politics and government today and to provide some tentative signposts to the future.

Who rules Britain?

Where is power to be found in British politics today? One lesson is that power does not necessarily lie where it appears to lie. Back in the 19th century Walter Bagehot wrote a brilliant book *The English Constitution* (1867, 1963 edn) in which he sought to strip away the illusions people had about British government. He distinguished between what he called the dignified and efficient parts of the constitution. His point was that some parts – the monarchy, and increasingly the House of Lords – were largely for show; they no longer involved real power. For Bagehot the efficient secret of the constitution was the Cabinet. This was the real centre of power. Bagehot's readers found his account so convincing that Cabinet government became the new orthodoxy. A book that began as an exercise in debunking old assumptions became the new received opinion.

Yet Bagehot, if he was right, had only provided a snapshot of British government at a particular moment in time. A century later, another sceptical observer of British politics, Richard Crossman, wrote an introduction to a new edition of Bagehot's work (1963) in which he argued that the Cabinet had joined the dignified elements of the British constitution. Cabinet government had been replaced by prime ministerial government. Again, of course, he was not necessarily right. Crossman himself soon had first-hand experience as a leading member of Harold Wilson's government from 1964–70, and his voluminous diaries provide rather ambivalent evidence on the issue of Cabinet government (Crossman, 1975, 1976).

From another perspective the arguments of Bagehot and Crossman on the role of the Cabinet tell us very little about real political power. Bagehot was a contemporary of another keen observer of politics, Karl Marx. Yet Marx was hardly concerned at all with constitutional theory and the relative importance of particular governmental institutions. For Marx, political power reflected economic power. Power in 19th-century Britain, he argued, lay with the capitalists (or bourgeoisie). The state and its political institutions served the interests of this ruling class. Parliament, for Marx, was simply a committee for discussing the common affairs of the bourgeoisie. It is a very different view of politics and power. Had a 19th-century Jeremy Paxman managed to get Bagehot and Marx into the same studio, the encounter might have been fascinating but perhaps not very illuminating, as they were proceeding from such different theoretical assumptions, with few if any points of contact. A similar encounter between a modern Marxist such as the historian Eric Hobsbawm and a modern Bagehot, perhaps Peter Hennessy, would in all probability be equally unproductive.

Top-down and bottom-up approaches to politics

Peter Hennessy's book *The British Prime Minister* (2000) exemplifies what might be called a top-down approach to politics. He is concerned with power at the centre. Thus in a series of diagrams and accompanying text he describes the changing circles of influence in Tony Blair's government – who's in and who's out. To some, this is the very stuff of politics. It reflects a widespread fascination with the men (and occasionally women) at the top of the greasy pole of politics, as demonstrated by the continuing market for the memoirs and biographies of dead and still-living leading British politicians. Nor is the interest necessarily misplaced. Personality matters. The decisions made (and sometimes ducked) by those at the top can have momentous consequences. If Churchill had not become prime minister Britain might well have made peace with Hitler, and the future of Britain and the world could have been very different. Margaret Thatcher's personal responsibility for the Falklands expedition and the poll tax, and Tony Blair's for the Iraq War, may not be quite of the same order of magnitude, but they did have important consequences for British politics (not least for their own reputation and future).

Yet a focus on great men and women has its limitations. For a start it grossly exaggerates their power to achieve change. Hitler's regime was not ultimately defeated by the 'big three' of Churchill, Roosevelt and Stalin, but by millions of ordinary combatants and civilians. The final allied victory had much more to do with the endurance of Russian soldiers or the productivity of American factory workers than Churchillian rhetoric. Moreover, the focus on leaders seems to restrict the scope of politics. Politics, we are told, is a universal human activity. It should concern us all, yet many people, especially the young, seem uninterested in politics, or worse still alienated by it. It may be because politics often seems to be about 'them' rather than 'us' – top people making decisions which, it often appears, we can do little to influence.

Other approaches to the study of history and politics focus on broader social and economic processes – on the masses rather than a handful of leaders, on the crowd rather than the individuals who seek to influence or control the crowd. E. P. Thompson (1963) charted the growth of a politically conscious English working class through the activities of small radical societies and groups of rural and urban artisans. Eric Hobsbawm (1984) began as a labour historian, examining groups and individuals who contributed to the rising political weight of trade unions and the labour movement.

It does not follow that one or other approach is necessarily right or wrong, although they are both inevitably partial. A full understanding of politics arguably has to involve the view from both the top and the grassroots. To an extent this is what most mainstream accounts of British politics (including this one) strive to provide. Thus we have sought to describe and explain both the broader political process in the earlier chapters of this book and the apparently rather narrower governmental process from Chapter 10 onwards. The final chapters on issues and policies bring together, to varying degrees, both the top-down and bottom-up approach to politics.

Participating in politics

One of the central concerns in the earlier chapters was over the scope for popular participation in the political process and for effective influence in the framing and implementation of public policy –

essentially the potential for effective democracy. While Chapter 4 reviewed various channels for citizen participation and possible reasons for alienation and apathy, Chapter 5 focused on elections and voting, central to the whole concept of representative as opposed to direct democracy. A key issue here was the extent to which the electoral system and participation through the ballot box enabled government and public policy to reflect the will of the people, or at least the will of the majority. Some questions were raised here over the fairness of the electoral machinery and over declining turnout levels.

The ideas and mainstream ideological perspectives that underpin British party-political debate and party differences over specific issues and policies were explored initially in Chapter 6. The roles of political parties and the British party system were examined in Chapter 7. British government still remains party government. However, the familiar British two-party system may be evolving into a more complex multi-party system, both at Westminster and in the council chamber, where there has been no reform of the voting system, and more particularly in other representative bodies, where new electoral systems have accelerated change. At other levels and even perhaps ultimately at Westminster, coalition government rather than single-party government may soon became the norm rather than the exception (thus bringing British politics into line with the general practice in most other democracies).

Yet although party remains important in British government, party allegiances and identities have weakened among the wider electorate. Once political parties provided a crucial link between the governors and the governed, for they offered a recognised and legitimate channel for participation by ordinary citizens in the political process, through their actively engaged mass membership. Of course, there were always questions about the effectiveness of that participation and the responsiveness of the leadership to the rank and file. Yet the problem today is not so much the extent of internal party democracy but the failure of the parties to engage with most people at all, for even the major parties have ceased to be mass parties in any meaningful sense.

Today, more people are prepared to engage in politics through organised groups than political parties. The scale and passion of some pressure group activity (discussed in Chapter 8) may be taken as an indication of a vibrant pluralist democracy. Some of the more dramatic or effective manifestations of pressure group politics have been cited earlier in this book. Thus anti-poll tax protests contributed to the downfall of Margaret Thatcher. The Snowdrop petition (following the Dunblane massacre) led to the ban on handguns. The fuel protests of September 2000, the Countryside Alliance demonstrations and the marches against war in Iraq all exerted serious pressure on the Blair government. It could be claimed that all these began as spontaneous popular protests from below. As one placard proclaimed at a Countryside Alliance march, 'The peasants are revolting'. Yet sceptics might respond that many participants in that demonstration did not look much like peasants. One problem with pressure group politics is that they almost inevitably involve minorities, even if they are often sizeable and vociferous minorities, who are not always representative of the majority.

Although parties and pressure groups both have some positive and negative characteristics (see Box 27.1), they perform different roles in the political process, and their contribution to democracy is perhaps best seen as complementary rather than competitive.

The role of political communication in the relationship between rulers and ruled, or elite and mass, most commonly today through the mass media (examined in Chapter 9), remains particularly contentious. The mass media can be seen as the voice of the people or alternatively as an elite instrument for manipulating and misrepresenting the views of the people, a crucial element in the democratic process or a key means by which the interests of the majority are negated or subverted. The answer to the question of media influence will tend to reflect assumptions derived from rival models of the role of the mass media in modern society, although some suggestive evidence on media ownership and case studies of media influence was reviewed in the chapter. The relationship between government and the media has also received more scrutiny lately. While the media can ruin the careers of individual politicians and damage the reputation of governments, government 'spin doctors' can use the media to shape the presentation of news and to boost the image of political leaders and parties.

Box 27.1

Parties and pressure groups: power, influence and democracy

Political parties seek power.

- They engage directly in the democratic process by pursuing the support of majorities to secure the election of party candidates, with the ultimate aim of establishing a party government and controlling public policy.
- Representative democracy would be virtually impossible without them.
- However, today they only engage the masses in the political process through elections.
- Few join parties and even fewer actively participate in them. Thus activists are unrepresentative of voters.
- Moreover, despite commitments to internal democracy, effective power is (perhaps inevitably) concentrated at the centre.

Pressure groups seek influence rather than power.

- While elections offer voters only an occasional highly limited and blunt choice, there is an almost limitless choice of groups for citizens to join.
- Group influence can be continuous in promoting specific interests and causes.
- Many more people are actively engaged in politics through groups than through parties.
- Groups thus play a crucial role in pluralist theories of democracy.
- However, groups serve sectional minority interests rather than the majority.
- There are significant inequalities in resources, organisational capacities and influence between groups.
- There are elitist tendencies within groups – leaders are generally unelected and may be unrepresentative of members.

Power in Whitehall and Westminster

Chapters 10 to 14 focused on those at the heart of government: prime ministers, ministers, top civil servants, MPs, members of the judiciary, those who form the cast lists of numerous memoirs and biographies. Here the emphasis was on the relationship between individuals and institutions among a small governing elite. Has prime ministerial government replaced Cabinet government? Are top civil servants more influential than elected politicians? Has the power of Parliament declined? Can the judiciary effectively restrain the executive? These questions are hardly new. They have figured in textbooks and in examination questions on British government for half a century or more. They are in one sense perennial issues at the heart of government. This does not mean that nothing new can be said about them. Constitutional change and changes in the machinery of government, as well as more subtle changes in assumptions and behaviour, are likely to alter the balance of arguments over time. Changes in domestic and even global political circumstances may alter the scope of particular posts. Beyond that, much inevitably reflects the personalities and interrelationships of individuals.

Some views are perhaps less fashionable than they were. To take one example, the bureaucratic model of power was influential 20 years or so ago, both among the political elite (partly through insider accounts and academic theories) and among the masses (through media images, such as those created by the comedy series *Yes, Minister*). The arguments seem less persuasive now, partly because the civil service did not seem particularly effective at defending its own interests in the face of Conservative reforms in the 1980s and 1990s, and partly because those reforms have further limited the power and influence of leading civil servants. Indeed, the *Yes, Minister* thesis became widely accepted at the very time when it was already effectively defunct. Today's political satire assumes that it is not the 'Sir Humphreys' of Whitehall who manipulate their elected leaders, but 'spin doctors' and press spokespersons, the Mandelsons and Campbells of New Labour (although this new cynical reality may too be already out of date). Yet if the power of the senior civil service now seems less obvious, the continuing interrelationship of elected politicians and appointed civil servants at the heart of government remains an important issue.

Fashions in politics (as in clothes) come and go. Debates over prime ministerial power have waxed and waned through successive governments. Thatcher's dominance appeared to confirm the prime ministerial power thesis, until her abrupt fall apparently refuted it. Major's government appeared to confirm prime ministerial impotence in the face of open Cabinet dissent and backbench revolt, and inspired some wider speculation about the weakness of the office and the hollowing-out of the centre of British government (Rhodes 1997). From 1997 some journalists and academics referred to a 'Blair Presidency' (Hennessy 2000), although by the time of the 2005 election campaign Blair's position appeared so much weaker that he was described as a 'lame duck', only for him to bounce back as a 'world statesman' only weeks later. The changes in perception perhaps reflect some substance: the different personality of the holder of the office, altered electoral and parliamentary circumstances, or simply political events and the passage of time. Fundamentally the issues and arguments are much the same as they always were. It has long been the case that much depends on what the holder makes of the office, and on domestic and international political circumstances.

All these issues and many more can be illuminated by a thorough survey of the different kinds of evidence, but it is virtually impossible to measure in any objective and effective way the distribution of political power. Sometimes it may appear from the focus on leaders that government is the concern of a limited elite – as indeed theorists like Pareto or Michels always maintained. Thus public policy can be explained largely in terms of the internal dynamics of government – who won which battle in Cabinet or Whitehall. Yet from another perspective the freedom of manoeuvre of governments can seem very limited. Wilson's government in 1967 and Major's in 1992 failed to defend the parity of the pound sterling, despite their best efforts. This might emphasise the impersonal power of the market, of currency dealers making their own assessment of the health and future of sterling, disregarding official government pronouncements. Other defining moments in post-war British political history may reflect the power of unions (for example, the failure of the Wilson and Heath industrial relations reforms), or business influence (see Box 27.2), or public opinion, expressed either through the ballot box or in some other way.

Figure 27.1 Still the centre of power?

Photograph: EMPICS

Government and governance

To an extent the new governance literature (described particularly in Chapters 17 and 18) transcends the traditional divide between the governmental and wider political process, or between governors and governed. Governance is an activity, not an institution. It is an activity in which ministers and civil servants may be involved but so also are often businesses, voluntary organisations and community groups. It emphasises cooperation rather than coercion, networks rather than hierarchies, inclusion rather than exclusion. Power, by implication, is diffused rather than centralised.

Where does the new governance leave old government? In some respects old government appears weaker. The shift towards 'governance'

Box 27.2

People power or business power?

Inevitably the answer to this question rests on initial assumptions. Much depends on the particular case studies selected, and even more on their interpretation. Business influence may be less visible and vocal than other interests, but may be more effective.

People power?

- **Replacement of poll tax** – 'people power' shown through demonstrations, tax evasion, the ballot box (local elections, parliamentary by-elections) and opinion polls.
- **Ban on handguns following Dunblane shooting** – 'people power' shown through 'Snowdrop petition', other pressure group influence and opinion polls persuaded the Major government to implement a partial ban and the Blair government a total ban.
- **The fuel protests of September 2000** – a more dubious case, but apparent public support for the protest influenced the government to abandon planned further increases in fuel duty. (Note also, however, the ambivalent role of the fuel companies, and the kid-glove treatment of blockades by the police.)

Business power?

- **The exemption of Formula One motor racing from the ban on tobacco advertising, 1997** – notorious because of the contribution of £1 million to the Labour Party by F1 boss Bernie Ecclestone, although other arguments may have swayed the decision.
- **The continued sale of arms to repressive regimes**, despite the announcement of a more ethical approach by Foreign Secretary Robin Cook, 1997 onwards. The arms industry could point to the loss of export earnings and loss of jobs resulting from restrictions on exports – arguments which would carry weight with the Treasury and Labour's trade union allies.
- **The growth of private sector involvement in public services** (for example through PFIs and PPPs) – this partly perhaps reflects a New Labour ideological commitment to partnership with the private sector, but it has provided highly profitable opportunities for the businesses concerned. The costs and benefits of private-sector involvement remain highly contentious.

partly reflects an ideological reaction against the growth of government on the one hand and an increased realisation of the practical constraints on government on the other. This no longer involves just the issue of the location of power within government, but the power of government or the state itself, and the balance between the public sector and the private sector, or between the state and civil society. There are limits to what governments can or should do. Governments should seek to enable rather than provide, 'steer' rather than 'row', and should work with the private and the voluntary sector in partnerships and networks. In the process the distinction between government and non-government is eroded. There is no clear dividing line between what is the state and what is not the state. Instead there is a subtle gradation running from government departments, through semi-autonomous public agencies, quangos, and formal public–private partnerships, and on to voluntary organisations and private firms working closely with some part of government (Rhodes 1997).

Moreover, there is no transparent chain of command, as there used to be in hierarchically organised departments. While it is possible to list those participating in formal partnerships and networks, it is much more difficult to be clear about the balance of power within and between them. Who calls the shots in the new governance? There is a considerable divergence of views. Some argue that the state has been 'hollowed out', others that it has been 'filled in' (by, among other developments, the proliferation of task forces). Some suggest an increased governmental capacity to deliver policies, others emphasise the relative impotence of ministers and government collectively, partly because so many executive activities have been 'hived off' to quasi-independent agencies. It could be argued that it is still too early to judge the results of some recent initiatives, such as the reforms in the NHS, or the increased reliance on PFI for new investment in the public sector. The balance of power and influence may be clearer in due course. Others would see enhanced business power or professional dominance behind the new more complex structures.

Multi-level governance

Arguments over the location of power in the new British politics are further complicated by the increased importance of new levels of governance, for governance operates not only across sectors but at an increasing number of levels. Once, power in British government was largely a matter of determining the current relationship between individuals and institutions at the centre of London, in the relatively small world of Westminster and Whitehall. The only other level of government that seemed to count at all was local government, in town and county halls. Although there was a continuing debate over 'central–local relations' and some apparent shifts over time, the general consensus was that local government was clearly subordinate and only enjoyed a very limited or qualified autonomy (see Chapter 17).

The position of local government may not have changed very much, or may even have grown more impotent, as many have argued. Its future remains clouded. However, there is no longer a simple bipolar relationship between British central and local government. On the one hand the European Union has become a steadily more important influence on British public policy since the UK joined in 1973. The power exercised in Westminster and Whitehall is increasingly constrained by decisions taken in Brussels, Strasbourg and Luxembourg. On the other hand, devolution within the United Kingdom has set up a number of national or provincial assemblies and executives, operating between Whitehall and town halls. The implications for the UK state are profound and contentious. If membership of the European Union may appear to undermine UK national sovereignty, devolution could lead to the end of 'British' government and politics. Alternatively it could lead to a quasi-federal Britain. Already there has been some shift in power away from Whitehall and Westminster to Edinburgh, to Cardiff (to a markedly lesser degree) and (briefly) to Stormont.

These changes are obvious and dramatic, even if their long-term implications remain far from clear. Yet multi-level governance is not just about the European Union and devolution, but also involves a host of other changes in the process of governance, of which much of the public is only dimly aware. This is sometimes referred to in rather pejorative terms as 'quangocracy', the 'new magistracy' or the 'regulatory state' (see Chapters 17 and 18). It certainly involves more managerial delegation, in keeping with the ideas of the new public management and theories of governance.

Sometimes managerial delegation involves geographical decentralisation. Giving more authority over decisions to those in the front line of delivering services implies some decentralisation in the health and education services. In the case of education this has meant giving more power to the governing bodies of institutions (but arguably in practice to heads or principals) at the expense of local elected authorities. In the case of health it involves a transfer of power away from the centre (in theory at least) to hospital trusts and more recently primary care trusts. There has been a proliferation of other local bodies – housing associations, learning and skills councils, effectively autonomous police authorities. All this may be regretted as involving a bypassing of local government, but it appears to be an aspect of the fragmentation of government (and power?) rather than its centralisation. It is another dimension of multi-level governance. Decisions affecting the lives of citizens of the United Kingdom can now be taken at a number of levels, some local or institutional.

The segmentation of public policy: policy communities

The fragmentation of governance makes it rather more difficult to discuss British politics in terms of a single system of decision making or a single model of power. It is feasible that policy making and the distribution of power vary between services or functions, some of which were reviewed in the later chapters of this book.

Each major public service or area of public policy involves its own distinctive cast of players

In Focus 27.1 Influences on UK government policy under multi-level governance

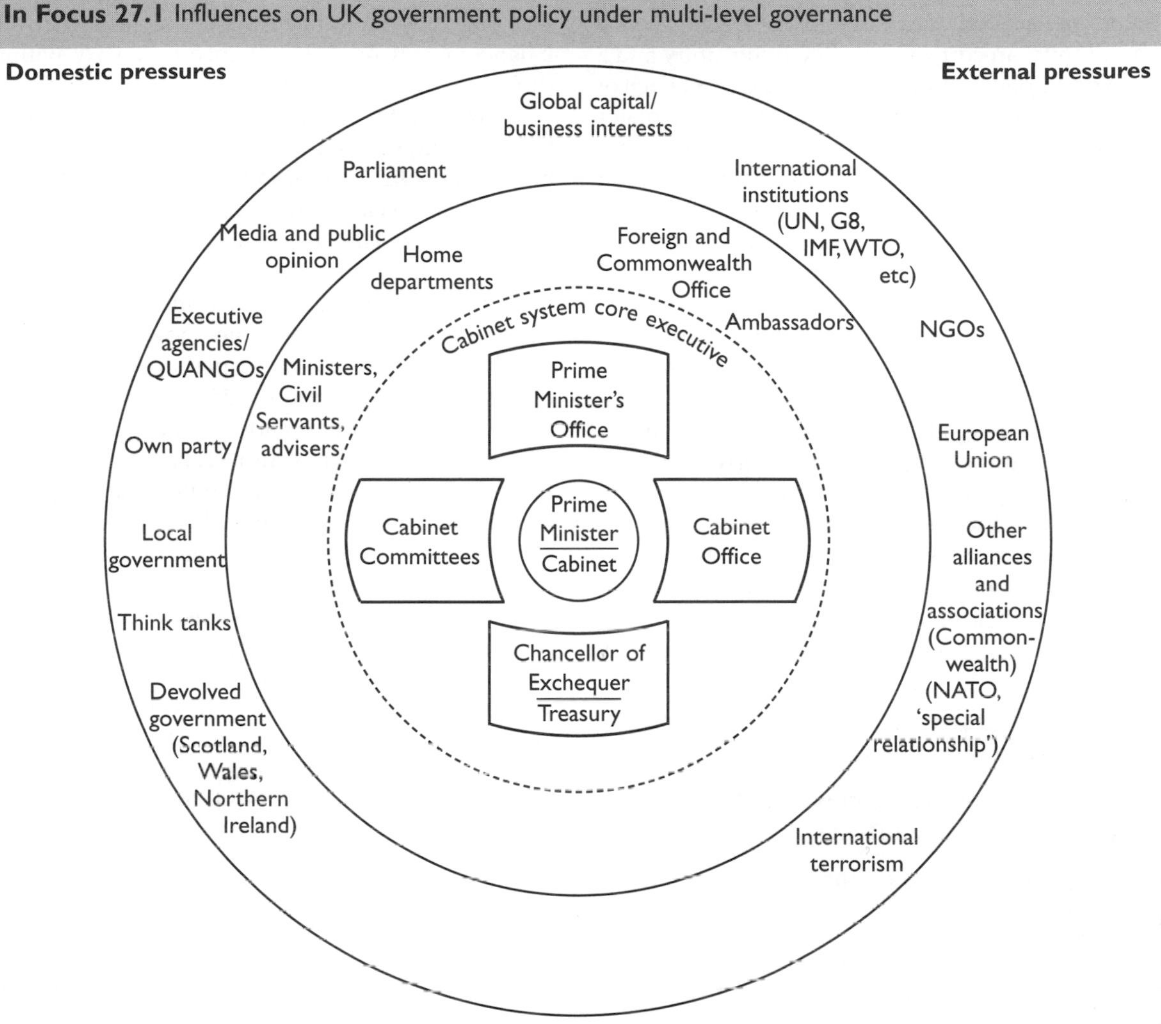

UK government policy today is formally determined within the core executive, but subject to a complex range of domestic and external pressures in a developing system of multi-level governance. While the Prime Minister and Cabinet (innermost circle) remain at the hub, Cabinet Committees, the Cabinet Office and Prime Minister's Office are integral to the UK core executive. Control of finance gives the Chancellor of the Exchequer and Treasury a key veto on policy, but also a significant positive influence on a wide range of economic and social issues (particularly under Blair). Individual ministers and their advisers and senior civil servants within their departments may play a crucial part in specific decisions. Yet many of these decisions will be influenced and constrained by other parts of the UK governmental system, by international institutions, the European Union and other alliances and associations to which Britain belongs, as well as by other foreign powers (well-disposed or hostile). Beyond the formal institutions of government, UK parties and interests, the media and public opinion may exert significant pressure. UK government policy is also inevitably constrained by world markets and global capital, and more specifically by the activities of particular transnational corporations (TNCs), as well as by a growing range of transnational interests represented by non-governmental organisations (NGOs). Particular governments may be more receptive to some influences than others, while opportunities and threats can change over time. Thus international terrorism is a relatively new threat to which the UK government and other governments have to respond.

which constitute a policy community. Thus it could be argued that there is a health policy community, an education policy community and a transport policy community (see Box 27.3). Each of these policy communities may contain a major government department, several executive agencies, a range of quangos, local elected and/or appointed bodies, as well as a range of pressure groups representing managers, professionals, workers, client groups, and private sector and voluntary organisations. While it is possible that there is a similar distribution of power and influence within all the major communities, and they all fit one particular model, it is also possible that there are some significant variations. For example, it has been argued (rightly or wrongly) that elite specialisms within the medical profession used to dominate decision making in the health service, that the old Ministry of Agriculture, Fisheries and Food, had been effectively captured by producer interests, or that the Department of Transport was dominated by motoring interests. Such judgements may be facile or perhaps outdated, but the fact that they have been made suggests that the balance of power and influence may vary within different policy communities.

However, the examples selected imply that there also may be significant changes over time in particular policy communities. An ostensible aim of the Conservative reforms of the health and education services under the Thatcher and Major governments was to give more power to patients and parents through market mechanisms. The extent of patient or consumer power in services like health or education is perhaps contentious, although it seems more significant than formerly. Moreover, it would be widely conceded that both managers and other health service professionals (such as nurses and paramedics) have gained influence in NHS decision making at the expense of the old medical elite. In the case of agriculture it is at least arguable that a series of damaging food scares have reduced the influence of producer interests and forced the government to pay rather more attention to consumer concerns. These were a significant factor in establishing the Food Standards Agency and replacing the old Ministry of Agriculture, Fisheries and Food in 2001 by the new Department of the Environment, Food and Rural Affairs.

If the distribution of power and influence varies significantly between policy communities and over time, then it is difficult to characterise British government and politics in terms of some single model – elitism, pluralism, consumer sovereignty, bureaucracy or whatever. Elected politicians may call the shots in one service, public sector bureaucrats in another, business interests in a third. More plausibly, however, there is a more messy and fluctuating balance of interests and influences in each policy community.

Box 27.3

The transport policy community in Britain: some key players

Government department, and associated agencies
Department of Transport
Highways Agency

Other government bodies
EU Transport Directorate (DG VII)
Scottish and Welsh transport departments
Regional English government (GOs, RDAs)
Local authorities

Road interests
Society of Motor Manufacturers and Traders, British Road Federation, Road Haulage Association, road builders and so on. Motoring organisations (AA, RAC and others)

Rail interests
Train operating companies, Network Rail, rail regulators, rail unions, passenger groups

Other transport and environmental interests
Transport 2000, British Waterways, Countryside Alliance, The Ramblers Association

Governance and democracy

If old-style British government seems to enjoy less power, what are the implications for democracy under new-style multi-level governance? Is government's loss the people's gain? Once more the answer depends to a degree on initial assumptions. For those who have always seen government and the state as a real or potential threat to the freedom of the individual, the fragmentation of government and the new emphasis on governance is an undoubted good. Instead of one over-mighty state staffed by a powerful and self-seeking central bureaucracy there is a diffusion of power and a pluralist plethora of competing public, quasi-public, private and voluntary bodies. Social democrats, by contrast, have generally assumed the state can be captured and effectively controlled to serve the interests of the majority. A weakening of the state thus weakens the capacity of the state to deliver services to the people, and particularly its capacity to achieve a significant redistribution of income and wealth. Yet this of course is precisely why free-market liberals welcome the weakening of the state – they do not believe redistribution is a legitimate function of the state, but rather see redistribution as an illegitimate interference with individual freedom and property.

The rhetoric surrounding governance suggests that it is all about engaging and involving the public, devolving and delegating power to ordinary people as voters, citizens, consumers or patients. However, administrative and geographical decentralisation by itself, even if actively and sincerely pursued (and there has been some room for doubt on this score in Britain) does not necessarily entail more influence and participation for ordinary people. Partly this is just a restatement of the argument (above) about quangocracy and the new magistracy. Power may have been transferred, and sometimes transferred downwards, but often to appointed businesspeople, professionals or middle managers rather than elected representatives or the people themselves. There may be no effective accountability to the public or democratic control. Delegating power to front-line workers or some local appointed body does not necessarily give more power to people as voters, consumers or service users. It may even have the opposite effect if producer or professional interests are strengthened.

The language of governance suggests consultation, cooperation and compromise rather than coercion, and appears highly compatible with public participation, which offers the prospect of a richer form of democracy than through the limited mechanism of the ballot box. Partnerships and networks provide more scope for individuals to get involved in services and policies that affect or concern them. Yet periodic attempts to secure wider public participation have generally met with limited success. Participation, of course, requires commitment, and can entail costs that are difficult to sustain on a longer-term basis. However, critics suggest that the public have generally been offered only token rather than genuine participation, and tokenism breeds apathy.

In the last resort other forms of public involvement in the process of governance can only supplement rather than supplant representative democracy through the ballot box, despite its shortcomings (amply documented in these pages). Multi-level governance has provided some additional opportunities for voting, and has led to the introduction of more proportional representation for devolved assemblies and the European Parliament. Yet despite, or conceivably partly because of, these reforms, voting turnout figures have generally declined. One possible explanation is that the proliferation of elections under the new multi-level governance has led to diminishing returns. Plausibly this is not just the result of apathy but of an understandable increasing confusion over who does what, exacerbated by the shifting boundaries and functions of public authorities. Devolution, delegation, the proliferation of agencies and task forces, the growth of networks and public–private partnership have all made it more difficult for ordinary members of the public to get to grips with government. Reforms intended to involve the public may sometimes have had the reverse effect. There are disturbing indications that a growing section of the electorate are becoming disengaged from mainstream politics.

Who gets what, when, how?

From a radical left-wing or Marxist perspective, little of the above analysis is particularly relevant to the real location of power in government and society. After all, if political power reflects economic power, the way the state is organised hardly matters very much. Those with economic power will continue to control the political process at every level: European, UK, devolved national, regional and local. Corporate power will continue to call the shots rather than the majority of voters at any level.

While both Marxists and social democrats favour some redistribution of income and wealth, unlike social democrats, Marxists simply do not believe that the state will be able to achieve it to any significant degree in a capitalist economy and society. They have some evidence on their side. How far effective redistribution was taking place in the decades immediately after the Second World War is a matter of some dispute. What would be widely conceded by neo-liberals, social democrats and Marxists alike is that over the last quarter of a century or so, British society has not become more equal, but if anything inequality of income and wealth has widened. This, Marxists would argue, reflects the continuing power of business.

Neo-liberals would not dispute the extent of inequality, but argue that this is functional to enterprise and growth. A more equal society would be a more impoverished society. The gap between rich and poor might be reduced but people on average would be worse off. As it is, neo-liberal advocates of the free market argue, the prosperity of the rich in a free capitalist society 'trickles down' to benefit the poor. Social democrats might dispute this optimistic assumption, but have some problems in explaining why they have not been more successful in creating a more equal society.

For British social democrats, exclusion from power for 18 years after 1979 provides an alibi, although some controversy surrounds the aims and achievements of New Labour from 1997. Critics argue that Blair and New Labour have substituted equality of opportunity for equality of outcome, that they have deliberately sought to woo business and this has ruled out redistribution. By contrast, both some New Labour apologists and some of its critics on the right have claimed that New Labour has pursued redistribution by stealth – that Gordon Brown's budgets have had a significant redistributive effect. It may be too early to judge whether the poor have significantly benefited even after more than two full terms of a Labour government. Yet how far a party in government is able to fulfil some of the aspirations of those who voted for it is one bench-mark for measuring the impact of representative democracy.

■ The future of British politics

It has long been assumed that modern politics revolves around economic issues, and government performance on the economy. Yet some of the most passionate political differences now seem to revolve around what has been called the politics of identity rather than the politics of materialism. Of course, it may be the case that some of the differences that have arisen over issues of national, ethnic, cultural or religious identity reflect economic differences and material deprivation. Yet this does not seem to be the whole answer. Today identity politics seem to be increasingly at the heart of some of the major problems confronting the British government and state.

The future of British politics has been a recurring question throughout this book. Until very recently only a handful of revolutionaries, fanatical Europhobes or optimistic Celtic nationalists would have thought to ask whether British politics has a future. The fortunes of parties might fluctuate, some institutions might be reformed, but it was widely assumed the British state would survive for the imaginable future. It may do, but it can no longer be taken for granted that it will.

It used to be widely assumed that Britain was a nation, and the United Kingdom some kind of nation state (albeit one with some peculiar features). Yet Britain and the symbol of Britannia were only reinvented in the 17th century, and more positively embraced in the 18th century after the Act of Union with Scotland. There is nothing particularly unusual about this. The forging of new national identities has been a feature of the modern world. Moreover, with the conspicuous exception of many Irish, allegiance to the British state was largely voluntary and enthusiastic, although it never fully replaced other older identities. Now the United Kingdom is itself a member of another much larger European Union, and rising support for Scottish and Welsh nationalism has led to meaningful political devolution to Edinburgh and Cardiff. Some fear that the European Union is developing into a superstate which will destroy British national sovereignty, others that devolution will prove a slippery slope towards the break-up of the United Kingdom. While disintegration is one possibility, another is that a federal Britain will become part of a federal Europe. At the very least, British politics and government has become more complex, and can no longer be related almost exclusively to the world of Westminster and Whitehall.

It may be argued that what is happening in Britain is happening in many other parts of the world. Other states too are faced with both global and supranational pressures, and internal pressures to devolve more power and autonomy to nations or regions within their borders. Perhaps the whole concept of a world of sovereign independent nation states is the product of a particular passing phase of historical development and has become outdated in the new world of global markets and global communications. Before the modern nation state emerged, much of the world was familiar with a hierarchy of authority. Multi-level governance may be seen as a return to this older state of affairs. Multiple allegiances to different levels of government may be seen as matching the multiple identities which many seem to feel. Yet, as has been noted, nationalism with its claims to a more exclusive identity and allegiance has proved a remarkably resilient ideology.

Old national borders are not the only fault lines within British politics. Newer ethnic divisions cut across these older national allegiances. The total non-white population of the United Kingdom (now over four million) already exceeds the total population of Wales and Northern Ireland, and is not far below that of Scotland. While the non-white population of England is relatively greater than that of Scotland, Wales or Northern Ireland, ethnic tensions and racial and religious prejudice are a feature of all the nations that form the United Kingdom. This has inhibited the development of a sense of British (or English, Scottish or Welsh) identity and allegiance among some at least of the ethnic minorities. The revelation that the London bombers of 7 July 2005 were 'British', at least in terms of their formal nationality, was a dramatic illustration of the failure of some British-born children of immigrants to feel part of the nation in which they have been brought up. Those who hate their 'fellow countrymen' enough to murder them may be a tiny very unrepresentative minority, although disturbingly 5 per cent of all Muslims in Britain and 7 per cent of Muslims aged under 35 apparently think further bomb attacks on Britain are justified (*Guardian*, 26 and 27 July 2005). This is even more of a problem for the vast majority of British Muslims who find such attitudes abhorrent and wholly inconsistent with their own Islamic faith than it is for the rest of the population. Those who are entirely guiltless fear they will suffer for the actions of fanatics. It is these ethnic, cultural and religious divisions that now seem to pose a more dangerous threat to the future of the British political system. The recognition and willing acceptance of the new reality of a multi-cultural and multi-ethnic Britain seems the only realistic alternative to corrosive inter-community tensions. Yet the old notion of Britain as a 'mongrel race' may make multi-cultural Britain an easier concept to accept than a multi-cultural England or even a multi-cultural Europe.

Summary

- There is no simple answer to the question 'Where does power lie in Britain?' Some suggest that power is highly concentrated in the hands of the few, others that it is relatively widely dispersed. The answers that are given depend in part on underlying assumptions.
- While some analyses of British politics focus on the handful of politicians and senior officials at the centre of British government, others emphasise the influence of the masses, of ordinary individuals and groups on the course of the history.
- Public opinion, exercised through the ballot box, through opinion polls or the media, or through the activities of organised groups, can constrain and influence government policy. However, some interests (particularly perhaps business interests) are clearly more influential than others.
- Views of power at the centre fluctuate with changing circumstances and academic fashion. However the traditional centre of British government at Westminster and Whitehall may have lost some power to other levels of governance above and below. Extensive delegation of managerial responsibility may have weakened the effective control of ministers and top civil servants.
- While the new multi-level governance may give people more opportunities for political involvement, participation and interest in politics has declined, perhaps because it has become more difficult to understand who does what.

- Changes in the party control of government and extensive changes in the structure of government seem hardly to affect the distribution of income and wealth in Britain. Some would conclude that political power substantially reflects economic power.
- The key issues in British politics today seem to revolve more around issues of identity and allegiance than economic interests. These issues could have momentous consequences for British society and the British political system.

Questions for discussion

- How far can ordinary people influence government decisions?
- Do great men (and sometimes great women) shape the course of history, or are they the instruments of wider economic and social forces?
- How far does influence and protest through pressure groups offer more chance of securing real political change than voting and involvement with political parties?
- Does pressure groups politics give too much influence to vested interests or angry minorities at the expense of the majority?
- Why has a Labour government pledged to serve the interests of 'the many not the few' failed to achieve a significant redistribution of income and wealth towards the many?
- Is it more difficult for ordinary people to understand who does what in British politics? If so, what might be the consequences?
- How far are issues of identity and allegiance more significant than economic and class divisions in modern British politics?

Further reading

It is difficult to recommend further reading here, as most of this chapter has been concerned with picking up on themes developed earlier in the book. Most of the sources cited have already been mentioned before, some several times over in different chapters. For one view of power at the top in Britain it may be worth dipping into Peter Hennessy's *The British Prime Minister* (2000). For a somewhat broader (but still essentially top-down) perspective, look at Anthony Sampson's *Who Rules This Place?* (2005). For the latest considered verdicts of some leading academics, see the most recent in the Palgrave series *Developments in British Politics* (for example, volume 7 edited by Dunleavy *et al.* 2003, and volume 8, 2006).

Bibliography

Note: where a much later edition of a book first published some time ago is cited, the original date of publication is given in square brackets.

Adams, I. (1998) *Ideology and Politics in Britain Today* (Manchester: Manchester University Press).

Adams, J. and Pyper, R. (1997) 'Whatever happened to the Scott Report?' *Talking Politics*, 9:3, Spring.

Adonis, A. (1993) *Parliament Today*, 2nd edn (Manchester: Manchester University Press).

Adonis, A. and Pollard, S. (1997) *A Class Act: The Myth of Britain's Classless Society* (London: Hamish Hamilton).

Alderman, K. (1995) 'The government whips', *Politics Review*, 4:4, April.

Allison, G. T. (1971) *Essence of Decision* (Boston: Little, Brown).

Almond, G. and Verba, S. (1965) *The Civic Culture* (Boston and Toronto: Little, Brown).

Almond, G. and Verba, S. (eds) (1980) *The Civic Culture Revisited* (Boston: Little, Brown).

Anderson, A. (1997) *Media, Culture and Environment* (London: UCL Press).

Anderson, B. (1991) *Imagined Communities* (London: Verso).

Annual Abstract of Statistics (London: HMSO).

Arblaster, A. (1987) *Democracy* (Buckingham: Open University Press).

Ascher, K. (1987) *The Politics of Privatisation* (Basingstoke: Macmillan).

Ash, T. G. (2005) *Free World* (London: Penguin).

Atkinson, R. and Durden, P. (1990) 'Housing policy in the Thatcher years', in S. Savage and L. Robins (eds), *Public Policy under Thatcher* (London: Macmillan).

Bachrach, P. and Baratz, M. (1970) *Power and Poverty: Theory and Practice* (New York: Oxford University Press).

Back, L. and Solomos, J. (2000) *Theories of Race and Racism: A Reader* (London: Routledge).

Bagehot, W. ([1867] 1963) *The English Constitution* (London: Fontana).

Baggott, R. (1990–1) 'The policy-making process in British central government', *Talking Politics*, 3:2, Winter.

Baggott, R. (1992) 'The measurement of change in pressure group politics', *Talking Politics*, 5:1, Autumn.

Baggott, R. (1995) *Pressure Groups Today* (Manchester: Manchester University Press).

Barberis, P. (ed.) (1996) *The Whitehall Reader* (Buckingham: Open University Press).

Barker, A. and Wilson, G. K. (1997) 'Whitehall's disobedient servants? Senior officials' potential resistance to ministers in British government departments', *British Journal of Political Science*, 27:2, April.

Barker, M. (1981) *The New Racism* (London: Junction Books).

Barker, R. (1997) *Political Ideas in Modern Britain*, 2nd edn (London: Routledge).

Barnett, A. (1997) *This Time: Our Constitutional Revolution* (London: Vintage).

Barnett, A., Eltis, C. and Hirst, P. (eds) (1993) *Debating the Constitution* (Oxford: Polity Press).

Barnett, H. (2002) *Britain Unwrapped: Government and Constitution Explained* (London: Penguin).

Barnett, H. (2004) *Constitutional and Administrative Law*, 5th edn (London: Cavendish).

Barry, B. (2001) 'Multicultural muddles', *New Left Review*, March/April.

Beer, S. (1982a) *Modern British Politics* (London: Faber & Faber).

Beer, S. (1982b) *Britain Against Itself: The Political Contradictions of Collectivism* (London: Faber & Faber).

Beetham, D. and Boyle, K. (1995) *Introducing Democracy: 80 Questions and Answers* (London and Paris: Polity Press and UNESCO Publishing).

Bell, A. (1991) *The Language of News Media* (Oxford: Blackwell).

Bell, D. (1960) *The End of Ideology* (New York: Free Press).

Benn, T. (1980) 'The case for a constitutional premiership', *Parliamentary Affairs*, 33:1, Winter.

Benn, T. (1982) *Parliament, Power and People* (London: Verso).

Bentley, A. F. ([1908] 1967) *The Process of Government* (Harvard: Belknap Press).

Berridge, G. R. (1992) *International Politics: States, Power and Conflict since 1945* (London: Harvester Wheatsheaf).

Berrington, H. (1995) 'The Nolan Report', *Government and Opposition*, 30:4, Autumn.

Beveridge, W. H. (1942) *Social Insurance and Allied Services*, Cmnd 6404 (London: HMSO).

Bilton, T. *et al.* (2002) *Introductory Sociology*, 4th edn (Basingstoke: Palgrave).

Birch, A. H. (1979) *Political Integration and Disintegration in the British Isles* (London: Allen & Unwin).

Birch, A. H. (1993) *The Concepts and Theories of Modern Democracy* (London: Routledge).

Birkinshaw, P. (1991) *Reforming the Secret State* (Milton Keynes: Open University Press).

Birkinshaw, P. (1996) *Freedom of Information*, 2nd edn (London: Butterworth).

Birkinshaw, P. (1997) 'Freedom of information', *Parliamentary Affairs*, 50:1, January.

Blackburn, R. and Plant, R. (eds) (1999) *Constitutional Reform* (London: Longman).

Blair, A. (2005) 'The 2004 European Parliament Elections', *Talking Politics*, 17:3.

Blair, T. (1996) *New Britain: My Vision of a Young Country* (London: Fourth Estate).

Blair, T. (1998) *Leading the Way: A New Vision for Local Government* (London: Institute for Public Policy Research).

Blumler, J. G. and McQuail, D. (1967) *Television in Politics* (London: Faber & Faber).

Bogdanor, V. (1984) *What is Proportional Representation?* (Oxford: Martin Robertson).

Bogdanor, V. (ed.) (1988) *Constitutions in Democratic Politics* (Aldershot: Gower).

Bogdanor, V. (1997) 'The politics of power', *Guardian*, 4 June.

Bolton, R. (1990) *Death on the Rock and Other Stories* (London: W. H. Allen).

Borthwick, R. L. (1997) 'Changes in the House of Commons', *Politics Review*, 6:3, February.

Bottomore, T. (1991) *A Dictionary of Marxist Thought* (Oxford: Blackwell).

Bradbeer, J. (1990) 'Environmental policy', in S. Savage and L. Robins (eds), *Public Policy under Thatcher* (London: Macmillan).

Bradbury, J. (2003) '2003 Scottish Parliament elections: Labour reclaims power', *Politics Review*, November.

Braybrooke, D. and Lindblom, C. (1963) *A Strategy of Decision* (New York: Free Press).

Brazier, R. (1988) *Constitutional Practice* (Oxford: Clarendon).

Brazier, R. (1991) *Constitutional Reform* (Oxford: Clarendon).

Breuilly, J, (1993) *Nationalism and the State*, 2nd edn (Manchester: Manchester University Press).

Briscoe, S. (2005) *Britain in Numbers: The Essential Statistics* (London: Politicos).

Brittan, S. (1968) *Left or Right: The Bogus Dilemma* (London: Secker & Warburg).

Bromley, C. and Curtice, J. (2002) 'Where have all the voters gone?' in A. Park, J. Curtice, K. Thomson, L. Jarvis and C. Bromley (eds), *British Social Attitudes: The 19th Report* (London: Sage).

Bromley, C., Curtice J. and Seyd, B. (2001) 'Political engagement, trust and constitutional reform', in A. Park, J. Curtice, K. Thomson, L. Jarvis, C. Bromley and N. Stratford (eds), *British Social Attitudes: The 18th Report* (London: Sage).

Brooke, R. (1989) *Managing the Enabling Authority* (Harlow: Longman/LGTB).

Bruce, S. (1986) *God Save Ulster: The Religion and Politics of Paisleyism* (Oxford: Oxford University Press).

Bryson, V. (1992) *Feminist Political Thought: An Introduction* (London: Macmillan).

Bryson, V. (1999) *Feminist Debates: Issues of Theory and Political Practice* (Basingstoke: Palgrave).

Bryson, V. (2000) 'Men and sex equality', *Politics*, 20:1.

Bryson, V. (2003) *Feminist Political Theory* (Basingstoke: Palgrave Macmillan).

Bullock, A. and Stallybras, O. (eds) (1977) *The Fontana Dictionary of Modern Thought* (London: Fontana).

Bulmer, M. and Solomos, J. (eds) (1999) *Racism* (Oxford: Oxford University Press).

Bulpitt, J. (1983) *Territory and Power in the United Kingdom. An Interpretation* (Manchester: Manchester University Press).

Burch, M. (1995a) 'Prime minister and Whitehall', in D. Shell and R. Hodder-Williams (eds), *Churchill to Major: The British Prime Ministership since 1945* (London: Hurst).

Burch, M. (1995b) 'Prime minister and Cabinet: an executive in transition?', in R. Pyper and L. Robins (eds), *Governing the UK in the 1990s* (London: Macmillan).

Burch, M. and Holliday, I. (1996) *The British Cabinet System* (London: Harvester Wheatsheaf).

Burch, M. and Wood, B. (1997) 'From provider to "enabler": the changing role of the state', in L. Robins and B. Jones (eds), *Half a Century of British Politics* (Manchester: Manchester University Press).

Burke, Edmund ([1790] 1975) *Reflections on the Revolution in France*, ed. B. W. Hill (London: Fontana/Harvester).

Butcher, T. (1995) 'A new civil service: the Next Steps agencies', in R. Pyper and L. Robins (eds), *Governing the UK in the 1990s* (London: Macmillan).

Butcher, T. (2004) 'The civil service under the Blair government', in S. Lancaster (ed.), *Developments in Politics*, vol. 15 (Ormskirk: Causeway Press).

Butler, D. and Butler, G. (2000) *Twentieth Century Political Facts 1900–2000* (Basingstoke: Palgrave Macmillan).

Butler, D and Kavanagh, D. (1992) *The British General Election of 1992* (Basingstoke: Macmillan).

Butler, D. and Kavanagh, D. (1997) *The British General Election of 1997* (Basingstoke: Macmillan).

Butler, D. and Kavanagh, D. (2001) *The British General Election of 2001* (Basingstoke: Palgrave Macmillan).

Butler, D. and Kavanagh, D. (2005) *The British General Election of 2005* (Basingstoke: Palgrave Macmillan).

Butler, D., Adonis, A. and Travers, T. (1994) *Failure in British Government: The Politics of the Poll Tax* (Oxford: Oxford University Press).

Butler, D. and Stokes, D (1969) *Political Change in Britain* (Basingstoke: Macmillan).

Butler, R. (2004) *Review of Intelligence on Weapons of Mass Destruction: Report of a Committee of Privy Counsellors*, HC898 (London: The Stationery Office).

Byrne, P. (1997) *Social Movements in Britain* (London: Routledge).

Byrne, T. (2000) *Local Government in Britain* (London: Penguin).

Cabinet Office (1999) *Modernising Government*, Cm 4310 (London: The Stationery Office).

Cabinet Office/Department of Transport, Local Government and the Regions (2002) *Your Region, Your Choice: Revitalising the English Regions*, Cm 5511 (London: The Stationery Office).

Cairncross, A. (1981) 'The post war years 1945–1977', in R. Floud and D. McCloskey (eds), *The Economic History of Britain since 1700*, vol. 2 (Cambridge: Cambridge University Press).

Cairncross, A. K. (1992) *The British Economy since 1945* (Oxford: Blackwell).

Callaghan, J. (1987) *Time and Chance* (London: Collins).

Campbell, J. (1993) *Edward Heath: A Biography* (London: Jonathan Cape).

Cantle, T. (2001) *Community Cohesion: A Report of the Independent Review Team* (London: Home Office).

Carson, R. ([1962] 1965) *Silent Spring* (Harmondsworth: Penguin).

Carter, A. (1988) *The Politics of Women's Rights* (Harlow: Longman).

Castle, B. (1980) *The Castle Diaries, 1974–1976* (London: Weidenfeld & Nicolson).

Cerny, P. (1996) 'What next for the state?' in E. Kofman and G. Youngs (eds), *Globalization: Theory and Practice* (London: Pinter).

Chadwick, A. and Hefferman, R. (2003) *The New Labour Reader* (Cambridge: Polity).

Chandler, J. (ed.) (1996) *The Citizen's Charter* (Aldershot: Dartmouth).

Chester, Sir N. (1979) 'Fringe bodies, quangos and all that', *Public Administration*, 57:1.

Childs, S. (2002) 'Parliament, women and representation', *Talking Politics*, 14:3.

Childs, S. (2004) *New Labour's Women MPs: Women Representing Women* (London: Taylor and Francis).

Clarke, M. (1988) 'The policy-making process' in M. Smith, S. Smith and B. White (eds) *British Foreign Policy* (London: Unwin and Hyman).

Clarke, M. and Stewart, J. (1988) *The Enabling Council* (Luton: Local Government Training Board).

Coates, D. (1984) *The Context of British Politics* (London: Hutchinson).

Coates, D. (2005) *Prolonged Labour* (Basingstoke: Palgrave).

Cochrane, A. (1993) *Whatever Happened to Local Government?* (Buckingham: Open University Press).

Cockburn, C. (1977) *The Local State* (London: Pluto).

Coleman, S. (2001) 'Online campaigning', *Parliamentary Affairs*, 54.

Colley, L. (2003) *Britons: Forging the Nation 1707–1837* (London: Pimlico).

Commission on Social Justice (1994) *Social Justice: Strategies for National Renewal* (London: Vintage).

Commoner, B. (1971) *The Closing Circle* (London: Jonathan Cape).

Cooper, M-P. (1995) 'Understanding subsidiarity as a political issue in the European Community', *Talking Politics*, 7:3, Spring.

Cowles, M. G and Dinan, D. (eds) (2004) *Developments in the European Union 2* (Basingstoke: Palgrave Macmillan).

Cowley, P. (1996–7) 'Men (and women) behaving badly? The Conservative Party since 1992', *Talking Politics*, 9:2, Winter.

Cowley, P. (2005a) *The Rebels: How Blair Mislaid his Majority* (London: Politicos).

Cowley, P, (2005b) 'Whips and rebels', *Politics Review*, 14:3.

Cowley, P. and Stuart, M. (2003) 'Shifting the balance: "modernising" the House of Commons', *Politics Review*, 12:4.

Cowling, D. (1997) 'A landslide without illusions', *New Statesman*, May special edn.

Coxall, B. (2001) *Pressure Groups in British Politics* (Harlow: Pearson Longman).

Coxall, B. and Robins, L. (1998) *British Politics since the War* (London: Macmillan).

Crafts, N. (1997) *Britain's Relative Economic Decline* (London: Social Market Foundation).

Cram, L, Dinan, D. and Nugent, N. (eds) (1999) *Developments in the European Union* (Basingstoke: Macmillan).

Crenson (1971) *The Un-politics of Air Pollution: A Study of Non-Decision Making in the Cities* (Baltimore: Johns Hopkins Press).

Crewe, I. and King, A. (1995) *SDP: The Birth, Life and Death of the Social Democratic Party* (Oxford: Oxford University Press).

Crick, B. (ed.) (1991) *National Identity* (Oxford: Blackwell).

Crick, B. (1993) *In Defence of Politics*, 4th edn (Harmondsworth: Penguin).

Crosland, C. A. R. (1956) *The Future of Socialism* (London: Jonathan Cape).

Crossman, R. (1963) 'Introduction' to W. Bagehot, *The English Constitution* (London: Fontana).

Crossman, R. (1975, 1976, 1977) *Diaries of a Cabinet Minister*, 3 vols (London: Hamish Hamilton and Jonathan Cape).

Curran, J. and Seaton, J. (2003) *Power without Responsibility: The Press, Broadcasting, and New Media in Britain* (London: Routledge).

Curtice, J. (1997) 'Anatomy of a non-landslide', *Politics Review*, 7:1, September.

Curtice, J. and Jowell, R. (1995) 'The sceptical electorate', in R. Jowell, J. Curtice, A. Park, L. Brook and D. Ahrendt (eds), *British Social Attitudes: The 12th Report* (Aldershot: Dartmouth).

Curtice, J. and Jowell, R. (1997) 'Trust in the political system', in R. Jowell, J. Curtice, A. Park, L. Brook, K. Thomson and C. Bryson (eds), *British Social Attitudes: The 14th Report* (Aldershot: Ashgate).

Dahl, R. A. (1961) *Who Governs?* (New Haven: Yale University Press).

Davies, A. J. (1996a) *We, The Nation: The Conservative Party and the Pursuit of Power* (London: Abacus).

Davies, A. J. (1996b) *To Build a New Jerusalem: The British Labour Party from Keir Hardie to Tony Blair* (London: Abacus).

Davies, N. (1996) *Europe: A History* (Oxford: Oxford University Press).

Davies, N. (2000) *The Isles* (London: Macmillan).

De Smith, S. A. and Brazier, R. (1994) *Constitutional and Administrative Law*, 7th edn (Harmondsworth: Penguin).

De Smith, S. A. and Brazier, R. (1998) *Constitutional and Administrative Law*, 8th edn (London: Penguin).

Dearlove, J. (1973) *The Politics of Policy in English Local Government* (Cambridge: Cambridge University Press).

Denenberg, R. V. (1996) *Understanding American Politics* (London: Fontana).

Denham, J. (2002) *Building Cohesive Communities: A Report of the Ministerial Group on Public Order and Community Cohesion* (London: Home Office).

Denver, D. (2003) *Elections and Voters in Britain* (Basingstoke: Palgrave Macmillan).

Denver, D. (2003) '2003 Scottish Parliament Elections: messages for unpopular parties', *Politics Review*, November.

Department of Health (1997) *The New National Health Service: Modern, Dependable* (London: The Stationery Office).

Dicey, A. V. ([1885] 1959) *An Introduction to the Study of the Law of the Constitution* (London: Macmillan).

Digby, A. (1989) *British Welfare Policy* (London: Faber & Faber).

Dobson, A. (ed.) (1991) *The Green Reader* (London: Andre Deutsch).

Dobson, A. (1993) 'Ecologism', in R. Eatwell and A. Wright (eds), *Contemporary Political Ideologies* (London: Pinter).

Dobson, A. (1995) *Green Political Thought*, 2nd edn (London: Routledge).

Donoughue, B. (1987) *Prime Minister* (London: Jonathan Cape).

Dorey, P. (1995) *British Politics since 1945* (Oxford: Blackwell).

Dorey, P. (2002) 'The West Lothian question in British politics', *Talking Politics*, September.

Dorril, S. (1992) *The Silent Conspiracy Inside the Intelligence Services in the 1990s* (London: Heinemann).

Dowding, K. (1995) *The Civil Service* (London: Routledge).

Dowds, L. and Young, K. (1996) 'National identity', in R. Jowell, J. Curtice, A. Park, L. Brook, and K. Thomson (eds), *British Social Attitudes: The 13th Report* (Aldershot: Dartmouth).

Downs, A. (1957) *An Economic Theory of Democracy* (New York: Harper and Row).

Downs, A. (1973) 'Up and down with ecology', in J. Bains (ed.), *Environmental Decay* (Boston: Little, Brown).

Drake, R. F. (2002) 'Disabled people, voluntary organisations and participation in policy making', *Policy and Politics*, 30:3.

Drewry, G (1988) 'Legislation', in M. Ryle and P. Richard (eds.), *The Commons Under Scrutiny* (London: Routledge).

Drewry, G. and Butcher, T. (1991) *The Civil Service Today*, 2nd edn (Oxford: Blackwell).

Driver, S. and Martell, L. (1998) *New Labour: Politics after Thatcherism* (Cambridge: Polity).

Driver, S. and Martell, L. (2002) *Blair's Britain* (Cambridge: Polity).

Dunleavy, P. (1991) *Democracy, Bureaucracy and Public Choice* (London: Harvester Wheatsheaf).

Dunleavy, P., Gamble, A., Heffernan, R., Holliday, I. and Peele, G. (2002) *Developments in British Politics 6* (rev. edn) (Basingstoke: Palgrave).

Dunleavy, P., Gamble, A., Hefferman, R. and Peele, G. (eds) (2003) *Developments in Politics 7* (Basingstoke: Macmillan).

Dunleavy, P., Gamble, A., Holliday, I. and Peele, G. (eds) (1997) *Developments in British Politics 5* (London: Macmillan).

Dunleavy, P. and Jones, G. W. (1993) 'Leaders, politics and institutional change: the decline of prime ministerial accountability to the House of Commons, 1868–1990', *British Journal of Political Science*, 23.

Dunleavy, P., Jones, G. W. and O'Leary, B. (1990) 'Prime ministers and the Commons: patterns of behaviour, 1868–1967', *Public Administration*, 68, Spring.

Dunleavy, P. and Margetts, H. (1997) 'The electoral system', *Parliamentary Affairs*, 50:4, October.

Dunleavy, P. and Weir, S. (1995) 'Media, opinion and the constitution', in F. F. Ridley and A. Doig (eds), *Sleaze: Politicians, Private Interests and Public Reaction* (Oxford: Oxford University Press).

Dunn, J. (ed.) (1992) *Democracy: The Unfinished Journey 508 BC to AD 1993* (Oxford: Oxford University Press).

Dutton, D. (1997) *British Politics since 1945: The Rise and Fall of Consensus* (Oxford: Blackwell).

Duverger, M. (1964) *Political Parties* (London: Methuen).

Duverger, M. (1972) *The Study of Politics*, trans. Wagoner (Sunbury on Thames: Nelson).

Eatwell, R. (1997) 'Britain', in R. Eatwell (ed.), *European Political Culture* (London: Routledge).

Eccleshall, R. (1986) *British Liberalism: Liberal Thought from the 1640s to the 1980s* (London: Longman).

Eccleshall, R. (1990) *English Conservatism since the Reformation: An Introduction and Anthology* (London: Unwin Hyman).

Eccleshall, R, Finlayson, A., Geoghegan, V., Kenny, M., Lloyd, M., Mackenzie, I and Wilford, R. (2004) *Political Ideologies: An Introduction* (London: Routledge).

Eckersley, R. (1993) *Environmentalism and Political Theory: Towards an Ecocentric Approach* (London: UCL Press).

Economist (1997) *Election Briefing, 1997* (London: Economist Publications).

Electoral Commission and Hansard Society (2004) *An Audit of Political Engagement* (London: Electoral Commission and Hansard Society).

Electoral Commission and Hansard Society (2005) *An Audit of Political Engagement 2* (London: Electoral Commission and Hansard Society).

Ellison, N. and Pearson, C. (2003) *Developments in*

British Social Policy, 2nd edn (Basingstoke: Palgrave Macmillan).

Etzioni, A. (1967) 'Mixed scanning: a "third" approach to decision-making', *Public Administration Review*, 27.

Etzioni, A. (1995) *The Spirit of Community* (London: Fontana).

Evans, M. (1997) 'Political participation', in P. Dunleavy, A. Gamble, I. Holliday and G. Peele (eds), *Developments in British Politics 5* (London: Macmillan).

Eysenck, H. J. (1957) *Sense and Nonsense in Psychology* (Harmondsworth: Penguin).

Farrell, D. (1997) *Comparing Electoral Systems* (London: Macmillan).

Fielding, S. (2003) *The Labour Party* (Basingstoke: Palgrave).

Figes, E. (1978) *Patriarchal Attitudes* (London: Virago).

Finer, C. J. (1997) 'Social policy', in P. Dunleavy, A. Gamble, I. Holliday and G. Peele (eds), *Developments in British Politics 5* (London: Macmillan).

Finer, S. E. (1979) *Five Constitutions* (Harmondsworth: Penguin).

Finer, S. E., Bogdanor, V. and Rudden, B. (1995) *Comparing Constitutions* (Oxford: Clarendon).

Fisher, J. (1996) *British Political Parties* (Hemel Hempstead: Prentice Hall/Harvester Wheatsheaf).

Flinders, M. (2002) 'Governance in Whitehall', *Public Administration*, 80:1.

Flude, M. and Hammer, M. (eds) (1990) *The Education Reform Act, 1988. Its Origins and Implications* (London: Falmer Press).

Foley, M. (1993) *The Rise of the British Presidency* (Manchester: Manchester University Press).

Foote, G. (1996) *The Labour Party's Political Thought* (London: Croom Helm).

Frankel, J. (1970) *National Interest* (London: Pall Mall).

Franklin, B. (1994) *Packaging Politics* (London: Edward Arnold).

Franklin, B. (2004) *Packaging Politics*, 2nd edn (London: Edward Arnold).

Franklin, M. (1985) *The Decline of Class Voting* (Oxford: Oxford University Press).

Freeden, M. (1996) *Ideology and Political Theory* (Oxford: Clarendon Press).

Freeden, M. (1999) 'The ideology of New Labour', *Political Quarterly*, 70:1.

Freedman, L. (1994) 'Defence policy', in A. Seldon and D. Kavanagh (eds), *The Major Effect* (London: Macmillan).

Freely, M. (1995) *What About Us? An Open Letter to the Mothers Feminism Forgot* (London: Bloomsbury).

Freeman, M. (1997) 'Why rights matter', *Politics Review*, 7:1, September.

Fukuyama, F. (1989) 'The end of history?' *National Interest*, 16, Summer.

Fukuyama, F. (1992) *The End of History and the Last Man* (London: Hamish Hamilton).

Gamble, A. (1997) 'Conclusion: politics 2000', in P. Dunleavy, A. Gamble, I. Holliday and G Peele (eds), *Developments in British Politics 5* (London: Macmillan).

Gamble, A. (1994) *The Free Economy and the Strong State: The Politics of Thatcherism*, 2nd edn (London: Macmillan).

Gamble, A. (2003) *Between Europe and America* (Basingstoke: Palgrave).

Game, C. (2001) 'The changing ways we vote', in S. Lancaster (ed.), *Developments in Politics*, vol. 12 (Ormskirk: Causeway Press).

Garner, R. (2000) *Environmental Politics: Britain, Europe and the Global Environment* (Basingstoke: Palgrave).

Garner, R. and Kelly, R. (1998) *British Political Parties Today*, 2nd edn (Manchester: Manchester University Press).

Garnett, M. (1996) *Principles and Policies in Modern Britain* (London: Longman).

Garnett, M, (2004) 'Judges versus politicians', *Politics Review*, 14:1.

Garnett, M. (2005) 'First among equals', *Politics Review*, 14:4.

Gavin, N. and Sanders, D. (1997) 'The economy and voting', *Parliamentary Affairs*, 50:4, October.

Geddes, A. (2003) *The European Union and British Politics* (Basingstoke: Palgrave Macmillan).

Gellner, E. (1983) *Nations and Nationalism* (Oxford: Blackwell).

George, S. (1998) *An Awkward Partner: Britain in the European Community* (Oxford: Oxford University Press).

Giddens, A. (1998) *The Third Way: The Renewal of Social Democracy* (Cambridge: Polity).

Giddens, A. (2001) *Sociology*, 4th edn (Cambridge: Polity).

Giddens, A. (2002) *Where Now for New Labour?* (Cambridge: Polity).

Gilmour, I. (1978) *Inside Right* (London: Quartet Books).

Gilmour, I. (1992) *Dancing with Dogma* (London: Simon and Schuster).

Gilmour, I. and Garnett, M. (1997) *Whatever Happened to the Tories? The Conservatives since 1945* (London: Fourth Estate).

Glasgow Media Group (1980) *More Bad News* (London: Routledge).

Glennerster, H. (1995) *British Social Policy since 1945* (Oxford: Blackwell).

Glennerster, H., Power, A. and Travers, T. (1991) 'A new era for social policy: a new enlightenment or a new Leviathan?', *Journal of Social Policy*, 20:3.

Golding, P. (1974) *The Mass Media* (London: Longman).

Goodin, R. (1992) *Green Political Theory* (Cambridge: Polity).

Goodlad, G. D. (2005) 'Devolution in the United Kingdom: Where are we now?' *Talking Politics*, 18:1 (September).

Graber, D. (1997) *Mass Media and American Politics* (Washington, D.C.: CQ/Press).

Grant, M. (1994) 'The rule of law – theory and practice', *Talking Politics*, 7:1, Autumn.

Grant, W. (1995) *Pressure Groups, Politics and Democracy*, 2nd edn (Hemel Hempstead: Prentice Hall/Harvester Wheatsheaf).

Grant, W. (2000) *Pressure Groups and British Politics* (Basingstoke: Palgrave).

Grant, W. (2001) 'Pressure politics: from "insider" politics to direct action?' *Parliamentary Affairs*, 54, pp. 337–48.

Grant, W. (2002) *Economic Policy in Britain* (Basingstoke: Palgrave).

Gray, J. (1986) *Liberalism* (Buckingham: Open University Press).

Greenaway, J. R., Smith, S. and Street, J. (1992) *Deciding Factors in British Politics: A Case-Studies Approach* (London: Routledge).

Greenleaf, W. H. (1973) 'The character of modern British conservatism', in R. Benewick, R. N. Berkh and B. Parekh (eds), *Knowledge and Belief in Politics* (London: Allen and Unwin).

Greenleaf, W. H. (1983) *The British Political Tradition, Vol. 2: The Ideological Heritage* (London: Methuen).

Greenwood, J. (2003) *Interest Representation in the European Union* (Basingstoke: Palgrave Macmillan).

Greenwood, J., Pyper, R. and Wilson, D. (2001) *New Public Administration in Britain* (London: Routledge).

Greenwood, J. and Robins, L. (2002) 'Citizenship tests and education: embedding a concept', *Parliamentary Affairs*, 55:3, pp. 505–22.

Greer, G. (1970) *The Female Eunuch* (London: MacGibbon and Kee).

Griffith, J. A. G. (1989) 'The Official Secrets Act 1989', *Journal of Law and Society*, 16:2, Autumn.

Griffith, J. A. G. (1997) *The Politics of the Judiciary* (London: Fontana).

Griffith, J.A.G. and Ryle, M. (1989) *Parliament* (London: Sweet & Maxwell).

Gyford, J. (1991) *Citizens, Consumers and Councils: Local Government and the Public* (London: Macmillan).

Hague, R. and Harrop, M. (2001) *Comparative Government and Politics* (Basingstoke: Palgrave).

Hall, M. (2004) 'Nationalism in the UK', *Talking Politics*, April.

Hall, P. A. (1999) 'Social capital in Britain', *British Journal of Political Science*, 29:3, pp. 417–61.

Hall, W. and Weir, S. (1996) *The Untouchables: Power and Accountability in the Quango State* (London: Democratic Audit/Scarman Trust).

Halsey, A. H. (ed.) (1988) *Trends in British Society Since 1900* (London: Macmillan).

Hames, T. and Rae, N. (1996) *Governing America* (Manchester: Manchester University Press).

Harrison, M. (1985) *TV News: Whose Bias?* (Hermitage: Policy Journals).

Harvie, C. (1994) *Scotland and Nationalism* (London: Routledge).

Hayek, F. A. von (1944) *The Road to Serfdom* (London: Routledge and Kegan Paul).

Hazell, R. (ed.) (1999) *Constitutional Futures: A History of the Next Ten Years* (Oxford: Oxford University Press).

Hazell, R. (ed.) (2000) *The State and the Nations* (Thorverton: Imprint Academic).

Hazell, R. (2001) 'Reforming the constitution', *Political Quarterly*, 72:1.

Hazell, R. (ed.) (2003) *The State of the Nations 2003: The Third Year of Devolution in the United Kingdom* (Exeter: Academic Imprint).

Heath, A., Jowell, R. and Curtice, J. (1985) *How Britain Votes* (Oxford: Pergamon).

Heath, A. and Park, A. (1997) 'Thatcher's children', in R. Jowell, J. Curtice, A. Park, L. Brook, K. Thomson and L. Bryson (eds), *British Social Attitudes: The 14th Report* (Aldershot: Ashgate).

Heath, A. and Topf, R. (1987) 'Political culture', in R. Jowell, S. Witherspoon and L. Brook (eds), *British Social Attitudes: The 5th Report* (Aldershot: Gower).

Hechter, M. (1975) *Internal Colonialism: The Celtic Fringe in British Colonial Development, 1536–1966* (London: Routledge & Kegan Paul).

Heclo, H. and Wildavsky, A. (1974) *The Private Government of Public Money* (London: Macmillan).

Hefferman, R. (2002) 'The possible as the art of politics: understanding consensus politics', *Political Studies,* 50.

Held, D. (1996) *Models of Democracy* (Cambridge: Polity Press).

Held, D., McGrew, A., Goldblatt, D. and Perraton, J. (1999) *Global Transformations: Politics, Economics and Culture* (Cambridge: Polity Press).

Henn, M., Weinstein, M. and Forrest, S. (2005) 'Uninterested youth? Young people's attitudes towards party politics in Britain', *Political Studies,* 53:3, pp. 556–78.

Hennessy, P. (1987) *Cabinet* (Oxford: Blackwell).

Hennessy, P. (1990) *Whitehall,* 2nd edn (London: Fontana).

Hennessy, P. (1993) *Never Again: Britain 1945–51* (London: Vintage).

Hennessy, P. (1995) *The Hidden Wiring Unearthing the British Constitution* (London: Gollancz).

Hennessy, P. (1998) 'The Blair style of government: an historical perspective and an interim audit', *Government and Opposition,* 33:1, Winter.

Hennessy, P. (2000) *The British Prime Minister: The Office and its Holders since 1945* (Harmondsworth: Allen Lane).

Heywood, A. (2000) *Key Concepts in Politics* (Basingstoke: Palgrave Macmillan).

Heywood, A. (2002) *Politics,* 2nd edn (Basingstoke: Palgrave Macmillan).

Heywood, A. (2003) *Political Ideologies: An Introduction,* 3rd edn (Basingstoke: Palgrave).

Hill, M. (1997a) *The Policy Process in the Modern State* (London: Harvester Wheatsheaf).

Hill, M. (1997b) *The Policy Process: A Reader* (Hemel Hempstead: Prentice Hall).

Himmelweit, H., Humphries, P. and Jaeger, M. (1984) *How Voters Decide* (Milton Keynes: Open University Press).

Hobsbawm, E. (1984) *Worlds of Labour: Further Studies in the History of Labour* (London: Weidenfeld and Nicolson).

Hogwood, B. W. and Gunn (1984) *Policy Analysis for the Real World* (Oxford: Oxford University Press).

Holland, R. (1991*) The Pursuit of Greatness: Britain and the World Role, 1900–1970* (London: Fontana).

Holme, R. and Elliot, M. (1988) *1688–1988: Time for a New Constitution* (London: Macmillan).

Holsti, K. J. (1967) *International Politics* (Englewood Cliffs, NJ: Prentice Hall).

Hood, C. and James, D. (1997) 'The Core Executive' in P. Dunleavy, A. Gamble, I. Holliday and G. Peele (eds), *Developments in British Politics 5* (London: Macmillan).

Hood-Phillips, O., Jackson, P. and Leopard, P. (2001) *Constitutional and Administrative Law* (London, Sweet and Maxwell).

Hopkins, S. (2001) 'Northern Ireland: a place apart', *Politics Review,* November.

House of Commons Select Committee on Public Administration (2001) *Fifth Report 2000/01 Mapping the Quango State* (London: House of Commons).

Huntington, S. P. (1996) *The Clash of Civilizations and the Remaking of World Order* (New York: Simon & Schuster).

Hutchinson, J. (1994) *Modern Nationalism* (London: Fontana).

Hutton, B. (2004) *Report of the Inquiry into the Circumstances Surrounding the Death of Dr David Kelly,* HC 247 (London: The Stationery Office).

Hutton, W. (1995) *The State We're In* (London: Jonathan Cape).

Hutton, W. (1996) *The State We're In,* new and rev. edn (London: Vintage).

Hutton, W. (1997) *The State to Come* (London: Vintage).

Ingle, S. (2000) *The British Party System* (London: Pinter).

Jackson, N. (2004) 'Marketing man', *Politics Review,* 13:4.

James, S. (1992) *British Cabinet Government* (London: Routledge).

James, S. (1995) 'Relations between prime minister and Cabinet: from Wilson to Thatcher', in R. A. W.

Rhodes and P. Dunleavy (eds), *Prime Minister, Cabinet and Core Executive* (London: Macmillan).

Jeffery, C. (2003) 'Devolution: what's it all for?' *Politics Review,* 13:2.

Jeffries, L. (2003) 'The judiciary', *Talking Politics,* 15:2.

Jenkins, J. and Klandermans, B. (eds) (1995) *The Politics of Social Protest* (London: University College London Press).

Jenkins, R. (1991) *A Life at the Centre* (London: Macmillan).

Jenkins, R. (2001) *Churchill* (London: Macmillan).

Jennings, I. (1966) *The British Constitution,* 5th edn (Cambridge: University Press).

John, P. (1997) 'Local governance', in P. Dunleavy, A. Gamble, I. Holliday and G. Peele (eds), *Developments in British Politics* 5 (London: Macmillan).

Johnson, N. (1977) *In Search of the Constitution* (London: Methuen).

Johnson, P. (ed.) (1994) *Twentieth Century Britain* (London: Longman).

Jones, B. (ed.) (1999) *Political Issues in Britain Today,* 5th edn (Manchester: Manchester University Press).

Jones, B. (2003) 'Apathy: why don't people want to vote?' *Politics Review,* April.

Jones, B. (2004) *Dictionary of British Politics* (Manchester: Manchester University Press).

Jones, H. and Kandiah, M. (eds) (1996) *The Myth of Consensus: New Views on British History, 1945–64* (London: Macmillan).

Jones, B. and Robins, L. (eds) (1992) *Two Decades in British Politics* (Manchester: Manchester University Press).

Jones, G. W. (1990) 'Mrs Thatcher and the power of the prime minister', *Contemporary Record,* 3:4.

Jones, G. W. (1995) 'The downfall of Margaret Thatcher', in R. A. W. Rhodes and P. Dunleavy (eds) *Prime Minister, Cabinet and Core Executive* (London: Macmillan).

Jones, N. (1996) *Soundbites and Spin Doctors* (London: Indigo).

Jones, N. (1999) *Sultans of Spin* (London: Gollancz).

Jones, P. (1997) *America and the British Labour Party: The Special Relationship at Work* (London: Tauris Academic Studies).

Jordan, A. G. and Richardson, J. J. (1987) *Government and Pressure Groups in Britain* (Oxford: Clarendon).

Jordan, G. (2001) *Shell, Greenpeace and Brent Spar* (Basingstoke: Palgrave Macmillan).

Jordan, G. (2004) 'Groups and democracy', *Politics Review,* 13:3.

Jordan, G. and Mahoney, W. (1997) *The Protest Business* (Manchester: Manchester University Press).

Jowell, J. and Oliver, D. (2000) *The Changing Constitution* (Oxford: Oxford University Press).

Jowell, J and Oliver, D. (2004) *The Changing Constitution,* 2nd edn (Oxford: Oxford University Press).

Jowell, R., Curtice, J., Park, A., Brook, L. and Thomson, K. (eds) (1996) *British Social Attitudes: The 13th Report* (Aldershot: Dartmouth).

Jowell, R., Curtice, J., Park, A., Brook, L., Thomson, K. and Bryson, C. (eds) (1997) *British Social Attitudes: The 14th Report* (Aldershot: Ashgate).

Judd, D. (1996) *Empire: The British Imperial Experience from 1765 to the Present* (London: Fontana).

Judge, D. (1993) *The Parliamentary State* (London: Sage).

Kagan, R. (2004) *Paradise and Power* (London : Atlantic).

Kampfner, J. (2004) *Blair's Wars* (London: Free Press).

Kavanagh, D. (1980) 'Political culture in Great Britain: the decline of the civic culture', in G. Almond and S. Verba (eds), *The Civic Culture Revisited* (Boston: Little, Brown).

Kavanagh, D. (1990) *Thatcherism and British Politics,* 2nd edn (Oxford: Oxford University Press).

Kavanagh, D. (1991) 'Prime ministerial power revisited', *Social Studies Review,* 6:4, March.

Kavanagh, D. (1995) *Election Campaigning: The New Marketing of Politics* (Oxford: Blackwell).

Kavanagh, D. (1997) 'The Labour campaign', *Parliamentary Affairs,* 50:4, October.

Kavanagh, D. and Morris, P. (1994) *Consensus Politics from Attlee to Thatcher,* 2nd edn (Oxford: Blackwell).

Kavanagh, D. and Seldon, A. (eds) (1994) *The Major Effect* (London: Macmillan).

Keating, M. (1998) *The New Regionalism in Western Europe* (Cheltenham: Edward Elgar).

Kegley, C. and Wittkopf, E. (1999) *World Politics* (New York: Worth).

Kellner, P. (1997a) 'PR paradox puts Paddy in a quandary', *Observer,* 21 September.

Kellner, P. (1997b) 'Why the Tories were trounced', *Parliamentary Affairs*, 50:4, October.

Kelly, G. (1997) 'Economic policy', in P. Dunleavy, A. Gamble, I. Holliday and G. Peele (eds), *Developments in British Politics 5* (London: Macmillan).

Kemp, P. (1996) 'Handling the machine: a memo to Labour', *Political Quarterly*, 67:14, October–December.

King, A. (ed.) (1985) *The British Prime Minister: A Reader*, 2nd edn (London: Macmillan).

Kingdom, J. (1995) 'The European context', in M. Mullard (ed.), *Policy-Making in Britain* (London: Routledge).

Klein, N. (2001) 'They call us violent agitators', *Guardian*, 23 March.

Klein, R. (1989) *The Politics of the NHS* (London: Longman).

Klug, F., Starmer, K. and Weir, S. (1996) *The Three Pillars of Liberty* (London: Routledge).

Laffan, B. (1992) *Integration and Cooperation in Europe* (London: Routledge).

Lancaster, S. (ed.) (2001) *Developments in Politics*, vol. 12 (Ormskirk: Causeway Press).

Lancaster, S. (ed.) (2004) *Developments in Politics*, vol. 15 (Ormskirk: Causeway Press).

Lasswell, H. (1936) *Politics: Who gets What, When, How?* (New York: McGraw Hill).

Layton-Henry, Z. (1992) *Immigration and 'Race' Politics in Post-War Britain* (Oxford: Blackwell).

Leach, R. (1998) 'Local government reorganisation RIP?', *Political Quarterly*, 69:1.

Leach, R. (2002) *Political Ideology in Britain* (Basingstoke: Palgrave).

Leach, R. and Percy-Smith, J. (2001) *Local Governance in Britain* (Basingstoke: Palgrave).

Leach, S. (ed.) (1998) *Local Government Reorganisation* (London: Frank Cass).

Lee, J. M. (1995) 'The prime minister and international relations', in D. Shell and R. Hodder-Williams (eds), *Churchill to Major: The British Prime Ministership since 1945* (London: Hurst).

Lee, S. (1994) 'Law and the constitution', *in* A. Seldon and D. Kavanagh (eds), *The Major Effect* (London: Macmillan).

Leftwich, A. (ed.) (1984) *What is Politics?* (Oxford: Blackwell).

Lilleker, D., Negrine, R. and Stanyer, J. (2003) 'Media malaise: Britain's political communication problems', *Politics Review*, 12:3.

Lindblom, C. (1959) 'The science of muddling through', *Public Administration Review*, 19.

Lloyd, J. (2004) *What the Media are Doing to Our Democracy* (London: Constable).

Loughlin, M. and Scott, C. (1997) 'The regulatory state', in P. Dunleavy, A. Gamble, I. Holliday and G. Peele (eds), *Developments in British Politics 5* (London: Macmillan).

Loveland, I. (1997) 'The war against the judges', *Political Quarterly*, April–June.

Lovenduski, J. (1997) 'Gender politics: a breakthrough for women?', *Parliamentary Affairs*, 50:4, October.

Lovenduski, J. and Randall, V. (1993) *Contemporary Feminist Politics* (Oxford: Oxford University Press).

Lowe, R. (1993) *The Welfare State in Britain since 1945* (London: Macmillan).

Lucas, J. R. (1985) *The Principles of Politics* (Oxford: Oxford University Press).

Ludlam, S. (1996) 'The spectre haunting Conservatism: Europe and backbench rebellion', in S. Ludlam and M. J. Smith (eds), *Contemporary British Conservatism* (London: Macmillan).

Ludlam, S. and Smith, M.J. (eds) (1996) *Contemporary British Conservatism* (London: Macmillan).

Ludlam, S. and Smith, M. (eds.) (2001) *New Labour in Government* (Basingstoke: Palgrave).

Ludlam, S. and Smith, M. (eds) (2004) *Governing as New Labour* (Basingstoke: Palgrave).

Lukes, S. (1974) *Power: A Radical View* (London: Macmillan).

Lupton, C. and Russell, D. (1990) 'Equal opportunities in a cold climate', in S. Savage and L. Robins (eds), *Public Policy under Thatcher* (London: Macmillan).

Lustgarten, L. and Leigh, I. (1994) *National Security and Parliamentary Democracy* (Oxford: Clarendon).

Lynch, P. (1996) 'Labour, devolution and the West Lothian question', *Talking Politics*, 9:1, Autumn.

Lynch, P. (2002) 'Goodbye ballot box, hello post box', *Talking Politics*, 15:1.

Mac an Ghaill, M. (1999) *Contemporary Racisms and Ethnicities* (Buckingham: Open University Press).

Maclean, M. and Groves, D. (eds) (1991) *Women's Issues in Social Policy* (London: Routledge).

Macpherson, C. B. (1977) *The Life and Times of Liberal Democracy* (Oxford: Oxford University Press).

Macpherson, Sir W. (1999) *The Stephen Lawrence Inquiry*, Cm 4262 (London: The Stationery Office).

Madgwick, P. (1991) *British Government: The Central Executive Territory* (London: Philip Allan).

Madgwick, P. and Rawkins, P. (1982) 'The Welsh language in the policy process', in P. Madgwick and R. Rose (eds), *The Territorial Dimension in United Kingdom Politics* (London: Macmillan).

Madgwick, P. and Woodhouse, D. (1995) *The Law and Politics of the Constitution* (Hemel Hempstead: Harvester Wheatsheaf).

Magee, E and Lynch, P. (2003) 'The changing British constitution', *Politics Review*, 13:2.

Mair, P. (1994) 'Party organizations: from civil society to state', in R. S. Katz and P. Mair (eds), *How Parties Organize: Change and Adaptation in Party Organizations in Western Democracies* (London: Sage).

Major, J. (1999) *The Autobiography* (London: Harper Collins).

Marr, A. (1992) *The Battle for Scotland* (Harmondsworth: Penguin).

Marr, A. (1996) *Ruling Britannia: The Failure and Future of British Democracy* (London: Penguin).

Marsh, D. (1995) 'The convergence between theories of the state', in D. Marsh and G. Stoker (eds), *Theory and Methods in Political Science* (London: Macmillan).

Marsh, D. and Rhodes, R. A. W. (eds) (1992a) *Policy Networks in British Government* (Oxford: Oxford University Press).

Marsh, D. and Rhodes, R. A. W. (eds) (1992b) *Implementing Thatcherite Policies* (Milton Keynes: Open University Press).

Marsh, D. and Rhodes, R. A. W. (1996) 'The concept of policy networks in British political science: its development and utility', *Talking Politics*, 8:3, Spring.

Marsh, D. and Stoker, G. (eds) (1995) *Theory and Methods in Political Science* (London: Macmillan).

Marshall, G. (ed.) (1989) *Ministerial Responsibility* (Oxford: Oxford University Press).

Marshall, T. H. (1950) *Citizenship and Social Class and Other Essays* (Cambridge: Cambridge University Press).

Maynard, G. (1988) *The Economy under Mrs Thatcher* (Oxford: Blackwell).

Mazey, S. and Richardson, J. J. (eds) (1993) *Lobbying in the European Community* (Oxford: Oxford University Press).

McAllister, I. (1997) 'Regional voting', *Parliamentary Affairs*, 50:4, October.

McCartney, M. (2005) 'Mayor Livingstone: an assessment', *Talking Politics*, 18:1.

McCormick, J. (1991) *British Politics and the Environment* (London: Earthscan).

McCulloch, A. (1988) 'Politics and the environment', *Talking Politics*, 1:1, Autumn.

McDowell, L. Sarre, P. and Hamnett, C. (eds) (1989) *Divided Nation: Social and Cultural Change in Britain* (London: Hodder and Stoughton).

McGrew, A. and Wilson, M. (eds) (1982) *Decision-Making: Approaches and Analysis* (Manchester: Manchester University Press).

McIlroy, J. (1989) 'The politics of racism', in B. Jones (ed.), *Political Issues in Britain Today* (Manchester: Manchester University Press).

McKee, V. (1996) 'Factions and tendencies in the Conservative Party since 1945', *Politics Review*, 5:4, April.

McKenzie, R. T. (1955) *British Political Parties* (London: Heinemann).

McLean, I and McMillan, A. (eds) (2003) *The Concise Oxford Dictionary of Politics* (Oxford: Oxford University Press).

McLellan, D. (1980) *The Political Thought of Karl Marx* (London: Macmillan).

McLellan, D. (1995) *Ideology*, 2nd edn (Buckingham: Open University Press).

McNair, B. (2003) *An Introduction to Political Communication* (London: Routledge).

McNaughton, N. (2002) 'Prime ministerial government', *Talking Politics*, 15:1.

McQuail, D. (1987) *Mass Communications Theory* (Beverly Hills: Sage).

McVicar, M. (1990) 'Education policy: education as a business?', in S. Savage and L. Robins (eds), *Public Policy under Thatcher* (London: Macmillan).

Meadows, D. H., Meadows, D. L., Randers, D. L. and Behrens III, W. ([1972] 1974) *The Limits to Growth* (London: Pan).

Michels, R. ([1911] 1962) *Political Parties* (New York: Free Press).

Milbrath, L. (1965) *Political Participation: How and Why People Get Involved in Politics* (Chicago: Rand McNally).

Miles, R. (1989) *Racism* (London: Routledge).

Miles, R. (1993) *Racism after Race Relations* (London: Routledge).

Miliband, R. (1972) *Parliamentary Socialism*, 2nd edn (London: Merlin Press).

Miliband, R. (1973) *The State in Capitalist Society* (London: Quartet).

Miliband, R. (1984) *Capitalist Democracy in Britain* (Oxford: Oxford University Press).

Miliband, D. (ed.) (1994) *Reinventing the Left* (Cambridge: Polity).

Mill, J. S. ([1859] 1972) *On Liberty*, ed. H. B. Acton (London: Dent).

Mill, J.S. ([1861] 1972) *Considerations on Representative Government*, ed. H. B. Acton (London: Dent).

Mill, J. S. ([1869] 1988) *The Subjection of Women*, ed. S. Okin (Indianapolis: Hackett).

Miller, C. (2000) *Politicos Guide to Political Lobbying* (London: Politicos).

Miller, W. *et al.* (1990) *How Voters Change* (Oxford: Clarendon).

Millett, K. (1977) *Sexual Politics* (London: Virago).

Mills, C. Wright (1956) *The Power Elite* (New York: Oxford University Press).

Milne, K. 'Rise of the press-protest axis', *Guardian*, 15 March, p. 23.

Minkin, L. (1992) *The Contentious Alliance; Trade Unions and the Labour Party* (Edinburgh: Edinburgh University Press).

Minogue, K. (1995) *Politics: A Very Short Introduction* (Oxford: Oxford University Press).

Mohapatra, U. (1999) *With Love, From Britain. A Mother Writes to her Children: Observations on Changing Overseas Indian Culture* (Mumbai: Bhavans Book University).

Moran, M. (2000) 'From command state to regulatory state' , *Public Policy and Administration*, 15:4.

Moran, M. (2001) 'Not steering but drowning: policy catastrophes and the regulatory state', *Public Policy and Administration*, 15:4.

Moran, M. (2005) *Politics and Governance in the UK* (Basingstoke: Palgrave Macmillan).

Morgan, K. (1990) *The People's Peace: British History, 1945–1989* (Oxford: Oxford University Press).

Morgan, K. and Owen, K. (2001) *Britain Since 1945* (Oxford: Oxford University Press).

Mount, F. (1992) *The British Constitution Now* (London: Heinemann).

Mowlam, M. (2002) *Momentum: The Struggle for Peace, Politics and People* (London: Hodder and Stoughton).

Mulhall, S. and Swift, A. (1996) *Liberals and Communitarians* (Oxford: Blackwell).

Nairn, T. (1981) *The Break-up of Britain* (London: NLB and Verso).

Nairn, T. (2000) *After Britain* (London: Granta).

Nairn, T. (2001) 'Post Ukania', *New Left Review*, January–February.

Neunreither, K. (1993) 'Subsidiarity as a guiding principle for European Community', *Government and Opposition*, 28:2.

Newman, J. (2001) *Modernising Governance: New Labour, Policy and Society* (London: Sage).

Newton, K. (1976) *Second City Politics* (Oxford: Oxford University Press).

Niskanen, W. A. (1971) *Bureaucracy and Representative Government* (Chicago: Aldine-Atherton).

Niskanen, W. A. (1973) *Bureaucracy: Servant or Master?* (London: Institute of Economic Affairs).

Nolan, Lord (Chair) (1995) *First Report of the Committee on Standards in Public Life* (Nolan Report) Cm 2850 (London: HMSO).

Norris, P. (1991) 'Gender differences in political participation in Britain: traditional, radical and revisionist models', *Government and Opposition*, 26:1.

Norris, P. (1997) 'Anatomy of a landslide', *Parliamentary Affairs*, 50:4, October.

Norris, P. (ed.) (2001) *Britain Votes, 2001* (Oxford: Oxford University Press).

Norris, P. (2004) 'The 2003 Northern Ireland Assembly Election', *Talking Politics*, 16:3.

Norris, P. and Lovenduski, J. (1995) *Political Recruitment: Gender, Race and Class in the British Parliament* (Cambridge: Cambridge University Press).

Norton, P. (1990) 'Public legislation', in M. Rush (ed.), *Parliament and Pressure Politics* (Oxford: Oxford University Press).

Norton, P. (1994a) 'The constitution in question', *Politics Review*, 3:4, April.

Norton, P. (1994b) 'Select committees in the House of Commons: watchdogs or poodles?', *Politics Review*, 4:2, November.

Norton, P. (1995a) 'Standing committees in the House of Commons', *Politics Review*, 4:4, April.

Norton, P. (1997) 'The United Kingdom: restoring confidence?', *Parliamentary Affairs*, 50:3, July.

Norton, P. (2004) 'The power of Parliament', *Politics Review*, 14:2.

Norton, P. (2005) *Parliament in British Politics* (Basingstoke: Palgrave Macmillan).

Nugent, N. (2002) *The Government and Politics of the European Union,* 5th edn (Basingstoke: Palgrave Macmillan).

Nugent, N. (ed.) (2004) *European Union Enlargement* (Basingstoke: Palgrave Macmillan).

O'Gorman, F. (1986) *British Conservatism* (London: Longman).

O'Neill, M. (ed.) (2004) *Devolution and British Politics* (Harlow: Pearson Longman).

O'Toole *et al.* (2003) *Political Quarterly*, 74:3.

Oakeshott, M. (1962) *Rationalism in Politics and Other Essays* (London: Methuen).

Oliver, D. (1993) 'Citizenship in the 1990s', *Politics Review,* 3:1, September.

Oppenheim, C. (1990) *Poverty: The Facts* (London: Child Poverty Action Group).

Orwell, G. and Angus, I. (1968) *The Collected Essays, Journalism and Letters of George Orwell, vol. II* (London: Secker & Warburg).

Outhwaite, D. (2004) 'How should parties be funded?', *Politics Review,* 14:2.

Osborne, D and Gaebler, T. (1992) *Reinventing Government* (Reading, Mass.: Addison-Wesley).

Parekh, B. (2000a) *The Future of Multi-Ethnic Britain: Report of the Commission on Multi-Ethnic Britain* (London: Profile Books in association with Runnymede Trust).

Parekh, B. (2000b) *Rethinking Multiculturalism: Cultural Diversity and Political Theory* (Basingstoke: Palgrave).

Parry, G. and Moyser, G. (1990) 'A map of political participation in Britain', *Government and Opposition*, 25:2.

Parry, G., Moyser, G. and Day, N. (1992) *Political Participation and Democracy in Britain* (Cambridge: Cambridge University Press).

Parsons, W. (1995) *Public Policy: Introduction to the Theory and Practice of Policy Analysis* (Aldershot: Edward Elgar).

Pateman, C (1970) *Participation and Democratic Theory* (Cambridge: Cambridge University Press).

Paxman, J (1998) *The English* (London: Michael Joseph).

Payne, G. (ed.) (2000) *Social Divisions* (Basingstoke: Palgrave).

Peston, R. (2005) *Brown's Britain: How Gordon Brown Runs the Show* (London: Short).

Peterson, J. (1997) 'Britain, Europe and the world', in P. Dunleavy, A. Gamble, I. Holliday and G. Peele (eds), *Developments in British Politics 5* (London: Macmillan).

Pierre, J. and Peters, B. G. (2000) *Politics, Governance and the State* (Basingstoke: Macmillan).

Pimlott, B. (1992) *Harold Wilson* (London: Harper Collins).

Pimlott, B. (1994) 'The myth of consensus', in B. Pimlott, *Frustrate Their Knavish Tricks* (London: Harper Collins).

Pinder, J. (2001) *The European Union* (Oxford: Oxford University Press).

Pliatzky, L. (1980) *Report on Non-Departmental Bodies,* Cmnd 7797 (London: HMSO).

Pliatzky, L. (1982) *Getting and Spending* (Oxford: Blackwell).

Plummer, J. (1994) *The Governance Gap: Quangos and Accountability* (London: Demos/Joseph Rowntree Foundation).

Pollard, S. (2004) *David Blunkett* (London: Hodder and Stoughton).

Porritt, J. and Winner, D. (1988) *The Coming of the Greens* (London: Fontana).

Prabakar, R. (2004) 'New Labour and Education', *Politics Review,* 14:1.

Pugh, M. (1994) *State and Society: British Political and Social History 1870–1992* (London: Edward Arnold).

Pulzer, P. (1967) *Representation and Elections in Britain* (London: Allen & Unwin).

Putnam, R (1995) 'Tuning in, tuning out: the strange disappearance of social capital in America', *PS: Political Science and Politics*, 28, pp. 664–83.

Putnam, R (2000) *Bowling Alone: The Collapse and Revival of American Community* (New York: Simon and Schuster).

Pyper, R. (1991) 'Governments, 1964–1990: a survey', *Contemporary Record*, 5:2, Autumn.

Pyper, R. (1994) 'Individual ministerial responsibility: dissecting the doctrine', *Politics Review,* 4:1, September.

Pyper, R. (1995) *The British Civil Service* (London: Harvester Wheatsheaf).

Pyper, R. and Robins, L. (1995) (eds) *Governing the UK in the 1990s* (London: Macmillan).

Quinton, A. (1978) *The Politics of Imperfection* (London: Faber & Faber).

Ramsden, J. (ed.) (2005) *The Oxford Companion to Twentieth Century Politics* (Oxford: Oxford University Press).

Randall, V. (1987) *Women and Politics*, 2nd edn (London: Macmillan).

Rathbone, M. (2001) 'The Freedom of Information Act', *Talking Politics*, 13:3.

Rathbone, M. (2002) 'Labour and the Liberal Democrats', *Talking Politics*, 14:3.

Rathbone, M. (2005a) 'The November 2004 referendum in the north east', *Talking Politics*, 17:2, January.

Rathbone, M. (2005b) 'The future of the Liberal Democrats', *Talking Politics*, 18:1.

Rawnsley, A. (2001) *Servants of the People: The Inside Story of New Labour* (London: Penguin).

Rentoul, J. (2001) *Tony Blair: Prime Minister* (London: Little, Brown).

Rex, J. (1986) *Race and Ethnicity* (Buckingham: Open University Press).

Reynolds, D. (1991) *Britannia Overruled: British Policy and World Power in the Twentieth Century* (London: Longman).

Rhodes, R. A. W. (1981) *Control and Power in Central–Local Government Relations* (Farnborough: Gower).

Rhodes, R. A. W. (1988) *Beyond Westminster and Whitehall: The Sub-Central Governments of Britain* (London: Allen & Unwin).

Rhodes, R. A. W. (1997) *Understanding Governance* (Buckingham: Open University Press).

Rhodes, R. A. W. (ed.) (2000) *Transforming British Government, Volume 1: Changing Institutions* (London: Macmillan).

Rhodes, R. A. W. and Dunleavy, P. (eds.) (1995) *Prime Minister, Cabinet and the Core Executive* (Basingstoke: Macmillan).

Richard, Lord (2004) *Report of the Richard Commission* (Cardiff: National Assembly for Wales).

Richard, I. and Welfare, D. (1999) *Unfinished Business: Reforming the House of Lords*.

Richards, S. (1996) 'New Labour – new civil service?', *Political Quarterly*, 67:4, October–December.

Richardson, J. J. (ed.) (1993) *Pressure Groups* (Oxford: Oxford University Press).

Richardson, J. J. and Jordan, G. (1979) *Governing Under Pressure* (Oxford: Martin Robertson).

Ridley, F. F. (1988) 'There is no British constitution: a dangerous case of the emperor's clothes', *Parliamentary Affairs*, 41:3, July.

Ridley, F. F. (1991) 'Using power to keep power: the need for constitutional checks', *Parliamentary Affairs*, 44:4, October.

Ridley, F. F. and Rush, M. (eds) (1995) *British Government and Politics since 1945* (Oxford: Oxford University Press).

Ridley, F. F. and Wilson, D. (1995) *The Quango Debate* (Oxford: Oxford University Press).

Ridsdill-Smith, C. (2003) 'Protest and the environment', *Politics Review*, 12:3.

Roberts, H. (2004) 'The last lord chancellor', *Politics Review*, 13:4.

Robins, L., Blackmore, H. and Pyper, R. (eds) (1994) *Britain's Changing Party System* (London: Leicester University Press).

Robinson, M. (1992) *The Greening of British Party Politics* (Manchester: Manchester University Press).

Rose, R. (2001) *The Prime Minister in a shrinking world* (Cambridge: Polity).

Rush, M. (ed.) (1990) *Parliament and Pressure Politics* (Oxford: Clarendon).

Ryan, M. (2004) 'A Supreme Court for the United Kingdom?', *Talking Politics*, 17:1.

Saggar, S. (1997) 'Racial politics', *Parliamentary Affairs*, 50:4, October.

Saggar, S. (1992) *Race and Politics in Britain* (London: Harvester Wheatsheaf).

Sampson, A. (2005) *Who Runs This Place?* (London: John Murray).

Sanders, D. (1990) *Losing an Empire, Finding a Role* (London: Macmillan).

Sanders, D. (1995) '"It's the economy, stupid": the economy and support for the Conservative Party, 1979–1994', *Talking Politics*, 7:3, Spring.

Sanderson, M. (1994) 'Education and social mobility', in P. Johnson (ed.), *Twentieth Century Britain* (London: Longman).

Saunders, P. (1980) *Urban Politics: A Sociological Interpretation* (Harmondsworth: Penguin).

Savage, S. and Atkinson, R. (eds) (2001) *Public Policy under Blair* (London: Palgrave Macmillan).

Savage, S. and Robins, L. (eds) (1990) *Public Policy under Thatcher* (London: Macmillan).

Saville, J. (1988) *The Labour Movement in Britain* (London: Faber and Faber).

Scarman, Lord (1981) *The Brixton Disorders 10–12 April,1981: Special Report* (London: HMSO).

Schumacher, E. F. (1973) *Small is Beautiful* (London: Sphere).

Schumpeter, J. (1943) *Capitalism, Socialism and Democracy* (London: George Allen & Unwin).

Scruton, R. (1996) *Dictionary of Political Thought* (London: Macmillan).

Sedgemore, B. (1980) *The Secret Constitution* (London: Hodder and Stoughton).

Seldon, A. (1994) 'Policy making and cabinet', in D. Kavanagh and A. Seldon (eds), *The Major Effect* (London: Macmillan).

Seldon, A. (ed.) (1996) *How Tory Governments Fall* (London: Harper Collins).

Seldon, A. (ed.) (2001) *The Blair Effect* (London: Little, Brown).

Seldon. A. (2004) *Blair* (London: Free Press).

Self, P. (1993) *Governing by the Market? The Politics of Public Choice* (Basingstoke: Macmillan).

Seliger, M. (1976) *Ideology and Politics* (London: Allen & Unwin).

Semetko, H. A., Scammell, M. and Goddard, P. (1997) 'Television', *Parliamentary Affairs*, 50:4, October.

Seyd, P. and Whiteley, P. (1992) *Labour's Grass Roots: The Politics of Party Membership* (Oxford: Clarendon).

Seymour-Ure, C. (1974) *The Political Impact of the Mass* Media (London: Constable).

Seymour-Ure, C. (1995) 'Prime minister and the public: managing media relations', in D. Shell and R. Hodder-Williams (eds), *Churchill to Major: The British Prime Ministership since 1945* (London: Hurst).

Seymour-Ure, C. (1997) 'Editorial opinion in the national press', *Parliamentary Affairs*, 50:4, October.

Shaw, E. (1996) *The Labour Party since 1945* (Oxford: Blackwell).

Simon, H. (1947) *Administrative Behaviour* (Glencoe, Ill. : Free Press).

Sked, A. and Cook, C. (1979) *Post-War Britain: A Political History* (Harmondsworth: Penguin).

Skelcher, C. (1998) *The Appointed State* (Buckingham: Open University Press).

Skellington, R. (1996) *'Race' in Britain Today* (London: Sage).

Smith, A. D. (1979) *Nationalism in the Twentieth Century* (Oxford: Martin Robertson).

Smith, A. D. (1991) *National Identity* (Harmondsworth: Penguin).

Smith, D. (1994) *North and South: Britain's Economic, Social and Political Divide*, 2nd edn (Harmondsworth: Penguin).

Smith, M. J. (1995) *Pressure Politics* (Manchester: Baseline Books).

Smith, M. J. (1999) *The Core Executive in Britain* (London: Macmillan).

Smith, M. J. and Ludlam, S. (eds) (1996) *Contemporary British Conservatism* (London: Macmillan).

Snyder, R. C., Bruck, H. W. and Sapin, B. (1960) 'Decision-making as an approach to the study of international politics', in S. Hoffman (ed.), *Contemporary Theory in International Relations* (Englewood Cliffs, NJ: Prentice-Hall).

Solomos, J. (2003) *Race and Racism in Britain* (Basingstoke: Palgrave Macmillan).

Solomos, J. and Back, L. (1996) *Racism and Society* (Basingstoke: Macmillan).

Souza, C. (1998) *So You Want to be a Lobbyist?* (London: Politicos).

Stanworth, P. and Giddens, A. (1974) *Elites and Power in British Society* (Cambridge: Cambridge University Press).

Stanyer, J. (2000) 'A loss of political appetite', *Parliamentary Affairs*, 55.

Steed, M. (1986) 'The core–periphery dimension of British politics', *Political Geography Quarterly*, supplement to 5:4, October.

Stoker, G. (1991) *The Politics of Local Government* (London: Macmillan).

Stoker, G. (2003) *Transforming Local Governance* (Basingstoke: Palgrave Macmillan).

Stoker, G. and Wilson, D. (eds) (2004) *British Local Government into the 21st Century* (Basingstoke: Palgrave Macmillan).

Stokes, J. and Reading, A. (eds) (1999) *The Media in Britain: Current Debates and Developments* (Basingstoke: Macmillan).

Stokes, W. (2005) *Women in Contemporary Politics* (Cambridge: Polity).

Stott, T. (1995–6) 'Evaluating the Quango debate', *Talking Politics*, 8:2, Winter.

Stubbs, R. and Underhill, G. (eds) (2000) *Political Economy and the Changing Global Order* (Oxford: Oxford University Press).

Sutherland, K (ed.) (2000) *The Rape of the Constitution* (Thorveton: Academic Imprint).

Tapper, T. and Bowles, N. (1982) 'Working class Tories: the search for theory', in L. Robins (ed.), *Topics in British Politics* (London: Politics Association).

Tarling, R. and Dowds, L. (1997) 'Crime and punishment', in R. Jowell, J. Curtice, A. Park, L .Brook, K. Thomson and C. Bryson (eds), *British Social Attitudes: The 14th Report* (Aldershot: Ashgate).

Taylor, A. (2000) 'Hollowing out or filling in? Task forces and the management of cross-cutting issues in British government', *British Journal of Politics and International Relations*, 2:1.

Theakston, K. (1995) *The Civil Service since 1945* (Oxford: Blackwell).

Theakston, K. (1999) *Leadership in Whitehall* (London: Macmillan).

Thomas, G. (1992) *Government and the Economy Today* (Manchester: Manchester University Press).

Thompson, E. P. (1963) *The Making of the English Working Class* (London: Gollancz).

Tomkins, A. (1996) 'The Scott Report: the constitutional implications', *Politics Review*, 6:1, September.

Tomkins, A. (1997) 'Intelligence and government', *Parliamentary Affairs*, 50:1, January.

Tonge, J. (2004) *The New Northern Ireland Politics* (Basingstoke: Palgrave).

Tonge, J. and Geddes, A. (1997) 'Labour's landslide? The British General Election of 1997', *ECPRN News*, 8:3.

Topf, R. (1989) 'Political change and political culture in Britain, 1959–1987', in J. R. Giddens (ed.), *Contemporary Political Culture* (London: Sage).

Townsend, P., Davidson, N. and Whitehead, M. (1990) *The Health Divide* (Harmondsworth: Penguin).

Toynbee, P. and Walker, D, (2005) *Better or Worse? Has Labour Delivered?* (London: Bloomsbury).

Travers, T. (2003) *The Politics of London* (Basingstoke: Palgrave Macmillan).

Trenaman, J. and McQuail, D. (1961) *Television and the Political Image* (London: Methuen).

Troyna, B. and Williams, J. (1986) *Racism, Education and the State* (London: Croom Helm).

Tunstall, J. and Maching (1999) *The Anglo-American Media Connection* (Oxford: Oxford University Press).

Van Mechelen, D. and Rose, R. (1986) *Patterns of Parliamentary Legislation* (Aldershot: Gower).

Vital, D. (1968) *The Making of British Foreign Policy* (Oxford: Oxford University Press).

Wade, H. W. R. (1988) *Administrative Law*, 6th edn (Oxford: Clarendon).

Wadham, J. and Mountfield, H. (2000) *Human Rights Act, 1998*, 2nd edn (London: Blackstone).

Waldegrave, W. (1993) *The Reality of Reform and Accountability in Today's Public Service* (London: Public Finance Foundation).

Wallace, M. and Jenkins, J. C. (1995) 'The new class, post-industrialism and neo-corporatism: three images of social protest in the western democracies', in J. Jenkins and B. Klandermans (eds), *The Politics of Social Protest* (London: University College London Press).

Wallace, W. (1994) 'Foreign policy', in D. Kavanagh and A. Seldon (eds), *The Major Effect* (London: Macmillan).

Wallas, G. ([1908] 1920) *Human Nature in Politics*, 3rd edn (London: Constable).

Waller and Criddle (2002) *The Almanac of British Politics* (London: Routledge).

Walter, N. (1999) *The New Feminism* (London: Virago).

Walsh, K. (1995) *Public Services and Market Mechanisms* (Basingstoke: Macmillan).

Watts, D. (1994) 'Europe's Bill of Rights', *Politics Review*, 3:4, April.

Watts, D. (1997a) *Political Communication Today* (Manchester: Manchester University Press).

Watts, D. (1997b) 'The growing attractions of direct democracy', *Talking Politics*, 10:1, Autumn.

Watts, D. (2004) 'The politics of the environment' in S. Lancaster, *Developments in Politics*, vol. 15 (Ormskirk: Causeway Press).

Webb, P. (2000) *The Modern British Party System* (London: Sage).

Weir, S. (1995) 'Quangos: questions of democratic accountability', in F. F. Ridley and D. Wilson (eds), *The Quango Debate* (Oxford: Oxford University Press).

Weir, S. and Beetham, D. (1999) *Political Power and Democratic Control in Britain: The Democratic Audit of Great Britain* (London: Routledge).

Weir, S. and Hall, W. (eds) (1994) *Ego Trip: Extra Governmental Organisations in the UK and their Accountability* (University of Essex: Human Rights Centre).

Welfare, D. (1992) 'An anachronism with relevance: the revival of the House of Lords in the 1980s and its defence of local government', *Parliamentary Affairs*, April.

Westlake, M. (1996–7) 'A unique constitutional experiment', *Talking Politics*, 9:2, Winter.

Whale, J. (1977) *The Politics of the Media* (London: Fontana).

Whiteley, P. and Winyard, S. (1987) *Pressure for the Poor* (London: Methuen).

Whiteley, P., Seyd, P. and Richardson, J. (1994) *True Blues: The Politics of Conservative Party Membership* (Oxford: Clarendon).

Widdicombe Report (1986) *The Conduct of Local Authority Business: Report of the Committee of Inquiry into the Conduct of Local Authority Business*, Cmnd 9797 (London: HMSO).

Wilding, P. (1989–90) 'Equality in British social policy since the war', *Talking Politics*, 2:2, Winter.

Wilding, P. (1993) 'Poverty and government in Britain in the 1980s', *Talking Politics*, 5:3, Summer.

Williams, R. (1976) *Keywords: A Vocabulary of Culture and Society* (London: Fontana).

Williams, T. and Abse, D. (1997) 'Birth of a nation', *Guardian*, 26 July.

Wilson, D. (1996) 'Quangos in British politics', *Politics Review*, 6:1, September.

Wilson, D. (1984) *Pressure: the A to Z of Campaigning in Britain* (London: Heinemann).

Wilson, D. and Game, C. (2002) *Local Government in the United Kingdom*, 3rd edn (Basingstoke: Palgrave).

Wilson, G. K. (1991) 'Prospects for the public service in Britain: Major to the rescue?', *International Review of Administrative Sciences*, 57.

Wollstonecraft, M. ([1792] 1995) *A Vindication of the Rights of Woman*, ed. A. Tauchert (London: Dent).

Wood, B. (1992) *The Politics of Health* (Manchester: Politics Association).

Woodhouse, D. (1994) *Ministers and Parliament: Accountability in Theory and Practice* (Oxford: Clarendon).

Woodhouse, D. (1997) 'Judicial/executive relations in the 1990s', *Talking Politics*, 10:1, Autumn.

Wright, A. (1983) *British Socialism* (London: Longman).

Young, H. (1990) *One of Us*, expanded edn with new epilogue (London: Pan in association with Macmillan).

Young, H. (1998) *This Blessed Plot: Britain and Europe, from Churchill to Blair* (London: Macmillan).

Index